CURRICULUM LEADERSHIP

Fourth Edition

⑤SAGE | 50 YEARS

SAGE was founded in 1965 by Sara Miller McCune to support the dissemination of usable knowledge by publishing innovative and high-quality research and teaching content. Today, we publish more than 750 journals, including those of more than 300 learned societies, more than 800 new books per year, and a growing range of library products including archives, data, case studies, reports, conference highlights, and video. SAGE remains majority-owned by our founder, and after Sara's lifetime will become owned by a charitable trust that secures our continued independence.

Los Angeles | London | Washington DC | New Delhi | Singapore | Boston

CURRICULUM LEADERSHIP

Strategies for Development and Implementation

Fourth Edition

Allan A. Glatthorn

Floyd Boschee
The University of South Dakota

Bruce M. Whitehead
Principal, Missoula School District #4;
University of Montana

Bonni F. Boschee
Principal, Volga Christian School

Los Angeles | London | New Delhi
Singapore | Washington DC | Boston

Los Angeles | London | New Delhi
Singapore | Washington DC | Boston

FOR INFORMATION:

SAGE Publications, Inc.
2455 Teller Road
Thousand Oaks, California 91320
E-mail: order@sagepub.com

SAGE Publications Ltd.
1 Oliver's Yard
55 City Road
London EC1Y 1SP
United Kingdom

SAGE Publications India Pvt. Ltd.
B 1/I 1 Mohan Cooperative Industrial Area
Mathura Road, New Delhi 110 044
India

SAGE Publications Asia-Pacific Pte. Ltd.
3 Church Street
#10-04 Samsung Hub
Singapore 049483

Printed in the United States of America

Cataloging-in-publication data is available from the Library of Congress.

ISBN 978-1-4833-4738-7

Acquisitions Editor: Theresa Accomazzo
Editorial Assistant: Georgia McLaughlin
Production Editor: Libby Larson
Copy Editor: Megan Markanich
Typesetter: C&M Digitals (P) Ltd.
Proofreader: Theresa Kay
Indexer: Sheila Bodell
Cover Designer: Gail Buschman
Marketing Manager: Terra Schultz

Brief Contents

Detailed Contents

Preface

*C*urriculum *Leadership: Strategies for Development and Implementation* (4th edition) is intended for those presently functioning as curriculum leaders and those preparing for such roles. Its central intent is to provide such readers with the knowledge and the skills needed to exercise leadership in curriculum at several levels and in many roles.

To that end, it begins by exploring the foundations of the field in the first part—Foundations of Curriculum—so that decisions are made from a broad perspective and with deep knowledge. The first chapter establishes the central concepts used throughout the work, explaining the general concept of curriculum and explicating its essential elements; the goal of this chapter is to provide the reader with a set of conceptual tools. The second chapter reviews the past 100 years plus of curriculum history, so that decision makers can see the problems and solutions of the present from an informed historical perspective. The third chapter surveys the several types of curriculum theory, since good theory provides deeper insight about the complex relationships involved in all curriculum work. The final chapter of the "foundations" section examines the politics of curriculum work—the way that power and influence affect curriculum decision making at the federal, state, and local levels.

The second part, Curriculum Processes, turns to procedures. The general goal of this section is to help the reader acquire skills needed to bring about major curriculum change. The section begins with an overview of curriculum—planning process. Then, separate chapters deal with the more specific processes involved in improving and developing the three levels of curricula—programs of study, fields of study, and courses and units of study.

The third part of the book, Curriculum Management, is concerned with the management of curriculum. If curricula are to be truly effective, they must be managed well. Chapter 9 suggests specific ways in which the leader can supervise both instructional processes and the selection and use of materials—the "supported" and the "taught" curriculum—to use the constructs employed in this work. Chapter 10 presents a how-to in developing and implementing a districtwide curriculum for the subject areas. The next chapter provides a rationale for and explains the processes used in aligning the curriculum—ensuring that the written, the taught, the tested, and the learned curriculum are brought into closer alignment. The last chapter in this section, Curriculum Evaluation, reviews several models for evaluating the curriculum and makes specific suggestions for developing and implementing a comprehensive evaluation form.

The book closes with Part IV on curricular trends—Current Trends in the Curriculum. Chapter 13 examines trends in the subject fields, and Chapter 14 trends across the curriculum, including the use of technology. The book ends with an examination of current approaches to individuals and adapt the curriculum for learners with special needs.

NEW TO THE FOURTH EDITION

A sample of the changes for the fourth edition of *Curriculum Leadership: Strategies for Development and Implementation* are based on the recommendations and revisions suggested by the reviewers:

Chapter 1 emphasizes a comparison of education before standards-based education, during the standards movement, and under the Common Core State Standards (CCSS). Also, another aspect of the hidden curriculum was added.

Chapter 2 adds a new educational era highlighting Technological Functionalism.

Chapter 3 presents organizational leadership models with an emphasis on technology.

Chapter 4 illustrates a principal's political view of schools.

Chapter 5 establishes a curriculum framework for the development of professional communities.

Chapter 6 focuses on professional development protocol and closing the student achievement gap.

Chapter 7 provides insight into technology and reconceptualizing 21st-century learning.

Chapter 8 assesses academic, social, and cultural needs.

Chapter 9 accentuates the supervision of the taught curriculum.

Chapter 10 presents curriculum game changers and global connections.

Chapter 11 includes alignment and assessment of the CCSS.

Chapter 12 discusses the purpose of evaluation and presents an example of measuring teacher effectiveness.

Chapter 13 highlights the CCSS as they relate to multicultural education.

Chapter 14 relates the impact of technological advances and acknowledges the value of accommodating diversity.

Chapter 15 offers a renewed focus on differentiated instruction and a new culture of 21st-century digital citizens.

ACKNOWLEDGMENTS

We benefited greatly from reviews by Lisa Hazlett, University of South Dakota; Robert Kladifko, California State University, Northridge; Lora Knutson, Governors State University; Linda Noel-Batiste, Virginia State University; and Jody Wood, Saint Louis University.

Special thanks must go to Georgia McLaughlin, editorial assistant intern at SAGE, for her continuing dialogue, assistance, and constant willingness to help with the production of the fourth edition of *Curriculum Leadership: Strategies for Development and Implementation.*

We also acknowledge the supportive help received from Marlys Ann Boschee and Charlotte Whitehead. They helped us give meaning and coherence in an age in which change and flux in education reign supreme. Also, a special thanks goes to Dr. Bonni F. Boschee for her continuing contributions made from her experience as a current school administrator.

UPDATES TO THE FOURTH EDITION

Changes to Chapter 1

- Comparison of Education Standards
- Mindset of 21st-Century Learners
- Dynamics of Global Education
- Hidden Curriculum

Changes to Chapter 2

- Seven Cardinal Principles of Education
- Technological Functionalism

Changes to Chapter 3

- Organizational Performance
- Open-Systems Principle

Changes to Chapter 4

- Myths About U.S. Schools
- Political, Cultural, and Socioeconomic Realities
- Modern Conservatism (2000–2009)
- Technological Functionalism (2010–present)
- Common Core State Standards
- National Accreditation and Teacher Preparation
- Guiding Preservice Teachers
- Increasing Role of the Courts
- The Principal
- Technology and Elements of Change

Changes to Chapter 5

- Goal-Based Model of Curriculum Planning
- Curriculum Framework
- Importance of Integrity
- Professional Development
- Technology: 21st-Century Learning
- Global Connections: Research and Practice

Changes to Chapter 6

- Improving Low-Performing Schools
- Closing the Achievement Gap
- Professional Development Protocols
- Developing Cultural Leadership
- Building 21st-Century Technology Culture
- Global Connections: Finland's Model

Changes to Chapter 7

- Role of the Principal in Curriculum Improvement
- Student-Centered Process
- Prepare to Teach Culturally Diverse Classrooms
- Make Professional Development Priorities
- Human Development: Importance of Teaching Ethics
- Technology: Reconceptualizing 21st-Century Learning
- Global Connections: Bridging Community and School in Belgium

Changes to Chapter 8

- Assess Needs: Academic, Social, and Cultural
- Regional Centers and Technology Hubs
- Preparing Schools for New Beginnings With Technology
- Global Connections: Dual Systems in Korea

Changes to Chapter 9

- Supervising the Taught Curriculum: Current Approaches
- Elements of Supervision
- Understanding Change
- Situational Awareness
- Dilemma for Supervisors

- Differentiated Supervision
- The Role of the Curriculum Supervisor
- Differentiated Professional Development
- Motivating Staff
- Instructional Rounds
- Culturally Relevant Teaching
- Going Deeper Into Teaching and Learning With Technology
- Digital Solutions for 21st-Century Learning
- Global Connections: French Partnership

Changes to Chapter 10

- Leadership Truths for Curriculum Leaders

Changes to Chapter 11

- Role of the Principal
- Aligning With Common Core State Standards
- Assessment and Common Core State Standards
- Focusing on Culture and Social Diversity
- Data-Driven Programs
- Professional Development and Curriculum Alignment
- Classroom Learning and 21st-Century Technology
- Global Connections: Russia's Common Core

Changes to Chapter 12

- Authentic Assessment
- Purpose of Evaluation: Measuring Effectiveness Versus Developing Teachers
- Leadership and Evaluation
- Role of the Principal in Evaluation
- Building Collaboration
- Common Core State Standards
- Bridging Cultural Knowledge
- Measuring for Success
- Technology and Evaluation: The Final Piece of the Puzzle
- Connectivity
- Integrated Systems Assessments
- Classroom Technology Environment
- Technology and Student Achievement
- Technology Plan Assessment
- Data Collection

- Professional Development and Evaluation
- Equity Issues
- Global Connections: Evaluation and Accountability

Changes to Chapter 13

- Realities in Reading
- Expanding a Culture of Writing
- Dual Immersion Programs in English Language Arts
- Common Core State Standards and Multicultural Education
- Technology and Exponential Change
- Global Connections: Teaching Content Across Cultures

Changes to Chapter 14

- Accommodating Diversity
- Leadership for Socially Diverse Groups
- Innovation and 21st-Century Learning
- Technology and Pedagogy
- Redefining the Culture of School
- Technology Linked to Student Achievement
- Impact of Technological Advances
- Professional Development and Technology
- Core Competencies for Digitally Literate Teachers
- Global Connections: Canada's Shifting Minds Model

Changes to Chapter 15

- Differentiated Instruction
- Enhancing Teaching and Learning
- Special Needs: Accommodations and Modifications
- Cross-Cultural Comparisons in Special Education
- PreK and Early Childhood
- Social and Economic Considerations
- Focusing on Social Media and Ethical Issues
- Social Ramifications of Cyberbullying
- Digital Citizens: A New Culture of the 21st Century
- Nine Themes of Digital Citizenship (digitalcitizenship.net)
- Global Connections: Positive Impact Worldwide

*This book is dedicated to Dr. Allan A. Glatthorn (1924–2007), who believed
deeply in sharing his love of education and curriculum. His unique understanding
of leadership and curriculum processes continues to be a key for successful leaders today.
As coauthors of* Curriculum Leadership: Strategies for Development and Implementation, *we hope this edition will continue to provide completeness in curriculum thought
and theory and enhance positive changes for the future.*

—Floyd Boschee
—Bruce M. Whitehead
—Bonni F. Boschee

PART I

Foundations of Curriculum

Curriculum planners have tried to characterize curriculum with very little guidance. The purpose of Part I is to present an overview of curriculum so that curriculum planners can begin to comprehend the essential elements for curriculum development and implementation and gain a fundamental foundation on which to firmly build a sound curriculum.

CHAPTER 1

The Nature of Curriculum

The intent of this introductory chapter is to provide curriculum leaders and teachers with a general overview of the curriculum field and a set of concepts for analyzing the field. To accomplish these related goals, the discussion that follows focuses on these outcomes: defining the concept of curriculum, examining the several types of curricula, describing the contrasting nature of curriculum components, and analyzing the hidden curriculum. Some fundamental concepts essential for understanding the comprehensive field of curriculum can be established at the outset.

Questions addressed in this chapter include the following:

- What is curriculum?
- What purpose does the curriculum serve?
- What are the types and components of curricula?
- What is the difference between state standards and the Common Core State Standards (CCSS)?
- What are mastery, organic, and enrichment curricula, and what roles do they play in the development of curriculum?
- Why is knowledge of the "hidden curriculum" important to curriculum leaders?

Key to Leadership

School administrators, curriculum leaders, and teachers should review and monitor curriculum policies to make sure the policies align with curricular goals and support student learning.

THE CONCEPT OF CURRICULUM

In a sense, the task of defining the concept of curriculum is perhaps the most difficult of all—certainly challenging—for the term *curriculum* has been used with quite different meanings ever since the field took form. *Curriculum,* however, can be defined as prescriptive, descriptive, or both.

> Prescriptive [curriculum] definitions provide us with what "ought" to happen, and they more often than not take the form of a plan, an intended program, or some kind of expert opinion about what needs to take place in the course of study. (Ellis, 2004, p. 4)

Analogous to **prescriptive curricula** are medical prescriptions that patients have filled by pharmacists; we do not know how many are actually followed. "The best guess is that most are not" (Ellis, 2004, p. 4). This is parallel to the prescribed curriculum for schools where the teacher, like the patient, ultimately decides whether the prescription will be followed. In essence, "the developer proposes, but the teacher disposes" (p. 4).

To understand the nature and extent of curriculum diversity, it is important to examine the prescriptive and descriptive definitions offered by some of the past and present leaders in the field. The prescriptive definitions in Exhibit 1.1, arranged chronologically, have been chosen for their representativeness.

The descriptive definitions of *curriculum* displayed in Exhibit 1.2 go beyond the prescriptive terms as they force thought about the curriculum "not merely in terms of how things ought to be . . . but how things are in real classrooms" (Ellis, 2004, p. 5). Another term that could be used to define the **descriptive curriculum** is *experience.* The experienced curriculum provides "glimpses" of the curriculum in action. Several examples, in chronological order, of descriptive definitions of curriculum are listed in Exhibit 1.2.

EXHIBIT 1.1 Prescriptive Definitions of Curriculum		
Date	*Author*	*Definition*
1902	John Dewey	"Curriculum is a continuous reconstruction, moving from the child's present experience out into that represented by the organized bodies of truth that we call studies . . . the various studies . . . are themselves experience—they are that of the race" (Dewey, 1902, pp. 11–12).
1957	Ralph Tyler	"[The curriculum is] all the learning experiences planned and directed by the school to attain its educational goals" (Tyler, 1957, p. 79).
2010	Indiana Department of Education	"Curriculum means the planned interaction of pupils with instructional content, materials, resources, and processes for evaluating the attainment of educational objectives" (Indiana Department of Education, 2010).

In your opinion, which prescriptive definition is appropriate today? Why?

EXHIBIT 1.2 Descriptive Definitions of Curriculum		
Date	*Author*	*Definition*
1935	Hollis Caswell and Doak Campbell	"Curriculum is all the experiences children have under the guidance of teachers" (Caswell & Campbell, 1935).
1960	W. B. Ragan	"Curriculum is all the experiences of the child for which the school accepts responsibility" (Ragan, 1960).
2013	Edward S. Ebert II, Christine Ebert, and Michael L. Bentley	"Curriculum is only that part of the plan that directly affects students. Anything in the plan that does not reach the students constitutes an educational wish but not a curriculum" (Ebert, Ebert, & Bentley, 2013, p. 2).

In your opinion, which descriptive definition is appropriate today? Why?

The definitions provided for *prescriptive* and *descriptive curricula* vary primarily in their breadth and emphasis. It would seem that a useful definition of *curriculum* should meet two criteria: It should reflect the general understanding of the term as used by educators, and it should be useful to educators in making operational distinctions. Therefore, the following definition of *curriculum* will be used in this work:

> The curriculum is a set of plans made for guiding learning in the schools, usually represented in retrievable documents of several levels of generality, and the actualization of those plans in the classroom, as experienced by the learners and as recorded by an observer; those experiences take place in a learning environment that also influences what is learned.

Several points in this definition need to be emphasized. First, it suggests that the term *curriculum* includes both a set of plans made for learning and the actual learning experiences provided. Limiting the term to the plans made for learning is not enough because, as will be discussed next, those plans are often ignored or modified. Second, the phrase *retrievable documents* is sufficiently broad in its denotation to include curricula stored in a digital form—that is, software and/or shared on the Internet. Also, those documents, as will be more fully explained next, are of several levels of specificity: Some, such as curricular policy statements, are very general in their formulation; others, such as daily lesson plans, are quite specific. Third, the definition notes two key dimensions of actualized curriculum: the curriculum as experienced by the learner and that which might be observed by a disinterested observer. Finally, the experienced curriculum takes place in an environment that influences and impinges on learning, constituting what is usually termed the *hidden curriculum.*

Although the definition for curriculum does not deal explicitly with the relationship between curriculum and instruction, an implicit relationship does exist. Instruction is viewed here as an aspect of curriculum, and its function and importance change throughout the several types of curricula. First, in the written curriculum, when the curriculum is a set of documents that guide planning, instruction is only one relatively minor aspect of the curriculum. Those retrievable documents used in planning for learning typically specify five components: a rationale for the curriculum; the aims, objectives, and content for achieving those objectives; instructional methods; learning materials and resources; and tests or assessment methods.

Consequently, instruction is a component of the planned curriculum and is usually seen as less important than the aims, objectives, and content at the actualized level; when the planned or written curriculum is actually delivered, instruction takes on a new importance. For that reason, administrators and supervisors should view the curriculum as the total learning experience for students and focus on instruction—how teachers are teaching.

THE TYPES OF CURRICULA

The definition stipulated previously suggests a major difference between the planned curriculum and actualized curriculum. Yet even these distinctions are not sufficiently precise to encompass the several different types of curricula. It is important to note that the word *curriculum* (as defined from its early Latin origins) means literally "to run a course." For example, if students think of a marathon with mile and direction markers, signposts, water stations, and officials and coaches along the route, they can better understand the concept of types of curriculum (Wilson, 2005).

As early as 1979, Goodlad and associates were perhaps the first to suggest several key distinctions. As Goodlad analyzed curricula, he determined there were five different forms of **curriculum planning**. The *ideological curriculum* is the ideal curriculum as construed by scholars and teachers—a curriculum of ideas intended to reflect funded knowledge. The *formal curriculum* is that officially approved by state and local school boards—the sanctioned curriculum that represents society's interests. The *perceived curriculum* is the curriculum of the mind—what educators, parents, and others think the curriculum to be. The *operational curriculum* is the observed curriculum of what actually goes on hour after hour in the classroom. Finally, the *experiential curriculum* is what the learners actually experience.

While those distinctions in general seem important, the terms are perhaps a bit cumbersome, and the classifications are not entirely useful to curriculum workers. It seems to be more useful in the present context to use the following concepts with some slightly different denotations: the **recommended curriculum**, the **written curriculum**, the **supported curriculum**, the **taught curriculum**, the **tested curriculum**, and the **learned curriculum**. Four of these curricula—the *written,* the *supported,* the *taught,* and the *tested*—are considered components of the **intentional curriculum**. The intentional curriculum is the set of learnings that the school system consciously intends, in contradistinction to the **hidden curriculum**, which by and large is not a product of conscious intention.

The Recommended Curriculum

The recommended curriculum is the one recommended by the individual scholars, professional associations, and reform commissions; it also encompasses the curriculum requirements of policymaking groups, such as the federal government with the No Child Left Behind Act (NCLB) and state governments such as the Common Core State Standards Initiative (CCSSI). Similar to Goodlad's ideological curriculum, it is a curriculum that stresses "oughtness," identifying the skills and concepts that ought to be emphasized, according to the perceptions and value systems of the sources.

Curriculum Tip 1.1	Recommended curricula are typically formulated at a rather high level of generality; they are most often presented as policy recommendations, lists of goals, suggested graduation requirements, and general recommendations about the content and sequence of a field of study, such as mathematics.

Today, as in the past, the prevailing decline of American education at the elementary, middle, and high school levels; its low international educational ranking; and the achievement gap between students of different races are undoubtedly factors that influenced several of today's reform reports. Many perceive the state of American education as a national embarrassment as well as a threat to the nation's future.

> In the spring of 2009, an effort unprecedented in the history of U.S. education, governors and state commissioners of education from across the United States formed the Common Core State Standards Initiative (CCSSI). The goal of this initiative was to develop a set of shared national standards ensuring that students in every state are held to the same level of expectations that students in the world's highest-performing countries are, and that they gain the knowledge and skills that will prepare them for success in postsecondary education and in the global arena. (Kendall, 2011, p. 1)

The Council of Chief State School Officers (CCSSO) and the National Governors Association (NGA) committed to the CCSSI and selected representatives from 48 states, two territories, and the District of Columbia. The task engaged the talents and expertise of educators, content specialists, researchers, community groups, and national organizations, including an advisory group of experts from Achieve, ACT, the College Board, the National Association of State Boards of Education, and the State Higher Education Executive Officers. However, the subject-area organizations for which the CCSS were written did *not* include the National Council of Teachers of English (NCTE) and the National Council of Teachers of Mathematics (NCTM) for which the standards were written. Nor were they asked to help draft or provide feedback to early drafts of the standards. They were, however, invited to critique drafts of the CCSS prior to their release for public comment. "In addition, the draft standards were [reviewed] and feedback [provided] from teachers, parents, business leaders, and the general public" (Kendall, 2011, p. 1).

It should be noted that 40 plus states adopted the CCSS; some rejected them at the outset; and others, such as Indiana, Oklahoma, South Carolina, and Louisiana, have nullified them through legislative action, while other states have pending legislation to nullify the CCSS. Ultimately, we may end up with a natural experiment in which we finally get the trials that the founders of the CCSS preferred to avoid. And we will be able to compare the progress of the states that are 100% CCSS aligned with other states. It should also be noted that the development of the CCSS continues to be entirely state-led and they are global in scope as well.

Curriculum Tip 1.2	First, we must define what we mean by standards. Second, we must create a set of standards that are "doable" in the classroom. Finally, teachers must view standards as an important part of their work. I call these the three Ds—definition, doability, and desirability.
	—Jim Cox, president of JK Educational Associates, Inc., in Anaheim, California

Although standards existed prior to the CCSS, a comparison of standards in different periods of time is shown in Figure 1.1.

Common Core State Standards

As part of a recommended curriculum, many states are now using **Common Core State Standards (CCSS)** to spur curriculum change in a number of schools across the country. According to Gardner and Powell (2013), CCSS promised to improve teaching and learning without being prescriptive about individual state content standards. Unlike previous standards, CCSS emphasizes a set of skills that students will truly need to be college and career ready.

Although controversial, the goal of the CCSS initiative is to draw from research to inform the development of a common core set of standards that meet the essential criteria: fewer, clearer, higher, and internationally benchmarked (Gardner & Powell, 2013). A primary focus of CCSS is to draw on the evidence of what it means to be college and workforce ready and will lead to the development of voluntary adoption of a common core of state standards in a variety of subject areas for Grades K through 12. Furthermore, the development of the CCSS continues to be entirely state-led but is global in scope.

It is important from a curriculum leadership, as well as a theoretical perspective, to note CCSS standards have been developed and initiated to have an impact on the achievement levels of individual students. Collaboration is the key to fast, efficient reform. Despite continued controversy at federal levels, it is a state's responsibility to implement reform efforts. Additionally, by collaborating with state officials and other educators, building level leaders can achieve significant curriculum change by forgoing some of the costly time-impact on student achievement. Naturally, a compendium of educators in participating states continue to influence and mold recommended standards as an ongoing process. With this in mind, curriculum leaders, principals, and teachers must be ready with solid facts and

FIGURE 1.1   A Comparison of Education Before Standards-Based Education, During the Standards Movement, and Under the Common Core State Standards

	Before Standards-Based Education	*During the Standards Movement*	*Under the Common Core State Standards*
Appropriateness of expectations to instructional time	Time available = time needed.	Varies by state; no explicit design criteria. Often not enough instructional time available to address all standards.	Standards are designed to require 85 percent of instruction time available.
Curriculum support	Curriculum is defined by the textbook.	Standards drive the curriculum, but curriculum development lags behind standards development.	Standards publication is followed quickly by curriculum development.
Methods of describing student outcomes	Seat time; Carnegie units (emphasis inputs over outcomes).	State standards; criterion-based.	Cross state standards; consortia of states.
Source of expectations for students	The expectations in textbooks or those described in Carnegie units; historical, traditional influences.	Varies by state; over time, moved from traditional course descriptions to college- and career-ready criteria.	The knowledge and skills required to be college and career ready; international benchmarks; state standards.
Primary assessment of purposes	Infrequent comparison of students against a national sample; minimum competency tests in the 1970s.	Accountability; to clarify student performance by subgroup (NSLB).	Accountability; to learn and improve teaching and learning.
Systemic nature of reform	Not systemic; reform is enacted through programs at the school or district level.	Reforms varies by state and within states; "local control" states are much less systemic.	Standards curriculum and assessment are shared among participating states and territories.

SOURCE: Kendall (2011). Reprinted with permission.

research to back up their reform agendas. State educational leaders and legislators will be looking for information and, thus, educators are in good position to provide the information and influence to create educational standards for improved student achievement to compete in a global society in the 21st century (Whitehead, Jensen, & Boschee, 2013).

In conjunction with CCSS, the widespread use of technology internationally is becoming critically important. To be sure, numerous schools are using globally generated data and management tools to help facilitate teaching and learning. Especially important is the ability of educators to easily access worldwide information databases (Chesley & Jordan, 2012). As part of this new international perspective on education, administrators, curriculum advisers, and classroom teachers are now sharing a variety of instructional strategies, cultural ideas, files, and videos with educators around the world.

Some students have access to technology at school and in their homes; however, many do not. Technology has become a basic tool of learning, and this tool must be available to all students so as not to deprive those who have no access to the opportunities that technology provides. However, simply placing technology in students' hands does not improve their education if educators do not guide students into learning experiences. Many students spend their digital resources in hours of texting, e-mailing, Web surfing, watching videos, listening to MP3s, instant messaging, and gaming. However, the digital divide we should fear the most is split between the educational and entertainment uses of the new technologies. Rauh (2014) postulated the following:

> The digital divide can have huge effects on classroom instruction. Students who have had early and frequent access to technology tend to be more comfortable with using it. Those who have little to no computing experience outside of school not only start behind their peers in skill and comfort but also tend to advance more slowly, since there is little practice time available outside of school.
>
> On the other hand, if technology in the hands of our young people end up focused on trivial pursuits, if they become defined by the society as grown-up Gameboys, and if we find ourselves as educators on the wrong side of the divide, we will have lost a major battle with the forces of ignorance.

Students need to learn not only how to use technology to access information but also to analyze and apply higher order thinking to analyze and process this information and how to use technology to present information and ideas to their world. To accomplish this, teachers, administrators, and students need both technical literacy and information literacy as part of the curriculum.

The Role of Professional Associations and Individuals

Along with CCSS, the role of professional associations and individuals will continue to have a major impact on schooling. First, the professional associations representing the several disciplines, such as the NCTM and the National Council on Teacher Quality (NCTQ), advocating reforms in a broad range of teacher policies, as well as those representing school administrators, such as the National Association for Secondary School Principals (NASSP), have been active in producing recommended curricula.

As noted by Cox as early as 2000, there is major difference between content standards—what students should know and be able to do—and performance standards—those identifying acceptable levels of performance.

Raising standards in the core curriculum subjects continues to gain momentum in states and school districts across the country. In this regard, many states have begun to use CCSS to make clear what students should learn and what teachers should teach. Basically, whatever curricula is eventually recommended by state governments, as well as learned societies, should help curriculum coordinators and teachers make decisions about developing their instructional programs.

In addition to recommendations for the core curriculum by the NGA Center, CCSSO, and learned societies, there continues to be a focus on curriculum social and cultural issues in our schools. For example, Paul Gorski (2013) believes the best a way to address diversity issues and eliminate the achievement gap is to eradicate poverty. He further noted that educators should be in the process of taking research-proven steps to foster equality of opportunity throughout all schools. Although some may find Gorski's position unrealistic, the fundamental point is for curriculum planners to meet CCSS, or state standards, and to recommend the very best curriculum for their school—more specifically, to develop a curriculum that meets the needs of all students.

This new movement toward developing social and cultural capital is being radically enhanced through major advances in technology. The role of new 21st-century learning is best evidenced by Monica Martinez (2010), president of New Tech Network, who noted that with the advent of digital media, network teaching, and learning platforms, we now have an unprecedented opportunity to reimagine teaching and learning. Obviously, good and reliable data can lead to amazing results, particularly if channeled through well-led teachers on a global scale.

New 21st-century learners are highly relational and demand quick access to new knowledge. They are voraciously hungry for knowledge and capable of engaging in learning at a whole new level. Likewise, with the world literally at their fingertips, they need immediate access globally to the most advanced technology available. This means educators worldwide are having to regroup, rethink, and re-envision the role of technology in today's schools.

As part of any school's recommended curriculum, technology capability is coming to the forefront of priorities. According to Nancy Blair (2012), this shift has already begun. The new mind-set of technology through technology involves providing discovery and exploration, creation and design, a focus on authentic audiences, and a device for every child.

Elements of 21st-century technology integration include the following:

- *Discovery and exploration.* Teachers need to act as a learning catalyst, orchestrating and facilitating activities that spark defining moments for students. Classroom instructors globally are spending less time on creating presentations and more time using technology to craft powerful learning activities, find challenging materials, and deepen understandings.
- *Creation and design.* Emerging technologies are used to craft problem-solving skills and display student mastery in profound and meaningful ways. Students readily become active partners in designing and constructing learning experiences in the classroom and beyond. Examples might include kindergartners creating image-based movies; first graders sharing digital projects; fourth graders writing digital storybooks; fifth graders collaborating to launch a Web Safety Wiki; middle school eighth graders cowriting a blog with African students; and high school students creating, designing, and implementing a successful solar energy project.
- *Authentic audiences.* Sharing and collaborating in a digital world is transforming today's classrooms. Authentic audiences are not just limited to traditional class presentations, but can also involve digitally based school news shows, school Web

sites, film festivals, literary publications, online publishing through blogs and other Web 2.0 books, contests, competitions, as well as using Skype with other classes around the world.

- *A device for every student.* Schools today have a greater responsibility to help innovatively harness the power of 21st-century technological resources. Along with affordable netbooks, handheld mobile devices and a plethora of apps are expanding the realms of e-learning and m-learning. The signs are all around us that advances in technology are continuing to connect us globally. Having a mobile learning device in every student's hands is certain to make this dramatic shift a reality sooner than later.

Global Education

Exploring the dynamics of global education is becoming of paramount importance—especially in light of recent technological advances. Such an endeavor involves recommending and designing cultures of innovation that foster student skills that matter the most in our new technologically driven world. According to Tony Wagner (2008), author of the international best-selling book *The Global Achievement Gap,* creating innovation-driven schools can be the answer. Wagner believes that to motivate today's students and prepare them for a world that will require them to innovate, educators must be far more intentional in designing cultures of globally relevant innovation within our schools. This involves accessing mobile learning and the development of authentic performance-based forms of assessment, such as digital portfolios, along with hands-on project-based interdisciplinary focus.

Not surprisingly, students want to change the world. But first they must be given skills they need to do so. Wagner believes schools wanting to become globally involved need to embrace five essential elements. They are as follows:

1. Collaboration Versus Individual Achievement
   Conventional schooling in the United States celebrates and rewards individual achievement while offering few meaningful opportunities for genuine collaboration. This is in contrast to other countries that place an emphasis on collaborative learning and team building.

2. Multidisciplinary Learning Versus Specialization
   Innovation requires knowing how to apply an interdisciplinary approach to solving problems or creating something new. Learning how to solve problems across disciplinary boundaries is one of the most important skills for globally focused students.

3. Trial and Error Versus Risk Avoidance
   The most innovative internationally based companies celebrate failure along with success. Most schools with a culture of innovation teach students to view trial and error—and failure—as integral to the problem-solving process.

4. Creating Versus Consuming
   Most schools in the United States rely heavily on direct instruction as well as lecture formats, especially at high school and college levels. In contrast, other

countries, such as Finland, are creating a culture of innovation that encourages students to acquire knowledge while solving a problem, creating a product, or generating new understandings.

5. Intrinsic Versus Extrinsic Motivation
   Conventional classes in U.S. schools rely on extrinsic incentives as motivators for learning. Research indicates that most young global innovators are primarily motivated by extrinsic incentives. Successful schools internationally are now focusing on more discovery-based learning that evolves a deeper sense of understanding and purpose.

As can be seen, Wagner's five essential elements are very reflective as to what is needed to enhance a culture of learning and innovation. As part of the process of demystifying global education, we need to radically break from old approaches and embrace new ways of visualizing teaching and learning.

The Written Curriculum

The written curriculum is intended primarily to ensure that newly adapted educational goals of the system are being accomplished and that the curriculum is well managed. This enables all students, regardless of ethnicity, cultural background, or challenges, to be able to graduate from respective high schools and be prepared for postsecondary education and careers. Typically, the written curriculum is much more specific and comprehensive than the recommended curriculum, indicating a rationale that supports the curriculum, the general goals to be accomplished, the specific objectives to be mastered, the sequence in which those objectives should be studied, and the kinds of learning activities that should be used. Curriculum leaders are thus able to develop well documented and technologically driven implementation plans, goals and objectives, as well as timelines that can be used as reference points for future change and improvement.

Curriculum Tip 1.3	The written curriculum is an important component of authentic literacy—the ability to read, write, and think effectively.

As school administrators, curriculum leaders, and teachers, the authors believe that the written curriculum must be authentic. Similarly, Steven Wolk (2010), associate professor at Northeastern Illinois University, believes that we need visionary educators who see bold purposes for school and who understand that what students read has profound, lifelong effects. From a historical perspective, Walker (1979) was one of the first to note that written curricula can be both generic and site specific. Let's review the concepts of generic and site-specific curricula.

Generic curricula are those written for use in various educational settings. Initially, during the 1960s, numerous generic curricula were produced by federally funded research and development laboratories; now, more typically, they are produced by state and federal education departments and intended for use throughout the individual states and/or country, with some local leeway provided. Site-specific written curricula are those developed for a specific site, usually for a local school district or even for a particular school.

Site-specific written curricula are influenced by several different sources. First, as will be explained more fully in Chapter 4, federal and state legislation and court directives play a role. The passage of Public Law 94–142, prescribing that schools provide the "least restrictive environment" for handicapped learners, undoubtedly precipitated much local curriculum work to help teachers work toward "inclusion." The textbooks and standardized tests in use in the district seem to influence decisions about the inclusion and placement of content. The expectations of vocal parent and community groups seem to have at least a constraining influence on what can be done.

In general, however, the guides seem to reflect the preferences and practices of a local group of elites: a director of curriculum, a supervisor of that subject area, a principal with a strong interest in curriculum, and experienced teachers. They, in turn, seem most influenced by the practice of "lighthouse" districts. It is important to note that we are entering a new kind of shared leadership in the 21st century.

Key to Leadership

It is important to note how managers seem only to manage while, in contrast, leaders actually lead. A major key to school success is focusing on the quality of leadership.

Supporting teacher–leaders continues to evolve as classroom teachers gain a "global" view of what affects their vision of good schools and good teaching (Hanson, 2010). The authors know that people will support what they help create; so all stakeholders, especially teachers, share the commitment of curriculum leadership.

Equally important as quality leadership is a need for quality written curricula. The chief functions of written curricula seem to be three: *mediating, standardizing,* and *controlling.* They first mediate between the ideals of the recommended curriculum and the realities of the classroom; in this sense, they often represent a useful compromise between what the experts think *should* be taught and what teachers believe *can* be taught. They also mediate between the expectations of administrators and the preferences of teachers. The best of them represent a negotiated consensus of administrative and classroom leaders. An example of the "how-to" in developing and implementing curriculum is illustrated in Chapter 10.

Written curricula also serves an important role in standardizing the curriculum, especially in larger districts. Often they are produced as a result of directives from a superintendent who is concerned that students in School A are studying a social studies curriculum or using a reading series quite different from those in Schools B and C.

To be sure, standardizing and centralizing curricula are generally used by district and school administrators as leadership tools to guide what is taught. With this in mind, many states are using CCSS to instill more challenging demands on students and prompt educators to take a hard look at the deep and transferable knowledge students will need in college or career

(Smith, Wilhelm, & Fredricksen, 2013). That said, focusing on standards and student achievement is not new. Waters, Marzano, and McNulty (2003) compiled more than three decades of research on the effects of instruction and schooling on student achievement and found a substantial relationship between leadership and student achievement (see Exhibit 1.3). The results of this study continue to provide practitioners with specific guidance on the curricular, instructional, and school practices that, when applied appropriately, can result in increased achievement.

EXHIBIT 1.3 Principal Leadership Responsibilities	
Responsibilities	*The Extent to Which the Principal Does the Following:*
Culture	Establishes a set of standard operating procedures and routines
Discipline	Protects teachers from issues and influences that would detract from their focus on teaching time
Resources	Provides teachers with material and professional development necessary for the successful execution of their roles
Curriculum, instruction, assessment	Is directly involved in the design and implementation of curriculum, instruction, and assessment practices
Focus	Establishes clear goals and keeps those goals at the forefront of the school's attention
Knowledge of curriculum, instruction, assessment	Is knowledgeable about current curriculum, instruction, and assessment practices
Contingent rewards	Recognizes and rewards individual accomplishments
Communication	Establishes strong lines of communication with teachers and among students
Outreach	Is an advocate and spokesperson for the school to all stakeholders
Input	Demonstrates an awareness of the personal aspects of teachers and staff
Affirmation	Recognizes and celebrates school accomplishments and acknowledges failure
Relationship	Demonstrates an awareness of the personal aspects of teachers and staff
Change agent	Is willing to and actively challenges the status quo
Optimizer	Inspires and leads new and challenging innovations
Ideals/beliefs	Communicates and operates from strong ideals and beliefs about schooling
Monitors/evaluates	Monitors the effectiveness of school practices and their impact on student learning
Flexibility	Adapts leadership behavior to the needs of the current situation and is comfortable with dissent
Situational awareness	Is aware of the details and undercurrents in the running of the school and uses this information to address current and potential problems
Intellectual stimulation	Ensures that faculty and staff are aware of the most current theories and practices and makes the discussion of these a regular aspect of the school's culture

In reviewing the research on the effects of instruction and schooling on student achievement, it becomes readily apparent that any written curriculum must be adapted to emerging technologies. Similarly, written curriculum should represent a useful synthesis of recommended curricula and local practice and be well conceptualized, carefully developed, and easy to use.

Unfortunately, many written curriculums still lack these qualities. Careful reviews of a large number of such **curriculum guides** reveal a series of common faults: Objectives are often not related to the stated goals, instructional activities are not directly related to the objectives, the activities do not reflect the best current knowledge about teaching and learning, and the guides are generally cumbersome and difficult to use.

The Supported Curriculum

The supported curriculum is the curriculum as reflected in and shaped by the resources allocated to support and deliver it. Four kinds of resources seem to be most critical here: the time allocated to a given subject at a particular level of schooling (How much time should we allocate to social studies in Grade 5?), the time allocated by the classroom teacher within that overall subject allocation to particular aspects of the curriculum (How much time shall I allocate to the first unit on the explorers?), personnel allocations as reflected in and resulting from class-size decisions (How many physical education teachers do we need in the middle school if we let PE classes increase to an average of 35?), and the textbooks and other learning materials provided for use in the classroom (Can we get by with those old materials for one more year?).

A harsh reality today lies with school leaders having minimal guidance when facing continued budget cuts for supported curriculum. Decisions dealing with economic conditions are generally represented by two distinct lines of thought. First, there is the response to cut back leadership or management. Second, there is a move toward crisis management such as advocating slashing budgets, reducing programs, and eliminating teachers and staff. Given these two limited options, school leaders need to explore all possibilities if they are to accommodate needed curriculum changes. Thus, with more waves of digital innovation on the way, school leaders are scrambling to find creative ways to finance and budget curriculum. This conundrum is of paramount importance and is clearly critical if future generations of children are to remain educationally, socially, and economically competitive on a global level (Whitehead, Boschee, & Decker, 2013).

Clearly, the patterns of influence bearing on the supported curriculum seem rather complex. First, both federal and state governments exercise a strong influence on the supported curriculum: State curriculum guidelines go even further by specifying minimum time allocation, as well as state-approved lists of basic texts that restrict the choice of textbooks to a relatively small number.

In addition, the local school board, under the leadership of its superintendent, seems to be playing an ever-increasing role in supporting curriculum. In many districts, boards will adopt curriculum policies specifying minimum time allocations to the several subjects, will approve district-purchased texts, and will make major budget decisions that strongly affect the personnel and material support provided. At the school level, principals also seem to have a major influence. They usually have some discretion in the allocation of funds for textbooks, media, and other learning materials. They often are given some latitude in their requests for additional staff.

With the classroom teacher being so vital to the process, it is not surprising that a key to strengthening and deepening what is taught relies largely on professional development. As a result, school leaders at all levels are now recognizing the critical importance of teacher growth and the role of professional learning communities (PLCs). Like students, it is best if educators remain in a consistent state of discovery and learning. For these reasons, curriculum leaders and classroom teachers need to work collaboratively if they are to set the direction for 21st-century learning. Innovative concepts like m-learning and e-learning don't just happen. It takes planning, strategy, and collegial reform to make it happen. This is largely due to educators being pivotal in determining or altering students' educational path (Espinoza, 2012). By building awareness and strategic alliances, teachers can, and often do, make a significant difference in the lives of their students. To be sure, one cannot sidestep the importance of high-quality professional training in today's globally changing society.

First, early studies indicate that time is an important factor. In a review of the research, Stallings (1980) concluded that "the body of knowledge emanating from the research on teaching in the 1970s suggests that teachers should allocate more time to academic subjects, keeping in mind ability levels, and students should be kept engaged in the tasks" (p. 12), which is relevant today as well.

During the 1980s, Berliner (1984) also cited examples of the dramatic differences in the way time is allocated in elementary school classrooms. One fifth-grade teacher devoted only 68 minutes a day to reading and language arts; another teacher, 137 minutes. Karweit (1983), however, questioned one aspect of this concern for time. In a review of the research on time-on-task, Karweit noted that, "by a variety of criteria for the importance of an effect, the most outstanding finding relating the effects of time-on-task to learning is that the effects are as small as they are" (p. 46).

Second, the National Education Association (NEA; 2011) noted that a class size of 15 students in regular programs and even smaller in programs for students with exceptional needs is a key to success. NEA officials noted that while many education reform proposals remain controversial, reducing class size to allow for more individualized attention for students is strongly supported by parents, teachers, and education researchers. It is believed that teachers with small classes can spend time and energy helping each child succeed. Smaller classes also enhance safety, discipline, and order in the classroom. When qualified teachers teach smaller classes in modern schools, kids learn more.

Third, the quality of the textbook and other learning resources as an aspect of the supported curriculum seems to play a central role.

Undeniably, problems with textbooks and materials are a recurring issue. It should be shared that current elementary school reading series appear to contain several flaws: Stories written for use in the primary grades do not give enough insight into characters' goals, motives, and feelings; many of the so-called stories do not actually tell a story; and textbooks lack a logical structure, often emphasizing a trivial detail rather than a fundamental principle. Harder textbooks, as well as media-related texts, unfortunately, have captured the attention of educators and policymakers who want to raise academic achievement.

Yet today, the concern over quality textbooks continues to grow. Dr. Gay Ivey (2010), professor of early, elementary, and reading education at James Madison University, noted, "When it comes to subject-area reading materials, we are stuck in a rut" (p. 22). Further, she stated the following:

> To create lifelong readers, we need to give them reading materials that leave them wanting to know more. . . . Instead of focusing on how to get students to *remember* what they read, our best bet is simply to provide texts that are more *memorable*. (p. 19)

Fourth is the advent of CCSS. These standards continue to impact textbooks by setting higher expectations for students in the areas of reading, writing, speaking, and listening. While standards and curriculum guide teachers in instructional planning, outcomes continue to play a critical role determining whether standards have been met (Mahurt, 2013).

Looking retrospectively, the provision of supportive curriculum and leading students to mastery in any subject entails creating scenarios in which learners see themselves in that subject—because they grasp its potential to extend their capacities and to benefit other people (Tomlinson, 2013–2014). In an earlier study, Tomlinson et al. (2002) noted that the supported curriculum should also involve the use of flexible options and the formation of a parallel curriculum model.

Tomlinson et al. (2002) shared in the book *The Parallel Curriculum* that parallels can be used to develop or support curriculum for individuals, small groups, and entire classes. The term *parallel* indicates several formats through which educators can approach curriculum design in the same subject or discipline. She and her colleagues referred to the four parallels as core curriculum, curriculum and connections, curriculum of practice, and curriculum of identity. These parallel processes can be deductive or inductive and can be used as catalysts to discover student abilities and interests or in response to student abilities and interests. They believe that these parallels act as support for thematic study and help connect content that might otherwise seem disjointed to learners. Using this model, a teacher might establish a definition of change, identify key principles related to change, and introduce students to key skills as well as specify standards that need to be covered. Tomlinson and colleagues' parallel model for curriculum development is only one of the many approaches that can be used to help support curriculum.

As can be seen, supported curriculum does play a central role at several stages of the curriculum cycle—first in developing curricula and second in implementing the curriculum. Either way, administrators should be sure that adequate support is provided. Next, as Chapter 11 indicates, those involved in aligning the curriculum should assess to what extent a good fit exists between the written, the supported, and the taught curricula. Finally, any comprehensive evaluation of the curriculum should assess the supported curriculum because deficiencies in support will probably be a major factor in student achievement.

The Taught Curriculum

The extent to which consonance exists between the written curriculum and the taught curriculum seems to vary considerably. At one extreme are those school systems that claim to have achieved a high degree of consonance between the two by implementing curriculum-alignment projects. At the other extreme are schools where a state of curricular anarchy exists: Each teacher develops his or her own curriculum, with all sorts of disparate activities going on across the school.

Curriculum Tip 1.4	The taught curriculum is the delivered curriculum, a curriculum that an observer sees in action as the teacher teaches.

How does the taught curriculum, regardless of its fit with the written curriculum, become established? The question is a complex and important one that can best be answered by synthesizing several studies of teachers' thinking, planning, and decision making.

To be sure, a teacher's decision relating to curriculum is basically a product of many interacting variables. Hence, the role and importance of classroom teachers cannot be understated. Statistical evidence provides a strong warrant that how we organize and operate a school has a major effect on the instructional exchanges in the classroom (Bryk, 2010). Bergman and Bergman (2010) agree, noting that good teaching is like good writing—the principles of good writing can help teachers improve their style.

The Tested Curriculum

The tested curriculum is that set of learnings that is assessed in teacher-made classroom tests; in district-developed, curriculum-referenced tests; and in standardized tests. To what extent are these tests related to the taught curriculum? The answers seem to vary. There were early problems in test preparation. Tests previously concentrated on assessing students' comprehension and memory of objective information, and their attempts to measure understanding of concepts resulted in multiple-choice items that really assessed students' guessing ability.

The evidence on the congruence between curriculum-referenced tests and instruction suggests a somewhat different picture. In districts using curriculum-referenced tests as a means of monitoring teacher compliance, the test seems to drive instruction. The result is a closer fit. Yet, here, the congruence is not reassuring to those who value higher order learning. An examination of a curriculum-referenced test used in a large district's alignment project indicated that the test items were concerned almost exclusively with such low-level objectives as punctuating sentences correctly, spelling words correctly, and identifying the parts of speech. Finally, the research suggests that a gap is widening between standardized tests and what some instructors are teaching. The consequences of inadequate alignment and poor testing are serious.

From a historical perspective, Berliner took the lead in 1984 to point out that achievement was lower in schools where there was not a close fit between what was taught and what was tested. Students were put at a disadvantage when the teaching and testing did not match, and their grades and scores were probably not a valid measure of what they had learned. Finally, there were serious legal consequences when poorly fitting tests were used to make decisions about promotion and graduation. The courts ruled that when tests were used for purposes that denied constitutional guarantees of equal protection or due process (as in retention or denial of graduation), schools needed to provide evidence that those tests assessed skills and concepts actually taught in the classroom. Author James Popham (2007) stated the following:

> If we plan to use tests for purposes of accountability, we need to know that they measure traits that can be influenced by instruction. . . . Instructionally insensitive tests render untenable the assumptions underlying a test-based strategy for educational accountability. (p. 147)

Within this milieu of court orders, schools eventually began facing greater problems with local testing. The result has been high-stakes testing for accountability of not only schools and school districts but also individual teachers (Zirkel, 2013). Not surprisingly, new court cases seem to suggest another level of high-stakes testing: state laws and local policies that provide for student test performance as one of the criteria for summative evaluation of educators. Likewise, test performance criterion may play a carefully circumscribed rather than exclusive role in value-added evaluations having disciplinary consequences.

Despite the many challenges facing teachers and schools, more teachers are using state-approved, online-based programs to ease the alignment of local testing to state and national standards. Classroom teachers are also using data analysis of student strengths and weaknesses. In furthering this endeavor, a series of Web-based programs now allow classroom teachers to create pre- and posttests online easily and quickly and thus be able to adjust instruction as needed. Equally helpful is the availability of valid and reliable test questions (aligned with state standards and CCSS) that can be selected from large banks of test items. These types of online-based programs also provide valuable teaching strategies that can address specific areas of need for individual students.

Curriculum Tip 1.5	Components of the curriculum determine the fit between what is taught and what is learned.

It might be useful at this juncture to note again that the four curricula discussed previously—written, supported, taught, and tested—might be seen as constituting the intentional curriculum, which comprises that set of learning experiences the school system consciously intends for its students.

The Learned Curriculum

The term *learned curriculum* is used here to denote all the changes in values, perceptions, and behavior that occur as a result of school experiences. As such, it includes what the student understands, learns, and retains from both the intentional curriculum and the hidden curriculum. The discussion here focuses on what is learned from the intentional curriculum; the last part of the chapter analyzes what is learned from the hidden curriculum.

What, then, do students learn and retain from the intentional curriculum? Obviously, the answer varies with the student, the teacher, and the curriculum. Some subtle transformations, especially between the taught curriculum and the learned curriculum, however, occur in most classrooms, regardless of the specific conditions. (The discussion that follows draws primarily from the review of the research on academic work.)

To achieve success in an accountability-oriented classroom, students invent strategies for managing ambiguity and reducing risk. They will restrict the output they provide teachers, giving vague and limited answers to minimize the risk of making public mistakes. They also attempt to increase the explicitness of a teacher's instructions, asking the teacher for more examples, hints, or rephrasing of the question. Furthermore, they pressure teachers to simplify curriculum complexity, strongly resisting any curriculum that forces them to think, inquire, and discover. Undoubtedly, NCLB tried to address many of these student and classroom issues through accountability and testing. In this regard, NCLB brought about an accountability culture in numerous districts that creates greater coherence through centralized control.

Although assessment and accountability continue to be in the forefront, the role of digital learning in schools today is tremendously exciting and is sparking creative innovations with instructional methodologies. For example, teachers are now using forms of *flipped instruction* in their classrooms (Saltman, 2012). Flipped instruction is not a new concept and is occasionally referred to as backward classroom, reverse instruction, or reverse teaching. Unlike a traditional classroom—where knowledge is conventionally delivered by a teacher—a teacher using a flipped instructional strategy might *first* have students studying a topic on their own utilizing a variety of technological mediums. Using this learning approach, the teacher becomes more of a tutor, resource, or facilitator, thus "flipping" the instructional process. In addition to techniques such as flipped instruction, schools are focusing on different ways to use mobile devices and are implementing BYOD or BYOT (bring your own device or bring your own technology) policies. In fact, mobile devices were recommended for use in schools by the U.S. Department of Education in the National Education Technology Plan (NETP) as early as 2010 (Scholastic Administrator, 2012). Nonetheless, some educators remain justifiably wary of BYOD or BYOT because of the potential for misuse of mobile devices that can create a host of security concerns, including data protection and compliance with the Children's Internet Protection Act (CIPA).

With new technological innovations and better security, online educational communities are springing up across the country (Dobler, 2012). According to Banchero and Simon (2011), the state of Virginia authorized 13 online schools—with more to come. Not to be undone, Florida is requiring all public high school students to take at least one class online, partly to prepare them for college cyber courses. Idaho soon will require two. In Georgia, a new app lets high school students take full course loads on their mobile devices. Thirty states now let students take all of their courses online. According to the International Association for K–12 Online Learning, a trade group, more than 250,000 students nationwide are enrolled in full-time virtual educational experiences. A general search indicated that there are at least 18 or more virtual high schools in Canada and 311 virtual high schools throughout the United States. All of these new ways to reach students have implications for learning. Whether there is a virtual or hybrid educational experience, technology is changing learning and the ways in which students ready themselves for the future.

Along with new developments in technology, systemic planning is melding with up-to-date technological advancements to create digital-aided schools across the globe. Moreover, systemic designs are redirecting educational technology away from its use as a mere tool toward its role in addressing the academic needs for a different generation of learners. The concentration of this approach makes implementation and regular use of technology even more student centered while providing a shared vision as well as awareness on how technology can advance teaching and learning (Whitehead, Jensen, et al., 2013).

COMPONENTS OF THE CURRICULUM

Although several texts in the field seem to treat curriculum development as if it were one undifferentiated process, the realities are quite different. The concept subsumes several distinct entities that might best be described as components of the curriculum. Each of these will be analyzed briefly next and then discussed more fully in the chapters that follow.

Curricular Policies

David Jacobson (2010), senior specialist at Cambridge Education in Westwood, Massachusetts, believes results-oriented approaches explicitly direct administrators to set a specific agenda for school-based teaching teams that have a tighter, more structured, and somewhat more top-down feel. If Jacobson is correct, it appears that few education reforms will be long lasting unless they become institutionalized. And the best way to institutionalize curriculum is to formulate sound curricular policies. Jacobson's views, however, are not intended to dismiss or minimize the importance of collaboration. It is through collaboration and teamwork that educational leaders will truly be able to maximize effective school change and reform.

The term *curricular policies,* as used here, designates the set of rules, criteria, and guidelines intended to manage curriculum development and implementation. In reviewing the literature, Kirst (as cited in Glatthorn, 1987) led the way by noting that there are macro policies, such as a board policy on courses required in high school, and micro-policies, such as a set of recommendations for a curriculum unit in mathematics. Policymaking, as he noted, is essentially the "authoritative allocation of competing values" (p. 15). Thus, as a board makes a policy requiring three years of science in the high school curriculum but does not require any study of art, it is perhaps unwittingly according a higher value to science as a way of knowing than it does to aesthetics. Saylor, Alexander, and Lewis (1981) made a useful distinction between de jure policymaking (as implemented in court decisions, national and state legislative acts, and local agency regulations) and de facto policymaking (as carried out by community networks, testing bureaus, accrediting associations, and advisory boards).

Curriculum Tip 1.6	Educators, administrators, and teachers are well advised to reexamine policies affecting curriculum and the accepted practices at their schools.

The decisions that a school makes regarding established policies and practices can affect students enormously. For example, school boards that prioritize learning for all students help telegraph positive messages to administrators and thus try to invest deeply in human resources, especially professional development (Mizell, 2010). In this regard, school boards and administrators have multiple policies and practices that can and do affect curriculum development. Some policies are deliberately set in place, while others evolve with time.

Curricular Goals

Local district curricular goals are often generated from individual state standards or CCSS. Established goals are generally long-term educational outcomes that the school system expects to achieve through its curriculum. Three critical elements are included in this definition. First, goals are stated much more generally than objectives. Thus, one goal for English language arts (ELA) might be this: Learn to communicate ideas through writing and speaking. One objective for fifth-grade language arts would be much more specific: Write a letter, with appropriate business-letter form, suggesting a community improvement. Second, goals are long-term, not short-term, outcomes. The school system hopes that after 12 years of formal schooling, its students will have achieved the goals the system has set.

Finally, curricular goals are those outcomes the school system hopes to achieve through its curriculum. Here, it is important to make a distinction between educational goals and curricular goals. Educational goals are the long-term outcomes that the school system expects to accomplish through the entire educational process over which it has control, as Brown (2006) found from a survey conducted with educators, parents, and employers as to what type of skills they believed students should be developing. The following is a prioritized list of survey responses:

1. Critical-thinking skills

2. Problem-solving strategies and effective decision-making skills

3. Creative-thinking processes

4. Effective oral and written communication skills

5. Basic reading, mathematics, and writing abilities

6. Knowledge of when and how to use research to solve problems

7.   Effective interpersonal skills

8.   Technology skills

9.   Knowledge of good health and hygiene habits

10. Acceptance and understanding of diverse cultures and ethnicities

11. Knowledge of how to effectively manage money

12. Willingness, strategies, and ability to continue learning

How do curricular policies and curricular goals interrelate? In a sense, the policies establish the rules ("Take three years of health education") and the goals set the targets ("At the end of those three years, you will have adopted constructive health habits"). In this sense, they should determine in a rational system the form and content of all the other components that follow. As will be evident throughout this work, however, educational organizations are usually not very rational. Typically, policies are not related to goals, and goals are not related to fields and programs of study.

Fields of Study

A **field of study** is an organized and clearly demarcated set of learning experiences typically offered over a multiyear period. In most school curricula, such fields of study are equivalent to the standard school subjects: ELA, mathematics, social studies, science, and so on. At the college level, fields are more narrowly defined; thus, students pursue majors in history or anthropology or sociology—not "social studies."

Programs of Study

A **program of study** is the total set of learning experiences offered by a school for a particular group of learners, usually over a multiyear period and typically encompassing several fields of study. The program of study is often described in a policy statement that delineates which subjects are required and which are electives, with corresponding time allocations and credits. Here, for example, is a typical program of studies for an elementary school:

Reading and language arts: Eight hours a week

Social studies: Three hours a week

Mathematics: Four hours a week

Art: One hour a week

Music: One hour a week

Health and physical education: One hour a week

At the college level, a student's program of studies includes all the courses he or she will take or has taken.

Courses of Study

A **course of study** is a subset of both a program of study and a field of study. It is a set of organized learning experiences, within a field of study, offered over a specified period of time (such as a year, a semester, or a quarter) for which the student ordinarily receives academic credit. The course of study is usually given a title and a grade level or numerical designation. Thus, "third-grade science" and "English II" are courses of study. At the college level, courses of study seem to be the most salient component for both students and faculty: "I'm taking Economics I this term"; "I'm offering Elizabethan Literature this quarter."

Units of Study

A **unit of study** is a subset of a course of study. It is an organized set of related learning experiences offered as part of a course of study, usually lasting from one to three weeks. Many units are organized around a single overarching concept, such as "Mythical Creatures" or "The Nature of Conflict." Units of study generally follow established standards.

Robert Marzano (as cited in Marzano, Pickering, & Pollock, 2001) noted that when developing units of study at any level, it is best to view the process as a series of phases. The planning phases of unit development include the following:

- At the beginning of a unit, include strategies for setting learning goals.
- During a unit, include strategies

  - for monitoring progress toward learning goals;
  - for introducing new knowledge; and
  - for practicing, reviewing, and applying knowledge.

- At the end of a unit, include strategies for helping students determine how well they have achieved their goals.

As can be seen, it is a best practice for teachers to present students with components and subcomponents of the unit process and then structure tasks to emphasize a specific component or subcomponent. Marzano's intent is for teachers to systematically utilize strategies that work. These are best-practice approaches and will eventually lead to mastery. As noted by Guskey and Anderman (2014), students who focus on mastery are more likely to persist at academic tasks, especially challenging ones.

Lessons

A **lesson** is a set of related learning experiences typically lasting 20 to 90 minutes, focusing on a relatively small number of objectives. Ordinarily, a lesson is a subset of a unit, although, as noted previously, the unit level is sometimes omitted by teachers while planning for instruction.

These distinctions among the several components of a differentiated curriculum have an importance that transcends the need for conceptual clarity. Each seems to involve some rather different planning processes. Thus, to speak generally about "curriculum planning," without noting the difference between planning a program of studies and planning a course of studies, is to make a rather serious mistake.

Improving and differentiating lessons based on current brain research and curriculum design is becoming a critical component in the search for best practices. Moreover, foundations of differentiated lessons include such strategies as curriculum compacting, flexible grouping, tiered activities, and individual student contracts (Parsons, Dodman, & Burrowbridge, 2013). Clearly, this is an exciting time in the classroom and in education. New learning spaces and innovative applications are providing teachers with instant access to up-to-date information. Teachers wanting to develop creative and exciting lessons are now able to readily reach out to a strong network of colleagues (Ferriter & Provenzano, 2013). Nonetheless, it remains prudent to tie new lessons to tried and true strategies that have proven effective over time.

Marzano and his colleagues (2001) identified the following nine categories of strategies that have a strong effect on student achievement:

1. Identifying similarities and differences

2. Summarizing and note taking

3. Reinforcing effort and providing recognition

4. Doing homework and practicing

5. Allowing for nonlinguistic representations

6. Enhancing cooperative learning

7. Setting objectives and providing feedback

8. Generating and testing hypotheses

9. Formulating questions, cues, and advance organizers

As can be seen from analyzing these nine strategies, students need a fair amount of guidance when learning complex processes.

Classroom teachers, therefore, need to realize that curriculum planning should *emphasize metacognitive control* of all processes. These processes are similar to skills in that they often produce some form of product or new understanding. Teachers intuitively recognize the importance of metacognition but may not be aware of its many dimensions. Metacognitive ability is central to conceptions of what it means to be educated. The world is becoming more complex, more information rich, and more demanding of fresh thinking.

THE MASTERY, THE ORGANIC, AND THE ENRICHMENT CURRICULA

One additional classification system first proposed by Glatthorn (1980) has proven useful, especially in developing and improving fields of study.

The three types of learning result from the following analytical steps. First, divide the learnings in that field between those that are basic and those that are enrichment. Basic learnings are those that, in the views of knowledgeable educators, are essential for all students (all, in this use, refers to the top 90% of learners, excluding the least able and those with serious learning disabilities [LD]). Enrichment learnings are the knowledge and skills that are interesting and enriching but are not considered essential; they are simply "nice to know." Thus, in fifth-grade social studies, curriculum workers might decide that the early settling of the Vikings in Iceland would be interesting enrichment content.

Nonstructured learning, on the other hand, includes all those skills, knowledge, and attitudes that can be mastered without such careful sequencing, planning, testing, and delineation. Structured and nonstructured learning yield the three types of curricula depicted in Exhibit 1.4: mastery, organic, and enrichment.

Once the first division between basic and enrichment is made, then further divide the basic learnings into those that require structure and those that do not require structure. *Structured learning,* as the term is used here, has four characteristics:

EXHIBIT 1.4   The Three Types of Curricula

	Basic	Enrichment
Structured	Mastery	Enrichment
Nonstructured	Organic	Enrichment

1. Sequencing

2. Planning

3. Measurable outcomes

4. Clearly delineated content

Mastery learnings are those that are both basic and structured. An example of a mastery objective for language arts, Grade 2, is the following: Use a capital letter for the first word in a sentence.

Organic learnings, however, are those that are basic but do not require structuring. They are the learnings that develop day by day, rather naturally, as the result of numerous interactions and exchanges. They tend not to be the focus of specific learnings. They are just as important as the mastery outcomes (if not more so), but they do not require sequencing, pacing, and articulating. Here is an example of organic learning for language arts, Grade 2: Listen courteously while others speak.

The teacher might emphasize learning on every occasion, not just devoting a specific lesson to it. And enrichment learnings, as noted previously, are those learnings that simply extend the curriculum; they are not considered basic.

This tripartite division is more than an interesting intellectual exercise. It has significant implications for curriculum development. In general, district curriculum guides and scope-and-sequence charts based on individual state and/or CCSS should focus solely on the mastery elements. The nurturing of organic components can be enhanced through effective professional development; such outcomes do not need to be explicated fully and carefully in guides. The enrichment components can be included in a supplement for those teachers who want to share enrichment activities.

Likewise, curriculum-referenced tests should focus only on mastery elements; organic elements should not be tested. This distinction also has implications for the purchase of texts: Textbooks should focus on the mastery objectives; the teacher can nurture the organic without the aid of textbooks.

Finally, the distinction helps resolve the issue of district versus teacher control. In general, the district should determine the **mastery curriculum**, to the extent of specifying objectives. The district emphasizes the important outcomes but gives the teacher great latitude of choice in nurturing them. In addition, the **enrichment curriculum** is the teacher's own: Here, the teacher can add whatever content he or she feels might be of interest to the students.

Brain Research

In addition to the discussion of mastery and enrichment curriculum, it is also important that teachers be aware of brain research and how students learn. A look into brain research may provide some insight and offer ways to help reduce distractions and increase student attention in the classroom (McDonald, 2010). Thus, rearranging priorities and bringing brain research into teaching is at the forefront of future schooling. According to Brown (2012), a child's brain structure and chemistry change every day and that environment and experiences in the classroom have a profound impact on these changes. By applying a Mind, Brain, and Education (MBE) model espoused by Harvard professor Kurt Fischer, instruction can be directed to make smart decisions in a systematic, intentional, and sequential way. The MBE model can be applied in one or more of four areas that include the following:

1. *Instructional strategies* increase the brain's capacity to learn and change the emotional state of learners.

2. *Enriched environments* encourage optimal learning conditions in school, at home, and in the community.

3. *Deficit correction and cognitive enhancement* builds the foundation for critical thinking.

4. *Evaluation tools* provide feedback to learners, teachers, parents, and community members.

Being mindful of current research on brain development, especially during this digital age, continues to change and evolve. Such findings help educators select the most successful and evidence-based approaches especially for instruction. It is hoped that instruction using phonemic awareness, phonics, fluency, vocabulary, and comprehension strategies will be enhanced with the feedback from neuroimaging research. Additionally, using real-life problem-solving scenarios via technology applications can assist in the process of developing the strongest brain networks that will be formed by actual experience. As a result, most schools are now using critical-thinking and problem-solving skills and strategies as a major part of the curriculum-development process.

| **Curriculum Tip 1.8** | The key to enriching curriculum is to involve students in real-life problem-solving scenarios. |

THE HIDDEN CURRICULUM

The concept of hidden curriculum expresses the idea that schools do more than simply transmit knowledge. In fact, the challenges one faces by a student *inside* the school can easily be connected to and compounded by things that are happening *outside* of school or in the community (Hatch, 2009). Thus, there are differences between written and hidden curricula in that teachers teach and students learn implicit concepts and patterns (Deutsch, 2004). Hidden curriculum, which is sometimes called the "unstudied curriculum" or the "implicit curriculum," might best be defined in the following manner: those aspects of schooling, other than the intentional curriculum, that seem to produce changes in student values, perceptions, and behaviors.

As the definition suggests, students learn a great deal in school from sources other than the intentional curriculum. Although the term *hidden curriculum* is often used with negative connotations, those learnings can be both desirable and undesirable from the viewpoint of one aspiring to optimal human development. In examining the specific nature of the hidden curriculum, it seems useful at this point to distinguish between what might be termed the constants (those aspects of schooling that seem more or less impervious to change) and the variables (those aspects that seem susceptible to reform).

| **Curriculum Tip 1.9** | The hidden curriculum might be seen as those aspects of the learned curriculum that lie outside the boundaries of the school's intentional efforts. |

Another aspect of the hidden curriculum is that of the extracurriculum or cocurriculum. This curriculum embodies all of the school-sponsored programs that are intended to supplement the academic aspect of the school experience: athletics, band/coral groups, clubs, drama, student government, honor societies and/or student organizations, school dances, and social events—all fall under the heading of extracurricular activities. However, participation in these activities is purely voluntary and does not contribute to grades or credits earned toward advancement from one grade to the next or to graduation. Extracurricular activities are typically open to all, though participation often depends on skill level (Ebert, Ebert, & Bentley, 2013).

The Constants of the Hidden Curriculum

Certain aspects of hidden curriculum are so intrinsic to the nature of schools as a cultural institution that they might be seen as constants. Historically, the depiction of those constants presented next has been influenced by a close reading of several early curricular reconceptualists such as Apple (1979), Pinar (1978), and Giroux (1979); sociologists such as Dreeben (1968); and educational researchers such as Jackson (1968) and Goodlad (1984). One of the constants of the hidden curriculum is the ideology of the larger society, which permeates every aspect of schooling. Thus, schools in the United States inevitably reflect the ideology of democratic capitalism.

A key component of the school as an organization is the classroom, where the most salient aspects of the hidden curriculum come into play. The classroom is a crowded place, where issues of control often become dominant. Control is achieved through the differential use of power; the teacher uses several kinds of power to control the selection of content, the methods of learning, movement in the classroom, and the flow of classroom discourse. Control also is achieved by the skillful use of accountability measures; teachers spend much time evaluating and giving evaluative feedback. In such a classroom, students unconsciously learn the skills and traits required by the larger society; they learn how to be punctual, clean, docile, and conforming. They learn how to stand in line, take their turn, and wait.

Even though the previously given features of the hidden curriculum are presented here as constants relatively impervious to change, it is important for curriculum leaders to be aware of their subtle and pervasive influence. Being aware of aspects and variables of the hidden curriculum is crucial for the success of our future administrators and teacher–leaders.

The Variables of the Hidden Curriculum

Several other important aspects of the hidden curriculum can be more readily changed by educators. The most significant of these can be classified into three categories: organizational variables, social-system variables, and social and culture variables.

Organizational Variables

The term *organizational variables* is used here to designate all those decisions about how teachers will be assigned and students grouped for instruction. Here, four issues seem worthy of attention: team teaching, promotion and retention policies, ability grouping, and curriculum tracking. The evidence on the effects of team teaching on student achievement is somewhat inconclusive. Even though many school systems have implemented "promotional gates" policies that promoted students solely on the basis of achievement, several syntheses of the research indicate that social promotion results in better attitudes toward school, better self-image, and improved achievement.

Grouping practices in the schools often have been attacked by critics as one of the most baleful aspects of the hidden curriculum. Here, the denunciation of Giroux and Penna (1979) is perhaps typical of the era then and now:

> The pedagogical foundation for democratic processes in the classroom can be established by eliminating the pernicious practice of "tracking" students. This tradition in schools of grouping students according to "abilities" and perceived performance is of dubious instructional value. (p. 223)

However, Cris Tovani (2010), a high school reading specialist in Colorado, shared, "when strugglers are grouped together, all the experts except the teacher are taken from the mix." She further added, "groups are fine—as long as the teacher frequently changes the configuration" (p. 28).

The chief problem with curriculum tracking, according to researchers, is the lack of challenge in the general curriculum. Many approaches to tracking have been developed to prevent an exodus of public school students to private schools as per NCLB and other government regulations. In contrast to tracking, cooperative heterogeneous learning allows students to be active and social in the pursuit of academic excellence. Learning groups within a heterogeneous classroom have been shown to result in higher achievement, little or no psychological harm to the students, and reduced segregation. Students also gain experience in individual accountability and responsibility, as well as acquiring skills in working with others. Few would argue that increased cooperative learning, along with advanced technology skills, can help to more evenly distribute students. Additionally, student interaction through the use of collaboration and technology promotes the use of higher-level thinking skills and enables students to apply knowledge in new ways (Larson, 2013).

Clearly, the weight of the research suggests educational leaders interested in improving organization should focus attention on promotion policies and curriculum tracking as the key variables. In this regard, they can ensure that the general curriculum is neither dull nor trivial.

Other organizational variables might include connections such as class size, better libraries, breakfast and lunch, noncategorical special help, and better assessment, as well as outside connections such as community activities. Each of these hidden curriculum variables can, and do, affect school change in various ways.

Much discussion has taken place regarding the impact of class size on curriculum planning and implementation. Many authors and researchers believe that smaller class sizes facilitate better teaching and more personalized instruction. Some authors and researchers do not. The key is that smaller class size may facilitate, but does not necessarily ensure, better teaching and learning. Most individuals do agree, however, that class size does affect how the curriculum is delivered, and thus, the curriculum's nature can be implicit.

Breakfast and lunch may lie outside the boundary of curriculum, but they still may have an important impact on planning. For example, classes have to be scheduled around these activities, especially if the cafeteria is located in the gymnasium. Children having to eat late or not having proper nutrition may also influence when and how the curriculum is delivered.

Noncategorical special help has a substantial and yet hidden impact on a school's schedule in that staff may have to adjust classes to compensate for students' being out of the room. Teachers also have to adjust their classroom organization to accommodate students' arriving back into a classroom after receiving special help in another setting.

Of particular interest are special phonics-based programs that can have an impact on curriculum as well. Most educators would agree that a student's knowledge of academic language is vital (Overturf, 2013). As a result of this emphasis on language arts, many classes are scheduled around special phonics-based programs such as Reading Recovery and Read Well. The hidden aspect of these special phonics-based programs is that primary teachers must now schedule their units and lessons around these intensive reading programs to accommodate high-risk children. Nonetheless, there is little doubt as to the positive impact these special programs have on students.

Another factor involves schools with better libraries and/or those providing students with better access to books; they may have an advantage over schools that do not. Getting reading and informational materials to students in a timely manner can be a key to learning. Albeit hidden, the ability of a teacher to access books and materials will make a big difference in how that teacher will teach.

Equally important is the issue of accountability. Assessment and accountability are becoming bywords with the advent of NCLB and Race to the Top, and assessment and data analysis are now becoming major determiners of what is taught, when it is taught, and how it is taught. Entire curricula are being changed based on the collection of assessment data and student test scores.

Although the impact of assessment is not totally understood and often goes unnoticed, extended days and after-school programs appear to be having a major impact on curriculum planning and implementation. Teachers are now being paid extra for extended days to complete in-service and professional development requirements. Additional professional development opportunities often mean that teachers will be learning new material and trying different approaches in their classrooms. The impact of this change on curriculum may be obscure to some, but it is often immeasurable in scope.

Social-System Variables

The concepts of school climate, social networking, and culture are becoming a huge part of the standard rhetoric in contemporary discussions of school effectiveness. School climate can have major implications for curriculum. America's commitment to equity will determine our future (Darling-Hammond, 2010). Darling-Hammond also noted that creating schools that enable all children to learn requires the development of systems that enable all educators to learn. In keeping with her viewpoint, a small but growing number of school leaders are reviewing their districts' social systems and considering the integration of students by socioeconomic status.

Other research findings were related to teacher–student relationships: Teacher–student interactions in general were positive and constructive; students shared in decision making; and there were extensive opportunities for student participation in activities. Obviously, all these factors can be influenced through effective leadership by both administrators and teachers. They are the building blocks of a strong and healthy organizational culture (Waters, 2009).

<table>
<tr><td>**Curriculum Tip 1.10**</td><td>Social and economic issues can affect aspects of the hidden curriculum.</td></tr>
</table>

Social- and economic-related programs such as Head Start and Even Start are designed to assist economically challenged preschool children. Head Start is a federal program that has been around since the 1960s. Some school districts are designing their school operation to have Head Start on campus. This allows a good transition for the Head Start children to matriculate into a kindergarten program. Having Head Start on-site in a school district also enhances opportunities for professional development and offers a way to improve staff relations. Head Start teachers and administrators have an opportunity to plan their curricula so that it threads unnoticed into the district curriculum. On-site Head Start teachers are, thus, better able to understand the goals and objectives of the school district and better able to correlate their programs with district primary teachers.

Two great achievements prevailed in the design of Head Start. First, the program highlighted social and emotional development—emphasizing health, comprehensive services, and social services to families. Second, Head Start introduced parent participation.

Even Start is a family literacy program that includes preschool children and their parents. Both children and parents go to school. Parents work to complete their high school education or receive adult literacy instruction (Michigan Department of Education, 2010). The implicit aspect of this program is that children are provided with an enriched preschool curriculum.

Another social aspect of curriculum that may be hidden is the involvement of parents and community. Although parents may not directly create a change in curriculum, their approval or disapproval can have a tremendous impact on how a school is operated, what is taught, and how it is taught. An example might be the involvement of parents at the primary level and their support of technology. When parents are in the school at the primary level and see the impact that technology is having on their children, they often become major supporters of educational technology. This support is generated in the passage of special levies and bonds that affect the use of technology at all grade levels—even high school.

The involvement of the community can have an impact on curriculum development in much the same way. If members of the community feel positive about what is happening in their schools, they are much more apt to support the schools financially. This financial support might include more staff, improved facilities, materials, and/or professional development. The connection to the curriculum may not be readily apparent to some, but it is definitely a major factor in the success of the school.

Equally important are concerns over social media and cyberbullying. As the shift of responsibility for safety and proper use of technology moves into a shared framework among educators, students, and families, curriculum and teacher–leaders have a variety of constructs they need to address. Often, in the form of mean or threatening text messages, e-mails, rumors, or gossip posted on Web site, cyberbullying is becoming a major concern. This misuse of social media can be devastating for any individual as well as very disruptive in any school setting (Whitehead, Jensen, & Boschee, 2013).

Social and Culture Variables

Developing understandings involving social, cultural, and gender bias is becoming increasingly important in education. According to Medlin and Bang (2013–2014), social and cultural issues exist throughout many, if not most, school districts and classrooms. Although sometimes hidden or unseen, cultural differences, gender bias, and individual socioeconomic circumstances often relate to student learning and academic performance as well as to how children see themselves with others. For this reason alone, it is paramount that curriculum leaders and teachers understand the importance and role of individual diversity. Of particular importance is the selection of materials. When reviewing possible texts and resources, educators need to be sensitive as to individual needs. According to Silva, Delleman, and Phesia (2013), a focus on skills should include the following:

1. Identifying support for main ideas

2. Recognizing bias

3. Distinguishing arguments and corresponding counterarguments

4. Evaluating relative strength of arguments

5. Drawing conclusions based on evidence

Creating and implementing instruction that supports social and cultural capital awareness is a major aspect of addressing hidden curriculum concerns. Likewise, formulating challenging units and lessons that meet the rigor of CCSS as well as state standards is a crucial step in providing equity for all students.

Although cultural differences, organizational factors, and social systems are often a part of any hidden curriculum, they are nevertheless a very real part of everyday school life and in every classroom. Because hidden curriculum is so prevalent, it can have numerous implications for student learning. With this in mind, Glatthorn and Jailall (2009) identified a number of key factors relating to hidden curriculum:

- *Time allocation:* For example, are health and physical education allocated sufficient time to change the behavior of children and youth?
- *Space allocation:* How much space is allocated for teacher conferring and planning?
- *Use of discretionary funds:* How are such funds expended, and who decides this?
- *Student discipline:* Do suspensions seem to reflect an ethnic bias?
- *Physical appearance:* Does the appearance of facilities suggest that those in the building care for the school? Are walls decorated with student artwork?
- *Student activities program:* Does this program reflect and respond to student talent diversity?

- *Communication:* Are most of the messages over the public address system of a positive nature? How often are student voices heard?
- *Power:* Do teachers have power in the decision-making process? Do students have any real power over the factors that matter? (pp. 115–116)

These aspects of the hidden curriculum can be greatly minimized by administrators and teachers working collaboratively. Identifying problem areas and addressing concerns together can move any school toward success.

To summarize, then, hidden curriculum is seen here as both constant and variable aspects of schooling (other than the intentional curriculum) that produce changes in the student. The constants—the ideology of the larger society, the way in which certain knowledge is deemed important or unimportant, and the power relationships that seem necessary in large bureaucratic institutions—seem unlikely to change. However, the variables—those

EXHIBIT 1.5   Relationships of Types of Curricula

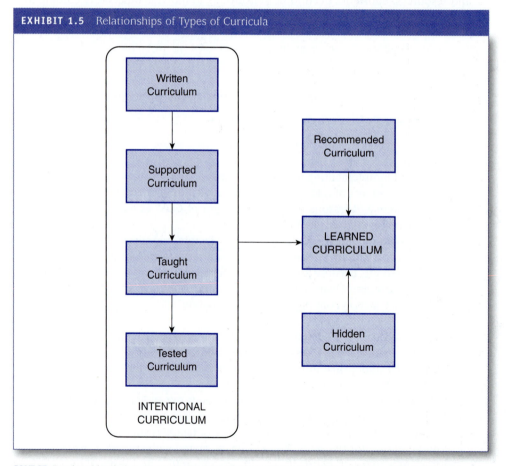

SOURCE: Developed by Mark A. Baron, Chairperson, Division of Educational Administration, School of Education, the University of South Dakota.

aspects of the organizational structure, the social systems, and the culture of the school that can be influenced—require the systematic attention and collaboration of curriculum leaders and teachers.

In reviewing the intentional, recommended, and hidden curriculums, a coming together of the three can be observed. Exhibit 1.5 illustrates how the intentional curriculum and the hidden curriculum extend into the learned curriculum.

SUMMARY

This introductory chapter provides a general overview of the curriculum field and a set of concepts for analyzing that field. The chapter defines the concept of curriculum and standards, examines the several types of curricula, describes the contrasting nature of curriculum components, and analyzes the hidden curriculum to provide some fundamental concepts essential for understanding the comprehensive field of curriculum. The chapter includes the topics of what curriculum is and why it is important; the types and components of curricula and how they have changed over the years; what mastery, organic, and enrichment curricula are and the roles they play in the development of curriculum; and why knowledge of the hidden curriculum is so important for school success.

APPLICATIONS

1. By reviewing the definitions of *curriculum* provided in this chapter and reflecting on your own use of the term, write your own definition of *curriculum*.

2. Some educators have suggested that the profession should use simpler definitions for *curriculum* and *instruction:* Curriculum is what is taught; instruction is how it is taught. Do these definitions seem to suffice, from your perspective? Why or why not?

3. Descriptive curriculum has numerous definitions, which can be slightly confusing. Based on the general definitions provided by educators and their operational distinctions, rank the three examples provided in Exhibit 1.2 and explain why your selection meets the criteria.

4. Some leaders have argued for a very close fit between the written and the taught curriculum, suggesting that teachers should teach only what is in the prescribed curriculum. Others have suggested teachers should have some autonomy and latitude, as long as they cover the essentials. What is your own position on this issue?

5. Although most curriculum texts do not make the distinctions noted here between programs of study, fields of study, and courses of study, those distinctions do seem to matter. To test this hypothesis, do the following: (a) List the steps you would follow in designing a program of studies for one level of schooling, such as elementary or middle school, and (b) list the steps you would follow in designing a field of study, such as social studies, K–12.

6. It has been suggested here that the "constants" of the hidden curriculum are not easily changed. Others would argue that they should be changed if we truly desire democratic and humanistic schools. As a school leader, would you attempt to change any of those constants, or would you give more attention to the "variables"?

7. Should the extracurriculum or cocurriculum be part of the hidden curriculum? Yes or no? Explain your reason(s).

8. Outline a change strategy you would use in attempting to improve the "culture" variables that seem to be associated with improved attitude and achievement.

9. It seems that in our profession, every year is the year of something—critical thinking, self-esteem, site-based management, portfolio assessment, outcome-based education, Goals 2000, NCLB, and on it goes. They come and they go. Now we have CCSS for ELA and mathematics adopted by many states. With this in mind, how will the CCSS standards movement move us ahead in some great way? Or will they not?

10. School district and state level education leaders are charged with developing and administering educational curricula to best prepare students for their future. Yet there can be tension between a curriculum that develops a well-rounded student and a curriculum that helps create a student who is career ready. Does tension exist? Yes or no? Why?

11. Do you agree or disagree with the states that have rejected or nullified the CCSS? Why or why not?

| CASE STUDY | Bridging the Gap Between Theory and Practice |

Dr. John Summers was hired to be the curriculum director to enhance the teaching and learning process for the Dover School District. Dr. Summers was the superintendent's choice for the position because he was highly qualified in the area of curriculum development, and his performance at a somewhat smaller school district with 5,000 students, in a neighboring state, was outstanding. The district Dr. Summers came from was known for its high academic achievement, which was attributed to a well-planned curriculum supported by the principals and teacher–leaders.

In contrast, the Dover School District was in curriculum disarray, and student achievement was low when compared with statewide achievement scores. As Dr. Summers soon discovered, some staff members and administrators in the Dover School District construed the curriculum as ideal because it met their standards. They also felt that if something was being taught, a curriculum existed. Others in the district, however, felt that a planned curriculum was vital for the district, but they were unable to generate the necessary leadership to bridge the gap between theory and practice.

The Challenge

How should Dr. Summers utilize administrators and teacher–leaders to help bridge the gap between curriculum theory and practice?

Key Issues or Questions

1. To what extent do you believe a written curriculum for the various disciplines plays a role in this case?

2. To what extent do you believe the supported, tested, and learned curricula for the various disciplines play a role in improving the intentional curriculum?

3. Do you think there is any hope of changing attitudes? If so, how would you attempt to do this? If not, why?

4. Do you feel that the intentional curriculum is prescriptive or descriptive, or a combination of both? Why?

5. What roles do the recommended curriculum and hidden curriculum play in developing the intentional curriculum?

6. In planning curricula, mastery curriculum should require from 60% to 75% of the time available. Do you agree that Dr. Summers should place an emphasis on mastery curriculum? Why?

WEBLIOGRAPHY

ASCD
www.ascd.org

Center for Research on Education, Diversity & Excellence (CREDE)
http://manoa.hawaii.edu/coe/crede/?p = 79

Common Core State Standards (CCSS)
www.corestandards.org

eSchool News
www.eschoolnews.com

Free Virtual Worlds for Kids
http://familyinternet.about.com/od/websites/tp/virtualworldskids.htm

Teaching for Change
www.teachingforchange.org

Teaching With Technology
www.bu.edu/jlengel and www.lengel.net

Textbooks Matching Common Core Standards
http://stateimpact.npr.org/florida/2014/02/26/studies-find-textbooks-are-a-poor-match-for-common-standards

REFERENCES

Apple, M. W. (1979, Winter). On analyzing hegemony. *Journal of Curriculum Theorizing, 1,* 10–43.

Banchero, S., & Simon, S. (2011, November 12). My teacher is an app. *The Wall Street Journal.* Retrieved from http://online.wsj.com/article/SB100 01424052970204358004577030600066250144.html

Bergman, D. J., & Bergman, C. C. (2010). Elements of stylish teaching: Lessons from Strunk and White. *Phi Delta Kappan, 91*(4), 28–31.

Berliner, D. C. (1984). The half-full glass: A review of research on teaching. In P. L. Hosford (Ed.), *Using what we know about teaching* (pp. 511–577). Alexandria, VA: ASCD.

Blair, N. (2012). Technology integration for the new 21st century learner. *Principal, 91*(3), 8–11.

Brown, B. L. (2012). Bringing brain research into teaching. *Principal, 91*(3), 34–35.

Brown, D. F. (2006). It's the curriculum, stupid: There's something wrong with it. *Phi Delta Kappan, 87*(10), 777–783.

Bryk, A. S. (2010). Organizing schools for improvement. *Phi Delta Kappan, 91*(7), 23–30.

Caswell, H. L., & Campbell, D. S. (1935). *Curriculum development*. New York: American Book Company.

Chesley, G. M., & Jordan, J. (2012) What's missing from teacher prep? *Educational Leadership, 69*(8), 41–45.

Cox, J. (2000). Are standards worth it? *Thrust for Educational Leadership, 29*(5), 5–8.

Darling-Hammond, L. (2010). America's commitment to equity will determine our future. *Phi Delta Kappan, 91*(4), 8.

Deutsch, N. (2004, November 9). *Hidden curriculum paper*. Retrieved from http://www.nelliemuller.com/HiddenCurriculum.doc

Dewey, J. (1902). *The child and the curriculum*. Chicago, IL: University of Chicago Press.

Dobler, E. (2012). Flattening classroom walls: Edmodo takes teaching and learning across the globe. *International Reading Association, 29*(4), 12–13.

Dreeben, R. (1968). *On what is learned in schools*. Reading, MA: Addison-Wesley.

Ebert, E. S., II, Ebert, C., Bentley, M. L. (2013, July 19). *The educator's field guide*. Thousand Oaks, CA: Corwin.

Ellis, A. K. (2004). *Exemplars of curriculum theory*. Larchmont, NY: Eye on Education.

Espinoza, R. (2012). Finding pivotal moments. *Educational Leadership, 69*(7), 56–59.

Ferriter, W. M., & Provenzano, N. (2013). Today's lesson: Self-directed learning for teachers. *Phi Delta Kappan, 95*(3), 16–21.

Gardner, N. S., & Powell, R. (2013). The common core is a change for the better. *Phi Delta Kappan, 95*(4), 49–53.

Giroux, H. A. (1979). Toward a new sociology of curriculum. *Educational Leadership, 37*(3), 248–253.

Giroux, H. A., & Penna, A. N. (1979). Social education in the classroom: The dynamics of the hidden curriculum. In H. A. Giroux, A. N. Penna, & W. F. Pinar (Eds.), *Curriculum and instruction* (pp. 209–230). Berkeley, CA: McCutchan.

Glatthorn, A. A. (1980). *A guide for developing an English curriculum for the eighties*. Urbana, IL: National Council of Teachers of English.

Glatthorn, A. A. (1987). *Curriculum leadership*. New York, NY: HarperCollins.

Glatthorn, A. A., & Jailall, J. M. (2009). *The principal as curriculum leader: Shaping what is taught and tested*. Thousand Oaks, CA: Corwin Press.

Goodlad, J. I. (1984). *A place called school: Prospects for the future*. New York, NY: McGraw-Hill.

Goodlad, J. I., & Associates. (1979). *Curriculum inquiry: The study of curriculum practice*. New York, NY: McGraw-Hill.

Gorski, P. C. (2013). Building a pedagogy of engagement for students in poverty. *Phi Delta Kappan, 95*(1), 48–52.

Guskey, T. R., & Anderman, E. M. (2014). In search of a useful definition of mastery. *Educational Leadership, 71*(4), 18–23.

Hanson, S. G. (2010). What mentors learn about teaching. *Educational Leadership, 67*(8), 76–80.

Hatch, T. (2009). The outside-inside connection. *Educational Leadership, 67*(2), 17–21.

Indiana Department of Education. (2010). *Definition of terms*. Indiana Accountability System for Academic Progress. Retrieved from http://www.doe.in.gov/asap/definitions.html

Ivey, G. (2010). Texts that matter. *Educational Leadership, 67*(6), 18–23.

Jackson, P. (1968). *Life in classrooms*. New York, NY: Holt, Rinehart & Winston.

Jacobson, D. (2010). Coherent instructional improvement and PLCs: Is it possible to do both? *Phi Delta Kappan, 91*(6), 38–45.

Karweit, N. C. (1983). *Time-on-task: A research review*. Baltimore, MD: Johns Hopkins University, Center for Social Organization of Schools.

Kendall, J. S. (2011). *Understanding common core state standards*. Alexandria, VA: ASCD.

Larson, R. (2013). Collaborate to integrate technology. *Principal, 92*(5), 44–45.

Mahurt, S. F. (2013). Developing the critical skills the new CCSS assessments will measure. *Reading Today, 31*(2), 22–24.

Martinez, M. (2010). Innovation: Imponderable or ponderables? *Phi Delta Kappan, 91*(5), 72–73.

Marzano, R., Pickering, D., & Pollock, J. (2001). *Classroom instruction that works: Research-based strategies for increasing student achievement*. Alexandria, VA: ASCD.

McDonald, E. S. (2010). A quick look into the middle school brain. *Principal, 89*(3), 46–47.

Medlin, D. L., & Bang, M. (2013–2014). Culture in the classroom. *Phi Delta Kappan, 95*(4), 64–67.

Michigan Department of Education. (2010). *Even start family literacy program.* Retrieved from http://www.michigan.gov/mde/0,4615,7-140-6530_6809-20426—,00.html

Mizell, H. (2010). School boards should focus on learning for all. *Phi Delta Kappan, 91*(6), 20–23.

National Education Association. (2011). *Class size.* Retrieved from http://www.nea.org/home/13120.htm

Overturf, B. J. (2013). Multiple ways to learn words: The keys to vocabulary development in the ELA Standards. *Reading Today, 31*(2), 14–15.

Parsons, S. A., Dodman, S. L., & Burrowbridge, S. C. (2013). Broadening the view of differentiated instruction. *Phi Delta Kappan 95*(1), 38–42.

Pinar, W. F. (1978). The reconceptualization of curriculum studies. *Journal of Curriculum Studies, 10*(3), 205–214.

Popham, W. J. (2007). Instructional insensitivity of tests: Accountability's dire drawback. *Phi Delta Kappan, 89*(2), 146–147.

Popham, W. J. (2009). A process—not a test. *Educational Leadership, 66*(7), 85–86.

Ragan, W. B. (1960). *Modern elementary curriculum* (Rev. ed.). New York, NY: Henry Holt.

Rauh, R. (2014). *Transcript of the copy of* The digital divide. Retrieved from http://prezi.com/fkkqwbgiemvy/copy-of-the-digital-divide

Saltman, D. (2012). Flipping for beginners: Inside the new classroom craze. *Harvard Educational Press, Tech Talk, 27*(6), 1, 2. Retrieved from http://www.hepg.org/hel/article/517

Scholastic Administrator. (2012). *BYOD to school?* Retrieved from http://www.scholastic.com/browse/article.jsp?id=3756757

Saylor, J. G., Alexander, W. M., & Lewis, A. J. (1981). *Curriculum planning for better teaching and learning* (4th ed.). New York, NY: Holt, Rinehart & Winston.

Silva, J., Delleman, P., & Phesia, A. (2013). Preparing English language learners for complex reading. *Educational Leadership, 71*(3), 52–56.

Smith, M. W., Wilhelm, J. D., & Fredricksen, J. (2013). Common core: New standards, new teaching. *Phi Delta Kappan, 94*(8), 45–46.

Stallings, J. (1980). Allocated learning time revisited, or beyond time on task. *Educational Researcher, 9*(4), 11–16.

Tomlinson, C. A. (2013–2014). One to grow on: Let's not dilute mastery. *Educational Leadership, 71*(4), 88–89.

Tomlinson, C. A., Burns, D., Renzulli, J. S., Kaplan, S. N., Leppien, J., & Purcell, J. (2002). *The parallel curriculum: A design to develop high potential and challenge high-ability learners.* Thousand Oaks, CA: Corwin Press.

Tovani, C. (2010). I got grouped. *Educational Leadership, 67*(6), 24–29.

Tyler, R. W. (1957). The curriculum then and now. In *Proceedings of the 1956 Invitational Conference on Testing Problems.* Princeton, NJ: Educational Testing Service.

Wagner, T. (2008). *The global achievement gap.* New York, NY: Basic Books.

Walker, D. (1979). Approaches to curriculum development. In J. Schaffarzick & G. Sykes (Eds.), *Value conflicts and curriculum issues: Lessons from research and experience* (pp. 263–290). Berkeley, CA: McCutchan.

Waters, T. (2009, Summer). Message from the CEO. *Changing Schools, 60.*

Waters, T., Marzano, R. J., & McNulty, B. (2003). *Balanced leadership: What 30 years of research tells us about the effect of leadership on student achievement* [Working paper]. Aurora, CO: McREL.

Whitehead, B. M., Boschee, F., & Decker, R. H. (2013). *The principal: Leadership for a global society.* Thousand Oaks, CA: Sage.

Whitehead, B. M., Jensen, D. F. N., & Boschee, F. (2013). *Planning for technology: A guide for school administrators, technology coordinators, and curriculum leaders* (2nd ed.). Thousand Oaks, CA: Corwin Press.

Wilson, L. O. (2005). *Curriculum: Different types.* Retrieved from http://www.uwsp.edu/Education/lwilson/curric/curtyp.htm

Wolk, S. (2010). What should students read? *Phi Delta Kappan, 91*(7), 8–16.

Zirkel, P. A. (2013). High-stakes testing: Administrator consequences. *Principal, 92*(5), 54–55.

CHAPTER 2

Curriculum History

The Perspective of the Past

It is history that establishes where we were, where we are, and how we got to where we are.

—Neil R. Fenske (1997, p. 4)

Understanding the history of curriculum development is useful for both scholars and practitioners. It results in a deeper awareness of the extent to which curricular changes are often influenced by and are a manifestation of larger social forces. It also offers a broader perspective from which to view so-called innovations and reforms, which often seem to reverberate with echoes of the past. For that reason, it is important that all children, regardless of their personal circumstances, have an equal opportunity to succeed as individuals and citizens in our rapidly evolving world (Connelly, 2010).

This understanding seems especially facilitated by a careful analysis of the past 100-plus years of that history. Such a demarcation results in a closer focus on the major developments affecting American schools while still providing the broader perspective that is so essential. Those developments perhaps can be better grasped if analyzed as parts of specific periods of history. Of course, an obvious fallacy occurs in delineating such periods. Historical periods become an artifact of the historian's analysis: People do not live and events do not occur in neat chronological packages called "periods." Given that caution, an analysis of the past century plus a decade of curriculum history seems to suggest that there were eight distinct eras, each with its own distinguishing features. Exhibit 2.1 is, therefore, suggested as a way of examining the past century plus a decade of curriculum theory and practice.

EXHIBIT 2.1	Educational Eras
1890–1916	Academic Scientism
1917–1940	Progressive Functionalism
1941–1956	Developmental Conformism
1957–1967	Scholarly Structuralism
1968–1974	Romantic Radicalism
1975–1989	Privatistic Conservatism
1990–1999	Technological Constructionism
2000–2009	Modern Conservatism
2010–Present	Technological Functionalism

Although the verity of the nine eras may be accepted by most individuals, it follows that any attempt to understand or instigate educational reform would be based on an inquiry of what has occurred in the past.

The following was described by Sarason (1990):

> The significance of the historical stance is not only in what it tells us about the manifestations of a particular problem over time, or what one learns about the efficacy of remedial actions, but also in what one learns about the system quality—that is, the features of the system in which the problem arises and recurs, or remains constant but unremarked until it is seen [again] as destabilizing the system. (p. 34)

Sarason also concluded that "one can write human history as a saga of the inability to recognize the obvious" (p. 146). "The important lesson is to keep reinventing the present in order to prepare for the future" (McCollum, 2010, p. 52).

Questions addressed in this chapter include the following:

- What were the periods of Academic Scientism, Progressive Functionalism, Developmental Conformism, Scholarly Structuralism, Romantic Radicalism, Privatistic Conservatism, Technological Constructionism, Modern Conservatism, and Technological Functionalism, and why was each important in the development of curriculum?
- How did the "temper of the times" for each period influence curriculum?
- What were some of the predominant trends that transcended each major period of curriculum development?

Key to Leadership

In reviewing curriculum history, two general observations should be made. The first is to note the pace of change. The second is to note the rhythms and directions of that change.

ACADEMIC SCIENTISM (1890–1916)

The term used here to identify the period from 1890 to 1916, **Academic Scientism**, derives from the two influences that seemed to predominate: the academic and the scientific. The academic influence was the result of systematic and somewhat effective efforts of the colleges to shape the curriculum for basic education; the scientific influence resulted from the attempts of educational theorists to use newly developed scientific knowledge in making decisions about the mission of the school and the content of the curriculum.

Curriculum Tip 2.1	There is an undeviating relationship between curriculum of the past and curriculum today.

The Temper of the Times

The educational trends of this period can perhaps best be discerned if viewed against the backdrop of societal changes. The turn of the century was characterized, first of all, by the post–Civil War growth of industry and the development of urban areas, stimulated primarily by the rapid growth of railroads.

The second distinguishing feature of the era was the impact of popular journalism. The linotype machine was introduced in 1890, the price of newspapers dropped to one cent, and the number of newspapers doubled. Magazines were also reaching larger audiences. Finally, it was a time when new immigrant waves were reaching these shores. The volume of immigrants increased, and their places of origin changed markedly. Whereas prior to the 1890s immigrants came chiefly from the Western European countries, during the turn-of-the-century decades, they were more likely to come from the Eastern European countries.

The Predominant Trends

As noted previously, the major educational influences of the period were both academic and scientific. The man who most clearly represented the academic influence of the colleges was Charles W. Eliot, president of Harvard University. In a perhaps immodest fashion, Eliot saw the entire curriculum as his purview, making specific recommendations for elementary, secondary, and higher education. In essence, Eliot's position was that a sound academic curriculum was best for all students, regardless of their college aspirations.

The scientific influence was perhaps stronger, even though less direct. One interesting sign of this scientific influence was the change of one of the major educational organizations: What had once been the Herbart Society changed its name in 1900 to the National Society for the Scientific Study of Education.

The scientific perspective seemed to influence educational thinkers in three important ways. First, science provided intellectual support for a rational and meliorist worldview, a view widely held by the educational thinkers of the period. Problems could be solved by the rational application of scientific processes: All that was needed was more knowledge and the ability to apply that knowledge.

Second, science provided a content focus for the curriculum. Flexner (1916) was one of several theoreticians who argued for the primacy of science. In his view, the central purpose of the school was to prepare children to cope in the real world—and that preparation would best be accomplished through a study of the physical and social world.

Finally, science provided a means for improving the schools. Scientific knowledge about the child yielded insights, proponents argued, about the desired nature of the curriculum—about what children could learn. Scientific knowledge also offered a rationale for the optimal methods of teaching.

The Exemplary Leaders

The major thrusts of this period were probably best represented by the careers and contributions of G. Stanley Hall and Francis W. Parker.

G. Stanley Hall

G. Stanley Hall (1904/1969) was an eminent psychologist who provided scientific support to the child-centered educators of the day. While earlier developmentalists had argued for the study of the child as the basis for curricular decision making, it was Hall who provided the charismatic leadership for the movement. As a social Darwinian, he believed in evolutionary social change, not radical transformation. The essential task of the school was to support this gradual change through the nurturing of the gifted, providing the gifted child with the opportunity to grow through individualized activities.

Francis W. Parker

Francis W. Parker seems to have had even more influence than G. Stanley Hall; in fact, John Dewey (1964) himself called Parker "the father of progressive education." Parker is significant for his contributions to both pedagogy and curriculum development. The pedagogical methods he advocated could perhaps best be described as natural, child-centered methods.

His contributions to curriculum theory were similarly comprehensive. In his *Talks on Pedagogics* (1894), he argued for a child-centered curriculum that builds on what the child instinctively knows. In contrast to Hall's essentially conservative orientation, Parker was in almost every respect a progressive who believed that the common school was the key to human advancement. In a chapter in his pedagogic work, he anticipated at least the rhetoric of more current social reformers: "This mingling, fusing, and blending [of children from all social classes] give personal power, and make the public school a tremendous force for the upbuilding of democracy" (p. 421).

The Major Publications

The major publications of the Academic Scientism period were perhaps the reports of two committees established by the National Education Association (NEA): one by the **Committee of Ten,** appointed to make recommendations for the high school curriculum, and the other by the **Committee of Fifteen,** for the elementary curriculum.

The Committee of Ten

Although many educators cite the work of the Committee of Ten as an example of the attempt of colleges to dominate the curriculum, the committee was appointed by the NEA at the request of members. There was so much variation in college preparatory curricula in schools across the country that school administrators themselves desired more uniformity.

The major recommendation of the committee report (NEA, 1893) was that four separate programs of study be offered to high school students: classical, Latin scientific, modern languages, and English. In essence, the Committee of Ten said to the profession and to the public, "A sound academic curriculum is the best preparation for life—for all students."

The Committee of Fifteen

The other committee appointed by the NEA at almost the same time was given the charge of making recommendations for elementary curriculum and instruction. Eliot had some influence with this committee, which accepted two of his recommendations: that the number of elementary grades be reduced from 10 to 8 and that algebra be substituted for arithmetic in Grades 7 and 8. However, it rejected his recommendation that the time devoted to grammar and arithmetic be reduced so that the program could be diversified and enriched (the committee's recommendations were outlined in the NEA 1895 report).

In its curriculum recommendations, the Committee of Fifteen advocated a rather conservative approach. Grammar, literature, arithmetic, geography, and history were seen as the central subjects for training the mind, and clear separation of those subjects was essential. The following subjects were to be taught every year, from first to eighth: reading, English grammar (except in the eighth year), geography, natural science and hygiene, general history, physical culture, vocal music, and drawing. Handwriting was to be taught in the first six years, and spelling lists in Grades 4, 5, and 6. Latin was to be introduced in the eighth year, and manual training (for boys) and sewing and cooking (for girls) in the seventh and eighth. In mathematics, arithmetic was to be studied in the first through the sixth years, followed by algebra in the seventh and eighth.

In addition to the required oral lessons in general history for all grades, U.S. history was to be taught in the seventh year and the first half of the eighth; the Constitution was to be taught in the second half of the eighth year. Thus, a pupil in the fourth year would be studying 11 separate "branches" or subjects: reading, handwriting, spelling lists, English grammar, arithmetic, geography, natural science and hygiene, general history, physical culture, vocal music, and drawing.

The ultimate impact of the Committee of Fifteen report was to sustain a somewhat fragmented and subject-centered curriculum.

PROGRESSIVE FUNCTIONALISM (1917–1940)

The era of **Progressive Functionalism,** which lasted from approximately 1917 to 1940, was characterized by the confluence of two seemingly disparate views: the progressive, child-centered orientation of the followers of John Dewey and the functional orientation of curriculum scientists.

The Temper of the Times

The decade of the 1920s was a time of seemingly unbridled optimism and growth in this country. Houses were being built at a record-making pace. By 1929, there were more than 26 million cars registered: one car for every five people.

All that optimism and growth was tragically destroyed in the Depression and the very slow recovery that followed. The human suffering of that period is difficult to exaggerate. At one point, it was estimated that 28% of the population was without any income at all. Many school systems simply shut down because there was no money to pay teachers.

The international picture was no less depressing, for the 1930s was the decade marking the rise of Hitler in Germany and Stalin in the Soviet Union, both of whom were ultimately responsible for the mass genocide carried out in both nations. Confronted with the global rapacity of the dictators in Germany, Italy, the Soviet Union, and Japan, the Western democratic governments seemed for many years to be confused and impotent.

The Predominant Trends

As noted previously, the term given this era derives from two forces—progressivism and functionalism—that, while seemingly antithetical in principle, often combined to influence both curriculum and instruction.

Progressivism in Education

It is obviously difficult in the brief space available to summarize a movement so complex and so often misunderstood as progressive education. Whereas in the prior decade the dominating influence of the curriculum was the academic subject, for progressive educators it was the child. The child-centered curriculum was based on a somewhat romantic and perhaps even naive view of child development: The child is innately curious and creative, with a thirst for learning and a need for self-expression. Such a view has clear implications for both the process and the content of the curriculum. In using a curriculum-development process, child-centered curriculum workers begin by determining the child's interests, assured that any desired content can be linked with those interests.

The content of the curriculum is similarly influenced. The arts are emphasized, because the nurturing of creativity is paramount. Subjects that have little immediate appeal to the child, such as mathematics and grammar, tend to be slighted.

Functionalism

Functionalism is the term given here to the educational theory of those whom Kliebard (1985) called "the social efficiency educators," who argued essentially that the curriculum should be derived from an analysis of the important functions or activities of adult life. As a curriculum theory, it was clearly influenced by two significant ideas current at the time: It was avowedly influenced by the stimulus response learning theory of Edward Thorndike that supported the importance of successful practice, and it reflected the concern for efficiency at the heart of the "scientific management" of Frederick Taylor (1911) and his followers. Taylor argued that any task could be analyzed for optimal efficiency by observing skilled workers, studying the operations they carried out, determining the time required, and eliminating wasted motion. Similarly, education could be made more efficient by analyzing learning tasks.

The Exemplary Leaders

Two figures seem to stand out in retrospect: John Dewey and Franklin Bobbitt. Although they espoused diametrically contrary views of the curriculum in particular, they both seemed to exert a strong influence on their contemporaries.

John Dewey

In a sense, it is fallacious to identify Dewey as a leader of this period alone, because his career as a philosopher and an educator spanned the eras of both Academic Scientism and Progressive Functionalism (Dewey, 1964).

Dewey's (1900) beliefs about the relationship of school and society are, of course, fundamental to his theories of the curriculum and are best understood at the outset. For Dewey, democracy was the ideal society, and he believed that the society can prevail only as it enables diverse groups to form common interests, to interact freely, and to achieve a mutual adaptation. Dewey (1916) pointed out in his book *Democracy and Education* that such a society needed schools for more than the superficial reason of producing an educated electorate.

It was this concern for the social nature of schooling and learning that led him to place so much emphasis on experience. Yet he did not advocate a mindless activity-centered curriculum in which any activity is considered worthwhile as long as it is perceived by the learners as interesting and relevant. In *Experience and Education,* Dewey (1938) noted that experience and education cannot be directly equated; some experiences are "mis-educative," to use his term. Desirable learning experiences had to meet certain stringent criteria: They had to be democratic and humane, they had to be growth enhancing, they had to arouse curiosity and strengthen initiative, and they had to enable the individual to create meaning.

Franklin Bobbitt

Franklin Bobbitt was the other curriculum theorist who seemed to exert a profound influence on the schools of his time and who still seems to affect indirectly even those who are not familiar with his work. The curriculum, in his view, was whatever was needed to process the raw material (the child) into the finished product (the model adult). He summarized in this early work the curriculum process as he saw it in the following manner:

1. We need first to draw up in detail for each social or vocational class of students in our charge a list of all of the abilities and aspects of personality for the training of which the school is responsible.

2. Next, we need to determine scales of measurement in terms of which of these many different aspects of the personality can be measured.

3. We must determine the amount of training that is socially desirable for each of these different abilities and state these amounts in terms of the scales of measurement.

4. We must have progressive standards of attainment for each stage of advance in the normal development of each ability in question. When these four sets of things are at hand for each differentiated social or vocational class, then we shall have for the first time a scientific curriculum for education worthy of our present age of science. (Bobbitt, 1913, p. 49)

Thus, while both Dewey and Bobbitt espoused a social meliorist view of the purpose of schooling, they differed sharply in their conception of the curriculum. From Dewey's (1902) perspective, the developing child was the beginning point for curriculum development; from Bobbitt's, the model adult was the starting point. Furthermore, while Dewey embraced an experience-centered program in which learnings emerged somewhat organically and informally from social interactions, Bobbitt seemed more concerned with a precise scientific matching of activity with outcome.

The Major Publications

Obviously, the writings of both Dewey and Bobbitt had an important influence on educational leaders of the time. However, two other works might be seen to have had a more direct impact: *The Cardinal Principles of Secondary Education* (Commission on the Reorganization of Secondary Education, 1918) and *The Foundations of Curriculum-Making* (Rugg, 1927b). While quite different in both their genesis and their intended audience, the two publications were surprisingly similar in their major emphases.

The Cardinal Principles of Secondary Education

In 1913, the NEA, perceiving a need to reconcile some important differences about the nature of secondary education, appointed the Commission on the Reorganization of Secondary Education. After five years of deliberation, the commission published its recommendations.

The commission was also instrumental in starting a standard of forming goals before reforming schools. Changes were needed because of increased enrollment in secondary schools. A new focus that would take into account individual differences, goals, attitudes, and abilities was adopted. The concept of democracy was decided on as the guide of education in the United States. Work on the Cardinal Principles was started in 1915 and finished in 1918. The seven Cardinal Principles of Secondary Education are as follows:

1. *Health.* A secondary school should encourage good health habits, give health instruction, and provide physical activities. Good health should be taken into account when schools and communities are planning activities for youth. The general public should be educated on the importance of good health. Teachers should be examples for good health and schools should furnish good equipment and safe buildings.

2. *Command of fundamental processes.* Fundamental processes are writing, reading, oral and written expression, and math. It was decided that these basics should be applied to newer material instead of using the older ways of doing things.

3. *Worthy home membership.* This principle "calls for the development of those qualities that make the individual a worthy member of a family, both contributing to and deriving benefit from that membership" (Raubinger, Rowe, Piper, & West, 1969, p. 108). This principle should be taught through literature, music, social studies, and art. Coed schools should show good relationships between males and females. When trying to instill this principle in children the future as well as the present should be taken into account.

4. *Vocation.* The objective of this principle is that the student gets to know himself or herself and a variety of careers so that the student can choose the most suitable career. The student should then develop an understanding of the relationship between the vocation and the community in which one lives and works. Those who are successful in a vocation should be the ones to teach the students in either the school or workplace.

5. *Civic education.* The goal of civic education is to develop an awareness and concern for one's own community. A student should gain knowledge of social organizations and a commitment to civic morality. Diversity and cooperation should be paramount. Democratic organization of the school and classroom as well as group problem solving are the methods that this principle should be taught through.

6. *Worthy use of leisure.* The idea behind this principle is that education should give the student the skills to enrich his or her body, mind, spirit, and personality in his or her leisure. The school should also provide appropriate recreation. This principle should be taught in all subjects, but primarily in music, art, literature, drama, social issues, and science.

7. *Ethical character.* This principle involves instilling in the student the notion of personal responsibility and initiative. Appropriate teaching methods and school organization are the primary examples that should be used. Although this report was published in 1918, it is just as apt today as it was then. Education must consist of more than just the three Rs for this great nation to exist for another 200 years.

Naming these seven objectives does not "imply that the process of education can be divided into separated fields" (Raubinger et al., 1969, p. 106). Thus, all of the seven principles are interconnected. In order for these principles to be successful, the student must have a willingness to follow these and an ethical character that will allow this learning to take place. In achieving these interconnected goals, schools were encouraged to construct programs of study around three elements: constants (required courses), curriculum variables (specialized subjects chosen in relation to the student's goals), and free electives (subjects chosen to develop the special interests of the student).

In addition to providing a useful framework for the secondary school curriculum, the commission accomplished two other important goals: It attempted somewhat successfully to free the secondary schools from the domination of the colleges, and it articulated forcefully a rationale for the comprehensive high school. In the commission's view, the U.S. high school should serve the needs of all youth, not just the college bound.

The Foundations of Curriculum-Making

In the midst of all the ferment resulting from the attempts to reshape the schools, the National Society for the Study of Education (Rugg, 1927a, 1927b) decided to bring together in two volumes the thinking of all the major experts in the field—as the preface noted, "making a special effort to bring together, and as far as possible to unify or to reconcile, the varying and often seemingly divergent or even antagonistic philosophies of the curriculum that were being espoused by leading authorities" (p. 6). It is obviously difficult to summarize adequately these two volumes produced by men whom Tyler (1971) called "pioneering leaders in curriculum development" (p. 28). Although the major weakness of the *Twenty-Sixth Yearbook,* according to Tyler, was its failure to recognize the importance of the classroom teacher, its major contribution was its achievement of a consensus by the experts in the field on two of the major issues that divided the profession. First, the committee articulated a balanced position on whether studies of the child or the adult should provide the grounding of the curriculum: "We would stress the principle that in the selection and validation of curriculum materials expert analysis must be made both of the activities of adults and interests of children" (Rugg, 1927b, pp. 12–13). The committee also recognized the importance of both individual and societal needs:

> The individual becomes an individual in the best sense only through participation in society. . . . The curriculum can prepare for effective participation in social life by providing a present life of experiences which increasingly identifies the child with the aims and activities derived from an analysis of social life as a whole. (p. 14)

DEVELOPMENTAL CONFORMISM (1941–1956)

The next period of educational history—the era of **Developmental Conformism** (1941–1956)— might be seen as a transition period, with the nation first embroiled in a cataclysmic war and then recovering from it to find a cold war on its hands.

The Temper of the Times

This period, of course, was in many ways a turbulent time. It was, first of all, a time of international conflict and tension. The United States entered World War II in 1941, and by 1945, the Allies had defeated the Axis nations. However, only three years after the war ended, tensions between the United States and the Soviet Union became critical with the Soviet blockade of Western Berlin—tensions that were to affect the nation for the next four decades.

It was also a time of racial unrest. For most of the period, this was a strongly segregated society, with deep-seated racial and ethnic biases. The U.S. Supreme Court outlawed school segregation in 1954, and in 1955, Rosa Parks refused to give her seat to a white man on a bus in Montgomery, Alabama.

Finally, it was the dawning of the atomic age. As several observers noted, the atom bomb profoundly changed the way the average person felt and thought about the world.

Most of the American people seemed to react to this societal turbulence by attempting to live lives of quiet conformity. As presidents, both Truman and Eisenhower seemed able to assure the American people that, despite these signs of unrest, the nation was essentially sound and its future bright.

The Predominant Trends

Here again, two trends are singled out as shaping educational efforts: the interest in the developmental abilities and needs of youth and a concern with conformity as an educational goal.

The Developmental Theorists

It was, first of all, a period marked by rather intensive interest in the educational implications of child and adolescent development. As noted previously, Dewey had long been concerned with delineating and responding to the stages of growth in children and youth.

As will be discussed next, Piaget's work was just becoming known by educators who perhaps sensed its importance but could not yet discern fully its implications. Yet, it was the theories and research of Havighurst that during this period seemed to make the most immediate difference to educators. Havighurst (1972) conceptualized need as a "developmental task," which he defined as the following:

> A task which arises at or about a certain period in the life of the individual, successful achievement of which leads to his happiness and to success with later tasks, while failure leads to unhappiness in the individual, disapproval by society, and difficulty with later tasks. (p. 2)

The importance of these developmental tasks for curriculum can be seen at once by examining just a few of the tasks that Havighurst identified for childhood and adolescence. Consider these examples:

Early Childhood

- Getting ready to read
- Learning to distinguish right from wrong
- Learning sex differences and sexual modesty
- Learning to talk

Middle Childhood

- Learning physical skills necessary for games
- Learning to get along with age-mates
- Learning an appropriate masculine or feminine social role
- Developing fundamental skills in reading, writing, and calculating

Adolescence

- Accepting one's physique and using the body effectively
- Preparing for marriage and family life
- Preparing for an economic career
- Desiring and achieving socially responsible behavior
- Developing intellectual skills and concepts necessary for civic competence

Conformity as an Educational Goal

Implicit in the conceptualization and language of Havighurst's developmental tasks is a strong sense of conforming to the status quo. Consider, for example, such tasks as these: "learning an appropriate masculine or feminine social role," "accepting one's physique and using the body effectively," "desiring and achieving socially responsible behavior," and "accepting and adjusting to the physiological changes of middle age." It is perhaps not unfair to say that such a strong emphasis on conformity was both a reflection of and a contribution to a prevailing educational view that held that one of the important responsibilities of the schools was to help children and youth conform to existing societal norms.

A second assumption was that the curriculum should emphasize functional outcomes— practical skills and knowledge that had immediate value for the student.

A concomitant assumption was that the disciplines themselves were not important as organizing bases for the curricula. Instead, schools were encouraged to develop "core curricula" that would minimize subject-matter distinctions and integrate learnings around major themes and issues. As Oliver (1977) noted, the primary objective of the core curriculum is "to develop unified studies based upon the common needs of the learners and organized without restriction by subject matter" (p. 246). Here, for example, are some of the "centers of experience" that Van Til, Vars, and Lounsbury (1961) recommended for structuring a core program: making and keeping friends, coming to terms with my body, money—magic or madness, meet your new school.

The recurring theme throughout much of this literature is that this is a good society that simply must be maintained. Also, the attempt to make education more relevant too often produced curricula that trivialized learning and overemphasized the needs of the present. Finally, in too many cases it provided a curricular excuse for tracking systems that imprisoned children from poor families in low-level programs that were banal and unimaginative and denied them the opportunity to pursue academic studies needed for success in college.

The Exemplary Leaders

Two curriculum theorists seem to have been important in this period: Ralph Tyler and Hollis Caswell. Although, like most exemplary leaders, their careers spanned several of the periods demarcated here, it seems most appropriate to examine their work within the framework of the period presently under discussion.

Ralph Tyler

Tyler first gained professional attention through his participation as research director of the "Eight-Year Study," sponsored by the Progressive Education Association, to evaluate and systematize the efforts of progressive schools to free their curricula from the domination of the colleges. The curriculum results of the study were summarized by Giles, McCutchen, and Zechiel (1942), who noted that curriculum development and evaluation involved attention to four basic issues: identifying objectives, selecting the means for attaining those objectives, organizing those means, and evaluating the outcomes. It seems apparent that their work influenced Tyler in his preparation of the syllabus for the graduate course he was offering at the University of Chicago. It is this syllabus for Education 305 (Tyler, 1950) that presents and explicates what has become known as the "Tyler rationale."

In the syllabus, Tyler noted that the first question that must be answered in developing any curriculum is, "What educational purposes should the school seek to attain?" These educational objectives can first be identified by examining three sources: studies of the learners themselves, studies of contemporary life outside of school, and suggestions from subject specialists.

The second question is, "How can learning experiences be selected that are likely to be useful in attaining these objectives?" Here, he argued for several general principles that should guide curriculum workers in selecting objectives.

The third question is, "How can learning experiences be organized for effective instruction?" In making determinations about the organization of experiences, the curriculum developer should consider three criteria: continuity, sequence, and integration.

The final question is, "How can the effectiveness of learning experiences be evaluated?" Valid and reliable curriculum-based tests should be developed and the results used to improve the curriculum.

Tyler's publication has had a lasting impact on curriculum leaders. By 1985, more than 100,000 copies of the syllabus had been purchased. It made a significant contribution by systematizing in a sequential manner, and curriculum workers seemed to value its clearness, its comprehensiveness, and its simplicity.

Hollis Caswell

Caswell was one of the first to understand the importance of staff development as a necessary foundation for curriculum work. To that end, he developed excellent study materials and bibliographies helping teachers perceive the larger issues of child development and curriculum ends and using those materials in educating the teachers of Florida and other states who were working with him in a comprehensive curriculum-revision project.

Second, he put into practice on a major scale the widespread belief that teachers should be involved in curriculum development. In developing state curriculum for Virginia, he involved 10,000 Virginia teachers studying and discussing curricular issues.

Third, he developed a useful set of organizing structures that integrated the three determiners of curricula—child interests, social meaning, and subject matter. He began by reviewing what was known about child development to identify important child interests.

The Major Publications

Two quite different publications are singled out here for attention: one by the distinguished Swiss psychologist Jean Piaget and one by a somewhat anonymous committee of American educators.

The Psychology of Intelligence

Because Piaget's publishing career spans several decades during which many seminal publications were produced, it is obviously difficult to select one work as most important. However, his 1950 book, *The Psychology of Intelligence,* seems to have been especially influential because it was one of the earliest to present in a systematic manner his comprehensive view of the nature of intelligence and the child's developmental stages.

Thus, the developmental stages he identified are organized around this essential principle. Four such stages are usually discussed in the extensive literature on Piaget: sensorimotor, preoperational, concrete operations, and formal operations. While these stages, in his view, are invariant in their sequence, they are also hierarchically related: Early stages are integrated into later ones.

The sensorimotor stage, which begins with conception and lasts until about age 2, is a preverbal period in which the child relies on sensorimotor information to adapt to the environment and to acquire new behaviors. The child begins with simple reflex actions, then makes responses modified by experience.

During the next stage, the preoperational, which lasts until about age 6 or 7, language and symbolic thought have their beginnings. The learner reconstructs the developments of the sensorimotor stage, integrating prior knowledge into the new intellectual structures.

During the stage of concrete operations, between ages 7 and 11, the child develops the cognitive ability to classify, order, and handle numbers, spatial operations, and all the operations of classes and relations. In a sense, the concrete operations are similar to those of the prior stage, except for the fact that the child is able to use representational thought instead of direct action on the object. In this stage, the child seems to have a well-integrated cognitive system through which he or she can act on the environment. However, the child is still able to deal effectively in a cognitive sense only with concrete objects, not with symbolic representations of those objects.

During the final stage of formal operations, the adolescent can think about both the real and the possible. Educators who first learned of the Piagetian stages in the late 1950s and early 1960s were initially impressed with the research data supporting this stage theory.

Historically, however, other researchers have been more concerned with conducting research to verify or challenge Piaget's stage theory. After reviewing all the pertinent research, Gelman and Baillargeon (1983) reached this conclusion: "In our opinion there is little evidence to support the idea of major stages in cognitive development of the type described by Piaget. Over and over again the evidence is that the preoperational child has more competence than expected" (p. 214).

Education for All American Youth

This influential volume was quite different from Piaget's work in both its genesis and substance. First, it was the product of a committee. The NEA, in 1935, established the Educational Policies Commission as a standing body to articulate a national policy for education. The commission first produced a policy statement advocating chiefly a social reconstruction role for the school. Their second volume was essentially a rewriting of the Cardinal Principles. Then followed three volumes, all published in the mid-1940s, that provided specific blueprints for the schools of the United States: *Education for All American Youth* (Educational Policies Commission, 1944), *Educational Services for Young Children* (Educational Policies Commission, 1945), and *Education for All American Children* (Educational Policies Commission, 1948). (In the discussion that follows, these volumes are considered as one report.)

In substance, the report was essentially an argument for Developmental Conformism. The main section of the report portrays two imaginary communities, Farmville and American City, and delineates model curricula for their schools. In developing such curricula, the commission members strongly endorsed the key role of the teacher, with laypeople serving in an advisory capacity. Those curricula were to be provided in a comprehensive system— the commission strongly recommended schooling for all children and youth from ages 3 through 20. There would be a public nursery school, followed by a six-year elementary school, and then an eight-year high school, including Grades 13 and 14.

SCHOLARLY STRUCTURALISM (1957–1967)

The Temper of the Times

In retrospect, the era of Scholarly Structuralism (1957–1967) seems to have been an interesting period of history. First, it was a time when the factors producing the turbulence of the previous period seemed to gather in strength. International tensions continued unabated.

The major event in education was the launching of *Sputnik,* the world's first artificial satellite, in 1957; it was an event that dramatized the need for strong programs in science and mathematics in American schools. Under the prodding of President Johnson, Congress responded with massive allocations of federal aid.

The Predominant Trends

The period under consideration was an interesting one from an educational perspective. This was the first time in American educational history that academic scholars decided that they had a key role to play in the development of specific curricula. Largely supported by federal funds channeled through the National Science Foundation, those scholars produced numerous curricula for every major discipline in both elementary and secondary education.

The Exemplary Leaders

During this interesting time, two curriculum theorists seem to have made major impacts—Jerome Bruner and Joseph Schwab.

Jerome Bruner

Bruner (1960) set forth rather cogently in *The Process of Education* a comprehensive rationale for Scholarly Structuralism. First, school curricula must be primarily concerned with effecting and facilitating the transfer of learning. Because school time is limited, educators must find the most efficient means of using the limited time available.

Understanding broad principles was especially important in the latter part of the 20th century. Bruner argued that increased scientific knowledge was able to clarify those structures in a way that perhaps was not possible before. The explosion of knowledge made it impossible for the student to learn everything. Therefore, learning the structures of a discipline resulted in a kind of curricular parsimony.

Joseph Schwab

Schwab's (1969, 1971, 1973, 1978, 1983) writings on curriculum span a period of at least 20 years and have proved to be rather influential in the field of curriculum theory. Like Bruner, Schwab was early concerned with the structure of the disciplines, yet it seems fair to say that his writings on the matter demonstrate a complexity and sophistication missing from Bruner's work.

Rather than insisting that there is only one way of understanding the world, Schwab argues for a "permissive eclecticism," which enables the inquirer to use any valid approach to understand natural and human phenomena. He noted that few disciplines have a single structure and that the scientists in a field are too diverse in their preferences to be unanimous about one right mode of attack.

Schwab's later writings on curriculum seem much more concerned with process and much less concerned with the structure of the disciplines. The outcome, he hoped, would be incremental change, and the process would be an eclectic one, drawing from several bodies of knowledge and from several perspectives.

The Major Publications

Three publications seem worthy of note: the "Conant Report," Physical Science Study Committee (PSSC) curriculum project, and the Coleman Report. One looked back; the other seemed to look ahead.

Conant Report

In 1959, James Bryant Conant, former president of Harvard University and high commissioner for Germany after World War II, was invited by John Gardner, head of the Carnegie Corporation, to undertake a major study of the U.S. high school. The result, known as the "Conant Report," put forth the following curricular recommendations, which were quite specific and somewhat conventional:

- All students should be required to complete four years of English, three years of social studies, one year of mathematics, and one year of science.
- Academically talented students should be required to take three additional years of mathematics, four years of one foreign language, and two additional years of science. If they wished, a second foreign language could be added.
- All students should be required to take a senior course in American problems, as part of their social studies requirement. In this course, students, heterogeneously grouped, would have free and open discussions of controversial issues.

Because the nation seemed to be searching for a new direction for its schools, the above recommendations were endorsed by most educators of the time. Principals and their faculties used the report as a set of criteria to judge their schools and changed their programs to bring them into line with Conant's recommendations.

PSSC Physics

This major curriculum project of the late 1950s and early 1960s (PSSC, 1961) claimed to involve students in discovery and inquiry as the basic pedagogical methods for identifying the structure of physics. Students "did physics" as physicists did, at least to the extent of their ability to do so. Although the implementation of the new course was supported by numerous federally funded teacher-training institutes, the developers had made a significant attempt to develop a "teacher-proof" curriculum that attempted to control all aspects of the instructional process.

Coleman Report

Written by James Coleman and others at Johns Hopkins University in 1966, the report focused primarily on equal educational opportunity. Of primary focus was the availability of equal educational opportunities to children of different race, color, religion, and national origin. The study was conducted in response to provisions of the Civil Rights Act of 1964 and concluded that disadvantaged black children learn better in well-integrated classrooms.

ROMANTIC RADICALISM (1968–1974)

The era of **Romantic Radicalism** (1968–1974) seemed to many observers to be a time of national fragmentation and upheaval, one in which the fabric of the society was stretched to its breaking point.

The Temper of the Times

It was, first of all, a time of rampant violence. It was also a time when youth seemed to be in the saddle. Popular writers trumpeted the glories of being young. A strongly vocal counterculture developed, espousing the virtues of drug-induced hallucinogenic visions, rock music, and spontaneous "openness" in all relationships—and at the same time rejecting the "bourgeois" values of work, punctuality, and bodily cleanliness.

The Predominant Trends

This period was obviously a time of experimentation in an attempt to develop child-centered schools and programs. The experimentation took three related but different forms: alternative schools, open classrooms, and elective programs.

Alternative Schools

The alternative schools were perhaps the most radical of all. While in later years alternative schools often seemed to be very similar to conventional schools, at the outset their faculties worked hard to make them different. Although these alternative schools ranged from completely unstructured "free schools" to mildly experimental schools that seemed different in only superficial ways, they did share certain characteristics (see Glatthorn, 1975, for a fuller account of the schools and their programs).

First, they were strongly teacher centered: Teachers often administered the schools without a principal, teachers determined the curriculum, and teachers offered many of the supportive services provided by specialists in the conventional schools. Second, the schools were in a real sense child centered: Curricula were shaped in response to the needs and interests of the children, and learning activities were selected primarily on the basis of their appeal to the children and parents. The most radical schools simply ignored the whole issue of evaluation; teachers in the more conventional alternative schools wrote anecdotal reports, basing their evaluations on students' self-assessments. Finally, of course, they were "schools of choice": students elected to attend the alternative, rather than being assigned to it.

Open Classrooms

The open classroom was perhaps an attempt on the part of the educational establishment to respond to the mood of the times. Largely influenced by developments in the best British primary schools, the open classroom movement in the United States was to a great extent a revitalization of a moribund progressivism. Although the term *open classroom* was often simply an ill-defined slogan, there were certain important characteristics. There was, first of all, an emphasis on a rich learning environment. Teachers in the open classroom typically began by provisioning the classroom with stimulating learning materials and activities—centers of interest that would immediately appeal to the child and at the same time help the child learn. Children were free to move from center to center, to work together, and to engage each other in discussion. Thus, there was little concern for order in the conventional sense of the term: The best discipline was the self-discipline that came from learning on one's own.

Elective Programs

The elective programs were perhaps an attempt on the part of secondary schools to capture the vitality and excitement of the open classroom, which to a great extent had been limited to the primary grades. The basic concept of the elective program was a relatively simple one: Instead of a student taking a general "10th-grade English," the student should be able to choose from a variety of short-term courses, such as Women in Literature, The Romance of Sports, and War and Peace. In this sense, of course, such electives are different in organizational function from a subject such as music, which students elect to study or not to study.

The Exemplary Leaders

It is symbolic that the two figures selected as representing this exciting period of innovation and experimentation were not educators in the conventional sense of that term. Carl Rogers was a psychologist, and John Holt was perhaps a professional gadfly.

Carl Rogers

Rogers was a psychologist whose name came to be used to identify a school of counseling psychology: A Rogerian counselor is one who attempts to enter into the client's world, adopt the client's frame of reference, and listen empathically without advising.

Although Rogers (1969) worked with several college and school faculties that were interested in a Rogerian approach to organizational revitalization, his chief contribution seems to have been his ability to articulate clearly and practice effectively what open educators and free-school advocates could only haltingly express and imperfectly implement.

John Holt

If Rogers was a counselor who did not believe in advising, then Holt might be characterized as a teacher who did not believe in teaching. In a sense, he is selected here as a representative figure of an influential group that included such other disenchanted teachers as Jonathan Kozol, James Herndon, and Herbert Kohl.

While it might seem surprising to identify a radical teacher as a major curriculum figure, Holt was selected because he and his associates represent a period of time when curriculum making itself was called into question. In Holt's (1964) view, the teacher *was* the curriculum. From his perspective, the schools did not need scope-and-sequence charts, clearly articulated objectives, or specified learning activities; the schools needed, instead, exciting and imaginative teachers who could provision a stimulating learning environment and involve learners in meaningful learning experiences.

The Major Publications

Two publications are selected here for quite different reasons: One heralded the promise of open education, and the other marked the end of federal involvement in curriculum making.

Crisis in the Classroom

In Ravitch's (1983) view, *Crisis in the Classroom* (Silberman, 1970) "projected open education into the public limelight as nothing previously had done" (p. 245). Its author, Charles Silberman, was an experienced journalist who had been commissioned by the Carnegie Corporation to conduct a study of teacher education. Silberman, however, realized that a more important story was breaking—open education might be the one movement that would revolutionize education.

Silberman was a highly skilled writer who knew how to personalize the dry stuff of educational change. He presented fascinating portraits of educators who seemed to be making a difference, and his own conviction made his message seem even more authentic.

Man: A Course of Study

This curriculum project (Curriculum Development Associates, 1972), usually identified by the acronym MACOS (Man: A Course of Study), had been developed at the Education Development Center with financial support from the National Science Foundation. As a social studies course designed for fifth or sixth graders, MACOS seemed, in many ways, to represent the best of federally supported curriculum work. It drew heavily from Brunerian curriculum theory, taking pains to provide interesting "discovery" experiences that would help young children understand some of the basic structures of the social sciences.

PRIVATISTIC CONSERVATISM (1975–1989)

The Temper of the Times

The period of **Privatistic Conservatism** (1975–1989) is generally recognized as the time when a strongly conservative philosophy permeated the national consciousness. It seemed that the American people were tired of violence, experimentation, and protest—and yearned for peace, stability, and traditional values.

It was also a time of increased religiosity. Fundamentalist groups, especially, became more active in the political arena, advancing their own candidates and giving large amounts of financial support to candidates who supported their agendas. Their agendas were concerned primarily with so-called family issues: elimination of abortion, restriction of the rights of homosexuals, and a return of Bible reading and prayer to the public schools. Interestingly enough, the resurgence of religiosity in this country seemed paralleled by an increase in religious fanaticism abroad.

This period was also a time when the information age fully arrived. More than 98% of American households owned one or more television sets—and most of those were color models.

Finally, it was a period of widespread immigration, especially of Hispanics and Asians. From 1971 to 1980, more than 44% of all immigrants were from South American or Central American nations, and more than 35% were from Asian countries. Subsequently, many schools in the 1970s had difficulty with the transition of multicultural populations. Some schools, however, eventually responded to the urban, multicultural student population by providing proactive support (Cuglietto, Burke, & Ocasio, 2007).

The Predominant Trends

As noted previously, this period seems to have been a time when a conservative view of both society and its schools held sway. Those espousing such a conservative educational view essentially argued that the chief function of the school was to transmit the culture and to prepare students for their roles in a technological society; in accomplishing such a mission, the curriculum should emphasize the scholarly disciplines, should be characterized by intellectual rigor, and should be closely monitored for its effectiveness. Emanating from this broadly conservative view of the school and its curriculum were several specific trends.

School Effectiveness and School Reform

The first significant development was a broad-based research effort to identify the key elements in effective schools, with a concomitant attempt to translate those elements into a plan for reforming the schools. Following some groundbreaking research, one of the most

---

EXHIBIT 2.2   Key Factors in Effective Schools

Organizational and Structural Variables

1. The leadership and staff of the school have considerable autonomy in determining the means they will use to improve academic performance.
2. The principal plays an active role as an instructional leader.
3. The staff remains relatively stable in order to maintain and promote further success.
4. The elementary curriculum focuses on basic and complex skills, with sufficient time provided and close coordination across grade levels and across disciplines; the secondary curriculum includes a planned and purposeful program without too many electives.
5. There is schoolwide staff development closely related to the instructional program of the school.
6. There is active parent involvement and support.
7. The school recognizes academic success, through symbols and ceremonies.
8. A greater portion of the day is devoted to academic subjects, with effective use made of academic time and with active involvement of students.
9. There is district support for school-based efforts.

Process Variables

1. There are collaborative planning and collegial relationships.
2. There is a pervasive sense of community.
3. Clear goals and high expectations are commonly shared.
4. There is order and discipline, with clear and reasonable rules fairly and consistently enforced.

SOURCE: Adapted from Purkey and Smith (1983).

useful reviews was performed by Purkey and Smith (1983), who, after reviewing, critiquing, and synthesizing all the research, were able to identify the key factors shown in Exhibit 2.2.

A More Rigorous Curriculum

Central to this reform effort was an emphasis on "curriculum rigor." In general, this slogan seemed most useful simply as a rallying cry for those who believed that a more academically challenging curriculum would best serve the needs of American youth. The most common expressions of this concern for curricular rigor were state laws and district policies mandating additional graduation requirements.

The Critical Thinking Movement

This concern for a new rigor in the curriculum also took the form of widespread interest in teaching critical thinking. Most of those in the forefront of the movement argued for the importance of critical thinking by stressing the need for better thinking in a technologically oriented information age. Typical of these arguments was the conclusion reached by the Education Commission of the States (1982). After analyzing the needs of the society in an information age, the commission concluded in a special report that these were the "basics of tomorrow": evaluation and analysis skills, critical thinking, problem-solving strategies, organization and reference skills, synthesis, application, creativity, decision making given incomplete information, and communication skills.

Accountability

Allied with the concern for more rigor in the curriculum was a demand that teachers and students be held more accountable. First, school districts eagerly embraced several programs that attempted to hold teachers more accountable for teaching and testing the prescribed curriculum. Such programs were usually identified as "**curriculum alignment** projects." Although they varied in detail, they attempted to align the written and the taught curriculum, usually by monitoring what was taught, and the written and the tested curriculum, ordinarily by matching the test with the instructional objectives.

These conservative responses noted some undesirable side effects: increased pressure on less able students, resulting in an unfavorable climate for growth, and overemphasis on the knowledge-transmission function, resulting from mandates and competency tests.

Vouchers

Historians credit Adam Smith for giving birth to the voucher system in 1778 when he argued that parents are in the best position to decide how their children should be educated and that the state should give parents the money to hire suitable teachers. The intent of the voucher or choice schema was to provide opportunities, supported by tax monies, to target populations. Advocates of the voucher or choice concept believed that competition improves the marketplace and enhances educational effectiveness. Adversaries of the voucher or choice concept for public school, however, argued the following points:

- Choice is a notion that flies in the face of the basic mission of American public education.
- Choice is a means to circumvent laws governing due process, religious activities, and desegregation.
- Choice is a means to express personal biases and to construct and reform society through political or religious beliefs.
- Choice lowers the quality of some schools, and lessened enrollments can threaten equal educational opportunity for the majority of the students.
- The focus ought to be on improving schools rather than directing funds from one school district to another. (Boschee & Hunt, 1990, p. 75)

In the 1980s, states that endorsed the voucher or choice concept with varied and different requirements included Alaska, Arizona, California, Florida, Iowa, Louisiana, Massachusetts, Missouri, New York, Vermont, Virginia, Washington, and Wisconsin. Taking issue with where people stand on educational choice and vouchers, Boschee and Hunt (1990) wrote the following:

> People take sides without really knowing what impact the concepts will have on the economies of daily life in a competitive marketplace; the organization and regulation of educational systems related to teaching, learning, and financial accountability; professional employment; cultural, social-psychological, and racial issues; parental choice; the state and federal laws; and values. (p. 86)

Having said that, they developed an instrument titled "Pros/Cons of Vouchers/Choice" to help people determine whether they really endorsed the concept, were neutral, or were opposed. The instrument addressed seven areas: regulation versus deregulation; effectiveness/efficiency of schooling; legal/constitutional issues; roles: local, state, regional, federal, student, teacher, parent; accountability/instability factors; society, values, and schooling; and research on schooling. (The instrument and score key are published in the March 1990 NASSP Bulletin.)

Multicultural Education

The 1980s saw the emergence of a body of scholarship on multicultural education by progressive education activists and researchers who refused to allow schools to address their concerns by simply adding token programs and special units on famous women or famous people of color.

Multicultural education activities for K–12 public schools among the states varied from having no requirements to Monoethnic Courses (Phase 1) to Multiethnic Studies Courses (Phase 2) to Multiethnic Education (Phase 3) to Multicultural Education (Phase 4; Banks, 1994). Several state mandates, models, and frameworks for multicultural education continued into the 21st century. For example, Iowa referenced its requirements as "The Legal Authority: Multicultural, Nonsexist Education" (Iowa Code, Chapter 256.11). Tennessee required that black history and culture be taught in all public schools. Hawaii had a natural setting for multicultural education, and Indiana requires public schools to incorporate world culture in the social studies curriculum. Nebraska compelled all school districts to submit a multicultural education program for approval by the Nebraska Department of Education.

From the survey results conducted by Boschee, Beyer, Engelking, and Boschee (1997) on K–12 multicultural education in the 50 U.S. states, a majority of the states did not mandate a multicultural education curriculum. Almost 30 years after the National Council for Accreditation of Teacher Education (NCATE) mandate, it appears that neither states nor teacher education programs have made substantial progress toward complying. Many, however, recommended that K–12 education be multicultural.

Goals 2000: Educate America Act

In 1989, the president of the United States, George H. W. Bush, and the nation's 50 governors came together for a historic summit on one of the most important issues affecting America's future: the education of our nation's children. Born of an urgent realization that America's future prosperity was at stake, the first Education Summit, cochaired by Governor Carroll Campbell and then Governor Bill Clinton, produced six ambitious goals for the nation's performance in education by 2000:

1. All children in the United States will start school ready to learn.

2. The high school graduation rate will increase to at least 90%.

3. American students will leave Grades 4, 8, and 12 having demonstrated competency over challenging subject matter including English, mathematics, science, history, and geography, and every school in America will ensure that all students learn to use their minds well, so they may be prepared for responsible citizenship, further learning, and productive employment in our modern economy.

4. U.S. students will be first in the world in mathematics and science achievement.

5. Every adult American will be literate and will possess the knowledge and skills necessary to compete in a global economy and exercise the rights and responsibilities of citizenship.

6. Every school in the United States will be free of drugs and violence and will offer a disciplined environment conducive to learning. (Goals 2000, 1994)

With the passage of Goals 2000 legislation in 1994, the U.S. Congress added to Goal 3 the subjects of foreign languages, civics and government, economics, and the arts and added two additional goals to be met by 2000:

1. The nation's teaching force will have access to programs for the continued improvement of their professional skills and the opportunity to acquire the knowledge and skills needed to instruct and prepare all American students for the next century.

2.   Every school will promote partnerships that will increase parental involvement and participation in promoting the social, emotional, and academic growth of children. (Goals 2000, 1994)

Knudsen and Morrissette (1998) made an analysis and critique of Goals 2000 and concluded that "although a gallant effort, Goals 2000 will be remembered as a reform movement that funneled millions, perhaps billions, of dollars into American public schools with little to show in return." The concept for Goals 2000 lacked agreement. It was a vision that did not reach the grassroots level. It can be argued that America was built from the grassroots level, and it appeared that American public education needed to be built from the grassroots level as well.

The Exemplary Leaders

Three figures stand out in this period for their pervasive influence: Benjamin Bloom, John I. Goodlad, and James Banks. Each in his own way made major contributions and influenced both research and practice.

Benjamin Bloom

Bloom was a psychologist and professor of education at the University of Chicago. He first attracted widespread attention from the profession with the publication of what quickly became known as "Bloom's taxonomy" (see Bloom, 1956). Bloom's taxonomy includes his famous educational objectives: knowledge, comprehension, application, analysis, synthesis, and evaluation. Several interpretations of Bloom's taxonomy of educational objectives, in the cognitive domain, include behavioral verbs that can be used to write higher level reasoning tasks (O'Shea, 2005, p. 53).

While his work on the taxonomy was obviously influential, Bloom's theory of and research on mastery learning had perhaps an even greater impact. In discussing his work on mastery learning, it is important to make a sharp distinction between three understandings of "mastery learning": what he himself has advocated, how his students have applied his ideas in developing curricula, and what some publishers have done in commercializing mastery learning.

Despite the fact that some have distorted his theory, Bloom made a major contribution to curriculum—one whose effects will probably endure for some time.

John I. Goodlad

Goodlad is another leading figure in the curriculum field whose career spans several periods. For more than 25 years, he conducted research, organized centers of educational change, and taught graduate courses in the field, publishing more than 20 books and some 200 articles. Educators tended to perceive him as a curriculum leader who understood schools, had a clear vision of what those schools could become, and had some tested ideas for helping them achieve their goals.

His analysis of the content of that balanced curriculum yielded a rather discouraging picture. By observing classes, interviewing teachers and students, analyzing texts and tests, and examining curriculum guides, he and his research team concluded that in all the academic areas—English language arts (ELA), mathematics, social studies, and science—the emphasis was on teaching basic skills and facts. Almost no attention in any grade was given to inquiry, critical thinking, or problem solving. The picture was especially dismal in lower-track classes.

James Banks

In *A Brief History of Multicultural Education,* Paul C. Gorski (1999), assistant professor in the Graduate School of Education at Hamline University and team member of EdChange, said the following:

> James Banks, one of the pioneers of multicultural education, was among the first multicultural education scholars to examine schools as social systems from a multicultural context. He grounded his conceptualization of multicultural education in the idea of "educational equality." According to Banks, in order to maintain a "multicultural school environment," all aspects of the school had to be examined and transformed, including policies, teachers' attitudes, instructional materials, assessment methods, counseling, and teaching styles.

The Major Publications

In 1983, nine national "school reform" reports were issued—so many that several educational publications saw fit to publish "scorecards" and "readers' guides" to help the profession make sense of the reform literature. Three of these reports seemed especially influential.

A Nation at Risk

This publication was produced by the National Commission on Excellence in Education (1983), appointed in 1981 by then secretary of education Terrel H. Bell. The report presented what it termed the "indicators of risk," carefully selected statistics purporting to demonstrate the gravity of the risk and to warrant the dramatic language.

Perhaps because the language was so dramatic, the picture portrayed so dismal, and the recommendations so clear and simple, *A Nation at Risk* seemed to have a pervasive and widespread impact, especially on the public. It became the subject of television and radio broadcasts, it was discussed at parent and citizen meetings across the nation, and legislators often made reference to it as they drafted their own reform legislation. In retrospect, perhaps the chief value of *A Nation at Risk* is that it dramatized the issue of educational reform and moved such reform into the arena of public debate. The report had a major impact on the continuing development of federal influence; however, in terms of curriculum, "the report's impact on schools and schooling is [an] illusion" (Hewitt, 2008, p. 579).

High School: A Report on Secondary Education in America

This book by Ernest Boyer (1983), while not getting the media attention of *A Nation at Risk,* was received much more favorably by educators and, thus, probably had a more pervasive impact. It was the result of a two-year study of the U.S. high school funded by the Carnegie

Foundation for the Advancement of Teaching. The research staff reviewed the literature, consulted with numerous educational leaders, and spent 20 days in each of 15 high schools. While the study perhaps lacked the breadth and comprehensiveness of the Goodlad study mentioned earlier, it resulted in some recommendations that in many ways seemed more useful to the profession.

Multiethnic Education: Theory and Practice

The two editions (1981, 1988) followed by three more editions (1994, 2001, 2006) of the book by James Banks helped preservice and in-service educators clarify the philosophical and definitional issues related to pluralistic education, design and implement effective teaching strategies that reflect ethnic diversity, and prepare sound guidelines for multiethnic programs and practices. Each edition described actions that educators could take to institutionalize educational programs and practices related to ethnic and cultural diversity.

TECHNOLOGICAL CONSTRUCTIONISM (1990–1999)

The Temper of the Times

The era of Technological Constructionism (1990–1999) can be viewed as a time when the net was cast more widely. Along with digital opportunity, it was an era when state content standards came into being, the "school choice" movement was given an intellectual boost, voucher legislation allowed students to attend religious schools at taxpayers' expense, students being homeschooled increased from 10,000 in the 1970s to nearly 1,000,000 in the 1990s, and Goals 2000 was adopted.

The decade also saw increased prosperity for Americans as the Dow Jones and NASDAQ stock markets reached all-time highs. Due to the prevalence of computers and Internet use, "dot-commies" became a new type of upper middle class. With that, 82% of the population had completed high school compared with 41% in 1960. Education subject guides appeared on the World Wide Web, and the Elementary and Secondary Education Act (ESEA) provided assistance to disadvantaged students and students with limited proficiency in English and also improved instruction in math, science, and drug use prevention. The nation also experienced extreme violence in the form of school shootings; according to the National School Safety Center, 255 school-associated violent deaths occurred during this decade (Center on Juvenile and Criminal Justice, 2000).

The appointment of Lamar Alexander, a prominent former governor from Tennessee, as secretary of education brought the Department of Education closer to the president. Another former governor, Richard Riley, succeeded Alexander when Bill Clinton began his first term as president in 1993. During Riley's eight-year term, the longest of any secretary to that time, he weathered congressional attacks on the Department of Education. Nonetheless, he initiated substantive policies (e.g., higher standards, accountability, and increased investments) that helped establish education as the key policy issue in the 2000 presidential election.

The Predominant Trends

This period followed an era, the 1980s, when the nation struggled mightily to improve public education. A report from InfoMedia, Inc. (1993) titled *Educational Reform: A National Perspective* indicated that "ten years have passed since the hoopla surrounding *A Nation at Risk.* Ten years of speechmaking and of handwringing" (p. 3).

Charter Schools

The **charter schools** movement originated from a number of other educational reform ideas—namely, alternative schools, site-based management, magnet schools, public school choice, privatization, and community–parental choice (US Charter Schools, 2008). This idea first became more noticeable in 1991 when Minnesota passed the first charter school law using the criteria of three basic values: opportunity, choice, and responsibility. California followed suit in 1992, and by 1995, there were 19 states that had signed laws allowing for the creation of charter schools. By 2003, that number had increased to 40 states, Puerto Rico, and the District of Columbia. States in which a charter school law still has not been passed are Alabama, Kentucky, Maine, Montana, Nebraska, North Dakota, South Dakota, Vermont, Washington, and West Virginia. Charter schools are one of the quickest-growing developments in education policy, benefiting from extensive bipartisan support from governors, state legislators, and past and present secretaries of education (US Charter Schools, 2008).

Charter schools were publicly funded, publicly controlled, and privately run. As noted by US Charter Schools (2008), the intent of most charter school legislation was to do the following:

- Increase opportunities for learning and access to quality education for all students.
- Create choice for parents and students within the public school system.
- Provide a system of accountability for results in public education.
- Encourage innovative teaching practices.
- Create new professional opportunities for teachers.
- Encourage community and parent involvement in public education.
- Leverage improved public education broadly.

Charter schools continue to be a cross between a public and private school and are seen by many as a halfway station between public school choice and voucher programs. Although details vary by state, charter schools in general are freed from some regulations that govern traditional schools in exchange for greater accountability for results (Ryan, 2009).

Murphy and Shiffman (2002) analyzed empirical evidence gathered over a period of time to determine the impact of charters—both on individual charter communities and on the larger educational system. They concluded that, "by and large, the picture that emerges from the data we compiled is probably disappointing to charter purists—those who hold that the central goal of charters is to overhaul the extant system of education in the United States" (p. 216). Further, "the data on student achievement and school accountability, while quite limited, are not nearly as positive as charter advocates had hypothesized" (p. 216).

Advent of Technology

The stability of the core tool and keystone of the educational system, the printed textbook, yielded significant ground to the astonishing storage and retrieval capacities of the computer. A new educational future was no longer inhibited and shaped by the exigencies of print- or textbook-based education. It was during this era that we experienced the first stages of humankind's third major change in the way we communicate with one another and with future generations yet unborn. In the same manner the alphabet and movable type changed everything about working and living in the decades after they were invented, the invention of the computer changed, and will continue to change, our lives and our children's lives dramatically.

The new technologies enabled a person with a computer and a phone line or cable in the remotest part of any state to connect to the equivalent of a million libraries worldwide. The use of an Internet browser and search engine allowed people to acquire within seconds the exact information they needed. Those same tools allowed people to organize and analyze huge quantities of acquired information to solve problems and create new opportunities. These technologies also enabled people to share information with one other person or with many millions of people worldwide (Whitehead, Jensen, & Boschee, 2013).

It was also during this decade that federal money was made available to take the country from a status of "digital divide" to one of "digital opportunity." In 1994, President Clinton and Vice President Gore bridged the digital divide by setting the goal of connecting every classroom and library to the Internet. In 1996, President Clinton unveiled his Technology Literacy Challenge and made a major commitment of resources to (a) connect every classroom to the Internet; (b) expand access to modern, multimedia computers; (c) make high-quality educational software an integral part of the curriculum; and (d) enable teachers to integrate technology effectively into their instruction. In retrospect, the 1990s provided a foundation for the unprecedented expansion and integration of technology in the classroom that we see today.

The Standards-Based Movement

The decade of the 1990s ushered in a wave of state educational standards. All the states, with the exception of Iowa, had adopted academic standards. Iowa required each school district to develop its own standards. Although the research on the value of state standards is fairly new—and much of it is still in progress—the findings, according to Jones (2000), offer the following unfaltering guidelines:

1. *Make academic standards everybody's business.* Everybody—students, parents, teachers, business, everybody—needs to know what the standards are and why they're important. Research shows that when students and teachers better understand what is expected of them, they perform better.

2. *Focus, focus, focus.* Each state's standards are different, but they all have one thing in common: They're not perfect. Some state standards are so vague that teachers aren't sure what they mean. Others are so specific and so numerous that it's

impossible to cover everything in the 13 years between kindergarten and high school graduation. Robert Marzano, senior fellow at the Mid-continent Research for Education and Learning (McREL) in Aurora, Colorado, studied the standards around the country and found it would take 23 years of schooling to cover all of the **benchmarks**. "Teachers can't teach it all and kids couldn't possibly learn it all."

3. *Make standards-based decisions.* If you want standards to work, researchers say, you have to work on standards. The simplistic-sounding advice means each decision, each program, each new hire should be examined with an eye toward its impact on helping students meet standards. Researchers say school districts should put their money where their standards are. If a district wants to improve students' performance in math, for instance, it should hire more qualified math teachers.

4. *Invest in teachers.* Numerous studies have identified the importance of teachers' credentials in determining students' academic achievement. Teacher quality is so important that some researchers are beginning to suspect that low student achievement often seen in low-income communities just might reflect the fact that the least qualified teachers are often assigned to schools in those communities.

5. *Demand helpful assessments that align with the curriculum.* If you want the curriculum to be taken seriously, you have to do something about assessments. In cases where there's concern about alignment between the test and the standards, districts ought to raise that with the state, and not assume that everything will work itself out. There can be real consequences if there's not good alignment.

6. *Approach accountability cautiously.* Most researchers recommend using test results and other standards-based data to make decisions about everything from textbooks to teachers.

7. *When students are in trouble, intervene.* Researchers have long touted the benefits of early intervention. Studies show that a few weeks of one-on-one tutoring aimed at teaching first-graders to decode words can save many children from special education.

SOURCE: Reprinted with permission from "Making Standards Work: Researchers Report Effective Strategies for Implementing Standards," by R. Jones, September 2000, *American School Board Journal, 187*(9), 27–31. Copyright 2000 National School Boards Association. All rights reserved.

With the development of state educational standards, and if public education is to be improved, teachers will require better training and staff development. Moreover, curriculum, instructional materials, and parental attitudes will have to change. As a result of these initial reform actions, early state standards helped set the tone for the unprecedented move to align standards in classrooms that we see today. Basically, over the past quarter century, a model for school standards and accountability has emerged in the United States that is now so locked into state and federal laws that its general shape seems here to stay. It can be said that where alignment between curriculum instruction and assessment is incomplete, the standards for validity are not being met (Barton, 2006).

The past quarter of a century also helped develop the long link between high school and college standards. High school administrators around the country are currently modifying their curricula so that students desiring to go to college are better able to succeed academically. This is evidenced by the number of tech prep courses being offered in secondary schools today that help make the link easier between high schools and colleges. For example, Idaho high school students could register to complete an approved tech prep course at any high school, which allows them an opportunity to earn college class credit and move from their high school to North Idaho State College without having to repeat tech prep courses (North Idaho State College, 2007).

The Exemplary Leaders

Three figures stand out in this period of change: Elliot W. Eisner, Robert J. Marzano, and Joseph S. Renzulli. Each of these individuals contributed his own special influence to the field of curriculum development.

Elliot W. Eisner

Eisner is a professor of education and art at Stanford University. He is widely considered a leading theorist on art education. Eisner has won wide recognition for his work internationally. Among his many awards is the Palmer O. Johnson Award from the American Educational Research Association. He has been a John Simon Guggenheim Fellow and a Fulbright Scholar and has served as the president of the National Art Education Association, the International Society for Education Through Art, the American Educational Research Association, and the John Dewey Society (Provenzo, 2003).

Eisner works primarily in three fields: arts education, curriculum studies, and qualitative research methodology (identifying practical uses of critical qualitative methods from the arts in school settings and teaching processes). His research interests have focused on the development of aesthetic intelligence and on the use of methods from the arts to study and improve educational practice. Originally trained as a painter, Eisner teaches ways in which schools might improve by using the processes of the arts in all their programs. He is considered one of the foremost leaders in the field of arts in education.

Robert J. Marzano

Marzano is a senior fellow at the McREL Institute in Aurora, Colorado, and has authored numerous books and articles. He is largely noted for translating research and theory into classroom practices. He heads a team of authors who developed *Dimensions of Learning* as well as *Tactics for Thinking*. One of his best works is the book *School Leadership That Works* (Marzano, Waters, & McNulty, 2005). He has developed programs and practices used in K–12 classrooms that translate current research and theory in cognition into instructional methods.

Joseph S. Renzulli

A professor of educational psychology at the University of Connecticut, Renzulli also served as director of the National Research Center on the Gifted and Talented. His research has focused on the identification and development of creativity and giftedness in young people and on organizational models and curricular strategies for total school improvement. He is a fellow in the American Psychological Association and was a consultant to the White House Task Force on Education of the Gifted and Talented. In addition, he was designated a Board of Trustees Distinguished Professor at the University of Connecticut.

The Major Publications

Educators at this time began focusing on individualized instruction, technology, and data analysis. Although there were many outstanding works during this period, two publications are obvious for their pioneering and innovative approaches.

Classrooms That Work

Patricia Cunningham and Richard L. Allington's 1994 publication *Classrooms That Work: They Can Read and Write* compiled some of the best strategies that work effectively in classrooms. The book was one of the first to put an analytical emphasis on classroom instruction and to focus on successful practices in schools from both research and teacher points of view. It is a positive resource containing practical ideas, activities, and organizational strategies. Five major components are noted in the book: engagement in real reading and writing, supported comprehension activities, supported writing activities, decoding and spelling activities, and knowledge-building activities. These components best describe the critical components of a balanced classroom program. In a supplement to the 1994 edition, Allington's 2005 book, *What Really Matters for Struggling Readers: Designing Research-Based Programs,* describes the characteristics of scientifically based reading research and some of its most significant subjects. He also discussed developing instruction for struggling readers, improving classroom instruction and access to intensive instruction, expanding available instruction time, and making support available for older struggling readers.

Data Analysis

The book *Data Analysis: For Comprehensive Schoolwide Improvement,* by Victoria Bernhardt (1998), had a vast impact on state officials, school district administrators, and teachers. As a result, it continues to play a major role in the school-improvement process nationally. It was written to help educators learn how to deal with data that will inform them of where they are, where they want to be, and how to get there. Bernhardt explained why data make the difference in quality school improvement. Also, depending on what data make the difference and how they are gathered, analyzed, and whether properly used, they make a difference in meeting the needs of every student in school. This book took data from schools and demonstrated how powerful data analyses emerge logically. It shows how to gain answers to questions and how to understand current and future impacts.

MODERN CONSERVATISM (2000–2009)

The Temper of the Times

The United States has undergone a period of modern conservative influence and control of its political system in the first decade of the 21st century. The range of persons identifying themselves as modern conservatives and the variety of sociopolitical beliefs that this group holds has increased in both number and diversity. Too, **Modern Conservatism** is an ideological shift that is due to the results of the 2004 presidential election.

Educational reform has become one of the most divisive issues in America, especially in the first decade of the 21st century. Concerns about our educational system are reverberating at the national, state, and local levels. A heated debate involving U.S. education has raged in the press over time but more since the passage of the No Child Left Behind Act (NCLB), Race to the Top, and Common Core State Standards (CCSS). Politicians, business leaders, educators, and parents are just some of the diverse groups of people engaged in the educational reform controversy. The intensity of the issues is accentuated by proponents across the political spectrum.

Added to the educational issues for U.S. public schools, the tea party, a grassroots movement of millions of like-minded Americans from all backgrounds and political parties, favors the elimination of the Education Department. Candidates for political office with tea party support believe that the 30-year-old agency, established during the Carter administration, should be abolished (Weber, 2010). In essence, the tea party's demand is that political power be returned to the states and the people so that the core principles of our Founding Fathers can become, once again, the foundation on which America stands.

The Predominant Trends

Americans increasingly recognize that the U.S. education system can and should do more to prepare our young people to succeed in the rapidly evolving 21st century. Skills such as global literacy, problem solving, innovation, and creativity have become critical in today's increasingly interconnected workforce and society.

No Child Left Behind Act

The biggest public school story in the 21st century was the 1,100-page NCLB Act signed into law by President George W. Bush in January 2002. Being that it was bipartisan legislation, a congressional coalition formed around the ambitious federal education bill. However, that unity dissolved as Democrats blamed Republicans for withholding funding and Republicans criticized Democrats for abandoning school reform.

According to Toch (2010), "we needed to restructure the accountability system in the NCLB to evaluate schools more comprehensively and give schools stronger incentives to embrace high standards" (p. 75). Surely, the logic of this transformation appeared to be clear and compelling at the time: National problems required national solutions. But it was not long before individuals who had been involved in promoting state academic standards, aligned assessments, and accountability for student performance began acknowledging that the ideas that had given rise to NCLB were failing (Colvin, 2013). Consequently, states across the nation began taking opposition to the law. For example, initially, the renewal of the oft-criticized NCLB federal law was supported by the nation's governors, but they wanted states to have far more authority in carrying out its mandates. Since the act repeatedly came under fire, the governors decried for such things as its focus on testing and punishments to be reauthorized.

Subsequently, several years later, the federal government released the NCLB waiver plan, which enabled individual states to craft their own accountability systems. Because NCLB was known as a flawed law that failed to deliver for schools and kids, Minnesota Education Commissioner Brenda Cassellius said, "Today is a great, great day for parents, teachers, schools, and most importantly students" (Staff and Wire Reports, 2011, p. A5). Although the requirement that all children be proficient in reading and mathematics (as early as 2014) was waived, states must still "meet conditions such as imposing their own standards to prepare students for college and careers and setting evaluation standards for teachers and principals" (Staff and Wire Reports, 2011, p. A5).

NCLB was a new federal law that provided an overall system for improving student achievement. The law's three goals were as follows:

1. To make sure that all students in a school, as well as students from low-income families, minority populations, limited English proficient students, and students with disabilities, perform well in the areas of reading and mathematics

2. To hold schools responsible if all children are not on grade level or above

3. To make sure that there is a highly qualified teacher in each classroom

Some other trends in education during the Modern Conservatism era besides NCLB include global education, **school vouchers,** homeschooling, P–16 education, the federal government's Race to the Top program, **diversity education** (replacing multicultural education), and CCSS.

School Privatization

Along with charter schools, there was a move toward private schools via school vouchers. In conjunction with the advent of a new Republican administration in 2001, educational reform moved away from technological structuralism and returned to a more modern and conservative nature. This is especially the case with former president George W. Bush's and President Obama's endorsements of vouchers.

As a move toward school choice, vouchers provide parents with tax-financed certificates or vouchers to pay tuition at schools, public or private, to which they choose to send their children. Basically, school vouchers can be considered a type of government grant that provides school tuition that can be used at both public and private schools and that could become a way to increase the option of school choice for low-income families. The concept behind school vouchers continues to focus on giving parents a wider choice of educational institutions and approaches.

The school voucher program has been controversial at best in that many individuals believe that such a program, if broadly applied, could destroy the American public education system. There is also debate over constitutional church–state issues related to vouchers being used to allow students to attend religious schools. This continues to be a controversial issue, and a federal court held that when a voucher system resulted in almost all recipients attending religious schools instead of public schools, the system violated the Constitution.

As can be seen, privatization remains a highly controversial issue today. According to Houchens (2012), school choice advocates are not suggesting that every charter or private school will naturally do a better job. But he added that if families are dissatisfied with the education their children receive, they should have the option to enroll elsewhere. Moreover, without options, poor families may have no other opportunity to evade a failing school. The U.S. Supreme Court agreed and ruled in *Zelman v. Simmons-Harris* that a Cleveland voucher program was constitutional.

In contrast, Harvey (2012) is concerned about charter schools and cites several Florida charters that came out badly in state investigations. Similarly, he shared problems of other charter schools involving sweetheart contracts, nepotism, conflicts of interest, and extravagant bonuses. Subsequently, the pros and cons debate on charter schools will continue.

Homeschooling

During the past 20 years, the general public's familiarity with homeschooling has evolved from a level of almost complete unawareness to one of widespread, if largely uninformed, awareness. Today, homeschooling parents are reinventing the ideas of school. Along with this movement, a growing body of literature on school choice has emerged. Despite legislative problems, regulatory hurdles, media attacks, and other affronts to the homeschooling movement, homeschooling has continued to gain in popularity and strength. Thomas Jefferson, the principal author of the Declaration of Independence, alleged that the price of freedom is vigilance (Gilmore, 2005). This has never been truer than in the case of freedom to homeschool in the United States in the 1980s and 1990s, when battles were fought in the courtrooms and state legislatures.

Reasons for Homeschooling. Although each family has its own value system and its own reasons for homeschooling, researchers have identified several reasons why families choose to homeschool their children. Ray (2006) found that the most common reasons given for homeschooling are to do the following:

- Teach a particular set of values, beliefs, and worldview
- Accomplish more academically than is achieved in schools
- Customize or individualize the curriculum and learning environment of each child
- Use pedagogical approaches other than those typical in institutional schools
- Enhance family relationships between children and parents and among siblings
- Provide guided and reasoned social interactions with youthful peers and adults
- Provide a safer environment for children and youth, because of physical violence, drugs and alcohol, psychological abuse, and improper and unhealthy sexuality

Along these same lines, parents may decide to homeschool their children simply due to school avoidance. According to Casoli-Reardon, Rappaport, Kulick, and Reinfeld (2012), school avoidance is a multifaceted problem but can be broken down into four groups. They include the following:

1. *Cultural factors.* For some students, the presence of gangs, guns, bullying, or poorly maintained facilities make school appear to be an unsafe place. Other students—especially recent immigrants—sometimes feel uncomfortable due to language barriers or differences in culture. This unease leads to students feeling isolated and anxious about attending school.

2. *Family factors.* Some families do not value the public education system or put education second to family personnel needs. Older children may be homeschooled in order to watch younger siblings or help earn money for the family.

3. *Peer factors.* Often students feel vulnerable to social factors that can contribute to anxiety and truancy. Social media and cyberbullying can extend beyond the school grounds and create major problems of harassment. For students who struggle with managing anxiety and have poor social skills, it is sometimes easier for the parents to simply homeschool their children.

4. *Neuropsychiatric factors.* Neurological and psychiatric factors can play a huge role in school avoidance. If not detected, students become withdrawn, which can lead to academic failure and truancy. Anxiety and mood disorders, such as social phobia, obsessive–compulsive disorder, generalized anxiety disorder, panic disorder, and post-traumatic stress disorder, can appear at any age. Other prevalent neurological factors that play a role in school avoidance include attention deficit disorder as well as learning disabilities (LD) such as dyslexia and nonverbal learning disorder. In addition, there are an increasing number of students being identified and diagnosed with autism spectrum disorders such as Asperger syndrome. That said, regardless of the reason for avoidance, some parents simply choose to homeschool their child, despite legal issues or the availability of quality public school services.

One cannot sidestep the impact of homeschooling on today's schools. As a result, public educators need to develop greater awareness as to medical, social, and cultural issues and then make some substantial changes, particularly if they want to minimize the impact of homeschooling, vouchers, charters, and private schools (McCollum, 2010).

P–16 Education

To bring about change in education via P–16 education, Gordon (Spud) Van de Water and Carl Krueger (2002) suggested the establishment of five central goals and recommended structural goals to achieve them:

1. Every child ready for school by age 6

2. Every child proficient in reading by age 8

3. Every child proficient in geometry and algebra by age 13

4. Every learner completing a rigorous core curriculum by age 17

5. Every learner expected to complete the first two years of college by age 21

To accomplish these central goals, recommended structural goals included the following:

- Starting universal public education at age 3
- Smoothing transitions from one level of education to the next
- Moving from a Carnegie-unit system to a competency-based system
- Creating more flexible learning opportunities for adolescent learners
- Moving the accepted endpoint of public education from Grade 12 to Grade 14

To achieve these goals, a P–16 system stresses these factors: the use of research to guide decisions about when and how children learn, a clearly articulated set of high expectations, improvement of teaching quality, and the use of data to measure progress.

A wave of educational reform has swept the nation over the first decade of the 21st century. For example, school choice, charter schools, NCLB, and standards-based instruction, among others, are highly debatable because the landscape of education in the United States has not undergone major change (Chamberlin & Plucker, 2008). Although the jury is still out, Chamberlin and Plucker believe that P–16 education has potential because it is more responsive to society's needs.

There is widespread agreement that all students in our schools and colleges need to learn more to lead successful economic and civic lives as adults in the 21st century. Implicit in this consensus is the notion that the current system is not capable of bringing this about. Consider these data points:

- Fewer than 3 in 10 teenagers think their school is "very academically rigorous."
- A students in high-poverty schools score at the same level as C and D students in affluent schools.
- Seventy-two percent of high school graduates go on to some form of postsecondary education, yet only 44% have taken a college-prep curriculum.
- Twenty-nine percent of college freshmen take one or more remedial courses in reading, writing, or math.
- By age 24, approximately 7% of young people from low-income families have graduated from college, versus 48% from high-income families. (Haycock & Huang, 2001)

The previously given signs would indicate that the educational system in the United States is under stress. A P–16 system could well smooth the needed transition from high school to college.

Race to the Top

According to U.S. Secretary of Education Arnie Duncan, the federal government is committed to reforming America's public schools to provide every child access to a complete and competitive education. Government officials recently presented states with an unprecedented challenge and the opportunity to compete in a "Race to the Top" designed to spur systemic reform and embrace innovative approaches to teaching and learning in America's schools. Backed by a $4.35 billion investment, the reforms contained in Race to the Top are hoped to prepare America's students to graduate ready for college and careers, and enable them to outcompete any worker, anywhere in the world.

Race to the Top emphasizes the following reform areas:

- *Designing and implementing rigorous standards and high-quality assessments* by encouraging states to work jointly toward a system of common academic standards that builds toward college and career readiness and that includes improved assessments designed to measure critical knowledge and higher order thinking skills (HOTS)
- *Attracting and keeping great teachers and leaders in U.S. classrooms* by expanding effective support to teachers and principals; reforming and improving teacher preparation; revising teacher evaluation, compensation, and retention policies to encourage and reward effectiveness; and working to ensure that our most talented teachers are placed in the schools and subjects where they are needed the most
- *Supporting data systems that inform decisions and improve instruction* by fully implementing a Statewide Longitudinal Data System (SLDS), assessing and using data to drive instruction, and making data more accessible to key stakeholders
- *Using innovation and effective approaches to turn around struggling schools* by asking states to prioritize and transform persistently low-performing schools
- *Demonstrating and sustaining education reform* by promoting collaborations between business leaders, educators, and other stakeholders to raise student achievement and close achievement gaps and also by expanding support for high-performing public charter schools, reinvigorating math and science education, and promoting other conditions favorable to innovation and reform

Diversity Education

The boundaries of diversity education are so immense that it is difficult to label which cultural groups should be the primary focus in curriculum, publications, or conventions. Increasingly, however, the term *diversity* (*equity* is another current term) is being used to refer to education related to race, gender, social class, exceptionality, and the interaction of these variables. In essence, "who we are includes the diversities that we are born to—that is, race, sexual orientation, and culture" (Starnes, 2010, p. 75). Likewise, regarding the new Indian education standards adopted by the South Dakota Board of Education, Governor Dennis Daugaard—speaking in favor of the standards before the board—said, "Students are more engaged when they find the curriculum relevant." Also, "it's important for Native students to have that relevancy, but it's also equally important for our non-Native students to have a better understanding of the cultural background of the state" (as quoted in Verges, 2011, p. A7).

In this time of cultural awareness, nations around the world are sharpening their focus on diversity and equity—often, with remarkable progress. The reality is that schools are not separate from the societies and culture in which they exist. Likewise, they need not be completely subservient to the negative aspects of those societies. Over the longer term, developing a quality and equitable education is one way societies improve. In leading and supporting differentiated education, for all students, regardless of background, educators not only embody the best principles of humanity, they also contribute to a better future for everyone (Levin, 2012–2013).

Common Core State Standards

CCSS continues to present a new challenge for many K–12 educators (Marzano, 2013). "For decades, the United States maintained various academic quality standards among states, resulting in wide disparities in student proficiency as measured under NCLB and highlighted by National Assessment of Education Progress scores" (ASCD, 2011). Here is the consequence:

> The Council of Chief State School Officers (CCSSO) and the National Governors Association (NGA) spearheaded the development of Common Core State Standards that should prepare our children for college, the workforce, and success in the global economy. The initiative's goal was to create K–12 English language arts and mathematics standards that are (a) fewer, higher, and clearer; (b) internationally benchmarked; (c) research-based; and (d) aligned with college- and career-readiness expectations. (ASCD, 2011)

The adoption of the CCSS by a number of states *is* the first step toward meaningful and comprehensive comparisons of student performance and achievement among states. Under these new standards, educators across the country will work under the same guidelines for what students need to know and are expected to do (ASCD, 2011). "*Assumingly* [emphasis added], the CCSS will provide a consistent, clear understanding of what students are expected to learn, so teachers and parents know what they need to do to help them" (ASCD, 2011).

CCSS was designed to help make every student college and career ready and is built on the well-founded expectation that students must do better than merely mastering basic skills (Sandler & Hammond, 2012–2013). Moreover, CCSS emphasizes prior knowledge and the growing body of literature about the neuroscience of learning. This focuses on how we as humans build interrelated networks of knowledge. As schools move toward full implementation of CCSS, we must make sure all students are able to leverage prior knowledge—both to help strengthen their analytical skills as well as to lay a solid foundation for further learning.

Technology and 21st-Century Learning

Similarly to CCSS, effectively implementing educational technology is a shared responsibility. From the onset, planning and implementation of educational technology continues to remain in uncharted territory. Many school leaders are just now trying to figure out how to best create good policies and rules about technology best practices and use. According to Johnson (2013), when it comes to 21st-century technology, better decisions require many perspectives. As part of those perspectives, Johnson notes five ways school leaders can approach future planning and implementation of 21st-century technology in their schools:

- Demand a voice, both formal and informal, in technology planning, budgeting, and policymaking.
- Have regular conversations with technology staff, and share challenges and goals with them (and community).
- Be knowledgeable about technology use in other school districts (as well as schools globally), learning what is possible and why.
- Participate in other formal technology advisory groups.

Developing a progressive technology-infused program is about developing a shared mission. To successfully implement 21st-century teaching and learning strategies, schools must be proactive (Wells, 2012). With this in mind, school leaders need to follow three basic steps. They include the following:

1. Make the needs of the new 21st-century learner a priority.

2. Deliberately empower teachers to innovatively craft digital learning experiences that promote discovery and creation.

3. Establish a shared vision and unique plan for both students and teachers.

Although the steps noted previously are a start to improving and enhancing a school's technology initiative, it is crucial for curriculum leaders and teachers to have an open dialogue about concerns, responsibilities, and priorities essential for successful technology integration. As will be covered extensively in subsequent chapters, having ongoing, informal conversations about technology resources is foundational to developing a global vision for 21st-century learning.

Global Education

As part of establishing new global insights, school leaders and teachers are working collaboratively to integrate 21st-century technology into classrooms today. From a national perspective, CCSS suggest students be able to effectively use technology in our globally connected world. As part of this process, Gail Connelly (2012), executive director of the National Association of Elementary Principals, shares four major focus areas for principals, curriculum leaders, and teachers. They include the following:

1. Develop a technology-rich culture that connects learning to our global society.

2. Make data a driver for school improvement.

3. Help adults and students use knowledge to make informed decisions.

4. Benchmark high-achieving schools with comparable demographics.

As Connelly aptly pointed out, one of the first and foremost goals for schools leaders and teachers is to use technology applications to connect learning in our global society. This is particularly important today in that expectations for education appear to be rising worldwide.

Focusing on real-world relevance, there is a growing presence of concern as to economic and social issues as well as the quality of education (Ferguson, 2013). Along with the macroeconomic pressures of increasing unemployment and social concerns, there is equally not enough schools or enough teachers in many countries.

In contrast, however, there have been many positive outcomes. According to Levin (2012–2013), access to schooling has improved dramatically across the world, with 80% of the globe's population considered to be literate as of 2002. This is the highest proportion in human history. It is believed this increase is a result of increased formal schooling, as well as highly successful efforts in adult literacy. For example, within schools and in adult education, more girls and women are now being educated. In addition, secondary and postsecondary education are expanding dramatically. Even countries that were already doing reasonably well (in educational terms) are experiencing sharp improvements over periods a short as a decade. Specific examples include Finland and Poland.

To be sure, many challenges will remain ahead for education—both here in the United States and worldwide. But, on a positive note, as cited by Levin, there is some improvement. And, along with this improvement, there will be more collaboration, more integration of technology, and, eventually, more globally connected learners. That is the future of globally connected education.

The Exemplary Leaders

Two major figures, Linda Darling-Hammond and Carol Ann Tomlinson, stand out from this unusual time of direct government involvement in individualized and differentiated learning, assessment, and school improvement. Never before has the federal government been so involved in making sure that schools apply standards and are held accountable.

Linda Darling-Hammond

Darling-Hammond is a Charles E. Ducommun Professor of Education at Stanford University School of Education. She has served as chief education adviser to President Barack Obama and is the author of the book *The Flat World and Education* (Darling-Hammond, 2010). She also served as executive director of the National Commission on Teaching and America's Future, which produced the widely cited 1996 blueprint for education reform, *What Matters Most: Teaching for America's Future*. Darling-Hammond's research, teaching, and policy work focus on teaching and teacher education, school restructuring, and educational equity. She has been active in the development of standards for teaching and served as a two-term member of the National Board for Professional Teaching Standards and as chair of the Interstate New Teacher Assessment and Support Consortium committee that drafted model standards for licensing beginning teachers. She is the author of *The Right to*

Learn (Darling-Hammond, 1997), *A License to Teach* (Darling-Hammond, Wise, & Klein, 1999), and *Professional Development Schools: Schools for Developing a Profession* (Darling-Hammond & Bransford, 2005) along with six other books and more than 200 book chapters, journal articles, and monographs on education.

Darling-Hammond has served as the faculty sponsor for Stanford's Teacher Education Program. As a leader in the charge for enhanced teacher education and teacher preparedness, she has been instrumental in redesigning programs to better prepare teachers to teach diverse learners in the context of challenging new subject matter standards (Glass, 2003).

Carol Ann Tomlinson

Tomlinson is a noted author whose work in the area of differentiated instruction is well known internationally. She is an associate professor of educational leadership, foundations, and policy at the Curry School of Education, University of Virginia. Her work has had a tremendous impact on the school-improvement process. Her books include information on curriculum and instruction for advanced learners and struggling learners, effective instruction in heterogeneous settings, and bridging the fields of general education and gifted education. She is the author of more than 100 articles, book chapters, and books. One of her best-known books is *The Differentiated Classroom: Responding to the Needs of All Learners* (Tomlinson, 1999). Another is *Integrating Differentiated Instruction and Understanding by Design* (2006), which she coauthored with Jay McTighe. Many school officials are turning to her work in their efforts to individualize classrooms and comply with new standards.

The Major Publications

No Child Left Behind Act

With the passage of NCLB in 2002, schools are continuing to turn to ways to enhance student achievement, align standards, and learn more about the brain and how children learn. There are seven authors—Charlotte Danielson, Patricia Wolfe, Michael Fullan, Rick Wormeli, William Bender, Thomas L. Friedman, and Temple Grandin—whose works have dramatically helped build a foundation in these areas.

Enhancing Student Achievement: A Framework for School Improvement

This book by Charlotte Danielson (2002) is fast becoming one of the most important books in education. Danielson's framework stresses the importance of aligning state and national standards and determining a means of assessing the school program as a whole. According to Danielson, when educators learn to "put it all together" to improve their schools, they will be bringing their entire expertise to bear on providing a first-rate education to all children.

Brain Matters: Translating Research Into Classroom Practice

The book by Patricia Wolfe (2010) continues to have a significant impact on classroom instructional strategies. Much of the research in this field confirms what experienced educators already know, and Wolfe's book helps functionally understand the brain and how it operates.

This allows teachers to critically analyze the vast amount of neuroscientific information arriving in the classroom daily. The book is divided into four parts. Part I is a mini-textbook on brain-imaging techniques and the anatomy and physiology of the brain. Part II introduces a model of how the brain processes information and explores some of the implications of this process for classroom practice. Part III presents examples of teaching strategies that match how the brain learns best: through projects, simulations, visuals, music writing, and mnemonics. Part IV shows how to make the curriculum meaningful with strategies.

Leading in a Culture of Change

Michael Fullan is the dean of the Ontario Institute for Studies in Education at the University of Toronto. An innovator and leader in teacher education, he has developed a number of partnerships designed to bring about major school improvement and educational reform. His powerful and pioneering book *Leading in a Culture of Change* (2001) integrates theory, research, case studies, and anecdotes to flesh out the dynamics of effective leadership in this era of Modern Conservatism. He identified and elaborated on five components of leadership that can affect sustainable and systemic change: moral purpose, understanding change, relationship building, knowledge creation and sharing, and coherence making. Fullan noted that in an increasingly complex and fast-changing world, it is crucial that we cultivate leadership at all levels of organization, business, and education.

Fair Isn't Always Equal: Assessing and Grading in the Differentiated Classroom

Rick Wormeli's 2006 book is meant to do four things: (1) be a catalyst for serious reflection on current grading and assessment practices in differentiated classes, (2) affirm effective grading and assessment practices, (3) provide language and references for substantive conversations with colleagues and the public, and (4) provide coherent and effective grading practices in a high-stakes, high-accountability world.

Response to Intervention: A Practical Guide for Every Teacher

William Bender's 2007 book addresses the issues and guidelines associated with **Response to Intervention (RTI)** key concepts and guidelines. RTI is now a mandated process. Bender's book assists educators with the basic and necessary steps to provide students with a free and appropriate public education in the least restrictive environment.

The World Is Flat: A Brief History of the 21st Century

Thomas L. Friedman's book—first released in 2005 and later as an "updated and expanded" edition in 2006, with additional updates in 2007—analyzes the progress of globalization, with an emphasis on the early 21st century. The title is a metaphor for viewing the world as flat or level in terms of commerce and competition, as in a level playing field—or one where all competitors have an equal opportunity. As the first edition cover indicates, the title also alludes to the historic shifts in perception once people realized the world was not flat but round and how a similar shift in perception—albeit figurative—is required if countries, companies, and individuals want to remain competitive in a global market where historical, regional, and geographical divisions are becoming increasingly irrelevant. Thus, a major emphasis on global education is included in the school curriculum today.

The Way I See It: A Personal Look at Autism and Asperger's

The Way I See It: A Personal Look at Autism and Asperger's is a book on the challenges of autism. Temple Grandin (2011), a professor at Colorado State University and behavioral consultant with high-functioning autism, is widely known as an advocate for children with autism. She has been included in the 2010 *Time* 100, the magazine's annual list of the 100 most influential people in the world.

The list, now in *its* seventh year, recognizes the activism, innovation, and achievement of the world's most influential *individuals.* Temple is listed among the 25 "Heroes" of 2010. The author of the article, a professor at Harvard University, wrote, "What do neurologists, cattle, and McDonald's have in common? They all owe a great deal to one woman . . . Temple Grandin . . . an extraordinary source of inspiration for autistic children, their parents—and all people" (Hauser, 2010).

TECHNOLOGICAL FUNCTIONALISM (2010–PRESENT)

The major thrusts of the Technological Functionalism era, thus far, are best represented by myths and hoaxes about the educational system in the United States, educational reform, the CCSS, and disruptive behavior. While the challenges to fostering literacy among today's students are growing, so is the power of the tools at educators' disposal.

The Temper of the Times

Starting with the second decade of the 21st century, educational reform continues to be one of the most divisive issues in America. As reported in a blog by Gene V. Glass (2014), concerns about the educational system in the United States are resonating because some of the crisis narratives expressed at the edXchange initiative at the Mary Lou Fulton College of Education at Arizona State University in a public meeting on March 22, 2014:

- Our nation is at risk because our children are dumber than Finland, because our teachers are tools of greedy unions, [and] because incompetent "ed school" trained administrators are incapable of delivering first-rate education.
- What public education needs is total reform: higher standards, more tests, brighter teachers uncorrupted by the wishy washy "education school" ideologies, and above all, choice and competition. This narrative serves a set of private interests that want to reform our schools.
- "We need more tests to keep incompetent kids from being promoted." "School uniforms will close the achievement gap." "Teachers are all-important in a child's development; that's why we should fire the bad ones immediately based on their students' test scores and without due process."

About ten years ago, Rupert Murdoch—the billionaire owner of Fox News—called public education a "$600 billion sector in the U.S. alone that is waiting desperately to be transformed." He might have more honestly said, "Public education is a half trillion dollar plum waiting to be picked." Here's one of the pickers: K12 Inc. is a profit-making corporation traded on the NYSE that supplies online virtual education to about 100,000 children nationwide. Its revenues exceed ¾ of a billion dollars annually and its CEO, a former banker, received total compensation last year of more than $1.5 million. All of their revenue comes from state-level charter school programs. To say that K12 Inc. is operating a substandard education factory is to give them more credit than they deserve.

The think tanks' mission is to get us all to believe that public education has failed and private, profit-making corporations hold the solution to restoring America to glory. Corporations enter into cozy relationships with politicians. Legislatures pass laws that create markets for private companies. This is called "crony capitalism," but its benefactors call it "free enterprise." It's the predominant mode of doing business in America today.

In summary, Glass alleged the purveyors of the mythology have been created by corporations and ideological interests that stand to gain from the coming great reformation. Enter the Koch brothers, Eli Broad, the Kaufmanns, Bill Gates, and their richly endowed ilk. In 2011 alone, the Koch Brothers donated $24 million to support free market and libertarian think tanks and academic centers.

The adoption of the CCSS in ELA and mathematics by a number of states is claimed to be the first step toward meaningful and comprehensive comparisons of student performance and achievement among states. Under these new standards, educators across the country will work under the same guidelines for what students need to know and are expected to do (ASCD, 2011). *Assumingly*, the CCSS will provide a consistent, clear understanding of what students are expected to learn, so teachers and parents know what they need to do to help them. Basically, the standards are designed to be robust and relevant to the real world, reflecting the knowledge and skills that our young people need for success in college and careers. The goal is to have American students fully prepared for the future, positioned to compete successfully in the global economy (ASCD, 2011).

Curbing disruptive behavior is a current issue in many U.S. schools (Young, 2014). The Sioux Falls School District in Sioux Falls, South Dakota, implemented a behavioral education program to the elementary school level on a trial basis to see whether it can curb a growing concern in the district. The focus of the two-year pilot program is to place teachers in those schools who are trained in breaking down behaviors into teachable skills that students don't have yet. In assigning another teacher to each of the two elementary schools in what the district calls its Tier 2 Program, the mission is to remove children who are acting or talking inappropriately out of their regular classroom for as short a period of time as is necessary to address their behavior (Young, 2014).

The goal of the district wouldn't be to provide a punitive place, a place where the child is just sitting. It is based on the Boys Town framework. Students are taken to a place in the same building where there would be teaching. When the child is calm and has de-escalated through a teacher's help or through their own coping strategies, then they go to teaching, talking about the challenges the child faces and breaking it down into teachable parts. A board member said, "When we teach kids skills they need to be more successful in the classroom, we then share those with the family at home." "We want these kids to practice these skills in multiple environments" (Young, 2014, p. 6). Interestingly, a person who has grandchildren in the district suggested to board members that the increased behavioral issues schools are seeing could be related to stress tied into the new CCSS.

The Predominant Trends

The 2013–2014 school year drew to a close in U.S. school districts and with it the final period in which white students composed a majority of the nation's K–12 public school population. When schools reopened in August and September 2014, black, Latino, Asian, and Native American students together made up a narrow majority of the nation's public school students (Ross & Bell, 2014). Broader demographic trends indicate that the new student majority, a collection of what have long been thought of as minority groups, will grow. In just three years, Latino students alone will make up nearly 28% of the nation's student population according to data from the National Center for Education Statistics (2004). Latino student population growth combined with a slow but steady decline in the number of white children attending public schools will transform the country's schools.

As public schools increasingly become institutions serving large numbers of students of color, some states with largely white state legislatures and aging electorates have already proven unwilling to raise taxes or divert needed funds to meet the needs of public schools. Further, school funding and other public resource needs will become increasingly critical as children of color go on to become the majority of the U.S. workforce and total population by 2042.

The Exemplary Leaders

It is symbolic that the leaders selected as representing this exciting period of innovation and experimentation are true educators who challenge unsound beliefs about U.S. public schools with sound research.

David C. Berliner is an educational psychologist, an emeritus professor and dean of the Mary Lou Fulton Teachers College at Arizona State University. He has authored more than 200 articles, books, and chapters in the fields of educational psychology, teacher education, and educational policy, including the bestseller *The Manufactured Crisis*. His recent publication, *50 Myths & Lies That Threaten America's Public Schools: The Real Crisis in Education* (Berliner, Glass, & Associates, 2014), challenges the myths and hoaxes about U.S. public schools with sound research.

Gene V. Glass is currently a senior researcher at the National Education Policy Center and a Regents' Professor Emeritus from Arizona State University. Trained originally in statistics, his interests broadened to include psychotherapy research, evaluation methodology, and policy analysis. His work on meta-analysis of psychotherapy outcomes (with M. L. Smith) was named as one of the *Forty Studies That Changed Psychology* in the book of the same name by Roger R. Hock (1999). His more recent contributions to the analysis of education policy include *Fertilizers, Pills and Magnetic Strips: The Fate of Public Education in America* (Glass, 2008) and *50 Myths & Lies That Threaten America's Public Schools: The Real Crisis in Education* with David C. Berliner and Associates (2014).

The Major Publications

50 Myths & Lies That Threaten America's Public Schools: The Real Crisis in Education

For example, Myth 1 in the book *50 Myths & Lies That Threaten America's Public Schools: The Real Crisis in Education* challenges the 2011 TIMSS results:

> The average U.S. score in mathematics, in both 4th and 8th grade, for the many millions of children in school where family poverty rates were less than 50% was higher than the mean scores of Finnish children in those grades. Furthermore, the state of Massachusetts participated in this TIMSS study as a separate entity from the United States as a whole. Massachusetts is ranked relatively high in unionization and in preschool attendance, has a relatively low unemployment rate, and has almost universal health care. In short, it is a progressive state with social policies and practices closer to Finland, than say Alabama. So how did Massachusetts do? It scored so high that only a few Asian countries beat it, and the mean 8th-grade scores in math and science for African American children in Massachusetts were higher than the mean scores of high-scoring Finland. Education systems in the United States obviously differ enormously, and average scores on international tests cannot capture that variation. (pp. 16–17)

Jonathan Kozol, in his review of the book, *50 Myths & Lies That Threaten America's Public Schools: The Real Crisis in Education,* so fittingly said, "this book is a powerful defense of public education and a discerning refutation of the reckless misimpressions propagated by a juggernaut of private-sector forces and right-wing intellectuals who would gladly rip apart the legacy of democratic schooling in America." Berliner et al. (2014) separated fact from fiction in this comprehensive look at modern education reform. In reality, the authors are able to sort through the discord of today's all too often ill-informed debate. The book is a true grit loaded with hard data and, as Linda Darling-Hammond in her review of the book said, "Anyone involved in making decisions about today's schools should read this book."

Planning for Technology: A Guide for School Administrators, Technology Coordinators, and Curriculum Leaders (2nd ed.)

The textbook *Planning for Technology: A Guide for School Administrators, Technology Coordinators, and Curriculum Leaders* (2nd ed.) provides educators with indispensable tools that engage learners and enhance learning. At the core of a successful education system is an effective technology plan that Whitehead et al. (2013) masterfully outline.

The authors noted that in the past 30 years, humanity has moved into a digital era where billions of people are connected via an ever-advancing technology boom. Technological growth has led to changes in the ways in which humans communicate with one another, and we are connecting in new ways on both physiological and emotional levels. Also, new neural pathways are created as a result of using the Internet and new relationships are being formed more quickly and by different avenues. Recent research suggests that the brain may interpret this digital interaction as the same as in-person interaction while others maintain that differences are growing between how we perceive one another online as opposed to in reality. Inevitably, as technology shows no signs of slowing its expansion into every facet of our lives, the authors note that these changes will become more pronounced. Still, while little is yet known about the extent and implications of these changes, this book attempts to highlight several of them.

Within the book, readers are shown that a modern technology plan respects that students are demanding a rich learning environment that utilizes their knowledge of complex social networks, instant information retrieval, and real-time feedback that provides up-to-the-minute performance evaluations. In the foreword to the book, Dr. Daniel J. Hoesing, superintendent of the Schuyler Community Schools in Schuyler, Nebraska, writes, "the formal educational background and practical experience of the authors make this book a real treasure." Also, "the authors use the term future proofing when talking about their technology infrastructure to assist readers in understanding the impact of an effective technology plan has on the quality and sustainability of today's learning environment" (pp. vii–ix).

Understanding Common Core Standards

John Kendall (2011) provided an in-depth analysis of the CCSS in his book titled *Understanding Common Core Standards*. To fully understand the CCSS, it is essential to comprehend how standards-based recommendations have transformed K–12 education in the United States. He describes the three phases of the standards movement by labeling them as before standards, during standards, and under the CCSS. Each chapter provides a learning experience for the reader. For example, Chapter 1 addresses the CCSS in context while Chapter 2 articulates "what the standards look like." Chapter 3 shows what benefits are derived from CCSS and what concerns exist. Ways on how to prepare for the CCSS are presented in Chapter 4, and Chapter 5 provides a worthy conclusion by looking ahead. It is a timely publication that blends argument and evidence.

A CENTURY PLUS OF CURRICULUM TRENDS IN RETROSPECT

In reviewing this century of curriculum history, two general observations might be made. The first is regarding the pace of change. Observe that after the first two 20-year periods, the remaining periods become increasingly shorter, each lasting 10 years. Having said that, it would seem that futurists who have commented on the rapid pace of change in today's society are probably correct.

The second observation is of the rhythms and directions of that change. Here, it might be useful to search for the best metaphor describing those rhythms and directions. Currently, when most educators speak about the general directions of the curriculum, past and present, they seize initially on the metaphor of the pendulum, which suggests short swings between extreme positions. Or they talk of cycles, a more abstract figure that suggests longer periods of recurring tendencies. Neither metaphor seems to portray the past century plus of curriculum history. Instead, it might be more appropriate and more insightful to speak of separate streams that continue to flow—at times swollen, at times almost dry; at times separate, at times almost joining.

In identifying such streams in our curricular history, some useful terms proposed by Eisner and Vallance as early as 1974 help delineate the five orientations in the curriculum: academic rationalism (foster intellectual growth in the subjects most worthy of study), personal relevance (emphasize the primacy of personal meaning), cognitive processes (help children acquire the basic skills and learn how to think), social adaptation reconstruction (derive educational aims from an analysis of the society), and technology (operationalize curricular outcomes by technological analysis of the observable behaviors sought). The nine curricular orientations—Academic Scientism, Progressive Functionalism, Developmental Conformism, Scholarly Structuralism, Romantic Radicalism, Privatistic Conservatism, Technological Constructionism, Modern Conservatism, and Technological Functionalism—are thus seen as streams that always have been present during the 20th century and the beginning of the 21st century of curricular history.

Exhibit 2.3 shows how these streams seem to have ebbed and flowed throughout the separate periods. It reflects how their strength has varied and how, during a given period, one or two have predominated. It suggests that the strength of a given orientation at a particular time seems to have resulted from powerful social forces impinging on the curriculum. It also makes clear that educators in general have typically espoused a pragmatic eclecticism, one in which all nine streams have at least some part to play.

EXHIBIT 2.3 The Streams of Curricular History

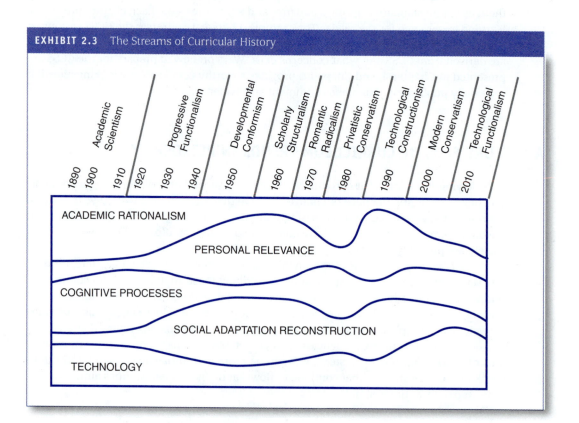

SUMMARY

This chapter provides a useful understanding of the history of curriculum development for scholars and practitioners and a careful analysis of the past 100-plus years of curriculum development history. A historical understanding results in a deeper awareness of the extent to which curricular changes are often influenced by and are a manifestation of larger social forces. Chapter 2 offers an expansive perspective from which to view so-called innovations and reforms. In addition, this chapter focuses on the major developments affecting American schools and provides an essential broader perspective. Specifically, the chapter addresses the periods of Academic Scientism, Progressive Functionalism, Developmental Conformism, Scholarly Structuralism, Romantic Radicalism, Privatistic Conservatism, Technological Constructionism, Modern Conservatism, and Technological Functionalism and why each was important in the development of curriculum. Finally, some of the predominant trends that transcended each major period of curriculum development are identified.

APPLICATIONS

1. Based on what you have learned about the history of curriculum and what you observe happening now, when do you think the period of Technological Functionalism will end, and what type of period will succeed it?

2. Some have argued that there are really no new ideas in education and that all so-called innovations are simply a refurbishing of old ideas. Based on your knowledge of curriculum history, would you agree or disagree? Please explain.

3. Most nationally disseminated reports recommending educational reform have very little impact. How, then, do you explain the seemingly profound impact made by the reform reports of the 1990s and the early years of the 21st century?

4. NCLB has had major impacts on how schools plan and implement curriculum, as well as on how students are assessed. What aspects of NCLB do you feel have been advantageous to the school improvement process? What aspects, if any, do you feel have been detrimental, and why?

5. Charter schools, school vouchers, and homeschooling movements are becoming commonplace in American education. How do you feel about each of these practices, and do you believe that they will continue in the future? Why or why not?

6. According to Van de Water and Krueger (2002), much more evidence is needed concerning what works in a P–16 system. Which element from the following list would be the most difficult to accomplish, and which one would be the easiest to accomplish? Why?

   o *Inclusiveness*—everyone expected to meet rigorous learning standards
   o *Alignment*—of standards, curricula, expectations, assessments
   o *Support*—for all learners as they strive to meet learning standards

○ *Removal of artificial barriers*—especially those surrounding the transition from high school to college (e.g., high school exit requirements, college entrance requirements, and college placement assessments)

○ *Reductions in level of remediation*—high expectations, clear standards, and strong support services leading to better-prepared students able to meet postsecondary expectations upon entry

7. School district and state-level education leaders are charged with developing and administering educational curricula to best prepare students for their future. Yet there can be tension between a curriculum that develops a well-rounded student and a curriculum that helps create a student who is career ready. Explain your opinion in detail.

8. Although the Seven Cardinal Principles were published in 1918, they are just as apt today as they were then. Do you agree or disagree that education must consist of more than just the three Rs for this great nation to exist for another 200 years? Why?

CASE STUDY | **Curriculum Approaches Can Challenge Administrators**

The new elementary school principal, Dr. Susan Davenport, was hired to replace Dr. Robert Edwards, who left Washington Elementary School for a professorship at a university in the same town. When she was hired, the superintendent told her that he expected the principal to get the school's staff on board to bring the curriculum into compliance with district, state, and federal standards.

With the superintendent's edict to bring the staff on board so that the standards could be met, Dr. Davenport felt that information was needed about the diverse faculty at Washington Elementary School. She arranged a meeting with the previous principal to get some insights about the faculty at the school. Dr. Edwards was pleased to meet with Dr. Davenport and share some information about the teachers.

In describing the six fourth-grade faculty members at Washington Elementary School, Dr. Edwards made reference to Mr. Anderson, who was a 40-year veteran at the school. He noted that Mr. Anderson is very conservative in nature and a blend of Academic Scientism and Progressive Functionalism. He also does not believe in individualizing or having students work in groups. Another teacher, Mrs. Ferrell, is less conservative than Mr. Anderson; however, she is not a big fan of technology and focuses on the social aspects of the child, a type of Developmental Conformism.

Mrs. Bardwell, a close friend of Mrs. Ferrell, is a far more structured teacher who has the desks lined up in rows. She does focus on fundamentals but uses an inquiry approach to teaching at times, especially in science. Dr. Edwards felt that Dr. Bardwell fit nicely into the era of Scholarly Structuralism—curriculum should be focused on discipline-based principles, concepts, and inquiry processes. Tammy Rabine, another fourth-grade teacher, Dr. Edwards noted, is right out of the Romantic Radicalism period. She is an exciting and imaginative teacher but does not follow the district curriculum scope and sequence and is not interested in clear and articulated objectives. Her philosophy is that learning is about student discovery and student self-esteem. In contrast, Tammy's colleague, Jack Duringer, is very much into critical thinking and the development of an academically challenging curriculum. He is also a stickler for assessment and accountability, as well as technology, which places him in the Privatistic Conservatism and Technological Constructionism eras.

Juanita Sanchez, the last fourth-grade teacher who Dr. Edwards talked about, has taught for two years and is a wiz with technology. Because she is interested in cultural diversity, she believes in teaching values through the curriculum. She is a strong proponent of standards for teaching and assessment and could well fit the Technological Constructionism, Modern Conservatism, and Technological Functionalism eras.

The Challenge

Analyze the behavior of the fourth-grade teachers in this case. How can the new principal get the thinking of teacher-leaders and the fourth-grade faculty working together to bring the curriculum into compliance with district, state, and federal standards?

Key Issues or Questions

1. Judging from your own experience, do you think it was ethical for Dr. Edwards to discuss his former teachers with the new principal? Why or why not?

2. Curricular changes are often influenced by and are manifestations of larger social forces. What societal changes are influencing curricular changes today?

3. Is it possible to bring a school facing the problem of unsatisfactory levels of student achievement to meet the current standards set by the district, state government, and federal government with a diverse faculty? Why or why not?

4. One of the major problems of this school was the lack of incentive to change, a situation not unique to Washington Elementary School. Tradition and goal ambiguity tended to make this school sluggish. How can the new principal initiate change efforts and find ways of providing help instead of "managing" school-level programs?

5. How might the principal use the diversity of faculty as strength to improve the teaching and learning process?

WEBLIOGRAPHY

Academic Scientism (1890–1916)

http://stevebarrington.blogspot.com/2008/06/week-one-compare-and-contrast.html

Brain Revolution (2012–present)

http://blogs.biomedcentral.com/bmcblog/2014/03/13/

advances-to-watch-in-brain-research-a-collection-of-editors-perspectives

Developmental Conformism (1941–1956)

www.proprofs.com/quiz-school/story.php?title = curriculum-i

Global Education

www.globaled.org/fianlcopy.pdf

Modern Conservatism (2000–2012)

www.huffingtonpost.com/sahil-kapur/key-difference-between-mo_b_175535.html

P–16 Education

www.ecs.org/html/issue.asp?issueID = 76

Privatistic Conservatism (1975–1989)

www.ecs.org/html/issue.asp?issueID = 76

Progressive Functionalism (1917–1940)

http://research-education-edu.blogspot.com/2009/01/theory-of-functionalism-in-education.html

Romantic Radicalism (1968–1974)

www.proprofs.com/flashcards/download.php?title = school-curriculum

Scholarly Structuralism (1957–1967)

www.filmreference.com/encyclopedia/Romantic-Comedy-Yugoslavia/Structuralism-and-Poststructuralism-THE-SCIENTIFIC-METHOD-STRUCTURALISM.html

Status of Charter School Legislation

www.charterschoolstoday.com/charter-school-legislation.php

Technological Constructionism (1990–1999)

www.bookrags.com/history/america-1990s-science-technology

REFERENCES

Allington, R. L. (2005). *What really matters for struggling readers: Designing research-based programs.* Boston, MA: Allyn & Bacon.

ASCD. (2011). *ASCD and common core standards resources.* Retrieved from http://www.ascd.org/public-policy/common-core.aspx

Banks, J. A. (1981). *Multiethnic education: Theory and practice.* Boston, MA: Allyn & Bacon

Banks, J. A. (1988). Approaches to multicultural curriculum reform. *Multicultural Leaders, 1*(2), 41–46.

Banks, J. A. (1994). *Multiethnic education: Theory and practice* (3rd ed.). Boston, MA: Allyn & Bacon.

Banks, J. A. (2006). *Cultural diversity and education* (5th ed.). Boston, MA: Allyn & Bacon.

Banks, J. A., & Banks, C. A. M. (2001). *Multicultural education: Issues and perspectives* (4th ed.). Boston, MA: Allyn & Bacon.

Barton, P. E. (2006). Needed: Higher standards for accountability. *Educational Leadership, 64*(3), 28–36.

Bender, W. N. (2007). *Response to intervention: A practical guide for every teacher.* Thousand Oaks, CA: Corwin Press.

Berliner, D. C., Glass, G. V., & Associates. (2014). *50 myths & lies that threaten America's public schools: The real crisis in education.* New York, NY: Teachers College Press.

Bernhardt, V. L. (1998). *Data analysis: For comprehensive schoolwide improvement.* Larchmont, NY: Eye on Education.

Bloom, B. S. (Ed.). (1956). *Taxonomy of educational objectives: The classification of educational goals; Handbook 1. Cognitive domains.* New York, NY: McKay.

Bobbitt, F. (1913). *The supervision of city schools (Twelfth Yearbook of the National Society for the Study of Education, Part I).* Chicago, IL: University of Chicago Press.

Boschee, F., Beyer, B. M., Engelking, J. L., & Boschee, M. A. (1997). *Special and compensatory programs: The administrator's role.* Lanham, MD: Rowman & Littlefield.

Boschee, F., & Hunt, M. M. (1990). Educational choice and vouchers—Where do you stand? *NASSP Bulletin, 74*(524), 75–86.

Boyer, E. L. (1983). *High school: A report on secondary education in America.* New York, NY: Harper & Row.

Bruner, J. S. (1960). *The process of education.* Cambridge, MA: Harvard University Press.

Casoli-Reardon, M., Rappaport, N., Kulick, D., & Reinfeld, S. (2012). Ending school avoidance. *Educational Leadership, 70*(2), 51–55.

Center on Juvenile and Criminal Justice. (2000). *School house hype: Two years later.* Retrieved from http://www.cjcj.org/pubs/schoolhouse/shh2.html

Chamberlin, M., & Plucker, J. (2008). P–16 education: Where are we going? Where have we been? *Phi Delta Kappan, 89*(7), 472–479.

Colvin, R. L. (2013). New "chief" will stay the course. *Phi Delta Kappan, 94*(5), 66–67.

Commission on the Reorganization of Secondary Education. (1918). *Cardinal principles of secondary education.* Washington, DC: Government Printing Office.

Conant, J. B. (1959). *The American high school today.* New York, NY: McGraw-Hill.

Connelly, G. (2010). Pay it forward. *Principal, 89*(3), 52.

Connelly, G. (2012). There's no time like the future. *Principal, 91*(3), 48.

Cuglietto, L., Burke, R., & Ocasio, S. (2007). A full-service school. *Educational Leadership, 64*(6), 72–73.

Cunningham, P. M., & Allington, R. L. (1994). *Classrooms that work: They can read and write.* New York, NY: HarperCollins.

Curriculum Development Associates. (1972). *Man: A course of study.* Washington, DC: Author.

Danielson, C. (2002). *Enhancing student achievement: A framework for school improvement.* Alexandria, VA: ASCD.

Darling-Hammond, L. (1997). *The right to learn.* San Francisco, CA: Jossey-Bass.

Darling-Hammond, L. (2010). *The flat world and education.* New York, NY: Teachers College Press.

Darling-Hammond, L., & Bransford, J. (2005). *Professional development schools: Schools for developing a profession.* New York, NY: Teachers College Press.

Darling-Hammond, L., Wise, A. E., & Klein, S. P. (1999). *A license to teach.* San Francisco, CA: Jossey-Bass.

Dewey, J. (1900). *The school and society.* Chicago, IL: University of Chicago Press.

Dewey, J. (1902). *The child and the curriculum.* Chicago, IL: University of Chicago Press.

Dewey, J. (1916). *Democracy and education.* New York, NY: Macmillan.

Dewey, J. (1938). *Experience and education.* New York, NY: Macmillan.

Dewey, J. (1964). *John Dewey on education: Selected writings* (R. Archambaust, Ed.). New York, NY: Random House.

Education Commission of the States. (1982). *The information society: Are high school graduates ready?* Denver, CO: Author.

Educational Policies Commission. (1944). *Education for all American youth.* Washington, DC: National Education Association of the United States.

Educational Policies Commission. (1945). *Educational services for young children.* Washington, DC: National Education Association of the United States.

Educational Policies Commission. (1948). *Education for all American children.* Washington, DC: National Education Association of the United States.

Eisner, E. W., & Vallance, E. (1974). *Conflicting conceptions of curriculum.* Berkeley, CA: McCutchan.

Fenske, N. R. (1997). *A history of American public high schools: 1890–1990.* Lewistown, NY: Edwin Mellen Press.

Ferguson, M. (2013). Economists' view of education is not all bad. *Phi Delta Kappan, 95*(3), 68–69.

Flexner, A. (1916). The modern school. *American Review of Reviews, 8,* 465–474.

Friedman, T. L. (2005). *The world is flat: A brief history of the twenty-first century.* New York, NY: Farrar, Straus, & Giroux.

Friedman, T. L. (2006 & 2007). *The world is flat: A brief history of the twenty-first century, expanded editions.* New York, NY: Farr, Straus & Giroux.

Fullan, M. (2001). *Leading in a culture of change.* San Francisco, CA: Jossey-Bass.

Gelman, R., & Baillargeon, R. (1983). A review of some Piagetian concepts. In P. H. Mussen (Ed.), *Handbook of child psychology* (Vol. 3, pp. 167–230). New York, NY: John Wiley.

Giles, H. H., McCutchen, S. P., & Zechiel, A. N. (1942). *Exploring the curriculum.* New York, NY: Harper.

Gilmore, J. (2005, August). Keep the home-school fires burning. *New American, 21*(17), 29–33.

Glass, G. V. (2008). *Fertilizers, pills, and magnetic strips: The fate of public education in America.* Charlotte, NC: Information Age Publishing, Inc.

Glass, G. V. (Ed.). (2003). *Education policy analysis archives.* Retrieved from http://epaa.asu.edu/epaa/board/darling-hammond.html

Glass, G. V. (2014). *BLOG. Remarks at the launch of "50 myths & lies . . ."* [Blog post]. Retrieved from http://ed2worlds.blogspot.com/2014/03/remarks-at-launch-of-50-myths-lies.html

Glatthorn, A. A. (1975). *Alternatives in education: Schools and programs.* New York, NY: Dodd, Mead.

Goals 2000: Educate America Act, H.R. 1804, 103d Cong. (1994). Retrieved from http://www.ed.gov/legislation/GOALS2000/TheAct/intro.html

Gorski, P. C. (1999, November). *A brief history of multicultural education.* Critical Multicultural Pavilion: Research Room. Retrieved from http://www.edchange.org/multicultural/papers/edchange_history.html

Grandin, T. (2011). *The way I see it: A personal look at autism and Asperger's* (2nd ed.). Arlington, TX: Future Horizons.

Hall, G. S. (1969). *Adolescence*. New York: Arno and the *New York Times*. (Original work published 1904)

Harvey, J. (2012). Response: School choice, a fix that fails. *Educational Leadership, 69*(6), 91–92.

Hauser, M. (2010, April 29). Temple Grandin: The 2010 Time 100. *Time*. Retrieved from http://www.time .com/time/specials/packages/article/0,28804, 1984685_1984949_1985222,00.html

Havighurst, R. J. (1972). *Developmental tasks and education* (3rd ed.). New York, NY: David McKay.

Haycock, K., & Huang, S. (2001). Are today's high school graduates ready? *Thinking K–16, 5*(1), 3–17.

Hewitt, T. W. (2008). Speculations on a *Nation at Risk:* Illusions and realities. *Phi Delta Kappan, 89*(8), 579.

Hock, R. R. (1999). *Forty studies that changed psychology: Explorations into the history of psychological research*. Upper Saddle River, NJ: Prentice Hall.

Holt, J. (1964). *How children fail*. New York, NY: Pitman.

Houchens G. (2012). Talking back on privatization. *Educational Leadership, 69*(6), 91–92.

InfoMedia, Inc. (1993). *Educational reform: A national perspective*. Ellenton, FL: Author.

Johnson, D. (2013). Power up! Good technology choices: A team effort. *Educational Leadership, 71*(1), 80–82.

Jones, R. (2000). Making standards work: Researchers report effective strategies for implementing standards. *American School Board Journal, 187*(9), 27–31.

Kendall, J. (2011). *Understanding Common Core Standards*. Alexandria, VA: ASCD.

Kliebard, H. M. (1985). What happened to American schooling in the first part of the twentieth century? In E. Eisner (Ed.), *Learning and teaching the ways of knowing* (pp. 1–22). Chicago, IL: University of Chicago Press.

Knudsen, L. R., & Morrissette, P. J. (1998). Goals 2000: An analysis and critique. *International Electronic Journal for Leadership in Learning, 2*(4). Retrieved from http://people.ucalgary.ca/ ~ huartson/iejll/vol ume2/Knudsen2_4.html

Levin, B. (2012–2013). Staying optimistic in tough times. *Phi Delta Kappan, 94*(4), 74–75.

Marzano, R. J. (2013). Art and science of teaching: Cognitive verbs and the common core. *Educational Leadership, 71*(1), 78–79.

Marzano, R. J., Waters, T., & McNulty, B. A. (2005). *School leadership that works*. Alexandria, VA: ASCD.

McCollum, J. (2010). With foresight comes success. *Principal, 89*(5), 52.

Murphy, J., & Shiffman, C. D. (2002). *Understanding and assessing the charter school movement*. New York: Teachers College Press.

National Center for Education Statistics. (2004). *Homeschooling in the United States: 1999*. Washington, DC: U.S. Department of Education, Office of Educational Research and Improvement.

National Commission on Excellence in Education. (1983). *A nation at risk: The imperative for educational reform*. Washington, DC: Government Printing Office.

National Education Association. (1893). *Report of the Committee on Secondary School Studies*. Washington, DC: Government Printing Office.

National Education Association. (1895). *Report of the Committee of Fifteen*. New York, NY: Arno and *The New York Times*.

North Idaho State College. (2007). *Tech prep leads from high school to technical training, college degrees, and high-demand careers*. Retrieved from http:// www.nic.edu/techprep/Region1

Oliver, A. I. (1977). *Curriculum improvement: A guide to problems, principles, and process* (2nd ed.). New York, NY: Harper & Row.

O'Shea, M. R. (2005). *From standards to success*. Alexandria, VA: ASCD.

Parker, F. W. (1894). *Talks on pedagogics*. New York, NY: E. L. Kellogg.

Physical Science Study Committee. (1961). *PSSC physics: Teacher's resource book and guide*. Boston, MA: D. C. Heath.

Piaget, J. (1950). *The psychology of intelligence*. New York, NY: Harcourt.

Provenzo, E. F. (2003). Contemporary educational thought. University of Miami School of Education. Retrieved from http://www.education.miami.edu/ep/ contemporaryed/home.html and http://www.educa tion.miami.edu/ep/contem poraryed/Eliott_Eisner/ eliott_eisner.html

Purkey, S. C., & Smith, M. S. (1983). Effective schools: A review. *Elementary School Journal, 83*(4), 426–452.

Raubinger, F. M., Rowe, H. G., Piper, D. L., & West, C. K. (1969). *The development of secondary education*. New York, NY: Macmillan.

Ravitch, D. (1983). *The troubled crusade: American education 1945–1980*. New York, NY: Basic Books.

Ray, B. D. (2006, July 10). *Research facts on homeschooling*. Retrieved from http://www.exploring homeschool ing.com/ResearchFactsonHomeschooling.aspx

Rogers, C. (1969). *Freedom to learn: A view of what education might become*. Columbus, OH: Merrill.

Ross, J., & Bell, P. (2014, July 1). School is over for the summer. So Is the era of majority white U.S. public schools. *National Journal*. Retrieved from http://www .nationaljournal.com/next-america/education/

school-is-over-for-the-summer-so-is-the-era-of-majority-white-u-s-public-schools-20140701

Rugg, H. O. (Ed.). (1927a). *Curriculum-making: Past and present (Twenty-Sixth Yearbook of the National Society for the Study of Education, Part I)*. Bloomington, IL: Public School Publishing.

Rugg, H. O. (Ed.). (1927b). *The foundations of curriculum-making (Twenty-Sixth Yearbook of the National Society for the Study of Education, Part II)*. Bloomington, IL: Public School Publishing.

Ryan, J. E. (2009). The big picture. *Phi Delta Kappan, 90*(10), 720–723.

Sandler, S., & Hammond, Z. (2012–2013). Text and truth: Reading, student experience, and the Common Core. *Phi Delta Kappan, 94*(4), 58–61.

Sarason, S. B. (1990). *The predictable failure of educational reform*. San Francisco, CA: Jossey-Bass.

Schwab, J. J. (1969). The practical: A language for curriculum. *School Review, 78*(1), 1–23.

Schwab, J. J. (1971). The practical: Arts of eclectic. *School Review, 79*(4), 493–542.

Schwab, J. J. (1973). The practical 3: Translation into curriculum. *School Review, 81*(4), 501–522.

Schwab, J. J. (1978). Education and the structure of the disciplines. In I. Westbury & N. J. Wilkof (Eds.), *Science, curriculum, and liberal education: Selected essays of Joseph T. Schwab* (pp. 229–270). Chicago, IL: University of Chicago Press.

Schwab, J. J. (1983). The practical 4: Something for curriculum professors to do. *Curriculum Inquiry, 13*(3), 239–265.

Silberman, C. (1970). *Crisis in the classroom*. New York, NY: Random House.

Staff and Wire Reports. (2011, September 24). States embrace education law change. *Argus Leader*, p. A5.

Starnes, B. A. (2010). Rethinking diversity. *Phi Delta Kappan, 92*(1), 75.

Taylor, F. W. (1911). *The principles of scientific management*. New York, NY: Harper.

Toch, T. (2010). The Sizer legacy. *Phi Delta Kappan, 91*(5), 75.

Tomlinson, C. (1999). *A differentiated classroom: Responding to the needs of all learners*. Alexandria, VA: ASCD.

Tomlinson, C. A., & McTighe, J. (2006). *Integrating plus differentiated instruction and understanding by design*. Alexandria, VA: ASCD.

Tyler, R. W. (1950). *Basic principles of curriculum and instruction*. Chicago, IL: University of Chicago Press.

Tyler, R. W. (1971). Curriculum development in the twenties and thirties. In R. M. McClure (Ed.), *The curriculum: Retrospect and prospects* (pp. 26–44). Chicago, IL: University of Chicago Press.

US Charter Schools. (2008). *US Charter Schools history and overview*. Retrieved from http://www .uschaarterschools.org/lpt/uscs_docs/309

Van de Water, G., & Krueger, C. (2002). *P–16 education*. Clearinghouse on Educational Policy and Management. Eugene: College of Education, University of Oregon. Retrieved from http://eric .uoregon.edu/publications/digests/digest159.html

Van Til, W., Vars, G. F., & Lounsbury, J. H. (1961). *Junior high years*. Indianapolis, IN: Bobbs-Merrill.

Verges, J. (2011, July 26). New Indian education standards aim for respect. *Argus Leader*, p. A7.

Weber, J. (2010, October 25). "Tea party" hopefuls target Education Department: Candidates renew call to abolish Carter-era agency. *The Washington Times*. Retrieved from http://www.washington times.com/news/2010/oct/25/tea-party-hope fuls-target-education-department

Wells, D. (2012). What if all the computers were broken? *Principal, 91*(3), 12–13.

Whitehead, B. M., Jensen, D. F. N., & Boschee, F. (2013). *Planning for technology: A guide for school administrators, technology coordinators, and curriculum leaders* (2nd ed.). Thousand Oaks, CA: Corwin Press.

Wolfe, P. (2010). *Brain matters: Translating research into classroom practice* (2nd ed.). Alexandria, VA: ASCD.

Wormeli, R. (2006). *Fair isn't always equal: Assessing and grading in the differentiated classroom*. Portland, ME: Stenhouse; Westerville, OH: National Middle School Association.

Young, S. (2014, June 24). Behavior in S. F. schools to receive amplified attention. *Argus Leader*, pp. A1, A6.

CHAPTER 3

Curriculum Theory

Curriculum theory is growing increasingly important in policy debates. Similarly, increased attention to educational research and the advent of Common Core State Standards has primarily focused on the relative merits of various research methodologies. With a renewed focus on curriculum theory and accessing technology on the basis of how well students are learning, these shifts, in turn, are leading to major transformational uses of technology in schools (Johnson, 2013–2014).

Questions addressed in this chapter include the following:

- What is the nature and function of curriculum theory?
- Why is it important to meld the theory and reality of school curriculum together as part of the planning process?
- What curriculum style(s) make conscious decisions about incorporating other styles into practice?
- What is the role of leadership in the development of curriculum theory?
- What are the major classifications of curriculum theory?
- How has technology been a catalyst for curriculum change?

Key to Leadership

Successful curriculum leaders realize educational theory serves as a catalyst for change.

Curriculum theory is fundamental component of curriculum studies. At its best, curriculum theory can provide a set of conceptual tools for analyzing curriculum proposals, for illuminating practice, and for guiding reform.

Melding theory and the reality of school curriculum together is an important step in the educational planning process. Not all curriculum theories translate smoothly into real-world practice. Educators have found it difficult to use theoretical approaches to make continual analyses, reevaluations, and revisions of curriculum in light of such fields as information technology and the sociology of knowledge. It is a daunting task to undertake the complexity of curriculum design given race, class, economic conditions, and cultural diversity—not to mention the continual changes evolving with technological advances in education. It is, therefore, essential to develop a fundamental understanding of curriculum theory by providing the tools necessary when analyzing curriculum proposals, illuminating practice, and guiding reform.

THE NATURE AND FUNCTION OF CURRICULUM THEORY

The concept of schooling and education has long been associated with the idea of curriculum and curriculum theory. With no definitive comprehensive theory that covers the field, a great deal of argument and discussion occurs in the field as to what curriculum theory is and what it is not. Today, with new intensity, educators, researchers, parents, and policymakers are working to create successful schools. Subsequently, no one has all the right answers.

More to the point, we are unlikely to get the practice right—unless we first get the theory right. Likewise, we must first agree on the purposes of education and among many valid purposes, which should be primary and have priority and, likewise, which should not (Sheppard, 2013). When approaching this conundrum, educational leaders must work collaboratively to strike a balance between the *how to get things right* verses *how to get things done*. Fortunately, with new intensity, educators, researchers, parents, and policymakers are working even harder and more collaboratively to create successful schools. This means more and more people in the field of education are collaborating—searching to blend philosophy and practice based on sound research that will result in a quality educational experience for every student.

Curriculum as Praxis

Upon reflection, the field of curriculum is complex, ramified, and highly multifaceted. To understand the concept of theory, it is essential to understand the nature of theory in general. Much disagreement exists among philosophers of science. On the one hand, some espouse what has come to be known as the traditional view of scientific theory.

Historically, the traditional view holds that a theory is a formalized, deductively connected bundle of laws that are applicable in specifiable ways to their observable manifestations. In the traditional view, a small number of concepts are selected as bases for the theory, axioms are introduced that specify the fundamental relationships among those concepts, and definitions are provided, specifying the remaining concepts of the theory in terms of the basic ones.

In reviewing the literature, Miller (2011) compiled the curriculum theories espoused by Ralph W. Tyler, Elliot Eisner, Peter Gray, and Paulo Freire to establish four curriculum styles. The four common schools of thought are linear, holistic, laissez-faire, and the critical theorist approach.

Linear Thinkers

Generally, the linear thinker favors structure, order, and maximum control of a particular environment. According to Miller (2011), "The linearist wants education to be as efficient as possible, both fiscally and empirically. In essence, this model mimics scientific management in the way that Frederick Taylor used science to manage business" (p. 34). In reality, scientific management is alive and well and diversity is not the ultimate goal because of fixed standards imposed on our public schools.

> It is a system that values procedure, routine, and the best way to do the job. Under the influence of such a design, standards control human effort, and predetermined outcomes require mastery, encouraging the worker or student to perform like a well-oiled machine. . . .
>
> We don't need to look far to see these influences in schools. Scope and sequence charts, bell schedules, grade-level designs, and Bloom's taxonomy. Furthermore, the prevalence of how-to books, social tendencies to rate performance against ideals, and our competitive spirit prove that linearism has permeated multiple aspects of life beyond school. Many of us find comfort in specifying content, articulating goals, following routines, and controlling variables. The more we value these elements, the more linear we are on the continuum. (Miller, 2011, p. 34)

Holists

This theory is very pragmatic in a Deweyan sense because it lets the teacher arrange the environment to stimulate student response. For example, by making suggestions, asking questions, and prompting student concern, teachers persuade students to join an educational experience. Such an arrangement, according to Miller (2011), demands more teacher awareness and knowledge in a wide variety of content to meet the varied interests of students. Also, a teacher must pay attention to each student and how that person interacts with the planned lesson.

Miller (2011) alleged the following:

> Holists don't divorce emotion from intellect; therefore, those espousing this philosophy honor a greater variety of learner references. In this model, power is more or less shared, boundaries are often crossed, and integrated learning experiences involve a quest for meaning. The holist pays attention to the emotional and creative components who are "productively idiosyncratic." (p. 34)

Justifiably, rather than seeing fun as the goal, the holistic teacher wants educational experiences that are expansive and substantive. Further, "the holist wants students to become masters of their environment and citizens who are equipped to live in a demo-cratic society" (p. 35). This conviction clarifies the holist's belief—sharing of power and engaging in genuine conversations to negotiate rules, influence policy, and effect cur-riculum change.

Laissez-Faire Advocates

This laissez-faire philosophy maximizes individual freedom without precipitating chaos and espouses no official curriculum. The fundamental belief is that "all people possess natural traits, like curiosity, that predispose learning; the most enduring and profound learning occurs when initiated and pursued by the learner" (Miller, 2011, p. 35). The phi-losophers who actually believe in the laissez-faire values "align their thinking with Piaget, who suggested that we don't learn something until we recognize that we need to know it" (p. 35). With the laissez-faire approach, the following occurs:

> Children freely explore ideas they wonder about. Learning stations provide student with options while allowing students to decide what they should do or why they should do it. The key word is access. Students have access to books, tools, and other resources that enable them to pursue their interests. In this participatory democracy, students initiate all their own activities and create their own environments. (Miller, 2011, p. 35)

Critical Theorists

As Miller (2011) explained, "The critical theorist believes in talking about the elephants in the room" (p. 35). Social justice is the major theme of this theory, which holds the following:

> Teachers should guide students to see social injustices, to make the chains visible, and to uncover subliminal messages. [For example], once students are aware of these external, constraining forces, knowledge might help them combat the hegemony. Any curriculum, then, would invoke critical consciousness, advocate for social and educational transformation, and promote the demonstration of respect, understanding, appreciation, and inclusion. [Further], with an equitable and rigorous curriculum design, teachers help students enter the world independently, preparing them for leadership. (Miller, 2011, p. 35)

This type of curriculum would provide what a person needs for health, comfort, and welfare.

> Critical theorists believe current schools reproduce the status quo—preserving race, gender, class, and social stratifications. They wish to offer an alternative vision through pedagogy of hope that instills the will, desire, knowledge, and skills needed to disrupt official meta-narratives and increase social justice. (Miller, 2011, p. 35)

Miller's (2011) analysis of the curriculum styles presented labels and described curriculum ideologies, which may do little more than provide a glimpse at a possible explanation for behavior. To a degree, however, "most of us possess a little of each of these habits of mind, but we generally espouse preferences that subconsciously or explicitly govern our actions" (p. 35).

Overall, it needs to be emphasized that curriculum as a process is not a physical thing but, rather, the interaction of teachers, students, and knowledge. In other words, curriculum is what actually happens in the classroom and what people do to prepare and evaluate.

NOTE: To conduct a self-examination of what your style is for curriculum theory and practice, use the "Miller Curriculum Style Indicator" (Miller, 2011, pp. 36–39). Miller grants permission to educators who wish to photocopy the survey for nonprofit purposes. Any other use requires written permission from the author, donnamiller@itstriangle.com.

LEADERSHIP IN CURRICULUM THEORY

Leadership involves entrusting the educational lives of children to their teachers and every moment in the classroom to learning (Bambrick-Santoyo, 2014). With that said, the need for leadership and theoretical planning in school curriculum is a common thread running through education on a global level. Not surprisingly, today's administrators and teachers currently face one of the most challenging and exciting times in educational history. New curriculum leaders now need to be familiar with a broad spectrum of curriculum theory ranging from behavioral to critical. They also need to fully understand the "mirrored" relationship between theory and practice and how each can be used to mold and define the other.

The role of leadership in reviewing the relationship between theory and practice will be a crucial element in the future success or failure of curriculum change and how it affects schools. It is, therefore, paramount for communities to encourage and recognize successful leaders who demonstrate an ability to make a difference in teaching and learning. No set rules or formulas exist for leaders to follow—only general guidelines, ideas, and generalities. In this age of technological reform, it is crucial that effective leaders formulate an understanding of curriculum theory if they are truly to evoke educational change in the future. Exercising leadership in these areas helps deepen a comprehension of "what works" and the "why" of curriculum development.

Leaders also need to be aware of the cyclical nature of curriculum theory. This is especially true when reviewing needs analysis, methodologies, evaluation, processes, and assessment procedures. Areas of review for curriculum leaders of the future should include the following:

- Historical development of curriculum studies (as found in Chapter 2)
- Current theory and practice in the field
- Macro and micro dimensions in curriculum
- Ethos and cultural considerations
- Process of curriculum change

- Impact of technology on curriculum
- Models and processes of instructional design
- Models and processes of developing learning strategies
- Identification and implementation of appropriate teaching methods
- Models and techniques of assessment and the evaluation process
- Staff development needs
- Practical application of curriculum design and product for student work programs

Quality leadership means having a thorough understanding of curriculum and being able to change administrative roles and responsibilities when needed to meet the new challenges of curriculum design. It is an art to know how and when to be flexible and yet at the same time be able to make important curriculum decisions. It is an art to be able to change administratively by shifting from a focus on the system to a focus on the learner. Such shifts in leadership style allow teachers to have more **input** in curriculum changes that will allow for the greatest impact on learning. Having educational leaders who understand the curriculum review process, are supportive of change, and are willing to formulate new instructional strategies is a definite key to the success of schools in the future.

CLASSIFYING CURRICULUM THEORIES

Numerous attempts have been made to classify curriculum theories in terms of maturity and complexity, as have attempts at categorization. Curriculum, however, continues to remain dynamic. Historically, McNeil (1985) set up what seems to be an unilluminating dichotomy: *soft curricularists* and *hard curricularists*. Soft curricularists, in his view, are those such as William Pinar and other **reconceptualists** who draw from the "soft" fields of religion, philosophy, and literary criticism; hard curricularists, such as Decker Walker and Mauritz Johnson, follow a rational approach and rely on empirical data. The difficulty with such a dichotomy seems obvious. It results in a grouping together of such disparate theorists as Elliot Eisner and Henry Giroux as soft curricularists simply because they draw from similar research perspectives.

A tripartite classification proposed by Pinar seems equally unsatisfactory: In his formulation, all curriculum theorists can be classified as **traditionalists**, **conceptual empiricists**, or reconceptualists. Traditionalists, in his formulation, are those such as Ralph Tyler, who are concerned with the most efficient means of transmitting a fixed body of knowledge in order to impart the cultural heritage and keep the existing society functioning (Pinar, 1978).

Traditionalists such as Tyler view curriculum as notions of class, teacher, course, units, lessons, and so forth. For example, Hirsch (1995), in *What Your Fifth Grader Needs to Know: Fundamentals of Good Fifth-Grade Education,* revealed his commitment to the concept of basic knowledge and cultural literacy in school curricula. He founded the core knowledge series to promote excellence and fairness in early education. Proponents of formal education are generally interested in the concept of schooling that emphasizes basic knowledge and a definitive structure of instruction that involves the classics. Common themes of formal education proponents might include the development of a syllabus, transmittal of data and knowledge via lecture, formulation of goals and objectives, assessment, and a focus on an end product.

Theorists who espouse an informal education reveal an entirely different perspective on how curriculum should be designed and implemented. Informal proponents such as conceptual empiricists and reconceptualists view education more as an existential experience. Conceptual empiricists, such as Robert Gagne, are those who derive their research methodologies from the physical sciences in attempting to produce generalizations that will enable educators to control and predict what happens in schools. The reconceptualists (a label Gagne applies to himself) emphasize subjectivity, existential experience, and the art of interpretation to reveal the class conflict and the unequal power relationships existing in the larger society. The basic difficulty with this tripartite formulation is that it mixes in a confusing fashion the theorists' research methodologies and their political stances as bases for categorizing theorists. Other theorists such as Elliot Eisner (1985) are equally informal in their approach and seem to be more interested in predicting what will happen in schools. Eisner, as a proponent of informal education, has been a leader in curriculum revision and new approaches for many years.

For example, one of the most widely cited classifications of curriculum theories was proposed by Eisner and Vallance (1974) in their *Conflicting Conceptions of Curriculum*. As they surveyed the field, they found five different conceptions of or orientations to the curriculum. A "cognitive-process" approach is concerned primarily with the development of intellectual operations and is less concerned with specific content. The "curriculum-as-technology" orientation conceptualizes the function of curriculum as finding the most efficient means of accomplishing predetermined ends. "Self-actualization" sees curriculum as a consummative experience designed to produce personal growth. "Social reconstruction–relevance" emphasizes societal needs over individual needs. Theorists with this orientation tend to believe that the primary role of the school is to relate to the larger society, with either an adaptive or a reformist stance. Finally, "academic rationalism" emphasizes the importance of the standard disciplines in helping the young participate in the Western cultural tradition.

While the Eisner and Vallance system seems to make more useful distinctions than either a dichotomous or tripartite system, it does seem to err in including "technology" as a basic orientation of the curriculum. All the other four seem to designate the major sources for determining curriculum content—the cognitive processes, the person, the society, and the subject. A technological orientation is, on the other hand, concerned primarily with advocating one process for developing a curriculum—a process that could be used with any of the other four types.

The basic error of all three formulations (Eisner & Vallance, 1974; McNeil, 1985; Pinar, 1978) is that they do not sort out curricular theories in terms of their primary orientation or emphasis. Here, Huenecke's (1982) analysis of the domains of curricular inquiry seems most productive. She postulates three different types of curricular theorizing: structural, generic, and substantive. Structural theories, which she claims dominated the first fifty years of the field, focus on identifying elements in curriculum and their interrelationships as well as the structure of decision making. Generic theories center their interests on the outcomes of curriculum, concentrating on the assumptions, beliefs, and perceived truths underlying curriculum decisions. Sometimes referred to as critical theories, they tend to be highly critical of past and present conceptions of curriculum. They seek to liberate the individual from the constraints of society, using political and sociological frameworks to examine issues of power, control, and influence. The substantive theories speculate about what subject matter or content is most desirable, what knowledge is of the most worth.

While Huenecke's typology seems useful, it may err in omitting one major domain—those theories such as Schwab's (1970) that are concerned primarily with the processes of curricular decision making. While Huenecke would probably argue that Schwab's work is primarily structural in its emphasis, the distinction between structure and process seems to be one worth maintaining.

It therefore seems most useful to divide curriculum theories into the following four categories, based on their domains of inquiry.

1. **Structure-oriented theories** are concerned primarily with analyzing the components of the curriculum and their interrelationships. Structure-oriented theories tend to be descriptive and explanatory in intent.

2. **Value-oriented theories** are concerned primarily with analyzing the values and assumptions of curriculum makers and their products. Value-oriented theories tend to be critical in nature.

3. **Content-oriented theories** are concerned primarily with determining the content of the curriculum. Content-oriented theories tend to be prescriptive in nature.

4. **Process-oriented theories** are concerned primarily with describing how curricula are developed or recommending how they should be developed. Some process-oriented theories are descriptive in nature; others are more prescriptive.

The rest of this chapter will use this categorization system for examining several major curriculum theories.

Structure-Oriented Theories

As indicated previously, structure-oriented theorists of curriculum are concerned with the components of the curriculum and their interrelationships. Primarily analytical in their approach, they seek to describe and explain how curricular components interact within an educational environment. Structure-oriented theorists examine questions such as the following:

- What are the essential concepts of the curriculum field, and how may they most usefully be defined? For example, what does the term *curriculum* mean?
- What are the levels of curriculum decision making, and what forces seem to operate at each of those levels? For example, how do classroom teachers make decisions about the curriculum?
- How may the curriculum field most validly be analyzed into its component parts? For example, how does a program of study differ from a field of study?

- What principles seem to govern issues of content selection, organization, and sequencing? For example, how can curricular elements be articulated?

In seeking answers to such questions, structure-oriented theorists tend to rely on empirical research, using both quantitative and qualitative methodologies to inquire into curricular phenomena.

Structure-oriented theorists seem to operate at what might be termed either a macro level or a micro level. Macro-level theorists attempt to develop global theories that describe and explain the larger elements of curricular structure.

Here, it is necessary to turn to the work of micro-level theorists who seem more concerned with describing and explaining curricular phenomena as they occur at the institutional instructional levels. George Posner seems most representative of the micro-level theorists. Over the course of several years, he identified and analyzed several microelements of curricular structure. Typical of his theoretical work is an article coauthored with Kenneth Strike in which they presented and explicated a "categorization scheme for principles of sequencing content" (Posner & Strike, 1976). By bringing to bear some useful epistemological distinctions and by analyzing the curriculum literature, Posner and Strike were able to identify five major types of content sequence.

They called the first principle for sequencing content "world related"—the content structure reflects the empirical relationships among events, people, and things. Subtypes here include sequences based on spatial relations, temporal relations, and physical attributes. The second principle is "concept related," in which sequences reflect the organization of the conceptual world. Thus, one subtype of concept-related sequences is "logical prerequisite"—when it is logically necessary to understand the first concept in order to understand the second. "Inquiry-related" sequences are those that sequence the curriculum in relation to a particular method of inquiry, such as Dewey's analysis of the problem-solving process. "Learning-related" sequences draw from knowledge of the psychology of learning in making decisions about sequence; thus, sequencing decisions based on such assumptions as "begin with content of intrinsic interest" or "start with the easiest skills" are learning related in nature. The final principle, "utilization related," sequences learning in relation to three possible contexts for utilization—social, personal, and career.

Value-Oriented Theories

Value-oriented theorists seem to be primarily engaged in what might be termed educational consciousness-raising, attempting to sensitize educators to the value issues that lie at the heart of both the hidden and the stated curricula. Their intent is primarily a critical one; thus, they sometimes have been identified as "critical theorists." Because many have argued the need for reconceptualizing the field of curriculum, they often are labeled as reconceptualists.

In their inquiries, value-oriented theorists tend to examine issues such as the following:

- In what ways do the schools replicate the power differentials in the larger society?
- What is the nature of a truly liberated individual, and how does schooling inhibit such liberation?

- How do schools consciously or unwittingly mold children and youth to fit into societal roles predetermined by race and class?
- As curriculum leaders determine what constitutes legitimate knowledge, how do such decisions reflect their class biases and serve to inhibit the full development of children and youth?
- In what ways does the schools' treatment of controversial issues tend to minimize and conceal the conflicts endemic to the society?

In examining these issues, most value-oriented theorists draw eclectically from several inquiry methodologies, such as psychoanalysis, philosophical inquiry, historical analysis, and political theory.

The Major Value-Oriented Theorists

Because many critical theorists seem to focus on the person, and many others on the socio-political milieu, it seems appropriate to select for examination one person-oriented theorist, James Macdonald, and one milieu-oriented theorist, Michael Apple.

James Macdonald. For a period of almost two decades, James Macdonald seemed to serve as a respected gadfly for the curriculum profession, challenging educators to question their assumptions, aspire to more worthy goals, and reconceptualize the enterprise of curriculum making. A prolific writer, his work is so multifaceted that it is difficult to summarize.

Basic to all his work is his view of the human condition. Central to that human condition is a search for transcendence, the struggle of the individual to actualize the whole self. Much influenced toward the end of his career by the writings of Carl Jung, Macdonald (1974) used almost mystical metaphors in "A Transcendental Developmental Ideology of Education" to speak of this journey toward transcendence as the primary concern of all humans.

Although Macdonald has been criticized for being too mystical and vague, the cumulative effect of his work has been to challenge curriculum leaders to rethink their basic assumptions and reconceptualize their field. In his view, the curriculum offered by most schools is seriously distorted in its emphasis. The goal of education should be to facilitate the development of autonomous and self-actualizing individuals. Macdonald (1977) put the matter cogently:

> Any person concerned with curriculum must realize that he/she is engaged in a political activity. Curriculum talk and work are, in microcosm, a legislative function. We are concerned with the goal of creating the good life, the good society, and the good person. If we curriculum talkers are to understand what we ourselves are saying, and communicate to others, those values must be explicit. (p. 15)

Michael Apple. Michael Apple is a critical theorist who seems to be concerned primarily with the relationship between the society and the school. Central to Apple's (1979) critique of the society and its schools is his use of the term *hegemony* to mean "an organized assemblage of meanings and practices, the central effective and dominant system of meanings, values, and actions which are *lived*" (p. 14). Hegemony in this sense permeates the consciousness of the society as a body of practices and a set of meanings determined by the dominant culture.

One crucial way in which this cultural hegemony influences educators is in their perception of science. In this telling critique of what might be termed *educational pseudoscientism,* Apple (1975) noted that almost all educators rely on a narrow and strict view of science, one that values only rationality and empirical data in the service of predictability and control and that ignores the close relationship between science and art, science, and myth.

Content-Oriented Theories

Content-oriented theorists are concerned primarily with specifying the major sources that should influence the selection and organization of the curriculum content. For the most part, their theories can be classified in terms of their views as to which source should predominate: child-centered curricula, knowledge-centered curricula, or society-centered curricula.

Child-Centered Curricula

Those who espouse child-centered curricula argue that the child is the beginning point, the determiner, and the shaper of the curriculum. Although the developing child will at some point acquire knowledge of subject matter, the disciplines are seen as only one type of learning. While the child develops in and is influenced by a social environment, the needs of the society are not considered paramount; that society will best be served by the kind of mature and autonomous individual that child-centered curricula attempt to develop. As Francis Parker (1894) expressed it many decades ago, "The centre of all movement in education is *the child*" (p. 383).

During the past three decades, three major **child-centered curriculum** movements have occurred: **affective education, open education,** and **developmental education.**

Affective Education. The affective education movement emphasized the feelings and values of the child. While cognitive development was considered important, it was seen only as an adjunct to affective growth. Thus, curriculum leaders were concerned primarily with identifying teaching and learning activities that would help the child understand and express feelings and discern and clarify values. For example, Brown (1975), who advocated "confluent education" (a curriculum approach that attempted to synthesize physical, emotional, and intellectual growth), recommended a "fantasy body trip" as a learning activity. In this activity, students are asked to close their eyes and "move into themselves"; each person is asked to concentrate on different parts of the body, beginning with the toes, and then all participants share their experiences.

Open Education. As previously noted, open education was a child-centered curriculum movement that emphasized the social and cognitive development of the child through informal exploration, activity, and discovery. Here the "whole child" was considered the beginning point and focus of curriculum work. Lillian Weber (1971), one of the foremost exponents of open education, stated the following:

These questions about children seem uppermost in developing plans for the classroom, for plans were not made from the vantage point of a syllabus of demand which a child had to meet, but with relevance to children in the most immediate way. A plan fitted itself to the child. (p. 169)

In fitting the plans to the child, the teacher provisioned a rich learning environment, one that emphasized the use of concrete and interactive materials organized in "learning centers."

The school day was not compartmentalized into subject periods, such as "language arts" and "mathematics." Instead, children experienced an "integrated day"; they were encouraged to solve problems that required the development of several skills and the acquisition of many kinds of knowledge.

Developmental Education. *Developmental education*, as the term is used here, refers to any curriculum theory that stresses the developmental stages of child growth as the primary determiners of placement and sequence.

Some current curriculum leaders use a Piagetian framework in selecting, placing, and structuring appropriate learning experiences. For example, Brooks (1986) described how the teachers in the Shoreham-Wading River (New York) schools first received extensive training in the theory and research on cognitive development. They then learned how to assess their students' cognitive development by using a variety of formal and informal measures. Finally, they were taught specific strategies for modifying and adapting predetermined curricula to match students' cognitive levels.

In the developmental perspective, curricula tend to be seen as instruments for facilitating child development. Certain general outcomes are postulated. The child's present developmental level is assessed. Then learning activities and content are selected that will challenge the student enough to produce growth but without overwhelming the student with impossible demands. In all developmental curricula, the teacher is seen primarily as an adapter of curricula, one who learns to modify predetermined content to fit the developmental needs and capabilities of the learner.

While it seems useful to consider the child's development in selecting and placing content, no conclusive evidence exists suggesting that developmental curricula are more effective than those not embodying such a perspective.

Knowledge-Centered Curricula

Those leaders who advocate a **knowledge-centered curricula** approach argue essentially that the disciplines or bodies of knowledge should be the primary determiners of what is taught. While they acknowledge that child-development research should affect decisions about placement, they pay greater attention to the structure of the disciplines or the nature of knowledge, even in matters of sequence. While they admit that the child lives and grows in a social world, they see society as playing only a minor role in developing curricula. In general, curricula based on a knowledge-centered approach might be divided into two groups: structures of the disciplines curricula and **ways of knowing** curricula.

Structures of the Disciplines. Two major attempts have been made to reform the curriculum so that it places greater emphasis on the subjects. During the period from 1890 to 1910, the concern of curriculum leaders was to standardize the school curriculum and to bring it into closer alignment with college requirements. During the period from 1958 to 1970, the curriculum-reform movement emphasized the updating of curriculum content by emphasizing the structures of the disciplines.

Ways of Knowing. This approach to the curriculum is of rather recent vintage. As Eisner (1985) noted, it grows out of several emerging research lines: cognitive science, human creativity, brain functioning, and conceptions of intelligence and knowledge. While Vallance (1985) saw this interest in ways of knowing as producing a radically different "curriculum map" that is quite distinct from the traditional disciplines, its emphasis on knowledge and knowing seems to warrant placing it in the broader category of knowledge-centered approaches.

Briefly, those espousing such a view argue that there are multiple ways of knowing, not just one or two. Further, they believe these multiple ways of knowing should be given greater attention in the school's curriculum.

Society-Centered Curricula

Several curriculum theorists agree that the social order, **society-centered curricula**, should be the starting point and the primary determiner of the curriculum. They differ sharply among themselves, however, about the stance the schools should take toward the existing social order; accordingly, they can best be understood by categorizing them on these bases: the **conformists**, the **reformers**, the **futurists**, and the **radicals.**

The Conformists. The conformists believe that the existing order is a good one—the best of all possible worlds. While problems obviously exist in that social order, in the eyes of the conformists those problems are of lesser consequence and can be handled by mature adults. Accordingly, the essential task of the curriculum is to indoctrinate the young: help them understand the history of this society, teach them to value it, and educate them to function successfully in it. Curriculum workers with a conformist intent begin curriculum development by identifying the needs of the existing society and its institutions; curriculum objectives are derived from those needs. The teacher is usually expected to serve as an advocate for the free-enterprise system, helping students understand why it is so much better than competing systems.

Curricula with a conformist thrust have been advocated in almost every period of curriculum history. Bobbitt (1918), in his basic work *The Curriculum,* argued for a social point of view, defining the curriculum as "that series of things which children and youth must do and experience by way of developing abilities to do the things well that make up the affairs of adult life; and to be in all respects what adults should be" (p. 42). In the eyes of many critics, the career education movement of the 1970s had a conformist thrust: Bowers (1977) saw its purpose as "designed to socialize students to accept the present organization of work and technology as the taken-for-granted reality" (p. 44). William Bennett, secretary of education during Ronald Reagan's second presidential term, advocated a brand of citizenship education that clearly had a conformist intent.

The Reformers. Those classified as reformers see society as essentially sound in its democratic structure but want to effect major reforms in the social order. The major vehicle is the curriculum: Courses should be developed that will sensitize students to emerging social issues and give students the intellectual tools they need to solve social problems. Thus, curriculum workers should begin the task of curriculum development by identifying social problems. Those social problems—such as racism, sexism, and environmental pollution—then become the center of classroom activity. The teacher is expected to play an active role in identifying the problems, in "raising the consciousness" of the young, and in helping students take actions to bring about the needed reforms.

The reformers seem most vocal during times of social unrest. During the 1930s, Counts (1932) challenged the schools to take a more active role in achieving his vision of a more liberal society: The title of his book—*Dare the School Build a New Social Order?*—conveys the tone of his work. During the late 1960s and early 1970s, liberal educators advocated curricula that would be responsive to what they perceived as a "cultural revolution." For example, Purpel and Belanger (1972) called for a curriculum that would institutionalize compassion and increase students' sense of social responsibility.

The Futurists. Rather than being attuned to the present problems of the society, futurists look to the coming age. They analyze present developments, extrapolate from available data, and posit alternative scenarios. They highlight the choices people have in shaping this coming age and encourage the schools to give students the tools to create a better future. In a sense, they might be described as reformers intent on solving the problems of the year 2020. In their view, the school curricula should have such a futurist orientation, focusing on the developments likely to occur and involving students in thinking about the choices they have and the consequences of the choices they make. Rapidly advancing and clear-cut new technologies will force schools to change rapidly. Gradual improvements of the educational process will not suffice. The education system of today will be completely transformed by 2020. Many factors will promote this change. The most important are the following:

- New management models from business will be applied to the educational system.
- Parents and students will promote change in the system.
- Private companies will play a larger role in the education process.
- Technology will influence the education landscape. (Imagitrends, 2000)

Technology can be used for learning. In an age of communication-rich technology environments, computers can be used for more than just communicating with other human beings (Foti, 2007).

Throughout the past few decades, technology has been viewed for improving student academic performance and increasing the flexibility of public schools. As a result, computer availability and use have increased, and programs addressing educational technology have gained attention (Franklin, 2008). Our schools thrive on information. In the ever-changing world filled with new technology, our teachers and students require the right information, from the right sources, today. Having direct access to industry information gives the competitive edge needed to succeed.

The Radicals. Radicals are those who regard the society as critically flawed and espouse curricula that would expose those flaws and empower the young to effect radical changes. Typically, reasoning from a neo-Marxist perspective, they believe the problems of the age are only symptoms of the pervasive structural inequities inherent in a technological capitalistic system. As a consequence, radicals want to reach the masses by revolutionizing education by "deschooling" the educational process.

One of the leading exponents of such an approach is Paulo Freire (1970), the Brazilian educator whose *Pedagogy of the Oppressed* made a significant impact on radical educators in this country. In Freire's view, the goal of education is *conscientization,* a process of enlightening the masses about the inequities inherent in their sociocultural reality and giving them the tools to make radical changes in that social order that restricts their freedom. He made the process explicit in explaining how he teaches reading. Adults learn to read by identifying words with power—words such as *love* and *person* that have pragmatic value in communicating with others in the community. They create their own texts that express their perceptions of the world they live in and the world they want. They learn to read to become aware of the dehumanizing aspects of their lives, but they are helped to understand that learning to read will not guarantee them the jobs they need.

Process-Oriented Theories

As curriculum theory seems to have reached its maturity as a systematic field of inquiry, several attempts have been made to develop conceptual systems for classifying curricular processes and products (see, e.g., Eisner & Vallance, 1974; Gay, 1980; Schiro, 1978). However, most of these categorization schemes are deficient on two grounds. First, they badly confuse what have been described above as value-oriented, content-oriented, and process-oriented theories. Second, they seem to give only scant attention to the curriculum-development process advocated by the theorist under consideration. Most suggest that there is some correspondence between the value or content orientation of the theory and the type of process espoused, although such connections do not seem apparent. Thus, one of Gay's (as cited in Eisner & Vallance, 1974) "conceptual models of the curriculum-planning process" is what she terms the "experimental model." Her description of the experimental model suggests that it gives predominant weight to the needs of the child as a determiner of content, is vaguely liberal in its value orientation, and emphasizes a planning process that she describes with such terms as *organic, evolving, situational,* and *inquiry centered,* but she does not provide much detail about the specifics of the planning process.

Thus, if we are asking about alternative planning models, we will have to turn to sources other than these widely known classification schemes. Historically, Short's (1983) article "The Forms and Use of Alternative Curriculum Development Strategies" seems to build on previous efforts. It reflects a comprehensive knowledge of both the prescriptive and descriptive literature and seems to offer the greatest promise for analyzing and generating alternative systems. Short's article has two explicit goals. One is to analyze what is known about the forms and use of alternative strategies of curriculum development, and the other is to organize this knowledge in a way that permits one to assess the policy implications of choosing and using one or the other of these strategies.

A System for Examining Curricular Processes

It would seem more pragmatic to both scholars and practitioners to have available for their use a systematic means for examining curricular processes. Such an analytic system should have the following characteristics: It would include all the process elements that the research would suggest are important, thus enabling curriculum researchers to make useful distinctions between sets of recommended and implemented processes; it would be open-ended in form, thus enabling practitioners to become aware of a comprehensive set of alternatives; and it would emphasize description and analysis, not evaluation, enabling both scholars and practitioners to reach their independent conclusions about desirability.

The set of descriptors presented in Exhibit 3.1 represents an initial attempt to formulate such an analytic system. Certain caveats should be noted here. First, the descriptors have been drawn from a preliminary analysis of the literature and the authors' personal experiences, but that analysis has not at this point been completely systematic and rigorous. Second, while there has been some initial success in using it to discriminate between development strategies that on the surface seem quite similar, it needs much more extensive testing and refinement. It is, thus, presented here as an initial formulation that invites criticism and improvement.

The first descriptor focuses on the participants in the process. The second descriptor is concerned with the general tenor of the discussions. A monologic discussion is one in which

---

EXHIBIT 3.1   An Analytic System for Examining the Curriculum Process

1. What groups, or constituencies, should be represented in the developmental sessions?
2. What type of participation structure is recommended for the sessions—monologic, participatory, or dialogic?
3. What shaping factors should receive significant consideration throughout the process?
4. Which curriculum element should be used as the starting point in the substantive deliberations?
5. Which curriculum elements should receive significant consideration—and in what sequence should such consideration occur?
6. Which organizing structures should receive significant consideration—and in what order: course structure, units, lessons, lesson components?
7. Should the progression from element to element or from structure to structure be predominantly linear or recursive?
8. What curriculum images and metaphors seem to influence the process?
9. What general type of problem-solving approach should be used throughout the process—technological, rational, intuitive, or negotiating?
10. What recommendations are made about the form and content of the curriculum product?
11. What recommendations are made for implementing the curriculum product?
12. What recommendations are made for assessing the curriculum product?
13. What criteria should participants use to assess the quality and effectiveness of the process?
14. To what extent should developers be sensitive to the political aspects of curriculum development?

only one person participates or makes decisions, such as a college instructor developing a new course independently. In a participatory discussion, one individual clearly is in control but makes a genuine effort to solicit the input of others. A dialogic discussion is one in which there is much open discussion in an attempt to achieve consensus on key issues.

The third descriptor identifies those elements that influence curriculum decision making, even though they may not be explicitly referred to in the final document. As Exhibit 3.2 indicates, several factors variously affect curriculum decisions. Thus, nursing educators who have been observed developing courses seemed most conscious of the requirements of accrediting bodies. On the other hand, teachers in a large urban district seemed chiefly concerned about "accountability procedures."

EXHIBIT 3.2   Shaping Factors in Curricular Deliberations

1. The developers: their espoused and practiced values, their knowledge and competence
2. The students: their values, abilities, goals, learning styles
3. The teachers: their values, knowledge, teaching styles, concerns
4. The organization: its ethos and structure
5. The administrators of that organization: their values and expectations
6. External individuals and groups (parents, employers, pressure groups): their values and expectations
7. Accrediting bodies: their requirements and recommendations
8. Scholars in the field: their recommendations, their reports of research, their perceptions of the structure of that discipline
9. The community and the larger society: what is required to maintain or change the social order
10. Other courses in that field of study, courses taken previously and subsequently
11. Courses in other fields that students are likely to take concurrent with the course being developed: their contents, impacts, and requirements
12. The schedule for the course: number of meetings, length of meetings, frequency
13. Accountability procedures: examinations, "curricular audits"

The fourth descriptor is concerned with the starting point for the substantive deliberations. As indicated in Exhibit 3.3, several curricular elements are in this formulation, any one of which might conceivably be a starting point. The obvious intent here is to challenge the conventional wisdom that curriculum development must begin with a clear statement of objectives.

As indicated in Exhibit 3.4, the fifth descriptor is concerned with those elements emphasized and the sequence in which they are considered.

The sixth descriptor focuses on the organizing structures of the course—the structural elements that give the course shape. Four structural components are included: the general structure and movement of the course itself, the units, the lessons, and the lesson components.

EXHIBIT 3.3 Curricular Elements

1. Rationale, philosophy, or statement of espoused values
2. Institutional goals or aims
3. Knowledge outcomes for the course, the units, the lessons: concepts, factual knowledge
4. Skill or process outcomes for the course, the units, the lessons
5. Affective outcomes for the course, the units, the lessons: values, attitudes
6. Content choices: elements of subject matter selected for their intrinsic worth (literary or artistic works, periods of history, important individuals, significant events, etc.)
7. Organizing elements: themes, recurring concepts, structures of linkage:
   a. Those used to link this course with courses previously or subsequently studied
   b. Those used to link this course with other courses studied concurrently
   c. Those used to link units in this course with each other
   d. Those used to organize units and relate lessons in a unit to each other
8. Teaching/learning activities
9. Instructional materials and media
10. Time allocations
11. Methods for assessing student learning

EXHIBIT 3.4 Analysis of Doll's (1986) Curriculum-Development Process

1. Groups represented: teachers, pupils, administrators, supervisors, school board, lay community
2. Participation structure: participatory
3. Shaping factors: organizational ethos; pupil needs; teachers' values, knowledge, teaching style, concerns
4. Starting point: institutional goals
5. Elements considered: goals, course objectives, evaluation means, type of design, learning content, interunit linkages, interlesson linkages
6. Organizing structures: not specified
7. Progression: linear
8. Images and metaphor: not used
9. Problem-solving approach: rational
10. Form and content of product: no specific recommendations
11. Implementation recommendations: no specific recommendations
12. Recommendations for evaluating product: extensive formative and summative assessments
13. Criteria in assessing process: 11 specific criteria offered
14. Political sensitivity: limited

The seventh descriptor examines the progression of the discussion. A linear progression would move sequentially from element to element or from structure to structure; a recursive discussion would move back and forth in some systematic fashion. The eighth descriptor asks the researcher to be sensitive to the curricular images and metaphors that seem to influence the process. Does the developer seem to conceptualize a curriculum as a mosaic or a patchwork quilt, as a journey or series of travel experiences, as a set of steps moving from the basement to the top floor? The obvious point, of course, is that such images and metaphors reveal the pervasive belief systems of the developers with respect to that field of study—and such belief systems subtly but profoundly influence their decision making.

The ninth descriptor examines the type of problem-solving process at work. Contrary to what some deliberative theorists assert, it seems in many respects that all curriculum making is a type of problem solving. Four types of problem-solving processes have been recommended by theorists: technological, rational, intuitive, and negotiating. A technological approach to curriculum problem solving argues for a tightly controlled process assessing needs, deriving goals from those needs, performing a task analysis to identify learning objectives, determining the sequential or hierarchical relationship among the objectives, specifying instructional activities, and identifying evaluation procedures.

A rational approach to curriculum problem solving describes the somewhat looser but still logical approach advocated by Schwab (1970) and others: Deliberators collect and examine pertinent data, formulate the curriculum problem, generate alternative solutions, and evaluate those solutions to determine which is best.

In an intuitive approach, participants are encouraged to rely on their intuition and tacit knowledge, like Schon's (1983) "reflective practitioners" who make wise choices but cannot explain how they make those choices. Moreover, in some processes, the problem solving is more like a negotiating exchange in which bargaining and trading and making compromises seem to be the predominant activities.

The 10th descriptor examines the decisions about the form and content of the final product. Again, there might be much variation here. For example, Glatthorn (1980) recommended that the final product should be a loose-leaf notebook that contains only a summary of pertinent research and a list of the required and testable objectives. Today, an electronic version would suffice. Teachers using the notebook or an electronic version have much latitude in how they organize the objectives and which methods and materials they use.

The 11th and 12th descriptors are concerned with the future—what plans are made for implementing and testing the product. The 13th descriptor examines the criteria that the participants seem chiefly to rely on in assessing the quality of their work, and the last descriptor examines the extent to which the process is sensitive to the political aspects of curriculum work.

If such an analytic system is at all valid, then it suggests, of course, that the Tyler rationale is not the only system for developing curricula; in fact, the system has been used in initial trials to analyze the significant differences between several distinct models of curriculum development. Exhibit 3.4 showed how the descriptors were used to analyze Doll's (1986) process, and Exhibit 3.5 shows how they describe the "naturalistic" process reviewed in Chapter 8 in this book.

EXHIBIT 3.5 Analysis of Glatthorn's (1987) Curriculum-Development Process

1. Groups represented: teachers
2. Participation structure: dialogic
3. Shaping factors: students, teachers, administrators, scholars, other courses, schedule
4. Starting point: knowledge and skill outcomes for course; starting point for unit planning varies
5. Elements considered: knowledge and skill outcomes for units and lessons, unit themes, teaching–learning activities, instructional materials and media, time allocations, student assessment
6. Organizing structures: units, lessons
7. Progression: recursive
8. Images and metaphors: not used
9. Problem-solving approach: intuitive
10. Form and content of product: open-ended "scenarios"
11. Implementation recommendations: no specific recommendations
12. Recommendations for evaluating product: emphasis on quality of learning experiences
13. Criteria in assessing process: none provided
14. Political sensitivity: extensive

Alternative Curriculum Approaches

Glatthorn's four curriculum categories still hold up to scrutiny today and continue to help provide a road map for curriculum theory. Nonetheless, Smith (2000) developed his own categories for understanding curriculum development:

- *Transmission of Information:* Curriculum as a body of knowledge to be transmitted via a syllabus
- *End Product:* Curriculum as an attempt to achieve certain ends (products)
- *Process:* Curriculum as a process
- *Praxis:* Curriculum as praxis (action that is committed)

Smith's categories reflect and synthesize the essence of curriculum theory into four easily understood approaches. With this in mind, the authors have taken the liberty of combining Smith's ideas into a figure that also includes categories noted by Glatthorn. Exhibit 3.6 is modified to reveal some clear links between Glatthorn and Smith. Areas of consideration include the body of knowledge and content to be transmitted, the process and value models to be conveyed, the focus on an end product, and the practical and technical deliberation. Most interestingly, Smith's categories mirror elements of Aristotle's characterization of the productive.

When reviewing the model using ideas from Smith and Glatthorn, it is important to note change results from several different perspectives. The model blends together the substantive nature of curriculum theory as well as the development of awareness and understanding. Next,

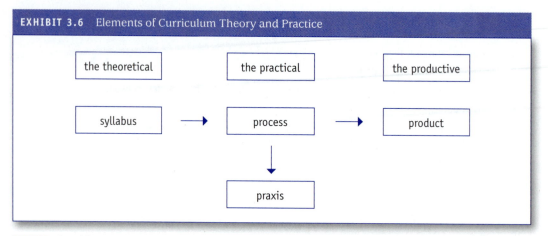

EXHIBIT 3.6 Elements of Curriculum Theory and Practice

SOURCE: Adapted from Smith (2000).

we expand on and compare the similarities between Smith's categories of transmitter of knowledge, end product, process, and praxis as they relate to Glatthorn's typology of structure-oriented theories, value-oriented theories, content-oriented theories, and process-oriented theories.

Curriculum as Transmission of Information

Smith views curriculum as a body of knowledge to be transmitted and equates it with the use of a syllabus. Some theorists believe that an overemphasis on the use of a syllabus as the sole foundation of curriculum is a dependence on content as well as an overdependence on a particular way of organizing a body of knowledge, content, and subjects.

The syllabus and transmitter-of-knowledge approach seems to follow closely with Glatthorn's *structure-oriented theories*. Structure-oriented theorists generally wish to transmit the body of knowledge but tend to rely on empirical research, using both quantitative and qualitative methodologies to inquire into curricular phenomena.

For example, macrostructural theorists are now more globally oriented and use technology to transmit information about curriculum. The use of technology is becoming a larger part of developing curriculum at this level. Educators are using the World Wide Web to share curriculum designs and syllabi. Larger, global forces of polity, economics, common cultures, and classics are becoming points of interest and are more evident when transmitting and sharing basic information. The transmitter-of-knowledge approach is often determined and manipulated to agree with the local interests, values, needs, and wants of the controlling agency, such as a state government educational agency, community, or school.

Curriculum as End Product

A second fundamental aspect of Smith's curriculum theory is that of *achieving an end product*. Goals and objectives become the common focus of theorists using this approach.

Educators using this approach are less concerned with how curriculum is taught than what the end product is and what the goals and objectives are that are used to achieve that product or result—for example, a science report, multimedia math project, piece of literature, poetry, or a speech. This follows with the concept of expanding and explaining curriculum. Themes often center on preparing the student for life, developing abilities, attitudes, habits, and appreciations. The focus of curriculum is generally that of systemic study, **needs assessment,** training, implementation, and evaluation with an emphasis on students' producing tangible results that reflect their potential.

End product approaches seem to follow closely with Glatthorn's *content-oriented theories*. As mentioned previously, content-oriented theorists are often concerned with determining and specifying the major sources as well as the details that influence the selection and organization of curriculum content.

Proponents of product-based curriculum usually focus on the following:

- *Real problems*. Real and relevant to the student and the activity
- *Real audiences*. Utilizing an "audience" that is appropriate for the product, which could include another student or group of students, a teacher (not necessarily the class teacher), an assembly, a mentor, a community or specific interest group
- *Real deadlines*. Encouraging time-management skills and realistic planning
- *Transformations*. Involving original manipulation of information rather than regurgitation
- *Appropriate evaluation*. With the product and the process of its development being both self-evaluated and evaluated by the product's audience using previously established "real-world" criteria that are appropriate for such products (Farmer, 1996)

An example of a product-based approach is Understanding by Design (UbD). UbD proponents Grant Wiggins and Jay McTighe (2005) noted that this approach often looks at instruction from a "results" orientation. They believe that UbD is a recursive process, not a prescriptive program. It targets achievement through a "backward design" process that focuses on assessment first and relevant instructional activities last. The design also uses a spiral of learning where students use and reconsider ideas and skills versus a linear scope and sequence. Individuals using the UbD approach have a tendency to view curriculum in terms of desired "performances of understanding" and then "plan backwards" to identify needed concepts and skills (Tomlinson & McTighe, 2006).

Researchers who espouse product-based curriculum commonly place an emphasis on case studies. Case studies help curriculum designers focus on the realities of classroom life. Teachers have long been aware of the increasing gap between the principles of education taught in university preservice programs and the classroom. The current burgeoning interest in educational case methods is testimony to the promise of case-based teaching as a way of bridging that gap and of easing the novice teacher's entry into the classroom. A case study holds attributes of both theory and practice, enabling teachers and students alike to examine real-life situations under a laboratory microscope. Case studies provide a piece of controllable reality, more vivid and contextual than a textbook discussion, yet more disciplined and manageable than observing or doing work in the world itself (Wiggins & McTighe, 2005).

Curriculum as Process

A third fundamental aspect of current curriculum theory noted by Smith focuses on *curriculum as process*. Viewing curriculum as process places the emphasis on the interaction among teacher, student, parent, and knowledge rather than on a syllabus or on an end product. The focus is on what is actually taking place in the classroom as well as the learning process itself. Critical thinking, listening, and communication are important components of process curriculum. Often, an emphasis is placed on thinking about planning, justifications of procedures, and actual interventions as well as providing feedback and changes during the curriculum process.

One of the earlier curriculum planning approaches involved the *instructional design process*. The instructional design process emerged from psychology laboratories and helped establish the first systematic approach to the development of instructional materials and teaching strategies. Instructional design is the systematic development of instructional specifications using learning and instructional theory to ensure the quality of instruction. It is the entire process of analysis of learning needs and goals and the development of a delivery system to meet those needs. It includes development of instructional materials and activities and tryout and evaluation of all instruction and learner activities (Shulman, 2003). Robert Gagne's (1985) *The Conditions of Learning and Theory of Instruction* and *Principles of Instructional Design* (Gagne, Briggs, & Wager, 1992) describe this approach. Gagne (as cited in Willwerth, 2003) once said the following:

> To know, to understand, to gain insight into, and so on are not useful as descriptions of relatively observable behavior; nor are their intended meanings easily agreed upon by individuals. . . . The action verbs which are used in the construction of the behavioral objectives for *Science: A Process Approach* are: identify, construct, name, order, describe, demonstrate, state a rule, and apply a rule.

The instructional design process continues to be an important part of the planning, implementation, and evaluation of curriculum.

Allan Glatthorn's concept of *value-oriented theorists* relates well to Smith's process and end product approach. It is primarily engaged in what might be termed *educational consciousness raising,* attempting to sensitize educators to the values and issues that lie at the heart of the stated curriculum. Advances in technology and the World Wide Web have provided value-oriented theorists with a global platform to access electronically and to share information on social reform, culture, and economics.

Curriculum as Praxis or Awareness

The fourth aspect of Smith's curriculum model is *praxis*. Praxis models deal primarily with continual reflection, practical deliberation, and differentiated curriculum. Through the use of technological advances, curriculum leaders can now access a body of knowledge; formulate content that is interdisciplinary; and provide a process of electronic communication that helps cut across cultural, economic, and social boundaries worldwide. The praxis concept encourages the student and teacher to reach a higher level of awareness through continual reflection and deepening understanding. It is here where the application of curriculum differentiation as well as advances in technology can help speed up the process. In support of the praxis model, Costa and Kallick (2008) felt that teachers who promote reflective classrooms ensure that students are fully engaged in the process of meaning making. They organize instruction so that students are the producers—not just the consumers—of knowledge. To best guide children in the habits of reflection, these teachers approach their role as that of "facilitator of meaning making" (Costa & Kallick, 2008, chap. 12).

Curriculum Tip 3.1	The art of teaching is the art of assisting discovery. —Mark Van Doren (cited in Costa & Kallick, 2008)

Praxis spotlights the importance of individual and cultural differences and the role of differentiated instruction. For most teachers, *curriculum differentiation* focuses on maximizing the potential of each student in their classrooms. At first glance, this seems basically straightforward, but in actuality, it is very difficult to accomplish. For example, the differences in student scores between Group A (say, low-income students) and Group B (middle-to high-income students) need to decline, with the goal of arriving at the point where scores between the two groups become equivalent (Murphy, 2009). Not surprisingly, this is a good thing if it can be made to happen.

Thus, as can be seen, there are many reasons for teachers to use differentiated instruction. Most notably, it helps teachers align instruction according to student characteristics of readiness and interest. To put it into perspective, students in differentiated classrooms can work on different tasks and are likely to finish their assigned work at different intervals. In conjunction with differentiated instruction, anchor activities are one method for the teacher to ensure that each student constantly has something productive to do. Anchor activities are tasks that students immediately begin working on when assignments are completed. Thus, teachers can create a list of anchor activities to accentuate differentiated instruction, some of which may be suggested by students.

Differentiation is a broad term referring to the need to tailor teaching environments and practices to create appropriately different learning experiences for different students. According to Hockett and Doubet (2013–2014) technology-savvy teachers need to design effective lessons differentiated for readiness. This follows the Common Core State Standards Initiative (CCSSI) and involves pre-assessments being designed to reveal significant differences in the knowledge, skills, or conceptual understandings of students. As a matter of record, however, it should be understood that differentiated curriculum is not a new concept. As early as the 1990s, Keirouz (as cited in Farmer, 1996) suggested the following procedures for enhancing differentiation:

- Deleting already mastered material from existing curriculum
- Adding new content, process, or product expectations to existing curriculum
- Extending existing curriculum to provide enrichment activities

- Providing coursework for able students at an earlier age than usual
- Writing new units or courses that meet the needs of gifted students

The focus here is to create a differentiated learning environment that encourages students to engage their abilities to the greatest extent possible, including taking risks and building knowledge and skills, in what they perceive as a safe, flexible environment. In that regard, Exhibit 3.7 describes what differentiated instruction *should* and *should not* look like.

EXHIBIT 3.7 Differentiated Instruction	
WHAT DOES DIFFERENTIATED INSTRUCTION LOOK LIKE?	
What differentiated instruction is:	*What differentiated instruction is not:*
1. Assessing students before a unit of instruction to determine what they already know	1. All students in the class completing the same work for a unit/chapter
2. Adjustment of the core curriculum by content (below to above grade level), process (concrete to abstract), and product (simple to complex)	2. Limiting how and what is taught by teaching to the average student
3. Providing assignments tailored for students of different levels of achievement	3. Assigning more work at the same level to high-achieving students
4. Having high expectations for *all* students	4. Focusing on student weaknesses and ignoring student strengths
5. Educational experiences that extend, replace, or supplement standard curriculum	5. Activities that all students will be able to do
6. Structuring class assignments so they require high levels of critical thinking and allow for a range of responses	6. Giving the same kind of problems or questions and expecting more
7. Students participating in respectful work	7. Creating more work—extra credit, do when done
8. Students and teachers collaborating in learning	8. Using higher standards when grading
9. Putting students in situations where they don't know the answer—often	9. Providing free-time challenge activities
10. Differing the pace of instruction	10. Using capable students as tutors
11. A blend of whole-class, group, and independent learning	11. Using individualized instruction

SOURCE: Parkway School District (n.d.). Used with permission from the Parkway School District, Chesterfield, Missouri.

Differentiated curriculum in enriched learning environments follows closely with a constructivist philosophy and focuses on making meaning of one's environment and becoming aware of the interaction between the enacted curriculum and the experienced curriculum. In reviewing the literature, Seymour Papert (1993) used the term *construction-ism* to brand his favored approach to learning. He stated the following:

> Constructionism is built on the assumption that children will do best by finding ("fishing") for themselves the specific knowledge they need. Organized or informal education can help most by making sure they are supported morally, psychologically, materially, and intellectually in their efforts. As such, the goal is to teach in such a way as to produce the most learning for the least teaching. (Papert, 1993, p. 4)

Constructionism differs from constructivism in that it looks more closely than other educationalisms at the idea of mental construction. Racer (2007) stated the following:

> Constructivist teachers too often skip the foundation, the discipline and practice of a subject. Because of the failings of the constructivist philosophy, educators have had to endure the back-to-basics movement, the accountability and standards movements, and now the imposition of NCLB [No Child Left Behind Act]. (p. 95)

Constructionism teachers, however, attach special importance to the role of constructions in the world as a support for those in the mind, thereby making this less of a purely mentalist doctrine. As historical examples of constructionist learning activities, Papert (1993) referred "to measuring quantities while making a cake, building with Lego or working with the computer programming language *LOGO* developed specifically . . . for educational use." As scientists study learning, they are realizing that a constructivist model reflects their best understanding of the brain's natural way of making sense of the world (Papert, 1993). Some educators in the field, however, become confused as to who are constructivists and who are behaviorists. In a behaviorist class, one focuses on the answers desired and tries to shape the responses until they resemble a prototype.

Constructivists and differentiated instruction do, however, require that teachers study differences in understanding, learning modalities, and interests. Conflicts between constructivists and those who favor high-stakes testing may be softened by the advent of technology. Advances in technology may hold the promise of providing a means to ameliorate the situation by allowing students to have an active, social, and creative learning environment as well as enabling educators to align the curriculum to state and national standards and assessments.

Through actual practice and activities in the classroom, students will be able to negotiate problems and analyze strategies on a case-by-case, situation-by-situation basis. This approach not only allows for description and explanation but also emphasizes prediction and problem solving at higher levels. It is a curriculum that makes teachers and students more introspective on a global level and allows teachers and students to see through each other's eyes. Learning involves exploration and is based on reflection, exploration, and physical experience. The praxis model becomes more metacognitively and activity centered and more personal in nature, allowing the development of real-life experiences to unfold. A greater chance exists for the dynamic interaction and reflection between student and teacher that drives the learning process. With the assistance of technological advances, a teacher today can be more involved in the process and is better able to capture the coveted "teachable moment."

ORGANIZATIONAL LEADERSHIP MODELS

A number of organizational models can be used to foster curriculum change. Some of these include the System 4 design, site-based management, transformational leadership, synergistic models, and many others. The authors have chosen the following organizational model (see Figure 3.1) in that it provides a novel example of how organizational theory relates to school systems and leadership styles (Shih, 2009).

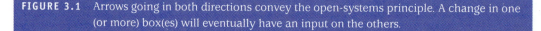

FIGURE 3.1 Arrows going in both directions convey the open-systems principle. A change in one (or more) box(es) will eventually have an input on the others.

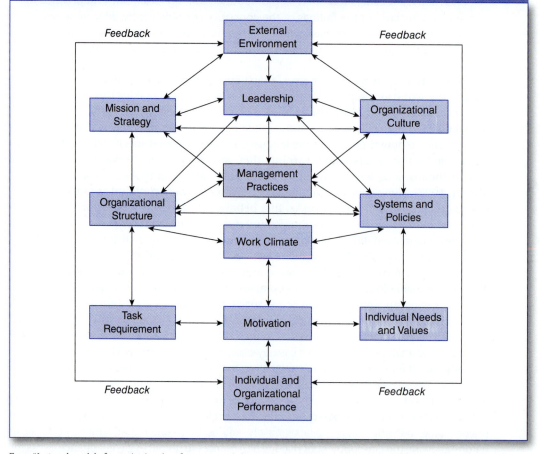

From "A causal model of organizational performance and change" by W. W. Burke and G. H. Litwin, 1992. *Journal of Management, 18*(3), 523–545. Copyright 1992 by Sage Publications, Inc. Reproduced with permission.

Burke–Litwin Model

As shown in Figure 3.1, the Burke–Litwin Model of organizational change and performance provides an overall institutional analysis and diagnosis of leadership. The model supports a link between an assessment of the wider institutional (school district) context and the nature and process of change within an organization. The model revolves around 12 organizational dimensions:

1. External environment
2. Leadership
3. Mission and strategy
4. Organizational culture
5. Management practices
6. Organizational structure
7. System and policies
8. Work climate
9. Motivation
10. Task requirement
11. Individual needs and values
12. Individual and organizational performance (Burke & Litwin, 1992)

The relationships between the variables are incorporated with seven factors, namely, *skills, structure, staff, systems, style, strategy,* and *shared values.* This model can be very useful for the transformation of the (school) organization to reflect the flow of leadership. The model also provides good support for the explanation of organizations to perform organizational change (Burke & Litwin, 1992).

RESEARCH THEORY INTO PRACTICAL APPLICATION

Theoretical leadership models can be awkwardly complex. One way of bridging the gap between theory and practice is raising awareness. School leaders need to accept and model new ideas if they are to address school reform. In the same fashion, school leaders must also be open to finding solutions—solutions that may be in one setting but may not be conducive in another.

Curriculum Tip 3.2

Theory is dynamic. Educators using research can change the culture of a school.

According to Fashola (2004), a window to school leadership reform is often based on three components: organizational programs, schoolwide reform programs with curricula, and combinations of organizational and curriculum-specific programs. It is up to the leadership team to explore each of these areas. In order to make the transition from the theoretical to best practice, **curriculum specialists,** principals, and teacher–leaders need to first establish clear goals for all projects. Second, curriculum, materials, and implementation strategies must be in place. And third, there must be high-quality professional development to solidify the process. The fourth and final capstone, however, is support from leadership.

In addition to Fashola's work as it pertains to leadership theory, it is also important to note the role of Howard Gardner's multiple intelligences as well as Daniel Goleman's contributions to emotional intelligence theory.

Gardner's (2011) *Frames of Mind: The Theory of Multiple Intelligences* helped lead the way in tying research to practical application as it relates to education. His work continues to mark a desire not just to describe the world but to help to create the conditions to change it. Gardner initially formulated a list of seven intelligences that includes linguistic intelligence, logical–mathematical intelligence, musical intelligence, bodily–kinesthetic intelligence, spatial intelligence, interpersonal intelligence, and intrapersonal intelligence. The primary focus here for curriculum specialists, principals, and teacher–leaders is that according to Gardner, intelligence has the capacity to impact leadership and thus solve problems valued in one or more cultural settings.

Multiple intelligences helped spawn other works related to practical applications of research. For example, author Daniel Goleman (1995) used the works of Mayer and Salovey and others to set the stage for his popular book *Emotional Intelligence: Why It Can Matter More Than IQ*. According to Goleman, emotional intelligence (EQ) describes the ability, capacity, or skill to identify, assess, manage, and control the emotions of one's self, of others, and of groups. Initially, EQ began impacting the business world. The *Harvard Business Review* (2011) listed Gardner as one of the 50 most influential management gurus and hailed it as a groundbreaking, paradigm-shattering idea. Eventually it found its way into education, and as can be imagined, the concept of EQ has had major ramifications on curriculum leadership as well as on research application.

Melding Theory and Research Into Best Practice

Referencing the melding of theory and research into best practice, Biddle and Saha (2006) gathered information on building-level leaders successfully using research through structured interviews and questionnaires from 120 school administrators (81 in the United States and 39 in Australia). Their findings have been adapted as the following:

1. *Most leaders hold positive opinions about educational research.* Roughly 90% of the respondents in both Australia and the United States rated building-level administrators high in research use.

2. *Most leaders are actively interested in education research that is relevant to their professional needs.* The typical respondent provided information regarding at least four different types of research.

3. *Most leaders are at least minimally familiar with a wide range of educational topics.* Building-level leaders were primarily interested in research and theory involving staff expectations, student achievement, time-on-task skills, and at-risk students.

4. *Most leaders are regularly exposed to information sources based on research.* Respondents noted they read one or two journals as well as one or more professional books annually.

5. *Most leaders believe that research knowledge plays an active role in policy decisions and instructional practice.* A number of building-level leaders used research applications in addressing school policy change and new instructional practices.

Both Biddle and Saha found in their study that most building-level leaders acquired much of their theory and research practices from secondary sources such as visiting other schools, meetings, conferences, and educational journals. Overall, the study showed that these leaders generally view research positively and it helped them in improving their schools.

On-the-Ground Connections

Theory is dynamic. Educators using research can change the culture of a school. As part of on-the-ground training, a curriculum leader's most important job is to assist others as well as to make connections both in and out of the classroom. Good leaders know they need to help organize schools in a manner that makes these theoretical connections possible. Making good things happen is fundamental to making a school successful.

Building theoretical connections means acquiring frontline experience. Successful team leaders have learned to apply new ideas in a practical straightforward fashion, and then, over time, augment these ideas. This allows the staff to self-organize and develop without being continually monitored. If given the support and freedom they need, staff members will make the right choices and the right connections. For example, if a building-level leader is introducing a new program, it is important to lay the groundwork with others and then to move slowly. Moving with deliberation from the abstract to the concrete, along with well-planned professional development, allows for a better transition toward change.

Curriculum Tip 3.3	Social networking is a crucial element in creating change.

Educators like and want new theoretical ideas if they work, save time, and produce tangible results. If they accept new ideas and develop ownership in the process, there is a good chance these ideas will be used in the classroom. Therefore, the key to curriculum leadership is developing necessary relations before embracing change. When others develop a deep understanding of what is expected, then needed change will follow. As can be seen, anchoring and reinforcing core concepts is paramount to the process of melding theory into practice. Moreover, in the end, making the right connections is the essence of quality leadership.

New and Aspiring Teacher–Leaders as Partners

Theory into practice means curriculum leaders become partners within the school community. Going solo does not help. In addition to building connections with other teachers and students, it is important to foster partnerships with superintendents, central office staff, and other administrators. Aspiring leaders need to understand that superintendents and central office staff have a limited amount of time and may not totally comprehend what is happening at other levels. Considering theory and practice, it is important for new and aspiring leaders to consider the following:

- Invite central office staff and other educators to your school. Try to include these individuals at gatherings when possible and make them feel welcome.
- View issues from a district level as well as building-level perspective. Having a better understanding of issues often gives curriculum leaders a greater chance to succeed.
- Schedule times to meet with others to review programs. Collaborating with other administrators and teachers, and even with central office staff, can be enlightening.
- Create networking opportunities. Joining local, state, and national groups can be enormously rewarding.
- Mentor new teacher–leaders. Building coalitions with others can be of benefit to all.

Logically, making connections with other aspiring administrators, teachers, students, parents, and community stakeholders can make or break communication. Involving as many individuals in the decision making process—before decisions are made—can and is a vast part of creating successful change.

Curriculum Tip 3.4	Tip for teacher–leaders: Trust doesn't just happen; it happens when individuals network and work together at all levels.

A primary ingredient in moving from theory into practice is developing trust. When formulating trust, teacher–leaders need to make an extra effort to reach out not only to administrators, staff, and students but also to parents as well. Trust does not just happen; it occurs when new and aspiring leaders network as well as work collaboratively at all levels. If individuals are struggling with trust issues, there is little hope for a positive school climate.

Team leadership at all levels is a major part of building trust. And, without trust, there can be no collaboration. Along with building trust, nurturing and sustaining shared leadership allows for a balance between theory and practical application of ideas. Aspiring teacher–leaders who share leadership with others are best able to develop a strong school culture because school culture often shapes who and what we represent. Not surprisingly, those who reach out to others are apt to be effective leaders. Thus, networking and building the right connections can make the difference in melding theory into best practices (Whitehead, Boschee, & Decker, 2013).

CURRICULUM AS CHANGE

It is believed that teachers will use more research when researchers fine-tune how they present their discoveries to teachers (Miller, Drill, & Behrstock, 2010). Keeping with this perspective, curriculum, whether it is hidden or apparent, seems to be changing even more to meet today's needs and realities. This is especially the case in that current instructional design based on brain research is becoming more common.

For example, processes involved in a student learning how to read are now being found to occur during dynamic states of brain development. According to McDonald (2010), "A quick look into a little brain research may provide some insight and offer ways to help reduce these distractions and increase student attention in the classroom" (p. 46).

In reviewing the literature, brain research completed by D'Arcangelo revealed that the brain changes physiologically as a result of experience and that an individual's environment may determine to a large extent the functioning ability of the brain (Brooks & Brooks, 1999). Work in the field of brain research is helping suggest strategies for teachers in the classroom. Research is helping teachers know how students learn and how they receive, process, and interpret information (Caulfield, Kidd, & Kocher, 2000).

The importance of a student's emotional intelligence (EQ) is also being considered. Daniel Goleman's (1995) *Emotional Intelligence* and Joseph LeDoux's (1996) *The Emotional Brain* have advanced our understanding of the role of emotions in learning. In addition, Howard Gardner's work in multiple intelligences and the dimensions of learning reveals that human intelligence encompasses a far wider and more universal set of competencies than a single general intelligence (Given, 2000).

Bransford, Brown, and Cocking (2001), in *How People Learn: Brain, Mind, Experience, and School,* noted that it is important for students to organize their knowledge around important ideas and concepts—that students "learn how to see" a problem like an expert and understand the "why" and "when" as well as the "what" and "how." They state that it is important for students to integrate their new knowledge with existing knowledge (constructivism) and to monitor their learning and problem solving (metacognition; Caulfield et al., 2000).

Metacognitive ability appears now to be central to conceptions of what it means to be educated. Martinez (2006) stated, "Metacognition is usually presented as a conscious and deliberate mental activity—*we become aware that we don't understand a paragraph we read or a statement we hear*" (p. 697, italics added).

With the advent of recent research and clinical observations, educators no longer have to apply a "one-size-fits-all" approach in helping struggling students. Brain-based research is providing new strategies for identifying and treating the many causes of slow learning.

Problems in reading and writing often originate from underlying neurodevelopmental dysfunctions. Levine and Barringer (2008) noted, "To better understand how students' neurodevelopmental profiles affect their learning and performance, eight constructs—groupings of related functions—help organize thinking and communication about learning differences" (p. 17).

These constructs are as follows:

- *Attention.* The ability to concentrate, focus on one thing rather than another, finish tasks, and control what one says and does
- *Temporal-sequential ordering.* The ability to understand the time and sequence of pieces of information is a key component to learning
- *Spatial ordering.* The ability to distinguish between a circle and a square, or to use images to remember related information
- *Memory.* The ability to understand, organize, and interpret complex information at the moment; their inability to store and later recall that information can dramatically affect their performance
- *Language.* The ability to develop language functions involves elaborate interactions between various parts of the brain that control such abilities as pronouncing words, understanding different sounds, and comprehending written symbols
- *Neuromotor functions.* The ability to coordinate motor or muscle functions, which is key to many areas of learning, including writing and keyboarding
- *Social cognition.* The ability to succeed in social relationships with peers, parents, and teachers. Students strong in other areas may have academic difficulties because of an inability to make friends, work in groups, or cope with peer pressure.
- *Higher order cognition.* The ability to understand and implement the steps necessary to solve problems, attack new areas of learning, and to think creatively. (Levine & Barringer, 2008, pp. 14–18)

With the advent of more innovative ideas and with the advancement of understanding and technology, curriculum is becoming more comprehensive and differential in nature. It is forcing change in order to meet new challenges and changes. Educational content and teaching–learning materials now appear to be more functional, diversified, and operational in nature. An increased emphasis is placed on relevance, flexibility, needs, and speed. Demographics, population, health, nutrition, and environment are becoming dominant factors in what appears to be a value-oriented instructional design process focused on the global community.

A case can be made that the very nature of educational structure and methodologies is undergoing a significant change. Web-based programs, educational technologies, multimedia capability, and distance education are changing the face of educational curriculum worldwide. Electronic media on a global level appear to be evolving their own pedagogical methodologies and strategies. These advancements in technology are leading to a multitude of approaches blending a milieu of curriculum that caters to the needs of interested, disinterested, and remedial learners worldwide.

Common Core State Standards: Theory Into Practice

The Common Core State Standards Initiative (CCSSI) is all about outcomes students should obtain. But moving from Common Core State Standards (CCSS) to local school classroom instruction requires a pathway of quality planning and implementation. McTighe and

Wiggins (2012–2013) suggested five major ways how curriculum planners and teachers can effectively use CCSS to design a coherent curriculum and assessment system for realizing their promise. These ideas are:

1. *CCSS has a new emphasis and requires careful reading.* As a result, educators need to determine what the new distinctions are in these standards and what they mean for putting theory into practice.

2. *Standards are not curriculum.* CCSS is about the outcomes that students should achieve.

3. *Educators must "unpack" the standards.* Educators need to interpret the standards as per three categories:

    a. *Long-term transfer goals.* What is it that we want students to do as they confront new complex problems in and outside of school?
    b. *Overarching understandings and essential questions.* What important themes will students encounter? Likewise, what questions must students ask to make meaning from what they are learning?
    c. *Cornerstone tasks.* What tasks should be embedded in the curriculum that encourage students to apply their knowledge and skills in authentic and relevant contexts, using creativity, technology, and teamwork?

4. *A coherent curriculum is mapped backward from desired performances.* Basically, the first questions curriculum planners and teachers need to ask are what will we teach, when should we teach it, and what will students be able to do with it? The focus, then, is not on scope and sequence as much as "autonomous transfers," which require a deliberate and transparent plan for helping the student rely less and less on teacher hand-holding and scaffolds.

5. *The standards come to life through assessments.* Standards shouldn't be tested one by one but rather by rich, complex performance tasks that can assess a number of standards. These kinds of assessments are being designed by groups such as Smarter Balanced Assessment Consortium (SBAC).

Complex Issues Involving Accountability

In moving from the theoretical to substantial academic change, curriculum leaders now need accurate data scores with meaningful references. With this in mind, school leaders now must be able to obtain accurate digital measures, especially student measures that align with standards and produce timely results.

Data should include the following:

- Norms for public accountability
- Curriculum references to focus instruction
- Prior scores to assess growth individually and collectively
- Benchmarks to measure yearly adequate progress

Providing accountability as part of reform continues to be a central pillar for curriculum change. For example, Web-based computerized achievement-level tests are now aligned with CCSS. Valued by most educators, electronic or Web-based adapted tests combine the benefit of technology with the integrity of level tests.

Mindful as to concerns over accountability and individual diversity, Web-based computerized tests draw from a bank of more than 30,000-plus calibrated test items. When individual students access a digitized adaptive test, the difficulty of the test is adjusted to the student's performance. The level of each question is based on how well the student has answered the questions up to that point. As the student answers correctly, the questions become more difficult. If the student answers incorrectly, the questions become easier. Each student then receives a personalized test specifically designed for them. An even more astonishing feature is the ability for students to stop at any point and go to lunch or recess and come back to start where they left off. Following this perspective, schools using these electronic formats are reducing test anxiety and at the same time are very accurate.

Thanks to fast-link online capabilities, when a student completes a computerized adaptive test, a student's score can be quickly retrieved, allowing for immediate analysis and feedback. Theoretically, a student's up-front score should show growth from year to year and can be correlated longitudinally to scores from previous years. This firsthand data has the ability of creating instantaneous and worthwhile changes in instructional direction for any principal, curriculum adviser, or teacher depending on information received. Accordingly, computerized adaptive tests (aligned with CCSS) are proving to be one of the fastest and easiest ways to assess individual student learner needs.

What is novel and really valuable is that principals, curriculum leaders, and teachers can download information about students and classes shortly after the test is completed. Results can be printed for individual teachers or parents as well. Another great feature involves the ability for teachers to assess student scores at any time throughout the year as well as obtain gains made in certain areas. The true test, however, is when curriculum and teaching strategies are positively altered based on immediate feedback.

Socioeconomic Challenges, Tolerance, and Cultural Capital

From a theoretical perspective, the importance of socioeconomic challenges, tolerance, and cultural capital cannot be understated. For educators, developing an awareness as to cultural, socioeconomic issues, and gender bias is paramount. How individuals interact not only can reflect cultural assumptions but can also have effects on how students see themselves in relation to school, communities, and nature itself. This observation represents both a challenge and an opportunity (Medin & Bang, 2013–2014).

Just as the CCSS set a high bar for students across subject areas, they set a high bar for subject-matter teachers. According to Yu Ren Dong (2013–2014), as teacher education programs, districts, and schools change their curriculums and instruction to meet these new standards, they must also design ways to address the needs of students for whom achieving the standards is especially challenging. In that larger numbers of **English language learners (ELLs)** are spending a significant amount of time in mainstream subject-matter classes, there is a greater potential for cultural concerns to emerge. To be sure, cultural issues are subtle and elusive, so teachers may not be aware of their individual students' cultural needs. It is here that the new CCSS standards can bring such needs to light. Most importantly, teachers need to recognize that the prior cultural knowledge of an ELL can be a major resource (a form of intellectual capital) in improving an individual's life.

In addition to standards and schools focusing on diversity, educational leaders must also focus on the importance social issues such as tolerance and how it relates to individual performance. According to Costello (2012), a lack of tolerance in schools is greatly impacting kids who look different, those with disabilities, the ones who follow a minority religion or have no religion, and the children whose parents do not have the means to keep up economically.

As many teachers have already witnessed firsthand, socioeconomic concerns can pose huge problems for students. This is especially true with poverty levels continuing to rise worldwide. Clearly, having school leaders focusing on unique challenges faced by low-income students could very well make the difference between educational achievement and dropping out (Ching & Steinberg, 2012).

In addition to socioeconomic concerns, school leaders must also take into account stereotypes and gender bias. Hynes and Bakal (2012) noted that lesbian, gay, bisexual, and transgender (LGBT) caucus teachers and students are still facing bigotry and difficulty in many schools. With this in mind, there needs to be a move to set aside bigotry and stereotypes through awareness and new forms of action. This can largely be done by emphasizing a classroom culture in which students and colleagues focus more on the individual than on any label or stereotype.

Social and emotional competencies are also a looming issue for schools. Educators and students seem to know intuitively what research has shown: Social and emotional competencies along with gender bias influence everything from teacher–student relationships to classroom management. Likewise, practices and policies that support and foster social and emotional competencies are fundamental in addressing many of the problems facing schools today (Jones, Bouffard, & Weissbourd, 2013).

In retrospect, then, a closer look at socioeconomic challenges, gender bias, and cultural diversity is bearing out findings that both confirm and expand a mounting body of international research about the efficacy of relationship in school engagement and performance. Keeping with this thought, a 2010 report of the Program for International Student Assessment (PISA) notes that "positive student-teacher relations" are described as key to improved outcomes (Reichert & Hawley, 2013). An important answer, then, to improving schools is taking into account the importance of cultural diversity, social issues, teacher and student relationships, tolerance of others, and how students feel about themselves and their school.

Technology as Catalyst of Change

With technology emerging as a catalyst for real change, school leaders are becoming more fervent about school reform and how students learn. This fervency includes greater insight into the power of technology and how it allows teachers to present information in ways students will more readily understand (Peterson, 2011). At the same time, students are coming into the educational environment with new ideas and intentions for connecting thought, knowledge, and achievement to technology. These students live in a world where technology is how they communicate, socialize, and create. For them, technology makes academic growth exciting.

As excitement builds over new ways to use and experience technology in schools, educators at all levels are also directing their attention toward global connections, differentiated curriculum, and evaluation strategies. This is best represented by the movement toward low-cost, portable devices for student use in all schools that assists teachers and students in redirecting learning on an international scale. Responding to this change, numerous classroom teachers are currently communicating and exchanging information worldwide with students via Web-based programs. In these environments, educators are no longer bound by classroom walls and are allowing students to work in multiple settings. These virtual communities and learning spaces are exciting ways for students, teachers, and schools to collaborate on a variety of educational projects and relationships. From a school leader's perspective, technology, with its overflowing waves of information and media, appears to be making a difference on *how* teachers teach and *how* students learn. Examples include technology applications promoting investigative skills, making learning more exciting, providing opportunities to apply knowledge, as well as preparing students for an increasingly diverse world. In addition, digital formats and applications are revolutionizing student assessment by allowing teachers and students to instantaneously enter and access pre- and post-assessment data. Information from these digital measures can be quickly graded and uploaded to various files for real-time analysis by both teachers and administrators. By and large, all of these changes and applications are providing a starting place for educators who want to channel energies toward technology-related schools and data-driven instruction.

Technology is also a catalyst for change in that it can provide administrators with access to digitized up-to-the-minute performance information challenging leaders to reconceptualize the meaning of data and how it impacts instruction (Nidus & Saddler, 2011). It is through the use of data-driven instruction that school leaders can now access data globally and readily analyze, chart, and graph every student, class, and school within a district—or multiple districts as needed. This is very helpful from an assessment, evaluation, and accountability perspective. In the confines of their offices, administrators can now instantly diagnose academic weaknesses and strengths in any school environment—as well as display, annotate, organize, import, capture, record, or share whatever information is provided with anyone across the world—in real time. Naturally, all of this uploaded information is encrypted allowing for data transactions that are private, secure, and safe. More importantly, with up-to-date instantaneous data results that are easy to read and understand, teachers have the resources they need to make data-driven changes. In particular, instructional action will hopefully lead to improved student achievement and create positive change (Whitehead, Jensen, & Boschee, 2013).

Technology Tip	More and more, the world is doing things in collaborative ways, at a distance. —Jack Stripling (2011)

As such, educational instructional practices and skills are currently blending with new developments in technology to help create the classroom of the future. Little doubt is evidenced that technology is serving as the catalyst for change. In addition, setting high expectations and appropriate, rigorous goals (CCSS) now for every student is an essential part of the job of effective school leaders, according to researchers at Vanderbilt University (Spiro, 2013).

As part of this transformational process, further advances in technology are now utilizing the cooperative learning and differentiated curriculum strategies and combining them with the use of a variety of mobile devices. Currently, a movement is under way to provide students at school with low-cost devices that can be connected through global networks and tailored for specific tasks or applications. Some classroom teachers now have the capability of communicating and exchanging information worldwide with students via classroom workstations and district servers.

THE THEORETICAL SCHOOL OF THE FUTURE

Schools can no longer ignore the importance of digital competencies or what children are already doing (Zhao, 2010). Moreover, educators are now envisioning schools as learning communities in which teachers and students succeed in infusing technology seamlessly into classroom practice worldwide. The hope is to have every teacher become proficient in using technology in all aspects of instruction as well as to create technological infrastructures that are future-proofed, self-sustaining, and self-renewing. This fact is best illustrated by the unprecedented opportunities for educators to share their expertise and collaborations, not only across state and national boundaries but also globally (Berry, 2013).

Likewise, teacher–leaders will work collaboratively with others to determine needs at every grade level as well as develop a Web-based system that will address those needs. Through self-evaluation and assessment tools, future educators can identify hardware and software needs, teacher proficiency levels, and teacher interest in integrating technology into the curriculum.

Professional training and staff development programs of the future will build a scaffold supporting plans of technology integration. Improvement plans will reflect professional development and technology models.

Funding sources in the future will be redirected to support a school's need for ongoing technology infusion. From those plans, each teacher will develop a personal growth plan indicating the training he or she will need.

As per the CCSSI, technology and 21st-century learning applications will help increase the emphasis on individuals as well as project-based learning. Students will shift to using technology in student-centered learning environments for research, collaboration, communication, presentation of knowledge, and multimedia production.

With this infusion of technology, the areas of greatest impact will be student and teacher interest, motivation, improved student behavior, increased technology skills for both students and teachers, and the developing of high-order thinking skills in students.

It will be the global mission for tomorrow's curriculum and teacher–leaders to support the implementation of technologies for high-quality and safe learning environments that will allow all students to achieve at their highest potential for future years to come.

Along these same lines, the National Association of Elementary School Principals (NAESP) commissioned the Institute for Alternative Futures to explore areas of uncertainty and opportunity for schools as part of its Vision 2021 Project. The institute crafted nine forecasts to start a dialogue with school principals, other educators, and the public about a preferred future:

1. *Schools become the learning portals to a global workplace.* This forecast explores what schools must become to align with the new requirements of a global society.

2. *Free-market forces favor school choice over educational equity.* This forecast probes social preferences for choice and the possibility for recommitting to educational equity.

3. *Hyperlinked learning explores meaning through multimedia.* This forecast examines new capabilities to enrich and transform the learning experience.

4. *Scientific knowledge brings new understanding to child development.* This forecast anticipates scientific research that clarifies individual differences and defines appropriate learning approaches for different students.

5. *Holistic standards expand expectations for achieving student potential.* This forecast explains how today's proficiency standards will necessarily morph into standards that support educating the whole child.

6. *Networks of learning innovation experiment with new learning strategies for children.* This forecast anticipates networks of research and development that link schools to centers of innovation in collaborating research and knowledge sharing.

7. *Surveillance society links schoolhouses into electronic safety network.* This forecast projects today's concerns about school safety into a future where surveillance is ubiquitous and welcome.

8. *Society's mounting debts compromise future investments in education.* This forecast takes a hard look at the limitations schools face and asks what it would take to create a tipping point where education is a priority.

9. *School leaders can set the standard for chief learning officers.* This forecast acknowledges that building-level leaders will be using continuous learning processes to engage students, teachers, parents, and the community in achieving learning outcomes for students.

As can be seen from the NAESP Vision 2021, the implications of *new theoretical constructs* embracing technology and schools on a global scale will be staggering. The implications of educational change in the future seem to be limitless.

SUMMARY

Chapter 3 explains that sound theory can be of value to both the scholar and the practitioner because curriculum theory can provide a set of conceptual tools for analyzing curriculum proposals, illuminating practice, and guiding reform. This chapter shows how melding theory and the reality of school curriculum is an important step in the educational planning process. Because it is difficult to use theoretical approaches to make continual analyses, reevaluations, and revisions of curriculum—especially in such fields as information technology and the sociology of knowledge—this chapter explains the necessity of developing a fundamental understanding of curriculum theory by providing the tools necessary when analyzing curriculum proposals, illuminating practice, and guiding reform. This chapter addresses the nature and function of curriculum theory. It also addresses why it is important to meld the theory and reality of school curriculum together as part of the planning process. This chapter explains the role of leadership in the development of curriculum theory and the major classifications of curriculum theory. Finally, it addresses how technology has been a catalyst for curriculum change.

APPLICATIONS

1. As noted in this chapter, much debate occurs in the field about the value of curriculum theory. As you understand the nature of curriculum theory, how much professional value does it seem to have for you?

2. Most of the theoretical work in the field would be subsumed under the headings of value-centered and content-centered theories. How do you explain the fact that structure and process matters have received much less attention from curriculum theorists?

3. Several experts who have analyzed process theories claim that all attempts to develop new process approaches turn out to be simply variations of the Tyler rationale. To what extent do you agree with this assessment?

4. Use the proposed descriptive system to analyze any article or book that describes a curriculum-development process.

5. As noted in this chapter, very little work has been done in applying ways-of-knowing approaches to curriculum-development projects. What do you think a school curriculum would look like, in general, if it attempted to embody a ways-of-knowing approach to the curriculum?

6. Looking at your school system, how have advancements in technology changed the roles of the education process?

7. Compose a self-examination of your style for curriculum theory and practice by using the "Miller Curriculum Style Indicator" (Miller, 2011, pp. 36–39). What is your style, and what relevancy does it have for curriculum development?

8. Exhibit 3.7 illustrates what differentiated instruction *is* and *is not*. Identify the differentiated-instruction activities that occur in your school district's classrooms.

CASE STUDY   Integrating Curriculum Theory

Bruce Novac has been a PK–5 elementary school principal in the Plentywood School District for the past two years. This is the beginning of his third year and the year in the district in which he will be up for tenure. He has a meeting scheduled with the school superintendent, Dr. Robert Kerr, and the curriculum director, Dr. Karla Johnson, to review test score data of the third-grade students in his school. The results revealed that the third-grade students' scores were well below state and federal guidelines for proficiency. In fact, second-grade students had higher achievement scores than the third-grade students in his school.

Mr. Novac was told by the two central office administrators that his theory of curriculum implementation was not working. In fact, what he was doing was held in low regard by the teachers in his school. In a panic, Novac begins to search for some answers on curriculum theories espoused by authors of curriculum textbooks and in educational journals. His focus is captured by structure-oriented, value-oriented, content-oriented, and process-oriented curriculum theories, which he hopes will provide answers to the third-grade low-achievement dilemma in his school.

The Challenge

Student achievement is often thought to be the result of curriculum theory that teachers support. How can Mr. Novac educate and motivate the third-grade teachers to integrate sound curriculum theory into their day-to-day work with students?

Key Issues or Questions

1. What are your impressions of the superintendent and curriculum director? Did they adequately address Mr. Novac's responsibilities in this incident? Why or why not?

2. What are your impressions of the third-grade teachers in this elementary school in the Plentywood School District?

3. If the principal meets with the third-grade teachers, what should be discussed?

4. What are some possible reasons why third-grade students in Mr. Novac's school are low achievers?

5. What are some theoretical curriculum approaches that Mr. Novac might use to increase student achievement scores? Identify the strategies and explain why you think they might be effective.

WEBLIOGRAPHY

ASCD
www.ascd.org/publications/educational-leadership
.aspx

Curriculum Theory and Practice
www.infed.org/biblio/b-curric.htm

Education Week's Research Center
www.edweek.org/rc/?intc = intst

Education World Article on Multiple
Intelligences
www.education-world.com/a_curr/curr054.shtml

Educational Theory
www.ed.uiuc.edu/EPS/educational-theory

Guide to Action Research
www.infed.org/research/b-actres.htm

Guide to Educational Research
http://guides.nyu.edu/friendly.php?s = education

Media Policy Center
www.mediapolicycenter.org

National Association of Elementary School
Principals (NAESP)
www.naesp.org/about

Phi Delta Kappa International
www.pdkintl.org

University of Maryland, Department of
Education: Educational Policy and Leadership
http://mdk12.org/instruction/curriculum

REFERENCES

Apple, M. W. (1975). Scientific interests and the nature of educational institutions. In W. Pinar (Ed.), *Curriculum theorizing: The reconceptualists* (pp. 120–130). Berkeley, CA: McCutchan.

Apple, M. W. (1979). On analyzing hegemony. *Journal of Curriculum Theorizing, 1*(1), 10–43.

Bambrick-Santoyo, P. (2014). Giving and getting feedback in real time. *Phi Delta Kappan, 95*(4), 72–73.

Berry, B. (2013). Bold leaders, inconvenient truths. *Educational Leadership, 71*(2), 15–16.

Biddle, B. J., & Saha, L. J. (2006). How principals use research. *Educational Leadership, 63*(6), 72–77.

Bobbitt, F. (1918). *The curriculum.* Boston, MA: Riverside Press.

Bowers, C. A. (1977). Emergent ideological characteristics of educational policy. *Teachers College Record, 79*(1), 33–54.

Bransford, J., Brown, A. L., & Cocking, R. R. (2001). *How people learn: Brain, mind, experience, and school.* Washington, DC: National Academy Press.

Brooks, M. (1986, April). *Curriculum development from a constructivist perspective.* Paper presented at the annual meeting of the American Educational Research Association, San Francisco, CA.

Brooks, M., & Brooks, J. (1999). The courage to be a constructivist. *Educational Leadership, 57*(3), 18–24.

Brown, G. I. (1975). Examples of lessons, units, and course outlines in confluent education. In G. I. Brown (Ed.), *The live classroom* (pp. 231–295). New York, NY: Viking.

Burke, W. W., & Litwin, G. H. (1992). A causal model of organizational performance and change. *Journal of Management, 18*(3), 523–545.

Caulfield, J., Kidd, S., & Kocher, T. (2000). Brain-based instruction in action. *Educational Leadership, 58*(3), 62–65.

Ching, J., & Steinberg, J. (Spring 2012). The poverty myth. *Teaching Tolerance, 41,* 44–45.

Costa A. L., & Kallick, B. (Eds.), (2008). *Learning and leading with habits of mind: 16 essential characteristics for success.* Retrieved from http://www.ascd.org/publications/books/108008/chapters/Learning-Through-Reflection.aspx

Costello, M. (2012 Spring). What's in a name? *Teaching Tolerance, 41,* 15.

Counts, G. S. (1932). *Dare the school build a new social order?* New York, NY: Day.

Doll, R. C. (1986). *Curriculum improvement: Decision making and process* (6th ed.). Boston, MA: Allyn & Bacon.

Dong, Y. R. (2013–2014). The bridge of knowledge, *Educational Leadership, 71*(4), 30–36.

Eisner, E. (Ed.). (1985). *Learning and teaching the ways of knowing* (Eighty-Fourth Yearbook of the National Society for the Study of Education, Part II). Chicago, IL: University of Chicago Press.

Eisner, E. W., & Vallance, E. (Eds.). (1974). *Conflicting conceptions of curriculum.* Berkeley, CA: McCutchan.

Farmer, D. (1996, January). *Curriculum differentiation: An overview of the research into the curriculum differentiation educational strategy.* Retrieved from http://www.austega.com/gifted/provisions/curdifferent.htm

Fashola, O. S. (2004). Being an informed consumer of quantitative educational research. *Phi Delta Kappan, 85*(7), 532–538.

Foti, S. (2007, May). Technology: Did we leave the future behind? *Phi Delta Kappan, 88*(9), 647–648, 715.

Franklin, C. A. (2008). Factors determining elementary teachers' use of computers. *Principal, 87*(3), 54–55.

Freire, P. (1970). *Pedagogy of the oppressed.* New York, NY: Herder and Herder.

Gagne, R. (1985). *The conditions of learning and theory of instruction* (4th ed.). New York, NY: Holt, Rinehart & Winston.

Gagne, R., Briggs, L., & Wager, W. (1992). *Principles of instructional design* (4th ed.). Fort Worth, TX: HBJ College.

Gardner, H. (2011). *Frames of mind: The theory of multiple intelligences.* New York, NY: Basic Books.

Gay, G. (1980). Conceptual models of the curriculum planning process. In A. W. Foshay (Ed.), *Considered action for curriculum improvement* (pp. 120–143). Alexandria, VA: ASCD.

Given, B. (2000). Theaters of the mind. *Educational Leadership, 58*(3), 72–75.

Glatthorn, A. A. (1980). *A guide for designing an English curriculum for the eighties.* Urbana, IL: National Council of Teachers of English.

Glatthorn, A. A. (1987). Analysis of Glatthorn's (1986) curriculum-development process. In A. A. Glatthorn (Ed.), *Curriculum leadership* (p. 120). New York, NY: HarperCollins.

Goleman, D. (1995). *Emotional intelligence: Why it can matter more than IQ.* New York, NY: Bantam Dell.

Harvard Business Review. (2011). *The 50 most influential management gurus.* Retrieved from http://hbr.org/web/slideshows/the-50-most-influential-management-gurus/37-gardner

Hirsch, E. D., Jr. (1995). *What your fifth grader needs to know: Fundamentals of good fifth-grade education.* Los Alamitos, CA: Delta.

Hockett, J. A., & Doubet, K. J. (2013–14). Turning on the lights: What pre-assessments can do. *Educational Leadership, 71*(4), 50–54.

Huenecke, D. (1982). What is curricular theorizing? What are its implications for practice? *Educational Leadership, 39,* 290–294.

Hynes, W., & Bakal, S. (2012 Spring). Class outing. *Teaching Tolerance, 41,* 44–45.

Imagitrends. (2000). *Future primary educational structure.* Retrieved from http://pages.prodigy.net/imagiweb/reports/file00/oct1.htm

Johnson, D. (2013–2014). Power up: Teaching above the line. *Educational Leadership, 71*(4), 84–85 & 87.

Jones, S. M., Bouffard, S. M., & Weissbourd, R. (2013). Educators' social and emotional skills vital to learning. *Phi Delta Kappan, 94*(8), 62–65.

LeDoux, J. (1996). *The emotional brain: The mysterious underpinnings of emotional life.* New York, NY: Touchstone.

Levine, M., & Barringer, M. (2008). Getting the lowdown on the slowdown. *Principal, 87*(3), 14–18.

Macdonald, J. B. (1974). A transcendental developmental ideology of education. In W. Pinar (Ed.), *Heightened conscience, cultural revolution, and curriculum theory* (pp. 85–116). Berkeley, CA: McCutchan.

Macdonald, J. B. (1977). Value bases and issues for curriculum. In A. Molnar & J. A. Zahorik (Eds.), *Curriculum theory* (pp. 10–21). Alexandria, VA: ASCD.

Martinez, M. E. (2006). What is metacognition? *Phi Delta Kappan, 87*(9), 696–699.

McDonald, E. S. (2010). A quick look into the middle school brain. *Principal, 89*(3), 46.

McTighe, J., & Wiggins, G. (2012–2013). Misconceptions about Common Core. *Phi Delta Kappan, 94*(4), 6.

McNeil, J. D. (1985). *Curriculum: A comprehensive introduction* (3rd ed.). Boston, MA: Little, Brown.

Medin D. L., & Bang, M. (2013–2014). Culture in the classroom. *Phi Delta Kappan, 95*(4), 64–67.

Miller, D. L. (2011). Curriculum theory and practice: What's your style? *Phi Delta Kappan, 92*(7), 34–35.

Miller, S. R., Drill, K., & Behrstock, E. (2010). Meeting teachers halfway: Making educational research relevant to teachers. *Phi Delta Kappan, 91*(7), 31–34.

Murphy, J. (2009). Closing achievement gaps: Lessons from the last 15 years. *Phi Delta Kappan, 91*(3), 8–12.

Nidus, G., & Saddler, M. (2011). The principal as formative coach. *Educational Leadership, 69*(2), 30–35.

Papert, S. (1993). *The children's machine: Rethinking school in the age of the computer.* New York, NY: Basic Books. Retrieved from http://www.stemnet.nf.ca/~elmurphy/emurphy/papert.html

Parker, F. W. (1894). *Talks on pedagogics.* New York, NY: E. L. Kellogg.

Parkway School District. (n.d.). *Principles of differentiation.* Chesterfield, MO: Author. Retrieved from http://www.pkwy.k12.mo.us/candd/Curriculum Areas/Gifted/PrinciplesofDifferentiation.htm

Peterson, T. (2011). Innovation in action: Leading by example. *EDTECH, 9*(3), 49–51.

Pinar, W. F. (1978). The reconceptualization of curriculum studies. *Journal of Curriculum Studies, 10*(3), 205–214.

Posner, G. J., & Strike, K. A. (1976). A categorization scheme for principles of sequencing content. *Review of Educational Research, 46,* 665–690.

Purpel, D. E., & Belanger, M. (1972). Toward a humanistic curriculum theory. In D. E. Purpel & M. Belanger (Eds.), *Curriculum and the cultural revolution* (pp. 64–74). Berkeley, CA: McCutchan.

Racer, C. E. (2007). Best of the blog: In response to "Engaging the Whole Child," summer online. *Educational Leadership, 65*(1), 94–95.

Reichert, M., & Hawley, R. (2013). Relationships play primary role in boys learning. *Phi Delta Kappan, 94*(8), 49–53.

Schiro, M. (1978). *Curriculum for better schools: The great ideological debate.* Englewood Cliffs, NJ: Educational Technology.

Schon, D. A. (1983). *The reflective practitioner: How professionals think in action.* New York, NY: Basic Books.

Schwab, J. (1970). *The practical: A language for curriculum.* Washington, DC: National Education Association.

Sheppard, V. (2013). Leadership helps turn around a troubled school. *Phi Delta Kappan, 94*(8), 32–39.

Shih, P. C. (2009). *Achieving chunghwa postal business sustainability through organizational learning.*

(Unpublished dissertation). University of Montana, Missoula.

Short, E. C. (1983). The forms and use of alternative curriculum development strategies: Policy implications. *Curriculum Inquiry, 13,* 45–64.

Shulman, J. (2003). *Institute for case development.* Retrieved from http://www.wested.org/cs/we/view/pj/173

Smith, M. K. (2000). *Curriculum theory and practice. The encyclopaedia of informal education.* Retrieved from www.infed.org/biblio/b-curric.htm

Spiro, J. D. (2013). Effective principals in action. *Phi Delta Kappan, 94*(8), 27–31.

Stripling, J. (2011, July 29). For two college leaders, 1,000-mile workplaces. *The Chronicle of Higher Education, p. B49.*

Tomlinson, C. A., & McTighe, J. (2006). *Integrating + differentiated instruction and understanding by design.* Alexandria, VA: ASCD.

Vallance, E. (1985). Ways of knowing and curricular conceptions: Implications for program planning. In E. Eisner (Ed.), *Learning and teaching the ways of knowing* (pp. 199–217). Chicago, IL: University of Chicago Press.

Weber, L. (1971). *The English infant school and informal education.* Englewood Cliffs, NJ: Prentice Hall.

Whitehead, B. M., Boschee, F., & Decker, R. H. (2013). *The principal: Leadership for a global society.* Thousand Oaks, CA: Sage.

Whitehead, B.M., Jensen, D. F. N., & Boschee, F. (2013). *Planning for technology: A guide for school administrators, coordinators, and curriculum leaders* (2nd ed.). Thousand Oaks, CA: Corwin Press.

Wiggins, G., & McTighe, J. (2005). *Understanding by design* (Expanded 2nd ed.). Alexandria, VA: ASCD.

Willwerth, D. (2003). *Heuristics and curriculum theory.* (Originally cited in Schiro, M. [1978]. *Curriculum for better schools: The great ideological debate* [pp. 7–16]. Englewood Cliffs, NJ: Educational Technology Publications.) Retrieved from http://www2.bc.edu/-evansec/curriculum/index.html

Zhao, Y. (2010). What children should know about technology and the virtual world. *Principal, 89*(3), 14–19.

CHAPTER 4

The Politics of Curriculum

School administrators and teachers with very different experiences teaching and very similar students continue to work through artificial boundaries of school politics to ask how they can better service students (Lam, 2014). In reviewing political and social influences, this chapter examines some of the myths about U.S. schools, cultural and socioeconomic realities, the role of federal and state governments, the courts, national organizations, Common Core State Standards (CCSS), as well as local internal and external factors impacting school principals and classroom teachers.

Questions addressed in this chapter include the following:

- What has been the role of the federal government in curriculum development, and how has this changed over the years?

- What is the general role of state governments in curriculum development today? How has this changed over the years?

- What are the roles of educational organizations, courts, educational leaders, and classroom teachers on current curriculum development?

Key to Leadership

Curriculum leaders are now realizing that we have entered a political era of global knowledge exchange and application.

MYTHS ABOUT U.S. SCHOOLS

Is the corporate and political movement taking us in the wrong direction in education? In a conversation conducted by Arnold Dodge (2011–2012) with Diane Ravitch, a noted education historian, she indicated that "Horace Mann was incredibly prescient in predicting what might happen if schools got into politics" (p. 54).

> Today you see a lot of governors enacting draconian laws that will damage public education and dismantle the teaching profession. You see it in Wisconsin, Ohio, Florida, Pennsylvania, and Indiana. And then you see President Obama and Secretary Duncan pushing charter schools and the evaluation of teachers by test scores. In so many cases, political figures are shaping education policy and not trusting professionals to make professional judgments. (p. 54)

Dodge (2011–2012) referenced a story told by David Berliner to make the point on opinion versus facts. Berliner said the following:

> Two doctors . . . are walking beside a river and see somebody drowning. They take the person out of the river and save his life and then all of a sudden they see another floating down the river. They pull him out and save his life, [and] then all of a sudden they see another person floating down the river. They pull him out, and they save his life, but then here comes another, and another, and another. Finally, one of the doctors starts running upstream. The other doctor says, "Where are you going?" The first replies, "I am going to find out why they are falling in." (p. 57)

Berliner used this story to point out that while the ostensible cause of student failure may be the teacher, are we looking upstream to find out what the problem is? Do we look into communities? Do we look at poverty? Do we look at the home life of children before we blame the teacher? (Dodge, 2011–2012, p. 57).

In essence, "children who are homeless, who don't speak English, who have preventable illnesses, and who live in communities where there is a lot of violence, have challenges. These challenges come with poverty and get in the way of high achievement" (p. 57). Likewise, "Race to the Top incentivizes schools to do all the wrong things—like open more privately managed schools and judge teachers by student test scores" (p. 57). Any time there is a race there are few winners and many losers.

In a conversation with Dodge, Ravitch contended that the corporate elite want the public to believe that teachers are using poverty as an excuse, but those individuals excuse themselves from having anything to do about poverty. "They don't worry about the effects of outsourcing jobs. They don't worry about the fact that 20 percent of the nation's children live in poverty" (Dodge, 2011–2012, p. 57). As a result, "they are left off the hook if the conversation continues to be about blaming teachers" (p. 57). And if this rhetoric continues, Ravitch said, "it is a poisonous narrative. If you so poison the *public mind* against teachers, then who will teach?" (p. 57).

Most educators are aware of the many arrows, daggers, and spears thrown at them for the failure of public education. The political and corporate pundits base their decisions on opinions that have a ring of accuracy and intelligence. However, the research found that those opinions are based on unfounded beliefs rather than facts driving beliefs. Bill Moyers (2011) told the History Makers at a convention in New York City the following:

> Most of us like to believe that our opinions have been formed over time by careful, rational consideration of facts and ideas and that the decisions based on those opinions, therefore, have the ring of soundness and intelligence, [however] the research found that actually we often base our opinions on our beliefs . . . and rather than facts driving beliefs, our beliefs can dictate the facts we chose to accept. They can cause us to twist facts so they fit better with our preconceived notions.

Based on facts and not on emotion or ill-conceived beliefs, Paul Farhi (2011) presented *five prevalent myths* espoused by the critics about U.S. schools. The five trendy myths and logic disputing the myths are as follows:

1. *Our schools are failing.* The percentage of Americans earning a high school diploma has been rising for 30 years. According to the Department of Education, the percentage of 16- to-24-year-olds who were not enrolled in school and had not earned a diploma or its equivalent fell to 8% in 2008.

2. *Unions defend bad teachers.* Unions have proved amenable to removing the bad apples in their ranks—with due process. Every new teacher and those flagged as "underperforming" by a principal are to be observed by a specialist over a school year. All teachers get support, advice, and a chance to do better; then they are reevaluated. Those that fall short lose their jobs.

3. *Billionaires know best.* Massive financial contributions were given to public schools to promote pay-for-performance programs, which reward teachers with bonuses when their students do better on standardized tests. They argue that merit pay creates the same incentives for public-sector employees that bonuses do in the private sector. In a three-year, $10 million study released last fall, Vanderbilt University researchers found no significant difference in performance between students who were taught by middle school teachers eligible for cash bonuses and those who were not.

4. *Charter schools are the answer.* A standard university study in 2009 concluded the following: "Nearly half of the charter schools nationwide have results that are no different from the local public school options and over a third, 37%, deliver learning results that are significantly worse than their student[s] who would have realized had they remained in traditional public schools."

5. *More effective teachers are the answer.* Let's be realistic. There's only so much they can do to address problems that troubled students bring to class every day, including neglect, abuse, and unaddressed medical and mental health issues. The obvious and subtle ways that poverty inhibits a child's ability to learn—from hearing, visual and dental problems, to higher asthma rates to diminished verbal interaction in the home—have been well documented. (p. 1)

To be sure, myths about American schools will continue to abound, but facts still matter to critical thinking. As Bill Moyers (2011) alleged, "If we respect and honor the facts, even revere them, they just might help us right the ship of state before it rams the iceberg."

POLITICAL, CULTURAL, AND SOCIOECONOMIC REALITIES

From a political, cultural, and socioeconomical perspective, an important lesson is for educators to be prepared for the future. As part of that preparation, we are learning that what is actually taught in the classroom results from a confluence of conflicting factors. For example, state and federal governments, professional organizations, local school boards, textbook and software companies, accrediting and international organizations, parent and community groups, school administrators, and classroom teachers all seem to make a difference on how we educate students. Add to the mix growing pressures of political parties, economists, and organizational lobbyists, and education can change dramatically.

Economic terms like *productivity, incentivizing, human capital,* and *resource reallocation* suddenly are becoming a part of the school reform conversation. Over the past 15 years, the influence of economic analyses on education reform has steadily grown, and today politicians and economists of varying degrees have become a vocal and powerful part of the education policy landscape. Not surprisingly, this has become particularly relevant as soon as education reformers began using test scores and tools like value-added assessments to evaluate teacher performance and determine consequences for failing student achievement (Ferguson, 2013).

Along with economics, the political process (especially elections) is becoming increasingly important. And this is as it should be. Democracy relies on an informed public and citizens—including educators—becoming involved. Interestingly enough, educators are becoming more involved in supporting candidates who are attuned to cultural and social issues and who value education. At times, political passion can be an issue. But, if held in a climate of respect, it can be beneficial (Hoerr, 2012). In the long run, the value of political diversity is too important to ignore. Likewise, the importance of the electoral process is too great to leave to chance.

For the most part, influences of political and economic lobbying seem to change in their strength from time to time, and their particular impact on a given classroom is often difficult to trace. However, any curriculum leader or teacher who wishes to develop or improve curricula needs to understand what political and economic pressures are being applied and the way organizations and individuals are attempting to influence what is taught in the schools.

Issues involving school reform are not new. For example, many reform books have been on the market, such as William Bender and Cara Shores' (2007) *Response to Intervention: A Practical Guide for Every Teacher,* Tomlinson and McTighe's (2006) *Integrating Differentiated Instruction and Understanding by Design,* Ruby Payne's (2002) *Understanding Learning,* John Holt's (1964) *How Children Fail,* and Ivan Illich's (1972) *Deschooling Society.* Jonathan

Kozol's (1991) *Savage Inequalities: Children in America's Schools* and Grace Llewellyn's (1991) *Teenage Liberation Handbook: How to Quit School and Get a Real Life and Education* are also examples of reform books that are still popular. As a result, this chapter presents an overview of the way influences are brought to bear and then examines in greater detail those agencies that seem to have the greatest influence.

AN OVERVIEW OF THE CURRICULUM-INFLUENCE PROCESS

Teachers who are changing the direction of instruction in their classrooms are now taking learning to a new level (Bergmann & Sams, 2013–2014). Thus, it is important at the outset to realize that instructional change does not take place in a vacuum. It occurs in a complex social and cultural environment—an environment that significantly determines which belief systems and practices will gain the widest audience.

In reality, school leaders face many of the same problems other (business) leaders face (Abbate, 2010). The key, however, is for educators to be particularly careful not to let regulations get in the way of leadership. The prevailing pressures of regulations and mandates can be especially dangerous to education leaders. Moreover, if these pressures are not handled, they will wear away at genuine educational excellence. With this in mind, educational leaders are constantly monitoring all programs.

In reviewing the literature on school reform, Schon (1971) is perhaps the most illuminating. As he sees it, ideas "in good currency" flow into the mainstream, mediated by certain roles. New ideas incompatible with the prevailing conceptions are suppressed within the social system but kept alive by people in vanguard roles until a crisis occurs. At that time, those new ideas might be released and spread by information networks and the mass media. Before they are accepted, however, these new ideas become issues in power struggles. As Schon sees it, only a limited number of "slots" are available for new ideas because these new ideas are attached to advocates competing for power positions. In this manner, inquiry around the ideas becomes politicized. Those that have the most powerful support become legitimated by the approval of powerful people. Only then can the new ideas become public policy.

On July 1, 1954, the National Council for Accreditation of Teacher Education (NCATE) was founded. Five groups were instrumental in the creation of NCATE: the American Association of Colleges for Teacher Education, the National Association of State Directors of Teacher Education and Certification, the National Education Association (NEA), the Council of Chief State School Officers (CCSSO), and the National School Boards Association. When NCATE was founded as an independent accrediting body, it replaced the American Association of Colleges for Teacher Education as the agency responsible for accreditation in teacher education. Although membership is voluntary, NCATE is the accrediting body for colleges and universities that prepare teachers and other professional specialists for work in elementary and secondary schools. Basically, the most pressing goal of the NCATE, now the Council for the Accreditation of Educator Preparation (CAEP), accreditation process continues to be raising the bar for teacher education programs nationwide (Connelly, 2010).

Curriculum Tip 4.1

This struggle for power in the curriculum-making process seems to occur most stridently at the federal, state, and local district levels, and differentially—in some cases positively—affects the recommended, the written, and the taught curricula.

The end of the 1970s signaled a dramatic change in the form and purpose of public schools. From an economic standpoint, individual income and state financial resources were falling and costs were spiraling upward. School enrollments were declining, with parents moving their children into private schools or into the suburbs. Financial struggles of public schools, especially large urban public schools, continued to be a problem. Budgets reflected a drop in local support from 60% to 30%, while the role of the state increased. Federal government educational assistance continued at around 10%. With an increase in state contributions to education, the role of politics intensified.

At the same time that states were gaining a firmer foothold in education, Ronald Reagan was elected to the presidency. This began a new era of conservative government at the federal level. Between a decline in enrollment and rising costs, school boards were having difficulty and began to take a more conservative stand. The code phrase of the conservative movement became "Back to the Basics," and accountability became the norm.

At the federal level, the struggle for power occurs chiefly behind the scenes, as several influence groups and individuals attempt to persuade members of both the executive and legislative branches. Bell (1986) described how the decision not to abolish the Department of Education during President Reagan's second term came about as the result of such behind-the-scenes maneuvering. First, the platform-drafting committee for the 1984 Republican National Convention decided to ignore pressures to abolish the department that came mainly from individuals whom Bell called movement conservatives, "ideologues of the far right." As Bell pointed out, key members of the platform committee were House Republicans running for office in 1984. They had read *A Nation at Risk* (National Commission on Excellence in Education, 1983), they had sensed the grassroots interest in education, and they did not want to be perceived by voters as being anti-education. Although the "movement conservatives" continued to attempt to persuade Reagan to exert leadership on the issue, Reagan was, in Bell's view, a pragmatist with different priorities. He cared deeply about tuition tax credits, vouchers, and prayer in the schools, but he saw the fate of the Department of Education as a matter of lesser consequence. Knowing there was no broad-based support to abolish the department and not caring enough to spend his political capital in fighting the battle, Reagan quietly put the proposal on the back burner and never again raised the matter with Bell.

Lobbying groups can play an important role in this hidden power struggle at the federal level. Levine and Wexler (1981) documented clearly how the Council for Exceptional Children and other interest groups representing the handicapped played a determining role in the passage of Public Law 94–142, the most important national legislation affecting the handicapped. These lobbyists had developed close relationships with the staff and members of the congressional education committees, had formed close alliances with leaders in the Bureau of Education for the Handicapped, and spoke authoritatively at every congressional hearing on the bill.

The same picture of policy being made in a highly charged and politicized environment with much behind-the-scenes lobbying is seen at the state level. A case in point is the way Pennsylvania adopted its new curriculum regulations. In 1981, a forward-looking secretary of education proposed a radical restructuring of the state's curriculum regulations, replacing lists of required courses with the specification of student competencies that could be developed in a variety of ways. For two years, these changes were discussed and debated by lobbyists (chiefly those from professional organizations) by the state board of education and by Department of Education officials. No action was taken; state legislators were indifferent. One legislative leader expressed it this way:

> The reaction of the legislature when they were talking about these learning outcomes—the competency-based curriculum proposal—was pretty much a hands-off thing. They realized it was an issue they didn't want to get involved in. . . . Then all the reports came out in the intervening time, and there was a kind of a rush to judgment to see who was going to address this serious problem . . . all of a sudden the national environment was "let's do these things," and so everyone wanted to have their stamp on them. (Lynch, 1986, p. 74)

The governor published his own recommendations for "turning the tide," the House passed legislation mandating increased curriculum rigor and an emphasis on traditional subjects (not competencies), the Senate passed a resolution directing the state Board of Education to take action, and the state board adopted revised curriculum regulations—all within six months' time.

In such a politicized environment at the state level, numerous groups and individuals have a differential impact. In her study of policymaking in one of the eastern states, Marshall (1985) identified 15 influence groups. The strongest of those include the governor and his or her executive staff, the chief state school officer, individual members of the state legislature, the legislature as a whole, the legislative staff, and education interest groups. Those with moderate influence are the teachers' association, the state Board of Education, and the administrators' organization. The courts, the federal government, the school boards' association, non-educator groups, and researchers had much less influence.

It was during this time that an attempt was made to introduce "international" achievement testing as a measure of excellence. There was concern that U.S. children were somehow behind the children in other countries. Berliner and Biddle's (1997) book *The Manufactured Crisis* soon put this argument to rest by noting that the top 10% of children in countries such as Germany were being compared to the upper 50% of U.S. children. Berliner and Biddle contended that the U.S. best and brightest children could compete with Europe's top children on any testing measure.

Nonetheless, this assault on progressive education worldwide has continued for more than a decade. Phillips (2007), professor of education at San Francisco State University, noted, "Within the policy sphere, education has been dominated by the No Child Left Behind Act (NCLB) and its closely related state-level mandates. The focus has been on standards, test scores and accountability" (p. 712). As such, it can be seen that education across the country is clearly being directed by state agencies as well as mandated programs such as NCLB, Race to the Top, and Response to Intervention (RTI; Toch, 2010). All of these programs, along with a new emphasis on early childhood and pre-K programs, begs this question: Does the locus of reform lie within schools, or must forces beyond schools promote change?

At the local level, there is the same interplay of conflicting and coalescing influences; only the key actors are different. As the local school board sets general curriculum policy, it also is sensitive to prevailing trends in the society; in this context, it makes general decisions that have been strongly influenced by the superintendent, who is responding to his or her own perception of the larger educational scene and local needs. At the same time, local pressure groups, often acting in concert with nationally organized lobbies, will attempt to influence the board's curriculum policy as it involves such specific controversial issues as sex education, evolution, creationism, and values education.

Once general policy has been determined at the district level, key decisions are made about the written curriculum by curriculum leaders, school administrators, and teachers. At the district level, the assistant superintendent for curriculum and instruction and several subject matter supervisors usually provide leadership in developing and improving a field of study, such as mathematics K–12. Typically, the assistant superintendent or a supervisor will appoint a committee made up of representatives of the major constituencies: a principal, department chair, two to five teacher–leaders, and perhaps a token parent. In making decisions about the scope and sequence of that field, the committee typically uses a variety of professional sources: It consults state guidelines and standards, checks mandated tests, reviews available texts, confers with consultants, reviews guides from other districts and from professional associations, and surveys classroom teachers. When conflicts arise in their deliberations, committee members typically resolve them through political processes—negotiating, compromising, and deferring to the most powerful.

The picture changes somewhat at the school level. In elementary schools, the principal and teacher–leaders seem to play a key role in determining curricular priorities and in monitoring the curriculum. If conflict arises, it will usually occur between the principal and a small group of teacher–leaders who are jealous of their curricular autonomy. At the secondary level, the principal will usually delegate that responsibility to a team leader or department chair, because subject matter expertise is more important at this level. In secondary schools, curricular battles are usually waged between departments as they compete for scarce resources.

It should be noted that in the past, when the classroom door closed, the teacher could, at times, become the curriculum. It used to be that behind closed doors a teacher would make decisions based on a somewhat unconscious response to several sources: the district guide, the textbook, curriculum-referenced and standardized tests, the teacher's knowledge and perception of the subject matter, and the teacher's assessment of pupil interest and readiness. Teachers of today, however, are not as independent. With new technologies and data-driven curricula, as well as charts and graphs of student achievement, it is far less easy for teachers to dictate their own curricula from behind closed doors.

Thus, at different levels of curriculum decision making, the major sources of influence vary considerably, yet at every level, the process seems to be a highly politicized one in which issues of power and control are resolved in curriculum decision making. At this juncture, a closer examination of certain key elements might be useful.

THE ROLE OF THE FEDERAL GOVERNMENT

Even though the Tenth Amendment to the U.S. Constitution states that "the powers not delegated to the United States by the Constitution, nor prohibited by it to the States, are reserved to the States respectively, or to the people," the federal government has established a role in public education (see Exhibit 4.1 for major federal government legislation). Federal legislation passed has impacted the educational system and has significantly provided direction that the federal government believes is in the best interest of society and the United States. With federal funds that are provided to public education, the government has demanded school districts to provide results for the federal money that has been expended on public education (Whitehead, Boschee, & Decker, 2013).

Curriculum Tip 4.2	Successful curriculum leaders are those who continually learn and follow the regulations of federal and state legislation.

EXHIBIT 4.1 Federal Government Legislation	
Elementary and Secondary Education Act (ESEA; April 11, 1965)	The act funds primary and secondary education while explicitly forbidding the establishment of a *national curriculum*. Funds are authorized for professional development, instructional materials, resources to support educational programs, and parental involvement promotion. The government has reauthorized the act every five years since its enactment. The current reauthorization of ESEA is NCLB, which also allows military recruiters access to 11th- and 12th-grade students' names, addresses, and telephone listings when requested.
Individuals with Disabilities Education Act (IDEA) (1975)	In 1990, this law was renamed IDEA from the Education for All Handicapped Children Act. The amendments of 1997 further clarified its provisions. Significant changes revolved around three main themes: strengthened parental participation in the educational process, accountability for students' participation and success in the general education curriculum and mastery of individualized education program goals and objectives, and remediation and rehabilitation of behavior problems at school and in the classroom. The act requires all participating states to offer to all children with disabilities a "free and appropriate public education" and that those children are educated with children who are not disabled "to the maximum extent appropriate." Source: Ubben, Hughes, and Norris (2007), p. 163.
A Nation at Risk: The Imperative for Educational Reform (National Commission on Excellence in Education, 1983)	This publication was considered a landmark event in modern U.S. educational history. It contributed to the ever-growing sense that U.S. schools were failing miserably, and it touched off a wave of local, state, and federal reform efforts. The report itself is perhaps best remembered for the language in the opening pages: "The educational foundations of our society are presently being eroded by a rising tide of mediocrity that threatens our very future as a Nation and a people" and for the statement, "If an unfriendly foreign power had attempted to impose on America the mediocre educational performance that exists today, we might well have viewed it as an act of war."

Goals 2000: Educate America Act (P.L. 103–227) (1994)	The act was based on the premise that students would reach high levels of achievement when more is expected of them. Goals 2000 established a framework to identify world-class academic standards, to measure student progress, and to provide the support that students needed to meet the standards.
No Child Left Behind Act of 2001 (replaces the Elementary and Secondary Education Act [ESEA] passed on April 11, 1965)	This act was a landmark in education reform designed to improve student achievement and change the culture of U.S. schools. The act embodied four key principles–stronger accountability for results; greater flexibility for states, school districts, and schools in the use of federal funds; more choices for parents of children from disadvantaged backgrounds; and an emphasis on teaching methods that have been demonstrated to work. The act also placed an emphasis on reading, especially for young children, enhancing the quality of the nation's teachers, and ensuring that all children in U.S. schools learned English.

Curriculum Tip 4.3	Take advantage of the Tenth Amendment right to take the lead on policy, remaining accountable to the people.

As shown in Exhibit 4.2, some of the latest developments in education with political implications for school principals include RTI, school vouchers, homeschooling, P–16 education, and the Common Core State Standards Initiative (CCSSI).

As shown in Exhibit 4.1, prior to the early 1960s, little federal involvement existed in curriculum. Other than the National Defense Education Act of 1958, activities of the federal government in education were being primarily limited to convening prestigious groups, creating professional societies, and disseminating the recommendations of prominent individuals. Upon reviewing the lengthy list of legislation, the discussion that follows examines the federal government's role in the five most recent periods discussed in Chapter 2 of this work: Scholarly Structuralism (1957–1967), Romantic Radicalism (1968–1974), Privatistic Conservatism (1975–1989), Technological Constructionism (1990–1999), Modern Conservatism (2000–2009), and Technological Functionalism (2010–present).

Curriculum Tip 4.4	In examining the role of the federal government in influencing the school curriculum, it is useful to bring to bear a historical perspective, because patterns of influence have changed over the past few decades.

Scholarly Structuralism (1957–1967)

This was the period of the national frenzy to "catch up with the Russians." Largely instigated by the launching of *Sputnik*, it was a time of intensive and extensive federal intervention in

EXHIBIT 4.2 Political Implications for Principals

Response to Intervention (RTI)	RTI is addressed through federal law and refers to a tiered approach to instruction. Students who do not make adequate academic progress and who are at risk for reading and other learning disabilities receive increasingly intensive instructional services. RTI can be conceptualized as providing a framework for systemic reform directed at improving all learners' outcomes as intended by the [NCLB] of 2001.
School vouchers	There have been various programs, with various names, designed for the purpose of using public funds to pay for all or part of the costs of students' tuition at private or religious schools. The American public foots the bill, but have no way of knowing how their tax dollars are being used because private and religious schools, unlike public schools, typically do not have to report to the public about how they spend their funds or how well their students are achieving.
Homeschooling	This educational practice has evolved from a level of almost complete unawareness to one of widespread uninformed awareness. Today homeschooling parents are reinventing the ideas of school. Along with this movement, a growing body of literature on school choice has emerged. Despite legislation problems, regulatory hurdles, media attacks, and other affronts to the homeschooling movement, homeschooling has continued to gain in popularity and strength. Even though exact numbers are hard to come by, homeschooling may be the fastest growing form of education in the United States. In 2005–2006 there were an estimated 1.9 to 2.1 million children home schooled. This represented an increase from the estimated 850,000 students who were home schooled in the spring of 1999 (National Center for Education Statistics, 2004).
P–16 education	This configuration of education has a growing body of interest in the 21st century. A wave of educational reform has swept the nation over the first decade of the 21st century. For example, school choice, charter schools, NCLB, RTI, and standards-based instruction, among others are highly debatable because the landscape of education in the United States has not undergone major change. Although the jury is still out, P-16 education has potential because it is more responsive to society's needs. There is widespread agreement that all students in our schools need further postsecondary education to lead successful economic and civic lives as adults. Implicit in this consensus is the notion that the current system is not capable of bringing this about.

| Common Core State Standards Initiative [CCSSI] | The [CCSSI] is a state-led effort coordinated by the National Governors Association Center for Best Practices (NGA Center) and the Council of Chief State School Officers (CCSSO).

Governors and state commissioners of education from 48 states [Alaska and Texas have not joined], 2 territories [Puerto Rico and the Virgin Islands], and the District of Columbia committed to developing a common core of state standards in English language arts and mathematics for grades K-12. A few states have passed legislation to withdraw. These sets of standards define the knowledge and skills students should have to succeed in entry-level, credit-bearing, academic college courses and in workforce training programs.

They will:

- Be aligned with college and work expectations
- Include rigorous content *and* application of knowledge through high-order skills
- Build upon strengths and lessons of current state standards
- Internationally benchmarked, so that all students are prepared to succeed in our global economy and society.
- Evidence and/or research based

In the twenty-six years since the release of *A Nation at Risk* [National Commission on Excellence in Education, 1983], states have made great strides in increasing the academic rigor of education standards. Yet, America's children still remain behind other nations in terms of academic achievement and preparedness to succeed.

An advisory group provides advice and guidance on the initiative. Members of this group include experts from Achieve, Inc., ACT, the College Board, the National Association of State Boards of Education, and the State Higher Education Executive Officers. |
|---|---|

SOURCE: National Governors Association (2009).

curriculum. During this period, education seemed to be dominated by what Atkin and House (1981) called a "technological" perspective. Educational leaders were convinced that rational, technological approaches could solve the schools' problems. Teaching was seen as a technological endeavor: The essential skills of teaching could be identified and taught through a step-by-step approach. Curriculum development similarly was viewed as a rational technological enterprise: The right content could be identified by the scholars and then delivered in tested packages. Even the change process was seen from this perspective: The agricultural model of conducting research and disseminating its results through "change agents" was viewed as the only proper means for changing the schools.

The primary intervention strategy adopted by the federal government was the development and dissemination of generic curricula. To use the constructs explicated in Chapter 1, the developers of the "alphabet soup curricula" attempted to fuse the recommended, the written, and the taught curricula; they sincerely believed that their idealistic recommendations would be embodied into district curriculum guides and that teachers would willingly and faithfully implement what they had produced.

The developers of these generic curricula seemed most concerned with course content: the National Science Foundation developed and supported the Course Content Improvement Program, which in turn strongly influenced a similar program adopted by the U.S. Office of Education, called the Curriculum Improvement Program. In the view of these leaders, curriculum and content were synonymous. That content, in their view, should be determined only by the scholars in the disciplines—not by "educationists." It was the scholars alone who understood the structures of the disciplines, who could identify the critical concepts, and who knew how to organize and sequence that content.

Once the scholars had developed these ideal curricula, the dissemination effort began. Large-scale publicity efforts were undertaken: Articles appeared in the professional journals touting the high quality of the products, and sessions were held at the major professional conferences advocating the adoption of the materials. Teachers were trained in summer institutes with rather generous stipends provided. More than 30 regional laboratories were funded to aid in the development and dissemination efforts, and the curriculum was translated into marketable packages—textbooks either produced by commercial entities or sold by the developers themselves.

Initially, these federally funded generic curricula seemed successful. The materials produced were significantly different from what had been developed before, especially in science and mathematics. Even the conventional textbooks produced by mainline publishing houses included concepts introduced by the scholarly curriculum projects. Early users, the most committed and knowledgeable of teachers, seemed enthusiastic.

However, resistance to these federal efforts to transform the curriculum through direct intervention began to increase at the end of this period. First of all, concern surfaced about what some termed the *federal curriculum,* a fear that these federally supported curriculum projects would reduce local curricular autonomy. Others pointed out, of course, that in some fields, at least, the effect was quite the opposite. Until Project Social Studies came along, there was in effect a nationally standardized curriculum in social studies—a curriculum that was limited almost solely to recurring courses in U.S. history, a little geography in elementary schools, and a smattering of civics in junior high schools and "Problems of

Democracy" in senior high schools. Project Social Studies offered more alternatives: Schools could now teach economics, anthropology, and sociology, using materials that had a scholarly cachet.

Objections also mounted as to the specifics of the content. Many teachers complained that the materials were too difficult for their students. Parents and lay critics argued that the "basics" were being slighted: Not enough attention was paid to computational skills in the mathematics curriculum projects or to spelling and grammar in the English curricula. There were also numerous protests about the values issues embedded in many of the social studies and science curricula; many individuals and organizations felt that these nationally disseminated projects espoused values they considered too liberal and permissive. As noted in Chapter 2, these complaints reached a crescendo in the bitter controversy over *Man: A Course of Study* (MACOS; Curriculum Development Associates, 1972).

Finally, it was obvious that these so-called teacher-proof curricula were doomed to fail because they were put in the hands of "curriculum-proof" teachers. The developers of these curricula seemed totally oblivious to the nature of schools as organizations and to the complexities of classroom life. They somewhat naively believed that their curricula would be adopted uniformly and implemented as designed. They foolishly expected teachers to acquire, internalize, and use teaching strategies that were radically different from those they already used and that were quite demanding in their complexity.

Romantic Radicalism (1968–1974)

During this period, the national agenda changed. While international issues such as the war in Vietnam continued to dominate the headlines, at the grassroots level people seemed more concerned with their own individual freedoms. It was a time when "rights," not responsibilities, was the dominant slogan: Black people, handicapped individuals, homosexuals, women, and nonnative groups all asserted their rights to liberation and to greater power.

In this seven-year period, educational thinking at the policymaking level seemed to be dominated by what Atkin and House (1981) called a political perspective, in contradistinction to the technological perspective that had dominated the previous period. A political perspective views educational reform essentially as a political process. The legitimacy of several conflicting views is recognized. Decisions are made primarily through a process of compromise and negotiation.

It was this political perspective that seemed to influence both Congress and the several federal agencies empowered to enforce compliance with federal legislation. Their intervention strategy seemed to be a "carrot-and-stick" approach: Develop specific policies mandating changes in the operation of schools and offer financial rewards to those who comply. Their impact on school curricula is perhaps best seen in an analysis of their response to pressures from two groups: those insisting on the need for bilingual education and those arguing for the educational rights of the handicapped.

English Language Learners

From a historical perspective, Ravitch (1983) pointed out that the demand for bilingual education (currently English language learner [ELL] programs) seemed to result from a surge of new ethnocentrism that argued for ethnicity as a basis for public policy. Initially, the demand seemed modest enough. As Ravitch noted, those advocating bilingual education in the congressional hearings of 1967 desired funding only for demonstration projects that would meet the special educational needs of Hispanic children; in their view, the aim of bilingual education was to help the Hispanic child master the English language. The Bilingual Education Act of 1968, which ultimately became Title VII of the Elementary and Secondary Education Act (ESEA), covered not just Hispanic children but all children of limited English-speaking ability, especially those from low-income families. The act was intentionally vague in key particulars: Bilingual education was not defined, and the purpose of the act was never made explicit.

Although the act itself did not require districts to provide **bilingual programs**, in 1970 the Office of Civil Rights (OCR) informed every school district with more than 5% "national origin–minority group children" that it had to take "affirmative steps" to rectify the language deficiency of such children or be in violation of Title VI of the Civil Rights Act. The OCR guidelines were sustained and supported by the Supreme Court in its *Lau v. Nichols* (1974) decision, which directed the schools to create special language programs for "non–English-speaking children," to correct what it called "language deficiency."

Also in 1974, Congress renewed and extended the 1968 act, making several important changes in response to pressures from lobbying groups representing ethnic minorities. First, the provisions of the act covered all children—not just those from low-income homes. Instead of being primarily concerned with teaching these children how to speak English, the act recognized the importance of maintaining the native language and cultural heritage. Ravitch (1983) added that the 1974 act was a landmark in that it marked the first time Congress had dictated a specific pedagogical approach to local districts.

Currently, ELL programs are becoming even more prevalent. In classrooms across the world, multilingual learning environments are helping students feel at home and are accelerating language learning (Agirdag, 2009).

Educating the Handicapped

In many ways, federal intervention in the education of the handicapped seemed to parallel its activities on behalf of nonnative children. What began as a relatively small effort became a major establishment supported with federal funds. Prior to 1965, there seemed to be almost no concerted effort to secure federal funds to aid the education of the handicapped. The leaders of organizations such as the National Association for Retarded Citizens and the Council for Exceptional Children, however, viewing the success of the civil rights movement, began to coordinate their lobbying efforts. Their efforts quickly paid off: In 1966, Congress established the Bureau of Education for the Handicapped, within the Office of Education, and in 1970 passed new legislation increasing the amount of aid for the education of the handicapped and expanding the definition of the term *handicapped* to include the learning disabled and the socially and emotionally disturbed.

Two important court decisions provided strong impetus for further efforts. In 1971, the federal courts issued a consent decree requiring Pennsylvania to provide a free public education to all exceptional children between the ages of 6 and 21; in 1972, the federal court in the District of Columbia held that every school-age child in the district had to be provided with a "free and suitable publicly supported education regardless of the degree of a child's mental, physical, or emotional disability or impairment" (*Mills v. Board of Education,* 1972).

Congress then responded by enacting the Rehabilitation Act of 1973, including Section 504, which Ravitch (1983) called "the handicapped person's equivalent of Title VI of the Civil Rights Act of 1964" (p. 307). The enactment of that legislation was quickly followed by the passage in 1975 of Public Law 94–142. In many ways, this particular law was the most prescriptive educational legislation ever passed by Congress. The law not only required that every child receive an individualized educational program but it even specified the content of these plans. They had to include a statement of present levels of performance, a statement of annual goals and short-term objectives, a statement of the educational services to be provided, and the extent to which the child would be able to participate in regular programs. Projected dates for initiation and duration, objective criteria and evaluation procedures, and schedules also determined whether the objectives were being achieved. Finally, the law required the **mainstreaming** of the handicapped: Such children were to be educated with the nonhandicapped "to the maximum extent appropriate."

Whereas the development of generic content-oriented courses did not seem to have a lasting impact, the carrot-and-stick approach of passing and enforcing legislation had a pervasive impact, to the extent that many educational leaders of the time expressed grave concern about the intrusion of the federal government and the courts into matters that they believed were better left to local control.

Privatistic Conservatism (1975–1989)

This period, of course, was dominated by President Ronald Reagan, who was elected on a conservative platform and who used his considerable leadership skills to implement that platform. As perceived by Terrel H. Bell (1986), then secretary of education, Reagan had in mind six goals relating to education: substantially reduce federal spending; strengthen local and state control; and maintain a limited federal role in helping states carry out their educational responsibilities, expand parental choice, reduce federal judicial activity in education, and abolish the Department of Education.

The Reagan administration's initiatives had clear implications for curriculum. To strengthen the state role in education and provide equitable services for private school students, Congress adopted under Reagan's prodding a program to award block grants to the states: Chapter 2 of the Education Consolidation and Improvement Act of 1981 consolidated more than 30 categorical programs into a single block grant to each state. An initial study by Hertling (1986) of the effects of this block-grant program indicated that, in general, the Chapter 2 money had been used to support computer-based education, curriculum development, staff development, and pilot development of new programs. Although inner-city districts tended to lose the largest amount of money under the block-grant approach, 75% of the districts gained funds under Chapter 2, and per-pupil spending for nonpublic schools increased.

Much of this curriculum development undertaken by the states seems to have responded to Secretary of Education William J. Bennett's agenda of "choice, content, character, and citizenship." In his initial distribution of more than $2.5 million in discretionary grants to 34 organizations, Bennett made 11 awards to organizations desiring to develop materials in character education and 7 to those interested in strengthening the academic content of the curriculum.

The most controversial of Bennett's initiatives was his attempt to modify the federal government's approach to bilingual education. He proposed several changes in the regulations governing the distribution of bilingual education funds: allow districts to increase the English-language component of bilingual programs, encourage them to mainstream limited-English-proficiency students more rapidly, and require districts to assume increased financial responsibility for the programs. His proposals were hailed by many who criticized the practice of teaching such students in their native language and attacked by those who saw the new proposals as jeopardizing the educational rights and opportunities of such students.

Technological Constructionism (1990–1999)

Throughout much of the 1990s, conservatives would address their concerns with education via teacher certification (national board certification), standards-based curriculum (America's Choice), and other similar programs. The standards-based and technological reform movement continued to gain support at the national, state, and local levels. This was especially true with regard to having chief state officers (politically elected state commissioners of education) disseminate and enforce tests and measures of educational competency. With more interest focused on standards and student achievement, the U.S. Department of Education and Congress began looking at more effective ways to close the achievement gap between students in wealthy and poor communities.

It was during this era that Jonathan Kozol's (1991) publication of *Savage Inequalities* exposed the gross disparities existing between public school districts serving the poorest of the poor and the most affluent sectors of American society. Kozol's work shed light on overlapping inequalities emergent in public education. Such disparities merely reflected the growing gap between rich and poor exacerbated by the Reaganomics of the previous decade (Schugurensky, 2003).

On March 26, 1994, President Clinton's Goals 2000: Educate America Act was passed by the U.S. Congress. This bill was intended to do the following:

> Improve learning and teaching by providing a national framework for education reform; to promote the research, consensus building, and systemic changes needed to ensure equitable educational opportunities and high levels of educational achievement for all American students; . . . [and] to promote the development and adoption of a voluntary national system of skill standards and certifications. (Schugurensky, 2003, p. 1)

Part A of the legislation outlined national goals for education, to be achieved by the year 2000. The goals were organized into eight categories: (1) school readiness; (2) school completion; (3) student achievement and citizenship (including access to physical and health education); (4) teacher education and professional development; (5) mathematics and science; (6) adult literacy and lifelong learning; (7) safe, disciplined, and drug-free schools; and (8) school and home partnership.

The Goals 2000 Technology Plan, built on local, state, and regional initiatives in technology and telecommunications, was a major part of the technological constructionism reform movement. Goals 2000 included such programs as the Star Schools project as well as the growing demand for and use of the Internet. The planning and implementation efforts of the Goals 2000 Technology Plan greatly helped the enhancement of telecommunications in education.

To help schools and communities, especially those with high concentrations of poor children, meet higher education standards, Congress and the U.S. Department of Education in 1997 also developed the Comprehensive School Reform Demonstration (CSRD) program (Partners in Education, 2003). The CSRD program was designed to give schools more flexible funding to adopt research-based models that focused on improving the whole school, not just specific students or subject areas. CSRD grants created a wave of interest among schools and districts, all seeking to improve teaching and learning and to meet higher education standards. The grants allowed schools to choose among a new and wider range of research-based models, many of which provided both strategies and technical assistance for school improvement and student achievement.

More and more communities began to realize the pressing needs and challenges of public schools as the nation increased its focus on new education reform strategies. School systems were being asked to aim higher academically and to do more for students and families, but many lacked the resources (financial, human, and administrative) needed to accomplish these ambitious goals. In light of this situation, partnerships emerged as a powerful strategy for strengthening and improving schools. For many communities, meeting higher education standards and special education needs was often dependent on finding more resources to apply to the task.

For example, new legislation in the 1990s restructured IDEA (the Individuals with Disabilities Education Act) into four parts: Part A, General Provisions; Part B, Assistance for Education of All Children With Disabilities; Part C, Infants and Toddlers With Disabilities; and Part D, National Activities to Improve Education of Children With Disabilities ("Summary of the Individuals with Disabilities Education Act [IDEA]," 2003). Affirmative-action programs were also becoming more prevalent during this time of technological constructionism. A new focus on children's rights and school safety emerged following the aftermath of such tragedies as the Columbine High School shooting. A move toward homeschooling was on the rise as well.

School leaders searched for new ways to use local resources to meet education goals and current challenges. Building on new coalitions of schools and communities forced a move away from individualism and toward partnerships at the end of the century. With the assistance of university and college programs, schools began providing much-needed training and professional development to teachers. In addition, partnerships with small and large businesses emerged to help school officials learn how better to leverage their human and financial resources. Through successful collaborations with community agencies, public schools started blending resources and offering a continuum of comprehensive and preventive services. A transition to a new, more federal conservative privatistic movement could be seen in the offing.

Modern Conservatism (2000–2009)

In 2001, educational reform moved away from technological constructionism and returned to a more privatistic and conservative nature. This was especially the case with President George W. Bush's move toward charter schools, vouchers, and tax credits. Supporters for charter schools, vouchers, and tax credits believed that the government should not be in the business of running schools. State-funded vouchers should pay for privately run education at private schools, parochial schools, charter schools, homeschooling, or whatever schools parents choose. Charter schools were generally considered publicly funded and publicly controlled schools that were privately run. They were usually required to adhere to fewer district rules than were regular public schools. Most assuredly, the strengths and weaknesses of these hybrid public schools came into sharp focus and charter schools became a cornerstone of the multibillion-dollar federal education reform agenda (Toch, 2010). But teachers became disillusioned when charters came to be seen as a way to turn over schools to outside operators. Now teachers are playing a key role in regaining momentum with the development of organizations such as the Minnesota Guild of Public Charter Schools. These guilds as teacher-led "single-purpose" charter school authorizers are able to closely monitor whether charters live up to the promises in approved agreements (Sundin, 2014).

Much like charter schools, vouchers became a means of implementing school choice. Basically, the school district gave parents a "voucher," which entitled them to choose their public school or private school. This same movement was initially called the School Choice Movement. "School choice" referred to a school district allowing parents to decide in which school within the district to enroll their children. The underlying philosophy of school choice appeared to be that parents should have the right to choose how their children were educated, regardless of income level.

Another aspect of the modern conservative movement arrived with the passage of NCLB in 2002. According to the 2003 Education Commission of the States, NCLB and the revised ESEA are blends of new requirements, incentives, and resources, and they pose significant challenges for states. The law sets deadlines for states to expand the scope and frequency of student testing, revamp their accountability systems, and guarantee that every teacher is qualified in his or her subject area. NCLB requires states to make demonstrable annual progress in raising the percentage of students' proficiency in reading and math and in narrowing the test-score gap between advantaged and disadvantaged students.

In addition, NCLB annual testing requirements pressured many schools to pump up the amount of time spent teaching math and reading—often at the expense of other subjects, such as history, art, or science. This appears to be the case in some districts, with elementary schools often requiring a block of 90 minutes for both reading and the mathematics courses. High school block class schedules for math and reading are also running around 90 minutes each. The problem is that most regular classes at the high school level are 55 minutes. As a result, middle and high school students often lose time in elective classes. Unfortunately, some of these elective classes provide technical or trade skills that students use after they graduate.

Even more mystifying was NCLB initially requiring states to set challenging student academic achievement standards without a set definition of proficiency. This led to disarray with some states setting lenient standards while others set stringent standards. For example, some states set standards such that 80% or more of their students will perform at the proficient level or above on their assessments, while other states set such stringent standards that 20% or less of their students will perform at that level. Therefore, if we look back since the NCLB inception, the act created quite a stir in the field of education. And clearly there is little doubt that a number of schools across the United States struggled in getting all subgroups to meet the expectations of the act. Not surprisingly, backers of NCLB may have had their hearts in the right place, but the amount of pressure and fear it has put on schools to reach minimum standards certainly has created some major unintended consequences.

In response to the many challenges and failures associated with NCLB, another approach— Race to the Top—was soon initiated. According to Jennings (2012), Race to the Top became a form of discretionary authority reflected in rewards states could receive for developing broadly supported plans to reform education and promote innovation. Individual states could apply for Race to the Top competitive grants if they could prove significant need as well as demonstrating changes in various education policies, such as adopting systems to evaluate teachers based on student test scores and removing caps on the number of charter schools.

Dietel (2011) noted that the U.S Department of Education's Race to the Top Assessment Criteria includes the following:

- Assessments should be aligned to a common set of college- and career-ready, K–12 standards at minimum in mathematics and English language arts in Grades 3–8 and at least once in high school.
- Assessments must be capable of measuring standards that have been traditionally difficult to measure.
- Assessments must include ELLs and students with disabilities and include appropriate accommodations.
- Assessment scoring must be consistent and ideally will include teachers in the scoring process, with the goal that the inclusion will help inform teaching and improve instructional practice.
- Colleges can use results. Students who meet achievement standards can be exempt from remedial courses and placed directly into college courses.
- Assessments must produce student achievement data and student growth data that can be used to do the following:
  ○ Measure and report school effectiveness
  ○ Measure individual principal and teacher effectiveness
  ○ Determine principal and teacher professional development and support needs
  ○ Improve teaching, learning, and programs
- Technology should be used in assessment design, development, administration, scoring, and reporting, and can be used by states not involved in the consortia.

Along with Race to the Top, and with a number of states signing on to CCSS, educators are turning their sights to assessments that will measure them—one by the Smarter Balanced Assessment Consortium (SBAC) and a second by the Partnership for Assessment of Readiness for College and Careers (PARCC) (Dietel, 2011, p. 32).

Some believe that by increasing competition through programs, government policies have increased the effectiveness of many sectors of the economy. But not education (Jensen, 2013–2014). Following Race to the Top, a new ruling was added allowing states to apply for *waivers* of key NCLB provisions. Waivers meant that a state could develop its own set of changes to NCLB, provided it could show intent to reform as well as some commonalities to NCLB provisions. As a result, a number of states developed accountability systems even more sophisticated than the one required by NCLB. In addition, these same states received permission to shift funds set aside by NCLB for underused tutoring services and choice options. These funds could then be used for such purposes as providing extra services for struggling students. As the South Dakota secretary of education said, "The waiver plan means that a state can focus its school improvement efforts at the bottom 15 percent of schools, instead of good schools judged as failing because of diverse student populations that create more opportunities to fall short" (Staff and Wire Reports, 2011, p. A5).

Looking back over the many years of NCLB-related changes, one could state that the act called for quality education and accountability for all children in U.S. schools. Huntsman (2010), however, disagrees. He noted that many educators still believe there are fundamental problems with NCLB—especially those representing curriculum changes and trends that may be deemed as unintended and harmful. The most serious problem noted by Huntsman and others is that NCLB expectations for student achievement are set unrealistically high. And, if that is not enough, schools' scores are expected to continually progress higher and higher.

Regardless of the downside, a number of positives have been gleaned since the passage of NCLB. For example, some schools have implemented new research-based programs and have made positive changes in their high school teaching sequence. And testing scores are increasing. Moreover, other schools have met their five-year plan and continue to evaluate district progress, as well as adding numerous after-school programs to continue trying to meet the original intent of NCLB. Along with a renewed interest in early childhood education, more states are implementing PreK programs and all-day kindergartens, both of which help the students continue to gain knowledge at a younger age.

Thus, some schools have to evaluate what teachers teach and the way they teach it. Most notable, however, are the achievement gains made by low-performing students who have too often been ignored in the past. Even opponents of NCLB grudgingly concede that the law has revolutionized how schools look at poor, minority, and disabled children in big cities, who often find themselves struggling academically.

Along with concerns and challenges with NCLB, a decision was made to target $100 billion in American Recovery and Reinvestment Act (ARRA) to education. The direct effect of the ARRA-funded School Improvement Grants initially was not readily apparent to school leaders and teachers, but they did help in developing better state assessments aligned with CCSS (Jennings, 2012).

In retrospect, then, NCLB as a nationally mandated accountability system has had both positive and negative impacts. Most importantly, it has ensured adequate attention to the reporting of results for subgroups including economically disadvantaged students, students with disabilities, limited-English-proficient students, and race or ethnicity groups. Such disaggregated reporting of results provides a mechanism for monitoring the degree to which the goal of improving achievement of these underserved student groups is being accomplished.

Obviously, there have been changes—and there will continue to be changes. The focus on annual yearly progress, narrow standards, and the NCLB political grip on education cannot totally reflect the shared vision that is needed for the future. Education reform, therefore, continues to be a major problem facing political administrations and organizations seeking to limit the role of the federal government in education.

Technological Functionalism (2010–Present)

Today, the functionalism of technology in school districts demands hard work to manage the needs of their constituents: students, parents, teachers, and taxpayers, not to mention local and statewide governing bodies and agencies. Now, more than ever, it is critical that schools function well as a cohesive system—from the classroom and the business office to the transportation department and the superintendent's office.

Technological Functionalism's view on education should be to have a consensus perspective: examine society in terms of how it is maintained for the common good. As such, it will put an emphasis on positive aspects of schools such as socialization: the learning of skills and attitudes in school. Too, education helps maintain society by socializing young people into values of achievement, competition, and equality of opportunity. The skills provision is also important: Education teaches the skills for the economy—for example, literacy, numeracy, and information technology for particular occupations (History Learning Site, 2014).

Michelle Exstrom (see Kardish, 2014), an education policy analyst at the National Conference of State Legislatures, said the following:

> The rollout of Common Core, the new state standards that demand more of students and teachers, as well as research on the changing needs of the workforce, are placing teacher preparation [and professional development] front and center in state houses.

Additionally, due to the lack of a small-scale pilot test, the CCSS seems to lose support because, as Schmoker (2014), in a made-up story, compared it to an experimental drug:

> In the early 20th century, medical scientists created an experimental drug with immense potential for preventing terminal illnesses. But before the drug was tested in trial runs, it was manufactured, distributed, and sold nationally in its raw form. Some might refer to this process as a "pilot." But it wasn't a pilot at all; in other words, it was not a small-scale, carefully studied trial. Thousands died, and countless others became ill. The drug was finally pulled from the market and properly tested. Once scientists refined it, the drug saved millions of lives.

If one replaces "drug" with the CCSS, we might have a good analogy for its increasingly troubled launch but also the opportunity to salvage it. Too, much of the trouble could have been avoided had the standards been piloted on a small scale. Further, Schmoker (2014) said the following:

A lot of the current public confusion and acrimony could have been avoided had we piloted the standards in a small-scale, publicly transparent fashion. They should have been piloted for clarity, economy, and alignment with the assessments with which they are now appallingly misaligned. Instead, the standards were launched, like an untested prescription drug, even as they were being used as the basis for expensive new textbooks, tests, and countless misconceived training sessions in dozens of states.

The authors, through experience and research, concur with Schmoker. School personnel have not had adequate time to determine if the standards are clear and concise enough to achieve their primary purpose: "facilitating the creation of appropriate and coherent curricula for English/language arts and math, by grade level, that make sense within the constraints of a nine-month school year" (Schmoker, 2014). Instead, the standards have been launched on a near-national scale before even a single district or school could pilot them.

The basic steps on "how to" develop and implement curriculum are illustrated in Chapter 10.

COMMON CORE STATE STANDARDS

In a politically charged atmosphere, CCSS continues to be controversial. At a time when many states are in the process of implementing CCSS, there is a renewed interest in contemporary vision, active thought, active expression, and active preparation for lifelong learning. Thus, engaging new standards as well as marshaling data is taking precedence over the acquisition of general knowledge (Meacham, 2013). What is at odds is standards-based curriculum and delivery. The idea of a standards-based curriculum and delivery system might seem simplistic, but at its core, teachers must teach the standards if students are expected to master them (Brown, 2011). This makes the issue of CCSS sometimes controversial. Of major concern is whether the federal government should make the receipt of federal funds contingent on states adopting common academic standards. Hence, accountability for improved student achievement lies at the heart of the matter. And with the federal government a more forceful player in education, Congress is more likely to debate recommended national standards in the future (Jennings, 2010–2011).

With the advent of CCSS, many district and school leaders are currently facing numerous decisions on curriculum adoption, assessment, and professional development. These decisions will have tremendous long-term impacts. Fortunately, according to Schifter and Granofsky (2012), CCSS can help address this situation in that it is both focused and coherent. It is focused because there are fewer CCSS than existing state standards. And it is coherent because it supports concepts as well as skills. For example, at the heart of K–12 mathematics, it considers how large conceptual issues develop from grade to grade.

A reality is that CCSS is requiring a new set of instructional competencies. As noted by Holliday and Smith (2012), the implementation of CCSS in Kentucky has brought about a major systems change. With CCSS changes, principals in Kentucky now must do the following:

- Set a new vision for learning based on CCSS
- Promote implementation efforts by nurturing school culture
- Support necessary instructional shifts
- Establish learning communities where teachers have adequate time to deepen their knowledge
- Act as coach, providing feedback and identifying exemplary practices to share best practices within their buildings
- Monitor and evaluate implementation efforts based on student work

Certainly, as evidenced previously, principals and teachers across the United States are focusing on new ways of teaching and learning due to the CCSS. In developing principal and teacher capacity, working collaboratively, and supporting district and school planning processes, many states, like Kentucky and Oklahoma, are now realizing the intended vision of the new standards.

STATE ROLE IN CURRICULUM

States are playing a key role in defining ways for schools and districts to increase student achievement. In this regard, many states are focusing on CCSS implementation as a recommended driver of school improvement. Yet, when examining the role of the states in curriculum, two problems present themselves. The *first* is the fact that the states differ significantly in the extent to which they are centralized, retaining authority at the state level, or decentralized, delegating authority to the local districts. The *second* is that the patterns of state influence have shifted in response to NCLB and CCSS. Most state departments of education are now playing their own expanded roles in ensuring compliance with federal mandates and CCSS.

According to Ferguson (2013), outsized attacks on the CCSS are not likely to derail the most significant education effort since desegregation. Successful implementation of the CCSS depends primarily on a state's adherence to concepts having an effect at scale (Wilhoit, 2012). In addition, it is important for state leaders to understand that the effort ahead is a systems issue. Any kind of reform depends on how it affects the vast majority of teachers, schools, and districts across the country. As such, implementation will certainly be about state systems addressing their shortcomings and about actionable plans that can be brought to scale. Unfortunately, from a historical perspective, previous standards have not necessarily led to improved student outcomes. Keeping this in mind, states today must challenge existing assumptions about inherited systems and be committed to graduate each and every student and ensure these students will be prepared for success in college, careers, or whatever they choose to pursue. By and large, this can only happen by cultivating the most promising examples created by teachers and leaders and helping schools and districts set up structures for continuous learning.

Curriculum Tip 4.5	"Tapping into teacher expertise can produce dividends in developing policies" (Eckert & Kohl, 2013).

Traditions and inherited systems at state levels often pose resistance and can be difficult to change. In some states, a series of constants prevail as to the nature of a states' influence over curricula. They include the following:

1. Specifying time requirements for the school year, for the school day, and for particular subjects

2. Mandating specific subjects and requiring instruction in such specific areas as alcohol and drug abuse, driver safety, and the American economic system

3. Setting graduation requirements

4. Developing programs for such special groups as the handicapped and those for whom English is a second language

5. Mandating procedures for the adoption of textbooks, software, and other instructional materials

6. Specifying the scope and sequence of topics to be covered in various subjects and grades

7. Mandating data-driven assessment to monitor student growth

Education Is a State Function

Because "the courts have consistently held that the power over education is an essential attribute of state sovereignty" (Alexander & Alexander, 2005, p. 99), resource and material selection are instrumental in defining both the written and taught curriculum at state levels. Even during this age of Web-based instruction, e-learning, and m-learning, many school districts are still relying heavily on textbooks. Thus, when selecting resources, whether they be online or texts, the end goal for every state should be to ensure all students strive to become quality citizens and productive in our globally competitive society. If this is going to happen, educators in all states must rethink and reexamine how they can improve student performance and close the achievement gap. Moreover, if we want students to learn and participate more effectively in society, then we must give them access to materials that open their eyes to new possibilities (Ivey, 2010).

THE ROLE OF PROFESSIONAL ORGANIZATIONS

When gauging the impact of professional organizations, many educators wonder at times who is really controlling public schools.

Monica Martinez (2010), president of New Tech Network, believes that with new skills, educators will come together to "amplify" new organizational capabilities and thus stretch current organizational boundaries.

It is therefore important to review the roles of international, national, and state professional organizations and their impact on public schools. The way professional organizations come together to influence schools often differs from the formalized and regulated procedures involved with governmental agencies.

The role of many *international* professional organizations should be to improve excellence in education. With this in mind, Erin Young (2008) listed some of the ideas originating from a Phi Delta Kappa Summit on global perspectives that are relevant today. They include the following:

- Acknowledge different learning styles.
- Celebrate and respect diversity.
- Instill a desire for continual, lifelong learning.
- Build partnerships with organizations such as Rotary and UNICEF.
- Develop students' skills in other languages at an early age.
- Develop proficiency in one other language.
- Develop a teacher education corps to work in other countries and communities.
- Model empathy and intercultural understanding.
- Create a heightened sense of cultural awareness.
- Provide cross-cultural experiences for students and teachers.
- Prepare students to live and work in a digital world.
- Overlay globalization on every course.
- Expand the diversity of the teacher education pool.
- Set standards for cultural competency to be integrated into curricula.
- Help students understand geography.
- Use popular media to highlight positive features of linguistic and cultural diversity at home and abroad.
- Integrate language learning and intercultural communication into business, technology, science, and arts programs.
- Model open-mindedness.
- Teach students to be strong communicators who can connect with others around the world.
- Prepare students to use technology effectively and responsibly.
- Make international awareness and understanding a focus.
- Promote international sister-school projects.
- Use video conferencing to cross borders. (p. 353)

With such an emphasis on worldwide issues, U.S. educators believe the best way to improve excellence in education is by studying excellence on a global scale. This means studying what other countries are doing well. It is crucial that we as educators understand global interdependence, global economics, global problems, and global conflicts if we are to succeed (Zhao, 2009).

At a national level, the role of professional organizations is becoming particularly noticeable. First, professional groups such as the Council for Exceptional Children, the NEA, National Council on Teacher Quality (NCTQ), and Council for the Accreditation of Educator Preparation are at times highly effective in lobbying for or against curriculum-related legislation. Second, in conjunction with CCSS, several professional organizations, such as the National Council of Teachers of Mathematics (NCTM), work to influence the written curriculum by publishing curricular guidelines or model scope-and-sequence charts. These professional publications seem to be effective in reaching only a limited audience of subject-matter curriculum specialists. School administrators and classroom teachers for the most part do not give them much attention: They are usually perceived as too "idealistic," insensitive to the realities of the classroom. Finally, they attempt to influence local practice by sponsoring institutes and workshops in which new programs and approaches are explained and demonstrated. Such show-and-tell sessions seem to have an impact on participants; they return to their schools often eager to share what they have learned.

Curriculum Tip 4.6	At one point, political and economic perspectives were not considered relevant to education policymaking and curriculum planning, but they are now.

At a state level, the role of professional organizations seems most influential as per large memberships and strong lobbyists—the teachers' and administrators' associations that fight to protect the interests of their constituencies. In many states, the state teachers' association is so active politically that it can be the determining factor in close elections and thus has significant influence with both office holders and candidates. At the local level, professional associations' attempts to influence curricula have been curtailed with the passing of NCLB and the adoption of CCSS by a majority of the states, as well as Race to the Top. Thus, many states are following explicit directives from their state boards of education or legislatures related to these federal programs.

National Accreditation and Teacher Preparation

Regarding teacher preparation programs, the NCATE merged with the Teacher Education Accreditation Council (TEAC) to form the CAEP (2014). One of the initial goals of CAEP is to enable the education profession to speak with a single voice about the preparation of teachers, administrators, and other P–12 professional educators. Other goals for CAEP are to raise the performance of candidates and practitioners in the nation's P–12 schools and to raise the stature of the profession by raising standards for the evidence the field relies on to support its claims of quality.

To accomplish these goals, accreditation is based on a set of common standards to ensure that accreditation decisions are reaching the same result based on similar evidence. In an effort to develop standards that are "fewer, clearer, and higher," three initial standards are noted in Exhibits 4.3 and 4.4.

The NCTQ is another advocate for reforms in a broad range of teacher policies at federal, state, and local levels. A major goal of the NCTQ is to lend transparency as well as increase public awareness about institutions having the greatest impact on teacher preparation programs, school districts, and teachers unions (NCTQ, 2014).

GUIDING PRESERVICE TEACHERS

Many preservice teachers believe their technology preparation in college and university teacher education programs is not compatible to meet state standards and assessments

---

EXHIBIT 4.3 Council for the Accreditation of Educator Preparation Standards for Teacher Preparation

Standard 1: Candidates demonstrate knowledge, skills, and professional dispositions for effective work in schools. Candidates preparing to work in schools as teachers or other school professionals know and demonstrate the content knowledge, pedagogical content knowledge and skills, pedagogical and professional knowledge and skills, and professional dispositions necessary to help all students learn. Assessments indicate that candidates meet professional, state, and institutional standards.

Standard 2: Data drive decisions about candidates and programs. The unit has an assessment system that collects and analyzes data on applicant qualifications, candidate and graduate performance, and unit operations to evaluate and improve the performance of candidates, the unit, and its programs.

Standard 3: Recourses and practices support candidate learning. The unit has the leadership, authority, budget, personnel, facilities, and resources, including information technology resources, for the preparation of candidates to meet professional, state, and institutional standards.

SOURCE: Council for the Accreditation of Educator Preparation. (2011). *CAEP pathways to accreditation for institutions.* Retrieved from http://www.ctc.ca.gov/educator-prep/coa-agendas/2011–03/2011–03-item-13.pdf

---

EXHIBIT 4.4 Accreditation Options of the Council for the Accreditation of Educator Preparation

Partial list of the pre-accreditation process. A pre-accreditation process will be developed for accrediting new programs, such as the many alternative providers that do not have a track record and new teacher educator programs in colleges and universities.

Commission A (NCATE/CAEP)	Commission B (TEAC)
Guiding framework Existing NCATE Standards and CAEP Standards	Guiding framework TEAC Quality Principles and CAEP Standards
Organizational Unit(s) Commission A accredits the professional education unit(s) that is responsible for educator preparation for accreditation purposes, programs are organized by initial teacher preparation and advanced preparation, which includes graduate programs for advanced teaching and other school professionals.	Organizational Unit(s) Institutions seeking accreditation through Commission B options can organize their work as best suits the evidence they bring forward. Program options (e.g., licensure areas, endorsements, etc.) can be organized into one or larger program units that share a common logic, structure, quality control system and similar and comparable categories of evidence. Educational leadership programs are general presented through a separate self-study.

(Continued)

EXHIBIT 4.4 (Continued)	
Formative Process Units submit evidence that they have a well-developed conceptual framework and assessment system. These documents are reviewed by a committee of representatives from stakeholders who write a report approving the intuition's readiness to host a site visit.	Formative Process Programs submit drafts of their self-study/studies that are reviewed by a staff evaluator and returned with comments. The formative evaluator and the lead auditor review a final draft of the self-study document to determine whether it is ready to be audited.
Focus on Research: Focus on Improvement: Transformation Initiative Continuous Improvement	Focus on Research: Focus on Improvement: Inquiry Brief Program Quality Audit Report

SOURCE: Council for the Accreditation of Educator Preparation. (2011). *CAEP pathways to accreditation for institutions.* Retrieved from http://www.ctc.ca.gov/educator-prep/coa-agendas/2011–03/2011–03-item-13.pdf

---

EXHIBIT 4.5   Model for Preservice Teachers to Integrate Technology in Education

Preservice teachers need the following:

1. Opportunities to observe how technology theory aligns with practice. Education students need to know the theory presented during class lectures, but need to see how this can be applied through real-world class examples.

2. Teacher educators as role models. Education students need to observe teachers and professors using technology in their instruction so they can imagine ways to use technology in their own teaching.

3. Opportunities to reflect on their attitudes about the role of technology in education. Education students need opportunities to dialogue with peers, professors, and teacher mentors about technology in the classroom so they can develop their own technological attitudes.

4. Specific direction on how to incorporate technology into their regular instructional design. Education students need opportunities to go through the planning and preparation process so they can see how to implement lessons incorporating technology.

5. Time to collaborate with peers. Education students need opportunities to work in groups when learning about technology use in the classroom so they can discuss and share concerns.

6. Develop ability to scaffold their technology learning experiences. Education students need opportunities to try out their ideas for incorporating technology into their lesson plans with appropriate supports to provide feedback and direction for improvement.

7. Opportunities to access appropriate technology resources. Education students need to see and have hands-on experience with resources essential to technology integration in the curriculum.

SOURCE: Tondeur et al. (2012).

(Plonczak, Brooks, Wilson, Elijah, & Caliendo, 2014). This perception alone confirms a general consensus among school leaders that preservice teachers, graduating from teacher education programs at both university and college levels, need to receive more experience. For example, there needs to be more awareness on the part of new teachers as to how to best integrate technology into various subject areas and across the curriculum. Likewise, preservice teachers must know how to acquire and best utilize the latest technological information, especially technology applications involving assessment. To meet these challenges many states are revising their teacher education program standards to require a course in technology applications as well as instruction in how to integrate and effectively use technology in an instructional setting. A useful model for preparing preservice teachers to integrate technology into education is shown in Exhibit 4.5.

INCREASING ROLE OF THE COURTS

Increasingly, courts in the United States have played an active role in education. Both federal and state courts have become so active in education that principals are advised to seek legal assistance for many historical routine decisions that were made in the past. Society and culture of many communities have changed or are changing, which has provided the need for principals and teacher–leaders to reevaluate their performance. Community's expectations for administrators have changed, and this has resulted in new practices for building principals and teachers. As shown in Exhibits 4.6 and 4.7, Perry A. Zirkel (2009) identified the top ten educational decisions from 1954 to 1985 and then the top ten decisions from 1986 to 2009. The following are the court cases and significant decisions that have impacted education today and for the foreseeable future. The reader is advised that the following are brief synopsis of the court cases and for in-depth understanding they should be referred to the full text of the court case (Whitehead, Boschee, et al., 2013).

Curriculum Tip 4.7	Ignorance is not a defense in a court of law.

LOCAL EDUCATION

The notion of local control runs deep. The U.S. Constitution left authority over education in the hands of the states under the Tenth Amendment, and the states passed that power to local school boards. For much of the nation's history, local boards were solely responsible for school funding, standards, instruction, and outcomes (Toch, 2012). According to Levin (2013), local governance of education can act as a useful countermeasure to central government policies that may be badly conceived or badly implemented. What one level sees as resistance to change may be seen by the other level as standing up for important principles.

At the local district level, central office administrators, school-building principals, and teachers continue to play key roles in influencing curriculum. At the same time, school superintendents across the nation are now becoming more involved in actual curriculum planning and implementation as well. Naturally, depending on the size of the district, many

EXHIBIT 4.6 Top Ten Educational Decisions, 1954–1985

Court Case	Decisions That Affected Education
1. *Brown v. Board of Education* (1954)	*The issue was that black children were denied admission to public schools attended by white children under laws requiring or permitting segregation according to the races.* The conclusion was that despite the equalization of the schools by "objective" factors, intangible issues foster and maintain inequality. Racial segregation in public school education has a detrimental effect on minority children because it is interpreted as a sign of inferiority.
2. Civil Rights Act of 1964	*The provisions of this civil rights act forbade discrimination on the basis of sex as well as race in hiring, promoting, and firing.* In the final legislation, Section 703(a) made it unlawful for an employer to "fail or refuse to hire or to discharge any individual, or otherwise to discriminate against any individual with respect to his compensation, terms, conditions or privileges or employment, because of such individual's race, color, religion, sex, or national origin."
3. *Tinker v. Des Moines Independent Community School District* (1969)	*The issue centered around three students who decided to wear black armbands in protest of the Vietnam War.* Fearing that this would provoke disturbances, the principals resolved that all students wearing armbands be asked to remove them or face suspension. On a decision for Tinker, the wearing of armbands was "closely akin to 'pure speech'" and protected by the First Amendment. The principals had failed to show that the forbidden conduct would substantially interfere with appropriate school discipline.
4. *Leman v. Kurtsman* (1971)	*The issue in this case was Rhode Island and Pennsylvania statutes violate the First Amendment's Establishment Clause by making state financial aid available to "church-related educational institutions."* The court found that the subsidization of parochial schools furthered a process of religious inculcation and that the "continuing state surveillance" necessary to enforce the specific provisions of the laws would inevitably entangle the state in religious affairs.
5. *San Antonio Independent School District v. Rodriguez* (1973)	*The question raised in this case was if the Texas public education finance system violated the Fourteenth Amendment's Equal Protection Clause by failing to distribute funding equally among its school districts.* The Supreme Court sided with the school district. The court refused to examine the system with strict scrutiny since there is no fundamental right to education in the Constitution and since the system did not systematically discriminate against all poor people in Texas. Given the similarities between Texas' system and those in other states, it was clear to the Court that the funding scheme was not "so irrational as to be invidiously discriminatory."

6.	Public Law 94–142 (passed November 29, 1975)	This law provided that handicapped students, ages 3–21, be educated in the "least restrictive environment" to the maximum extent appropriate, meaning that they are educated with children who are not handicapped and that special classes, separate schools, or other removal of children from their regular educational environment occurs only when the severity of the handicap is such that education in regular classes cannot be achieved.
7.	Goss v. Lopez (1975)	The issue in this case questioned the imposition of the suspensions without preliminary hearings. Did this violate the student's due process rights guaranteed by the Fourteenth Amendment? The court held that students facing suspension should at a minimum be given notice and afforded some kind of hearing.
8.	Mt. Healthy School District v. Doyle (1977)	The issue is whether a public employer can defend itself in a First Amendment retaliation claim by proving that it would have made the same employment decision in the absence of the employee's protected First Amendment activity. The Court held that an employer can successfully defend itself in First Amendment employee litigation by showing that it would have made the same decision in the absence of the protected speech activity.
9.	Board of Education v. Rowley (1982)	The issue here was a claim of a deaf student suing local school officials, claiming that the administrators' denial of a qualified sign-language interpreter in all of the student's academic classes constituted a denial of the "free appropriate public education" guaranteed by the Education for All Handicapped Children Act of 1975. The Supreme Court decision was that a state that receives federal funds to educate handicapped children need not provide a sign language interpreter for a deaf student who is receiving an adequate education and personalized instruction and related services calculated by local school administrators to meet the child's educational needs.
10.	New Jersey v. T.L.O. (1985)	The question in this case centered on whether the search of a student purse violated the Fourth and Fourteenth Amendments. The Supreme Court decision abandoned its requirement that searches be conducted only when a "probable cause" exists that an individual has violated the law. The Court used a less strict standard of "reasonableness" to conclude that the search did not violate the Constitution.

EXHIBIT 4.7 Top Ten Educational Decisions, 1986–2009

Court Case	Decisions That Affected Education
1. *Hazelwood School District v. Kuhlmeier* (1988)	*The question in this case was whether the principal has the right to withhold articles in the school newspaper if the principal deems the articles inappropriate.* The court held that schools must be able to set high standards for student speech disseminated under their auspices and that schools retained the right to refuse to sponsor speech that was "inconsistent with 'the shared values of a civilized social order.'" Educators did not offend the First Amendment by exercising editorial control over the content of student speech so long as their actions were "reasonably related to legitimate pedagogical concerns."
2. *Missouri v. Jenkins II* (1990) and *Missouri v. Jenkins III* (1995)	*The question centered on whether the court order to increase property taxes violated Article III, the Tenth Amendment, or principles of federal or state comity.* When a constitutional justification existed, courts had the authority to order tax increases despite statutory limitations. The Court reasoned that "to hold otherwise would fail to take account of the obligations of local governments, under the Supremacy Clause, to fulfill the requirements that the Constitution imposes on them."
3. Americans with Disabilities Act (ADA; 1990) and ADA Amendments (2008)	*Signed into law, the ADA is a wide-ranging legislation intended to make American society more accessible to people with disabilities.* While the employment provisions of the ADA apply to employers of fifteen employees or more, its public accommodations provisions apply to all sizes of business, regardless of number of employees. State and local governments are covered regardless of size.
4. *Lee v. Weisman* (1992)	*The case determined whether the inclusion of clergy who offer prayers at official public school ceremonies violates the Establishment Clause of the First Amendment.* The Court held that government involvement in this case creates "a state-sponsored and state-directed religious exercise in a public school." Such conduct conflicts with settled rules proscribing prayer for students. The school's rule created a subtle and indirect coercion, forcing students to act in ways that established a state religion.
5a. *Vernonia School District 47J v. Action* (1995)	*The issue determined whether random drug testing of high school athletes violates the reasonable search and seizure clause of the Fourth Amendment.* The court sided with the district. High school students who are under state supervision during school hours are subject to greater control than if they were free adults. The privacy interests compromised by urine samples are negligible since the conditions of collection are similar to public restrooms, and the results are viewed only by limited authorities.

5b.	Santa Fe Independent School District v. Doe (2000)	*The question addressed whether the Santa Fe Independent School District's policy permitting student-led, student-initiated prayer at football games violated the Establishment Clause of the First Amendment.* The court concluded that the football game prayers were public speech authorized by a government policy and taking place on government property at government-sponsored school-related events and that the district's policy involved both perceived and actual government endorsement of the delivery of prayer at important school events. Such speech is not properly characterized as "private."
5c.	Board of Education v. Earls (2002)	*Another drug testing Fourth Amendment case faced the Supreme Court.* In favor of the Board of Education, the Court held that because the policy reasonably serves the school district's important interests in detecting and preventing drug use among its students, it is constitutional.
6a.	Gebser v. Lago Vista School District (1998)	*A student has a secret sexual issue with a teacher.* After being caught having sex, the teacher was arrested and fired. Claiming she was harassed in violation of Title IX of the Education Amendments of 1972, providing that no person "being subject to discrimination" under any federally funded education program or activity, Gebser sought damages against Lago Vista. At the time, Lago Vista had no official procedure for reporting sexual harassment or any formal anti-harassment policy, as required by federal law. The court held that two minimal criteria must be met in order for an aggrieved party to recover sexual harassment damages under the amendments. First, the party must show that a school district official with the ability to institute corrective measures knew of the forbidden conduct. Second, a showing must be made that despite having knowledge of the forbidden conduct, the educational establishment deliberately failed to respond in a proper manner. The court concluded that Lago Vista never showed indifference to Gebser's relationship since it never knew, either formally or informally, of its existence. Lago Vista was not liable for sexual harassment damages.
6b.	Davis v. Monroe County Board of Education (1999)	*This case determined whether a school board could be held responsible, under Title IX of the Education Amendments of 1972, for allowing "student-on-student" harassment.* A parent alleged that school officials failed to prevent her daughter from receiving sexual harassment at the hands of another student. The parent claimed that the school's complacency created an abusive environment that deprived her daughter of educational benefits promised her under Title IX. The Court noted that because there is an implied private right to education under Title IX, private damage action may lie against schools that act with deliberate indifference to harassment that is severe enough to prevent victims from enjoying educational opportunities. The Court observed that the board acted with deliberate indifference, since it ignored several complaints by the parent, and that the harassment in question was serious and systematic.

(Continued)

EXHIBIT 4.7 (Continued)

7.	No Child Left Behind Act (2001)	*Coming at a time of wide public concern about the state of education, the legislation sets in place requirements that reach into virtually every public school in the United States.* It takes aim at improving the educational lot of disadvantaged students. At the core of NCLB are a number of measures designed to drive broad gains in student achievement and to hold states and schools more accountable for student progress. This act has expanded the federal role in education and becomes a focal point of education policy.
8.	Zelman v. Siommons-Harris (2002)	*Ohio's Pilot Project Scholarship Program provides tuition aid in the form of vouchers for certain students in the Cleveland City School District to attend a participating public or private school of their parent's choosing.* A group of Ohio taxpayers sought to enjoin the program on the ground that it violated the Establishment Clause. Chief Justice Rehnquist wrote that the "Ohio program is entirely neutral with respect to religion. It provides benefits directly to a wide spectrum of individuals, defined only by financial need and residence in a particular school district. It permits such individuals to exercise genuine choice among options public or private, secular and religious. The program is therefore a program of true private choice."
9.	Morse v. Frederick (2007)	*The question in this case was twofold. (1) Does the First Amendment allow public schools to prohibit students from displaying messages promoting the use of illegal drugs at school-supervised events? (2) Does a school official have qualified immunity from a damages lawsuit under 42 U.S.C. 1983 when, in accordance with school policy, she disciplines students for displaying a banner with a drug reference at a school-supervised event?* The court ruled that school officials can prohibit students from displaying messages that promote illegal drug use.
10.	Parents Involved in Community Schools v. Seattle District No. 1 (2007)	*The Seattle School District allowed students to apply to any high school in the district.* When too many students chose a school, the district used a system of tiebreakers to decide which students would be admitted to a school. A nonprofit group, Parents Involved in Community Schools, sued the district arguing that the racial tiebreaker violated the Equal Protection Clause of the Fourteenth Amendment as well as the Civil Rights Act of 1964 and Washington state law. The Court applied a "strict scrutiny" framework and found the district's racial tiebreaker plan unconstitutional under the Equal Protection Clause of the Fourteenth Amendment.

superintendents delegate curriculum duties to an assistant superintendent or to a curriculum director. Despite a variety of extenuating circumstances, the assistant superintendent for curriculum and instruction in most districts is the sole individual exercising general supervision over the entire curriculum.

Curriculum Tip 4.8	"An important lesson is for us to keep reinventing our schools to prepare for the future" (McCollum, 2010).

As previously noted, the role of principals and classroom teachers in curriculum planning and implementation seems to vary with the level of schooling. It is now commonplace for principals and teacher–leaders in the most effective elementary schools to take a very active role in curriculum leadership. They play the central role in articulating educational goals and curricular priorities, in influencing teacher perceptions about curricular approaches, in helping colleagues use test results, and in aligning the curriculum. At the secondary level (especially in larger schools), however, administrators are more likely to delegate these roles to department heads, whose subject-matter expertise enables them to influence the curricular decision making of secondary teachers.

Just as the roles of administrators are changing, the role of teacher–leaders in curriculum development is becoming more evident. Considering changes in technology and the need for curriculum alignment, teacher–leaders are now playing an ever-greater role in changing the makeup of schools. With higher stakes placed on the performance of all students, teachers must play an increasingly vital role in curricular and instructional leadership. And, through the development of effective collaborative teacher teams, schools are becoming even more successful (Paige, 2010).

THE PRINCIPAL

Highly successful principals have an ability to create and reinforce cultures of high expectations for student learning and behavior. Research backs this up by noting that with the development of a consistent schoolwide approach to behavior, higher expectations can lead to increased student achievement levels (Goodwin, 2012). But, as middle managers, principals are often caught in the middle of many internal and external situations that have political implications. They work at the will of the superintendent and board of education in following policies and procedures officially adopted by the school district and at the same time receive pressure from business and community members, parents, faculty, and staff. If those issues and situations are not enough, there are also federal regulations, state legislative mandates, as well as state board of education requirements. Additionally, the National Leadership Standards such as Interstate School Leaders Licensure Consortium (ISLLC) and the Educational Leadership Constituent Council (ELCC) provide guidance for principals and other educational leaders. A visual of the political role of the principal is illustrated in Diagram 4.1 (Whitehead, Boschee, & Decker, 2013).

DIAGRAM 4.1 Principal Balancing Political Issues

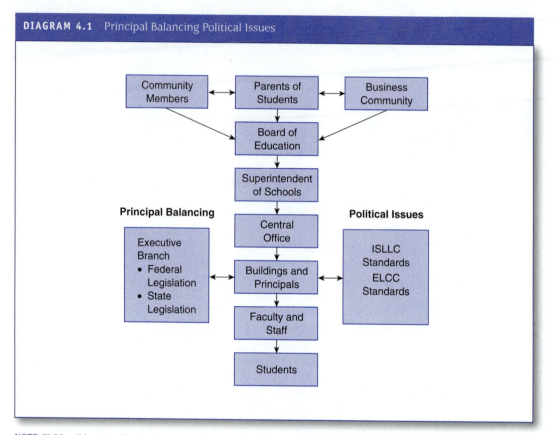

NOTE: ELCC = Educational Leadership Constituent Council; ISLLC = Interstate School Leaders Licensure Consortium.

A Principal's Political View of Schools

The role of the principal is clearly changing as well as the expectation of the community, both internally and externally. With federal and state legislative mandates along with CCSS, building-level principals are taking a *collaborative role* in establishing a multitude of achievement expectations. To meet these new challenges, principals are seeking assistance from teacher–leaders, team leaders, and data specialists. Each of these positions can provide needed assistance to the principal to further efforts on assisting faculty on instructional leadership initiatives.

In the past, curriculum leadership was often put on the back burner as many principals were pressured on management concerns and disciplinary issues. Likewise, from a historical perspective, colleges of education and more specifically departments of educational administration emphasized the management side of the position, minimizing the importance of helping teachers improve instruction. It was well understood that principals would be fired for poor management skills, but very few were ever dismissed for lack of instructional leadership skills. With the advent of federal and state legislation, as well as with issues of student achievement on a global level, the position has now changed. Currently, building-level principals are expected and required to help their faculty improve their teaching skills that will make a positive difference for students in the classroom.

To accomplish this task, practicing principals are heading back to college campuses, enrolling in professional development programs, and receiving assistance in learning instructional strategies and skills to further assist teachers to be more effective. Principals today are realizing the complexity of their position and have complained about the lack of time to accomplish this new job description that started in the political arena, but now has become a reality throughout the educational field. The successful principal has become a collaborative leader who works with other building leaders and provides the leadership for successful instructional and curriculum initiatives.

THE CLASSROOM TEACHER

Great teachers know how to focus on helping students learn how to savor their newfound expertise as consumers of knowledge (Gardner & Powell, 2013–2014). Research suggests that teachers providing positive relationships with students have a tendency to promote higher engagement, have fewer resistant behaviors, and are able to improve achievement. Clearly, then, successful teachers are finding positive attitudes and reinforcement to be extremely beneficial and effective in the classroom. In short, top-notch classroom teachers are finding ways to motivate students and catch them doing the right things (Goodwin, 2012).

With this in mind, it stands to reason that teachers who meaningfully incorporate technology-rich experiences into the classroom are able to provide learners with greater opportunities in developing skills that are needed for the 21st century (Leh, Kouba, & Davis, 2005). In addition, mobile technology is now proving great opportunities for classroom teachers to address individual student needs such as multicultural issues, academic challenges as well as the enhancement of higher order thinking skills. Basically, the trend for modern classrooms to utilize the Internet, social networks, and mobile technology continues to increase along with an emphasis of using the latest cutting edge technology (Keane, 2010). As teachers become more versatile in their practices, classroom learners are storing more information in the Internet cloud, sending and receiving text messages, streaming more audio and video, and creating a bundle of applications on handheld devices.

Power and Responsibility

Teachers and students need to recognize that their views matter.

To be sure, a classroom teacher is key to unlocking the mysteries of learning for individual students. It is for this reason that developing teacher–learning communities can be one of the best ways for teachers to break the cycle of poverty and inequity. This is why it is so important to develop and support classroom teachers who handle both internal and external pressures in today's global world.

Internal Pressures

In a school of any size, anywhere in the world, teacher–leaders are an invaluable asset (Williams, 2012). Although high-quality teachers are a key to success, a variety of political and socioeconomic issues loom as barriers to teaching and learning. Creating conditions under which teachers can be effective requires strategies and partnerships that address both in-school as well as out-of-school concerns.

Curriculum Tip 4.9	"How teachers and students see themselves in relation to school and community is paramount" (Medin & Bang, 2013–2014).

As far as internal concerns, teachers assume a wide range of roles to support school and student success. Along with building an entire school's capacity to improve, they must formulate their own sense of independence and be able to make important decisions. They know that what works for one teacher may not work for another. Dealing with a lack of recourses, poor facilities, internal staff disagreements, and administrative political intrigue can be ongoing. Likewise, dealing with individual student social and cultural issues can become heart rending. But, if teachers feel valued and truly believe their students need them—these same teachers will rise to the occasion.

External Pressures

Besides responding to personal and professional needs, classroom teachers are also susceptible to numerous external pressures. According to Gordon Donaldson (2007), professor of education at the University of Maine, administrators, school boards, and state and federal policymakers can do the following to help ease external pressures:

- First, identify and support those clusters of teachers in which professional relationships and commitments are fostering instructional innovation.
- Second, respect the judgment of the teachers and be willing to adjust strategies to complement teacher innovations.
- Third, put resources behind the efforts of teacher–leaders by supporting shared practice, planning, and professional learning focused on improvement of practice.
- Fourth, acknowledge that goals and initiatives can best be addressed by treating teacher–leaders as vital and powerful partners.

As can be seen, regardless of internal or external pressures, it is the classroom teacher who basically holds the power to improve student learning. The bottom line is that there will have to be major changes in our educational system to accommodate societal and political pressures in the classroom if our students are to remain competitive in this new global age. Moore and Berry (2010) support this concept and believe that achieving school success with quality teachers is possible. They shared that teachers are increasingly turning to one another to expand both professional knowledge and teacher voice to induce change. The greatest challenge, therefore, is to accommodate this effective change politically.

Looking back retrospectively, the rationale for learning has been politically dominated by the desire of government and educators to have students acquire content or knowledge. The new rationale will have to be that of students developing a value of knowing as well as requiring a belief that learning is a continuous process defined by individual needs and experiences. Therefore, the key to improving education worldwide is sharing a vision of teaching and learning—especially through the use of 21st-century technology.

TECHNOLOGY AND ELEMENTS OF CHANGE

Along with a focusing on internal and external issues, it is important to review some of the *key elements* impacting 21st-century learning today. As noted in Whitehead, Jensen, and Boschee (2013), a partial list of key elements includes the following:

- *Time.* Teachers and students in our schools today perceive *working, learning,* and *activities* as being interconnected. As a result, 21st-century schools must implement curricula where working, learning, and activities converge allowing learning to occur at any time, any place, and anywhere.
- *Relationships.* Students of this century are beginning to reestablish strong interconnections to community and linkages with other cultures via handheld mobile technology. This creates a somewhat fluid society vastly different from that of their parents. Today's tech-age students are now learning and growing in communities that are becoming highly diverse in age, religion, culture, language, and location. Within these newly emerging digital communities, collaboration is surfacing as a primary expression of experience, and the working realities of life are becoming focused on being connected.
- *Technology.* Students in schools today are living in a reality of reform and changing technologies. Moreover, these students are preparing and constantly waiting for the next level of advancement that will provide them with new ways of learning as noted by standards developed by the International Society for Technology Education (ISTE). Developed as early as 2008, the ISTE domains for teachers focused on facilitating and inspiring students to learn; designing digital-age learning experiences and assessments; modeling digital-age career and work learning; promoting digital citizenship, responsibility, and ethics; and engaging in professional growth.
- *Learning style.* Digitally savvy students are now effectively using state-of-the-art technology. This does not mean individual students are spending time working alone but are reinforcing learning through memberships in a network of social groups—even if those groups are thousands of miles away. As such, students want

to solve real problems with hopes they can make a contribution to their school, city, and community. With information and knowledge acquisition expanding and changing, students also desire to formulate analysis skills that will help them succeed in our digitally transforming world.

- *Flexibility.* Students participating in the global shift to mobile technology can no longer depend on the stable and unchanging reality of school buildings and classrooms; therefore, they desire a curriculum open to a diverse range of options and educational choices. This is especially true with learning opportunities and knowledge acquisition expanding so rapidly. As a result of these transformative changes, school leaders, curriculum designers, and technology planners are taking note. Not surprisingly, these educators are now looking for flexibility in allowing students to learn in multiple settings—public and private schools, homeschooling, travel, community groups, as well as cloud computing groups.

GLOBAL CONNECTIONS: PRESERVICE TEACHERS IN CHINA

As noted by Scott (2014), immersing preservice teachers in an unfamiliar culture helps prepare them to teach children from cultures different from their own. Student teachers from the University of North Carolina are experiencing a new culture in foreign settings. For example, they are given an opportunity to learn about life in China, experience the culture, and network with professional educators. Preservice teachers spend their first ten weeks in the United States and then travel to China for four more weeks of being immersed in another school setting. Professors from the United States are on location to support the student teachers, work with faculty at the host site, and conduct classroom observations.

An exposure to different perspectives on learning helps expand participants' thinking about education and themselves as educators. Developers of the program note that visiting cultures that are vastly different from the United States gives students an appreciation for the struggles that immigrant students go though trying to learn a second language. Preservice teachers learn what it feels like to be completely unable to read, to need help doing basic assignments.

Clearly, changing classroom demographics on a global level means preservice teachers learn to understand and work with children from other cultures. Student teaching abroad is a type of catalyst that starts many of these beginning teachers down a path of learning that expands their cross-cultural knowledge. Moreover, this short-term international experience enhances their perspective of global education many times over.

SUMMARY

International organizations, countries, federal and state governments, professional organizations, local school boards, textbook publishers, accrediting organizations, parent and community groups, school administrators, teacher–leaders, and classroom teachers all pose conflicting influences that seem to change in their strength from time to time and in their particular impact on education. This chapter provides curriculum leaders who wish to develop or improve curricula an understanding of the politics of curriculum and the way organizations and individuals attempt to influence what is taught in schools. This chapter presents an overview of the way influences are brought to bear and then examines in greater detail those groups or agencies that seem to have the greatest influence. In addition, this chapter addresses the role of the federal government in curriculum development and how it has changed over the years. Chapter 4 also gives an overview of the general role of state governments in curriculum development today and how this has changed over the years. Finally, this chapter explains the roles of educational organizations, courts, educational leaders, and classroom teachers in current curriculum development.

APPLICATIONS

1. Some experts have argued that the difficulty of finding sufficient fiscal resources will shortly reduce state activity in the curriculum field. If that development does occur, and if the federal government continues to take a less active role, which sources of influence do you believe will increase in power?

2. Based on what you now know about the sources of curriculum influence, what advice would you give a superintendent who posed this question to you: "Does our district really need central office curriculum specialists?"

3. Some analysts have reached this conclusion: "All curriculum making is essentially a political process." Would you agree or disagree? Prepare a well-thought-out response to the question.

4. As the conclusion in Application 3 suggests, the federal government has for the most part abandoned the change strategy of funding the development of exemplary generic curricula. Some have argued that such abandonment was premature—that given greater insight into the change process, such a strategy might be effective. Consider two related issues: Under what circumstances would you recommend that this strategy be reintroduced? What modifications in the approach would you recommend?

5. What advice would you give this fourth-grade teacher: "My principal and the district science supervisor do not agree about what I should emphasize in teaching science. The principal wants me to spend more time on practical applications; the supervisor, on science processes."

6. Less than half the institutions of higher education are CAEP/NCATE accredited, but they prepare two thirds of new teachers yearly. Should school administrators hiring first-year teachers give preference to applicants who graduated from CAEP/NCATE-accredited institutions? Defend your answer.

7. Various individuals and groups influence curriculum in our states. Complete the following chart to identify the relative influence that you feel individuals or groups have on curriculum in your state.

Perceptions Regarding Curriculum Influence in Your State

The following chart is designed to explore your perceptions regarding the relative influence exerted by various individuals and groups on the curriculum process within the state in which you work. Please identify the state in which you work, and rate the relative influence you feel that each individual or group within the state exerts by placing a check in the most appropriate column.

State	*Level of Influence*				
	None	*Little*	*Some*	*Great*	*Don't Know*
1. Governor					
2. State Department of Education					
3. State Board of Education					
4. Chief state school officer					
5. State and local courts					
6. State legislature					
7. Local Board of Education					
8. Local superintendent					
9. Local principal(s)					
10. Local teachers					
11. Local community members					
12. State administrators' organization(s)					
13. State teachers' association(s)					
14. State special interest groups					
15. Local teachers' organization(s)					
16. National professional (subject area) organizations					
17. Federal government					
18. National Council for Accreditation of Teacher Education (NCATE)					
19. Other					

CASE STUDY   Being Politically Correct

Richard F. Elmore (1997) wrote that "U.S. elementary and secondary education is a vast and extraordinarily complex enterprise that seems to defy simple generalizations. However, the two central imperatives of U.S. educational governance are dispersed control and political pluralism" (p. 1). He believes that control of education is not decentralized in the United States and that "local control of schools is largely inaccurate and outmoded, especially in the light of the direction education reform has taken in the past decade" (p. 2). In essence, "the idea of political pluralism is more straightforward. It captures a fundamental principle of U.S. politics—that political decisions and actions are the result of competing groups with different resources and capacities vying for influence" (p. 2).

According to Elmore (1997), "The story of U.S. education reform since the 1980s is worthy of either a Gilbert and Sullivan operetta or theater of the absurd, depending upon your tastes" (p. 2). Consider the following, which called for major educational reform: *A Nation at Risk* (National Commission on Excellence in Education, 1983), Goals 2000 in 1989, and NCLB, which was signed into law in 2002. Intermittent interventions resembled a "horse trade—greater flexibility and less regulation for schools and school systems in return for tangible evidence of results, reckoned mostly in terms of student achievement" (p. 2).

> Control of education . . . is only local when schools and school systems appear to be doing the right thing; when they're not, they are fair game for elected officials, at whatever level of government, with a political interest in their performance. (p. 3)

The Challenge

How can educators—especially curriculum specialists looking for the cutting edge of curriculum and instructional practice—deal with the virtual blizzard of leading-edge advice on curriculum and pedagogy?

Key Issues or Questions

1. Various groups compete for resources and thus require school districts to prioritize their needs to gain political influence and resources. How do politics influence what is included or excluded in curriculum and determine what is funded?

2. What measures can a school district take to leverage resources to enable the district to achieve higher curriculum standards?

3. If the federal government allocates 6% of a district's budget but mandates a specified curriculum, how do you justify the discrepancy?

4. What questions should curriculum leaders ask before addressing state and federal mandates and embarking on a course of major change within their school districts?

5. What role does politics play in the development of state and national education regulations?

6. What are the differences between internal political pressures and external political pressures?

WEBLIOGRAPHY

eSchool News
www.eschoolnews.com

National Association of Elementary School Principals (NAESP) Federal Legislative Action Center
www.naesp.org/advocacy/action

National Conference of State Legislatures
www.ncsl.org

National Council for Accreditation of Teacher Education (NCATE) Accredited Institutions
www.ncate.org/tabid/176/Default.aspx

Organisation for Economic Co-operation and Development
www.oecd.org

Schooling in America
http://c2.com/cgi/wiki?AmericanSchoolSystem

Southern Regional Education Board
www.sreb.org

UNICEF
www.unicef.org

United Nations Educational, Scientific, and Cultural Organization
http://unesco.org

Urban Excellence Framework
www.nlns.org/uef

U.S. Department of Education
www.ed.gov

U.S. House Education and the Workforce Committee
http://edworkforce.house.gov

The Wallace Foundation
www.wallacefoundation.org

REFERENCES

Abbate, F. J. (2010). Educational leadership in a culture of compliance? *Phi Delta Kappan, 91*(6), 35–37.

Agirdag, O. (2009). All languages welcomed here. *Educational Leadership, 66*(7), 20–24.

Alexander, K., & Alexander, M. D. (2005). *American public school law* (6th ed.). Belmont, CA: Thomson West.

Atkin, J. M., & House, E. R. (1981). The federal role in curriculum development, 1950–80. *Educational Evaluation and Policy Analysis, 3*(5), 5–36.

Bell, T. H. (1986). Educational policy development in the Reagan administration. *Phi Delta Kappan, 67,* 487–493.

Bender, W. N., & Shores, C. (2007). *Response to intervention: A practical guide for every teacher.* Thousand Oaks, CA: Corwin Press.

Bergmann, J., & Sams, A. (2013–2014). Flipping for mastery. *Educational Leadership, 71*(4), 24–29.

Berliner, D. C., & Biddle, B. J. (1997). *The manufactured crisis: Myths, fraud, and the attack on America's public schools.* White Plains, NY: Longman.

Brown, L. M. (2011). Standards-based curriculum and delivery. *Principal, 91*(1), 38–39.

Connelly, G. (2010). Pay it forward. *Principal, 89*(3), 52.

Council for the Accreditation of Teacher Preparation. (2011). *CAEP pathways to accreditation for institutions.* Retrieved from http://www.ctc.ca.gov/educator-prep/coa-agendas/2011–03/2011–03-item-13.pdf

Curriculum Development Associates. (1972). *Man: A course of study.* Washington, DC: Author.

Dietel, R. (2011). Testing to the top: Everything but the kitchen sink? *Phi Delta Kappan, 92*(8), 32–36.

Dodge, A. (2011–2012). Changing the poisonous narrative: A conversation with Diane Ravitch. *Educational Leadership, 69*(4), 54–57.

Donaldson, G. A., Jr. (2007). What do teachers bring to leadership? *Educational Leadership, 65*(1), 26–29.

Eckert, J., & Kohl, K. (2013). Beyond buy-in. *Phi Delta Kappan, 95*(2), 80.

Elmore, R. F. (1997, Fall). The politics of education reform [Electronic version]. *Issues in Science and Technology Online,* 1–3.

Farhi, P. (2011, Fall). *Five myths about America's schools.* Port Ludlow, WA: The Horace Mann League.

Ferguson, M. (2013). Economists' view of education not all bad. *Phi Delta Kappan, 95*(3), 68–69.

Gardner, N. S., & Powell, R. (2013–2014). The common core is a change for the better. *Phi Delta Kappan, 95*(4), 49–53.

Goodwin, B. (2012). Research says: For positive behavior, involve peers. *Educational Leadership, 70*(2), 82–83.

Hertling, J. (1986, March 12). Block grants found to achieve gains. *Education Week,* p. 8.

History Learning Site. (2014). *Functionalism and education.* Retrieved from http://www.historylearningsite.co.uk/functionalsim_education.htm

Hoerr, T. R. (2012). "Your candidate sucks!" *Educational Leadership, 70*(2), 86–87.

Holliday, T., & Smith, F. C. (2012). Leading common core implementation. *Principal, 92*(1), 12–15.

Holt, J. (1964). *How children fail.* New York: Dell.

Huntsman, B. (2010). *Impact of NCLB on curriculum* (Unpublished paper). University of Montana, Division of Educational Leadership, Phyllis J. Washington College of Education and Human Sciences, Missoula.

Illich, I. (1972). *Deschooling society.* New York: Harper & Row.

Ivey, G. (2010). Texts that matter. *Educational Leadership, 67*(6), 18–23.

Jennings, J. (2010–2011). The policy and politics of rewriting the nation's main education law. *Phi Delta Kappan, 92*(4), 44–49.

Jennings, J. (2012). What has President Obama done? *Phi Delta Kappan, 94*(2), 50, 52–57.

Jensen, B. (2013–2014). Can schools compete? *Phi Delta Kappan, 95*(4), 76–77.

Kardish, C. (2014, June 25). *States are strengthening teacher preparation laws.* Retrieved from http://www.governing.com/topics/education/gov-teacher-prep-report.html?utm_source = The + HM L + POST + for + September + 29 % 2C + 2014& utm_campaign = hml&utm_medium = email

Keane, M. (2010). The uncertain journey. In *The QUT creative industries experience* (pp. 61–65). Retrieved from http://eprints.qut.edu.au/39735/1/16684_QUT_CI_Experience_Lres.pdf

Kozol, J. (1991). *Savage inequalities: Children in America's schools.* New York, NY: Crown.

Lam, D. (2014). Charter, private and public schools work together in Boston. *Phi Delta Kappan, 95*(5), 356–39.

Lau v. Nichols, 414 U.S. 563 (1974).

Leh, A. S. C., Kouba, B., & Davis, D. (2005). Twenty-first century learning: Communities, interaction and ubiquitous computing. *Educational Media International, 42*(3), 237–250.

Levin, B. (2013), Do we need school districts? *Phi Delta Kappan, 94*(5), 74–75.

Levine, E. L., & Wexler, E. M. (1981). *P.L. 94–142: An act of Congress.* New York, NY: Macmillan.

Llewellyn, G. (1991). *Teenage liberation handbook: How to quit school and get a real life and education.* Eugene, OR: Lowery House.

Lynch, K. L. (1986). *School finance policy formulation in Pennsylvania: A case study* (Unpublished doctoral dissertation). University of Pennsylvania, Philadelphia.

Marshall, C. (1985, March). *Policymakers' assumptive worlds: Informal structures in state education policymaking.* Paper presented at the meeting of the American Educational Research Association, Chicago, IL.

Martinez, M. (2010). How a new generation of teachers will change schools. *Phi Delta Kappan, 91*(7), 74–75.

McCollum, J. (2010). With foresight comes success. *Principal, 89*(5), 52–53.

Meacham, J. (2013). Special college report, Class of 2005: How they'll learn and what they'll pay. *Time Magazine, 182*(15), 42–43.

Medin, D. L., & Bang, M. (2013–2014). Culture in the classroom. *Phi Delta Kappan, 95*(4), 64–67.

Mills v. Board of Education, 348 F. Supp. 866 (D.D.C. 1972).

Moore, R., & Berry, B. (2010). The teachers of 2030. *Educational Leadership, 67*(8), 36–39.

Moyers, B. (2011, February 14). Bill Moyers: "Facts Still Matter . . ." *Truthout.* Retrieved from http://www.truth-out.org/bill-moyers-facts-still-matter67571

National Commission on Excellence in Education. (1983). *A nation at risk: The imperative for educational reform.* Washington, DC: Government Printing Office.

National Council on Teacher Quality. (2014). *Training our future teachers: Classroom management.* Retrieved from http://www.nctq.org/about

National Governors Association. (2009, July 01). Common Core State Standards development work group and feedback group announced. Retrieved from http://www.nga.org/cms/home/news-room/news-releases/page_2009/col2-content/main-content-list/title_common-core-state-standards-development-work-group-and-feedback-group-announced.html

Paige, P. (2010). Advocate or adversary. *Principal, 90*(1), 54.

Partners in Education. (2003). *Partnerships 1990–2000: Ten years of supporting education.* Retrieved from http://www.napehq.org/d.pdf

Payne, R. K. (2002). *Understanding learning: The how, the why, the what.* Alexandria, VA: ASCD.

Phillips, M. (2007). Backwards into the future—again. *Phi Delta Kappan, 88*(9), 712–714.

Plonczak, I., Brooks, J. G., Wilson, G. L., Elijah, R., & Caliendo, J. (2014). STEM studio: Where innovation generates innovation. *Phi Delta Kappan, 95*(5), 52–56.

Ravitch, D. (1983). *The troubled crusade: American education, 1945–80.* New York, NY: Basic Books.

Schifter, D., & Granofsky, B. (2012). The right equation for math teaching. *Principal, 92*(2), 16–20.

Schmoker, M. (2014, October 18). The common core is not ready. *Education Week.* Retrieved from http://www.edweek.org/ew/articles/2014/09/24/05schmoker.h34.html

Schon, D. A. (1971). *Beyond the stable state.* New York, NY: Random House.

Schugurensky, D. (2003). *History of education: Selected moments of the 20th century.* Retrieved from http://fcis.oise.utoronto.ca/~daniel_schuguren sky/assignment1/1994goals2000.html

Scott, C. E. (2014). Preparing to teach culturally diverse classrooms. *Phi Delta Kappan, 95*(5), 2.

Staff and Wire Reports. (2011, September 24). States embrace education law change. *Argus Leader,* p. A5.

Summary of the Individuals with Disabilities Education Act (IDEA). (2003). Retrieved from http://edwork force.house.gov/issues/108th/education/idea/idea.htm

Sundin, L. (2014). Teachers creating and leading schools . . . is union work! *Phi Delta Kappan, 95*(5). 31–34.

Toch, T. (2010). Reflections on the charter school movement. *Phi Delta Kappan, 91*(8), 70–71.

Toch, T. (2012). The fallacy of "local control." *Phi Delta Kappan, 93*(5), 66–67.

Tomlinson, C. A., & McTighe, J. (2006). *Integrating differentiated instruction and understanding by design.* Alexandria, VA: ASCD.

Tondeur, J., van Braak, J., Sang, G., Voogt, J., Fisser, P., & Ottenbreti-Leftwich, A. (2012). Preparing pre-service teachers to integrate technology in education: A synthesis of qualitative evidence. *Computers & Education, 59*(1), 134–144.

Ubben, G. C., Hughes, L. W., & Norris, C. J. (2007). *The principal: Creative leadership for excellence in schools* (6th ed.). Boston, MA: Pearson Education.

Whitehead, B. M., Boschee, F., & Decker, R. H. (2013). *The principal: Leadership for a global society.* Thousand Oaks, CA: Sage.

Whitehead, B. M., Jensen, D. F. N., & Boschee, F. (2013). *Planning for technology: A guide for school administrators, coordinators, and curriculum leaders* (2nd ed.). Thousand Oaks, CA: Corwin Press.

Wilhoit, G. (2012). Make-or-break state action. *Phi Delta Kappan, 94*(2), 47–49.

Williams, T. (2012). Supporting rural teachers. *Principal, 92*(2), 26–29.

Young, E. (2008). Focus on global education: A report from the 2007 PDK summit. *Phi Delta Kappan, 89*(5), 349–353.

Zirkel, P. (2009). School law all-stars: Two successive constellations. *Phi Delta Kappan, 90*(10), 704–708.

Zhao, Y. (2009). Needed: Global villagers. *Educational Leadership, 67*(1), 60–64.

PART II

Curriculum Processes

Understanding the history and process of curriculum development is useful for both scholars and practitioners. The purpose of Part II is to help curriculum leaders acquire the skills needed to bring about major curricular change. Curriculum change is often based on specific details involved in improving and developing three levels of curricula—programs of study, fields of study, and courses and units of study.

CHAPTER 5

Curriculum Planning

Decades of research indicate that holding mastery goals is related to a host of beneficial outcomes (Guskey & Anderman, 2013–2014). This is especially the case with an increasing focus on curriculum planning. To be even more specific, details of the curriculum-planning process are determined by the following: *the level and nature of curriculum work as well as designing a field of studies, improving a program of studies,* and *developing a course of study.* Each of these components involves quite different processes, and will be addressed throughout the book.

Questions addressed in this chapter include the following:

- What is a goal-based model of curriculum planning, and how does one determine the locus of planning decisions and organizational structures that are needed?
- What is the importance of establishing a curriculum framework?
- How can we identify and allocate leadership functions as well as align goals with curricular fields?
- How can community members be involved in curriculum planning?
- How do we organize, evaluate, change, and provide curriculum resources?

Key to Leadership

Curriculum planning is the specification and sequencing of major decisions to be made in the future with regard to the curriculum.

Certainly, curriculum planning is at the heart of school reform, and thus, everyone wants to know "what works" to help schools improve student achievement (Weinbaum & Supovitz, 2010). But before addressing individual components in subsequent chapters, it might be useful at the outset to define curriculum planning.

Within this context and from a historical perspective, curriculum planning is often represented as a cycle involving, but not limited to, a series of steps: *analysis, design, development, implementation,* and *evaluation,* or ADDIE design model (Design Theories and Models, 2014). Moreover, curriculum planning and development also touches upon five foundational areas of understanding that include society, knowledge, human development, technology, and learning (Wiles & Bondi, 2011). Certainly, as noted here, any discussion involving collaborative curriculum planning quickly becomes complex. It is with this in mind, and for the sake of deepening understanding, the authors have chosen to focus in this chapter on one particular model—the **goal-based model** of curriculum planning.

GOAL-BASED MODEL OF CURRICULUM PLANNING

Curriculum models used to plan and implement curriculum are becoming increasingly popular. That said, developing curriculum models as part of a school improvement plan can be challenging but also tremendously rewarding (Bryk, 2010). The use of standards-based teaching as part of the goal-based process is now becoming common practice. Although several planning models are available to educators, one that seems effective for curriculum planning is the goal-based model.

Developing a goal-based model requires some preliminary planning. School leaders must first begin the process by initializing three organizing strategies.

Organizational Strategies

School leaders need to do the following:

- Distinguish between district- and school-based responsibilities to clarify the locus of decision making.
- Decide what organizational structures are needed, appointing the needed advisory groups and task forces.
- Allocate specific leadership functions to district and school staff.

Following these initial steps, a **curriculum framework** should be developed.

CURRICULUM FRAMEWORK

Formulating a curriculum framework is one of the initial tasks of curriculum planning. It is important to note that a curriculum framework is an organized plan, set of standards, or list of outcomes defining recommended curricula. Initiating a curriculum framework first involves defining clear goals to be achieved by all students. In the past, many schools used a traditional approach based primarily on delivering content. Today, most schools are developing and aligning frameworks to new standards. For example, Common Core State Standards (CCSS) currently include a number of very important goals such as critical thinking and other key skills development, a tolerant and multicultural school environment, and civic competencies (Lenskaya, 2013). Much of the work in aligning these state mandated standards and benchmarks to local school curriculum is often done by administrators and teachers working collaboratively with a committee or task force.

Curriculum Tip 5.1	Giving a curriculum committee a special title can be an important part of the process. For example, some school districts call their select group "The Vision Alive Committee."

The purpose of any curriculum framework is to guide the formation of a curriculum aligned with standards and benchmarks. In addition, the framework spotlights the need for continuous improvement through the alignment of all district initiatives as well as the maximizing of student achievement. Serving as an outline, the framework can help focus on the importance of incorporating research-supported teaching and learning into daily practice, the use of student achievement data in making decisions about continuous school improvement, and the development of a professional learning community (PLC).

How to Use a Framework

District and schools often use a curriculum framework as a reference to state standards or CCSS. Serving as an outline, it can be particularly helpful when making decisions about professional development strategies as well as targeting student achievement goals. Once a framework is in place, an analysis can be made as to what needs to be done, tasks can be assigned, and the planning calendar set. The number of subcommittees may vary depending on school district.

Of particular importance is the notation of benchmarks and outcomes mandated by state standards and CCSS. Resources and materials are to be listed as well. School leaders should make an extra effort to relate district level goals and objectives to career and employability skills, technology education, human development, and citizenship as well as living in a global society. Naturally, changes to the framework can be made periodically depending on data analysis and feedback. Once everything is in place, the goal remains the same—to align coursework, assessment, and professional development with an intent of improving instruction and increasing individual student achievement.

Framework Planning Cycle

For the purposes of developing a goal-based framework, phases for curriculum development are generally cyclical in nature and may include the following: *analysis*—content relating to standards and benchmarks; *design*—planning strategies; *development*—professional development;

implementation—teaching and learning; and *evaluation*—formative and summative assessment. These phases are adapted from an ADDIE design model (Design Theories and Models, 2014):

Analysis—Content relating to standards and benchmarks

As part of the overall analysis, standards and benchmarks are an essential part of the curriculum framework. Each standard or benchmark (as per individual state standards or CCSS) describes what students should know and be able to do in each subject area.

Design—Planning strategies

The design is an essential component of the framework. The overall design can act as a reference guide for curriculum change. As part of the design process, planning strategies reflect the importance of collaboratively involving stakeholders and highlights the need for alignment. It also emphasizes the need for continuity in a K–12 curriculum.

Development—Professional development

Professional development is instrumental to successful implementation. This section can list standards for the context, content, and process of professional development experiences and may involve the designing of PLCs as well as other approaches that focus on school improvement, curriculum content, student learning, and assessment needs.

Implementation—Teaching and learning

Teaching and learning is the heart of the curriculum planning process. It describes the rigorous standards forming the foundation to successful learning in all content areas. These standards (aligned with state standards and CCSS) include deep knowledge, higher order thinking, cultural awareness, and communication skills. This section also discusses the importance of incorporating strategies for using technology, learner connections, interdisciplinary learning, special education, and maximizing career-related and college skills in a global society.

Evaluation—Formative and summative assessment

Evaluation describes the need for both formative and summative evaluations. As part of this process, Web-based assessments (aligned with state standards and CCSS) can be used to monitor student growth and program effectiveness. Included as well is a rationale for why data-driven assessment is important; how teachers can develop and use performance assessments based on the content standards and benchmarks; and why the district's student performance system should be aligned with state assessment or CCSS.

ELEMENTS OF GOAL-BASED PLANNING

Reflecting a core element to curriculum development, thoughtful planning and close tracking of how it plays out in schools is key to the process (Goodwin, 2013). Once a planning framework is in place and possible instructional design models are reviewed, curriculum committees will be ready to move forward. It should be noted here that as for larger districtwide curricular projects, task forces can be appointed to carry out the development and improvement suggested by the needs assessment. Their work is evaluated, and appropriate plans are made to implement the new or revised programs effectively. Exhibit 5.1 provides an overview of the cyclical process of curriculum planning.

Obviously, depending on the school or district, different models will have a variety of components. But, to be true to the process, the model should be basically goal-based, ensuring that curriculum revisions are collaboratively made with general outcomes clearly in mind. It should also emphasize feasibility and thus assist schools and districts in undertaking only priority projects that leaders believe can be accomplished effectively. Finally, it should be systematic, meaning that planning decisions will be cast in a rational framework emphasizing orderly progression.

EXHIBIT 5.1 Goal-Based Curriculum Planning Cycle

Organize for Planning

1. Develop awareness and knowledge of state standards or CCSS.
2. Determine the locus of planning decisions: Differentiate between district and school planning responsibilities.
3. Determine the organizational structures needed to facilitate planning, and set up those structures.
4. Identify leadership functions, and allocate those functions appropriately.

Establish a Planning Framework

1. Align the district's educational goals with appropriate curricular fields as recommended by learned societies as well as with mandated state standards or CCSS.
2. Develop a curriculum database.
3. Review possible models of instructional design.
4. Develop a planning calendar based on leaders' assessments of organizational priorities.

Carry Out Specific Planning Activities

1. Conduct needs assessment in high-productivity areas by standardized tests, curriculum-referenced tests, and other measures and data sources (aligned with state standards or CCSS); use assessment results to determine the need for curriculum development or improvement.
2. Organize task forces to carry out development or improvement projects, and monitor the work of the task forces.
3. Provide professional development needed for effective implementation.
4. Evaluate development or improvement projects.
5. Link outcomes back to initial goals, benchmarks, and standards.
6. Make necessary organizational changes and provisions for effective implementation.
7. Secure resources needed for new or revised curricula.

Curriculum Tip 5.2	Sharing common goals is key to making curriculum changes in a classroom, school, or district.

In retrospect, leading change and implementing a goal-based approach often go hand in hand. The key to success in both is a thorough, inclusive curriculum-planning process. The process described and tools provided in this book will assist you in leading change and guiding you through the curriculum-planning process. The following sections provide even more insight into the basic elements of goal-based planning and will focus on the locus of planning decisions, organizational structures, identification and allocation of leadership, alignment of educational goals, curriculum database, planning a calendar, conducting a needs assessment, organizing and evaluating resources, and developing PLCs.

LOCUS OF PLANNING DECISIONS

There is no single plan or one style of leadership that will make every school successful (Bridges, 2010). Therefore, curriculum planning obviously needs to occur at several levels: at the federal level, when policy decisions and their implementation are planned; at the state level as per CCSS, or when state offices of education plan for major changes in graduation requirements; at the district level, when the district plans to revise a field of study; at the school level, when the school revises its program of studies or adds a new course; and at the classroom level, when the teacher plans a unit of study.

The rationale for standardization, whether CCSS or an individual state initiative, speaks in terms of achievement, equity, and efficiency. The first argument is that standardized curricula will result in higher achievement. The second is that standardization ensures equity: Every student gets the same curriculum, regardless of school and teacher assignment. Critics would point out that equity does not equal uniformity. The final argument is that the standardized curriculum is more efficient and, thus, more economical: The district can offer the same type of staff development, order large quantities of the same materials, and develop a single set of curriculum-referenced tests. This claim of efficiency is probably a reasonable one; the issue is whether other considerations are more important. Regardless of the approach, individual school districts must still adopt a set of goals and objectives that align to state standards (see Exhibit 5.2).

ORGANIZATIONAL STRUCTURES

With district and school delineations made, school leaders can next determine which organizational structures are needed to provide ongoing curriculum leadership (Jaquith, 2013). For example, given the dynamic context of schools, central offices have an important role to play as well as the local building level principal. Whichever is the case, it is desirable to

---

EXHIBIT 5.2   Issues in District or School Curriculum Decision Making

1. What goals are more appropriate for students in a particular school?
2. How should school leaders reconceptualize and reorganize fields of study, using such approaches as interdisciplinary courses and "broad fields" curricula?
3. How will a school develop its own instructional objectives or modify district objectives, as long as those objectives are consonant with district goals and state standards?
4. What instructional processes and activities are to be used?
5. What recommendations will involve instructional pacing?
6. How will the school develop and select assessments for evaluating student achievement?
7. How will a school select instructional materials, provided materials meet district guidelines and align to state standards?
8. How will a school evaluate its own program of studies and make needed changes, including the addition or elimination of specific courses?

---

have a simple and flexible committee structure that can provide the continuity required and also respond quickly to changing needs. An examination of both the research and reports of effective practice suggests that the following structures would accomplish those goals.

District Curriculum Advisory Council

The District Curriculum Advisory Council is a standing committee, with members appointed by the superintendent of schools. Its membership will vary with the size of the school district, but the following members or constituencies should be represented:

- The school superintendent or assistant superintendent
- The school district curriculum directors or supervisors
- Secondary school principals
- Elementary school principals
- Teachers
- Parents and other community representatives
- Secondary school students

The advisory council, as its name suggests, serves in an advisory capacity only, recommending to the superintendent what problems require systematic attention and what processes might be used to solve those problems. Typically, it meets four times during the school year to collaboratively identify problems, review planning calendars, receive evaluation reports, and review curriculum proposals. Its members serve for a stated period of time; a rotating three-year term of office would ensure both continuity and fresh ideas.

Larger districts may wish to establish a separate community advisory council composed of parents and representatives of the business and professional community. Most superintendents, however, seem to feel that such separate councils complicate the work of the curriculum advisory group and may even attempt to usurp certain board functions.

Local School Advisory Council

Each school should also have a standing advisory group, especially if individual schools are to have a large measure of curricular autonomy. Its members should be nominated by the faculty and appointed by the principal. The school advisory council includes the principal; subject-matter specialists; or grade-level leaders, teachers, and parents. Students from upper grade levels might also be included. One of the teachers and one of the parents on the school advisory council should represent the school on the district council to ensure good communication and collaboration between the two advisory groups. The school advisory council advises the principal on school-based curricular issues, in a manner similar to the district advisory council. Its members also serve for a specified term, like those on the district council.

In smaller school districts, there might not be a need for separate school councils; the district council could be composed so that it has representatives from each school. In either case, these standing groups provide the continuity required for effective planning.

Curriculum Task Forces

In addition to these two standing committees, the superintendent may appoint a task force to deal with any major issues that need attention. Task forces are seen as working groups, numbering from perhaps 6 to 12 members, depending on the nature of the problem. Members are appointed on the basis of the technical skills required for the job; at the same time, the superintendent should make sure membership is representative of the types of professional roles that exist in the district. Thus, most task forces might include a curriculum specialist, a principal, and several knowledgeable teachers. If a task force needs additional technical assistance, it can request approval from the superintendent to secure a qualified consultant. Each task force can be given a specific problem to solve, a deadline for developing and implementing the solution, and the resources required to do the job. Ordinarily, a task force remains in existence only until a problem is solved. These ad hoc groups give the school system the flexibility and generally complement the standing bodies. An example might be the formation of a technology task force committee. A technology task force committee can be made up of administrators, teachers, parents, and community members. At least six of the members of this larger committee can be asked to form a special steering committee.

Community Participation–Cultural Awareness

The importance of participation in school and community is a notable point of agreement in the literature. For example, community trust, especially from a cultural perspective, is definitely becoming an essential ingredient in school success (Schlechty, 2011). The idea that individuals or groups with compelling interests in schooling should be involved in changes affecting them or their multicultural families is increasingly popular. Within a school community, a number of major groups and subgroups have interests in the school or are affected by the educational system. These groups can be considered the major stakeholders in the community of interest. They include the political, multicultural, and commercial leaders, as well as the social service and educational personnel, along with student and parent populations.

An example of community participation as per the development of a district health curriculum in the author's school district is provided next:

> The revision of our health curriculum (K–12) was relatively easy; however, incorporating sex education into the curriculum was bound to create a quandary in the community. The author—in this case, the curriculum director—formulated a committee that included a member of the clergy (priest), a nurse and mother, a father of 12 children, a mother/grandmother, and a female high school senior who had a baby out of wedlock. The district writing committee for the health curriculum included representatives from the various grade levels—elementary, middle, and high school. Issues for sex education were openly discussed, with significant input from the community participants. The end result was a health curriculum that included sex education supported by the invited and respected participants and accepted by the community.

Curriculum Tip 5.3	Involving stakeholders is a key to success—especially in that communities often support a curriculum they help create.

As can be seen, the select committee, noted previously, can assist with the development of the district's vision and curricula mission statements as well as assist with the development of guidelines for a health curriculum. The committee can also help formulate guidelines for equipment and programs designed to enhance communication and awareness. This type of committee is representative of how a school district special subcommittee might be organized. Developing an effective select committee can be a crucial part of the process of curriculum planning.

IDENTIFICATION AND ALLOCATION OF LEADERSHIP

From a historical perspective, in small school districts, the building principal (or superintendent) is expected to be involved in curriculum planning and staffing. As such, they learn the value of trust as they assume and share responsibilities for instructional leadership tasks (Gill & Hendee, 2010). In larger school districts, an assistant superintendent (or curriculum director) is expected to provide systemwide curriculum leadership. Depending on the size of district, the central office staff might also include several subject-matter coordinators (usually responsible for coordinating the K–12 curriculum in a designated content area). At secondary levels, the building-level principal or assistant principal is expected to provide leadership. Department chairs also provide subject-matter leadership. At middle school levels, principals and assistant principals often rely on grade-level team leaders as well as department heads. In large elementary school districts, principals, along with grade-level leaders or teacher specialists (especially in reading and mathematics), help guide the curriculum process.

The key is to identify and analyze leadership functions required at both the district and school levels (depending on size of district) and then allocate functions to those best able to perform them. This specification and allocation process can begin by having the district curriculum advisory council develop a form like the one shown in Exhibit 5.3. It lists all the leadership functions relating to curriculum, organizing them into four categories based on the level and focus of the responsibility.

Simply setting a high bar is inadequate; all participants, including students, need the will to achieve established goals (Goodwin & Miller, 2013). Keeping with this perspective, as part of their leadership task, an advisory council needs to first review the form to ensure that it includes all the goals and functions they consider important and uses language that communicates clearly to everyone in that district. At this point (especially in larger districts), the superintendent or the assistant superintendent, with input from central office staff, principals, and teacher–leaders, can take over the complex and sensitive task of reallocating and reassigning functions for maximum effectiveness. Before any decisions are made, school district leaders might want to first analyze which individuals in the district are presently

EXHIBIT 5.3 Functions of Curriculum Leadership			
Function	Now	Assign	New
At the district level—for all areas of the curriculum			
1. Articulate district curriculum goals and priorities.			
2. Chair district advisory council.			
3. Develop and monitor curriculum budget.			
4. Develop and implement plans to evaluate curricula and use evaluative data.			
5. Identify and prioritize curricular problems to be solved.			
6. Develop a curriculum-planning calendar.			
7. Appoint task forces and review their reports, proposals, and products.			
8. Develop and monitor processes for materials selection and evaluation.			
9. Plan districtwide staff development programs required by curricular changes.			
10. Represent district on curricular matters in relationships with state and intermediate unit curriculum offices.			

(Continued)

EXHIBIT 5.3 (Continued)

Function	Now	Assign	New
11. Evaluate district-level curriculum staff.			
12. Develop general district guidelines for aligning curricula at the school level.			
At the district level—for special areas of the curriculum			
1. Develop and implement plans to evaluate curriculum, as specified in the district planning calendar.			
2. Use evaluative data to identify specific curricular problems, and develop proposals to remedy them.			
3. Evaluate articulation of the curriculum between elementary and middle schools and between middle and high schools.			
4. Provide leadership in developing and improving K–12 curriculum materials in that special area.			
5. Implement district guidelines in selecting and evaluating texts and other instructional materials.			
6. Provide leadership in implementing K–12 staff development programs for that specific area.			
At the school level—for all areas of the curriculum			
1. Implement plans to monitor and align the curriculum.			
2. Evaluate curricula at the school level, and use evaluative data to identify school-level problems.			
3. Ensure that important skills that cut across the disciplines are appropriately taught and reinforced in those disciplines.			
4. Monitor coordination of the curriculum between those content areas where close coordination is important.			
5. Develop school-based budget for curriculum needs, reflecting school priorities.			
At the school level—for special areas of the curriculum			
1. Supervise teachers with respect to curriculum implementation.			
2. Assist teachers in developing instructional plans based on curriculum guides.			
3. Implement school-based staff development required by curriculum change.			
4. Select instructional materials.			
5. Help teachers use student evaluation results to make needed modifications in curriculum.			

responsible for specific functions. Once this is determined, they can enter role designations in the "Now" column. In many instances, they will indicate that no one is presently performing those functions.

After assessing how effectively functions are being performed and how equitably they are distributed, the advisory council can then determine where changes can be made in present assignments, entering those decisions in the "Assign" column. Entries in this column yield a clear picture as to which functions can best be discharged by reassigning them to present role incumbents. In some cases, however, it will be apparent that a new role is needed: It is possible that several important functions are not being performed successfully, and no one among the present staff is available and competent to assume those critical functions. Allocation of functions to a newly conceived role is reflected by placing the new role title in the "New" column.

Final allocations become the basis for reconceptualizing present roles and creating any new positions needed. This process enables a local district to develop its own staffing pattern, one that reflects its special needs and resources.

As can be seen by working through this process, leadership and planning are often common threads invariably found in the curricula design of any successful K–12 program. That said, today's school administrators and teacher–leaders must exercise a level of leadership required to ensure the successful integration of planning into the curriculum. Additionally, principals, curriculum coordinators, superintendents, and teacher–leaders must reach clear answers to four basic questions:

1. What is required to make the improvements we wish to see in the student-centered learning environments of our schools?

2. Why do we want to commit a great deal of time and money to a curriculum initiative for change, and how are our motives focused on improving student learning?

3. Who is the best person to lead the curriculum initiative we are considering?

4. Who will be best suited to assess and maintain the quality of curricular programs after the initial stages of implementation are completed?

IMPORTANCE OF INTEGRITY

As part of this process, *integrity* should be a major criteria when identifying and allocating curriculum leadership. This is particularly important when considering Interstate School Leaders Licensure Consortium (ISLLC) standards. With a gap sometimes between theory and action, translating ethics and integrity into action is an important part of becoming an effective curriculum leader. According to Darden (2014), school leaders facing ethical dilemmas have three main guideposts to help choose between right and wrong: laws, professional codes of ethics, and personal values and beliefs. All three interact—and sometimes conflict—as the impetus for action or inaction as school personnel fulfill day-to-day responsibilities. The question is not whether an individual can lead but more appropriately can they lead with integrity, compassion, and good judgment? Along with developing integrity, the ability of school leaders to provide a supportive climate is key to the process. Such discussions can also build a platform for shared decision making when opportunities are appropriate. Likewise, involving more teachers in curricular deliberations may well make the difference in a positive outcome (Whitehead, Boschee, & Decker, 2013).

Results from the research from the schools of integrity project by Mirk (2009) identified openness, honesty, relationship-building, and constant rigorous reflection as key elements in schools that successfully balance academic rigor with ethical development. The Institute for Global Ethics translated those findings and interviewed six secondary school leaders—who were recommended on their solid reputations of integrity—to learn how ethics and values contribute to leadership effectiveness. Those leaders offered five key recommendations.

1. *Lead from your core values.* Deeply held values become an operating platform that works in two directions: compelling constant internal alignment and driving outward actions. In an age of increasing transparency, both functions are essential.

2. *Have the courage to connect.* As a leader of a school community, it can take a measure of courage to stick to ideals and share vulnerabilities. A commitment to fairness leads a leader to suspend preconceived ideas or assumptions as they go into potentially tough meetings. Having a strong set of beliefs falls short and often backfires without the courage and humility to share and connect with others. Effective leaders resist the temptation to impose their beliefs; instead, they opt for a slower and perhaps less convenient route that seeks common ground and mutual respect and, ultimately, leads to meaningful connections. The focus on positive, authentic relationships sets the tone for what the leader wants their building culture to become.

3. *Do your homework.* As part of developing relationships, an ethical leader needs to understand how others think and operate in certain situations. With this understanding, the leader has an understanding and respect for the person as well as the issue at hand. Remembering details and giving specific feedback help others to understand that you paid attention. The point of not talking jargon but being able to communicate in ways that anyone could understand with clarity was a huge difference maker for the leader.

4. *Model your outcomes.* School leaders can establish trust with their willingness to be open and transparent with faculty and staff. The need to model your openness and give of yourself is a key ingredient of **modeling** of what you expect your faculty to do with students. As a school leader, the modeling of experimentation and welcoming feedback is a risk but is also a huge modeling technique as well as opening the channels for feedback for discussion and working toward future improvement.

5. *Lean on others for support.* Bringing the faculty and staff into conversations provides a learning and growth process. This concept recommended building values-driven relationships within a school community. Asking the question "What would you do?" opens the door to talk about different points of view and then sharing your point of view allows the faculty and staff to start to understand your view and decision-making process on issues of concern for all.

ALIGNMENT OF EDUCATIONAL GOALS

Understanding that standards and accountability reforms can permeate the educational system and change educator beliefs is fundamental to school improvement (Desimone, 2013). Thus, determining goals and an alignment of goals in each field of study remains the key step in the goal-based model. Several methods are available to accomplish this task. This chapter explains one method for allocating goals to curriculum fields as an aspect of the planning process; the next chapter explains a somewhat different process for aligning and assessing the several fields for goal conformance as part of the program-improvement process. However, when creating an alignment of educational goals with curricular fields, the following guidelines will be helpful:

1. *Specify district educational goals.* An educational goal is a general long-term outcome to be accomplished through the total educational program. Most districts are developing goals aligned with CCSS. In addition to the core curriculum, educators today are focusing on more than just district and state curriculum issues. They are also focusing, to a larger extent, on goals having a global perspective. Generating a clear narrative of a school district's basic mission and fostering a shared sense of purpose among students and school personnel can be a major factor in generating a positive school climate and an engaging academic curriculum.

2. *Determine which of the educational goals should be accomplished primarily through the courses of study.* Many school leaders neglect this important step; they assume that every educational goal is a curricular goal. Thus, educators, noting that the state board specifies the development of self-esteem as an educational goal, sometimes mistakenly assume that they need to develop courses and units in self-esteem. Numerous educational goals, like this one, can better be accomplished through other means, such as instructional methods or programs, the organizational climate, the activity program, or the guidance program.

For this reason, the curriculum leadership team should carefully analyze each educational goal and make a preliminary determination of whether that goal will be accomplished primarily through organized courses of study or through some other means. In this manner, they identify a shorter list of curriculum goals—those general long-term outcomes that are to be accomplished primarily through the organized curriculum. Advisory councils should review their tentative decisions. The input from those groups should then be used to make any needed modifications so that the resulting list represents a broad consensus.

3. *Allocate the curricular goals to the several fields of study.* Once the curricular goals have been identified, the leadership team can allocate those goals to appropriate fields of study. A system such as this seems to work. This process is one that begins with the district's educational goals and ends with individual student goals. The process can be reversed: Each field or subject area can help develop its own list of curricular goals, and these can be synthesized into one comprehensive district list. The outcome, not the process, is important: Each field or subject area should have a clear list of curricular goals.

Along with this process, school district administrators along with the curriculum committee can collaboratively establish district-level technology goals. Classroom teachers can then use this template to create an even more detailed plan for how they are going to incorporate technology into their individual classrooms.

Curriculum Tip 5.4	Continuous monitoring and feedback links outcomes back to initial goals, benchmarks, and standards. This phase both completes and renews the curriculum cycle.

Technology Planning Goals

- Align technology resources with CCSS, district curricula programs, and planning.
- Facilitate integration of technology with the instructional program as to be consistent with the district's curriculum.
- Implement technologies that support a high-quality and safe learning environment and allow all students to achieve at their highest potential.
- Develop teacher and student interest and motivation in utilizing technology to develop higher order thinking skills (HOTS).
- Teachers work to create technology standards and share best practices.
- Develop authentic, problem-based use of technology that becomes self-renewing for teachers.
- Transform every classroom into a digitally based learning environment.

FORMULATING A CURRICULUM DATABASE

A second key aspect of the planning framework is the development of a comprehensive curriculum database. With increasing technological innovations, new tools are making it easier for educators to use digital data (Johnson, 2013). Using a system's instructional tools, teachers can search for a particular theme or standard, click on items addressing that area, and incorporate them into their lesson plans. Moreover, looking at data should never be an isolated activity. The argument here is that good curriculum work and good data analysis require extensive knowledge about resources, inputs, and constraints. To that end, school leaders and teachers need to develop technology-based skill levels that can be used in assessing needs and developing curricula. What should be included? The temptation is to collect too much information, just because it is available or seems interesting. It makes more sense to collect and organize only that information likely to be used. Exhibit 5.4 lists the kinds of information that seem most essential in the needs-assessment process; as will be explained in Chapter 8, a shorter list of information needs can be useful in the course-planning process.

Large varieties of student information stored in databases can greatly facilitate the work of any curriculum planning committee. Consider, for example, how the database can be used by a committee appointed to develop a new personal well-being course for middle school students that would combine health and physical education. They would first get

EXHIBIT 5.4   Information for the Curriculum Database

Community Resources

1. People with knowledge, expertise, and influence

2. Organizations and places useful as resources

Students

1. Date of birth, sex, and ethnic identity

2. Eligibility for federal or state assistance programs

3. Parents' occupations and marital status

4. Verbal and mathematical abilities and IQ score

5. Talents, skills, and special interests

6. School achievement: standardized test scores and curriculum-referenced test scores

7. English proficiency; native language if other than English

8. Limitations: physical, emotional, and learning disabilities (LD)

9. Learning styles and cognitive levels

10. School record: subjects studied, grades, and attendance

11. Career and educational plans

12. Extracurricular activities

13. Community activities

Faculty

1. Subjects and grades certified to teach

2. Present assignment

3. Special interests and competencies

4. Recent professional development: courses, workshops, etc.

School

1. Courses offered and enrollments

2. Extracurricular activities and student participation

Other Resources

1. State curriculum guides

2. Curriculum guides from other districts

3. Other sources of learning objectives

4. Professional materials and resources for teachers

comprehensive data about the students likely to take the course and to become aware of students' needs, limitations, and capacities: "About 15% of the students will have **limited English proficiency (LEP)**; we may need a separate section or special materials for them." Next, they would get data on student participation in extracurricular activities and note that very few students participate in activities that require a high level of physical exercise: "We should include a unit that deals explicitly with the value of and opportunities for in-school aerobic activities." They can then retrieve information about other professional resources available—state curriculum guides, CCSS recommendations, guides from other districts, as well as banks of learning objectives.

Having a curriculum database team can be very beneficial to the process. The team then has the task of translating individual state or CCSS and benchmarks into academic performance indicators from prekindergarten to Grade 12, which can then be adopted as official achievement targets for the district. Assessments can be administered every eight weeks, and the tests can then measure every standard that had been taught up to that date. Thus, the first step on the path to high student achievement is to establish a series of Web-based transparent, common, rigorous assessments. This enables teachers to make solid, root-cause analyses from data, which in turn facilitates far more effective action plans. Even with high-quality interim assessments and effective analysis of data, student achievement will not improve without targeted follow-through. The key is to provide a seamless connection between assessment analysis and teaching. To this degree, then, the question is not whether to integrate the use of data in school improvement efforts, but how (Protheroe, 2010).

Clearly, developing an effective data-analysis program to improve curriculum is a vitally important component. As part of planning curriculum, school leaders will find that databases, as well as a system of data analysis, can be used to facilitate systemic curriculum changes: regarding issues between teachers and administrative personnel; between administrators and parents; and among administrators within the same district or throughout a region. For example, databases in the area of curriculum can be used to determine professional development interests and needs, develop a background of skills and usage, and identify individuals willing to share ideas and techniques, as well as being used to inventory the type and level of materials and resources used in the classroom. Conducting an in-depth analysis of your curricular needs is, therefore, a crucial part of any program.

PLANNING A CALENDAR

One of the central leadership functions is to collaboratively develop and monitor the district's curriculum-planning calendar, a master schedule that assists district leaders in making systematic plans for **curriculum evaluation** and development. For example, aligning the master schedule with building-level principal schedules frees up administrators to participate in collaborative grade-level team meetings (Hewson, 2013).

The planning calendar, as shown in Exhibit 5.5, can include the six steps listed as "specific planning activities" in Exhibit 5.1. Note that a distinction is made between major and other fields simply to assist in the planning process, not to depreciate the importance of

EXHIBIT 5.5 Curriculum-Planning Calendar			
Major Projects	*2015–2016*	*2016–2017*	*2017–2018*
1. Needs assessment, major fields	Language arts	Math	Science
2. Needs assessment, other fields	Industrial arts	Art	
3. Needs assessment, programs	Elementary School	Middle School	High School
4. Task forces appointed, at work		Language arts Industrial arts	Math Art
5. Projects evaluated		Language arts Industrial arts	Math Art
6. Organizational provisions		Language arts Industrial arts	Math Art
7. Resources selected and provided		Language arts Industrial arts	Math Art
8. Staff development			Language arts Industrial arts

such areas as art and industrial arts. Provision is also made for evaluating the several programs of study. Note that, in this example, the district has chosen to do a needs assessment each year of one major and one other field and of one program level. With such a schedule, the district would be able in a five-year period to assess all major fields, five other fields, and every program level.

A curriculum leadership team can begin developing a calendar by tentatively mapping out a five-year plan that will indicate year by year the major projects to be undertaken. The committee can make collaborative decisions based on their own analysis of district needs and their own priorities for improvement. The decision about how many projects can be initiated will, of course, be influenced by their perception of district needs and resources. A large school district with well-staffed curriculum and evaluation offices can obviously plan for many more projects than a smaller district with an overextended staff. These tentative decisions can be shared with the district advisory council for its input before a final form of the calendar is developed. The final form of the calendar can then be used to develop budget requests, appoint subcommittees and task forces, as well as monitor progress.

Administrators and teachers must work collaboratively to construct a practical calendar for any curriculum project. Realistic target dates are a key ingredient, and committee

Curriculum Tip 5.5	A planning calendar can mark important reference points for the planning committee to reach in order to keep a project on schedule.

members should be included, as this is really the only way to ensure a workable schedule of events. In this respect, it is important to remember that committee members are usually chosen because they know how to get tasks done, and they are also the ones who usually have the best idea of how long it will take to accomplish these tasks.

CONDUCTING A NEEDS ASSESSMENT

A reality is that new technologies require a new set of instructional competencies (Holliday & Smith, 2012). Thus, another major step in the curriculum planning process is to conduct a needs assessment (see Exhibit 5.6). An example of a *classroom needs assessment* might include the following questions:

EXHIBIT 5.6 Establishing a Data-Driven School Culture Checklist

What does the district want to know?

Where to look:

- Current district goals
- Patterns in data
- Upcoming district decisions
- Questions raised by teachers, administrators, or the community

How will the district find out?

What to do:

- Form a data team.
- Conduct inventory of data currently compiled in the district and determine format (electronic or paper).
- Assess technological capacity of the district to manage and analyze data.
- Determine the extent to which personnel in the district have time, skills, and willingness to engage in data-driven projects.
- Identify indicators of input, process, and outcome variables related to goals.
- Determine which additional data are reasonable to collect.
- Train staff to collect and use data.
- Analyze and disaggregate data.

What does the district do next?

How to proceed:

- Establish goals and benchmarks (aligned with state standards).
- Measure progress by linking objectives (outcomes) back to goals, benchmarks, and standards.
- Develop action or school improvement plans.
- Communicate findings.

SOURCE: From "Creating Data-Driven Schools," by P. Noyce, D. Perda, and R. Traver, 2000, *Educational Leadership*, 57(5), pp. 52–57.

- What analysis is needed?
- Do I have just-right learning targets?
- Do I use a planning schema?
- How can I best incorporate technology?
- Do I vary assessment data?
- Will feedback improve student performance?

As part of the process, curriculum leaders and teachers may need to use multiple data regarding inputs, processes, products, outputs, and outcomes. In addition, planners should be sensitive to both the internal organization and external society. This may involve socio-economic, socioemotional, or multicultural issues.

A simpler needs-assessment model can be built on several of the elements explained in this chapter and in Chapter 12 (note that this section explains the needs-assessment process in developing a field of study; Chapter 6 explains how to assess needs in improving a program of studies). First, the district can collaboratively develop a comprehensive curriculum database, as noted previously. This provides information on two major "inputs"—the classroom instructors and the learners. Next, the district can develop for each field or subject area a clear set of curricular goals (aligned with CCSS, using the processes described previously). These specify the ends to be accomplished. Then the district can evaluate selected fields of study, assessing the major components of the field explained in Chapter 1: *the written curriculum, the supported curriculum, the taught curriculum, the tested curriculum,* and *the learned curriculum.* Theoretically, it should also parallel the district's *curriculum cycle* involving the ADDIE design model. Thus, if a planning committee is concerned with assessing curricular needs in a single field of study, the process is a rather straightforward one.

On the other hand, if a district wishes to make a needs assessment that focuses on a general curriculum goal (not a single field), then the process is slightly more complex. The more complex process uses a broader assessment component, such as the guidance and activity programs. A special committee or task force can then be appointed to identify those fields of study that emphasize or contribute to a specific goal.

Any newly developed committee or task force can proceed to examine the written curriculum in those fields. Questions might include the following: Do the written guides give sufficient and explicit attention to the goal of enhancing creativity? Does the district provide sufficient funds for creative materials? Do texts, digital programs, and applications, as well as other instructional materials, emphasize creativity in their approach and content? Are these fields of study allocated sufficient time to include creative activities?

Members of the select group can then consider a tiered or more complicated approach of the taught curriculum. Here, they can focus on critical issues. Questions might include the following: Are instructors actually teaching units in the written guide that were initially designed to enhance creativity? Are instructors teaching in a manner that fosters creative thinking? Obviously, these questions will require supervisors and evaluators to use great care and observe a representative sample of as many lessons as possible.

Overall, the tested curriculum (assessment) must be closely monitored as well. Questions might include the following: Do curriculum-referenced and teacher-made tests make adequate provisions for assessing creativity? Finally, do assessments attend to the learned curriculum: Are students actually learning to think creatively and to produce creative works? These questions can be answered through several data sources: results from tests of creativity; results from surveys of teachers, parents, and students; and an evaluation of a representative sample of student creative products.

The results of this process can then be used to determine which elements of the curriculum need strengthening and/or to suggest the possibility of a new course to be added to the curriculum.

Looking back retrospectively, a curriculum needs-assessment format can be used for a series of multilevel purposes. Through the use of a needs-assessment program, the district curriculum specialist, along with staff members, can examine curriculum goals and objectives to identify instructional opportunities. Information derived from a quality needs-assessment program can then be used to infuse change directly into the classroom. The result is a major improvement in the teaching and learning process and a major improvement in the learning environment. Effective and collaborative curriculum planning, therefore, should always include some type of needs assessment. Thus, it is through the development of quality needs-assessment programs that administrators, curriculum leaders, and teachers can best facilitate systemic educational change and reform in our schools.

ORGANIZATION AND EVALUATION OF RESOURCES

It has been said that when we focus on possibilities, we get more possibilities (Tschannen-Moran & Tschannen-Moran, 2014). Keeping with this thought, the next step in the planning process involves developing and implementing strategies (these are more fully explained in subsequent chapters). After determining whether to strengthen existing programs and courses, or add new ones, school leaders can appoint another committee or task force. The select committee's work is evaluated by expert review and systematic field testing. Any necessary organizational elements are changed, such as the school schedule, teacher assignments, or grouping practices. Then plans can be made to secure the necessary material resources required by the new or improved program.

Curriculum Tip 5.6	It is critical to avoid implementing change for change's sake.

It is important to reemphasize that state regulations and standards have a major influence on curriculum planning. Many school districts today use standards as a reference point in establishing benchmarks, goals, and objectives; developing plans; driving instruction; and prescribing assessment. That said, evaluating curriculum on a systemwide basis, as part of the planning cycle, focuses on the premise that school systems must set benchmarks (aligned with standards), goals, and objectives as well as provide the means for supervision as per teacher performance to enable students to meet targeted achievement levels.

Through the use of data analysis, checklists, and system-to-system discussions to review progress, school leaders are able to link outcomes back to the original written curriculum. This feedback loop places attention on the most important task: deciding where the schools and districts are going (goals, benchmarks and standards), how they will get there (planning and strategies), and whether they are making progress (formative and summative evaluation). It is this process that completes and renews the curriculum cycle (Benjamin, 2011).

Not to be forgotten, another important piece to the curriculum planning process is the power of professional development. The curriculum-planning committee, along with district administration, should collaboratively determine (based on their goals and resources) the extent to which a PLC can be infused into the daily operation of the curriculum, classroom, or school.

PROFESSIONAL DEVELOPMENT

Radoslovich, Roberts, and Plaza (2014) pose the following question: How can schools create a process that inspires teacher to develop throughout their careers, see feedback from peers and students, and collect accurate data about student learning? Keeping with that perspective, a major aspect of curriculum planning focuses on the timing of professional development as it relates to curricular change. Although there are many strategies as per the specifics of this issue, the authors provide several models that have been used successfully in educational settings.

In the first model, professional-development sessions are held prior to any major curriculum change. The intent here is to update teachers' knowledge about new developments in the field, to give them the skills they need for writing curriculum and instructional materials, and to provide an opportunity for them to exchange and try out such materials. The chief advantage of a pre-professional development model is that it tends to result in a teacher-produced curriculum of high quality. Teachers collaboratively involved in professional development become local experts who have a better understanding of the field, and the materials they produce have usually stood the test of rigorous trials in the classroom. The chief drawback to this model is that it can result in piecemeal change. Thus, the curriculum becomes a collection of interesting exercises but lacks an integrating conceptual framework.

In the second model, professional development sessions are held subsequent to the curriculum change. The new curriculum is developed, and then those who developed the curriculum identify the new knowledge, skills, and attitudes required for successful implementation. Those new learnings then become the basis for a series of professional development programs offered immediately prior to the introduction of the new program and during its implementation stage. This essentially is the model used in many traditional curriculum development and implementation projects. The chief advantage of this model is its close fit between curricular change and professional development. If planned and executed well, this professional development model equips teachers with the skills they need to implement a new curriculum. The chief drawback is that it can place the teacher in a passive role: "Here is your new curriculum—and this is how you teach it."

The third, and more contemporary, is the **community-based learning model.** Examples are professional learning communities (PLCs) as well as teacher–leader networks. These are community-based independent networks, both physical and virtual, that make it possible for teachers to draw on external communities that promote divergent thinking. Such networks support the view that teachers have unique insights that can improve education and accelerate student achievement. These networks are especially important because they enable some of the best teaching minds in a state, region, or nation to bond together into influential PLCs.

Curriculum Tip 5.7	"The strength of a professional learning community model relies on its flexible implementation. Professional learning communities are the engine of high-quality work" (Lovely, 2010).

A community-based learning model is a broad framework that includes service learning, experiential learning, school-to-work, youth apprenticeship, lifelong learning, and other types of learning experiences that are beneficial to the local community. A problem with these individual approaches is that each focuses on only a portion of the learning outcomes that potentially can be achieved through community-based learning. For example, implementing PLCs requires educational leaders to communicate the essential components of the plan. Curriculum leaders must be able to provide faculty and staff members as well as related publics with a clear framework of the concept they desire to implement. To give an idea of how PLCs are organized, the following information, as well as questions and responses, is provided by Slater (2010).

Question 1: What are the essential components to implementing the PLC concept in schools?

Response: PLCs help address the concepts of reflection, experimentation, analysis, and learner.

Reflection is a basis for actions. Actions and habits create character, and character channels teaching and learning.

Experimentation is the willingness to be innovative.

Analysis means using multiple data sources, not just test scores, to get a more comprehensive analysis of what is happening; checklists and walk-throughs can provide real-time data.

Learner means focusing and designing lessons on the learner. The focus is always on learning and achievement.

Question 2: Who conducts the walkthroughs?

Response: Some PLC models require walk-throughs completed by a principal or vice principal.

Question 3: What is the greatest barrier to implementing PLCs?

Response: Safety, climate, and culture. Teaching methods of the past involving cultural insensitivity and isolation must change. A common practice for staff is to go into the lounge and say, "I tried this, and I tried that—but it didn't work." Traditionally, teachers sometimes feel threatened and are not used to sharing failure with fellow staff members.

Question 4: What is the building principal's role in the PLC concept?

Response: The principal must model the concept and act as a facilitator. Moreover, building leaders must be collaborative in their approach. Holding to high ethical values, they must be honest as to what decisions they are willing to share and what they are not. Their role is to initiate the process and then withdraw when appropriate or as participants gain more confidence.

Once the essential components of a PLC are understood, a building administrator can develop a strategic plan to put the change in place. However, the plan must be clearly communicated. The PLC plan must also exist on a continuum by constantly being assessed, adapted, and changed while maintaining the core components.

To be sure, ongoing PLCs are quickly becoming the bedrock of the work that creates a whole school of effective teachers. According to author Reggie Routman (2012), as teachers take ownership in a PLC they begin asking questions about theory, research, and practice. Likewise, when they are able to examine work with a goal of improving teaching as well as assessing data across grade levels, they begin changing beliefs and practices into more effective teaching. Clearly, then, the PLC model can be a transformative factor in school change and a positive move for education.

TECHNOLOGY: 21st-CENTURY LEARNING

More individuals are recognizing our current education system is not set up to prepare students perfectly for a world that no longer exists. As a result, they are encouraging the establishment of virtual schools (Jukes, McCain, & Crockett, 2010–2011). One of the largest—the Florida Virtual School—enrolls over 150,000 students a year (Schneider, 2013–2014). Along with larger numbers of virtual schools, new advances in mobile learning and a plethora of applications is allowing classroom teachers to readily access information across the globe as well as be able to address the individual academic needs of each student. But, that said, schools still have a long ways to go. If educators want to see the

Technology Tip	Effective integration of technology is achieved when students are able to select technology tools to help them obtain information in a timely manner, analyze and synthesize the information, and present it professionally. The technology should become an integral part of how the classroom functions—as accessible as all other classroom tools. (edutopia, 2014)

kinds of changes necessary to bring schools in line with a new reality of 21st-century technology and learning, then leadership will have to radically reprioritize and restructure how they approach teaching and learning.

Thinking about a school that is ready for the future requires school leaders and teachers to work together to see the school in a different way. It is not about seeing classroom technology as a stable entity but one that is prepared to evolve and adapt to changing educational contexts and pedagogies. As has been stated throughout this book, designing and conceptualizing a 21st-century school is about understanding that the educational processes we engage in today are the ones that are going to prepare students to live, work, and interact in a world they haven't experienced yet. In this sense, today is linked with tomorrow. So when thinking about the curriculum planning, it is about learning how to connect the future vision of education with past and present school and district-level assets. Very few schools are in a situation where they can start from scratch with a new building that is linked with a new curriculum that is linked with new technology. Educational leaders need to be considerate of their legacy technology and the continued purpose it can serve within your school and also how that legacy infrastructure can be used to aid in the advancement of a 21st-century technology plan. Some of the legacy infrastructures that school administrators will need to be respectful of can include the following:

- Low, medium, or high bandwidth Internet connectivity
- Types of cable or fiber-optic lines bringing connectivity to the school
- Standardized infrastructure systems such as networking equipment, wireless routers, school-level telephones, or projection systems
- Existing WLAN infrastructure
- School's current voicemail, e-mail system, types of remote access, or storage databases
- District-level technology safety and protection protocols

As can be seen, there is a great deal of work ahead for educational leaders to ready schools for an even faster paced world. With centers of learning gravitating toward a reality of online and virtual schools, it will be paramount for leadership to focus on the integration of technology as part of curriculum planning and implementation in an ever-expanding interconnected global society (Whitehead, Jensen, & Boschee, 2013).

GLOBAL CONNECTIONS: RESEARCH AND PRACTICE

Bridging the knowledge gap between research and practice on a global level remains a difficult challenge. According to Levin (2012), over the past few years, interest in using research to support good policy and practice worldwide has grown significantly. The appetite for reliable and practical research finding has never been high but most educators and many countries now see research playing a vital role in their work.

Accumulated findings of research across the globe now offer substantive guidance to educators and education policymakers. Levin noted a few examples:

- John Hattie's ratings of the effect of various education interventions based on more than 800 research meta-analyses
- A series of reviews of research on professional development, leadership, social studies, and others produced by the New Zealand Ministry of Education's Best Evidence Synthesis
- A series of books by the National Academy of Education reporting research findings on a range of issues such as student engagement, mathematics, and science (p. 72)

An important part of the getting more countries to use research for curriculum development lies in the work of universities, since virtually everywhere in the world universities are the main producers of educational research. Worldwide, universities are struggling with how to share their research more effectively with schools and school systems. In addition, countries differ in how they link research enterprises to policy and practice. In Korea and China, for example, there are very close links between senior researchers, university leaders, and senior policy officials. This contrasts with the United States and England where there are few such links. To remedy this situation, 10 countries met as part of the International Alliance of Leading Educational Institutions in 2011. Countries represented included Australia, Brazil, Canada, China, Denmark, Korea, Singapore, South Africa, the United Kingdom, and the United States. Each of these countries openly shared political and cultural attitudes toward improving the use of research in education (Levin, 2012).

SUMMARY

Throughout this chapter, the authors have noted that curriculum planning should guide and direct the specification and sequencing of major decisions to be made in the future with regard to the curriculum. As part of that process, a goal-based model of curriculum planning provides organizing strategies to determine the locus of control in decision, focuses on what organizational structures are needed, and enables a targeted allocation of functions to teacher–leaders. Additionally, quality curriculum planning provides schools and districts with an opportunity to identify and allocate leadership functions and align goals and benchmarks with individual state standards and CCSS. In the process of initiating transformative change, curriculum planning entails organizing, evaluating, changing, and providing curriculum resources as an integrated process. As part of forging a more vibrant system of reform, long-range curriculum planning combined with strong leadership, a shared vision, and a successful professional development model can be a powerful tool to support student learning and increase staff productivity. It remains, therefore, vitally important that educational leaders realize the importance of implementing and enforcing a successful curriculum plan. By doing so, our future educational leaders will help ensure that all teachers will be able to teach and all students able to learn.

APPLICATIONS

1. In the school district about which you are most knowledgeable, would you recommend a separate community advisory council rather than appointing representatives to a general council? Explain the reasons behind your decision to set up a separate council or appoint a general one.

2. In the school district you know best, how would you balance the need for school autonomy? Use the questions in Exhibit 5.2 as guidelines for resolving this issue.

3. How would you allocate leadership functions in that same district? Use the form shown in Exhibit 5.3 to answer this question, indicating how you think functions should be allocated.

4. Develop a planning calendar you would use in a district you know well. Use the form shown in Exhibit 5.5.

5. Some experts in the field have recommended a more complex needs-assessment model—one that would make extensive use of such measures and processes as parent interviews, community surveys, student interviews, and futures forecasting techniques. If you were in a district leadership position, would you recommend using one of these more complex processes instead of the more sharply focused model described here? Justify your answer.

6. Regarding the PLC concept, how could it be implemented in the school district where you are employed?

7. In what program or subject area in your school or school district do you feel community members should be invited to participate in planning a curriculum change? Why?

8. Why is it important to have a standard curriculum to improve a district's lagging student achievement scores?

CASE STUDY   Involving Community Leaders

A Kentucky school district superintendent appoints David Smith, a local businessperson, to the district's curriculum committee. The businessperson is viewed as an influential person who can get things done in the community—a "mover and shaker."

"Thanks for being able to attend our meeting, Mr. Smith," says Principal Powers.

"Glad to be here. What are some things you want to do with the curriculum?" he asks.

"Well, we were just discussing some options—but the concern is that a number of committee members don't have a good understanding of what is needed. That means that we should develop an extensive needs-assessment component as well as draft some surveys as part of the process."

"I understand," says the businessperson. "Education is changing pretty rapidly these days. I happen to be on the boards of several banks here in town—perhaps I can bring a business as well as community perspective to some of the questions on some of the needs-assessment surveys."

"That would be great!" says the superintendent enthusiastically.

Principal Powers can feel the excitement in the room. "We really appreciate your help, Mr. Smith," he says, smiling. "We want to involve the community in our decision-making process. I'll talk to the superintendent and begin setting up a meeting and check on surveys as soon as possible. This will make it a lot easier for the committee to have a better understanding of how our community feels about the school and about our curriculum."

The Challenge

Reaching out to the community and developing a school-to-community connection is becoming a vital component of the curriculum-planning process. What are some possible criteria that Principal Powers can use to select other community members who are similar to Mr. Smith and who can lend their expertise to his school?

Key Issues or Questions

1. In planning curricula, most administrators agree that determining the locus of planning is crucial. To what extent should Principal Powers involve community member David Smith?

2. Do you think the decision to involve businessperson David Smith in the curriculum-planning process should have been made by the district superintendent? Why or why not?

3. What are some other strategies that the district superintendent or Principal Powers can use to involve more community members in the curriculum-planning process?

4. Do you think there might have been any resistance from staff or teachers unions in having community members such as David Smith on the curriculum committee? Why or why not?

5. How might a businessperson such as David Smith help in developing a curriculum-planning calendar?

6. What roles might David Smith play in organizing, evaluating, and providing resources for curriculum programs?

WEBLIOGRAPHY

Coalition for Community Schools
www.communityschools.org

Curriculum-Planning Resource for
Administrators and Teachers
www.cie.org.uk/images/134557-implementing-the-curriculum-with-cambridge.pdf

National School Public Relations Association
www.nspra.org

Northwestern University Distributed
Leadership Study
www.sesp.Northwestern.edu/dls

The Parent Institute
www.parentinstitute.com

Quia Online Educational Plans, Activities, and
Web-Based Workbooks and Textbooks
www.quia.com

SEDL
www.sedl.org

REFERENCES

Benjamin, S. (2011). Simple leadership techniques: Rubrics, checklists, and structured collaboration. *Phi Delta Kappan, 92*(8), 25–31.

Bridges, S. (2010). Data use + community building = student success. *Principal, 90*(1), 50–51.

Bryk, A. S. (2010). Organizing schools for improvement. *Phi Delta Kappan, 91*(7), 23–30.

Darden, E. C. (2014). Ethics at school: Let your conscience be your guide. *Phi Delta Kappan, 95*(5), 70–71.

Design Theories and Models. (2014). *ADDIE Model.* Retrieved from http://www.learning-theories.com/addie-model.html

Desimone, L. M. (2013). Reform before NCLB. *Phi Delta Kappan 94*(8), 57–61.

edutopia. (2014, September 29). *What is successful technology integration?* Retrieved from http://www.edutopia.org/technology-integration-guide-description

Gill, J., & Hendee, R. (2010). Leading others into leadership. *Principal, 89*(5), 16–20.1

Goodwin, B. (2013). Research says teacher leadership: No guarantee of success. *Educational Leadership, 71*(2), 78–79.

Goodwin, B., & Miller, K. (2013). Research says: Grit + talent = student success. *Educational Leadership, 71*(1), 74–75.

Guskey, T. R., & Anderman, E. M. (2013–2014). In search of a useful definition of mastery. *Educational Leadership, 71*(4), 19–23.

Hewson, K. (2013). Time shift: Developing teacher teams. *Principal, 92*(3), 14–17.

Holliday, T., & Smith, F. C. (2012). Leading common core implementation. *Principal, 92*(1), 12–15.

Jaquith, A. (2013). Instructional capacity: How to build it right. *Educational Leadership, 71*(2), 56–61.

Johnson, D. (2013). 7 updated rules for securing data. *Educational Leadership, 71*(3), 82–84.

Jukes, I., McCain, T., & Crockett, L. (2010–2011). Education and the role of the educator of the future. *Phi Delta Kappan, 92*(4), 15–21.

Lenskaya, E. (2013). Russia's own Common Core. *Phi Delta Kappan, 95*(2), 76–77.

Levin, B. (2012). Research and practice: Using what we know. *Phi Delta Kappan, 93*(6), 72–73.

Lovely, S. (2010, January). Generations at school: Building an age-friendly workforce. *American Association of School Administrators, 67,* 10–16.

Mirk, P. (2009). Ethics by example. *Principal Leadership, 9*(2).

Noyce, P., Perda, D., & Traver, R. (2000). Creating data-driven schools. *Educational Leadership, 57*(5), 52–57.

Protheroe, N. (2010). School as effective data users. *Principal, 90*(1), 24–28.

Radoslovich, J., Roberts, S., & Plaza, A. (2014), Charter school innovations: A teacher growth model. *Phi Delta Kappan, 95*(5), 40–46.

Routman, R. (2012). Mapping a pathway to schoolwide highly effective teaching. *Phi Delta Kappan, 93*(5), 56–61.

Schlechty, P. C. (2011). The threat of accountabalism. *Educational Leadership, 69*(1), 80–81.

Schneider, J. (2013–2014). Cyber skepticism. *Phi Delta Kappan, 95*(4), 80.

Slater, J. (2010). *Implementing professional learning communities* (Unpublished paper). University of Montana, Division of Educational Leadership, Phyllis J. Washington College of Education and Human Sciences, Missoula.

Tschannen-Moran, M., & Tschannen-Moran, B. (2014). What to do when your school's in a bad mood. *Educational Leadership, 71*(5), 36–41.

Weinbaum E. H., & Supovitz, J. A. (2010). Planning ahead: Make program implementation more predictable. *Phi Delta Kappan, 91*(7), 68–70.

Whitehead, B. M., Boschee, F., & Decker, R. H. (2013). *The principal: Leadership for a global society.* Thousand Oaks, CA: Sage.

Whitehead, B. M., Jensen, D. F. N., & Boschee, F. (2013). *Planning for technology: A guide for school administrators, technology coordinators, and curriculum leaders* (2nd ed.). Thousand Oaks, CA: Corwin Press.

Wiles, J. W., & Bondi, J. C. (2011). *Curriculum development: A guide to practice, eighth Edition.* Upper Saddle River, NJ: Pearson Education.

CHAPTER 6

Improving the Program of Studies

A key to school success is to strengthen and quicken efforts to improve the program of studies and help all students engage deeply in productive learning (Moreno, Luria, & Mojkowski, 2013). This is particularly poignant due to an ever-widening focus on individual state as well as Common Core State Standards (CCSS). With the advent of a standards movement, an increase in governmental regulations continues to remain a key issue for curriculum planners. Interestingly enough, many of the concerns are not with the regulations or standards themselves, especially in that individuals are finding the regulations and standards to be central in defining excellence. In contrast, the primary issue remains on how to best plan, as well as how best to implement, the standards.

With a major focus on standards and benchmarks, it is useful for school leaders to begin implementing a process of systematic change to assess and improve the program of studies offered at one or more levels. This chapter suggests such a process, after reviewing some recent attempts to reconceptualize programs of study. It should be noted here that the chapter focuses on improving an existing program, rather than developing a completely new program, because few educators have the opportunity to develop new programs of study.

Questions addressed in this chapter include the following:

- What basic attempts have been made in the past to reconceptualize programs of study?
- What can current curriculum leaders do best to improve programs of study?
- What is Finland doing in education that the U.S. educators should consider?
- What should be done to close the achievement gap?

Key to Leadership

Effective school leadership provides a critical bridge between most educational-reform initiatives, and having those reforms make a genuine difference for all students.

RECONCEPTUALIZING PROGRAMS OF STUDY

Historically, attempts to reconceptualize curriculum were generally motivated by concerns over **discipline-based curriculum.** This approach focused primarily on standard disciplines as the fields or organizing centers of learning.

In reviewing the literature, one of the by-products of the progressive era was widespread interest in developing a curricular mode that transcended or ignored the traditional discipline-based approach. An example of this change was the **core curriculum movement**, which flourished in the 1940s and still persists as a curricular model for many middle schools. In one widely disseminated model of the core curriculum, a ninth-grade student would have two periods a day of learning experiences related to personal interests, three periods a day of "common learnings" (one continuous course that would help students develop life competencies), and one period of health and physical education (Educational Policies Commission, 1952). The organizing center of the common learnings course was not the disciplines but the needs of youth. That said, some of the basic principles of the core curriculum along with **interdisciplinary courses** still continue to influence current attempts to reconceptualize the curriculum.

Interdisciplinary Courses

Interdisciplinary courses are courses of study that either integrate content from two or more disciplines (such as English and social studies) or ignore the disciplines totally when organizing learning experiences. Integrated approaches often take the form of "humanities" courses that include content from literature, history, art, and music. Such humanities courses can be organized in terms of cultural epochs (the Renaissance), area studies (American Studies), ethnic identity (the Black Experience), or themes (the Utopian Vision). While such courses include material from several disciplines, there is still a strong sense of the disciplines' informing the decisions about content and sequence. At the elementary level, while not concerned with "humanities courses," innovative teachers have always developed interdisciplinary units, such as Our Animal Friends, that draw from such subject areas as language arts, social studies, science, and art.

Courses or units that ignore or transcend the disciplines are almost always thematically structured. Thus, a team of teachers might develop a course called The Nature of Conflict, which would embody concepts from literature, biology, anthropology, philosophy, and psychology. The planning focuses on key concepts and skills, with no regard for their disciplinary sources. Alternatively, an elementary team might cooperatively develop an integrated unit called Families First, which would integrate content from social studies, reading, and language arts. In reality, interdisciplinary courses usually begin when one or two people get a good idea and then seek the appropriate ways and means to carry it out.

Interdisciplinary courses of both types can be offered either as a substitute for the standard required courses ("take U.S. Studies instead of junior English and U.S. history") or as enrichment electives ("take our new humanities course in addition to junior English and U.S. history").

The research on interdisciplinary courses has been neither extensive nor deep. However, the few well-designed studies available suggest that such interdisciplinary courses are as effective as the standard courses in teaching basic skills.

Restructured Programs of Study

In exploring the dynamics of the CCSS, schools are beginning to restructure programs of study. Undeniably, as educators begin to translate the standards into practice, they have a new opportunity to think about what is important and new ways to restructure education. According to Conley (2011), a potential sea change is underway in U.S. education. This new focus on standards is designed to improve learning by identifying key knowledge and skills, organizing these elements sequentially and progressively into the knowledge-acquisition process. Likewise, as educators design and implement curriculum aligned to the new standards and assessments, they can focus and organize their programs of instruction toward the goal of preparing more students for college and careers. For example, educators might prepare students for opportunities in international affairs and diplomacy or similar careers that foster a multicultural understanding (Zirkel, 2009–2010). With this new move toward career development and college, digital assessments and mobile learning continue to help lay out a new road map of major ideas, concepts, knowledge, and skills. This futuristic process of reconceptualizing schools and possible career choices through standards and technological innovation is allowing current school leaders to redesign curriculum and instruction in ways that fully engage students at all levels.

IMPROVING THE PROGRAM OF STUDIES

A key to improving programs of studies is to prepare students to live in an increasingly interconnected global society. From this perspective, Ferrero (2011) shared that we need to recognize the three broad purposes of schooling: personal, economic, and civic. At the personal level, schools need to help students discover and cultivate individual interests, talents, and tastes. From a socioeconomic perspective, schools should prepare students to contribute productively to society and allow them to pursue a vocation or further study leading toward some profession. Likewise, schools can achieve civic goals by equipping students with the knowledge and skills necessary to be good citizens. Along this same line, Wiggins (2011) believes students should prepare for adult life by studying subjects that suit their talents, passions, and aspirations.

As part of reimagining education, improving programs of study will therefore require more than simply having good ideas. According to Hatch (2013), educators must focus on developing technical, human, and social capital both inside and outside schools. Similarly, schools must create the conditions for individuals, groups, and organizations to adapt, innovate, and improve all the time. Developing these conditions begins with rethinking what is really required to build capacity for educational improvement and recognizing the social and systemic aspects of learning. Effective education takes more than individual effort. It takes an entire system to enable every child to reach high standards of learning. Thus, through collective effort and a common understanding comes a central building capacity to create significant improvements in programs of studies.

Improving Low-Performing Schools

According to Sandler and Hammond (2013), students do not learn in a vacuum. Nor is high knowledge built on prior knowledge. Research seems to confirm this by noting that connections between new information and what is already experienced plays a central role in learning. With that said, low-performing schools, many with students from low socioeconomic backgrounds and little prior experience, are facing challenges in making school-improvement changes as mandated by both state and federal programs.

University of Montana research professor Conrad W. Snyder (2004) shared early on how this situation is a problem for many schools trying to achieve state and federal student achievement guidelines. Snyder notes how low-performing schools with a large number of nonproficient and novice students continue to face several formidable tasks: to change and improve their curriculum process, streamline their political institutions, and reform their education systems. He further noted that schooling, in these settings, is often dominated by memorization and lecture. Moreover, educators are confronting serious problems such as low salaries, uncomfortable or unsuitable classroom conditions, lack of books, apathetic teachers, and disinterested students. All too often, students only memorize, without having to think and develop knowledge on their own.

Curriculum Tip 6.1	Two major factors for school improvement are cooperation and buy-in of state and local educational agencies and the development of some type of specialized district curriculum planning team.

For any project involving curriculum improvement to succeed, several factors need to be addressed. One is the cooperation of state and local educational agencies. Another is the development of some type of specialized district curriculum team that is dedicated to combining the best of the school's current curriculum with enhancements based on modern approaches to knowledge development, curriculum design, and teacher education. The formation of a **curriculum-development team (CDT)** is an example of how some school districts are helping improve the program of studies.

A model CDT is often made up of about six members who are highly interested in helping schools improve curricular programs. A district administrator and/or building principal selects and leads the team. If the model is to be successful, team members selected must be creative, innovative, contemporary, and visionary. All participants on the team should have prior experience in teaching and in writing instructional materials. School districts can recruit a combination of specialists and educators as well as a member of the community for this important committee.

A major purpose of the CDT is to provide briefings on the status of curriculum within the district. It is best if these briefings and meetings are held with organizations working in the education arena, the state educational agency, teachers, students, and so forth. Members of the CDT can then visit various schools and begin the process of assessing all relevant documents.

An early goal of any curriculum team is to visit selected schools, interview teachers and students, and review materials. This is necessary to conduct preliminary needs assessments. Schools selected for participation in the CDT process should have a means of providing data collection and Internet accessibility. Having access to digitized survey data will be important when noting differences between teaching methods, student involvement, and the like at schools where only traditional teaching methods are utilized. It is best if CDT members are linked via interactive Internet connections to maintain communication throughout the process.

After data have been collected and analyzed by the CDT, the role of the committee is to select specific topics or subtopics for which curriculum materials and accompanying units in the teacher's guide can be developed or enhanced. The CDT, then, has the ability to send different examples of textbooks, supplemental materials, visual aids, curriculum guides, teacher's guides, video media, evaluation forms, and more to individual schools and teachers.

Topics to be covered might include examples of other school curricula, contemporary approaches to knowledge development, new approaches to curriculum design and development, evaluation and assessment, and educational leadership, as well as hands-on training in computers and Internet use and new technologies for classrooms. Interviews with students, teachers, and administrators can be arranged throughout the process. Meetings and interviews with specialists in state agencies and other educational organizations can be organized as well.

The process for developing a draft of curricular materials and a teacher's guide is primarily the responsibility of the committee. CDT members can meet with each selected school's principal and teacher(s) to review new concepts and programs to be introduced. They can also reaffirm the CDT's readiness to provide support throughout the school year and emphasize its need for feedback, and they can reaffirm that CDT members will regularly visit the schools to talk with teachers and sit in on classes to view progress, reaction, interaction, receptivity, and so forth. Information collected and shared with participating schools and individuals is often invaluable. Intensive interactions among all members often lead to strong mentoring relationships and personal ties between the individual administrators and teachers. These ties can be sustained throughout the project and into future years as well, assisted by communications via the Internet.

Common Findings at Low-Performing Schools

As noted by Stein (2012), a study done by the Thomas B. Fordham Institute revealed that barely 1 % of the low-performing schools dramatically improved their academic performance over a five-year period. Likewise, fewer than 10% made even moderate gains. One universal theme emerged from the study—that being, many of the low-performing schools had a complete and utter breakdown in instructional and organizational leadership. The leaders of many of these schools provided no clear direction, teachers and staff were demoralized, and students were apathetic toward learning. The most commonly used form of instruction basically centered on declarative knowledge, facts, and concepts. In essence, a number of these schools generally focused on low student expectations reflecting a culture of failure.

In contrast, ample evidence exists that with visionary leadership, supported by motivated and highly qualified teams of teachers, underperforming schools are very capable of transforming into successful schools. Thus, with new state standards and CCSS, along with excellent curriculum planning and new instructional strategies, low-performing schools can become successful turnaround schools.

Using Pacing Guides

As part of the urgency to help low-performing schools meet state standards and CCSS, a growing number of school leaders and public policy experts are finding that pacing guides might just be "the missing element." With this in mind, the following information is provided by Bonnie Perry (2010), an elementary teacher, who can readily testify to the success of pacing guides in her school.

A pacing guide is a standardized format for long-range planning that groups learning objectives into units, allocates time to each unit, and sequences units on a calendar. Pacing guides provide a plan to teach the relevant curriculum before administering state-mandated assessments.

Pacing guides are known to cover a wide range of curriculum. Basically, they attempt to do the following:

- Address content in a sequential manner.
- Create a "snapshot" of the curriculum needed to be covered.
- Focus on content, skills, and assessments taught by every teacher within grade level.
- Organize information into an easily accessed visual timeline that is easy to use.

One of the most reliable features of pacing guides is that they follow a preset school calendar, and there is a timeline for all teachers to follow. The precision of a timeline is site specific to each district, school, grade level, or even teacher.

An important aspect of the process is that there is no single format for a pacing guide. They may be as simple as a list of topics organized by week or as comprehensive as to include instructional strategies, assessments, materials, and alignment to a set of standards. Thus, individual teachers, departments, and/or teachers across a district might collaborate to design a pacing guide. This makes pacing guides easily accessible to everyone. Nonetheless, pacing guides can vary greatly. In addition, they note how research on new teachers, for example, points to their need for curricular guidance. One study finds that new teachers can benefit from resources such as pacing guides designed to help them figure out what to teach and how to teach it. As a result, the best pacing guides emphasize curriculum guidance instead of prescriptive pacing; these guides focus on central ideas and provide links to exemplary curriculum materials, lessons, and instructional strategies.

Are pacing or instructional guides the answer to 100% student success? Probably not. In fact, if a teacher is required to cover too many concepts by a particular date, there is a possibility of the teacher becoming a "steamroller," moving on and covering material regardless of the performance, or lack thereof, of students. When teachers are forced to continue covering new material, they may feel that they have no time for remediation.

Effective teachers pace instruction to the level of their students. Moreover, they evaluate their success based on the success of their students. The key is for administrators to believe in the teachers, allow them to think, and allow them to teach.

Overall, for a new teacher, the benefits of a pacing guide far outweigh the negative drawbacks perceived by some colleagues and administrators. If the instructional guides can be developed through teacher, administrator, and board collaboration, student needs can be met in a meaningful and comprehensive, yet flexible, guide. There is a catch, however. In some cases, teachers must be given the authority to "stray" from a developed guide in order to meet students' zone of proximal development (ZPD) and relevance (buy-in). This should not be a concern in that good administrators realize building a relationship and understanding students' abilities, desires, and interests will drive instruction. Couple this teacher knowledge with a comprehensive guide to standards-based teaching, and student success will surely follow. As many principals and teachers of underperforming schools can attest, pacing guides do work.

Therefore, to meet high standards and increase student achievement, schools must have accountability that is shared and embraced by colleagues who understand and support one another's work. In the process, colleagues must also share information, opinions, and expertise. Through this collaborative, team-oriented approach, teachers and administrators can partner to regain control of student success and tailored education.

Closing the Achievement Gap

As for closing the achievement gap, there is indisputable evidence that improvements in schooling have a significant effect on student learning (Schmoker, 2012). In attempting to better understand the link between school improvements and technology innovation, the Milken Exchange on Education Technology conducted a meta-analysis of 700 empirical research studies. This findings revealed that students who had access to technology showed positive gains in achievement on researcher constructed tests, standardized tests, and national tests (Whitehead, Jensen, & Boschee, 2013).

Areas with students showing the most improvement in student achievement include the following:

- Technology assisted instruction
- Integrated learning systems technology
- Software that teaches higher order thinking
- Collaborative networked technologies
- Design and programming technologies

Much like the Milken study, research on closing the achievement gap continues to become more prevalent. Future measures of school accountability in all states are likely to rely on longitudinal data systems. As grant money becomes available, such systems will be able to automatically link student and teacher data, measure the growth students make each year, and evaluate which curriculum reforms make a difference in the classroom. By using longitudinal data systems, questions that a state and local school district will be able to answer are as follows:

- Which teachers consistently get the most individual student growth in their classrooms?
- What percentage of students requires remedial courses in college?
- Which education colleges produce the most effective teachers?
- How does student performance in traditional courses compare to those enrolled in online courses? (descriptors by Verges, 2011, p. 10A)

The Statewide Longitudinal Data Systems (SLDS) Grant Program, as authorized by the Educational Technical Assistance Act of 2002, Title II of the statute that created the Institute of Education Sciences (IES), is designed to aid state education agencies in developing and implementing longitudinal data systems. These systems are intended to enhance the ability of States to efficiently and accurately manage, analyze, and use education data, including individual student records. The data systems developed with funds from these grants should help States, districts, schools, and teachers make data-driven decisions to improve student learning, as well as facilitate research to increase student achievement and close achievement gaps. (U.S. Department of Education, Institute of Education Sciences, 2011)

Developing Dynamic Knowledge

Dynamic knowledge refers to metacognitive strategies, cognitive processes, thinking skills, and content-area procedural knowledge. In dynamic knowledge, curricula and teachers no longer serve solely as static knowledge options but assist in the development of a knowledge base that is student centered and enhances effective thinking on the part of the individual learner. Lessons are comprehensively planned and developed, and both the teacher and the materials become key resources in the instructional strategy menu to build the cognitive base for greater student understanding and application.

Curriculum Tip 6.2	A goal of curriculum planning is to increase the knowledge and levels of understanding that students take from the instructional events embedded in learning and instructional materials.

Developing Learner Interaction and Curriculum Integration

Improving school studies involves the interaction of teachers, students, and instructional materials with an integrated knowledge base; an extended understanding of that knowledge in the ability to use the knowledge meaningfully; and the proper development of attitudes, perceptions, and effective habits of cognition that enable complex reasoning and effective applications of that reasoning. How can this happen? Piaget (1977) long ago characterized this as formal operations, especially when students begin to think more abstractly and meta-cognitively, including asking an all-important question: Why must I learn this? "When teachers fail to answer that question satisfactorily, student engagement suffers" (Goodwin, 2014, p. 14). Further, Goodwin cited the following research on student engagement and motivation:

- A long-term study by Gottfried, Fleming, and Gottfried (2001) found that interest in core academic subjects peaks around age 9 and slips downward as children grow older. By the time students reach high school, most are hopelessly bored.
- A national survey of 81,000 students found nearly two thirds (65%) reported feeling bored in class on a daily basis (Yazzie-Mintz, 2010).
- A survey of high school dropouts by Bridgeland, Dilulio, and Morrison (2006) found that 81% said they would have stayed in school had they been able to see the purpose of real-life application of what they were being asked to learn.

After compiling decades of research on student motivation, Goodwin referred to Brophy's finding:

In his synthesis of research on student motivation, Jere Brophy (2004) [reduced] the findings down to a simple formula: *expectancy x value;* that is, for students to commit to learning, they need some expectation they can be successful at it and also be able to see *value* in its outcome. [In essence], when students don't value what they're being asked to learn, they tend to react with frustration and anger, which itself creates cognitive strain and diminishes focus on re-directing mental energies to thinking about how much they resent being coerced into learning something. (p. 14)

Curriculum Tip 6.3	"Before every learning opportunity, teachers ought to spend time helping their students (and themselves) understand not only what students will learn, but why they should learn it" (Goodwin, 2014, p. 14).

These processes are embedded in declarative knowledge but enable the student to extend that base and operate successfully in an increasingly complex world where learning is a lifelong endeavor. The key to effective thinking about problems of history, civics, and government (including law and constitutions) is the development of deep understanding, in terms of both declarative and procedural knowledge.

Educators can help students understand the reasons for learning by helping students to think with their whole brains. Daniel Pink (2005) has popularized the argument that while the 20th century belonged to workers who were paid for applying book-smarts, logic, and analysis to work—all left-brain functions. Automation and global competition have reduced the premium paid for this work and elevated the value of right-brain functions—seeing the big picture, making meaning from piles of data, and thinking creatively.

The goal is not to define intelligence in terms of the apprehension of truths or fact in these areas but to explicate instead the apprehension of truths in terms of intelligence. Under this type of approach, students develop the capacity to find and organize facts and to exploit them in application. Understanding, then, is more than mere knowledge.

Operationalizing Change and Reform

A crucial part of the problem of disengaged students is that classroom curriculum is often disconnected from the real world (Smith & Sobel, 2010). When curriculum questions are operationalized in an effective package, the roles of a teacher, textbook, and other instructional materials are changed from the articulated, comprehensive curriculum framework to an outline of possibilities. Both the teacher and the materials are more of a resource and reference book that lies in the background of the instructional program. Lecturing teachers and printed materials, by their very nature, provide linear presentations, and due to the inherent development limitations—both time and finance—they reflect the sequential perspective of one or a few people (and not that of the student). For this reason, not much is covered in textbooks and other materials that is part of a content area. A successful classroom can add the richness needed to build deeper understanding and encourage effective habits of the mind by including important and uncovered aspects as an intentional part of the instructional strategy.

Developing the Assessment Agenda

The first step is to develop the program of studies assessment agenda. District administrators, school administrators, key faculty members, and parent leaders should meet to discuss these issues:

- How often should program assessment be undertaken?
- Which program-assessment issues should be addressed?
- What levels of schooling should be examined?
- What resources are available?

These questions should be answered, of course, by weighing assessment priorities ("Are we most concerned with our middle school?"), by noting any forthcoming external reviews ("When is the high school scheduled for its next accreditation visit?"), and by reflecting on the importance of program assessment ("How much time and effort should we really be putting into this process?").

One of the key components of the assessment agenda is the set of assessment issues. The five major issues that might be considered are listed briefly here and then discussed at length in the following sections:

1. *Goal–curriculum alignment:* To what extent does the program of studies reflect and respond to the school district's goals?

2. *Curriculum correlation:* To what extent do learning experiences in the various subjects correlate with one another at a given grade level?

3. *Resource allocation:* To what extent does the district's allocation of resources to the program of studies reflect district priorities and provide for equity of opportunity?

4. *Learner needs:* To what extent does the program of studies respond to present and future needs of the students?

5. *Constituent satisfaction:* To what extent are teachers, students, and parents satisfied with the program of studies?

The decisions about the assessment agenda can be formalized in a program-assessment calendar, such as the one shown in Exhibit 6.1.

EXHIBIT 6.1 Program-Assessment Calendar		
Year	*Level*	*Assessment Issues*
2015–2016	Elementary schools	Goal–curriculum alignment; resource allocation; learner needs
2017–2018	Middle schools	Goal–curriculum alignment; resource allocation; constituent satisfaction
2019–2020	High schools	Goal–curriculum alignment; resource allocation; curriculum correlation

Using Standards and Outcome Statements

A challenge for school administrators today is to create an effective balance between bottom-up and top-down change (Jacobson, 2010). Some believe we need to establish a no-excuse attitude for students not achieving the education they deserve. Practically speaking, this approach involves turning content **standards and outcome statements** into a question form and then designing assignments and assessments that evoke possible answers. Only by framing our teaching around valued questions and worthy performances can we overcome activity-based and coverage-oriented instruction and the resulting rote learning that produces formulaic answers and surface-level knowledge. The benefit of a modern curriculum development training model is that it serves as the core of the content coverage for topics while tending to uncover concerns. Reinterpreting textbook and Web-based information within the same instructional objectives will add to instructional effectiveness by taking students into the realm of cognitive understanding. The curriculum materials and teachers guide will help structure learning episodes that include both declarative and procedural knowledge and that enable students to think thoroughly and deeply about enduring and changing schemas. What is learned in the classroom will relate to life and enhance individual students' understanding of their world. Interactive learning and the incorporation of standards, outcome statements, and data-based forms of assessment will give students the ability to think for themselves and generate a better understanding of how what has been learned relates to their lives.

Aligning District Goals and the Curriculum

In the previous chapter, the process of aligning goals with specific fields of study was explained as a critical step in the goal-based planning model. This chapter suggests a slightly different procedure when the focus is on improving a program of studies.

The first step is to identify the school's curriculum goals—those educational goals to which the curriculum is expected to make a major contribution.

Consider this goal, one found in many goal statements: *The student will develop a positive self-image.* In general, the research suggests that self-image is chiefly affected by the expectations of others—such as peers, parents, and teachers—and by the role one chooses for oneself. Because the curriculum makes only a relatively minor contribution, this educational goal probably should not be identified as a curriculum goal.

One useful way of making such a determination is to survey the faculty, using a Web-based application or traditional form such as the one shown in Exhibit 6.2. Following the survey, time should be provided at a faculty meeting for a general discussion of results and issues. Teachers and administrators can meet in small groups for fuller discussions. In general, any educational goal that at least half the faculty believes should be met primarily through the curriculum should be considered a curriculum goal for the school.

The next step is to determine to what extent and in what subjects these curriculum (or educational) goals are being met. The objective here is to develop a matrix that shows in graphic form each goal and the contributions of each subject, grade by grade.

EXHIBIT 6.2   Identification of Curriculum Goals

To the Faculty: Listed here are the educational goals of the school. In your opinion, to which of these educational goals should the school's curriculum make a major contribution? Write the letter *C* after each educational goal to which you think the curriculum should make a major contribution. We should note here that not all these educational goals necessarily have to be curriculum goals. Some goals, for example, might be achieved primarily through the extracurricular program, with the curriculum making only a minor contribution.

1. Develop a positive self-image. _____
2. Value own ethnic identity and accept people of other ethnic groups. _____

Part of such a matrix is shown in Exhibit 6.3 to illustrate the format and content desired here. Curriculum (or educational) goals are listed down the left-hand side. Across the top are the required subjects offered by the school (note that only required subjects are listed; because not all students take electives, the contributions of electives should not be assessed here). Each subject column is further subdivided into grade levels because it is important to analyze grade-level progression. The entries note major curriculum units, which make a major contribution to each goal.

EXHIBIT 6.3 Curriculum (Educational) Goals and Subject Contributions		
	English Language Arts	
Goal	*Grade 4*	*Grade 5*
Think critically and solve problems creatively	Solving personal problems	Solving school problems

If survey is Web-based, data can be easily retrieved and organized. But if using a standard approach, one method is to do a goal analysis of the curriculum guides for all major subjects. A member of the leadership team can go through a guide systematically, entering in the matrix the titles of units that relate to a particular goal and listing any units that do not seem directly related to any of the goals. One drawback to this process is that the matrix reflects only what is in the written guides, not what is actually taught. For that reason, districts may prefer to build the matrix by surveying teachers. The form can be a simple one, with these directions:

Listed here is a sample of our school's curriculum goals. Consider each goal. If you teach a unit of study that relates directly to or makes a major contribution to that goal, enter the title of the unit. Please keep in mind that we are trying to identify only major units of the curriculum that make major contributions; therefore, you should not note any incidental attention you give to this goal.

Because the objective is to get valid data from individual teachers, individuals should probably complete this survey without consultation or discussion with colleagues.

The results collated in the matrix should then be reviewed by the leadership team, keeping these questions in mind:

- *Is each curriculum goal reflected in state standards or CCSS?*
- *Is each curriculum goal adequately addressed in at least one of our required subjects?* This question examines the basic goal–curriculum relationship to ensure that every goal is dealt with in at least one subject.
- *Are complex curriculum goals reinforced appropriately in two or more subjects?* This question is concerned with reinforcement across the curriculum. A complex goal, such as the development of critical thinking, should appear as a focus in several subject areas.

- *Is each goal appropriately developed and reinforced from grade to grade?* This question examines the developmental sequence from grade to grade to be sure that each goal is sufficiently reinforced.
- *Are we avoiding unnecessary duplication and overlap from subject to subject and from grade to grade?* This question focuses on the particular units to be sure that unnecessary duplication is avoided.
- *Does each required subject seem to be making an adequate contribution to the curriculum goals of the school?* This question focuses on a given subject and examines its contributions to all the goals.

The results of the alignment process can lead to several responses. One response is to reconsider the set of curriculum goals making sure they align with state standards and CCSS. If it turns out that a curriculum goal is not adequately treated in at least one of the required subjects, then perhaps that goal might be better assigned to some other aspect of the educational program, such as the activity program. A second response is to add a new required course or sequence of courses specifically designed to address a particular goal. Thus, if it appears that critical thinking is not sufficiently stressed in any of the subjects, a required course could be developed that students would have to take at some point in their program. The third response to a perceived deficiency—and perhaps the most effective— would be to determine with teachers in each department how they could develop new units in their courses that would specifically relate to goals not receiving adequate treatment.

Curriculum Tip 6.4	With fewer, clearer, and higher standards (aligned with state standards and CCSS), correlating curricula can be as easy as aligning the contents of two or more subjects.

Correlating Curricula

Correlating curricula is most essential in schools with a departmentalized structure. An elementary teacher in a self-contained classroom is probably able to achieve whatever correlation is necessary without special intervention. In the same way, a group of teachers working closely together in an interdisciplinary team are probably able, in their own way, to effect the correlation they consider desirable.

Some good reasons exist for a closely correlated curriculum, as long as the integrity of individual disciplines is not violated. Teachers in one subject can call on and develop the skills students have learned in another discipline, without having to take the time to teach those skills themselves. For example, the chemistry teachers know they can expect students to be able to handle quadratic equations. Important skills that transcend a given discipline, such as retrieving and evaluating information, can be reinforced from subject to subject without excessive repetition. The sense of isolation that seems endemic to departmentalized teaching can be reduced as teachers discuss their curricula and develop correlated units of study. Consequently, students begin to see more clearly how their learning is interrelated.

There are some obvious drawbacks, however, to excessive or misdirected correlation. In some cases, misdirected efforts to correlate can impose unduly restrictive constraints on teachers. Consider, for example, the problems in trying to correlate U.S. history and U.S. literature. The period of the American Revolution is vitally important in U.S. history, deserving intensive treatment from a historical perspective, but the literature of that period is considered by most experts to be insignificant as literature and merits only brief consideration. A second drawback is that some attempts to impose correlation can result in a situation in which one subject is perceived as a "service" subject that exists chiefly to serve the needs of other disciplines. English often suffers this fate: "That's the English teacher's job" is the common cry across the disciplines.

For these reasons, a problem-solving approach to correlation is emphasized, where school leaders work with classroom teachers in determining subject by subject how much correlation is needed. The process begins with a survey, using a form such as that shown in Exhibit 6.4. Notice that it first asks about five general sets of skills and concepts that seem to have applicability across the curriculum: library and study skills; reading skills other than basic comprehension; academic writing skills, such as summarizing an article; mathematics skills; and English grammar. The data from this section of the survey can be collated and shared with the faculty to help them determine how to proceed.

EXHIBIT 6.4 Curriculum-Correlation Analysis

Department/Team

Directions: Our school has decided to undertake a study of curriculum correlation to determine what is taught in the various subjects that can be mutually reinforcing. Consider the subject you teach and answer the following questions based on your knowledge of your own subject.

1. What library or study skills do you think your students should have in order to perform more successfully in your subject?

   Grade 10 _____

   Grade 11 _____

   Grade 12 _____

2. What special reading skills (other than comprehension skills) do you think your students should have?

   Grade 10 _____

   Grade 11 _____

   Grade 12 _____

3. What academic writing skills do you think your students should have?

   Grade 10 _____

   Grade 11 _____

   Grade 12 _____

4. What mathematics skills do you think your students should have?

   Grade 10 _____

   Grade 11 _____

   Grade 12 _____

5. What knowledge of English grammar do you think your students should have?

   Grade 10 _____

   Grade 11 _____

   Grade 12 _____

6. List any units of study you presently teach that you think could be correlated profitably with units in other subjects or any new units with a correlated approach that you might be interested in developing.

   Grade 10 _____

   Grade 11 _____

   Grade 12 _____

These data will usually indicate two sorts of problems in correlation. One problem occurs when one or more departments indicate that the curriculum requires the intensive development of one of the basic skills. Suppose, for example, that several departments indicate that their students should know certain basic library skills. There are essentially three options available to administrators. One would be to develop a new course that teaches the required skills; such a new course would serve the needs of all departments. A second option would be to ask one department (in this case, reading/language arts) to assume primary responsibility, with each department then adding its own special content. The third option would be to decide that each department should teach in its own way the library skills its students need. A fuller discussion of these options as they relate to academic writing and critical thinking is presented in Chapter 14.

In some cases, the problem is misalignment of content: The 9th-grade science curriculum requires a mathematics skill that the mathematics curriculum places in 10th grade. In such instances, the two departments should confer to determine which adjustment seems more feasible—to change the science curriculum so the skill is not required until the later grade, or to change the mathematics curriculum so the skill is taught in the earlier grade.

In the same manner, the responses to the last question, dealing with the possibilities of developing correlated units, can be shared with the appropriate departments or teams to see if such units might be cooperatively planned. It might happen, for example, that the mathematics teachers, learning about a unit in logical thinking taught by the English teachers, suggest a correlated unit that would include an analysis of valid and invalid uses of statistics in reasoning.

Thus, correlation is achieved through a problem-solving process of determining need, assessing the options, and making decisions that seem best for the students.

Analyzing Resources Allocated to Curricula

The third process for assessing and improving the program of studies is to analyze the resources allocated to the several curricula. The resource allocation analysis provides data relevant to these related issues:

- *Does the school's allocation of resources reflect its educational priorities?* The assumption here is that the manner in which resources are allocated should reflect the system's priorities.
- *Does the school's allocation of resources seem adequate for achieving the outcomes desired?* If certain important educational outcomes are desired, then those classes will need adequate time, appropriate staffing, and suitable class size.
- *Does the allocation of resources seem to be cost effective?* This question essentially examines the relationship between the number of students served and the resources required to serve them.
- *Is the allocation of resources equitable?* This question is concerned with whether the needs of all students are being met in an equitable fashion. In too many instances, less able students receive less than their share.

The examples shown in Exhibit 6.5 illustrate the types of data that might be analyzed in answering those questions. Obviously, additional data could be included, such as classroom space, instructional costs, noninstructional costs, and overhead and indirect costs. However, that additional information would contribute only some refinements to the basic data presented in Exhibit 6.5 and, therefore, might be omitted without harm to the analysis.

A special note might be made about the importance of analyzing time allocations.

EXHIBIT 6.5 Analysis of Curriculum Resources

Subject	Required or Elective	Enrollment	Number of Sections	Faculty Assigned	Minutes per Week
Art	Elective	250	14	1.0	80
Physical Education	Required	1,500	50	6.0	120
Russian	Elective	36	3	0.6	200

Several studies, both old and new, indicate quite clearly that the time allocated to a particular area of the curriculum is directly related to student achievement in that area. After reviewing the literature and assessing their own extensive experience in curriculum development, the authors of this book concluded that the following allocations would be desirable for the upper three grades of elementary school:

- Language arts: 1.5 hours a day
- Mathematics: 1 hour a day
- Social studies: 2.5 hours a week
- Science: 2.5 hours a week
- Health and physical education: 2.5 hours a week
- Arts: 3.5 hours a week

In many states, of course, minimum time allocations are stated in the school code; where the district has some flexibility, however, allocations should be closely examined.

In examining those data in relationship to the questions noted previously, the leadership team might decide that certain reallocations would strengthen the overall program. Such reallocations might take several forms: increasing or decreasing time allotments, increasing or decreasing section size, or increasing or decreasing the number of teachers assigned.

Curriculum Tip 6.5	In the current world of technology and education, data analysis is a critical component toward improving programs of study.

Importance of Data Analysis in Assessment

School leaders are coming to know the importance of data-driven instruction (Ravitch, 2010). Without a doubt, data collection and analysis continues to provide curriculum leaders with the power to make good decisions, work intelligently, work effectively and efficiently, change in better ways, understand the impact of hard work, help prepare for the future, and know how to make work benefit children. The collection of data can make a major difference in school reform by accomplishing the following tasks:

- Replacing hunches and hypotheses with facts concerning changes that are needed
- Identifying root causes of problems
- Assessing needs to target curriculum services and issues
- Aligning school and district data with state databases
- Providing security policies
- Determining if goals are accomplished

The key is that schools gather data correctly and use the data appropriately. With data mining, data-driven decision making, and big data analysis becoming standard education practices, schools are collecting and digitally storing more and more information, both academic and personal. This requires school leaders to take privacy and security seriously and thus develop good security policies (Johnson, 2013).

Assessing Learner and Cultural Needs

One of the most important aspects of developing curriculum involves the extent to which the curriculum seems to respond to both present and future diversity of the learners. Keeping with this perspective, Bathina (2013) noted that students will only be able to fully use the academic knowledge they gain in school if they have a firm grip on who they are. Thus, assessment of learners and their individual needs must be done carefully and conscientiously. How this is done will obviously vary with the local situation; however, the process explained next is one that should work well in most systems.

School leaders can initiate this process by forming a committee composed of key stakeholders—especially in multicultural as well as economically challenged communities. The primary task of the committee is to develop a tentative draft of present learner needs. As part of their mission, this select committee should rely heavily on research, data analysis, and best practices. The committee can then undertake a systematic examination of current research dealing with various age groups. For each age level—children in elementary schools, preadolescents, early adolescents in middle schools, and youth in high schools—numerous sources synthesize the research on the psychological, physical, social, and intellectual needs of that population. The committee may want to limit itself to a careful study of a smaller number of the best sources (perhaps no more than five or six) rather than attempt a comprehensive survey. Members should also use whatever expert advice they can get from both district personnel (such as school nurses, counselors, social workers, and psychologists) and professionals in the community.

Their draft report might take the form of the one shown in Exhibit 6.6. This document synthesizes the most current and reliable information about middle school learners and can be shared with faculty as part of a digital or standard format. Observe that it first states the need and then suggests a curricular response.

The committee's next major task is to identify future needs of the learners. Here, the intent is not to play the role of futurist and attempt to develop elaborate scenarios; instead, the goal is to identify rather predictable features of the next 20 years that might influence the kind of education provided for today's students (for example, global and socioeconomic implications). By identifying learner needs, linking state standards and CCSS and projecting possible outcomes, educators can best move instruction toward productive pathways.

Improving the Program of Studies

To improve schools is to improve curriculum through commitment and a compelling vision (Gonzalez, 2013). With a strong vision and comprehensive curriculum, as well as a fair assessment and evaluation program in place, teachers will be able to teach the curriculum as planned. Furthermore, a draft report on present and future needs, shown in Exhibit 6.7, should be analyzed and discussed by the faculty, meeting in small groups. Out of these discussions should emerge a final draft reflecting faculty consensus. This process results

EXHIBIT 6.6 Adolescent Needs and Curricular Responses	
The research suggests that young adolescents have these needs:	*The program of studies for young adolescents should provide the following to meet their needs:*
1. Understanding the physical changes occurring and the special nutritional needs that result	1. Health education units and science units emphasizing that these physical changes are normal and stressing the importance of good nutrition
2. Developing greater physical coordination in a nonthreatening environment	2. Physical education experiences that build coordination without overemphasizing competition
3. Increasing level of cognitive development, moving from semiformal to formal operations	3. Units in all appropriate subjects that include a mix of concrete and abstract learnings
4. Becoming more sophisticated in their political reasoning	4. Units in social studies that help students examine complexities of current political issues
5. Increasing level of moral development	5. Units in social studies, science, and English that help students examine complex moral issues
6. Developing clear sense of personal identity	6. Units in English that explore issues of personal identity and self-awareness
7. Maintaining balance between growing sense of autonomy and continuing need for peer approval	7. Units in social studies that explore the nature of peer influence from a sociological perspective

in a final document that can then be used in assessing the programs of study. Not only will the faculty have produced a highly useful document but teachers will also have had an opportunity to analyze and discuss some critical social or multicultural issues.

How can this document be used in assessing the program of studies? Two processes might be considered. The first is a mapping of what may be called the "needs-responsive curriculum"—those aspects of the curriculum that specifically respond to the needs that have been identified. A form (digital or standard) similar to the one shown in Exhibit 6.8 can be distributed to departments or teams of teachers, who can then meet in small groups (or videoconference) to discuss the questions. As a follow-up, the leadership team can review the results to determine areas of strength and weakness.

It might be useful here to distinguish between the goal-curriculum alignment process and the mapping of the needs-responsive curriculum. Goals are usually general statements that apply to all levels of schooling and are ordinarily produced at a local level. The goal-curriculum alignment process attempts to align larger curriculum entities, such as units of study, with these general outcomes. The statement of needs is produced at the school level and focuses on the more specific needs of a given age level, and the mapping process seeks detailed evidence of how a given curriculum responds to those needs. Because the alignment

EXHIBIT 6.7 The Future and the Curriculum

The experts predict that the future will be marked by the following developments:	*The curriculum should respond to future developments by offering the following:*
1. The world becomes an "interconnected global society."	1. Units in social studies and English that increase students' awareness of global connections; foreign language study made available to all students
2. New immigrant groups continue to arrive in this country in large numbers.	2. Units in English and social studies that emphasize multicultural themes
3. The information age arrives: a glut of information made available by technology innovations.	3. Units in all appropriate subjects on information retrieval, evaluation, and application
4. Mobile devices become increasingly dominant as a medium of communication and entertainment.	4. Units in English that emphasize critical viewing
5. The family continues to change: more family instability, more one-parent families.	5. Units in social studies that put such changes in perspective
6. The technology continues to change, with frequent global socioeconomic implications	6. Units in English and social studies that emphasize career-mobility skills, rather than examining particular careers

EXHIBIT 6.8 The Needs-Responsive Curriculum

Directions: The following curriculum characteristics have been suggested by our analysis of our students' present and future needs. Consider each characteristic. If you feel that the curriculum in your subject in some way reflects that characteristic, then indicate specifically how it does.

Department: English language arts (ELA)

A needs-responsive curriculum should have this characteristic:	*Our curriculum reflects these characteristics with the following guideline:*
1. Helps students develop a global perspective	1. Students read some contemporary literature written by European and Asian writers.

and mapping processes are somewhat similar in approach, however, it might be desirable to use only one, not both, during a given assessment project.

The other process for assessing the needs-responsive curriculum takes an entirely different approach. Each homeroom or adviser or room teacher is asked to identify a select number of students from that homeroom and conduct an in-depth interview with them to ascertain the students' perceptions of how well the program of studies responds to the needs identified. If the homeroom group is heterogeneous in abilities, the teacher should choose at least one student from each ability level.

Each teacher then should be asked to prepare a written summary of results of the interviews. Time also should be provided for small groups of homeroom advisers to meet to discuss their findings. The written summaries should be reviewed by the leadership team to identify specific ways in which the program of studies does not seem sufficiently responsive to learner needs.

Both of these processes will have identified certain needs-based deficiencies in the existing program of studies. The leadership team can then decide how to respond to those deficiencies. One response, obviously, is to determine that a particular need should not be addressed in the curriculum. Upon further reflection, the leaders might determine that a particular need can better be satisfied through some other educational means or through some other agency. The more likely response is to suggest to appropriate teams or departments that they spend more time deciding how they could make the curricula more responsive. Thus, if it is apparent that none of the school's courses is concerned with, for example, the need to develop a global socioeconomic perspective, several departments might be asked to examine how their curricula might be suitably modified. Other faculty and stakeholders can be involved as well.

Curriculum Tip 6.6	Curriculum leadership teams should be aware that instructional knowledge, not content knowledge, is a more frequent cause of instructional ineffectiveness.

Assessing Constituent Satisfaction

Because schools do not operate in isolation, a final assessment process might involve measuring constituent satisfaction; the term *constituent* is used here as an umbrella term that includes students, teachers, and parents as constituents whom the curriculum serves. This is especially important in multicultural settings and economically challenged communities. Clearly, this is not to suggest that all groups need to be surveyed, especially at the elementary level. With this in mind, curriculum leaders might decide to survey all teachers, a stratified sample of 20% of the students, and all parents. Although no example of a survey (digital or standard format) is provided here, any sampling should focus on the entire program of studies, not on individual subjects or just the instructional processes. It should be emphasized that constituent satisfaction is only one standard by which a program of studies should be assessed. The leadership team and the faculty should use one or more of the measures discussed above to supplement this particular analysis.

The goal, then, for improving programs of studies is primarily framed around meeting state standards and CCSS by increasing the quality of individual instruction for students. Taken together, the five assessment processes—developing the assessment agenda, aligning district goals and the curriculum, analyzing resources allocated to curricula, assessing learner needs, and assessing constituent satisfaction—can yield some highly useful data that the leadership team and the faculty can use in improving the program of studies.

PROFESSIONAL DEVELOPMENT PROTOCOLS

A key to improving programs of studies is the development of quality professional development protocols. Teachers often have preferences and interests that need to be addressed if schools are considering improvement and reform. This is especially true for those teachers wanting change. Research in the field focuses on seven professional development protocols that have proven to enhance curriculum implementation. According to Fogarty and Pete (2009–2010), these protocols are as follows:

1. *Sustained professional learning.* Teachers are self-directed learners. They need options and support to develop best practices.

2. *Job-embedded professional learning.* When support is visible, available and accessible all day, every day, the rate of success for implementing new initiatives increases phenomenally.

3. *Collegial professional learning.* Teachers want to work with colleagues. This preference calls for collaboration among peers.

4. *Interactive professional learning.* Teachers desire hands-on active, engaged, interactive learning.

5. *Integrative professional learning.* Teachers want face-to-face, Internet, Web-based, collegial kinds of learning opportunities.

6. *Practical professional learning.* Teachers are pragmatic learners. They want to know what will help them succeed.

7. *Results-oriented professional learning.* Teachers are goal-oriented. It is best if there are measurable results to maintain and sustain interest and commitment.

The seven protocols of professional development noted previously can be used as a checklist by school leaders planning to improve curriculum studies. Moreover, these protocols are particularly helpful when developing professional learning communities (PLCs).

Designer

A school leader as designer needs to understand the creative process of transforming a plan or vision into reality. Making change possible, and making it work, may be the best way to describe a school leader's role as designer. The skills necessary for school leaders to become designers are as follows:

- Have a workable familiarity with bureaucratic processes.
- Know how to translate a vision or idea into a policy.
- Be able to reconceptualize how to improve programs of studies (how they will look).
- Understand the persuasive strategies necessary to bring multicultural groups together in the process of change.

DEVELOPING CULTURAL LEADERSHIP

The dynamics and logistics of most schools are such that building-level leaders have an enormous impact on the multicultural environment in which they participate. The traditional view of the lone principal as an authoritarian decision maker is becoming obsolete. The principal and teacher–leaders of the 21st century now work as a team—and as such, they sometimes make unpopular and difficult decisions. But, that said, they can, and often do, make these decisions as part of a *collaborative process*.

Curriculum Tip 6.7	Culture building requires school leaders to give attention to informal, subtle, and multicultural aspects of school life. These social and cultural aspects of school tend to shape the beliefs and actions of each employee and each student.

From a historical perspective, Senge (1990) identified future generations of (school) leaders as having a threefold model for their rethinking of their role. These three roles are applicable today and now see school leaders as designers, teachers, and stewards. Senge is quick to acknowledge that these changes are still difficult to process. Future change still requires recognition of power relationships between the principal and other aspiring leaders within any school. It also requires the attention of school leaders as to current roles in the decision-making process. That said, 21st-century principals must be willing to relinquish some authority and control over the administrative and creative processes if change is truly to occur. Senge has given us some ideas for reflection on this topic with his threefold mode.

Leading Cultural Change

Becoming effective cultural leaders will require individuals to pay attention to language, both verbal and nonverbal. This process includes framing the boundaries of discussion and remembering a shared sense of values in the negotiation process. At the same time, school leaders need to have skills and ability to recognize implicit elements as they pertain to the discussion (such as administrative processes, historical contexts, traditional practices, or cultural and gender differences). Most importantly, effective school leaders will have an ability to make all participants aware of acceptable guidelines used to direct such dialogues.

By establishing clear boundaries, cultural leaders allow participants to reach agreement that reflects the core values of the school, district, and a diverse community. In this way, faculty, staff, and members of a multicultural community feel a sense of empowerment and take ownership of goals they help define.

Cultural Steward

For 21st-century schools, cultural leadership will become a defining moment. A cultural leader, as a steward, operates on two levels: stewardship for the people they lead and stewardship for the larger purpose or mission that underlies the building or district. Both are important and both are critical to success. The key lies in understanding that these two elements always work together: first, stewardship for individuals by recognizing the impact of decisions on diverse members of a school's social culture; second, an understanding of the larger mission or purpose of the school. In this regard, participants sense when leaders (principals and teacher–leaders) lose focus, interest, or direction. True cultural leaders, then, are responsible for the aims implicit in the values and policies of the district as well as for individuals within a district. Stewardship makes the enactment of this mission an act of both compassion and commitment as part of a larger multicultural community.

| **Curriculum Tip 6.8** | Changing school culture into a healthy culture inspires learning at all levels. |

BUILDING 21st-CENTURY TECHNOLOGY CULTURE

The wise use of technology engages students in rigorous and meaningful learning (Tucker, 2014). Beyond the reality of having the actual technological devices and systems in public schools, educational leaders should be aware of a new educational culture and responsibility that come with 21st-century learning and schools. As has been discussed, one of the core realities associated with 21st-century learning is that technology is interwoven into the educational experience and that there is a close relationship among technology, pedagogy, and the content. Consequently, if school principals and teacher leaders get too focused on the "tools" of technology, they will be missing out on the essence of 21st-century learning and how to improve programs of study. In this new educational paradigm, educators are helping their students with developing essential competencies, dispositions, and literacies that will enable students to navigate an increasingly technological and changing world. Through further consideration, we come to realize that we should not be basing our school infrastructure around a specific piece of technology but should instead be future-proofing our schools. This means that the actual infrastructure of the school is adaptable to changing devices and concepts of teaching, learning, and processing information. So, too, is the reality with students and technology. Twenty-first-century learning is about helping young learners be adaptable and literate in the cultural, societal, and technological aspects of their world. It is not about the device itself but more about the ability to be responsive, responsible, and innovative in technological use no matter the device. This is the culture of technology, and school principals and teacher–leaders have an integral responsibility in its creation. The reality for schools that are integrating technology into school practices and educational activities is that the process is going to impact administrators, teachers, students, and families in both positive and negative ways. There is going to be excitement over the educational opportunities and the potential for real learning change. There is also going to be frustration over just how to incorporate technology into daily learning and how technology is actually going to be used in the classroom. It is one thing to have the vision for one-to-one learning, and it is another thing to plan it and do it. Educators need to embrace the opportunities and try to be creative in working through the frustrations because the educational reality is that

21st-century learning is really not a choice. It is educational reform that needs to happen (Whitehead, Boschee, & Decker, 2013).

GLOBAL CONNECTIONS

At the turn of the 21st century, there has been a movement for educational reform (improving the program of studies) with numerous research studies and articles looking at different educational systems worldwide. Resulting out of this movement were several interesting reports and articles. A McKinsey report titled "How the World's Most Improved School Systems Keep Getting Better" (Mourshed, Chijioke, & Barber, 2010) and articles by Ravitch (2012), Abrams (2012), and Goodwin (2012) have identified issues and concerns that school leaders need to consider as they prepare for a global educational experience for students.

So the nagging question becomes this: What can curriculum leaders learn from Finland's magical turnaround? Perhaps an answer to this question lies with the disappointing results born out of the No Child Left Behind Act (NCLB), the Elementary and Secondary Education Act (ESEA), and Race to the Top (CCSS was not emphasized). It should be noted that each of the previous governmental mandates posed a heavy focus on improving test scores in certain subjects but at the expense of other subject areas. The unfortunate by-product of these regulations has been the deprecation of principals, teachers, and the creation of lifeless classrooms (Goodwin, 2012). Moreover, the ever-present spotlight continues to fall on failing schools.

McKinsey's report (Mourshed et al., 2010) found the top performing educational systems worldwide indicated that the success of their system was the training of their teachers in applying the best practices as well as training principals to create them. Rigorous management and leadership training programs were available for both teachers and principals. Top performing school systems *worldwide* recognized that the only way to improve outcomes is to improve instruction. The report concluded that lessons learned were as follows:

- The quality of an education system cannot exceed the quality of its teachers.
- The only way to improve outcomes is to improve instruction.
- High performance requires every child to succeed.
- Every school needs a great leader.

Teacher quality is the most important lever for improving student outcomes. The underlying conclusion basically states that it is easy to create a few good schools, but the real challenge is to create a system that can deliver the same quality to all children.

Finland's Model

Abrams (2012) addressed his research of looking at the *Finnish Educational System* that is being viewed around the world as a leader in educational systemic reform. Finland has implemented a very different model of educational reform than many of the more industrialized countries, including the United States. The Finnish model is based on balanced curriculum and professionalism and *not* on testing. In Finland, elementary students receive 75 minutes a day in recess time compared to an average of 27 minutes in the United States. The Finnish curriculum also mandates a great deal of arts and crafts with more learning by doing. The reform movement in Finland has also established rigorous standards for teacher certification with higher pay and attractive working conditions.

The result of a 2009 Program for International Student Assessment (PISA), an exam in reading, math, and science given every three years to 15-year-olds per nation around the world, revealed that for the fourth consecutive time, Finnish students posted some of the highest scores. The United States meanwhile lagged in the middle of the pack.

In *50 Myths and Lies That Threaten America's Public Schools: The Real Crisis in Education*, Berliner, Glass, and Associates (2014) indicate that a high rate of poverty negatively impacts the national average test score. "Comparatively, Finland boasts the best education system in the world . . ., but has a child poverty rate of less than 5%" (p. 15). In the United States, however, "if we looked only at the students who attend schools where poverty rates are under 10%, we would rank as the number one country in the world, outscoring countries like Finland, Japan, and [South] Korea" (p. 15).

Ravitch (2012), in a Horace Mann League article titled "Schools We Can Envy," discussed in part the history of U.S. school reform and then identified Finland as a nation who is doing things right and for the following four good reasons:

1. Finland has the highest performing school system in the world as measured by the PISA examination. Ravitch stated that "unlike our domestic tests, there are no consequences attached to the tests administered by the PISA. No individual or school learns its score. No one is rewarded or punished because of these tests. No one can prepare for them, nor is there any incentive to cheat" (p. 3).

2. Finland's reform efforts and philosophy are very different from those of the United States. Ravitch stated, "It rejects all of the 'reforms' currently popular in the United States, such as testing, charter schools, vouchers, merit pay, competition, and evaluating teachers in relation to the test scores of their students" (p. 3).

3. Finnish schools have the least variation in quality, meaning that they come closest to achieving equality of educational opportunity—a U.S. educational goal as well.

4. The fourth and final reason identified by Ravitch stated that Finland borrowed many values from the United States, such as equality of educational opportunity, individualized instruction, portfolio assessment, and cooperative learning. Most of this is derived from the work of John Dewey.

Finally, to stress another significant difference between Finland's reform movement and that of the United States' is that Finland's students do not take any standardized tests until the end of high school (Abrams, 2012; Mourshed et al., 2010; Ravitch, 2012). Finland students do take tests; however, these tests are developed by their own teachers, not by national or multinational testing corporations. A major emphasis of the Finnish comprehensive school is where children are encouraged to know, to create, and to develop and sustain natural curiosity and not to be nationally tested, even periodically.

The McKinsey report (Mourshed et al., 2010) identified eight significant factors. They include the following:

1. A system can make significant gains from wherever it starts—student outcomes in a large number of systems have either stagnated or regressed over the last ten years. A sampling of systems show that substantial improvement can be achieved relatively quickly.

2. There is too little focus on "process" in the debate today. Improving systems generally spend more of their activity on improving how instruction is delivered than on changing the content of what is delivered.

3. Each particular stage of the school system improvement journey is associated with a unique set of interventions. The research suggests that all improving systems implemented similar sets of interventions to move from one particular performance level to the next, irrespective of culture, geography, politics, or history. The research also showed that systems cannot continue to improve by simply doing more of what brought them past success.

4. A system's context might not determine what needs to be done, but it does determine how it is done. There is little or no evidence of a "one-size-fits-all" approach to reform implementation. The research suggests that one of the most important implementation decisions is the emphasis a system places on mandating versus persuading stakeholders to comply with reform.

5. Six interventions occur equally at every performance stage for all systems. The research suggests that all interventions are common to all performance stages across the entire improvement journey. The interventions are as follows:

    o Building the instructional skills of teachers and management skills of principals
    o Assessing students
    o Improving data systems
    o Facilitating improvement through the introduction of policy documents and educational laws
    o Revising standards and curriculum
    o Ensuring an appropriate reward and remuneration structure for teachers and principals

6. Systems further along the journey sustain improvement by balancing school autonomy with consistent teaching practice. Collaborative practice becomes the main mechanism both for improving teaching practice and for making teachers accountable to each other.

7. Leaders take advantage of changed circumstances to ignite reforms. All systems studied identified one or more of three circumstances that produced the conditions that triggered significant reform:

- ○ Socioeconomic crisis
- ○ High-profile critical report of system performance
- ○ A change in leadership

8. The most common event to spark the drive to reform is a change in leadership. It was reported that every system studied relied upon the presence and energy of a new leader, either political or strategic, to jumpstart the reform. Critically being new in and of itself is insufficient for success. Successful leaders tend to have a vision and plan upon entering their position as a foundation for their improvement journey.

9. Leadership continuity is essential. Leadership is essential not only in sparking reform but in sustaining it. Two things stand out about the leaders of improving systems. First is their longevity: the median tenure of the new strategic leader is six years and that of the new political leader is seven years. Second, improving systems actively cultivate the next generation of system leaders, ensuring a smooth transition of leadership and the longer-term continuity in reform goals. The stability of reform direction is critical to achieving the quick gains in student outcomes (Mourshed et al., 2010).

As educational preparation programs prepare tomorrow's leaders in the area of improving a program of studies, there is a need to reflect on current research on global educational systems that continue to perform at high levels. The most current research indicates that there is no one best way to reform schools, but there is a relation to the tenure of school leaders both at the building and district levels. Therefore, successful educational leaders for the 21st century need to have a vision and plan to collaboratively implement any new programs of study in the future.

SUMMARY

Educational leaders periodically need to implement a systematic process to assess and improve each program of studies. The process usually involves improving an existing program rather than investing in developing new programs of study. Value is gained from examining past attempts to reconceptualize programs of study. Curriculum leaders can improve existing programs of study by developing an assessment agenda, aligning district goals and the curriculum, correlating curricula, analyzing resources allocated to curricula, and assessing constituent satisfaction.

APPLICATIONS

1. Compare a process from this chapter with a process recommended by one of the accrediting bodies. What do you perceive to be the advantages and disadvantages of each? List at least two advantages and two disadvantages. What local factors might affect the one you would recommend to a school district?

2. Some educators believe students will be unmotivated toward organized school because of advancements in technology. Is this a future problem? Why or why not?

3. There is a concern that schools are leaving out the involvement of student ideas as well as how, what, and when they learn. List and discuss at least three operational steps that you would take as a curriculum leader to ensure this does not happen.

4. Try your hand at reconceptualizing the curriculum. Choose a level of schooling you know best (elementary, middle, high). Identify the way you would organize learning (using some of the disciplines, if you wish), and indicate what percentage of time would be devoted to each broad field.

5. What is your reaction to using longitudinal data systems for measuring teacher effectiveness and student growth?

6. Develop a detailed program-assessment calendar for a school you know. Include the following: the program-assessment issues to be analyzed, the individuals primarily responsible, and the dates by which the final assessments should be made.

7. As you look at the future and the curriculum, what developments would you add to the items in Exhibit 6.7, and how should the curriculum respond?

8. Researchers argue that a more equitable ranking of international test performance could be achieved by comparing average test scores for all students attending public schools with poverty rates that are less than 10%. Do you agree or disagree? Explain your position.

CASE STUDY   Data Before Concepts

As part of a mentoring workshop, Craig Barrows, an experienced Vermont administrator, visits with a group of novice principals about instructional leadership and importance of focusing on data before concepts. One of the participants, Barbara Holloman, raises her hand and shares that her professors advised her to focus on the big ideas first before mapping out curriculum. Her professors used the analogy of laying down big rocks before paving a road.

Barrows listens politely and then speaks to the group in general. "I fully understand the analogy of 'The Big Rock Theory,'" he says reassuringly. The veteran principal then adds, "Having worked in road construction in the past, I found it essential to focus not only on placing big rocks when building a new road but to also focus on data and terrain. For example, the type of big rocks needed . . . can and do vary when building a road in a swamp as opposed to building a road on the side of a hill. Thus, I learned from my engineering friends that analyzing data can be very important whether building roads or building educational curriculum." The group leans forward—curious as to how all this applies to curriculum.

Principal Barrows continues, "Just like road building, we as school administrators need to focus on data before committing to large ideas—i.e., big rocks. This parallel has always helped me when mapping out curriculum, scheduling, or adding new courses."

The room becomes quiet. Many of the novice principals begin pondering the whole notion of putting data before concepts—especially when improving educational programs of study. For the first time, these new leaders are realizing that "big rocks" and "big ideas" may be important—but equally important are the data behind them.

The Challenge

Focusing on data before concepts can be a crucial component of improving school curriculum. Consider this process, and explain why it is important to analyze data before applying concepts.

Key Issues or Questions

1. Judging from your own experience, how do you feel about the importance of focusing on data before concepts?

2. Restructuring curriculum may involve a great deal of resistance. What types of problems might new principals experience when applying concepts and big ideas before actually analyzing data?

3. What are some innovative ways curriculum leaders can use technology to acquire data?

4. How do you feel about data analysis? How might you, as an administrator, use data before applying concepts when planning curriculum?

WEBLIOGRAPHY

Annenberg Learner: Free Video Course and Workshops for Teachers
www.learner.org

Educational Research Services
http://bearcats.dadeville.k12.mo.us/school-board-policy/instructional-services

Statewide Longitudinal Data Systems (SLDS) Grant Program
http://nces.ed.gov/programs/slds/stateinfo.asp

Teachers.net: Teaching Strategies and Lesson Plans
www.teachers.net

Trilemma Solutions Education Consulting: Information on Teacher Improvement
www.trilemmasolutions.com

REFERENCES

Abrams, S. (2012). *The children must play.* The Horace Mann League. Retrieved from http://horacemann league.blogspot.com/2012/02/children-must-play .html

Bathina, J. (2013). Before setting a course to learn, know thyself. *Phi Delta Kappan, 95*(1), 43–47.

Berliner, D. C., Glass, G. V., & Associates. (2014). *50 myths and lies that threaten America's public schools: The real crisis in education.* New York, NY: Teachers College Press.

Bridgeland, J. M., Dilulio, J. J., & Morrison, K. B. (2006). The silent epidemic: Perspectives of high school dropouts. Retrieved from http://files.eric.ed.gov/fulltext/ED513444.pdf

Brophy, J. (2004). *Motivating students to learn* (2nd ed.). Mahwah, NJ: Lawrence Erlbaum.

Conley, D. T. (2011). Building on the common core. *Educational Leadership, 68*(6), 16–20.

Educational Policies Commission. (1952). *Education for all American youth—A further look.* Washington, DC: National Education Association.

Ferrero, D. J. (2011). The humanities: Why such a hard sell? *Educational Leadership, 68*(6), 22–26.

Fogarty, R., & Pete, B. (2009–2010). Professional learning 101: A syllabus of seven protocols. *Phi Delta Kappan, 91*(4), 32–34.

Gonzalez, R. (2013). Emerging leader builds a high school. *Phi Delta Kappan, 95*(2), 79.

Goodwin, B. (2012). Make standards engaging. *Educational Leadership, 69*(5), 79–81.

Goodwin, B. (2014 Spring). Student engagement starts with asking why. *Changing Schools, 71,* 14–15.

Gottfried, A. E., Fleming, J., & Gottfried, A. W. (2001). Continuity of academic intrinsic motivation from childhood through late adolescence: A longitudinal study. *Journal of Educational Psychology, 93*(1), 3–13.

Hatch, T. (2013). Innovation at the core. *Phi Delta Kappan, 95*(3), 34–38.

Jacobson, D. (2010). Coherent instructional improvement and PLCs: Is it possible to do both? *Phi Delta Kappan, 91*(6), 38–45.

Johnson, D. (2013). 7 updated rules for securing data. *Educational Leadership, 71*(3), 82–84.

Moreno, C., Luria, D., & Mojkowski, C. (2013). The latest twist in spreading innovation. *Phi Delta Kappan, 95*(3), 8–11.

Mourshed, M., Chijioke, C., & Barber, M. (2010). *How the world's most improved school systems keep getting better.* McKinsey & Company. Retrieved from http://mckinseyonsociety.com/how-the-worlds-most-improved-school-systems-keep-getting-better

Perry, B. (2010). *A blueprint for increasing student achievement: Effectiveness of pacing guides* (Unpublished paper). University of Montana, Division of Educational Leadership, Phyllis J. Washington College of Education and Human Sciences, Missoula.

Piaget, J. (1977). In H. E. Gruber & J. J. Voneche (Eds.), *The essential Piaget.* New York, NY: Basic Books.

Pink, D. H. (2005). *A whole new mind: Why right-brained learners will rule the future.* New York, NY: Riverside Books.

Ravitch, D. (2010). Why public schools need democratic governance. *Phi Delta Kappan, 91*(6), 24–27.

Ravitch, D. (2012 February). Schools we can envy. The Horace Mann League. Retrieved from http://horacemannleague.blogspot.com/2012/02/schools-we-can-envy.html

Sandler, S., & Hammond, Z. (2013). Text and truth: Reading, student experience, and the common core. *Phi Delta Kappan, 94*(4), 58–61.

Schmoker, M. (2012). Can schools close the gap? *Phi Delta Kappan, 93*(7), 70–71.

Senge, P. M. (1990). The leader's new work: Building learning organizations. *Sloan Management Review,* (7–23).

Smith, G., & Sobel, D. (2010). Bring it on home. *Educational Leadership, 68*(1), 38–43.

Snyder, C. W. (2004). *Calendar of activities/itinerary narrative* (Unpublished paper). University of Montana International Studies program, Missoula.

Stein, L. (2012). The art of saving a failing school. *Phi Delta Kappan, 93*(5), 51–55.

Tucker, C. (2014). Five musts for mastery. *Educational Leadership, 71*(4), 56–60.

U.S. Department of Education, Institute of Education Sciences. (2011). *Statewide Longitudinal Data Systems Grant Program.* Retrieved from http://nces.ed.gov/programs/slds

Verges, J. (2011, July 3). S.D. will follow data to see gains in schools. *Argus Leader,* pp. 1A, 10A.

Whitehead, B. M., Boschee, F., & Decker, R. H. (2013). *The principal: Leadership for a global society.* Thousand Oaks, CA: Sage.

Whitehead, B. M., Jensen, D. F. N., & Boschee, F. (2013). *Planning for technology: A guide for school administrators, technology coordinators, and curriculum leaders* (2nd ed.). Thousand Oaks, CA: Corwin Press.

Wiggins, G. (2011). A diploma worth having. *Educational Leadership, 68*(6), 28–33.

Yazzie-Mintz, E. (2010). *Charting the path from engagement to achievement: A report on the 2009 high school survey of student engagement.* Bloomington, IN: Center for Evaluation & Education.

Zirkel, P. A. (2009–2010). Multicultural (Mis) understandings. *Phi Delta Kappan, 91*(4), 70–71.

CHAPTER 7

Improving a Field of Study

When a school district decides to improve a field of study, it typically is concerned with strengthening one subject area, such as English language arts (ELA), across several grade levels. Such a decision typically emerges from an awareness of a deficiency: Poor articulation exists between the various levels of schooling, teachers are no longer using existing guides, or the present curriculum has become outdated. As a result, connections have to be made between the present and the evolution of what is possible, and from there, educators have to make their best predictions. Providing professional development for teachers along with encouraging them to make new connections to teaching and learning is the key. This chapter describes a process for making these connections after noting some attempts to reconceptualize fields of study.

Also, it is important to believe that collaboration among students, parents, and teachers assures an innovative, culturally rich learning environment where differences are supported and celebrated (Johnson, 2014). Thus, if we are to improve cultural understanding and narrow the achievement gap, school leaders and teachers must become adept at linking the

Questions addressed in this chapter include the following:

- What basic attempts have been made in the past to reconceptualize fields of study?
- What can current curriculum leaders do best to improve fields of study?

Key to Leadership

School district leaders need and deserve accurate measures that align with individual state standards and CCSS and produce timely results.

present to what is possible in the future, and from there, they can make their best predictions. This effort can be enhanced by developing a deeper understanding as to the implementation of individual state standards or Common Core State Standards (CCSS).

RECONCEPTUALIZING FIELDS OF STUDY

While attempts to reconceptualize programs of study usually are concerned with proposals for minimizing the rigid demarcations between the disciplines, those involving fields of study ordinarily focus on eliminating rigidity often imposed by graded curricula. Therefore, schools must reflect the needs of society and offer coherent curriculum focused on performance across grade levels. Furthermore, it is critical that state and federal efforts to recognize success and remedy failure be based on thoughtful, educationally sound means for identifying schools that are successful (Darling-Hammond, 2010).

Proponents of reconceptualization of programs of study argue that curricula organized by grade level (Grade 10 English, Grade 6 mathematics) militate against individualization and result in "batch processing" that ignores individual differences. They argue for curricula that are not bound to grade levels but instead are mapped for individual progress.

Curriculum mapping is definitely an invaluable tool that can be used to help teachers and students cross imposed grade levels and reach students at their levels of interest. More importantly, it is a means of improving **integrated curriculum.**

The idea of minimizing the importance of grade levels in designing curricula is not new, of course. As early as 1919, Carleton Washburne, working in the Winnetka (Illinois) schools, developed an individualized program that emphasized self-paced progress. The pupils worked as long as they needed on self-instructional and self-correcting materials, progressing to subsequent units on the basis of teacher-administered tests (see Washburne & Marland, 1963, for a fuller discussion).

While several current models for a nongraded curriculum are available, most seem to be varieties of two basic ones: the diagnostic–prescriptive model and the elective model.

Diagnostic–Prescriptive Models

Due to changes emanating from the CCSS, diagnostic data can seem like pieces of a jigsaw puzzle that must be ordered in a way that feels cohesive and then ultimately benefits students (Tucker, 2014). As a result, there has been a greater call for diagnostic–prescriptive models that work and are easy to use.

Diagnostic–prescriptive models of the curriculum begin by structuring the field of study as a series of sequential nongraded levels of learning. These models may or may not use differentiated instruction.

Differentiated instruction is a collection of best practices strategically employed to maximize students' learning at every turn, including giving them the tools to handle anything that is undifferentiated. It requires teachers to do different things for different students, some, or a lot, of the time in order for them to learn when the general classroom approach does not meet student needs. It is not individualized instruction, though that may happen from time to time as warranted. It's whatever works to advance the students. It's highly effective teaching. (Wormeli, 2006, p. 3)

The diagnostic–prescriptive approach, therefore, can be labeled as an approach to instruction of students on an individual basis—with special attention to strengths or weaknesses, followed by teaching prescriptive measures to remediate the weaknesses and develop strengths. Additionally, elementary mathematics might be organized into 18 levels instead of six grades. Each level, in turn, comprises several sequential modules or units. Thus, in Level 3 mathematics, 16 modules might be arranged in a developmental sequence so that Module 2 builds on Module 1 and leads to Module 3. The curriculum can then be conceptualized as a linear series of tightly sequenced learning experiences, ordered without respect to grade level. The student moves through this linear sequence at an individualized pace. The teacher diagnoses the student's present level of achievement, prescribes the appropriate placement ("begin with Module 4, Level 3"), and monitors the student's progress through a series of formative and summative tests.

How effective are the diagnostic–prescriptive models? The answer is difficult to determine because it is almost impossible to sort out the effects of the curricular structure itself from those of the instructional system.

Elective Models

Elective models are quite different in concept from diagnostic–prescriptive models. Whereas developers of diagnostic–prescriptive models conceptualize the curriculum as a linearly ordered sequence, those advocating elective models view the curriculum as a multipath network. It is believed that the more aware teachers become of their capacity to drive change, the more likely it is that deep change will occur (Reason & Reason, 2007). The contrast is illustrated next. The elective curriculum is usually delivered as an array of mini-courses typically lasting 6, 9, 12, or 18 weeks (see Oliver, 1978, for a useful description of the various elective options). Because those mini-courses usually are offered to students from several grade levels, they achieve nongrading in their own way.

Individualized and Elective Systems Contrasted

The content of a given elective course is usually determined by an individual teacher or a team of teachers who draw on their own special interests and perceptions of student interest. Thus, an English department might offer electives with titles such as the following:

The Black Experience

Hispanic Literature

The Dialects of the South

Conflict: Literature of Battle

Examining Social Media With a Critical Eye

Communicating With Mobile Devices

Utopias, Real and Imagined

The historical review of research on the effectiveness of the elective model is even less conclusive than assessing the diagnostic–prescriptive models. Although several writers have blamed the elective program for the "educational crisis" of the early 1980s, no hard evidence supports such a conclusion (see Copperman, 1978, for one such attack). In fact, only a handful of studies have even attempted to assess electives systematically. Hillocks's (1972) study of English electives is one of those few. After reviewing more than 100 such programs, he concluded on a rather optimistic note:

> Given the time to study, plan, and evaluate their work, English teachers, with their newly awakened sense of professional dignity, may manage to revolutionize the teaching of English. . . . For that reason alone, elective programs will have been worth the effort. (p. 123)

While most objective observers tend to agree that electives were often poorly designed, the issue of whether well-designed programs could be as effective as the standard curriculum must still be considered unresolved.

What is the future of diagnostic–prescriptive and elective models? First, the diagnostic–prescriptive model has been enhanced in the past few years, mainly because of the extensive use of technology in the classroom. Technology integration facilitates diagnosis, prescription, and assessment. Therefore, technology-based programs help the teacher modify curriculum for each student's individual needs.

The elective model, however, seems to be a short-lived fad; its openness and lack of structure are considered suspect by those concerned with standards and rigor. Most leaders in the field seem to take for granted that the graded curriculum will persist because it is so deeply entrenched in the ways in which schools are organized, teachers are assigned, students are grouped, and materials are written. However, the process described next for improving the field of study can be applied in a way that will permit nongrading, if local administrators and teachers decide that such an option is desirable.

ROLE OF THE PRINCIPAL IN CURRICULUM IMPROVEMENT

More and more, the principalship is becoming less of an isolated executive activity and more of a flexible leadership endeavor that draws upon the best skills and assets of an entire school leadership team (Markle & VanKoevering, 2013). A key, then, to reforming schools continues to be for principals to keep and maintain a larger picture of the entire process. This follows closely with Educational Leadership Constituent Council (ELCC) Standard #6 that emphasizes that school leaders understand the importance of political, social, economic, legal, and cultural contexts. With this in mind, principals and teacher–leaders have found there is no "one-best-way" to improve instruction. And yet, fostering change is allowing creative school leaders to achieve and garner some ground in educational reform. "Real change" needs to move beyond the principal's office and penetrate the walls of the classroom (Trilling, 2010). Trilling suggested new inquiry- and design-based projects rooted in driving questions and real world problems to be used as keys in unlocking education. He also shared how students need to learn more deeply when applying classroom-acquired knowledge to real-world problems. In addition, students are most successful when they are taught *how* to learn as well as *what* to learn. In addition, Trilling recommended the following critical elements be infused into schools of change:

- Critical thinking and problem solving
- Communications and collaboration
- Creativity and innovation
- Information, media, and technology literacy
- Flexibility and adaptability
- Initiative and self-direction
- Social and cross-cultural interactions
- Leadership and responsibility

As can be seen, highly successful school leaders are acknowledging leadership and responsibility as critical factors in running schools. Principals in the future need to address *how* schools will interface with large global networks where big issues in one part of the world instantaneously affect another part of the world. These same principals will have to assist students in "learning how to learn" as well as how to meet a multitude of new, and never before imagined, careers. Finally, it will be up to these building leaders to assist students in facing new challenges of learning to work in a multitude of international settings.

Meaningful change requires whole-system reform (Fullan, 2009). For principals to evoke this type of transformation, it will take leadership development to be job embedded. Fullan related how school leadership consists of cultivating, developing, and continuously supporting individual leaders in real on-the-job settings. In tackling the challenge of reform, new leadership must focus directly on the organization—that is, its culture, structure, and processes. Subsequently, change is not just adoption and implementation. Real change involves nurturing such improvement strategies as collaboration, actively shared leadership, data-driven decisions, high-quality instruction, teacher commitment, and student effort as well as student engagement. In addition, Fullan believes job-embedded leadership requires the following:

- Recruiting dynamic teachers and leaders
- Creating a theoretically rich and practice-sensitive curriculum linking theory to practice
- Wrapping relevant course work around field-based experiences
- Blending coaching techniques
- Creating cohorts of professionals
- Securing financial support

Concisely, schools do not operate in isolation. Building leadership means building ongoing interactions, trust, as well as confidence across the board. With focused vision, school principals can hopefully provide a transition to high-yielding instruction, distributed leadership, as well as the formation of effective learning networks. Through this collectively responsible process, principals and teacher–leaders will be able to ensure and solidify the idea of 21st-century change.

IMPROVING THE FIELD OF STUDY

Although building-level principals remain technically in charge of their schools, the process described next is teacher centered and relies on teacher input. It is only one of many ways that a field of study might be improved; however, it has been used successfully by several school districts and seems to achieve the results desired without requiring excessive time or money. The phases in the process include the following:

1. Establish project parameters.
2. Orient for mastery.
3. Map the desired curriculum.
4. Refine the map.
5. Develop curriculum materials.
6. Suggest time allocations.
7. Select and develop tests.
8. Select instructional materials.
9. Provide for professional development.

Each of these steps will be explained in detail in the sections following the rationale. Although the ELA curriculum is used for most of the examples, the process has worked equally well with several other fields of study.

Curriculum Tip 7.1	Teacher-centered planning should reflect the formal, perceived, or operational curriculum.

Teacher-Centered Process

According to a study by the Organisation for Economic Co-operation and Development (OECD; 2013–2014), Americans are slipping in comparison to their peers around the world. This study involved 24 countries and focused on literacy, numeracy, and problem solving. Keeping with this perspective, Weisberg, Sexton, Mulhern, and Keeling (2009) noted early on that our national failure to acknowledge and act on differences in teacher effectiveness might be attributed to how our public education system treats teachers as interchangeable parts, not individual professionals, causing schools to ignore both excellence and ineffectiveness. This is called the "widget effect." Clearly, then, a great unfinished task in U.S. education could be to eliminate the widget effect and create conditions to better support teachers as well as teacher creativity. Moore and Berry (2010) claimed that what is needed is a form of "teacherpreneurism" (a form of educational entrepreneurship), which will create pathways for effective teachers to lead in their profession without giving up on teaching.

From a historical perspective, the teacher-centered process has been developed as a solution to a problem and was perhaps first identified by Goodlad (1977). As discussed in Chapter 1, his studies of school curricula indicate that there are, in fact, five different curricula that exist almost as separate entities: the ideal curriculum (in this work termed the *recommended curriculum*), that set of recommendations proposed by the scholars and experts in the field; the formal curriculum (identified in this work as the *written curriculum*), the curriculum embodied in the school district's curriculum guides; the perceived curriculum (in this work called the *taught curriculum*), the curriculum that the teachers believe they are teaching; the operational curriculum, which an observer would observe; and the experiential curriculum (in this work called the *learned curriculum*), the curriculum that students are learning.

Goodlad felt the ideal curriculum rarely influences either the written or the taught curriculum. However, as per the written curriculum, a teacher and an observer may not agree as to what the teacher actually taught, nor might students learn all that a teacher attempts to teach. His conclusions have been supported by several subsequent studies focusing on the teacher as curriculum maker (see, e.g., Cusick, 1983). Those studies present this general picture: Classroom teachers (especially secondary teachers), in making decisions about what to teach, rely primarily on their knowledge of the subject, their teaching experience and their perceptions of their students. Moreover, when teachers agree on the essentials and intervene until they believe students really understand them, both students and the school grow (Leane, 2014).

A process, then, is needed for teachers in the classroom that will at least bring the recommended, the written, and the taught curricula into closer alignment. The recommended curriculum should be followed: What teachers teach should reflect the best current knowledge about that subject, tempered by the realities of the classroom.

The process described next attempts to accomplish these objectives. It begins with the teachers determining what should be taught. It reviews their decisions along with the best current knowledge of state standards and CCSS and benchmarks. Observe that this improvement process, therefore, is not concerned primarily with improving the written materials; it is concerned with the much larger issue of improving teaching and learning in that field throughout the district. When discussing curriculum that is recommended, written, and taught, it is perhaps best to view the process of improving curriculum as a series of steps.

Curriculum Tip 7.2

Curriculum plans are often set up as content matrices, and the lessons or units are described in terms of key content. Piecing together the matrices in such a way that concepts build and overlap through transitions produces the most effective learning.

Developing ways to instill tolerance and the ability to thrive in a series of settings, as well as in ambiguity, can be an important part of the planning process. According to University of Montana research professor Conrad W. Snyder (2004), the first step in determining the development of a desirable curriculum for schools entails identifying and understanding what is enduring and needed, what is important to know, and what would be good to be familiar with (for students to encounter). This information may already exist in the curriculum created by a state educational agency or local school district, but it needs to be checked for comprehensiveness and expansiveness. Four criteria are often used to sort content listings and begin the development of generative questions around which the instructional events of materials can operate.

As an example, to what extent does the idea, topic, or process do the following:

1. Represent a big idea that has enduring value beyond the classroom in everyday life and reality?

2. Reside at the heart of the discipline?

3. Require coverage through other instructional events in the classroom, extending the textbook?

4. Offer potential for engaging students, keeping their attention, and encouraging their interest in the topic?

In the second step, it is important to develop each unit framed around the enduring understandings and essential questions. Once a unit is established, the question is this: What evidence exists to support acceptance of this as an understanding? At this point, the design criteria or filters for the assessments are (a) validity, (b) reliability, (c) sufficiency, (d) authenticity, (e) feasibility, and (f) friendliness. These criteria are instructional events, with the difference that the student produces all the required responses in order to diagnose or check his or her status in the areas of importance. Standard measurement criteria apply, but we make allowances because the effects are only remedial, which probably does not hurt as continuing thoughtful practice. The better the evidence, however, the better the decisions made for instructional strategies. Quality of measurement is an essential feature of quality instruction.

It is here that one should introduce technology to enhance the process, enable continuous connection among the educational colleagues, and allow substantive work to be ongoing and sustainable. The objective is to get administrators and teachers to think about technology from a new perspective. Unfortunately, change is not always easy and incorporating new technology changes can become somewhat challenging. Thus, the importance of professional development directly related to any new technology implementation changes (Tarte, 2014).

In the third step, it is important to attend to research-based teaching strategies to implement an intended curriculum. These strategies are guides to effective approaches. The problem with modern instructional design for school improvement lies in the level of teacher training and practicing expertise. The ideal project requires a teaching cadre that is trained in modern approaches to knowledge development, as well as mandated programs such as Response to Intervention (RTI) and corresponding teaching methods. Teachers do not always know how to use instructional material to provide a rich classroom learning experience; this requires considerable expertise. Therefore, it is important to combine the curriculum in understandable terms—including the more didactic approaches (i.e., improving on the direct instruction methods already in place) along with structured instructions in the newer teaching strategies. At first, teachers may find this restrictive, because every step in the process is standardized and fixed. As inquiry methods are explored, there should be adequate structure to assist classroom teachers. This occurs in the third step: planning of the teaching strategies. In typical curriculum development, the teacher is given only the barest of instructions, and the final enactments are creative products of the teacher, not the designer. In the approach to teacher education under this project, the designer would provide complete strategic scaffolding for teacher enactments. Student instructional materials, whether textbooks, Web-based, or otherwise, will reflect an inquiry approach, but the teacher's guide will spell out the specific instructional events and behaviors. Various teacher's guides developed by current curriculum publishing and software companies should help in providing teachers with some new ideas and strategies that can be used as beginning building blocks.

Preparation of curricular materials and teacher's manuals seeking to combine the best parts of a district's current curriculum with modern approaches will require many steps to complete. Each step needs to be negotiated in terms of progress and effectiveness as the process continues from initial selection of curriculum-development team (CDT) members to review of existing materials and methods to training, preparation of first and final drafts, pilot testing, and evaluation. Each step also constitutes professional development on the part of the team members themselves. The steps we envision are as follows:

1. Study local school district's curriculum. The local school district may have special needs and emphases different from those of other schools, so it is important to be sure that these are given attention and appreciation in the design process.

2. Select certain topics or subtopics in the school's curriculum, and match with both state and federal standards to ascertain areas of coverage and uncoverage.

3. Merge these plans to look for emphases and gaps.

4. Identify text and other printed or Web-based material from a wide range of sources to serve as exemplars of good instructional content and approaches in terms of the selected essential questions.

5. Review content by teachers in consultation with team members. Create collaborative teams to work through development details, using interactive international video and special curriculum links to provide for simultaneous connection to the materials.

6. Enhance materials, and write the text for selected curriculum portions and teacher's manual.

7. Identify educational assessments from a wide range of sources.

8. Study assessments provided by state educational agencies at relevant grade levels that have proven to be effective guides to instruction.

9. Compare and contrast the school's assessment material to other assessment material. Enhance and rewrite using various methods for demonstration and creating an item bank of assessments for reference.

10. Prepare initial drafts of written materials; obtain feedback from other curriculum members, trainers, and mentors; and revise and prepare final draft versions.

11. Select pilot test and assessment sites in the school district (with current classes) to ascertain level of difficulty and usefulness of responses.

12. Check to see that material exists for those areas where deficits are apparent in the current school district instructional program. (Use a small sample evaluation.)

13. Create pictures, illustrations, and video used in the curriculum subtopics. Identify new materials or retain old ones as appropriate. Work again with the collaborative teams.

14. Identify other media resources needed for each topic.

15. Create enhancement and revision materials using multimedia and Web-based materials. Pictures and media will be drawn from many sources of materials and resources.

16. Develop student and teacher assessment instruments for pilot pre- and posttests: Evaluate and incorporate feedback into preparation of final versions; print and distribute school district sample copies of curriculum and teacher's manual as required.

SOURCE: Snyder (2004). Used with permission.

| **Curriculum Tip 7.3** | Assessment alone cannot improve student learning. Defining the scope of a project and setting budget parameters are crucial to the success of curriculum planning. |

Student-Centered Process

More teachers are considering shifting from a teach-centered process to a student-centered one. As noted by Tucker (2013–2014), arranging the furniture in classrooms to foster interactions among students is a starting point. Likewise, weaving technology into methodology to create more opportunities for communication, collaboration, and transparency is also a step to driving deeper learning and engagement.

In student-centered classrooms, technology can create opportunities for students to not only pursue their passions but also help decide how to approach activities and assignments. Some teachers even use a crowd sourcing strategy to collect ideas from students about what they think will make the class successful, what skills they might like to learn, and what topics interest them. Students can post ideas on Web-based programs such as Survey Monkey or use sticky notes on a classroom board.

Transitioning to paperless classroom with Google docs can be incredibly freeing. Students share work with the teacher the day it is assigned, while the teacher provides continual formative feedback at any time. Detailed rubrics anchored in the CCSS using Google forms work well and are efficient. Communication can be made with students via e-mail and feedback using Google spreadsheets and scripts, such as FormEmailer, Flubaroo, and Doctopus. Google form rubrics for essays can easily be read and assessed. Data can be collected on a Google spreadsheet. Each of these applications can play a pivotal role in assessing student performance, providing grades, and keeping parents informed.

Because current education systems largely group students by age, not ability, teachers can benefit from a wide range of technology supports. To be sure, making a shift to student-centered teaching will be challenging for those individuals who prefer a teacher-centered process, but, for those teachers who decide to make the shift, the rewards are there.

Prepare to Teach Culturally Diverse Classrooms

Whether using a teacher-centered process or a student-centered process, educators need to prepare to teach in culturally diverse classrooms. This especially is the case when establishing projects or mapping out a new curriculum. Changing classroom demographics means teachers must understand and work with children from cultures other than their own. Scott (2014) noted that with about 20% of school-age children speaking a language other than English at home, today's teachers must be ready to address the needs of culturally diverse populations. Unfortunately, most current teachers have little intercultural experience, which means that schools have a tremendous gap to fill.

Exposure to different perspectives on learning helps expand teachers' thinking about education and themselves as educators. The benefit is creating a community of students who work together and are comfortable with each other. Working with other cultures and diverse students gives teachers an appreciation for the struggles that immigrant students go through while trying to learn a second language.

Establish Educational Project Parameters

A first task toward educational change is to define the scope and sequence of educational reform projects. In addition to providing for the necessary budget support, administrators need to answer several questions.

What Grade Levels Will Be Included?

The usual answer here is to improve the entire field, from prekindergarten to Grade 12. However, other options might be considered: Improve elementary, and then add middle and high school levels; improve the middle and then add elementary and high; improve the high school and then build backward to middle and elementary. Regardless of which field is to be targeted, there should always be a consideration of cultural and social issues.

What Ability Levels Will Be Included?

According to Tovani (2010), "when students experience success each day, they will take the risks they need to take in order to learn" (p. 28). Thus, if the school district groups by ability levels, then school leaders have to decide whether they will produce a different guide for each level or one basic guide that will then be supplemented with other materials. The mastery-curriculum theory posits a curriculum that can be mastered by most students. It makes more sense to produce one basic mastery guide, which is then supplemented with special materials for more able students.

Who Will Direct the Improvement Project?

Nearly all districts have found that a small task force is most efficient and effective. It should include one district administrator, one or two school administrators, the district supervisor for that field, at least one teacher–leader from each level to be addressed, and one parent representative. The task force should probably be led by one of the district administrators or the district supervisor.

How Much Time Will Be Needed?

Although the answer will vary with the size of the district, the scope of the project, and the resources available, most districts have found that one school year is sufficient for the entire project.

Orient for Mastery

Once the project parameters are set, the process begins with an orientation and buy-in for all teachers who will be affected by the improvement program. However, buy-in or engagement alone doesn't does not necessarily increase the ability of school staffs to make complex change. The kind of learning that induces change, especially with cultural and social considerations, requires ongoing support (Weinbaum & Supovitz, 2010). With this in mind, the project leader should prepare materials summarizing the project and stressing two basic features: First, the improvement program will rely heavily on teacher input, and second, the improvement program will focus on the mastery curriculum only. As explained in Chapter 1, the mastery curriculum is that part of a field of study that meets two criteria: It is considered essential for all students, and it requires careful structuring and organization for optimal learning. District curriculum efforts, then, should primarily focus on the mastery curriculum, while organic curriculum and the enrichment curriculum should be strengthened at the school level.

MAPPING THE DESIRED CURRICULUM

There is little doubt that if change is going to occur, the entire school community—including administrators, teachers, students, parents, and school board and community members—must speak the same language about any changes purposed (McAssey, 2014).

With this said, curriculum mapping is a great tool for planners as per improving communication and understanding. It can also help identify gaps in the curriculum between what is intended and what is actually taught. The best way to map the desired curriculum is to survey the teachers class by class and grade by grade. This should include a focus on both formative and summative assessments to ensure students are mastering objectives. The survey instrument is a crucial element here because the content and structure of the instrument will very much affect the kinds of data elicited. An expert in the field (either someone from the district or an external consultant) should develop a draft of the form by considering several crucial issues (Exhibit 7.1 shows a portion of a form used to map the social studies curriculum in a suburban school district):

- What elements of the mastery curriculum will be mapped? The objective is to elicit only essential information, not to clutter up the process with unnecessary detail. English teachers, for example, might decide that they do not want to get specific data about punctuation or usage items because those matters are extensively covered in most English textbooks.
- What strands will be used for the mapping process? The strands are the elements that make up a given field of study—the divisions of that field. Any given field of study could be analyzed differently in terms of its strands. Some, for example, would argue that ELA comprises only three strands: language, literature, and composition. The objective is to identify strands that make sense to the teachers— to conceptualize the field as they do, not as the experts do.
- How detailed should the mapping data be? Some who use mapping prefer to get very detailed data—long lists of specific objectives. Extensive experience with mapping suggests that more general data at this stage of the process are desirable. The specific objectives can be produced at a later stage of the process.
- Will the survey form include a summary of the recommendations of experts so that teachers can make more informed decisions? One advantage of including such information is that the process of completing the mapping form also serves to educate teachers about recommended practice. A remaining concern is that summaries might influence teachers to recommend content they would probably not really want to include. Someone who knows the teachers well should make this decision.

The final draft of the survey form should be tested with a small group of teachers to be sure that the directions are clear, that the strands seem appropriate, and that the structure of the form will elicit the kinds of information desired.

Teachers should then have an opportunity to complete the survey (online or standard format) during an in-service day or a faculty meeting. They should be notified in advance about the mapping process in case they wish to bring mobile devices, textbooks, lesson plan books, or existing curriculum guides. Should the teachers complete the form together in small teams, or should they work alone? Either approach can be used.

The returns can be digitally collated and displayed on an electronic whiteboard or be noted on a traditional scope and sequence chart. These charts can highlight the strands,

EXHIBIT 7.1   Mapping the Social Studies Curriculum: Skills

Recommendations From the Experts

1. Skill development is an important aspect of social studies goals. A skill is the ability to do something well—"knowing how."

2. Social studies skills are best developed through sequential instruction and practice, from prekindergarten through Grade 12.

3. The social studies curriculum should emphasize the important skills of acquiring information: reading skills, study skills, reference and information-searching skills, and the use of technology in acquiring information.

4. The social studies curriculum should emphasize the skills of organizing and using information: critical thinking and decision-making skills.

5. The social studies curriculum should emphasize the skills needed for effective interpersonal relationships and social participation: personal skills, group skills, and social and political participation skills.

What information-acquiring skills do you think should be taught for mastery at your grade level?

1. _____
2. _____
3. _____

What information-organizing skills do you think should be taught for mastery at your grade level?

1. _____
2. _____
3. _____

What interpersonal and social skills do you think should be taught for mastery at your grade level?

1. _____
2. _____
3. _____

the grade levels, and teachers' responses. Exhibit 7.2 shows a portion of such a chart. Note in this example the scope and sequence chart also shows responses school by school, because such information can help leaders identify special professional development needs.

| **Curriculum Tip 7.4** | As part of the beauty of any professional learning structure, teachers should have an opportunity to critique curriculum revisions. |

EXHIBIT 7.2 Results of the Mapping Process: Grade 7 English

The following chart shows how the English language arts (ELA) teachers in our three middle schools responded in indicating where they believe the parts of speech should be taught for mastery. The tallies indicate the number of teachers so responding for each part of speech.

Grammar: Parts of Speech

North	South	Central
Noun: 2	Noun: 3	Do not wish to teach parts of speech in Grade 7
Verb: 2	Verb: 3	
Adjective: 2	Adjective: 3	
Adverb: 2	Adverb: 3	

Refine the Map

When moving toward implementation, it is important to develop common talking points as well as share experiences and views. With this in mind, the next phase of the process is refining the map—reviewing the first version of the scope and sequence chart and making the necessary modifications. However, before refining the map, a few components need to be in place. First, there needs to be a thoughtful quality assessment of incoming students' strengths and weaknesses. Assessing thoughtfully means keeping a continual focus on each learner's needs (Chappuis, 2014). Using assessment in this manner serves as the baseline for skill development. Second, the instructor needs to appropriate resources to differentiate materials to support students' baseline skills, as well as to challenge individual student abilities. Third, a quality formative assessment (online or standard format) will allow instructors to understand whether improvement is occurring and what needs to be changed. Finally, there needs to be quality summative assessment at the end of the unit to demonstrate each student's skill development. This can serve as a baseline as well. Once these elements are accomplished, the process of refining the map can begin. At this point, the advice of an expert in the field might be needed—unless, of course, any local leaders have a deep and current knowledge of that field. The results should be reviewed with these questions in mind:

- What important skills and concepts have been omitted and should be included? What less-important content has been included that might be dropped to reduce the overall content load? What skills and concepts seem to be misplaced by level and might better be taught at some lower or higher level? Does placement reflect current knowledge about cognitive development?
- Where is there unnecessary duplication and repetition? Should some concepts and skills be taught for mastery at more than one grade level?

- Does each strand show a desirable development from grade to grade? What do the data indicate? Is there good progression in relation to difficulty and complexity?
- Is there good balance from grade to grade? Are some grades overloaded?
- Does the scope and sequence chart respond adequately to state and district mandates concerning student competencies?

During this phase, especially, the influence of the ideal curriculum is paramount.

The results of that critique are then reflected in a revised scope and sequence chart, which should be distributed to all administrators and classroom teachers involved.

Develop Curriculum Materials

Because researchers and practitioners are generating knowledge about what works in education, it is now time to step up collaboration for the good of all students (Dynarski, 2010). As part of the collaboration process, it is important for any curriculum select committee to revise a scope and sequence chart to show grade-level placement of major skills and concepts, strand by strand. Moreover, the select committee needs to resolve this important issue: What curriculum materials are needed to help teachers implement the improved curriculum?

Three likely options are available for the curriculum materials: a curriculum guide, a **curriculum-objectives notebook,** and a **curriculum-scenario book** (*Any of these can be displayed online or in standard format*).

The **standard curriculum guide**, outlined in Chapter 8, is perhaps used most often by districts. Its main components are the specific learning objectives and the activities suggested for each objective. If it is decided that a standard curriculum guide is needed, then a team of teachers should first use the general skills and concepts identified in the scope and sequence chart to develop the specific objectives. Thus, if the scope and sequence chart includes "nouns" as a concept in the grammar strand for Grade 8, then the team might develop this list of objectives:

- Define *noun.*
- Identify nouns in sentences.
- Define *concrete noun* and *abstract noun.*
- Identify concrete and abstract nouns in sentences.
- Use concrete and abstract nouns appropriately in sentences.
- Define *proper noun* and *common noun.*
- Identify proper and common nouns in sentences.
- Use proper nouns in sentences, capitalizing correctly.

That list of specific objectives is developed by analyzing the general skill or concept and determining what specific knowledge would be most appropriate for a given grade level. For each objective or set of objectives, the team would then identify the necessary learning activities.

Basically, the goal of a curriculum guide is to formulate a new model or new knowledge rather than trying to find different grease for an already squeaky wheel. For this reason, the distinguishing feature of any good guide is its comprehensiveness. Moreover, it ordinarily covers every grade level. And it not only details objectives and activities but also contains a statement of the philosophy, suggestions for evaluation, and lists of materials.

The second option is to produce a curriculum-objectives notebook (*online or text*). This notebook contains the following: a summary of the research on how to teach a given subject, a copy of the scope and sequence chart in reduced form, and a list of the objectives for those grade levels taught by the teacher to whom the guide is issued. Thus, a seventh-grade teacher would have a copy of the seventh-grade objectives only. The objectives are developed through the process that was just described.

The distinguishing features of the curriculum-objectives notebook are its simplicity and flexibility. Only the essentials are included for only the relevant grade level. Learning activities are not suggested; it is assumed that teachers can develop their own activities or be trained how to use varied educational activities from professional development programs. An important message is implied by this format: "Achieve these mastery objectives in any reasonable way you wish." The flexibility is of two sorts. First, the loose-leaf format (or data-entry format) makes it easy for teachers to add, delete, and modify. They are encouraged to make the notebook their own: to include their own learning materials, to insert their lesson plans, to add professional articles they find useful. The second type of flexibility results from listing only the objectives. Teachers thus have a great deal of freedom both in how they organize those objectives for teaching and in how they teach. If some teachers wish to teach integrated units, they may; if some wish to focus on discrete skills, they may.

The curriculum-scenario book is the term given here to describe a collection of **learning scenarios.** The team takes each general concept or skill and asks, "What mix of learning activities, learning materials, and learning objectives can result in quality learning experiences?" Thus, the team working on the concept "noun" might produce these scenarios, among others:

- Have students read the section from Helen Keller's autobiography where she first learns that things have names. Introduce the concept of nouns as names. Discuss the importance of naming as an aspect of using language. Discuss as well the danger of reification—of believing that whatever is named is real.
- Have students write noun poems—poems made of lists of very specific nouns. Discuss the importance of specificity. Ask students to think about the usefulness of general nouns. Advanced students may be interested in the "abstraction ladder" of the general semanticists.

Notice that the scenarios emphasize the holistic nature of the learning experience; the objectives are there, but they are implicit and do not dictate what occurs. In addition to the learning scenarios, the scenario book would also include a copy of the scope and sequence chart and a summary of the research.

Which of these three choices is best? The answer depends on the needs of the system and the maturity and competence of the teachers. The curriculum guide probably best serves the needs of a school district in which administrative direction is important. The curriculum-objectives notebook is perhaps best in a district wishing to give mature and competent teachers a great deal of freedom while still emphasizing the importance of the mastery learning objectives. The scenario book perhaps best serves the needs of those districts whose leaders feel they can be more concerned with the quality of the learning experiences and less concerned with the specification of objectives.

Curriculum Tip 7.5	Time allocated to a particular area of the curriculum often relates directly to student achievement in that area.

Suggest Time Allocations

Mastering time management is a key to school success (Jordan [as cited in "Time-Saving Teacher Evaluation Solutions"]). With CCSS and other programs affecting change, the leadership team should suggest time allocations to be used in teaching specific subject areas. This is because time allocation can become a huge factor in teaching.

Time allocations can be set several ways. One method uses several strands as the basis for establishing time allocations at a district level. For example, the curriculum-improvement select committee reviews the recommendations of experts, reflects on district curricular goals, and recommends time allocations for each strand of the curriculum. These recommendations are then made part of the final curriculum report.

A variation of this method relies more on teacher input about time and strands and sets allocations level by level. A district supervisor poses the question to all teachers in the district who teach that subject at a given level of schooling: "As you think about the students in our middle schools, what percentage of time do you think we should allocate to each strand of this curriculum?" The supervisor helps the teachers agree on time allocations that reflect their perceptions and at the same time are responsive to district priorities. Here is how one group of middle school social studies teachers answered the question:

History: 50%

Map and study skills: 20%

Geography: 15%

Civics: 10%

Other: 5%

A third method focuses on unit planning at the school level. At every grade level in each school, teachers are asked to submit at the start of every marking period a unit-planning proposal, indicating for each unit the unit objective, the important concepts and skills emphasized, and the number of instructional periods allocated. The principal reviews these plans and discusses with the teachers any proposals that seem to reflect unwise allocations of time.

A fourth method relies on professional development. Rather than specifying school district guidelines or checking on unit plans—or organizing "sit-n-git" affairs—administrators need seriously to address in-service needs. Keeping this in mind, a member of the leadership team uses professional development sessions to raise issues of time allocation and achievement with teachers, to encourage instructors to discuss openly with one another how they allocate time, and to assist them in making decisions about time.

Obviously, these methods can be used together, because, in effect, they complement one another.

Select and Develop Assessments

Curriculum-based tests, as aligned with individual state or CCSS assessments—for example, the Partnership for Assessment of Readiness for College and Career (PARCC) and the Smarter Balanced Assessment Consortium (SBAC)—are paramount to the process. Moreover, locally developed examinations (Web-based assessments) can be useful as well. If classroom teachers know their students will be tested on specific content, they are more likely to emphasize that content. Because CCSS is intended to be "fewer, higher, and deeper" than previous standards, they have created a natural opening for the development and adoption of better assessments of student learning (Darling-Hammond, 2014). These assessments are helping schools move toward more informative systems that include formative as well as summative elements—evaluating content that reflects instruction and includes some challenging open-ended tasks.

How many curriculum-based tests are needed at each grade level? The answer seems to vary with the district and the level. In many high schools, curriculum-based tests are usually administered as semester and final examinations. The key is balance. It is important to understand that one size does not fit all.

Because tests are so often used as measures of student progress, school success, and even teacher performance, it is essential that they be developed with the utmost care to ensure reliability and validity. Keeping testing and assessment in perspective is crucial. Thus, the advice of measurement specialists should be required, and every form of the tests should be used in pilot studies before the tests are administered throughout the district.

Curriculum Tip 7.6	Web-based assessments can provide quick and accurate measures that can be aligned with state and/or national standards.

Web-Based Testing

Developing valid digital assessments is an important element. To be sure, there is little doubt that school districts need and deserve accurate measures that align with state and CCSS and produce timely results. Districts also need scores that have meaningful references. With this in mind, the Northwest Evaluation Association (NWEA; 2014) provides an array of digital assessments. Aligned with local curriculum, as well as state and CCSS, NWEA assessments provide accurate information about student academic performance. Basically, these Web-based adaptive tests combine the benefit of technology with the integrity of on-level tests in that student assessments draw from a bank of thousands of calibrated test items. Thus, as individual students take the adaptive test, it adjusts to each student's performance. Likewise, the difficulty of each question is based on how well the student has answered the questions up to that point. As the student answers correctly, the questions become more difficult. If the student answers incorrectly, the questions become easier. Each student, in this way, receives a personalized test. Schools using the NWEA Measures of Academic Progress (MAP) system find that it reduces test anxiety and is accurate. Individuals taking the assessment can stop at any point and go to lunch or recess and come back to start where they left off.

When a student completes the adaptive test, the MAP system reports the student's score on the screen, allowing for immediate feedback. A student's score should show growth from year to year and can be correlated longitudinally to scores from previous years. Test administrators can download information about students as well as classes and distribute to teachers or parents as needed. Teachers and administrators can assess individual student information at any time to obtain gains made in certain areas. Curriculum and teaching strategies can be altered, depending on immediate feedback. This type of online adaptive test has proven to be one of the fastest and easiest ways to assess student learning and learner needs.

Select Instructional Materials

Any new or improved curriculum generally requires new instructional materials—many of which are now online. Furthermore, advancement in technology applications will allow us to individualize education in a whole new way in the 21st century. For example, technology allows us to accomplish more in less time and exposes us to information and items that were unimaginable years ago (Walmsley, 2014). Using digital tools that make customized learning possible, a teacher can be better prepared for the ranges that will define his or her classroom in the future.

Keeping with this perspective, and regardless of which tools are used, the select committee should develop guidelines for evaluating materials, pointing out any special features that the improved curriculum might require (e.g., "All language arts texts, as well as online resources, must give special attention to the composing process"). The group can then use these guidelines in reviewing and selecting materials that will provide the best support for teachers implementing the improved curriculum. It should be stressed here that textbooks, as well as any Web-based learning approaches, including applications, should align with state standards and CCSS.

Make Professional Development Priorities

When you listen to what educators want and partner in ways that help them achieve their own well-informed goals, amazing things happen (Gassenheimer, 2013). A key, then, to

Curriculum Tip 7.7	With education in a perpetual process of change, professional development is the key to successful curriculum implementation.

school success is making professional development a priority from the onset. For example, being able to integrate mobile learning, multimedia, and other Web-based technology as a tool along with the traditional resources is now one of the essential elements of any classroom curriculum experience. As noted in Chapter 5, establishing a professional learning community (PLC) can be critical to planning and to the success of linking technology to the curriculum. It is imperative to remember that technology is a tool, and like any educational tool, teachers need to be trained in its appropriate use. See Exhibit 7.3.

Curriculum Tip 7.8	As part of the "game of choosing what to leave in, and what to take out," the formation of a sound plan at a local level will determine success or failure of any quality professional development program.

EXHIBIT 7.3 Summary of Research on Effective Professional Development

Duration

1. The program should be ongoing and continuous.

Management

1. The principal should participate actively but should not dominate.
2. Teachers and administrators should plan the program jointly.
3. There should be regular project meetings in which participants review progress and discuss substantive concerns.

Content

1. The program should provide a necessary theoretical base for the new skills.
2. The program should give primary attention to the specific skills teachers believe they need.
3. The content should be timely, directly related to job needs.

Learning Activities

1. The program should make extensive use of hands-on activities and demonstrations of new skills.
2. The program should provide for the trial of those new skills in simulated or real settings.
3. The program should make it possible for teachers to get structured feedback about their use of those skills.
4. The program should provide opportunities for observation in other classrooms and schools.

Site

1. The program should be school-based, not university-based.
2. Local teachers should be the instructors, with minimal use of outside consultants.

CREATING PROFESSIONAL DEVELOPMENT STRATEGIES

Spurred by new state standards and CCSS as well as calls for more accountability, developing a creative mix of ideas and strategies can be instrumental for school leaders in reconceptualizing fields of study. Subsequently, many schools are fortunate in having a number of community members who are willing to become a part of a PLC and add their expertise and ideas. With this in mind, the authors have included a variety of *tried-and-true* professional development ideas that have proven successful over time.

The Rule of Three

Teachers and staff are encouraged to help one another before going to a principal, supervisor, curriculum leader, or technology coordinator. The simple rule is this: *Ask three and then me.* This little rule helps take pressure off of supervisors and coordinators and improves professional development and cooperation. Teachers can also use the rule with their students. If students ask three other students for help before going to the teacher, the teacher will have more time for curriculum-related instruction.

Early-Out Time for Students

Numerous schools have found ways to adjust schedules and provide planning and/or in-service for teachers while maintaining state requirements for student contact time. Teachers have agreed to start earlier and end later each day as well as give up some recess time in order to develop blocks of time per week, or every other week, for in-service and planning. A key is to make sure part of that earned block of time is devoted to in-service. It is also important to make sure that state requirements for student contact time are met.

Send Pairs of Individuals to Workshops and Seminars

A minimum of two individuals should attend workshops, seminars, and conferences. Teachers feel more comfortable working and training in a cooperative and supportive environment. Having at least two teachers (preferably from the same grade level) obtain the same in-service background goes a long way in increasing the success of any new program. Many programs have failed because only one teacher received the training and did not have the time or energy to carry the program through all the implementation stages.

Substitute Rotation

School leaders have freed blocks of time by having a set of substitutes rotate through the schedule. For example, a set of five substitutes are able to release five teachers in the morning, and the same five substitutes can release another set of teachers in the afternoon. Because this procedure diminishes regular teacher–student contact time, it is recommended that it should be used sparingly. It is beneficial when scheduling a special consultant for a certain period of time.

Free Consulting Services

Innovative school districts are collaborating to obtain free services of national consultants as per the adoption of textbooks and online materials. Some textbook and software companies are happy to provide consultants without obligation in the hopes that their materials and programs will be selected. Naturally, not all companies provide such services; it is up to creative administrators and teachers to search out these services. A key, here, is to work with company representatives and collaborate, if possible or necessary, with several adjoining school districts, in hopes of bringing a consultant into an area.

Schedule Adjustment

There never seems to be enough time to fit in every aspect of expected curriculum. But creative leaders are finding ways to adjust and align scheduled prep times—such as music, art, library, and physical education classes—to provide in-service to new teachers. For example, it is beneficial to align an experienced teacher's prep times with a new teacher's schedule so they can visit and share ideas. The experienced teacher can assist and model effective uses of technology during these times.

College and University Preservice Programs

Higher education is always looking for ways to extend learning on campus as well as beyond. Recent restructuring efforts have led to major changes in preservice and student teaching programs. Additional core classes now address curricular change as well as professional leadership projects. An innovative program now being used by a number of universities includes the use of online professional development opportunities. Another involves the development of a collaborative master's degree to be delivered from regional sites via interactive video and conferencing.

School, University, or College Partnerships

Both college and university faculty are always looking for ways to integrate their students into local schools, whether small or large. Many schools are using college and university students to help in-service faculty on technological innovations or model teaching strategies involving technology in the classroom. Local school faculty members learn new ideas, and the university student receives a grade and credit for the experience.

Curriculum and Technology Cooperatives

With educators across the country reconceptualizing ideas about purpose, organization, and teaching, more small and rural school districts are realizing the benefits of developing cooperatives. What cannot be achieved singly can be achieved through a collaboration of resources. School districts have banded together and hired curriculum and technical coordinators who can provide the training and professional development needed at a local level.

Some school district cooperatives have joined with colleges and universities to provide credit to experienced teachers acting as instructors, as well as providing credit to participants.

Community Resources

Both small and large school districts across the country have found valuable resource people within their communities. Individual community members who have a great deal of technical experience can provide both equipment and knowledge to school districts. Many individuals in the private sector are especially good at providing in-service in the areas of e-learning and m-learning as well as other technical applications. The key is that school leaders seek out and involve community members who can make these types of contributions to the district in the area of technology.

Management Planning Matrix

The Management Planning Matrix has been one of the most successful tools used by school leaders in designing effective professional development programs. The Northwest Regional Educational Laboratory in Portland, Oregon, has developed a Management Planning Matrix that can be used to plan, implement, and evaluate an effective professional development program. The matrix design encourages planners not only to develop technology professional development goals but also to formulate measurable indicators of successful in-service. The matrix also forces planners to detail activities and leadership roles and to set implementation and evaluation dates (Whitehead, Boschee, & Decker, 2013).

HUMAN DEVELOPMENT: IMPORTANCE OF TEACHING ETHICS

In focusing on real-world relevance, Darden (2014) noted that ethics occupies the space between the law and human behavior. Basically, a true ethical dilemma is not just a choice among competing alternatives. It is the kind of knotty problem that makes one stop, forces introspection, and requires a searching look at one's deepest tenants. That said—and from a curriculum foundation perspective—ethics needs to be woven into the practice of teaching. According to Sternberg (2011), eight fundamental principles that can help guide educators in planning and teaching ethical reasoning in the context of school curriculum include:

1. *Recognizing there is an event.* The teaching of ethics needs to be infused with actuality.

2. *Defining the event.* Students learn more by defining the event and being actively involved in ethical decision making.

3. *Deciding ethical dimension.* Seeing principles embodied in concrete case examples, rather than learning them by rote, is a key to awareness.

4. *Taking personal responsibility.* Applying principles and self-application to problems in their own lives allows students to gain ownership and develop deeper understandings.

5. *Dealing with abstract rules.* The best way to teach ethical reasoning is in the context of critical classroom conversations.

6. *Applying abstract rules.* Conversations relating to ethical situations can be followed up by assigning students to write papers or blogs, which allows them to internalize what they have learned.

7. *Preparing for possible repercussions.* Accepting risk and challenge is inherent in the process.

8. *Enacting ethical solution.* Carrying out an ethical solution and making it happen is a key part.

When dealing with competing perspectives, a primary goal of incorporating the teaching of ethics (in any subject area) is that of providing students with ways to formulate both problems as well as solutions to daily life situations. Teachers can guide conversations on ethics by helping students through a series of questions: Are there issues that need to be addressed? Do these issues involve ethics? Are these issues important enough to matter? Should one take personal responsibility for these issues? In retrospect, these questions represent a short sample that can be used by teachers to initiate classroom discussions. From a curriculum planning perspective, ethical reasoning does not appear on statewide mastery tests—and yet, educators and students still find it important in their daily lives, as do the lives of others in our globally connected society.

TECHNOLOGY: RECONCEPTUALIZING 21st-CENTURY LEARNING

Answer the "What" and "Why"

A key to improving student achievement and learning through 21st-century technology involves understanding that student engagement is a current topic of interest on many educational fronts (Whitehead, Jensen, & Boschee, 2013). If educators think student engagement is only about technology, they will miss the boat. For this reason, one needs to ask the following questions: Why do I want to put course materials online or in an application, and what are the materials I want to include? For example, you may want to make lecture notes or presentation materials accessible to your students. You may want to provide an online resource directory to assist your students' research or information gathering. Or you may simply want to make a course syllabus available to your students. Whatever the reason, you should start small. Online forms, video or animation clips, and many other types of interactive feedback can be challenging but also rewarding.

Learn the "How"

How are you going to take what you have—printed material, documents, slides, transparencies, graphics—and get it on the Web? Plus, how do you present it so your students can easily find what they are looking for? Is learning in sync with expectations? And, finally, is learning being connected globally?

Determine the "Where"

Where will you publish your course materials? You have more than one choice here as well. There are specialized companies that faculty members can use for their Web sites.

Distribute Your Web Address

How will your students find your site? You might want to consider posting your Web address (URL) in the classroom, on class handouts, and on a specialized Web site.

Whatever the classroom scenario, the key is keeping technology use in perspective. It seems many schools continue to have the *focus* and *fruit* of technology backward. The focus should be on student learning—whereas the fruit of student learning is often higher scores. Thus, the use of the Web-based technology, mobile devices, electronic whiteboards, or videoconferencing needs to focus on learning.

GLOBAL CONNECTIONS: BRIDGING COMMUNITY AND SCHOOL IN BELGIUM

From a global perspective, often the quality and equity of schools depend greatly on the quality of the cultural relationships among teachers and student families within the community. Agirdag and Van Houtte (2011) shared two innovative programs in Belgium that promote educational quality and equity as they reach out to ethnically diverse families. Programs are located in the city of Ghent, Belgium, as well as a school in nearby Zicht. The Ghent project is an intervention program titled *brugfigurenproject* (Bridge-Person Project). This program aims to reach low-income, socially disadvantaged (mostly immigrant) families. In contrast, the project in Zicht (*School in Sight Project*) primarily focuses on middle-class families and attendance concerns. The two programs share the same objective: to create more equal opportunities in education.

Ghent Bridge-Person Project Characteristics:

- *Home visits.* Bridge-persons visit the homes of all newly enrolled students. Parents may initiate a home visit in the event they have a concern about their child.
- *Organized school visits.* Informal social gatherings are made at school.
- *Basic social service support.* Social services and assistance are provided as requested.
- *Parents attend school activities.* Parents are encouraged to attend various school activities either in the evening or during the day.

- *Parent information*. Parents are informed as to possible consequences relating to social-economic disadvantages.
- *Feedback*. Teaching methods and approaches are validated through feedback.
- *Translation*. Translations are provided to parents at any time throughout the process.

School in Sight Project Characteristics:

- *Evidenced-based approach*. It determines that ethic concentration is only harmful when accompanied by socioeconomic school segregation.
- *Voluntary action*. Neither parents nor teachers are forced to participate. Participation has increased over time.
- *Collective action*. This approach not only helped decrease barriers but also reflects a more natural enrollment process. Attendance has increased over time.

Each of these projects reflects how educators can bring schools and families together on a global level. It is hoped that due to overwhelming success of the program, and support from policymakers, these programs will be replicated elsewhere across the world.

SUMMARY

This chapter describes a process for reconceptualizing fields of study and emphasizes that professional development is becoming an increasingly integral and critical part of our schools. With the advent of state standards and CCSS, along with technological advancements and globally connected classrooms, schools are now making significant inroads into enhancing individual student learning. Thus, finding creative ways to support current reforms is becoming a major part of reconceptualizing fields of study—not only nationally but also worldwide.

APPLICATIONS

1. If you wanted to develop a series of elective English courses for high school students, how could you ensure that all students would develop their reading and writing skills, regardless of the electives they chose?

2. Design a mapping form for a subject you know well. In designing the form, consider the issues presented in this chapter's discussion of such forms.

3. Develop a detailed planning schedule that you could follow in improving a field of study in a local school district. Note strengths and weaknesses of the planning schedule and why you chose this approach.

4. How do you account for the fact that the ideal curricula of scholars and experts have had such little impact on the written or the taught curriculum? As an administrator, how would you counteract this problem?

5. Suppose you are part of a Grade 5 team of teachers. You decide you would like to give the pupils some choices about the social studies content by offering elective units. How would you ensure that all pupils mastered the requisite skills, regardless of the content emphasis? How would you incorporate technology to achieve this goal?

6. Discuss why professional development that is characterized by collective participation of educators (in the form of grade-level teams or school-level teams) is most likely to affect teacher instruction positively.

7. Analyze professional-development activities in your school or district, and compare them to the research findings. How does your school or district compare?

CASE STUDY   Providing Diverse Teaching Strategies

The following case study is an example of how an Ohio principal is able to use professional development and differentiated instruction strategies to improve school curriculum.

"We have a situation whereby the fourth-grade teachers are fearful of meeting state guidelines and feel they are restricted to teaching only the basics," states principal Art Mandel. "Parents of the higher-level students are grumbling."

Susan Gibbons, a fourth-grade teacher–leader, listens and nods her head in agreement. "Yes, you are right," she says. "Martha and Bob are concerned their students will not make state mandates."

Principal Mandel is frustrated. "How can we help them?"

"Well," says Susan, smiling, "why don't you arrange for some professional development on compacting and differentiated instruction? That way, Martha and Bob can see some different ways to align their teaching with state standards and still reach all their students."

"That sounds like a great idea," says Principal Mandel approvingly. "I'll contact the district office as well as the local university to see if we can get some help in setting up an in-service on differentiated instruction as well as some other strategies."

The Challenge

Formulating strategies to improve fields of study and enhance professional development is a major goal for many school administrators. What can Principal Mandel do to get more teachers, like Susan Gibbons, involved in leadership roles?

Key Issues or Questions

1. What are your impressions of how Principal Mandel handled the situation involving Martha and Bob at his school?

2. Do you feel that Principal Mandel might have used or manipulated teacher Susan Gibbons to solve his problem?

3. How do you think other teachers will react when they find out that Susan Gibbons is providing professional development suggestions to the principal? What should be discussed?

4. What are some other possible ways that Principal Mandel can enhance professional development and improve fields of study at his school?

5. How would you feel about Principal Mandel asking Susan Gibbons, Martha, and Bob to attend a differentiated instruction conference together? Do you think this would be useful? Why or why not?

WEBLIOGRAPHY

All Kinds of Minds

www.allkindsofminds.org

Brown University Knowledge Loom

www.brown.edu/academics/education-alliance/sites/
brown.edu.academics.education-alliance/files/
publications/KLoom_Guidebook.pdf

Center on Innovation and Improvement: School Turnarounds

www.centerii.org/survey/downloads/
Turnaround%20Actions%20and%20Results%20
3%2024%2008%20with%20covers.pdf

Institute of Education Sciences (IES) What Works Clearinghouse

http://ies.ed.gov/ncee/wwc/

McREL: Professional Staff Development

http://files.eric.ed.gov/fulltext/ED491305.pdf

National Library of Virtual Manipulatives

http://nlvm.usu.edu/en/nav/vlibrary.html

Northwest Evaluation Association (NWEA)

www.nwea.org/

Public Impact

www.publicimpact.com

REFERENCES

Agirdag, O., & Van Houtte, M. (2011), A tale of two cities: Bridging families and schools. *Educational Leadership, 69*(8), 42–46.

Chappuis, J. (2014). Thoughtful assessment with the learner in mind. *Educational Leadership, 71*(6), 20–26.

Copperman, P. (1978). *The literacy hoax.* New York, NY: William Morrow.

Cusick, P. A. (1983). *The egalitarian ideal and the American high school: Studies of three schools.* New York, NY: Longman.

Darden, E. C. (2014). Ethics at school: Let your conscience be your guide. *Phi Delta Kappan, 95*(5), 70–71.

Darling-Hammond, L. (2010). America's commitment to equity will determine our future. *Phi Delta Kappan, 91*(4), 9–14.

Darling-Hammond, L. (2014). Testing to, and beyond the common core. *Principal, 93*(3), 8–12.

Dynarski, M. (2010). Connecting education research to practitioners—and practitioners to educational research. *Phi Delta Kappan, 92*(1), 61–65.

Fullan, M. (2009). Leadership development: The larger context, *Educational Leadership, 67*(2), 45–49.

Gassenheimer, C. (2013). Best practice for spreading innovation: Let the practitioners do it. *Phi Delta Kappan, 95*(3), 39–43.

Goodlad, J. I. (1977). What goes on in our schools. *Educational Researcher, 6*(3), 3–6.

Hillocks, G., Jr. (1972). *Alternatives in English: A critical appraisal of elective programs.* Urbana, IL: National Council of Teachers of English.

Johnson, K. (2014). Practitioner's corner: Arts-science approach for gifted learners. *Principal, 93*(3), 42–43.

Leane, B. (2014). How I learned the value of a true PLC. *Phi Delta Kappan, 95*(6), 44–46.

Markle, B., & VanKoevering, S. (2013). Reviving Edward Bell. *Phi Delta Kappan, 94*(8), 8–12.

McAssey, L. (2014). Common Core assessments: A principal's view. *Principal, 93*(3), 14–17.

Moore, R., & Berry, B. (2010). The teachers of 2020. *Educational Leadership, 67*(8), 36–39.

Northwest Evaluation Association. (2014). Retrieved from http://www.nwea.org

Oliver, A. I. (1978). *Maximizing mini-courses: A practical guide to a curriculum alternative.* New York, NY: Teachers College Press.

Organisation for Economic Co-operation and Development. (2013–2014). Highlighted & under-lined: A notebook of short but worthy items. *Phi Delta Kappan, 95*(4), 6. Originally cited in OECD skills outlook (2013). Paris, France: Author. Retrieved from http://skills oecd.org/skillsoutlook .html

Reason, C., & Reason, L. (2007). Asking the right questions. *Educational Leadership, 65*(1), 36–40.

Scott, C. E. (2014). Preparing to teach culturally diverse classrooms. *Phi Delta Kappan, 95*(5), 80.

Snyder, C. W. (2004). *Calendar of activities/itinerary narrative* (Unpublished paper). University of Montana International Studies Program, Missoula.

Sternberg, R. J. (2011). Ethics from thought to action. *Educational Leadership, 68*(6), 34–39.

Tarte, J. (2014). 10 tips to avoid tech integration frustration. *Principal, 93*(3), 50–51.

Time-saving teacher evaluation solutions. (2014). *Principal, 93*(3), 26–30.

Tovani, C. (2010). I got grouped. *Educational Leadership, 67*(6), 24–29.

Trilling, B. (2010). Learning in our times: Make way for age-old skills with a 21st century twist. *Principal, 89*(3), 8–12.

Tucker, C. (2013–2014). Five musts for mastery. *Educational Leadership, 71*(4), 56–60.

Tucker, K. (2014). From the editor, Data: Putting the pieces together. *Principal, 93*(3), 4.

Walmsley, A. (2014). Unplug the kids. *Phi Delta Kappan, 95*(6), 80.

Washburne, C. W., & Marland, S. P., Jr. (1963). *Winnetka: The history and significance of an educational experiment.* Englewood Cliffs, NJ: Prentice Hall.

Weinbaum, E. H., & Supovitz, J. A. (2010). Planning ahead: Make program implementation more predictable. *Phi Delta Kappan, 91*(7), 68–71.

Weisberg, D., Sexton, S., Mulhern, J., & Keeling, D. (2009). *The widget effect: Our national failure to acknowledge and act on differences in teacher effectiveness.* Brooklyn, NY: The New Teacher Project. Retrieved from http://widgeteffect.org

Whitehead, B. M., Boschee, F., & Decker, R. H. (2013). *The principal: Leadership for a global society.* Thousand Oaks, CA: Sage.

Whitehead, B., Jensen, D. F. N., & Boschee, F. (2013). *Planning for technology: A guide for school administrators, technology coordinators, and curriculum leaders* (2nd ed.). Thousand Oaks, CA: Corwin Press.

Wormeli, R. (2006). *Fair isn't always equal: Assessing and grading in the differentiated classroom.* Alexandria, VA: ASCD.

CHAPTER 8

Processes for Developing New Courses and Units

With today's student population being more mobile than ever, educational standards shared across geographical lines can, and will, help students develop increasingly complex skills regardless of what state, school district, or classroom they attend (Gardner & Powell, 2013–2014). This is certainly the case as it relates to the development of Common Core State Standards (CCSS)—especially with its focus on collaboration and integration of mobile technology. It is in this regard that CCSS is very specific about skills and processes that students should be able to demonstrate. As a result, teaching with CCSS continues to change how we think about improving schools. It is not only just about developing quality courses and units but also how students acquire the skills for success in life after high school. The CCSS language ultimately helps improve teaching, elevates student success, and encourages teachers to lead national reform through a sharing of ideas. Because of the emphasis on skills, the built-in rigor, the vertically aligned standards, and the expertise needed to reach the CCSS, this focus has greatly elevated the teaching profession as well as education in general.

Questions addressed in this chapter include the following:

- What is the technological process of curriculum planning?
- What is the naturalistic process of curriculum planning?
- How can curriculum leaders develop new courses that involve both the technological and naturalistic processes of curriculum planning?

Key to Leadership

Successful curriculum leaders realize collaborative curriculum planning is part of an ongoing cycle linking outcomes back to a shared vision, standards, and goals.

With an abundance of school change due to CCSS and a focus on collaboration and standards and testing, we need to exercise care in valuing what we measure rather than measuring what we value (Tashlik, 2010). It is for this reason that administrators, supervisors, and teachers must carefully decide what new courses and new strategies are needed. In some instances, they will see the need for a new course to fill a gap perceived in the existing program (e.g., "We need a course in career planning"). Likewise, elementary teachers might sense the need for a new integrated unit. In other cases, administrators, supervisors, or teachers may decide that an existing course should be completely redeveloped with a fresh perspective (e.g., "Let's rewrite our U.S. history course. The old course just isn't working anymore").

In keeping with the concept of school change, this chapter explains how to develop a new course or unit using two contrasting processes: the standard **technological process** and what is termed here a **naturalistic process**. The intent, it should be noted, is not to suggest that one process is better than the other but only to contrast two divergent processes that might be used in different subject areas, at different grade levels.

THE TECHNOLOGICAL PROCESS OF CURRICULUM PLANNING

While the technological process has many variations, it tends to be a rational, systematic, ends-oriented model. It is the process that is important.

Curriculum Tip 8.1	The term *technological process* describes any curriculum development model that emphasizes the importance of defining terminal learning objectives early in the process and then identifies the steps needed to accomplish those objectives.

Historically, basic principles were perhaps most clearly articulated by Tyler (1949), and the model's details are probably most clearly explained in manuals written for industrial training. Its systematic nature and its efficiency make it the preferred process in most industrial and military training. While details of the process will vary from specialist to specialist, in general, it moves in an orderly sequence through certain specified steps (for a useful explication of the technological process, see Wulf & Schave, 1984):

1. Determine the course parameters—a rationale for the course, its general goals, and its probable time schedule.

2. Assess the needs of the learners.

3. On the basis of those needs and the goals previously specified, identify the course objectives—the terminal outcomes desired.

4. Determine the optimal sequence for those course objectives and cluster related objectives into unified learning experiences.

5. For each objective, identify learning activities that will enable the learners to achieve those objectives.

6. Select instructional materials that will support the learning activities.

7. Identify methods by which the attainment of those objectives will be assessed.

8. Systematize all these decisions in a curriculum guide. (Wulf & Schave, 1984, as cited in Glatthorn, 1987, p. 198)

It should be noted that the steps identified previously are usually followed in that sequence; the most competent technological developers use them in a recursive, iterative fashion and do not apply them in a mechanistic, unthinking manner.

Each of these steps will be described in detail, using as an example a course for high school students in career planning.

Curriculum Tip 8.2	A statement of principles guiding curriculum development and an argument for any new course is an important step in developing parameters of curriculum projects.

Determine Course Parameters

It is significant to note that core concepts, and the value of research, puts information in a format that allows teachers to easily put it to use. In fact, teachers may be more likely to believe research that supports their current instructional pedagogy than research that might require them to change their practice substantially (Miller, Drill, & Behrstock, 2010). Henceforth, the first step for teachers is to collaboratively determine course parameters by establishing a rationale for a specific course. Moreover, there needs to be a statement of the principles guiding the developers and an argument for the course. With a rationale established, the curriculum specialist then makes a determination about the goals of the course—the general outcomes desired. It should be noted the term *curriculum specialist* is used here to designate any administrator or supervisor with responsibility for and training in curriculum development. He or she, as part of a collaborative process in building relationships, might organize a team of colleagues to assist in the process. For the purposes of the reader, a course goal is a general statement of the intended outcomes; typically, a one-semester course would have no more than three goals. Thus, the goal for the career course might be stated in this fashion:

This course will help students develop their career-planning skills.

A new integrated unit for fourth grade might have this as its goal:

This unit will help the pupils understand that there are many different kinds of careers and that each career has value to society.

With the course or unit goal established, the developers then consider the matter of the course schedule—how long it will last, how often it will meet, and for how many minutes per session.

Curriculum Tip 8.3	Building relationships and working collaboratively creates understanding and can alleviate possible multicultural or socioeconomic issues.

Assess Needs: Academic, Cultural, and Social

The next step is needs assessment; a need is perceived as a gap between a present and a desired state. To help address this need, schools must take deliberate actions to teach students how to become responsible for their own learning (Martinez & McGrath, 2013). This is especially important not only from an academic perspective but also in regards to cultural and social needs. Furthermore, the needs-assessment process evaluates the present state of the learners in relation to the general outcomes expected. The data for the needs assessment can come from several sources: achievement scores, surveys, observations, interviews, and measures of performance.

In reality, the key is collaboratively linking needs assessment to data collection and analysis. In this regard, it is best if school leaders and teachers develop action plans to design targeted tutoring sessions and differentiated small groups. Allowing for collaboration and the formation of seamless coherence among testing instruments, analysis, and action can create an ideal classroom environment for significant gains in student learning.

In addition, school districts can begin by making better use of existing data and by choosing a specific area of focus. Keeping with this approach, research tells us that more effective schools typically use data differently than less-effective ones (Protheroe, 2010).

Curriculum Tip 8.4	An important step to developing new courses and units is linking instructional objectives to established benchmarks as well as to individual state standards or CCSS.

Identify Course Objectives

As per effective implementation of individual state standards or CCSS, school leaders and teachers can work collaboratively to identify specific course objectives. Part of the process is connecting course objectives to specific goals or benchmarks—most of which are based on new standards. Doing so helps avoid selecting units of study posited in the same old material and approaches—but now possibly displayed with a new look in a different wrapper. Demystifying this deception can be accomplished by first performing a task analysis of various outcomes desired. In the case of the career-planning course, school leaders and teachers can collaboratively ask, "Given what is known about career choices, what specific skills must be mastered?" The results of the task analysis can then be checked against needs-assessment data, as well as established standards and benchmarks, as a means of determining which skills should be stressed for an intended population. The result is often a substantiated, as well as comprehensive, list of course objectives, stated in measurable terms. Exhibit 8.1 shows a list that might be developed for this course in career planning.

Sequence and Cluster Course Objectives

A problem for schools today is not specifying clearly how much improvement is needed, but how to collaboratively develop needs assessment to ensure improvement targets that are attainable (Martineau, 2010). Once standards-based improvement targets and benchmarks are specified, the next step is to work with staff in determining the optimal sequence in which objectives should be mastered. This can be accomplished by having curriculum leaders use technology as well as data analysis to determine the optimal sequence by examining the relationships among the objectives and then assessing the entry-level skills, knowledge, and attitudes of the learners. In the case of the career-planning course, the order in which the objectives are listed in Exhibit 8.1 is one that many curriculum specialists would use as the optimal sequence in a

---

EXHIBIT 8.1   Course Objectives for Career Planning

1. Define these three terms in a way that distinguishes them from one another: *job, career, vocation.*
2. Define these terms correctly: *talent, skill, value.*
3. Describe two career-related talents that you believe you possess to a high degree.
4. List four career-related skills that you possess.
5. Explain three ways in which you might acquire additional career-related skills.
6. Explain the two career values that seem most important to you.
7. In a well-organized essay, explain at least two factors that have influenced your career values.
8. In a well-organized paragraph, explain how you would distinguish between a highly reliable source and a less reliable source of career information.
9. Identify three reliable sources that provide current information about career opportunities and requirements.
10. Using those sources, identify three careers for which you possess the necessary talents and that would adequately respond to your career values.
11. Identify the education and experience you would need for securing an entry-level position in each of those three careers.
12. Describe the processes by which you would obtain the required education and experience.
13. Explain three sources of information you would use in locating an entry-level vacancy in one of the three careers selected.
14. Write a career résumé that you could use in applying for one of those positions.
15. Demonstrate that you know how to handle a job interview by role-playing such an interview.
16. In a well-organized essay, explain three factors that might cause you to change careers.

course of this sort. The sequence establishes a conceptual basis, moves to the student's awareness of self, and orders the rest of the objectives in what seems to be chiefly a temporal sequence.

Once the specific objectives are sequenced appropriately, the next step is to cluster related objectives into unified learning experiences, such as units of study or instructional modules. The specialist examines the entire list, assesses the constraints of the schedule, reflects on student interest and attention span, and determines which objectives should be placed together in a unified set of learning experiences. Thus, the specialist may determine that Objectives 1 and 2 in Exhibit 8.1 might make a good, brief introductory unit, which would establish the conceptual base for what follows.

Identify Learning Activities

As noted by Young (2013), school leaders and teachers working in collaboration can identify one or more learning activities for each stated objective that can be specifically shaped to help the learners master the objective. Moreover, this may involve the creation of high functioning collaboration teams that help guide collective work and learning activities. The learning activities are usually seen as an ordered set of learning experiences that move the learner step-by-step toward the objective. Consider, for example, Objective 7 in Exhibit 8.1:

> In a well-organized essay, explain at least two factors that have influenced your career values.

The following learning activities could be prescribed:

- Identify several possible factors that might influence career values: culture, ethnic group, family, peers, gender, region in which you were reared, school experiences, and physiological factors.
- In reflecting on yourself and your values, identify two of those having the greatest influence.
- Check your perceptions, and gather supporting information by discussing the question with parents and friends.
- Develop a plan for your essay; have the preliminary plan reviewed by your teacher and a classmate.
- Use the revised plan to write the first draft of the essay.
- Ask a classmate to edit your essay and give you feedback.
- Write a revised draft of the essay.

Note that learning activities are chosen primarily on the basis of their fit with the objective; only those activities that move the student step by step toward the objective are prescribed.

Select Instructional Materials

With the objectives and activities identified, the next step is to select the instructional materials that will help accomplish the objectives and support the learning activities. A systematic search would be made for texts, computer software, video media, and other instructional media.

Curriculum Tip 8.5	Selecting instructional materials that help accomplish the objectives and support the learning activities is key to the process.

Identify Assessment Methods

It is occasionally difficult to know exactly what staff *really* thinks about testing (Buck, Ritter, Jensen, & Rose, 2010). For this reason, a specialist might best determine which assessment methods are needed. Some assessment is done to evaluate readiness for a unit and to diagnose learner needs; some is done to provide the student and teacher with formative feedback to determine whether remediation is needed; and some is done to make summative judgments for grading purposes. In addition to the usual written tests, the specialist might decide to make use of other assessment methods, such as interviews, observations, or performance tests.

Curriculum Tip 8.6	School personnel need to regard data collection as a fundamental tool in obtaining immediate feedback, enhancing analysis, and organizing continuous improvement.

When planning a career course, a curriculum specialist, after consultation with staff and measurement specialists, might decide on the following assessments (standard or digital format): one diagnostic test to determine specific learning needs of each student, one short formative test for each lesson, one longer formative test for each group of five lessons, and one final summative test covering the entire course.

Whatever assessment teachers decide to use, the following guidelines can be considered:

- Understanding and articulating *in advance of teaching* the achievement targets their students are to hit
- Informing their students about those learning goals, *in terms that students understand,* from the very beginning of the teaching and learning process
- Becoming assessment literate and thus able to transform their expectations into assessment exercises and scoring procedures that *accurately reflect student achievement*
- Using classroom assessments to *build students' confidence* in themselves as learners and help them take responsibility for their own learning, so as to lay a foundation for lifelong learning
- Translating classroom assessment results into frequent *descriptive feedback* (versus judgmental feedback) for students, providing them with specific insights as to how to improve
- Continuously *adjusting instruction* based on the results of classroom assessments

- Engaging students in *regular self-assessment,* with standards held constant so that students can watch themselves grow over time and thus feel in charge of their own success
- Actively involving students in *communicating* with their teacher and their families about their achievement status and improvement (Stiggins, 2002, p. 761)

Curriculum Tip 8.7	"Curriculum guides often follow a school district's curriculum cycle. As noted in Chapter 5, most curriculum cycles generally include (but not limited to) five basic components: analysis, design, development, implementation, and evaluation" (ADDIE design model; Design Theories and Models, 2014).

Develop a Curriculum Guide

While formats vary from district to district, most guides developed from the processes described previously include some variation of the following:

- A rationale for the course or a statement of the philosophy that guided the course planners
- A list of the objectives, ordered in the desired sequence
- The recommended learning activities, displayed graphically so that their relationship to the objectives is very clear—in some cases, activities are described under each objective; in some guides, the objectives and activities are arranged in parallel columns
- A list of recommended instructional materials
- Copies of tests and suggestions for other assessment activities

Curriculum Tip 8.8	Regarding the foundational area of human development, integration of up-to-date transformative technology most likely will be critical for future school success. In addition, it will be crucial for schools to engage students in addressing real-world problems, issues, and questions that matter (Devine, 2012). When focusing on school reform, the reality is that developments in educational technology are changing societal and career needs as well as challenging the very nature of schools.

The Technological Model Summarized

Integrating technology into instruction has made good schools even better. The key, then, is to involve students in inquiry- and design-based projects that are rooted in driving questions and real-world problems (Connelly, 2010). Moreover, students must be successful in employing objectives, outcomes, and technological advances to facilitate processing of information in meaningful ways. Teachers planning new courses can now do Web-based research to locate current technological applications available to enable students to better collect and analyze "real-time, virtual, real-world" data in the field. For example, teachers could design an action plan for an ecosystem field trip that incorporates current technological equipment for gathering, analyzing, and sharing data.

Many curriculum planners now believe that it is important to get as many people on board as possible when developing new courses via the use of technology. They note that opinions can be dangerous if not buttressed by facts and believe that technology should be a learning aid or it will become an educational barrier. The bottom line is that new courses need to be developed on the basis of fact, not fiction. It is, therefore, crucial to get accurate data before making generalizations as to what is needed in the curriculum and before developing new courses.

Researcher Conrad Wesley Snyder (2004) noted advancements in educational technology that were helping transcend both the technological curriculum-planning model and the naturalistic planning model. Snyder's research is still applicable today. He states that there are six objectives for understanding that can also serve as criteria for lesson development using technology:

1. *Explanation:* knowledgeable and justified accounts of events, actions, and ideas

2. *Interpretation:* narratives and translations that provide meaning

3. *Application:* using knowledge effectively in new situations and diverse contexts

4. *Perspective:* critical and insightful points of view

5. *Empathy:* identification with another person's feelings and worldview

6. *Self-knowledge:* wisdom to know one's ignorance and one's patterns of thought and action

These criteria help ensure that understanding is not trained explicitly but is "awakened more than trained by design, not exhortation." The goal is for students to come to the realization that they are responsible for making meaning of ideas rather than waiting for teacher explanations. The "design" part is similar to a highly structured curriculum approach (sometimes referred to as Instructional Systems Design), and it includes didactic or direct instruction while emphasizing coaching and reflective or facilitative instruction. The latter are fostered by explicit attention to the creation of generative instructional events, created from what can be called an "inverse design"—from basic understandings and essential or generative questions.

THE NATURALISTIC PROCESS OF CURRICULUM PLANNING

An awareness of the limitations of the technological process and extensive work with curriculum specialists and teachers has led to the development of a special version of the naturalistic process.

Curriculum Tip 8.9	The naturalistic process attempts to embody the following characteristics: • Sensitive to the political aspects of curriculum making • Greater emphasis placed on the quality of the learning activities • More accurately reflects the way curricula actually have been developed • Cognizant of the way teachers really plan for instruction

In the following discussion, the steps in the process are described in the order in which courses ordinarily would be taken, although other sequences could just as well be followed. The process has been conceptualized as an interactive and recursive one, in which flexibility is emphasized. To illustrate these steps and to highlight comparisons with the technological approach, the discussion again uses the development of a new course for high school students in career planning. It then shows how an elementary team would use the same process in developing an integrated unit.

Assess Alternatives: Academic, Cultural, and Social

Even with state standards and CCSS, the naturalistic process begins with a systematic examination of the alternatives to a new course. Although many of those using a technological approach begin in the same manner, some technological developers seem to move too quickly from the identification of need to the development of the course.

To understand why this assessment of alternatives is important, consider how the initiative for a new course usually develops. Someone with a stake in the outcome, such as a principal, department head, teacher–leader, or teacher, assumes that a new course is needed.

Most advocates of the naturalistic process believe that only in rare instances does conviction emerge from a rational analysis of the data available. Even though most experts urge curriculum supervisors to use such information sources as test scores, parent surveys, and student interviews, such data are often sought to justify a predetermined solution, not to establish the need for a given response.

For this reason, it is important for a director of curriculum, or building principal, to examine alternatives before offering a new course or moving ahead too quickly (Whitehead, Boschee, & Decker, 2013). With that said, any new course can be costly. Cost in this case involves what economists call "opportunity cost"—every student who takes the new course loses, in the process, the opportunity for some other educational experience. It also involves substantial development cost—the time and effort of those responsible for planning it. Finally, it involves significant implementation costs—the funds needed to staff the course, provide facilities, and secure the necessary equipment and materials.

What are the alternatives to offering a new course? Several alternatives are available for those interested in a new course in career planning:

- Ignore the need, based on the assumption that somehow adolescents will acquire the career-planning skills they need without organizational intervention.
- Ask some other agency to respond to the need. Decide that helping adolescents make wise career choices is the responsibility of the family, the business community, or the YMCA—not the school.
- Provide for the need through the activities program. Arrange for assemblies, career-planning days, or career clubs; develop programs for the homeroom.
- Use noncurricular methods of responding to the need. Put career materials in the library; buy computer software on career planning and make it available in the guidance suite; and increase the guidance staff, adding specialists in career planning.
- Integrate the skills into existing courses. In each existing subject, include units in the careers that emphasize career-planning skills.

It is not suggested here that any of these alternatives are necessarily better than another as per offering a new course. The point is simply that the alternatives can be collaboratively examined before finally deciding that a new course is needed.

Curriculum Tip 8.10	The process of staking out territory is very similar to that of identifying course parameters.

Stake Out the Territory

Public schools thrive when parents see the needs of their children being met. Offering new courses and choices within the public school system while ensuring the strength and success of all students is the best policy (Foster, 2014). If a new course is the most desirable option, then the next step is to stake out the territory. The planning team considers the students for whom the course is intended, makes some initial determinations about the schedule, and tentatively identifies the coverage of the course. Note that the active parties in the naturalistic process are identified as a planning team—in contradistinction to the curriculum specialist—because teams of teachers are generally involved in using the naturalistic process.

However, there is an important difference between identifying the course parameters and staking out the territory—a difference connoted by the metaphors used. The identification of course parameters tends to be more definitive and final; the staking out of territory is a more tentative and open-ended boundary-setting process.

To assist in further development, the course territory should be described in a course prospectus. The course prospectus presents the answers to possible questions—and does so in a manner that will both guide planners and inform others. In the case of the career course, the prospectus might read as follows:

We're thinking about offering a new course tentatively titled Thinking About Careers. As we see the course now, it would be an elective offered to all juniors and seniors, although our hunch is that it would probably appeal most of all to those not presently interested in higher education. It would probably run for one term and meet three times a week for a total of about 40 classroom hours. As we presently conceptualize the course, it would help students examine their career values, assess career skills, learn how to retrieve career information, and do some systematic career planning. It would probably deemphasize the study of particular careers and focus on processes instead. Our written materials will include only the mastery component, not enrichment or organic content. All these notions are tentative; we need the advice of anyone competent and interested.

Observe that the description is general and the language tentative. The intent is to identify broad boundaries that will be flexible enough to accommodate the ideas of all those who will later be involved in the more detailed planning.

Develop a Constituency

School systems must have support when successfully planning and implementing high standards and assessments (Maunsell, 2014). But, as with most changes, curriculum planning often comes with a political twist. For example, there is a possibility that school leaders developing any new course may very well try to wield power and advance their own interests. While genuinely concerned with improving the education of students, they are also motivated by personal and cultural interests: to enhance their reputations, to make their positions more secure, to win the attention of superiors. For this reason, it is important throughout the naturalistic process for course planners to build a constituency for the new course—to mobilize support and neutralize likely opposition. How much time and energy are devoted to such politicking will depend, of course, on the likely impact of the proposed change and the extent to which the course seems to have broad-based support.

Win the Support of the Powerful

According to Toch (2010), the best change strategy for schools promotes reform from both the outside in and the inside out. With this in mind, a system of coordinated services should be established in every district. If the principal supports a curriculum change and works closely with governmental agencies, the process moves along well. If the principal opposes the change, major problems can develop: meetings are canceled, requisitions are delayed, and space is unavailable. Thus, central office supervisors who try to impose curricular changes on resistant principals soon discover the folly of such attempts.

Curriculum Tip 8.11	Opening up the planning process to all those who want to participate is an important component of the process.

Share the Power and the Glory

Having the student, parent, and school working in rhythm for the same long-term goal and dreams is essential for sustaining long-term, powerful relationships (Dillon & Nixon, 2014). With that being said, it is important to make the new course "our course," not "my course." Make a special effort to involve the undecided. Spread the credit around in all public discussions.

Collaborating with the international community is also important. Private academies such as the Global Village Academy seek to create curriculum that is rigorous and responsive to the global community's needs yet unbound to legislative pressures that sometimes undermine student development (Murray, 2010).

Be Prepared to Negotiate

The process of getting a new course approved often requires the art of negotiating. Especially when the opposition seems strong, course planners should give themselves room to bargain by asking publicly for more than they hope to get: asking for four periods, hoping to get three; asking for two classrooms in the expectation of getting one.

All these strategies will require time. For this reason, the process of developing a constituency is not initiated and then dropped; instead, it should continue throughout both the planning and implementation stages.

Curriculum Tip 8.12	Course planners should begin with a cursory "data-driven needs assessment" of the students.

Build the Knowledge Base

Zhang, Lundeberg, and Eberhardt (2010) suggested that, given the inherent complexity of teaching, one teacher research project or strategy is not likely to solve all problems in practice. As noted in Chapter 5, another fundamental step that should be initiated early is building a knowledge base—retrieving and systematizing information about the students, making social and cultural considerations, assessing faculty readiness, analyzing the relevant research, and identifying available materials and programs. Too often, those using the technological process neglect this crucial step: Course planners often ignore those who will be teaching the course, slight the research, and act as though nothing else has been done in the field before.

The questions listed in Exhibit 8.2 can guide the development of the knowledge base as it relates to course development. Note that the questions here are not as comprehensive as those suggested in Chapter 5; because local course planners usually have limited resources, only the most important questions are listed.

The student questions are designed to help planners understand the constraints imposed by the characteristics of those likely to take the course. In contrast to the usual "needs assessment," this component of the knowledge base reminds developers of the reality they face in implementing the course successfully. Will the course attract less able, unmotivated

EXHIBIT 8.2   Questions to Answer in Building the Knowledge Base

The Students

Consider the students likely to take the course:

1. What are the students' interests?
2. What is known about their academic achievement?
3. What levels of cognitive development are represented?
4. What are their predominant values and attitudes?
5. What similar learning experiences have they already had?

The Teachers

Consider the teachers likely to be assigned to the course:

1. What is their experience and background?
2. How much do they know about the content likely to be covered by the course?
3. What special skills and technology background can they bring to the course?

The Research

Consider the course territory:

1. What research is available that will help planners determine course content?
2. What research is available that will help curriculum planners select teaching–learning activities?

What Is Available?

Consider the course territory:

1. Have similar courses been developed by national curriculum centers?
2. Have similar courses been offered by other schools?
3. What materials (texts, multimedia, software, and Web-based resources) are readily available in the field?

students? Will many of them have serious reading problems? Will they have trouble understanding abstract concepts?

Teacher questions should be intended to guide developers in deciding how detailed the course planning should be and how much professional development will be required. Comments illustrate how answers might impinge on the planning process:

- We will need experienced teachers with a strong background in the subject area.
- This is a new field; we need to be rather explicit as to what resources are needed.
- The course will involve a great deal of technology and mobile learning applications.

Developing a wide range of questions allows for the development of efficient and effective ways to use research, which in turn, can contribute to significant improvements (Bauer & Brazer, 2012). For the most part, research questions can focus on course content and teaching–learning methods. Stated generally here so they can apply to any new course, they should be rephrased more specifically by the planners so they can be answered more readily. For example, individuals developing the career-planning course might seek answers to these more specific questions:

- What do we know about the career values of adolescents?
- What do we know about general patterns of career choice? How stable are career decisions?
- What do we know about changing occupational trends?
- What do we know about the skills needed for career decision making?
- What instructional methods seem to be most effective in developing decision-making skills?

Finally, the questions on "what is available" help the planners profit from the experience and work of others. If they locate an excellent program developed by a major curriculum center, they may decide to adopt it with modifications.

Block in the Unit

Ivey (2010) strongly advocates that students cannot learn much from materials that are not relevant, and they cannot learn much from just one book or one Web-based program. Thus, with a knowledge base developed, the next step is to block in the units—to determine the number and focus of each unit of study that will make up the new course. Note that while the recommended direction is (general to specific, from unit to lesson), in some cases it might be desirable to reverse the flow—to identify lessons and then cluster lessons into units.

In blocking in the units, planners make tentative decisions about these issues:

- How many units of study are planned?
- How many lessons will there probably be in each unit?
- What is the general objective of each unit?
- What is the optimal sequence of the units?

One specific unit-blocking process that seems to work well in most disciplines is as follows: First, identify the probable number of units by reviewing the course territory and assessing the interest span of the learners ("We're planning a one-semester course that will meet or digitally conference three times a week, and many of the learners will probably have some academic challenges, so perhaps we need seven to nine units—some two weeks long, some three weeks long.")

Second, identify the general objective of each unit. The *unit objective,* as the term is used here, is the one general outcome desired at the end of the unit. How can the tentative unit objectives be produced? One method that seems to work well is to assemble the planning team (or videoconference with team members), and review the course prospectus as well as the knowledge base. Then ask, "What do we really want the students to learn?"

Here is a list of tentative unit objectives that might be produced by those developing a career course:

- Understanding your career values
- Learning about your skills and aptitudes
- Thinking about the education you need
- Retrieving and using career information
- Gaining career-mobility skills

Once the list of unit objectives has been developed, the planning team can review the list in order to refine it. The refining process attempts to reduce the number of unit objectives to match the number of units previously identified and to ensure that the final list closely matches the course territory. Questions of the following sort can be asked:

- Which unit objectives might be combined?
- Which unit objectives are of low priority and might be eliminated?
- Which unit objectives are tangential to the central thrust of the course and might be eliminated?

The refining stage is also the best time to make a tentative decision about the number of lessons. In making this decision, the team should reflect on the complexity and importance of the unit and the attention span of the learners, realizing, of course, that the decision is only preliminary.

Thus, the team planning the career course might produce a final list such as the following, in which both the unit objectives and the probable number of lessons are indicated:

- Careers, jobs, and vocations: 6
- Looking at yourself—skills, aptitudes, values: 6
- Changing occupational needs: 6
- Retrieving and using career information: 9

The final step in blocking out units is determining the optimal sequence. Again, as with technological applications, course planners can have multiple sequences available to them. However, those using the naturalistic process ordinarily combine several types of sequence, giving considerable weight to student interest and the rhythms of the school year.

Plan Quality Learning Experiences

We now know that good teaching matters more for student outcomes than any other school-based factor (Coggins, Zuckerman, & McKelvey, 2010). With this in mind and with units blocked out, the next stage in the process is planning quality learning experiences—designing a set of learning experiences that together will lead to the unit objective. It is perhaps at this stage that the naturalistic process differs most significantly from the standard model; it therefore might be useful at this point to clarify the distinction.

Curriculum Tip 8.13	In the technological model, objectives drive the planning process. In the naturalistic model, objectives are set to produce desirable student experiences or outcomes.

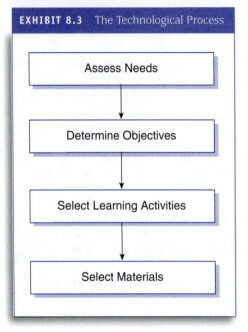

EXHIBIT 8.3   The Technological Process

Assess Needs → Determine Objectives → Select Learning Activities → Select Materials

In the technological model, the objectives determine the activities and influence the choice of materials. The intent is to control the learning process to ensure that a predetermined end is achieved. The process is linear and unidirectional, as Exhibit 8.3 suggests.

The intent is to develop plans for quality learning experiences—meaningful learning transactions, monitored through an assessment of goals and objectives and mediated by the teacher. Keeping this in perspective, Moore and Berry (2010) believe a number of "levers of change" will need to be in place to advance a 21st-century teaching profession. Some of these levers of change will require hard work—such as expanding writing or solving highly complex math problems as per CCSS. Student learning is facilitated through continuous feedback derived from an assessment of goals and objectives relating back to the written curriculum. (See Exhibit 8.4.)

In the naturalistic process, the planners attempt to design quality learning experiences—stimulating teaching–learning transactions that will produce several desirable outcomes, some of which might occur serendipitously. They think about the learners—their learning styles, their motivations, and their abilities. They keep in mind the unit objective, as well as the general outcome to be attained, and reflect on the more specific objectives it comprises. They search for materials or applications that will have high-interest value and good instructional payoff. They reflect on learning activities that will appeal to the learners, will challenge them to think, and will give them an opportunity to be creative.

Sometimes, specific objectives will dominate their thinking, as is the case with the technological approach. At other times, planners might begin to think about a range of materials and options and will derive an objective from a multitude of sources. In a naturalistic model then, objectives, materials, and activities are all examined in an interactive and recursive manner as components of a quality learning experience.

Develop the Course Examination

The naturalistic process places less emphasis on assessment. Rather than developing in advance several detailed assessment devices, course planners ensure that teachers are given the professional development needed to make their own ongoing assessments.

EXHIBIT 8.4   The Naturalistic Model

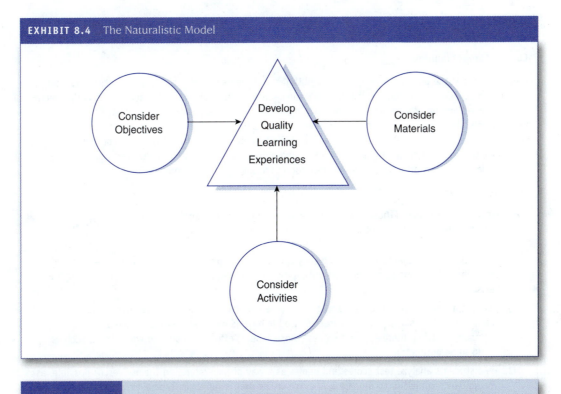

Curriculum Tip 8.14	A learning scenario is a more flexible and open-ended guide that assists the teacher in implementing a new course of study.

Develop the Learning Scenarios

Instead of using the standard curriculum guide, the naturalistic process culminates in the production and dissemination of **learning scenarios** for each unit of study.

Learning scenarios usually include these components:

- A clear and detailed statement of the unit objective
- A suggested number of lessons
- A list of recommended quality learning experiences, phrased in a way that integrates objectives, activities, and materials
- Reprints of articles, maps, photographs, and Web-based resources that teachers could use in making lesson plans; observe that materials are not just listed—they are included (the copyright law allows such professional use in a teacher's guide if three conditions are met: proper credit is given, the guide is not sold for profit, and the articles are not reproduced for student use)

An example of a learning scenario is shown in Exhibit 8.5.

EXHIBIT 8.5 Learning Scenario: Self-Understanding and Career Planning

Course: Career Planning

Unit objective: At the end of the unit, it is hoped that the students (notably those with multicultural and varied socioeconomic backgrounds) will have a clearer sense of their talents, skills, and values as they relate to the career-planning process. This is especially important in that social and income inequality issues affect families, neighborhoods, and schools in a manner that undercuts the effectiveness of schools serving disadvantaged populations (Duncan & Murnane, 2014). The goal, then, is to help students become somewhat more realistic as they think about careers. By focusing on their talents, hopefully they can acquire new skills and experience new opportunities to ready them for an increasingly global competitive world.

Suggested number of lessons: 6 to 8

Quality learning experiences (These are listed in what seems to be a desirable sequence, but you should feel free to modify the order as you see fit.):

1. Have students write an article or blog they can share with peers, parents, and counselors titled "My Ideal Career." Provide some good prewriting discussion, and allow time for expanded writing and revision.

2. Conduct a discussion of the nature of talents (the general aptitudes that we possess, such as a talent for music), skills (specific career-related behaviors we have mastered, such as being proficient in using interests), and values (those aspects of life we consider worthwhile, such as liking to be outdoors).

3. Help students analyze test scores and grades as a way of understanding themselves. If possible, ask the guidance counselor to prepare a test-and-grade profile for each student and to discuss the uses and limitations of test scores and school grades in assessing talents, skills, and values.

4. Have each student develop a talent profile. Identify the range of talents people possess—mechanical, verbal, mathematical, scientific, musical, physical, artistic, interpersonal, and managerial.

5. Help each student develop a skills inventory. Most students will probably believe that they have few career-related skills.

6. Ask students to interview one or both parents about parental career values. Emphasize that the goal here is not to intrude on parents' privacy (the results will not be shared with classmates or the teacher) but to get a broader understanding of parents and to see whether parent values have influenced student values.

7. As a culminating activity, ask students to write a final article or blog on the topic "Seeing Myself in Relation to Careers." They will probably need some prewriting help in organizing all the information they have collected.

8. As an enrichment activity for those with special interest in the subject, discuss how culture shapes career values. Ask them to speculate about the career values of a rural farmer and those of an urban factory worker.

Curriculum Tip 8.15

The naturalistic model can be used effectively, especially at the elementary level as well.

The Naturalistic Model Summarized

The naturalistic model is characterized by several features that set it off from the technological model. It is looser, more flexible, and less rational. It is more responsive to the political realities of curriculum making. It tends to be a top-down process, moving from the larger unit to the smaller lesson. It seems to be more in accord with the way teachers actually plan and gives equal weight to objectives, activities, and materials, rather than giving primary attention to objectives.

Its advantages seem clear. It should result in curricula that are more likely to be implemented, rather than shelved. Because it addresses the political reality of schools and because it is in accord with teachers' actual planning styles, it should have greater appeal to both principals and teachers. It should also result in more interesting and challenging learning experiences because it emphasizes the intrinsic quality of the experience.

Its main drawback is its looseness. Especially in the hands of the inexperienced, it can result in a seemingly random collection of entertaining activities that appear unrelated to the intended outcomes.

THE INVERSE DESIGN PROCESS OF CURRICULUM PLANNING

The inverse design process can be a valuable tool in the ongoing battle to determine what needs to be taught versus what is actually taught. Much like the backward design process noted in Chapter 3, an inverse design entails three steps: (1) Identify the desired results in terms of understandings and questions—that is, develop the essential questions; (2) determine the acceptable evidence to meet the standards specified in the desired results—that is, specify how learning will be assessed; and (3) plan learning experiences and instruction. This includes the following questions:

- What enabling activities will lead to the needed knowledge and skills?
- What needs to be taught and coached, and how should it best be taught, in light of the performance goals?
- What materials and resources are needed?
- Is the overall design coherent and effective?

Each of these steps reflects an important aspect of both the technological and naturalistic approaches. Subsequently, administrators and teachers are stepping back and gaining a perspective of the curriculum processes that allows them to embody each of the characteristics listed previously.

| **Curriculum Tip 8.16** | An alternative for addressing governmental regulations and formulating new courses can be the development of a distance learning component. |

DISTANCE LEARNING

In an era of mobile technology, when adolescents are online and actively consuming social media, schools need to be taking advantage of new technologies (Journell, Ayers, & Beeson, 2014). For example, distance learning can help in urban multicultural settings or in isolated frontier schools—basically anywhere that a teacher believes their classroom to be like an island. In addition, the Internet and related communications technologies, along with political, social, and economic changes in our society, continue to spawn an unprecedented growth of interest in distance education and the number of courses and programs available through distance learning. Research findings increasingly show that high school students who take college coursework while in high school (dual enrollment) are more likely to go to college. Dual enrollment provides high school students with significant opportunities to challenge themselves academically as well as to explore career and academic options not available in high school. When the distance-delivered course is provided for high school students only, it is important for the teacher to know and be able to meet the instructional, curricular, and legal expectations for teaching in that setting.

According to Montana high school teacher Bart Hawkins (2010), Web-based tools are becoming increasingly sophisticated and user-friendly for more educators—especially rural educators. Among the meeting place tools available online are Hangouts (www.google .com/hangouts) and GoToMeeting (www.gotomeeting.com) as well as a host of others. The authors have used Hangouts, finding it applicable to education and having specific tools designed for streamlining education processes. As such, it is extremely attractive as an option for Web conferencing. This simplicity is a must in the world of education where not all users will have the same level of access, knowledge, or assistance in the use of technology. Course management systems (CMS) are also an important component of distance education. These systems continue to become widespread and include Blackboard (www .blackboard.com) and Moodle (www.moodle.com), to name only two.

Regional Centers and Technology Hubs

Regional Technology Development Centers, sometimes called technology hubs, have the capability of serving as informational resource centers, information management systems, professional development centers, procurement centers, and research and evaluation centers, as well as grant-writing centers (Whitehead, Jensen, & Boschee, 2013). Technology service centers can help with new course or unit development, make the transfer of student records easier, as well as enhance the opportunity for state agencies and schools to share reports on student achievement, attendance, enrollment, demographics, and budget.

Most learning centers should have the capacity to train both urban and rural teachers in how to integrate technology into their classrooms, develop new courses and units, as well as how to evaluate instructional resources. School leaders now agree that training and content knowledge will become more important as faculty and students have regular access to technology. Regional centers will thus act as professional development centers or learning academies that offer courses for teachers on how to address individual learning needs as well as develop a closer link between technology and curriculum. Teachers and other educators can be provided with workshops and conferences at regional centers with the expectation that they will return to their districts and share what they have learned with their peers. The National Science Foundation uses regional technology centers as a base of operations for electronic learning.

Some regional centers have the capability of housing sophisticated distance learning classrooms. Participants using these interactive classrooms will be able to see, hear, and interact with other educators, classes, and presenters within their state as well as around the world. Centers can provide avenues for multicultural students to gain access to new courses, individualized instruction as well as participate in collaborative groups. Likewise, high school dropouts will be able to obtain credits needed to graduate. For example, a full menu of classes, such as foreign language, art, anatomy, and advanced math, can be accessed through interactive television networks linked to regional technology centers. Thus, using Internet and telecommunications strategies, technology hubs can go a long way to "filling in the holes of school curriculum" when necessary.

All these options—combined with increased availability of new software, increased bandwidth capabilities, and increasing comfort with technology—will likely drive the development of distance and online learning. In addition, distance education systems will be bolstered by policy developments from various state governments as well as the use of CCSS. The implications here are important. As we move forward, school leaders will be able to find ways to adopt distance learning strategies, use them to enhance student success, and keep our education system viable and strong throughout the 21st century.

Curriculum Tip 8.17	Using mobile devices along with a variety of applications (in the classroom) is one way technology can be meaningfully incorporated into the curriculum.

PREPARING SCHOOLS FOR NEW BEGINNINGS WITH TECHNOLOGY

Modern learners need to share their ideas, receive feedback about them, and participate in discussions surrounding academic topics (Johnson, 2014). In this regard, mobile technology offers teachers unique opportunities to link students with real-time information and diverse multicultural perspectives. Clearly, then, as we prepare students for new beginnings and shifting global dynamics in the 21st century, the need for more creative ideas and solutions is becoming even more pressing. With varying prescriptions being purported, most seem to point to the importance of technology innovations as well as a need for students to become active and successful citizens in our technologically interconnected world.

Clearly, any move toward the successful integration of technology in schools will likely be based on increased student achievement. Along these lines, any effort to integrate mobile technology into the teaching and learning process will hinge on an individual teacher's technology skills. According to Matt Clausen (2010), a traditional approach for evaluating teachers' basic technology skills has been gauging teacher readiness and planning at the early stages of professional development. In the long run, however, this is insufficient for developing a more comprehensive approach to assessment that moves a teacher's use of technology beyond the basics. What is really needed is a way to move teachers toward a fully integrated, student-centered model of learning. This is where the *Three-Dimensional Assessment Matrix* can prove invaluable.

A Three-Dimensional Assessment Matrix

The Three-Dimensional Assessment Matrix, developed by Washington's Educational Technology Support Center (2008), is not new but is still very much relevant today (Clausen, 2010). The matrix defines three tiers of use: (1) Teacher Productivity Station, (2) Instructional Presentation and Student Productivity, and (3) a Student-Centered Learning Classroom. For each tier, the matrix provides examples of best practices, professional development possibilities, required conditions, technology resources, and estimated costs. In total, the matrix provides schools with a clear picture of the resources and support necessary to achieve the desired outcomes. Districts looking to move beyond teacher productivity (Tier 1) to a more enhanced (Tier 2) or transformative (Tier 3) learning experience have a clear picture of the increasing sophistication of technology-facilitated learning experiences and the requisite supports. But locating quality information and assessing the depth of how technology is used in the classroom presents a variety of challenges at all tiers. Users need to be able to sort through the multitude of information to locate the most relevant pieces.

In addition to programs like the Three-Dimensional Assessment Matrix, teachers can also improve their understandings by utilizing WebQuest. WebQuest is often used by teachers to enhance a classroom unit or a particular curriculum area and engage their students in meaningful research work. (WebQuest is located at http://www.webquest.org.)

Looking back retrospectively at technology integration and distance learning, it is important for teachers to find that "learning must be developed around learner needs." While this may be self-evident to many, this message is ignored with surprising frequency. To some extent, this is because our established postsecondary institutions have evolved as teacher- and subject-centered institutions with little emphasis on the students' needs and interests. It is also because—just as anyone can be a publisher on the Internet—anyone can be a distance educator on the Internet. Many educators and subject specialists are newly involved in distance education, with little or no awareness of some of the important principles that have been developed over the years for creating new online distance courses.

GLOBAL CONNECTIONS: DUAL SYSTEMS IN KOREA

As part of charting new developments on a global level, evidence reveals that low-income students are more likely than higher-income students to be taught by highly qualified teachers in Seoul, South Korea. According to Levin (2013), Seoul has supported low-achieving schools through two main programs. First, schools with 5% or more students who are below national academic achievement standards are designated as Achievement Improvement Target Schools. As a result, twenty-seven schools receive funds for programs that impact academically vulnerable students. Principals in these schools may choose up to 20% of the teachers, many of whom will receive incentives such as additional salary, smaller class sizes, less instruction time, and additional credit toward promotion. The result is that students in these schools will most likely be taught by highly qualified teachers.

A second major project in Seoul involves another 350 schools. These specifically chosen schools receive additional funds under the Korean Educational Welfare Investment Priority School Project to address socioeconomic inequality. Students in these selected schools have access to after-school programs, counseling, mentoring, cultural programs, and health education. Moreover, the program is especially designed to involve families, schools, community agencies, and colleges in building an integrated support system for selected economically vulnerable students.

As can be seen, both projects in Seoul, South Korea, provide interesting approaches to improving educational practice and are well aligned with current research. Likewise, both programs focus on helping students improve—not punishing them for their limitations. Nonetheless, making these changes real and effective in all South Korean schools remains a daunting challenge. But, that said, it certainly poses a global challenge worth looking into.

SUMMARY

This chapter compares and explains how to develop a new course or unit using two contrasting processes: the standard technological process and what is termed here a *naturalistic process*. The chapter also explores how curriculum leaders can develop new courses that involve both the technological and naturalistic processes of curriculum planning. Also covered is how to improve and sustain academic achievement.

APPLICATIONS

1. Consider this issue: Should the choice between the technological or naturalistic process be influenced by the nature of the educational organization? If so, in what types of organizations should each be used?

2. To test your ability to use the technological model, do the following:
   a. Identify the parameters of a new course you might develop.
   b. Describe the purpose of data in regard to assessing the needs of the learner.
   c. List the learning objectives for the course.
   d. Identify the learning activities you would recommend for one of the objectives.

3. To test your ability to use the naturalistic model, do the following:
   a. Describe the territory of a new course.
   b. Describe the advantages of school-based curriculum development.

    c.   List all unit objectives.

    d.   Write at least four quality learning experiences for one of the units.

4.   Some who have used the naturalistic process have suggested that it is more suitable for elementary grades than for secondary. If you were an elementary school principal, would you recommend that your teachers use the naturalistic process? Discuss in detail your rationale for using the naturalistic process rather than a technological process approach.

5.   Which process, naturalistic or technological, is best suited for special education? List at least three reasons why one might be more applicable than another in a special education classroom.

6.   More educators are now recommending a combination of naturalistic and technological processes—especially at elementary levels. Explain in detail how you would incorporate both processes in an elementary school setting.

CASE STUDY   When Trivial Becomes Tragic

In visiting with one of her teachers, a California middle school principal discusses the problem of sixth- and seventh-grade students not meeting state standards in the area of mathematics.

"Thank you for stopping by my office," shares Principal Margaret Paine. "As part of our data-analysis program, I was looking at our sixth- and seventh-grade math scores—and I'm concerned they are so low."

"Yes," reluctantly admits seventh-grade teacher Nita Kaplan. "I'm highly concerned as well. We're finding many of our students missed some fundamental skills in the lower grades." Kaplan pauses and then adds, "These skills may seem trivial, but in math, they are critical to success in middle school."

"I totally agree," interrupts the principal, sounding frustrated. "The administration is examining both naturalistic as well as technological processes as a way to improve our elementary math curriculum. It seems these students are doomed to failure. It's tragic."

"You're correct on that one," grouses the seventh-grade teacher. "We've got to do something—and soon. It's a case of what might look trivial becoming tragic."

The Challenge

Determine whether the naturalistic or technological process, or both, should be used at elementary levels in math. How can Principal Paine educate and motivate elementary administrators and teachers to use online data-analysis strategies to ensure basic skills are being taught?

Key Issues and Questions

1. What steps can administrators take to ensure fundamental skills are taught and assessed in schools? Should online assessment have a role in this process?

2. What might happen if Principal Paine discusses the problem with her superintendent?

3. Determining alignment of online assessment programs with district, state, and national standards is crucial to the curriculum process. What actions can middle school and high school principals take to make sure feeder schools are aligned with district curricula?

4. The expense of online assessment programs can be challenging for many school districts. How can these costs be addressed?

5. Determining to use either a naturalistic or technological process in improving curriculum can be a daunting task—especially with the advent of CCSS. Such changes often affect the development of new courses and units. What measures can be taken to reduce teacher opposition to such radical curriculum changes?

WEBLIOGRAPHY

Discover Magazine
www.discovermagazine.com

James Madison University: Steps for Developing New Courses and/or Units
www.jmu.edu/curriculum/development.shtml

Northwestern University Leadership Study
www.sesp.northwestern.edu/msed/index.html

School Leadership and Student Outcomes
www.sesp.northwestern.edu/msed/index.html

Teachers.net: Chatboards and Lesson Plans
www.teachers.net

Teachers on Target: On-the-Job Strategies
www.teachersontarget.com/index.htm

REFERENCES

Bauer, S., & Brazer, D. (2013). Navigating your way through the research jungle. *Principal, 92*(2), 22–25.

Buck, S., Ritter, G. W., Jensen, N. C., & Rose, C. P. (2010). Teachers say the most interesting things: An alternative view of testing. *Phi Delta Kappan, 91*(6), 50–54.

Clausen, M. (2010). *Three-dimensional assessment of technology integration* (Unpublished paper.) University of Montana, Division of Educational Leadership, Phyllis J. Washington College of Education and Human Sciences, Missoula.

Coggins, C., Zuckerman, S., & McKelvey, L. (2010). Holding on to Gen Y. *Educational Leadership, 67*(8), 70–74.

Connelly, G. (2010). An unknown future. *Principal, 89*(3), 4.

Devine, P. A. (2012). A technology enabled journey. *Principal, 91*(5), 4.

Dillon, R., & Nixon, M. (2014). Building powerful parent relationships. *Principal, 93*(3), 48.

Duncan, G. J., & Murnane, R. J. (2014). Growing income inequality threatens American education. *Phi Delta Kappan, 95*(6), 8–14.

Educational Technology Support Center. (2008). *Technology use in classrooms.* Retrieved from http://www.edtech.wednet.edu/Tiers/TechUseIn Classrooms.cfm

Foster, A. (2014). Time for détente between charter and traditional schools. *Phi Delta Kappan, 95*(5), 18–22.

Gardner, N. S., & Powell, R. (2013–2014). The common core is a change for the better. *Phi Delta Kappan, 95*(4), 49–53.

Glatthorn, A. A. (1987). *Curriculum leadership.* New York, NY: HarperCollins.

Hawkins, B. (2010). *The advance of distance education* (Unpublished paper). University of Montana, Missoula.

Ivey, G. (2010). Texts that matter. *Educational Leadership, 67*(6), 18–23.

Johnson, D. (2014). Power up! Why Facebook belongs in your school. *Educational Leadership, 71*(5), 82–83.

Journell, W., Ayers, C. A., & Beeson, M. W. (2014). Tweeting in the classroom. *Phi Delta Kappan, 95*(5), 63–67.

Levin, B. (2013). Shanghai and Seoul plan higher achievement. *Phi Delta Kappan, 94*(8), 74–75.

Martineau, J. A. (2010). The validity of value-added models: An allegory. *Phi Delta Kappan, 91*(7), 64–67.

Martinez, M. R., & McGrath, D. (2013). How can schools develop self-directed learners? *Phi Delta Kappan, 95*(2), 23–27.

Maunsell, P. A. (2014). Communication is key to common core. *Phi Delta Kappan, 95*(6), 61–65.

Miller, S. R., Drill, K., & Behrstock, E. (2010). Meeting teachers halfway: Making educational research relevant to teachers. *Phi Delta Kappan, 91*(7), 31–34.

Moore, R., & Berry, B. (2010). The teachers of 2030. *Educational Leadership, 67*(8), 36–39.

Murray, M. (2010). *Curriculum foundations for the Global Village Academy* (Unpublished paper). University of Montana, Missoula.

Protheroe, N. (2010). Schools as effective data users. *Principal, 90*(1), 24–28.

Snyder, C. W. (2004). *Calendar of activities/itinerary narrative* (Unpublished paper). University of Montana International Studies Program, Missoula.

Stiggins, R. J. (2002). Assessment crisis: The absence of assessment for learning. *Phi Delta Kappan, 83*(10), 758–765.

Tashlik, P. (2010). Changing the national conversation on assessment. *Phi Delta Kappan, 91*(6), 55–59.

Toch, T. (2010). The Sizer legacy. *Phi Delta Kappan, 91*(5), 74–75.

Tyler, R. W. (1949). *Basic principles of curriculum and instruction.* Chicago, IL: University of Chicago Press.

Whitehead, B. M., Boschee, F., & Decker, R. H. (2013). *The principal: Leadership for a global society.* Thousand Oaks, CA: Sage.

Whitehead, B. M., Jensen, D. F. N., & Boschee, F. (2013). *Planning for technology: A guide for school administrators, technology coordinators, and curriculum leaders.* Thousand Oaks, CA: Corwin Press.

Wulf, K. M., & Schave, B. (1984). *Curriculum design: A handbook for educators.* Glenview, IL: Scott, Foresman.

Young, D. A. (2013). From a teacher to principal: Five effective tools. *Principal, 92*(5), 30–33.

Zhang, M., Lundeberg, M., & Eberhardt, J. (2010). Seeing what you normally don't see. *Phi Delta Kappan, 91*(6), 60–65.

PART III

Curriculum Management

Many curriculum leaders focus unduly on the written curriculum, neglecting the taught curriculum and the supported curriculum. The purpose of Part III is to incorporate ways to supervise instructional processes and the selection of materials, recommend specific processes for developing and implementing curriculum, provide a rationale for curricular alignment, and make specific suggestions for developing and implementing a comprehensive evaluation plan.

Supervising the Curriculum

Teachers and Materials

Evaluation and supervision are now becoming center stage—pushed there by the larger accountability movement (Murphy, Goldring, & Porter, 2014). Keeping with this perspective, Chapter 9 highlights supervision as it establishes a foundation for future thought and reflection. With a better understanding of past and present supervision approaches, school leaders will be better able to establish an evaluative process allowing for faculty input, collaboration,

Questions addressed in this chapter include the following:

- Who are some of the major leaders who have been concerned with supervision, and what are some of the current approaches to curriculum supervision?
- What are some of the issues and problems related to supervision that are facing curriculum leaders today?
- What are some of the major roles associated with curriculum supervision?
- Why is motivating staff an important component of supervision?
- Why are some of Abraham Maslow's theories on supervision still relevant today?
- What are the elements that make up supportive curriculum, and why is the supportive curriculum important?

Key to Leadership

One of the most important aspects of a quality supervision program is the area of assessment. No program can be significantly improved without assessment of both teacher and instructional programs.

and the promotion of individual professional growth and development. The terms *leadership* and *supervision*, as discussed in this chapter, focus on numerous research findings as well as identify specific skills and practices school leaders can develop if they are going to be successful in reforming schools in our ever-changing globally competitive world.

SUPERVISING THE TAUGHT CURRICULUM: CURRENT APPROACHES

The best measure of teaching effectiveness is a teacher's ability to identify a student performance challenge, to collect evidence that systematically addresses this challenge, and to adjust instruction based on the evidence (Radoslovich, Roberts, & Plaza, 2014). To reach this level of excellence, principals need to work with teachers to supervise and coordinate decisions within and between grade levels. Doing so will help align the school's curriculum with state and Common Core State Standards (CCSS), both horizontally and vertically. Additionally, a well-aligned and supervised curriculum ensures students are taught the necessary skills and standards that will be assessed on statewide exams.

Curriculum Tip 9.1	Helping teachers improve curriculum is about best practice, collaboration, and trust.

Leaders concerned with supervising the taught curriculum have available to them a number of historical approaches to supervision. In reviewing the literature, five seem to have had the greatest impact. These are Hunter's (1984) "Knowing, Teaching, and Supervising"; Farrell's (2005, 2006) "Teaching Backwards"; Glickman, Gordon, and Ross-Gordon's (2003) *Supervision and Instructional Leadership: A Developmental Approach;* Costa and Garmston's (2002) *Cognitive Coaching: A Foundation for Renaissance Schools;* and Glatthorn's (1984) *Differentiated Supervision.*

The following provides a review of the supervision models of Hunter; Farrell; Glickman, Gordon and Ross-Gordon; as well as Costa and Garmston.

Hunter's "Essential Elements"

During the middle of the 1980s, the work of Madeline Hunter seemed to be the dominant mode of supervision: Several state offices of education, in fact, had given the "Hunter approach" their official blessing and encouraged its adoption through workshops for administrators, supervisors, and teachers. Although Hunter herself advocated a number of "templates" that could be used to analyze and improve teaching, her **elements of lesson design** attracted the most attention. By reviewing the theory of and research on learning, Hunter was able to identify the elements of good lesson design shown in Exhibit 9.1.

What made the Hunter "elements" so popular with practitioners? First, they were based on sound theory, even though the research base seemed thin to some critics. Second, they

EXHIBIT 9.1	Hunter's Elements of Lesson Design
Element	*Description*
Anticipatory set	A mental set that causes students to focus on what will be learned. It may also give practice in helping students achieve the learning and yield diagnostic data for the teacher. Example: "Look at the paragraph on the board. What do you think might be the most important part to remember?"
Objective and purpose	Not only do students learn more effectively when they know what they're they are supposed to be learning and why that learning is important to them, but teachers teach more effectively when they have that same information. Example: "Frequently, people have difficulty remembering things that are important to them. Sometimes, you feel you have studied hard and yet do not remember some of the important parts. Today, we're going to learn ways to identify what's important, and then we'll practice methods we can use to remember important things."
Input	Students must acquire new information about the knowledge, process, or skill they are to achieve. To design the input phase of the lesson so that a successful outcome becomes predictable, the teacher must have analyzed the final objective to identify knowledge and skills that need to be acquired.
Modeling	"Seeing" what is meant is an important adjunct to learning. To avoid stifling creativity, showing several examples of the process or products that students are expected to acquire or produce is helpful.
Checking for understanding	Before students are expected to do something, the teacher should determine that they understand what they are supposed to do and that they have the minimum skills required.
Guided practice	Students practice their new knowledge or skill under direct teacher supervision. New learning is like wet cement; it is easily damaged. An error at the beginning of learning can easily "set" so that correcting it later is harder than correcting it immediately.
Independent practice	Independent practice is assigned only after the teacher is reasonably sure that students will not make serious errors. After an initial lesson, students frequently are not ready to practice independently, and the teacher has committed a pedagogical error if unsupervised practice is expected.

SOURCE: Adapted from Marzano (2003).

gave educators a common vocabulary to discuss teaching: Everyone could talk about the **anticipatory set** and know what was meant. Finally, they seemed "teacher-friendly": They did not require teachers to adopt new behaviors but, instead, helped teachers systematize what they already had been doing.

Hunter's approach, however, was not without critics, most of whom were university professors, not practitioners. Those critics faulted the model, first of all, because it offered a narrowly constricted view of teaching. Sergiovanni (1985) made the point that Hunter conceived teaching and learning only as an instructional delivery system, a conception that saw teaching as sending information through a pipeline to passive students. Others were unhappy because the elements seemed to be derived from the direct instruction model of teaching and slighted other models, although Hunter argued that the elements could be used flexibly in any model of teaching.

Although many administrators who had adopted the Hunter "elements" approach reported enthusiastic reception on the part of teachers and noted many positive effects, the early research on its impact on achievement indicated that it was not more effective than standard approaches to supervision (see Stallings, 1986).

Farrell's "Backwards Model"

Jack Farrell (2005), once a consultant teacher in the Conejo Valley Unified School District, California, took issue with Madeline Hunter's elements of lesson design. As a consultant teacher, Farrell had the opportunity to watch many hours of instruction. He believed that regardless of grade level or content area, certain pedagogical practices, for the most part, are systemic and unassailable. Besides, he believed that education at the time was experiencing the first generation of teachers who were themselves taught this way and who were products of teacher-training programs for which Hunter's strategies were nearly sacrosanct. With that said, specific aspects of Farrell's Elements of Lesson Design Model are noted in Exhibit 9.2.

As can be seen in a comparison of Hunter and Farrell's lesson designs, both models represent examples of forward and backwards design. The condensed practices of Hunter's model, the forward model, are (a) oral instruction, followed by (b) **permanent scaffolding,** to be followed by (c) front-loading prior knowledge. The condensed premises for the backwards model, proposed by Farrell, are (a) all learning begins in the text, (b) the teacher's job is to engage his or her reader and activate his or her prior knowledge, (c) multiple readings of academic text should be routine, (d) independent mastery of text is crucial for academic success, (e) writing not only records thought but it creates thought, (f) teachers should frequently communicate their ideas through writing, and (g) rhetoric is as important as the concept. Interestingly enough, both Farrell's model and Hunter's model are still used in schools today.

Glickman, Gordon, and Ross-Gordon's "Developmental Supervision"

In contrast to Hunter's model (and later Farrell's model), Carl Glickman and colleagues' (2003) "developmental supervision" model is characterized by two important features. First, Glickman and colleagues argued that the development of teacher thought should be the focus of supervisors' work with teachers—helping them increase their conceptual level of development. They posited three levels of development: low abstract (the teacher is confused, lacks ideas, wants to be shown, gives habitual responses to varying decisions), moderate abstract (the teacher depends on authority, identifies one dimension of

EXHIBIT 9.2 Farrell's Elements of Lesson Design

Element	Description
Independent practice (all learning begins in text)	As much as possible, learning should begin with students engaging the text. It then becomes the writer's responsibility to orient his or her readers and access their prior knowledge, if necessary. In the absence of a suitable text, the teacher can write it. This is no small point. It is crucial for students to glean ideas by decoding text and correctly deducing voice and tone, rather than for them to listen to these same ideas orally or visually presented by the teacher.
Guided practice	The independent practice precedes the guided practice. Not only should all learning begin in text but students should routinely reread any text they have difficulty with. The guided practice begins only after teachers have given students every chance to independently master text, or at least to proceed as far as they can on their own.
Check for understanding	The initial class discussion of the lesson concepts follows a student's deep immersion in text-based learning. This is where the teacher can use questioning techniques to find out what his or her students understand. All discussions should be text based. Displaying of text is more valuable than culling ideas from the text and transforming them into a visual display. It is at this point in the lesson that the teacher offers scaffolds to the students who need them. These scaffolds should be for targeted and temporary use. The teacher should continually test for independence by attempting in future lessons to remove the scaffolds.
Modeling	Only after the teacher has pulled all he or she can from the students regarding their understanding of the text does he or she model how this might be done differently or more deeply. This modeling can be oral or visual. It can even be the sharing of a critical piece about the reading from a secondary source, or written by the teacher.
Application	Students are exposed to new, or similar, concepts in new texts and asked to transfer skills acquired during the lesson. The main purpose of reading any text is to become a better reader of the next text.
Application/ independent practice	The last step of a lesson becomes the first step of the next lesson.

SOURCE: Farrell (2005).

instructional problem, generates one to three ideas about solutions, needs assistance from experts), and high abstract (the teacher uses various sources to identify problems, generates multiple ideas, chooses for self the action to be taken).

This "thought-oriented" approach permeates the four ways supervisors can help teachers grow: by offering direct assistance (what is usually called "clinical supervision"), providing in-service education, working with teachers in curriculum development, and helping them carry out action research.

Although Glickman et al. (2003) admitted that the results on developmental supervision have been "predictably mixed," both features make the model seem useful for curriculum leaders. They recognized the fact that teachers are different and require contrary approaches. They also broadened the prevailing understanding of supervision by emphasizing the importance of in-service, curriculum development, and action research.

Costa and Garmston's "Cognitive Coaching"

Similar to Glickman et al. (2003), Costa and Garmston (2002) emphasized the importance of teacher thinking, although their approach seems quite dissimilar. Rather than using all the approaches Glickman et al. (2003) advocated, they gave their attention exclusively to direct assistance, or clinical supervision; however, it is clinical supervision with a profound differential. Costa and Garmston were not concerned initially with skills; they believed it more productive to emphasize teacher thinking. As the supervisor works with teachers in this "cognitive coaching" mode, the supervisor has these goals: to create and manage a trusting relationship, to facilitate teacher learning by restructuring teacher thinking, and to develop teacher autonomy. These goals are achieved primarily through in-depth conferences in which the supervisor listens actively, questions insightfully, and responds congruently.

Although the authors indicated that their approach was based on current theory and sound research on adult development, they did not offer any empirical evidence for its effectiveness. Its emphasis on teacher thinking and its concern for teacher autonomy both seem to be useful from the standpoint of curriculum leaders.

ELEMENTS OF SUPERVISION

Having identified and previewed some of the earlier models, it is perhaps best to note the actual elements of supervision. This involves shifting focus from influencing singular teacher actions through individual classroom observations to increased involvement via supervision of teacher teams. In this regard, principals can have greater impact on the actions of the teacher—as well as on student learning (Hewson, 2013). Keeping with this perspective, many unsolved problems can be associated with the need for better supervision practices and the formation of an effective instructional program.

A major problem that has been facing school leaders and supervisors historically is the inability of instructional programs to reach students and to meet their needs. This situation led to the passage of the No Child Left Behind Act (NCLB), which is responsible for holding schools more accountable for student learning levels and student achievement. Regrettably, some scholars (e.g., Maleyko & Gawlik, 2011) posit that NCLB has narrowed the curriculum

Curriculum Tip 9.2	Three main influences that appear to thread their way through the supervised curriculum are students, classroom climate, and informational resources.

and discouraged the use of instructionally useful forms of assessment that involve extensive writing and analysis. This has evolved into a growing concern over skills and school climate and is revolutionizing the way schools are developing curriculum from preschool years through high school. In addition, the lack of real understanding in various subject areas has led to CCSS as well as a series of mandates from the federal government requiring strict proficiency levels and adequate yearly progress goals.

In the quest to address these issues, curriculum planners, principals, and classroom teachers are finding new and innovative ways via technology to deliver subsequent stages of educational development for students. As school leadership transitions into the 21st century, and with an outcry for accountability, there becomes a reality check that takes place among administrators and teachers. With this in mind, the question then becomes this: As a school leader, how can I initiate the needed improvements for improved student success and at the same time create an atmosphere of community for faculty and staff? This seemingly simple question has created problems and issues for school administrators all across the United States. Moreover, it is a question that needs to be acted upon, immediately, if building-level leaders are to ensure the success of the educational process.

Understanding Change

As school leaders struggle for answers to educational reform, they are finding a review of the literature (on change) to be a foundational piece to the puzzle. School principals and others, then, will need to develop knowledge and skills in managing the change process. This will entail future building-level leaders being skilled in the different orders of change and how these changes will affect faculty, students, and community members.

As new curriculums are developed, best practices identified, and state standards applied to education, there will be a need for skilled administrators to monitor and evaluate the implementation process. Without proper change management, as well as an understanding the implementation of change, the process will not be voluntarily accepted and in the end possibly fail because of lack of ownership on the part of the faculty.

Situational Awareness

With so many changes emerging on the horizon, school leaders are discovering that the most important tool for learning is the development of positive relationships between teachers and students (LaPoma & Kantor, 2013–2014). Likewise, communication is becoming the key to making these relationships work. Keeping with this perspective, school leaders are needing to become "situationally" aware of their surroundings at all times—especially due to imposed changes on education, either at the local, state, or national level. Thus, any successful supervisor of the 21st century needs to acquire the skill of "looking around the corner" as a way of anticipating implications that can induce change in their building or district. Likewise, any supervisor who has acquired the skill of "looking around the corner" will be able to develop strategies and answers to questions that will arise with the result of moving into the future and away from the status quo. In the end, it will be the building-level leaders who will be the students of best practice and research-based learning and who will be able to provide a back support and foundation for faculty, students, and community—especially those who are not convinced of the need to look at different practices and initiatives that provide evidence for a need to change.

School leaders who have not developed the skill of being situationally aware will be caught in the quagmire of faculty debate concerning best practice about teaching and learning. Thus, principals, as well as other supervisors, need to arm themselves with data and evidence to counter nonbelievers and those who believe we need to provide the education that we received when we were in school. Without data and evidence, change will not happen, and the educational experience that students will receive will be status quo and not geared to the global society in which they will function.

Curriculum Tip 9.3	Teacher evaluation and supervision are defined as the following: • Teacher evaluation is a summative organizational function to make a comprehensive judgment concerning a teacher's performance and competence for the purpose of continuing employment. • Supervision is a formative organizational function concerned with providing information to the teacher for personal growth in their teaching practice.

Dilemma for Supervisors

Clearly, there is a perceived dilemma between supervision and evaluation that continues to confuse the world of educational practice. Some school leaders misguidedly define *supervision* and *evaluation* as the same function—in both policy and practice. Other school leaders make a distinction between teacher supervision and evaluation in policy and yet use the same procedures for both functions, with the result of the teachers viewing the process as evaluative.

This educational dilemma has inadvertently created a lack of commonly accepted definitions of terms and concepts. With this in mind, the authors define *teacher evaluation* as a summative organizational function to make a comprehensive judgment concerning a teacher's performance and competence for the purpose of continuing employment. In contrast, *teacher supervision* is a formative organizational function concerned with providing information to the teacher for personal growth in teaching practice.

Differentiated Supervision

In a differentiated supervision setting, school leaders can conduct a series of coordinated observations as well as provide for cooperative professional development that allows for small teams of peers working together to obtain mutual growth. For the most part, the concept of differentiated supervision weighs heavily on the shoulders of each building principal, or supervisor, to understand the different professional models within a particular school building and to be able to provide support for a variety of professional development models. Regardless of the process, the revised Interstate School Leaders Licensure Consortium (ISLLC) Standards (2008) indicate the need for the principal to take on significant responsibility of being an instructional leader. ISLLC Standard 2 states the following:

> An educational leader promotes the success of every student by advocating, nurturing, and sustaining a school culture and instructional program conducive to student learning and staff professional development.
> Functions of Standard 2 include the following:

- Nurture and sustain a culture of collaboration, trust, learning, and high expectations.
- Create a comprehensive, rigorous, and coherent curricular program.
- Create a personalized and motivating learning environment for students.
- Supervise instruction.
- Develop assessment and accountability systems to monitor student progress.
- Develop the instructional and leadership capacity of staff.
- Maximize time spent on quality instruction.
- Promote the use of the most effective and appropriate technologies to support teaching and learning.
- Monitor and evaluate the impact of the instructional program.

As can be seen, through this differentiated supervision effort, the district, schools, and teachers can work together to reach a goal of successful instruction that will improve student achievement. This systemic effort can create an environment where district instructional goals are implemented, monitored, and evaluated.

THE ROLE OF THE CURRICULUM SUPERVISOR

Developing ways to get to the heart of curriculum programming and bring about educationally significant change lies largely with individual school principals. As noted by Gail Connelly (2013), executive director of the National Association of Elementary School Principals (NAESP), building-level principals, as local facilitators of change, are largely responsible for steering their schools though the numerous implementation hurdles as related to CCSS. NAESP polled over 1000 principals in 14 states and found most building-level principals have curricular modifications and supervision plans already in place. In addition, these same administrators are currently gathering evidence to assess the effects of the standards on teaching.

Curriculum Tip 9.4	The role of the principal has grown from that of a manager to that of a change agent, an administrative-organizational specialist.

Clearly, in today's world of new standards and change, school principals along with other building-level leaders need to be aware and knowledgeable about workable approaches to curriculum supervision. Likewise, they have to know how to write and direct curriculum, as well as have the ability to find needed supportive materials during a time of declining budgets. Even more importantly, these same school leaders must have a new sense of direction as to how to improve teaching and learning. This involves creating a quality classroom-learning environment based on an effective well-planned **differentiated professional development** program.

DIFFERENTIATED PROFESSIONAL DEVELOPMENT

As part of the supervision process, it is critical for teachers to discover new ways of teaching and learning (Plonczak, Brooks, Wilson, Elijah, & Caliendo, 2014). Each school possesses its own traditions, values, culture, and willingness to accept change. It is in this light of multiple variables affecting school climate that differentiated professional development should be considered. Differentiated professional development is essentially a reconceptualization of the supervisory function, one that attempts to broaden the practitioner's view of supervision.

Curriculum Tip 9.5	Leaders who wish to improve the taught curriculum need to reconceptualize the supervisory process—to see it more broadly and to differentiate its use in relation to teacher need.

In an attempt to reconceptualize and revamp the supervision process, it seems useful to substitute the term *professional development* for those activities ordinarily subsumed under the heading of *supervision*. The advantage of using new terminology is that it facilitates the task of reconceptualizing the field by distancing users from the restrictive assumptions implicit in the old language. In this reconceptualization, teacher development is used in this sense: All systematic processes used by school administrators, supervisors, and teachers to help teachers grow professionally are divided into four distinct yet related tasks. These are professional development, informal observations, **rating,** and individual development.

Professional Development

The term *professional development* is used here to designate all those district- and school-sponsored programs, both formal and informal, offered to groups of teachers in response to organizational needs. The importance of professional development and professional learning communities (PLCs) has been noted in Chapter 5, as an aspect of the planning process, and in Chapter 7, as a critical ingredient in improving a field of study.

The ability of teachers to develop and guide curriculum requires a sophisticated set of judgments about the content, students, learning, and teaching. It should be noted that professional development can be both formal and informal. Formal professional development programs have a specific agenda, a set schedule, and a structured set of experiences. Typically, such formal programs are skill focused. The research on such skill-focused programs suggests that they will be more effective if they embody the tested practices recommended in Chapter 7. As noted in previous chapters, professional development of both the formal and informal type is essential throughout the curriculum development and improvement process. If professional development has helped teachers change their perceptions of a subject, to develop the materials to be used in implementing the new curriculum, and to acquire the skills needed to deliver it, then it is quite likely that the written, the taught, the tested, and the learned curricula will be in much closer congruence.

Informal Observations

Informal observations are brief, unannounced classroom visits, lasting from perhaps 5 to 15 minutes. Some term these informal visits **walkthroughs**; some experts in the corporate world call such informal observations "management by walking around." To make accurate decisions based on short observations in the walkthrough, principals should ask six questions, which are posed and defined in Exhibit 9.3.

EXHIBIT 9.3 Seeing the Trees and the Forest	
Questions to Ask Oneself	*Answers*
1. Are teachers using research-based teaching strategies?	1. It is important to look for teachers' use of instructional strategies. No single "right way" to teach exists, but great teachers use myriad teaching strategies, understand the instructional purposes of each, and use each strategy intentionally.
2. Do student grouping patterns support learning?	2. "Cooperative learning" is one of the nine categories of effective instruction in *Classroom Instruction That Works*. It includes supporting student learning using large groups, small groups, pairs, cooperative groups (each member has an assigned role), or working individually. Determining whether teachers are intentional in their use of grouping patterns is key.
3. Are teachers and students using technology to support student learning?	3. Educational technology is more prevalent in today's classrooms, but many teachers still do not put these tools to their best use. During walkthroughs, principals should note the technology being used and how it is being used.
4. Do students understand their goals for learning?	4. While conducting a walkthrough, principals should go beyond conducting a checklist of teacher practices; they also should observe what students are doing and learning. Are students able to explain what they are doing in terms of their learning goals? Are students involved in true learning objectives, or are they just focused on activities? Over time, student responses will tell how well teachers are communicating these goals and whether students are engaged and deliberate about their own learning.

Questions to Ask Oneself	Answers
5. Are students learning both basic and higher order levels of knowledge?	5. Classroom observation also should reveal if students are learning at the lower rungs of Bloom's taxonomy (e.g., remembering, understanding, and applying) or at the higher levels (analyzing, evaluating, and creating). All of these forms are necessary and appropriate in different contexts. If the majority of student learning, however, is focused on lower-level learning, principals should have conversations with teachers about the levels of student learning they observed.
6. Do student achievement data correlate with walkthrough data?	6. Principals should also view classrooms through the lens of student achievement data. When principals conduct their classroom observations within the context of student achievement data, they can dramatically increase the acuity of their observations and discover ways to improve teaching and learning.

SOURCE: Adapted from Pitler & Goodwin (2008).

There are a number of misconceptions on how to use the data generated from classroom walkthroughs. Likewise, some teachers' resistance to walkthroughs is because they or their principals, or both, are unclear about how observation data is or should be used. The walkthrough data should be used in the following ways:

- *Coaching, not evaluating.* The purpose of a walkthrough is not to pass judgment on teachers but to coach them to higher levels of performance. Walkthroughs are *not* teacher evaluations; they are a method for identifying opportunities for improvement and supporting the sharing of best practices across the school.
- *Measuring the impact of staff development efforts.* In its best use, the walkthrough process will provide strong data to schools and districts regarding the extent to which their professional development initiatives are actually making it into the classroom. . . . By systematically collecting and analyzing data from classroom observation, school leaders can determine whether staff development efforts are making a difference and guide real-time adjustments to the professional development they are offering teachers.
- *Supporting PLCs with walkthrough data.* Savvy principals also understand the power of sharing their aggregated observation data with school staff to support PLCs. (Pitler & Goodwin, 2008, p. 11)

For walkthroughs to be highly successful, the data collected must be aggregated over a period of time. "One or two, or even 10 observations of an individual teacher, do not provide a clear picture of the quality of instruction within a school. But 10 visits each to 40 teachers' classrooms does provide a more accurate picture" (Pitler & Goodwin, 2008, p. 11). Pitler and Goodwin see the walkthroughs as a mosaic. "Looking at one tile in isolation tells you almost nothing. But when you see 400 of those tiles laid out in an orderly manner, a picture begins to emerge" (p. 11). Thus, when principals or supervisors know what to look for and understand the purpose of their observations, "the power of walkthroughs lies not only in seeing the trees, but also the forest" (p. 11).

Instructional Rounds

Instructional rounds involve teacher observations and help enhance pedagogical skills as well as develop a culture of collaboration. The primary purpose of instructional rounds is for observing teachers to compare their own instructional practices with those of the teachers they observe (Marzano, 2011). The rounds are generally facilitated by a lead teacher, although an administrator might lead the rounds as well. Observed teachers are volunteers, or selectively asked to participate, and normally are drawn from a pool of master teachers. To help move things along, groups conducting instructional rounds are kept small.

Often, a focus area, strategy, or topic of interest is identified prior to the instructional rounds. Visiting teachers spend 10 to 15 minutes observing in a classroom and then reconvene to reflect on their experience. Ideally, observing teachers will be able to identify instructional practices that they use in their own classrooms. The goal at that juncture is for teachers to have an opportunity to observe and interact with their colleagues in a non-evaluative way regarding instruction.

Rating

Specific, accurate, and timely feedback is often a missing element in leadership encounters (Reeves, 2007). This is especially significant when related to decision making. In the reconceptualization, the term *rating* is used in this sense: the process of making formative and summative assessments of teacher performance for purposes of administrative decision making. The term is chosen to distinguish this formal assessment function from a more general act of evaluation, which is often construed to mean a judgment about the quality of performance made on any occasion for a variety of purposes. This distinction between *rating* and *evaluation* is intended to clarify the conceptual confusion so prevalent in our professional discourse. In reviewing the literature, one interesting example of the conceptual confusion is McGreal's (1983) monograph titled *Successful Teacher Evaluation,* which really seems to be a treatise on teacher supervision.

Perhaps some examples of the two concepts would provide more clarity. You make an informal observation of a teacher with a disorderly class; you decide you do not like what you see. You observe a teacher for the purpose of diagnosing teaching style; you try your best to be objective, but you find yourself smiling in approval. You conduct a professional development session and ask one of the teachers to demonstrate a particular skill; you are not happy with the demonstration. In each instance, you have made an evaluation—a judgment about quality. Despite all attempts to be objective, it is probably impossible to observe the act of teaching without making judgments. Most teachers would not want an observer to pretend that he or she had not made any judgments about their performance. In addition, there is some evidence that supervisors who are candid about their assessments are deemed more effective than those who do not provide evaluative feedback (see Gersten, Green, & Davis, 1985).

Now consider a contrary example. You visit a teacher's class in September with a rating form in hand in which explicit criteria are stated along with the standards of performance. You observe the class and complete the rating form. You confer with the teacher and say, "Your performance in that class was not satisfactory; I hope your supervisor will be able to help you improve before the next rating observation." You have made a formative rating. You make several more formative rating observations throughout the year. Then, in May, you make a summative assessment based on all your data and say to the teacher, "Your performance this year was unsatisfactory; your contract will not be renewed."

Perhaps one more analogy will help. The gymnast performs a set of exercises at a meet. The coach watches and says, "Your approach was faulty; we'll have to work on that." The coach has made an evaluation. The judges were also watching. They hold up their score-cards with numerical scores on each. The judges have made a rating.

What rating systems are most effective? After studying 32 school districts reported to have effective rating systems, Wise, Darling-Hammond, McLaughlin, and Bernstein (as cited in Glatthorn, 1987) reached five conclusions (their term *teacher evaluation* is used next instead of the narrower term *rating* because many of the systems included processes that in the reconceptualization are considered primarily developmental):

1. To succeed, the teacher-evaluation system must suit the goals, management style, conception of teaching, and community values of the school district.

2. Top-level commitment to and resources for evaluation are more important than the particular kind of checklist or procedures used.

3. The school district should decide about the main purpose of the rating system and then match the process to the purpose.

4. The evaluation process must be seen to have utility: It is cost effective, fair, valid, and reliable.

5. Teacher involvement in and responsibility for the process improves the quality of teacher evaluation. (p. 229)

Obviously, these conclusions suggest that several types of rating systems can be effective. However, if the purpose is administrative decision making, then a criterion-based system using multiple observations seems preferable. One process that has been used effectively in several districts is described next.

Together, administrators, supervisors, and teachers analyze the job of teaching and the research on effective teaching. From those reviews, they develop a comprehensive set of criteria dealing with the three important aspects of the teacher's role. First, they define the noninstructional aspects of the teacher's role. In most cases, a short list of noninstructional responsibilities is all that is necessary: Supervise students in noninstructional settings, communicate with parents, attend faculty meetings and professional development sessions as required, and carry out other assigned duties.

By reviewing the research, supervisors can identify the essential instructional skills that can be directly observed, such as providing a clear lesson structure. Finally, they identify

Curriculum Tip 9.6	The research-based list of the "essential observables" and the "essential nonobservables" plays a crucial role in both rating teachers and helping them grow professionally.

the essential instructional skills that are not always directly observable, such as making valid tests. Therefore, care should be taken to ensure that the list includes only those skills well supported by the research. One formulation of these skills is shown in Exhibit 9.4.

EXHIBIT 9.4   Essential Skills of Teaching

The following list of essential skills is intended to provide general guidelines for administrators, supervisors, and teachers. While based on a careful review of the literature and a reflective analysis of shared experience, it is not intended as a definitive prescription of the "best way to teach." Other cautions need to be noted:

1. The list focuses on the instructional role of the teacher; it does not address the important noninstructional responsibilities.
2. The list does not speak directly to the skills of lesson planning and communicating. As will be noted next, effective planning and clear communication lie behind several of the skills listed.

Essential Skills Observable in Classroom Instruction

Lesson Content and Pace

1. Chooses content for the lesson that relates directly to curriculum goals, is at an appropriate level of difficulty, and corresponds with assessment measures
2. Presents content of lesson in a way that demonstrates mastery of subject matter
3. Paces instruction appropriately

Climate

1. Creates a desirable environment that reflects appropriate discipline and supports the instructional function
2. Communicates realistically high expectations for students
3. Uses instructional time efficiently, allocating most of the time to curriculum-related instruction
4. Keeps students on task
5. Provides organizing structure for classroom work: reviews, gives overview, specifies objectives, gives clear directions, summarizes, makes relevant assignments
6. Uses instructional strategies, learning activities, and group structures that are appropriate to objectives; responds to student needs; and reflects sound learning theory
7. Ensures active participation of students in learning activities

Assessment

1. Monitors student learning and uses evaluative data to adjust instruction
2. Questions effectively: asks clear questions, asks questions at appropriate level of difficulty, varies types of questions
3. Responds effectively to student answers: allows sufficient wait time, gives prompt and corrective feedback, praises appropriately

Essential Skills Not Directly Observable in Classroom Instruction

1. Develops long-term plans that reflect curricular priorities and adequately deal with all aspects of written curriculum
2. Uses tests that are consistent with instructional objectives
3. Grades student learning fairly, objectively, and validly

NOTE: This list of skills has been synthesized from several reviews of the research on teaching effectiveness. Three sources have been especially useful: Berliner (1984), Brophy and Good (1986), and Rosenshine and Stevens (1986).

The essential observable skills become the basis of a "rating observation" form, which identifies each skill and specifies several indicators of performance for each one. A portion of one such form is shown in Exhibit 9.5. That form is then used in making a rating observation. The rater tells the teacher that he or she will be observing the class sometime in the next week to rate performance. The teacher is familiar with both the criteria and the indicators and understands clearly that the purpose of the observation is to rate, not to improve instruction. The rater arrives with the rating observation form in hand. The rater observes solely to rate: He or she makes careful notes throughout the lesson about the teacher's performance in relation to each of the criteria and then makes a holistic rating of the entire class. Then the rater holds a rating observation conference to inform the teacher of the general rating, review the specific strengths and weaknesses, and with the teacher lay out a professional development plan for remedying any perceived deficiencies.

All these formative data are drawn together in a summative rating conference: The rater reviews with the teacher his or her performance of the noninstructional responsibilities, summarizes the results of all the rating observations, synthesizes the results of the conferences at which the nonobservable skills were assessed, and provides a final holistic rating of the teacher's performance for that year. The conference ends with a view to the future: How will the teacher build on strengths and remedy any deficiencies?

Obviously, such a rating system will require a great amount of administrator and supervisor time if it is to be thorough—much more time than is perhaps warranted in relation to the value of the process for teachers who are known to be highly competent. Therefore, the reconceptualized model proposes two rating tracks: standard rating and intensive rating. The standard rating is used for career teachers whose performance is clearly satisfactory; it is a pro forma compliance with the state school code, usually involving one observation and one final conference. An intensive rating is used for all probationary

---

EXHIBIT 9.5 Portion of Rating Observation Form

Teacher's name _____   Rater _____

Class _____   Date and time _____

Rating Code: 1 = unsatisfactory; 2 = satisfactory; 3 = more than satisfactory; NA = not able to make a judgment

☐   1.   Chooses content that relates directly to curriculum goals and assessment measures, at appropriate level of difficulty

☐   2.   Chooses unrelated content, too difficult or too easy

☐   3.   Chooses related content, with appropriate difficulty

☐   4.   Chooses related content, with appropriate difficulty, relates content to student needs and interests

☐   5.   Integrates technology effectively

Rating

Observations supporting rating:

Teacher comments:

Overall rating for this class:

1. Which essential teaching skill(s) does this teacher seem to use most successfully?
2. Which essential teaching skill(s) does this teacher need to improve?

---

teachers, for any teachers being considered for special promotion, and for teachers whose level of performance is questionable. The intensive rating involves several observations by two or more observers, with a conference following each observation.

Individual Development

In contrast to professional development, individual work is with a single person, not the group; and the needs of the individual, not those of the organization, predominate.

Curriculum Tip 9.7	Individual development includes all the processes used by and with individual teachers to help them grow professionally.

For two reasons, a differentiated system of professional development is recommended—one that gives teachers some options in the type of developmental processes used. First, as noted previously, most principals are too busy to provide clinical supervision to all teachers.

Second, teachers vary significantly in their conceptual development, learning styles, and professional needs; thus, they should be provided with different types of developmental services. Accordingly, the differentiated system offers three options for individual development: intensive, cooperative, and self-directed.

Intensive development is ordinarily called "clinical supervision," although it is more broadly construed. It is an intensive and systematic process in which a supervisor, administrator, or expert teacher works closely with an individual teacher in an attempt to effect significant improvement in the essential skills of teaching. While intensive development is most needed by inexperienced and struggling teachers, it can be provided for any teacher who wants to work with a skilled educational leader to bring about significant improvement in teaching performance. In providing intensive development, the leader works closely with the teacher in determining which of several processes will be used. Rather than relying solely on planning conferences, observations, and debriefing conferences, they examine together a wide array of commonsense processes to determine which ones might be most effectively employed:

- *Planning conferences:* conferring with the teacher on yearly planning, semester planning, unit planning, and daily planning
- *Student assessment conferences:* conferring with the teacher about assessing student progress, testing, grading, and record keeping
- *Diagnostic observations and diagnostic feedback:* observing all significant transactions in a classroom to diagnose priority developmental needs and then providing appropriate feedback
- *Focused observations and feedback:* observing one particular aspect of teaching and learning (such as classroom management) and providing appropriate feedback
- *Video analysis:* making a video of teaching and analyzing it with the teacher to complement direct observation
- *Coaching:* developing a particular teaching skill by providing a rationale, explaining the steps, demonstrating those steps, providing a supportive environment in which the teacher can use the skill, and giving the teacher feedback
- *Directed observation of a colleague:* structuring and guiding an opportunity for the teacher to observe a colleague using a specific skill

Although some administrators would say that certain teachers do not need mentoring but they need to be dismissed, intensive development does provide a variety of supportive services; to be most effective, these services should be provided in a systematic manner. First, after an initial orientation session, the supervisor makes a diagnostic observation, one in which all-important classroom interactions are recorded and analyzed to determine patterns of behavior. The supervisor analyzes those diagnostic data and tentatively identifies which skills can best be developed over the next two to three months. The supervisor and the teacher then confer about the observation. They review together those observational data and any other information they have and decide together on the skill development agenda for the months ahead. They formalize this decision in a professional development plan, which lists the skills to be developed, the resources to be used, and the deadlines to be met.

The key, then, is engaging expert teachers to help the district build systems that link evaluation, professional development, and collegial learning (Darling-Hammond, 2013). Once teachers are engaged, they can begin to work together on the first skill. The supervisor coaches the teacher in the use of that skill. Then the supervisor makes a focused observation of one of the teacher's classes, gathering data on only the skill being developed. They confer again to decide whether more coaching and observing for that skill is needed or whether they should move to the next skill. It is an intensive process of diagnosing, developing a growth plan, coaching, holding a focused observation, and then assessing the next move. Obviously, this takes a great deal of time to implement effectively; the hope is, however, that only a few teachers in each school will be involved in such intensive development.

Cooperative development is an option usually provided only to experienced and competent teachers; it enables small groups of teachers to work together in a collegial relationship for mutual growth. It is intended to be a teacher-centered, teacher-directed process that respects the professionalism of competent teachers. While it requires administrative support, it does not require inordinate amounts of administrator or supervisor time; the expectation is that the cooperative groups can direct their own growth. In doing so, they may decide to use a variety of processes: observing and conferring about one another's classes, exchanging classes, collaborating on action research, and developing curricular and instructional materials.

Self-directed development is an option usually provided to experienced and competent teachers who wish to work on their own, rather than as part of a cooperative team. Teachers who choose this option identify a small number of professional growth goals for the year and work independently in attempting to accomplish those goals. In a sense, the self-directed model is akin to the management-by-objectives assessment process, except that it is completely nonevaluative. The administrator or supervisor simply acts as a supportive resource for the teacher in the self-directed mode.

Albeit many school districts mandate evaluative policy as dictated by state boards of education or state departments of education, teachers should be able to choose which of these options they prefer, with the understanding that all probationary teachers will be involved in the intensive mode and that the principal will be able to identify tenured teachers who should also be involved in this mode. A form facilitating these choices is shown in Exhibit 9.6. These three individual development options provide teachers with a choice and enable supervisors and administrators to focus their supervisory efforts on those teachers in the intensive mode who most need their skilled services.

MOTIVATING STAFF

Without a doubt, professional development, informal observations, rating, and individual development are all crucial parts of the supervision component. This is especially important in that we, as a nation at large, have a collective stake in ensuring that teachers have a voice in shaping the teacher profession (Wise & Usdan, 2013).

For the most part, evidence reveals that motivated teachers require less supervision and are willing to accomplish teaching and learning goals. They accept teaching goals as personal

EXHIBIT 9.6   Options for Professional Development

Teacher's name _____   School _____   Date _____

Basic Assumptions

1. All teachers will participate in system-based and school-based professional development.
2. All teachers will be observed informally several times during the year.
3. All teachers will be rated by an administrator.

Teacher's Preferred Option (check one)

___ For this year, I prefer not to participate in any special professional development activities other than those outlined above.

___ For this year, I prefer to work cooperatively with colleagues using the processes identified below.

___ For this year, I prefer to work in a self-directed mode using the processes identified below.

Preferred Developmental Processes (check all those that seem desirable at this point)

___ Observe a colleague and confer about observation.

___ Exchange classes with a colleague and confer about exchange; develop a new course of study.

___ Develop and try out new instructional materials; improve an advanced teaching skill.

___ Conduct action research.

___ View and analyze video of your own teaching.

___ Plan and implement an independent study program.

___ Enroll in a graduate course or special workshops.

___ Other _____

goals. They have a sense of confidence, enjoy teaching, are loyal, and are more committed to education as a whole. In contrast, unmotivated teachers are less apt to achieve their curricular goals, have more student discipline problems, and are less interested in change. With strict evaluation strategies, prodding, clear instructions, and close supervision, they often do a satisfactory job at best (Weiss & Pasley, 2004).

| **Curriculum Tip 9.8** | A primary factor for curriculum success is motivating teachers to work. |

Effective supervisors, therefore, should focus on the interrelationship of the four processes with an interest in motivating teachers to invest themselves in their work to obtain desired returns and rewards. Taking an interest in teachers, helping build their confidence, assisting in preparing unique lesson plans, and providing new learning programs can make the difference between a good teacher and a great teacher. Greatness in teaching always has been a result of a mentor helping an individual teacher go the extra mile. The key is to motivate teachers and show them how to exceed normal expectations when developing an interrelationship among the four processes of professional development, informal observations, rating, and individual development.

The Interrelationship of Processes

How do processes for professional development interrelate? Obviously, they are closely related.

Curriculum Tip 9.9	Data derived from informal observations can be used to supplement the information derived from rating other observations and can play an important part in assessing professional development needs.

The rating process can help the supervisor or administrator identify those teachers who need intensive development. The activities undertaken in all the options for individual development can be linked with ongoing in-service programs. In addition, a professional development program can provide needed support for the individual development. All the processes obviously play key roles in improving the taught curriculum.

Having administrators and supervisors examine these processes separately and analytically has clear advantages, because each requires different skills, provides different kinds of information, and employs different processes. In such an examination, it is most useful to work with individual school districts to assist them in developing their own model, rather than presenting them with a formulaic solution. Thus, some districts link rating and individual development rather closely; others keep them quite distinct. Some emphasize curriculum alignment in the informal observations; others focus on instructional processes. Some offer teachers only the cooperative and intensive options; others provide the full array. Because such matters are much affected by district size, administrative philosophy, and available resources, they are best resolved at the district level.

One particular local option needs to be emphasized here. As each district develops its own model, it determines who will be primarily responsible for each of the four approaches. Some districts limit the informal observations to administrators; others expect supervisors to be involved. Some require that rating be done only by administrators; others expect input from the supervisory staff. Some districts use assistant principals for the intensive development; others use supervisors or expert teachers. Some expect administrators to direct professional development; others see this as a supervisory function. Rather than beginning with a set of foreordained conclusions about these important matters, the professional development approach suggested here enables local districts to resolve these issues in a way that makes the most sense to their administrators, supervisors, and teachers.

Although the differentiated model has been found to be feasible and acceptable to teachers (see Glatthorn, 1984), again, no empirical research proves it to be more effective than other approaches. Curriculum leaders, therefore, would be well advised to study all four approaches carefully (along with any others that seem useful) and choose or develop a model that seems to respond best to their own district's needs.

MASLOW'S THEORY OF HUMAN NEEDS

Any discussion of supervision, professional development, and/or teacher motivation would not be complete without noting the work of Abraham Maslow.

Maslow's need hierarchy is arranged in pyramidal form, with physiological needs at the bottom and self-actualization at the top. Curriculum and instructional leaders need to interact with teachers and others whose support will be needed to accomplish the objectives for the school district. To gain support, curriculum or instructional leaders must be able to understand and motivate these people. To understand and motivate people, you must know human nature. Human nature is the common quality in all human beings. People behave according to certain principles of human nature. These principles, as noted in Exhibit 9.7, govern our behavior.

Maslow's taxonomy specifies that needs at the lower levels of the hierarchy must be reasonably satisfied before one can be interested in needs at the next higher level. For example, teachers who are working at a lower-based need, such as the social-need level, are primarily concerned with obtaining acceptance from administrators, other teachers, and parents. These teachers are less apt to be concerned with self-esteem, autonomy, and/or self-actualization. They could, however, abandon the need for social acceptance if a lower need, such as security or safety, presented itself.

Critics argue as to whether Maslow was practicing a rigorous scientific study of personality and whether it relied too heavily on case studies and not enough on experimental work. Another common criticism is that Maslow's classification of self-actualized individuals related only to highly educated white males. Regardless of these criticisms, it is important

EXHIBIT 9.7	Maslow's Hierarchy of Needs
Needs for self-actualization	The needs for self-actualization are activated when all the preceding needs are satisfied.
Needs for self-esteem	The needs for self-esteem can become dominant when the first three needs are satisfied.
Needs for love, affection, and belonging	When the needs for safety and for physiological well-being are satisfied, the needs for love, affection, and belonging can emerge. The key word is *belonging*: "People will support what they help create."
Safety needs	When the physiological needs are satisfied and no longer control thoughts and behaviors, the needs for security can become active.
Physiological needs	These are biological needs—oxygen, food, water, and a relatively constant body temperature—that come first in a person's search for satisfaction.

for students of curriculum supervision to have some basic understanding of his taxonomy as a historical reference when reviewing curriculum development.

MCGREGOR'S THEORY X AND Y

McGregor's (1960) work was based on Maslow's hierarchy of needs. He grouped Maslow's hierarchy into "lower order" (Theory X) needs and "higher order" (Theory Y) needs. He suggested that management could use either set of needs to motivate employees. As management theorists became familiar with Maslow's work, they soon connected higher level needs to worker motivation. If organizational goals and individual needs could be integrated so that people would acquire self-esteem and, ultimately, self-actualization through work, then motivation would be self-sustaining. Today, his Theory Y principle influences the design of personnel policies, affects the way some school districts conduct performance reviews, and shapes the ideas for supervision and professional development. The idea that people are assets was unheard of before McGregor developed this theory in the 1960s.

HERZBERG'S MOTIVATION AND HYGIENE FACTORS

The Motivation to Work, written by Frederick Herzberg, Bernard Mausner, and Barbara Bloch Snyderman (1959), first established his theories about motivation in the workplace. Many decades ago, Herzberg, like Maslow, understood well and attempted to teach the ethical management principles that many leaders today, typically in businesses and organizations that lack humanity, still struggle to grasp. In this respect, Herzberg's concepts are just as relevant now as when he first suggested them, except that the implications of responsibility, fairness, justice, and compassion are now global.

Although Herzberg is noted for his famous "hygiene" and motivational factors theory, he was essentially concerned with people's well-being at work. Underpinning his theories and academic teachings, he attempted to bring more humanity and caring into the workplace. He and others did not develop their theories as "motivational tools" purely to improve organizational performance. They sought instead primarily to explain how to manage people properly, for the good of all people at work.

Herzberg's research proved that people strive to achieve "hygiene" needs because they are unhappy without them, but once satisfied, the effect soon wears off—satisfaction is temporary. Then as now, poorly managed organizations fail to understand that people are not motivated by addressing "hygiene" needs. People are motivated by enabling them to reach for and satisfy the factors that Herzberg identified as real motivators. Examples of Herzberg's hygiene needs (or maintenance factors) in the workplace are as follows:

- Policy
- Relationship with supervisor
- Work conditions

- Salary
- Company car
- Status
- Security
- Relationship with subordinates
- Personal life

Herzberg's research identified that true motivators were other completely different factors, notably the following:

- Achievement
- Recognition
- Work itself
- Responsibility
- Advancement

Understanding the basic theories of motivation that affect organizations, principals, supervisors, and other educational leaders will develop patterns of behavior that will have an impact on faculty. Teachers are professionals, and in the workplace, principals who work at building trust and cooperation and establishing a sense of trust and accountability must meet their needs. The organization (school district) has the obligation to provide for the lower needs as identified by Maslow's higher hierarchy of needs. The principal and other supervisors through their use of professional development, observations, formative and summative evaluations, and individual development will motivate teachers to perform at the higher levels of the theoretical pyramid.

Much like McGregor and Herzberg, other motivational theories appear to focus on involving an organization of needs and goals within an individual's personality. Just prior to the turn of the century, Deci, Ryan, and Koestner (1999) characterized motivation as an individual moved to do something. With this in mind, an individual's underlying motivations are often based on goals and attitudes giving rise to selected actions. Simuyemba (2008) also described motivation as a reason for action or that which gives purpose and direction. The motivation then becomes "why" one chooses to behave a certain way or take a particular action. This type of analysis gives a clearer picture of "why and how" highly motivated principals are often more successful as supervisors than others. Thus, a better understanding of motivational factors can assist school administrators in pinpointing possible internal and external dimensions that may or may not stimulate desire and energy as well as success in the classroom.

CONTEMPORARY RESEARCH

Basically, years of motivational research reveal an emergence of individual responsibility and perpetual assessment due to numerous changes across time, place, and people (Hegarty, 2010). This form of "self-determination theory" has generated a considerable amount of data and research requiring principals as supervisors to continually assess an individual's current state of internal motivation. For example, Vallerand and Losier's (2001) study supported the stated notion that perceptions of competence are often conducive to higher levels of motivation. Likewise, perceived competence is generally improved by positive verbal feedback, which can enhance intrinsic motivation levels. The reverse, however, is true as well. For example, negative feedback, when consistently applied, can reduce intrinsic motivational levels of individuals (O'Neill, 2012). Subsequently, school administrators at all levels are finding that being positive and gaining better understanding of how to motivate teachers and students is paramount. Moreover, the path to inner growth and school success is different for each individual. The key is for school principals to become even more knowledgeable about best supervisory practices, especially if they wish to ensure their schools' success.

As noted by current research, the distinct and most significant aspect of a motivation and self-concept is the element of perceived competence. Assessing competence relative to self-concept is often dependent on an individual's relative standing in his or her school as well as his or her relevant standing in the community. For example, perceptions of self-efficacy are often formed by gauging one's capability against the standards of any given task. Following various theories of motivation, Kinicki (2010) suggested individuals are motivated by two factors: how much they want something and how likely they are to get it. Thus, it is likely that a principal's characteristics such as locus of control, ability, need for achievement, and experience as well as goal clarity might very well determine one's persistence and success.

Regardless of what motivational theory is applied, principals and other supervisors do seem to develop patterns of behavior having an impact on faculty. For this reason, it is important for principals to have a larger understanding of all ramifications, whether they be political, social, economic, or cultural in nature. Teachers are professionals, and in the workplace, principals who work at building trust, cooperation, and accountability must meet their needs. The organization (school district) has the obligation to provide for the lower needs as identified by Maslow's hierarchy of needs. The principal and other supervisors, through their use of professional development, observations, formative and summative evaluations, and individual development, will motivate teachers to perform at the higher levels of the theoretical pyramid.

SUPERVISING THE SUPPORTED CURRICULUM

Clearly, to improve teaching and learning, teachers must take advantage of all the instructional resources in their schools (Jaquith, 2013). Because time and personnel allocations are discussed in Chapter 6, this chapter focuses on the commonsense application of instructional materials as a central aspect of the supported curriculum. Thus, the importance of developing an effective system for selecting and using instructional materials cannot be overemphasized. As noted in Chapter 4, materials play a central role in what teachers select to teach and how they teach it. Textbooks and software are often used to provide structure for the course of study and the sequence of instruction.

Given that importance, it is especially discouraging to note how little systematic attention is given to the selection process. What is needed, obviously, is a sound process for supervising the selection and use of materials—one that recognizes the central importance of the supported

Curriculum Tip 9.10	*Supported curriculum* is defined as all the resources provided to ensure the effective implementation of the curriculum: the time allocated, the personnel assigned to plan and implement the curriculum, and the instructional materials required.

curriculum. The procedures outlined next, drawn from a review of the literature on materials selection, provide a useful beginning for local leaders and teachers who wish to review their current selection and adoption procedures. The discussion that follows uses the terms *text* and *software* to refer, in general, to any instructional materials (standard or digital format, including mobile learning applications) that play a central role in the curriculum.

Develop a Statement of Board Policy and Administrative Procedures

The board policy needs to delineate the functions of instructional materials and specify the roles of the board, school administrators, and teachers in selecting particular materials. That policy should be supplemented with a more specific set of administrative procedures for implementing those specifications. The administrative procedures can also specify how materials will be selected, how citizens can register complaints, and how administrators should respond to such complaints.

Appoint the Materials Selection Adoption Committee

The adoption committee can be representative—large enough to include broad representation and small enough to work efficiently. At a minimum, the committee needs to be composed of one school principal, a supervisor in that field, one teacher from each school that will be using materials, an instructional materials specialist, as well as a parent.

Prepare the Committee

Because the committee will play such a central role in the adoption process, its members need to be trained in the following skills: understanding board policy and district procedures, maintaining ethical and professional relationships with publishers, understanding current research in the field, assessing district and teacher needs, evaluating instructional materials, and monitoring the implementation and use of instructional materials.

Provide the Committee With Selection Resources

The committee should also have easy access to selection resources. Two types of resources are especially needed. First, the committee should have access to catalogs of available materials and media. Several catalogs of print materials are now computerized, making it possible to conduct sharply focused searches for materials. Second, the committee should have access to objective reviews of materials. Periodicals and journals (standard or online) published by the several subject-centered professional groups (such as the National Council of Teachers of English [NCTE]) can be included in such reviews.

Determine How Teachers Will Probably Use the New Materials

To make a wise decision, the adoption committee needs good information about how teachers will likely make use of the materials. Here, the committee can survey, interview, and observe teachers to secure answers to these questions:

- For which groups of students will the materials be used?
- Will the materials be used primarily in class or outside of class?
- Will the materials be used chiefly to teach skills and concepts or to provide guided and independent practice?

To understand the importance of this information, contrast two groups of teachers teaching mathematics in elementary school. One team comprises specialists in a departmentalized setting; they have been well trained in modern approaches to mathematics and are highly skilled in explaining concepts. They want a mathematics text or software to be used primarily as a source of problems for pupils to work on in class and at home. The other teachers are teaching several subjects in a self-contained classroom. They do not have a deep or current understanding of mathematics. And, they want a mathematics text or software that can explain concepts clearly and can reduce their preparation time. These two contrasting uses of materials require quite different choices. It should be stated, however, that with the implementation of CCSS the contrasts between these two groups should not be as great.

Determine How Teachers Will Allocate Space

Teachers working collaboratively are often better able to generate a series of questions that help facilitate learning. For example, how are students and teachers assigned to space in the school in relation to the implementation of new materials? Where will materials be stored? Is it possible to situate instructional teams adjacent to one another? Which classrooms are nearest to the library or media center? Is there a learning support center, and if so, where is it located? Some of these decisions are essentially arbitrary, but others are more purposeful and can further the goals of the selection process.

Develop a Sharply Focused and Weighted Set of Criteria for Selection

Textbook and software selection practices are continually under review for several reasons. This can include a lack of inadequate criteria for evaluation, a lack of time devoted to the review process, possible political and social issues, as well as inadequate or nonexistent training for those charged with making recommendations.

One useful way of summarizing all these matters is to record them in a set of specifications similar to those shown in Exhibit 9.8. Also, an example of a selection guide to be used by a review committee is illustrated in Chapter 10.

EXHIBIT 9.8   Specifications for Elementary Language Arts Texts

For Which Pupils

All pupils (except those with limited English proficiency [LEP]) in Grades 1 through 6

How Selections Will Probably Be Used

Most teachers will use them in class, as the primary source for language arts instruction. Pupils will frequently read the materials independently, discuss what they have read, and then do practice exercises.

Basic Requirements

1. Free of racial, ethnic, and sexist stereotyping
2. Written so that they can be read by all pupils who will use them but should not be too simple or childish

Major Selection Criteria (Listed in Order of Importance)

1. Emphasize a process approach to writing, giving special attention to prewriting, expanded writing, and revision.
2. Include a number of integrated units that show the interrelationships of writing, speaking, listening, and reading.
3. Reflect an informed view of language learning: Good form is stressed as an aid to clarity, not as a set of rigid rules; pupils are encouraged to value their own language and to accept the languages of others; grammar is presented as a system of language structures, not a collection of abstract terms and rules.

Ancillary Materials Required

1. Testing program

Base Selection on Research

Along with a focus on accountability, there are concerns of educators not basing their selections of materials on research. Realistically, school districts need to review selections based on scientific research as well as on recommended state standards and CCSS. With that said, other national educational organizations and panels are moving in the same direction. For example, in the area of reading, CCSS is the major literacy instructional challenge of the day. Also, text complexity, close reading instructional texts, and writing from sources are just a few of the requirements playing out in classrooms across the country (International Reading Association, 2014).

Identify Programs That Best Meet the Requirements and the Criteria

The committee should then use the set of specifications to identify five programs (standard or digital format) that meet the criteria, and rank these five in order of **merit**. From these initial five programs, the committee will narrow the selection down to a final three.

Get Teacher Input on the Top Three Programs

At this point, all teachers who will be using the text or software should be given an opportunity to review the top three series or programs identified by the committee and give their own input. Perhaps the best way to do this is for the committee members representing a specific school to meet with the teachers from that building, explain the requirements and criteria, and discuss the three programs that have passed the initial screening. The teachers can then be encouraged to discuss the merits of each program and express their own preferences—with the understanding that the final decision will be made by the committee and administration, not by a majority vote.

Select the Best Program, Series, or Materials

The committee can then meet; review teacher input; take a fresh look at the three programs, series, or materials; and make its final choice. One of the authors of this book successfully used this process in selecting a textbook series for his school district. The textbook selection committee was formed in a manner similar to the one previously mentioned; however, the final selection of the textbook differed slightly. The major difference in this selection process came in the final stage, before a service contract was developed with the publisher. The committee selected three companies whose textbooks closely matched the requirements and criteria the committee had identified. The companies were then asked to send a representative to the school district to demonstrate how their company's textbook correlated with the requirements and criteria of the school district. The committee members attended the presentation, but only those members who attended all three presentations were allowed to vote on the selection of the final textbook. Basically, the presentations served to affirm the committee's confidence in the company's ability to meet the needs of their school district and curriculum. The committee then used this presentation along with teacher input to make its final choice.

Have a Service Contract With the Company or Provider

Services that can be requested include the following: giving the district a right to reproduce certain portions; in-servicing administrators, teachers, and staff in use of the materials; guiding teachers in placing pupils appropriately in the program; correlating the materials with the district curriculum; assisting schools in ordering other resources; and providing follow-up assistance when problems develop. Obviously, such services will be costly to a company or provider, but the amount of service contracted will likely be contingent on the size of the order.

Monitor the Use of Selection Materials

Experts in the field point out the necessity of closely monitoring the process to be sure selected materials are being used appropriately and to identify possible problems. Not using technology appropriately, as well as misuse and loss of textbooks, soon becomes expensive and should be addressed.

CULTURALLY RELEVANT TEACHING

When selecting materials for schools, multicultural and diversity issues should be considered. Keeping with this perspective, helping teachers understand culturally relevant ways of learning is a step toward addressing multicultural issues in local communities. Having a knowledge of learners, learning in social contexts, knowledge of teaching, and a knowledge of curriculum is paramount to success. This means teachers understand how life is organized in the communities where their students live; their students' values, beliefs, and cultures; how students use knowledge; and how these characteristics affect learning.

Knowledge and understanding of multicultural student backgrounds is of particular relevance in large urban areas. Formulating a better understanding of social justice approaches holds promise for developing a broader perspective of education (Gimbert, Desai, & Kerka, 2010). Teacher educators who develop an understanding of culturally rich and diverse backgrounds view schooling as a crucial element in creating a more just society. Culturally knowledgeable teachers, then, are better able to challenge the structural barriers that inhibit student success. Along these same lines, teacher education should include partnerships between schools of education and local community organizations so that teachers are prepared to be community advocates. Current research highlights six interrelated factors through which supervisors can help implement these ideas. The six factors as noted by Gimbert et al. include the following:

1. Knowledge base for teaching
2. Knowledge of students as learners
3. Culturally relevant teaching
4. Learning cohorts within learning communities
5. Mentors and teaching models
6. School–university–community partnerships

As can be seen, ensuring that all teachers understand the sociocultural, economic, and political factors of their communities is key to school success. To be sure, supporting culturally relevant teaching is a critical component of any supervision program.

GOING DEEPER INTO TEACHING AND LEARNING WITH TECHNOLOGY

We should assess technology use on the basis of how well students are learning (Johnson, 2013–2014). Subsequently, along with sociocultural, economic, and political factors, it is critical that school leaders no longer view technology as just a tool of educational practice. The reality, then, is that technology has become the means through which we interact, engage, and create in our world. With that in mind, the following questions might apply.

As an educator, state how much technology impacted the way you do the following:

- Communicate and interact with others
- Plan and organize your day

- Perceive teaching and learning
- Monitor and evaluate student achievement

As part of the supervision process, school leaders need to help teachers create 21st-century classrooms whereby technology is infused into the teaching and learning experience and will need to reflect on the actual pedagogies used to create the learning context. The nature of our educational methodologies and theories are shifting to pedagogies that require learning in a technological space. It is easy to do some basic Internet searches and find research that explores specific instructional strategies, communication techniques, and learning methodologies related to bringing technology into the classroom. But there is limited discussion as to how technology is actually challenging the educational pedagogies of the teaching and learning experience.

Clearly, from a supervision standpoint, technology is becoming a major factor in the classroom. While the theories behind much of what takes place in the classroom are well grounded in a firmly established body of literature, the theories behind how best to utilize forms of mobile technology in the classroom is still to be determined. Just as instructional and educational technology programs are grappling with a rapid infusion of new devices, so, too, are researchers coming to terms with a rapidly changing social cultural revolution when it comes to educational technology.

DIGITAL SOLUTIONS FOR 21st-CENTURY LEARNING

School leaders are finding that use of technology greatly increases motivation and student engagement (Beninghof & Blair, 2014). But, just as importantly, technology can also enhance assessment and supervision. The range of technology models, programs, and applications are too numerous to cover here—but the authors have chosen several examples to highlight. The first example is The Pearson SuccessMaker, which has proven to be an effective technology-based program focusing on differentiated learning. According to Brown (2011), teachers use the Pearson digital aspect of SuccessMaker to set student benchmark levels corresponding with state assessments (aligned with state standards and CCSS). Based on grade and initial placement, the program designates a level of instruction and assessment for each individual student. The program then isolates areas of difficulty and offers prescriptive scheduling to ensure maximum effectiveness. From a curriculum perspective, this program allows principals and teachers to make on-site adaptive instructional decisions based on individual student data.

Another tried and true program is Silverback Learning's Mileposts program (Silverback Learning Solutions, 2014). One of this book's authors has personally used Mileposts and found it to be extremely helpful. This unique program empowers educators to improve PK–12 education with better access to data; shared accountability; and a culture of collaboration for teachers, administrators, students, and parents. Silverback's Mileposts program makes it easy to access students' test data as well as place new students in various programs and courses. In addition, it has been very beneficial in sharing charted student data with parents. Practical aspects of the program for teachers, principals, and district administrators include the following:

Teacher

- Data defines student needs
- Informs teachers about instruction and interventions
- Documents interventions/Focuses instruction
- Writes individual student plans when appropriate

Principal

- Instant sort for whole school reports
- Teams with teachers
- Data drives professional development
- Data focuses areas of instructional need

District Administrators

- Instant sort for whole district progress
- Drives future professional development
- Identifies area of curriculum needs
- Keeps public informed of progress

Technology advantages of the program include:

- Centrally stored data system (SaaS Cloud)
- Web-based
- Integrates readily with district systems
- Automatically synchronizes with SIS systems
- Designed to integrate with SLDS
- Provides Sate and District student assessment results
- State and District benchmarks embedded
- Daily class differentiation of instruction support
- Sort capability within program, class, school, district

SOURCE: Silverback Learning Solutions (2014).

As can be seen by the previously given information, these types of data solution programs are designed to provide data at the point of instruction where teachers need it. Just as importantly, they help identify subject strand support needs, identify areas of curriculum concern, indicate areas of teacher strength and areas of concern, create a whole staff focus, and help create intentional collaboration and team cohesiveness.

GLOBAL CONNECTIONS: FRENCH PARTNERSHIP

As part of an international exchange between American building-level leaders and French principals, educators are sharing the meaning and application of transformational leadership across Franco-American contexts. Although France has a national system of inspectors who review teacher performance, it is considered to have a weak accountability system (Supovitz, 2013). This is particularly the case when compared to the amount of attention paid to accountability in the U.S. system. In France, the principal's job is largely administrative, with very little formal influence or supervision regarding teacher classroom practices. Likewise, teachers in the upper grades are subject specialists, and principals in France are not considered to have a requisite level of content expertise across diverse subjects. Moreover, the French consider teaching to be the transfer of content knowledge; what is taught is valued over pedagogical content knowledge or techniques to effectively transfer learning.

To help remedy this situation, the French developed a series of international supervision teams of principals who began sharing information and experiences with American principals as a way of planning curriculum and sparking instructional improvement. Now, selected principals from both the United States and France continue to share ideas on supervision, empowering staff, gaining visibility through focused walks, establishing PLCs, and creating structures that support learning. Given the substantial differences between the French and U.S. systems, the value of exchanging ideas across a centralized and a decentralized educational system are proving to be very worthwhile—especially in the area of supervision. Thus, making global connections in the area of supervision and accountability is assuredly a step in the right direction toward worldwide understanding and peace.

SUMMARY

This chapter examines problems and issues in supervision as well as how to improve two often-slighted aspects of curriculum: the taught curriculum and the supported curriculum. The chapter addresses major leaders who have been concerned with supervision and some current approaches to curriculum supervision. Major roles associated with curriculum supervision are discussed, including an important component of supervision: motivating staff. It is perhaps important to note that regardless of democracy in the selection process, final decisions are often made based on people's judgments and biases. It is the hope of the authors that educational leaders will make every attempt possible to eliminate arbitrary judgments and biases when selecting and developing supportive curriculum.

APPLICATIONS

1. On the basis of your experience in schools, do you believe that teachers should have some options regarding the types of supervisory services they receive? Give examples and support your position with well-reasoned arguments.

2. Carol Jago (as cited in Farrell, 2005) once defined schools as "places where young people go to watch old people work." Rank the lesson design models presented, and explain why your number one choice was selected.

3. Glatthorn (1984) recommended that each district develop its own differentiated system of professional development. Sketch out the main components of a system that you think would work well in a district with which you are acquainted. Which components would you emphasize (professional development, rating, informal observations, individual development)? Which options would you provide to teachers? Who would be responsible for the several components?

4. The list of essential teaching skills presented in this chapter is only one way of describing and analyzing effective teaching. Review the research on teacher effectiveness, and develop your own list of essential teaching skills—one that you could use in supervising teachers. Discuss in detail your list of skills and why you chose them.

5. Using a materials selection evaluation form such as the one shown in Chapter 10, evaluate a textbook, program, or software in a subject field you know well and discuss your findings.

6. One of the issues that confront larger districts is whether all the elementary schools in that district should use the same reading series. What position would you take on this issue? What reasons would you advance in support of your position?

7. With more and more small schools consolidating, give examples of how distance learning technology can improve your curriculum.

CASE STUDY   Improving Professional Development

An Illinois school district superintendent is looking for ways to make sure that all his teachers are using the same textbook series. He decides to meet with a group of principals for ideas.

"I need to find a way to make sure our staff follows the text in each of our curriculum subject areas," states Superintendent Stanford.

Karen Carpenter, principal of a K–5 elementary school, offers an example of what she is doing in her school. "I found that my teacher–leaders do best if they receive professional development in smaller bands of time using the same textbook series, rather than trying to learn everything at once. Whenever I've tried to take a 'one-long-in-service-fits-all' approach, I find that the staff begins to wander away from the text."

"So how do we change our professional development schedule?" asks the superintendent.

"I try to set up in-service by grade level, for only half a day. I do a substitute rotation plan," says Carpenter. "I also schedule a lot of my early outs for in-service relating to the text. Whenever I have a series of short in-services spread out over the year, the staff seems to stick with the text. I find that shorter and more frequent professional development programs keep the reading material lively and interesting."

Principal Carpenter continues, "I like to use this format because the teachers don't become so overwhelmed with information. It is also great because it is a better use of their time. My staff has been very happy with the whole process."

"Well, let's take a look at this as an option for our professional development program," says Superintendent Stanford with a smile. "I'll schedule another meeting to discuss it in more detail."

The Challenge

Substitute rotation plans proved to be effective for Principal Carpenter. What are some other supervisory strategies that she can use to support curriculum and free up teachers for professional development?

Key Issues or Questions

1. What are some supervisory steps to consider before adopting any professional development program?

2. How do you feel about Principal Carpenter's use of a substitute rotation to enhance in-service? Is this something you might use in your school? Why or why not?

3. To what extent could Principal Carpenter's substitution rotation plan lend itself to differentiated professional development?

4. What other innovative supervision strategies can be used to aid the supported curricula?

5. How do you think Principal Carpenter's substitute plan would lend itself to the selection and adoption of textbooks or online programs for a school district? What other strategies could be used in the selection and adoption of materials?

WEBLIOGRAPHY

Curriculum Change Process
www.ecoliteracy.org/change/changing-curriculum

Lesson Plans and Teaching Tips for English language learners (ELLs)
http://everythingESL.net

Supervising the Curriculum
www.ascd.org/publications/jcs/winter1995/Exploring-Supervision-History@-An-Invitation-and-Agenda.aspx

REFERENCES

Beninghof, A. M., & Blair, D. (2014). Transforming learning with tech co-teaching. *Principal, 93*(3), 44–45.

Berliner, D. C. (1984). The half-full glass: A review of the research on teaching. In P. Hosford (Ed.), *Using what we know about teaching* (pp. 51–85). Alexandria, VA: ASCD.

Brophy, J. E., & Good, T. L. (1986). Teacher behavior and student achievement. In M. C. Wittrock (Ed.), *Handbook of research on teaching* (3rd ed., pp. 328–375). New York: Macmillan.

Brown, L. M. (2011). Standards-based curriculum and delivery. *Principal, 91*(1), 38–40.

Connelly, G. (2013). Postscript: Relationships are key to common success. *Principal, 93*(3), 56.

Costa, A. L., & Garmston, R. J. (2002). *Cognitive coaching: A foundation for renaissance schools.* Norwood, MA: Christopher-Gordon.

Darling-Hammond, L. (2013). When teachers support & evaluate their peers. *Educational Leadership, 71*(2), 24–29.

Deci, E. L., Ryan, R., & Koestner, R. (1999). A meta-analysis review of experiments examining the effects of extrinsic rewards on intrinsic motivation. *Psychological Bulletin,* 627–668.

Farrell, J. (2005). *The failure of McREL.* Retrieved from http://www.readfirst.net/mcrel.htm

Farrell, J. (2006). *Teaching backwards.* Retrieved from http://www.readfirst.net/backwards.htm

Gersten, R., Green, W., & Davis, G. (1985, April). *The realities of instructional leadership: An intensive study of four inner city schools.* Paper presented at the annual meeting of the American Educational Research Association, Chicago, IL.

Gimbert, B., Desai, S., & Kerka, S. (2010). The big picture: Focusing urban teacher education on the community. *Phi Delta Kappan, 92*(2), 36–39.

Glatthorn, A. A. (1984). *Differentiated supervision.* Alexandria, VA: ASCD.

Glatthorn, A. A. (1987). *Curriculum leadership.* New York, NY: HarperCollins.

Glickman, C. D., Gordon, S. P., & Ross-Gordon, J. M. (2003). *Supervision and instructional leadership: A developmental approach.* Boston, MA: Allyn & Bacon.

Hegarty, N. (2010). *An examination of motivation levels in graduate school students.* New York, NY: St. John's University Press.

Herzberg, F., Mausner, B., & Synderman, B. (1959). *The motivation to work.* New York, NY: Wiley.

Hewson, K. (2013), Time shift: Developing teacher teams. *Principal, 92*(3), 14–17.

Hunter, M. (1984). Knowing, teaching, and supervising. In P. L. Hosford (Ed.), *Using what we know about teaching* (pp. 169–193). Alexandria, VA: ASCD.

International Reading Association. (2014). Institute offerings provide immersive enrichment on critical topics related to research and common core. *Reading Today, 31*(4), 30–32.

Interstate School Leaders Licensure Consortium. (2008). Council of Chief State School Officers (CCSSO). Retrieved from http://coe.fgcu.edu/faculty/valesky/isllcstandards.htm

Jaquith, A. (2013). Instructional capacity: How to build it right. *Educational Leadership, 71*(2), 56–61.

Johnson, D. (2013–2014). Power up! *Educational Leadership, 71*(4), 84, 85, 87.

Kinicki, A. W. (2010). *Management: A practical approach.* New York: McGraw-Hill.

LaPoma, J., & Kantor, H. (2013–2014). It's all about relationships. *Phi Delta Kappan, 95*(4), 74–75.

Maleyko, G., & Gawlik, M. A. (2011). No child left behind: What we know and what we need to know. *Education, 131*(3), 600–624.

Marzano, R. J. (2003). *What works in schools: Translating research into action.* Alexandria, VA: ASCD.

Marzano, R. J. (2011). Art and science of teaching: Making the most of instructional rounds. *Educational Leadership, 68*(5), 80–81.

McGreal, T. L. (1983). *Successful teacher evaluation.* Alexandria, VA: ASCD.

McGregor, D. (1960). *The human side of enterprise.* New York: McGraw-Hill.

Murphy, J., Goldring, E., & Porter, A. (2014). Principal evaluation takes center stage. *Principal, 93*(3), 20–24.

O'Neill, T. L. (2012). *Dissecting "why." A study focusing on the relationship between freshman and senior business students' academic motivation, academic self-concept, and ultimate impact on academic achievement at Montana Tech* (Unpublished doctoral dissertation). University of Montana, Missoula.

Pitler, H., & Goodwin, B. (2008). Classroom walkthroughs: Learning to see the trees and the forest. *Changing Schools, 58,* 9–11.

Plonczak, I., Brooks, J. G., Wilson, G. L., Elijah, R., & Caliendo, J. (2014). STEM studio: Where innovation generates innovation. *Phi Delta Kappan, 95*(5), 52–56.

Radoslovich, J., Roberts, S., & Plaza, A. (2014). Charter school innovations: A teacher growth model. *Phi Delta Kappan, 95*(5), 40–46.

Reeves, D. B. (2007). Coaching myths and realities. *Principal, 65*(2), 89–90.

Rosenshine, B., & Stevens, R. (1986). Teaching functions. In M. C. Wittrock (Ed.), *Handbook of research on teaching* (3rd ed., pp. 376–391). New York, NY: Macmillan.

Sergiovanni, T. J. (1985). Landscapes, mindscapes, and reflective practice in supervision. *Journal of Curriculum and Supervision, 1,* 5–17.

Silverback Learning Solutions. (2014). Retrieved from www.silverbacklearning.com

Simuyemba, D. M. (2008). Motivation-for-dreamers. Life Coaching Ltd. Retrieved from http://www.motivation-for-dreamers.com

Stallings, J. (1986, April). *Report on a three-year study of the Hunter model.* Paper presented at the annual conference of the American Educational Research Association, San Francisco, CA.

Supovitz, J. A. (2013). Leadership lessons for French educators. *Phi Delta Kappan, 95*(1), 74–76.

Vallerand, R.J., & Losier, G. F. (2001). The temporal relationship between perceived competence and self-determined motivation. *Journal of Social Psychology,* 793–801.

Weiss, I. R., & Pasley, J. D. (2004). What is high-quality education? *Educational Leadership, 61*(5), 24–28.

Wise, A. E., & Usdan, M. D. (2013). The teaching profession at the crossroads. *Educational Leadership, 71*(2), 31–34.

CHAPTER 10

Curriculum Development and Implementation

Previous chapters have discussed the processes used in developing new courses and improving programs and fields of study. Each of these processes represents a type of curriculum change, and the literature on educational change suggests that those new and improved curricula will require support throughout stages to be successful.

The dialogue that follows examines several questions as well as the critical stages for curriculum development and implementation.

Questions addressed in this chapter include the following:

- What is the procedure for developing a program philosophy and rationale statement?
- What is the procedure for developing a program scope and sequence, goals, objectives, learning outcomes, and authentic tasks?
- What methods can be used for choosing teacher representation? What procedures should be followed for developing program elements?

Key to Leadership

Leadership for curriculum development and implementation involves working with multiple people to ensure that the curriculum for each subject area or discipline is aligned both horizontally and vertically.

SOURCE: Excerpts from Baron, Boschee, and Jacobson (2008) were used for most of the content in Chapter 10. Permission was granted by Rowman & Littlefield, Lanham, MD.

DEVELOPING A PROGRAM PHILOSOPHY AND RATIONALE STATEMENT

When educators focus on equitable practices, risk taking, and a rich curriculum, schools can accomplish great things (Burris & Murphy, 2013–2014). With this in mind, previous chapters have discussed the processes used in developing new courses and improving programs and fields of study. Each of these processes represents a new type of curriculum change. Moreover, the literature on educational change suggests that these new and improved curricula will require a *collaborative effort,* as well as careful teacher and student support, to be successful.

Curriculum Tip 10.1	Building collaborative relationships is essential to making the curriculum planning process a success.

The dialogue that follows examines critical stages for curriculum development and implementation as they relate to state standards and Common Core State Standards (CCSS). The *philosophy* and rationale statement for a school program, also known as a subject-area curriculum or discipline, must augment a school district's philosophy, vision, mission, and exit (graduation) outcomes.

A variety of philosophies of education abound, including those by Dewey, Adler, Bestor, Hirsch, and others (Wiles & Bondi, 2011).

Philosophy of Education—Traditional education consists of bodies of information (subjects) and of skills that have been worked out in the past. Progressive education cultivates individuality and acquiring skills to make the most of the opportunities of the present life.

—John Dewey (1916)

For the purposes of this book, the authors focus on Dewey's philosophy of education that is predicated on cultivating individuality and acquiring necessary skills needed for life. With this in mind, school leaders facilitating the development of curriculum hold the responsibility of guiding the planning and implementation process. Much of this vision, for many schools, is based on a three-prong approach involving implementation of CCSS or individual state standards, using technology and data analysis to guide and monitor instruction, and finally, implementing a strong supervision or evaluation system to drive the movement forward (McAssey, 2014). Just as importantly, and to secure success, it is crucial to build collaborative relationships through professional development.

As part of putting all of these elements into place, schools need to establish a district-wide *curriculum council* that meets on a monthly basis during the school year. A curriculum council can consist of professional staff in leadership positions—that is, the curriculum director, building principals, department heads, teacher–leaders, and others in leadership positions. Council members need to be cognizant of the school district's mission, vision, philosophy, exit outcomes, program philosophies and rationale statements, program goals, program objectives, learning outcomes, learning activities, assessment, and textbooks (standard or digital), including publication year, edition, and condition, and so on.

A major function of the curriculum council is to *develop a scope and sequence as well as review the cycle* for districtwide curriculum development. For example, a typical five-year cycle is illustrated in Exhibit 10.1.

EXHIBIT 10.1 Typical Five-Year Curriculum Development Cycle		
2015–2016	English language arts	2020–2021
2016–2017	Science and social studies	2021–2022
2017–2018	Fine arts	2022–2023
2018–2019	Mathematics and health	2023–2024
2019–2020	All others	2024–2025

NOTE: Technology and business or vocational subjects may need a shorter development cycle.

The curriculum council should also select teacher representation for curriculum development. The representatives should be chosen using one of five methods: voluntary, rotation, evolvement, peer selection, or administrative selection.

The procedure for developing a districtwide English language arts (ELA) program philosophy and rationale statement and examples of the declarations follow.

Procedure

To develop a sound philosophy for an ELA program (or any school program), an ELA program committee (also known as a subject-area committee) must be established for the initial phase. The steps for structuring, along with responsibilities for the committee, are as follows:

Step 1

- The school district superintendent and board of education must approve the process for districtwide curriculum development. *Special note:* J. Timothy Waters, CEO of McREL, and Robert J. Marzano, a senior scholar at McREL, found a statistically significant relationship (a positive correlation of .24) between district leadership and student achievement (Waters & Marzano, 2006).
- As part of a collaborative process, a newly created curriculum council needs to form an ELA program committee composed of ELA teachers representing all grade levels (pre K–12), preferably two teachers from each grade level. In smaller districts, however, one teacher per three grade/course levels is satisfactory (with feedback from those teaching the other grade/course levels). In smaller districts, a curriculum director could be hired by the cooperative (if such a co-op exists) to

lead this process (a cooperative is a consortium of school districts cooperatively working together toward common goals). Co-op superintendents would need to support this approach to curriculum development. The superintendents, building principals, and content-area teachers would need to see the value of receiving input from other teachers in the cooperative and embrace the idea of a similar curriculum in cooperative schools. It should be noted that the principal's input is a major key to making the process work. According to a research report from the Wallace Foundation, a building principal's influence on teachers' motivations also impacts student achievement (Protheroe, 2011). And although there may be resistance to adopting a first-grade curriculum throughout the co-op, most classes would benefit from a standard curriculum. Distance learning classes (e.g., foreign languages) would benefit from a co-op curriculum coordinator helping the schools set up a common curriculum. This common curriculum (including the textbook or software) would give the co-op schools much more flexibility in creating a schedule. Schools would not be tied to one school in the co-op. If School A could not fit its students into the schedule of the school that usually offered the class, the students could receive the same class from another school in the cooperative and be confident that the materials and content are the same. In this process, the curriculum coordinator could use the distance learning equipment to facilitate meetings. Staff from each school could sit in their own distance learning rooms and share with the other members of the co-op. This would eliminate travel and make the possibility of meeting more often realistic.

- Building principals (or designees) from the elementary, middle-level or junior high school, and senior high school must be members of the committee as well (preferably with one principal or designee from each level).
- The school district curriculum director (or designee) should serve as chairperson and be responsible for organizing and directing the activities of the ELA program committee.
- The school district's board of education should be informed by the board curriculum committee about the process used for program (curriculum) development.
- All ELA program committee members must have a thorough understanding of the school district's philosophy, vision, mission, and exit (graduation) outcomes to enable committee members to blend them into the ELA program philosophy and rational statement.
- The Dialogue Technique, the Delphi Technique, the Fishbowl Technique, the Telstar Technique, or the Nominal Group Technique could be used to guide the ELA program committee in developing a program philosophy.
- The number of meetings by the ELA program committee to complete the task of writing a program philosophy should be limited to three or four during the school year.
- The curriculum meetings should be held in a comfortable environment—in other words, comfortable work seats, circular seating arrangement, tables with room for participants to spread their papers out, and good acoustics. Name tents for the participants should be made by folding a piece of paper so it will stand on its own.

Step 2

- Immediately after completion of the ELA program philosophy, disseminate it to the ELA staff and building administrators throughout the school district for their input. Grade- and department-level meetings should be organized by the building principals to peruse the program philosophy developed by the committee.
- The timeline is one week for return of the program philosophy with additions, corrections, or deletions from noncommittee ELA staff and administrators.

Step 3

- After the ELA program philosophy is returned to the curriculum director, the original ELA program committee should reassemble to consider the additions, corrections, and deletions suggested by noncommittee ELA staff and administrators.

Step 4

- The completed ELA program philosophy is now ready to be given to the school superintendent and board of education for approval.
- After approval by the school superintendent and board of education, the ELA program philosophy is given to the ELA writing committee responsible for developing the ELA program scope and sequence, program goals, objectives, learning outcomes, and **authentic tasks.**

This step-by-step process should be used to develop a program philosophy, followed by the same procedure to develop a program rationale statement (see Exhibit 10.2, which represents this top-down as well as bottom-up process). Further, the process heightens the district ELA staff's, building administrators,' central administration's, and board of education's commitment to the ELA program.

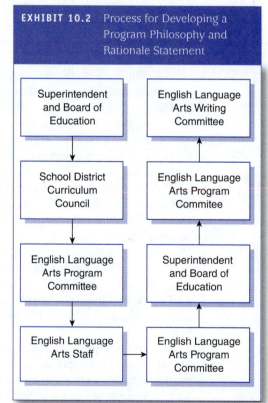

EXHIBIT 10.2   Process for Developing a Program Philosophy and Rationale Statement

Superintendent and Board of Education

School District Curriculum Council

English Language Arts Program Committee

English Language Arts Staff

English Language Arts Writing Committee

English Language Arts Program Commitee

Superintendent and Board of Education

English Language Arts Program Committee

Sample: English Language Arts Program Philosophy

Learning is a complex process of discovery, cooperation, and inquiry and is facilitated by the ELA program. The language processes of listening, speaking, reading, writing, viewing, and representing are interrelated and interdependent. Language is not only systematic and rule governed but also dynamic and evolving, facilitating communication with others and flexibility of meaning. Through interaction with the social, cultural, intellectual, emotional, and physical components of the environment, the learner acquires language developmentally along a continuum.

Language learning thrives when learners are engaged in meaningful use of language. The process of constructing meaning is influenced by the learners' previous knowledge, attitudes, experiences, and abilities. All forms of communication, oral and written, expressive and receptive, are equally valuable. The ELA program utilizes an integrated approach that treats skills as part of all subject areas. Through the study of language, literature, and media, students broaden their experience; weigh personal values against those of others; and become appreciative of the past, sensitive to the present, and inquisitive about the future.

The ELA program accommodates each learner's abilities, interests, and background by allowing for a range of learning styles, teaching styles, instructional strategies, and resources. The program supports a classroom environment that encourages mutual respect, risk taking, and experimentation. Effective evaluation is an integral part of the learning process. Continual evaluation that encompasses both process and product and both cognitive and affective domains allows each learner to take ownership of and responsibility for learning. The learner is already processing information and constructing meaning when formal schooling begins and continues to refine the processes of communication throughout the years of formal education and beyond.

SOURCE: The ELA rationale statement was adapted from the *Language Arts English Primary–Graduation Curriculum Guide* (Canadian Ministry of Education, 1992, p. 13).

Sample: English Language Arts Program Rationale Statement

The language skills and processes developed collaboratively through the ELA program are central to successful achievement in all subject areas and equip students with skills necessary to pursue learning throughout life. Likewise, problem-based tasks in the classroom are central to instruction and are linked to social roles, jobs, or professions (Plonczak, Brooks, Wilson, Elijah, & Caliendo, 2014). Students who read, write, speak, represent, view, and listen with intelligence, empathy, respect, and discrimination will develop the skills in thinking and communication, as well as the attitudes and knowledge, that will prepare them for active participation in a complex society.

The ELA program allows students to better understand themselves and others. The reading and study of literature enhance the aesthetic, imaginative, creative, and affective aspects of a person's development. Literature preserves and extends the imaginative power of individuals. It allows young people to explore imaginatively the places where they live and provides them with an understanding of cultural heritage and a historical perspective, exposing them to points of view other than the present and personal.

- Through fiction, the reader has the power to be transported in time and place to experience vicariously places, people, and events otherwise unavailable.
- Through poems, the reader may achieve heightened perceptions of the world, sharpened senses, clarified thoughts, and broadened emotions.
- Through drama, the participant continually renews a sense of the vitality and complexity of human actions.
- Through nonfiction, the reader accesses a wide range of possibilities, opinions, and interpretations.

The electronic media provides a similar range of possibilities and furnishes material for experience and study. In addition, the study of literature and media provides models of effective and varied language use for students to draw on in their own compositions.

The ELA program encourages students to develop meaning, both through active response to others' work and through their own speaking and writing. As part of this process, students need to maintain a respect for other ideas, artifacts, and cultures, understanding that classrooms and the things in them are culturally important and relevant (Medin & Bang, 2013–2014). Through speaking and writing, students learn to clarify thought, emotion, and experience and to share these ideas, emotions, and experiences with others. Like reading, writing is a source or pleasure, enjoyment, and knowledge. It is a way to experience the delight and wonder of everyday life.

Curriculum Tip 10.2	"In a truly aligned system, four things connect in an integrated way: what you teach, how you test it, what's the best curriculum to achieve that, and what are the best methods to teach it" (Richardson, 2010, p. 32).

Writing provides the opportunity for careful organization of one's picture of reality and stimulates development of the precision, clarity, and imagination required for effective communication. According to Gallagher (2014), we need to teach students to read like writers and write like readers. Basically, deeper writing leads to deeper reading. In this way, writing is socially valuable, one of the ways individuals engage in and contribute to the activities and knowledge of society. Writing is personally valuable and is also an important means of learning within this program and all other subject areas. It allows students to create personal meaning out of the information offered in and out of school.

In essence, education today increasingly emphasizes collaboration, evaluation and analysis skills, critical thinking, problem-solving strategies, organizing and reference skills, synthesis, application of ideas, creativity, decision making, and communication skills through a variety of modes. All these skills and processes are based in language use; all are the material of a language program; all are developed through the ELA program at Any Town School District in the United States.

SOURCE: The ELA program philosophy statement was adapted from the *Language Arts English Primary–Graduation Curriculum Guide* (Canadian Ministry of Education, 1992, pp. 18–30).

Methods for Choosing Teacher Representation

The five methods for choosing teacher representation for curriculum development have advantages and disadvantages. Discussion of each selection method and recommendations as to when it should be used are shown in Exhibit 10.3.

The five group techniques shown next can be described for sensitizing school-focused issues by enabling each practitioner's perspective to be uncovered and, if relevant, systematically

EXHIBIT 10.3 Methods for Choosing Teacher Representation for Curriculum Development		
Method	*Advantages*	*Disadvantages*
Voluntary	• People who volunteer are interested in the program. • The use of volunteers is an open, democratic process.	• Incompetents may volunteer. • Calling for volunteers may indicate unimportance of the task.
Recommended use: When everyone is acceptable		
Rotation	• All possible participants can eventually be involved. • Rotating eliminates the need for selection.	• There is little or no continuity. • There is an assumption that all eligible participants have equal ability.
Recommended use: When the rotating membership will not hinder the development of an acceptable process or product		
Evolvement	• It provides leadership from the group. • Cooperation from committee is high because it chooses the leader or representative through its own process.	• The evolvement process is feasible only in a long-term situation. • Emerged leaders exist without recognized authority.
Recommended use: When determining who the most competent teachers are in curriculum development		
Peer selection	• Committee members feel that they have control over their own destiny. • Cooperation is more likely.	• Committee representatives may be chosen for the wrong reasons. • Groups do not always know the kind of leadership or representation they need.
Recommended use: When the group has maturity and experience		
Administrative selection	• It tends to legitimize a committee member's position. • Administrators generally know who the best-qualified people are.	• Administrators may not know who is best qualified for curriculum development. • It can have negative implications if the selections were based on politics rather than reason.
Recommended use: When peer selection is not practical		

incorporated into curriculum development and implementation. The procedure is often based on building relationships through small-group discussions and involves specific procedures, sampling, timing, and methods of recording. The techniques not only permit teachers and administrators to collaboratively articulate their views and practice in a manner relatively undistorted by rhetoric, but they also result in data that readily inform the design of a working curriculum aimed at enhancing the teaching and learning. Clearly, then, collaboration, political awareness, and advocacy are skills that educators must master if they hope to build and sustain public schools that students deserve (Prichard, 2013–2014).

The main characteristic of the Dialogue Technique is that participants in the process are expected to rely more on dialogue to make decisions and less on individual preparation.

- Participants do not deal with content decision making until they are in the actual development process with other participants.
- The dialogue approach gives participants the opportunity to listen to other views that will either contradict or support their positions.
- The dialogue approach gives participants the opportunity to acquire ownership of a group product.

The Delphi Technique is a method for reaching consensus without the need for face-to-face meetings of all participants.

- Each member of the program committee writes a philosophy statement that they submit to the curriculum director.
- The philosophy statement written by each committee member is copied and distributed to all members on the program committee.
- Each committee member reviews the written philosophy statements and indicates which ones are germane.
- The curriculum director places the philosophy statements into two columns, one for those that are mostly agreed on and one for those for which general agreement was not found.
- The most-agreed-on philosophy statements are resubmitted to committee members and the process repeated until consensus is reached.

The Fishbowl Technique is one in which representatives from each of a large number of subgroups meet to reach consensus on a list of philosophy statements.

- Subgroups of six to eight participants meet and develop a philosophy statement.
- One elected representative from each subgroup meets with representatives from the other groups, who will bring their own group's philosophy statement.
- The representatives sit in a circle facing one another while all others remain seated outside the circle.
- Representatives within the circle discuss each of the subgroup's philosophy statements until consensus is reached.

The Telstar Technique is similar to the Fishbowl Technique but differs in its method of involving all committee members and in their degree of involvement.

- The large group is divided into subgroups, with each group representing specific grade-level groupings (e.g., primary grades, intermediate grades, middle level or junior high school, and senior high school).
- Two representatives are elected from each group to represent that group and bring their respective group's completed philosophy statement to the other group representatives.
- Each two-member delegation may be joined by a small advisory committee from its constituency.
- Any member of an advisory committee can stop the discussion at any time to meet with his or her representatives regarding the issue at hand.
- This procedure continues until a general consensus among all representatives is reached.

The Nominal Group Technique is a process that encourages divergence by individuals.

- A small group convenes to focus on a program philosophy. Members of the group work on an identified task, which is to develop a program philosophy, in the presence of one another but without any immediate interaction.
- Once the task of developing a program philosophy is explained by the curriculum director, group members are given time (20 to 30 minutes) during which each individual writes a program philosophy.
- After the time has expired, the committee members present the program philosophies one at a time. The program philosophies are posted. No discussion of alternative philosophies takes place until all program philosophies have been disclosed.
- Following disclosure, committee members rank the program philosophies presented and start the process again, considering the top three program philosophies.
- After individual committee members have chosen and modified one of the three program philosophies, the committee selects one to adopt as the program philosophy.
- A disadvantage of the process is that during the initial brainstorming, no interaction exists for one idea to inspire another. However, because committee members know that each member is developing a program philosophy and that everyone's philosophy will be displayed, the competitive pressure establishes impetus.

DEVELOPING A SCOPE AND SEQUENCE, PROGRAM GOALS, OBJECTIVES, LEARNING OUTCOMES, AND AUTHENTIC TASKS

Grant Wiggins (2013–2014), president of Authentic Education, noted that to help all students reach high standards, educators need to ask what level of performance is required for mastery. The issue of getting students to mastery must be addressed locally but calibrated to keep them with wider-world standards. Keeping with this perspective, to make a scope and sequence for a program, program goals, objectives for the program goals, learning outcomes for the objectives, and authentic tasks for the learning outcomes that are practical and results centered for students, they must be correlated with the district's philosophy, vision, mission, and exit (graduation) outcomes and with the program's philosophy and rationale statement (based upon individual state standards or CCSS).

Curriculum Tip 10.3	A writing committee should be selected to assume primary responsibility for writing the ELA curriculum.

The following sections present procedures for developing these program elements.

The Committee Structure

To develop a scope and sequence, program goals, objectives, learning outcomes, and authentic tasks for any school program, a subject-area writing committee must be established. The steps for structuring the committee, along with its responsibilities, follow.

Step 1

- The writing committee is selected by and from the program committee members. It must be made up of teachers representing all grade levels (K–12) and preferably two staff members from each grade grouping: primary, intermediate, middle-level or junior high school, and high school. In smaller school districts, one teacher per three grades or course level is satisfactory as long as there is feedback from those teaching the other grade or course levels.
- A building principal or designee from the elementary, middle-level or junior high school, and senior high school must chair or at least be represented on the committee.
- The school district curriculum director or designee should serve as chairperson and be responsible for organizing and directing the activities of the writing committee.
- The school district's board of education must be apprised of the process used to write curricula by the board curriculum committee.
- The writing committee workspace must be in a comfortable environment: comfortable work seats, tables to spread their papers out on, good acoustics, access to the district's curriculum lab containing sample courses of study and program textbooks or software, and clerical assistance.
- The ideal time to develop and write the program scope and sequence, program goals, objectives, learning outcomes, and authentic tasks is after the school year is completed. One week to 10 days is a normal timeline for a writing committee to complete the writing exercise for a program or subject area.

- Reasonable stipends or an extended contract should be given to members of the writing committee.
- All writing committee members must understand and be able to write meaningful program goals and objectives.
- The writing committee must be informed that the process for developing a course of study—the ELA program, for example—entails the following sequential tasks:

1. Review and use the school district's philosophy, vision, mission, and exit (graduation) outcomes for developing a course of study for the specified program.

2. Review and use the specified program philosophy and rationale statement developed by the ELA program committee for developing a course of study for the ELA program.

3. Develop an ELA program **scope and sequence matrix** for the K–12 grade levels (for an example, see Exhibit 10.7).

4. Develop ELA program goals (usually seven to nine) that are driven by the exit (graduation) outcomes (discussed later in this chapter).

5. Develop ELA program objectives (usually six to nine) for each program goal (discussed later in this chapter).

6. Develop ELA program learning outcomes for the objectives (i.e., primary, elementary intermediate, middle level or junior high, and high school; discussed later in this chapter).

7. Develop ELA program authentic tasks for the learning outcomes (discussed later in this chapter).

8. Develop criterion-referenced test items for the developed program (curriculum). If this is not possible, an item analysis of the standardized tests used should be made.

9. Correlate the program scope and sequence, program goals, objectives, learning outcomes, and authentic tasks with textbooks or software and learning materials.

10. Include learning materials for each learning outcome and authentic task.

The Dialogue Technique should be used to guide the ELA writing committee. Also, an example of action verbs for the six levels of learning is useful in developing new programs (see Exhibit 10.4 for categories and cue words).

Step 2

- After the program scope and sequence, program goals, objectives, learning outcomes, and authentic tasks have been written, they must be distributed to all ELA teachers and building administrators throughout the school district for additions, corrections, and/or deletions during the school year. Teachers and administrators should be given four to six weeks to return the document to the curriculum director or designee.

EXHIBIT 10.4 Levels of Action Verbs

Categories	Cue Words	
	Knowledge	
Recall Remembering previously learned information	Cluster	Observe
	Define	Outline
	Label	Recall
	List	Recognize
	Match	Record
	Memorize	Recount
	Name	State
	Comprehension	
Translate Grasping the meaning	Cite	Locate
	Describe	Paraphrase
	Document	Recognize
	Explain	Report
	Express	Review
	Give examples	Summarize
	Identify	Tell
	Application	
Generalize Using learning in new and concrete situations	Analyze	Manipulate
	Dramatize	Organize
	Frame	Sequence
	How to	Show or demonstrate
	Illustrate	Solve
	Imagine	Use
	Imitate	

Analysis		
Break down or discover Breaking down an idea into component parts so that it may be more easily understood	Analyze	Infer
	Characterize	Map
	Classify or categorize	Outline or no format given
	Compare or contrast	Relates to
	Dissect	Select
	Distinguish or differentiate	Survey
	Examine	
Synthesis		
Compose Putting together to form a new whole	Combine	Hypothesize
	Compose	Imagine or speculate
	Construct	Invent
	Design	Plan
	Develop	Produce
	Emulate	Propose
	Formulate	Revise
Evaluation		
Judge Judging value for a given purpose	Appraise	Justify
	Argue	Judge
	Assess	Prioritize or rank
	Compare and give pros and cons	Recommend
	Consider	Support
	Criticize	Value
	Evaluate	

SOURCE: Adapted from Boschee (1989, pp. 89–90).

- During the four- to six-week districtwide review period for the program scope and sequence, program goals, objectives, learning outcomes, and authentic tasks, grade-level and department meetings at the building level must be utilized to peruse the document. Members of the writing committee should be used as consultants (to provide clarification) at the grade-level and department meetings.

Step 3

- After receiving the corrected program documents from districtwide, noncommittee ELA grade- and course-level teachers and administrators, the curriculum director (or designee) must reassemble the writing committee to consider the additions, corrections, and/or deletions suggested.

Step 4

- After the ELA program course of study (curriculum resource guide) is completed with suitable additions, corrections, and/or deletions suggested, the document should be given to the school superintendent and the school board curriculum committee for presentation to the board of education for districtwide adoption and implementation.

Step 5

- Once the ELA program course of study (curriculum resource guide) is adopted, a textbook- or software-review committee, encompassing members from the ELA writing committee, is selected by that committee. Membership must include one person representing each grade and course level.
- Using a similar textbook- or software-selection guide (see Exhibit 10.5), members of the textbook or software review committee must evaluate and rank for their grade level each ELA series from the various publishing companies.
- The entire ELA staff should consider for review the three highest-ranked textbook or software series selected by the textbook- or software-review committee.
- The ELA program scope and sequence, program goals, objectives, learning outcomes, and authentic tasks should be submitted to the three highest-ranked publishing companies selected by the textbook- or software-review committee for their review and presentation to the districtwide ELA staff.
- The presentations by the three selected publishing company representatives should be scheduled during the school year, preferably with no more than one presentation each day.
- All ELA staff and school principals must participate. Voting rights are granted only to those who attend all three presentations by the publishing company representatives.
- The textbook or software series preferred by a majority of staff in the ELA program must be submitted, with rationale for the selection and cost to the district, to the school superintendent and the school board curriculum committee for presentation to the school board for adoption.

Curriculum Tip 10.4

"Consistent use of defined behavioral verbs in composing, rewriting, or selecting learning objectives can lead to improvement in efforts to change and reform education in general and curriculum in particular" (Kizlik, 2011).

EXHIBIT 10.5   Textbook or Software Selection Guide

ANY SCHOOL DISTRICT NO. 3

Any Town, USA

TEXTBOOK /SOFTWARE SELECTION GUIDE

Textbook/ Software _____ Company _____ Grade level _____

Reading level: _____ (Should be at or above grade level. Use the Flesch-Kincaid Grade Level Readability Formula to determine the readability of textbooks.)

Rate each characteristic listed for the textbook or software program on a scale from 1 to 5. Circle your choice and total your ratings to obtain a single overall measure for each reviewed.

Content	Low				High
1. Aligns with state standards or Common Core State Standards (CCSS)	1	2	3	4	5
2. Matches program goals and objectives	1	2	3	4	5
3. Avoids stereotyping by race, ethnicity, and gender	1	2	3	4	5
4. Stimulates student interest	1	2	3	4	5
Organization and Style					
1. Presents up-to-date, accurate information	1	2	3	4	5
2. Uses language and style appropriate for students	1	2	3	4	5
3. Develops a logical sequence	1	2	3	4	5
4. Contains useful practice exercises	1	2	3	4	5
5. Provides thorough reviews and summaries	1	2	3	4	5
6. Includes clearly outlined table of contents and index	1	2	3	4	5
7. Includes helpful student aids such as illustrations, charts, etc.	1	2	3	4	5
8. Provides practical teacher aids such as lesson plans, test questions, etc.	1	2	3	4	5

(Continued)

EXHIBIT 10.5 (Continued)

Physical Features					
1. Has attractive layout	1	2	3	4	5
2. Presents up-to-date, interesting illustrations and graphics	1	2	3	4	5
3. Is well designed	1	2	3	4	5
4. Uses clear text appropriate for students	1	2	3	4	5
5. Can be replicated	1	2	3	4	5

Subtotals =

TOTAL = _____

Evaluator _____   Grade level/subject _____

The Flesch-Kincaid Grade Level Reading Formula, used by the authors, can be used to determine the reading level of textbooks (http://www.readabilityformulas.com/flesch-grade-level-readability-formula.php)

The Flesch-Kincaid Grade Level Readability Formula

Step 1: Calculate the average number of words used per sentence.
Step 2: Calculate the average number of syllables per word.
Step 3: Multiply the average number of words by 0.39, and add it to the average number of syllables per word multiplied by 11.8.
Step 4: Subtract 15.59 from the result.

The specific mathematical formula is:

FKRA = (0.39 x ASL) + (11.8 x ASW)—15.59

Where does this fit?

FKRA = Flesch-Kincaid reading grade level

ASL = average sentence length (i.e., the number of words divided by the number of sentences)

ASW = average number of syllables per word (i.e., the number of syllables divided by the number of words)

Analyzing the results is a simple exercise. For instance, a score of 5.0 indicates a grade school level; i.e., a score of 9.3 means that a ninth grader would be able to read the document. This score makes it easier for teachers, parents, librarians, and others to judge the readability level of various books and texts for the students.

Theoretically, the lowest grade level score could be -3.4, but since there are no real passages that have every sentence consisting of a one-syllable word, it is a highly improbable result in practice.

Step 6

- Appropriate professional development activities must be planned for the ELA staff to accommodate the newly developed ELA course of study (curriculum resource guide). Some in-service activities may need to take place before the program is implemented, and some should take place after teachers have implemented the program.

Step 7

- Evaluation of the ELA program must be an ongoing process, and in-flight corrections should be made until the next five-year cycle. The curriculum director should have expertise in program (curriculum) evaluation.

The collaborative step-by-step process should be used to develop a course of study (curriculum resource guide) for all programs in the public schools. To further this process, principals can use their time effectively and encourage collaboration by working with teacher teams (Hewson, 2013). As illustrated in Exhibit 10.6, this top-down, bottom-up model will engage the process of planning, implementing, and evaluating in such a way that the work of content experts—the teachers—will be facilitated.

The process described will consolidate the efforts of staff, district administrators, and the board of education. Teachers, especially, will be advocates of a program if the process permits them to be the decision makers.

EXHIBIT 10.6 A Process for Developing a Course of Study for the ELA Program

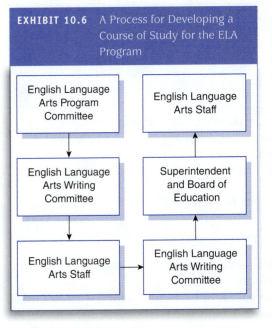

Samples: Program Scope and Sequence, Program Goal, Exit Outcomes Met, Objectives, Learning Outcomes, and Authentic Tasks

Bambrick-Santoyo's (2014) reason to increase persistence and graduation is that schools must become better at teaching students "on-the-ground skills" needed to be successful. Keeping with this perspective, the following are examples of a scope and sequence matrix, a program goal, objectives for the program goal, learning outcomes for the objectives, and authentic tasks for the learning outcomes of an ELA curriculum (see Exhibits 10.7 and 10.8 and the pages that follow). The program goal is driven by exit (graduation) outcomes, and the objectives, which constitute the program goal illustrated, are given specific implementation direction (scope and sequence) at the proposed groupings of primary, elementary intermediate, middle level or junior high, and high school.

Continue to the program goal and outcomes that follow.

Program Goal 1

To develop the knowledge, skills, and processes needed to communicate effectively by listening, speaking, reading, writing, viewing, and representing.

EXHIBIT 10.7		Sample Scope and Sequence Matrix for the Objectives of an ELA Program		
P EI ML/JH HS				These indicate the proposed groupings, which are primary, elementary intermediate, middle level or junior high, and high school.
0				Indicates an orientation stage. Preparatory activities are undertaken prior to the explicit teaching and learning activities suggested in the learning outcomes related to the objective. Refer to learning outcomes at the next stage if appropriate.
E				Indicates an emphasis stage. Learning outcomes are suggestions in this course of study (curriculum resource guide) as examples of appropriate authentic tasks (activities) and observable behaviors. Explicit teaching and learning activities are expected.
M				Indicates a maintenance stage. Provisions are made to reinforce learning outcomes and authentic tasks related to the objective.

Exit Outcomes Met

1. A purposeful thinker

   ○ uses strategies to form concepts, make decisions, and solve problems;
   ○ applies a variety of integrated processes, including critical and creative thinking, to accomplish complex tasks;
   ○ evaluates the effectiveness of mental strategies through meaningful reflection; and
   ○ demonstrates flexibility, persistence, and a sense of ethical considerations.

2. A self-directed learner

   ○ directs own learning;
   ○ sets well-defined goals and manages the process of achieving them;
   ○ acquires, organizes, and uses information;
   ○ initiates learning activities in the pursuit of individual interests;
   ○ applies technology to specific tasks;
   ○ applies realistic self-appraisal in selecting the content, method, and pace for learning; and
   ○ integrates knowledge and skills in both familiar and new situations.

3. An effective communicator

   ○ conveys messages through a variety of methods and materials,
   ○ adapts messages to various audiences and purposes,
   ○ engages the intended audience to understand and respond, and
   ○ receives and interprets the communication of others.

4. A responsible citizen
   o understands diversity and the interdependence of people in local and global communities,
   o demonstrates a respect for human differences,
   o makes informed decisions, and
   o exercises leadership on behalf of the common good.

EXHIBIT 10.8 Objectives Chart				
Objectives	*P*	*EI*	*ML/JH*	*SH*
Students will be able to demonstrate the following:				
1.1 Identify reasons for communicating.	E	E	E	E
1.2 Communicate ideas with clarity and precision.	E	E	E	E
1.3 Experience satisfaction and confidence in the communication skills and processes.	E	E	E	E
1.4 Produce, explore, and extend ideas and information.	E	E	E	E
1.5 Read and examine independently by choosing appropriate strategies and processes.	O	E	E	E
1.6 Comprehend that the communication skills and processes are interrelated avenues for constructing meaning.	E	E	M	M

Learning Outcomes and Authentic Tasks for an English Language Arts Program

Objective 1.1: Students will be able to identify reasons for communicating.

Primary Grades

Students will be able to demonstrate the following:

1.1.1. Recognize why they are communicating.
Authentic task: Students will express feelings, solve problems, or confirm the meaning of a message.

1.1.2. Discuss the purposes of communicating.
Authentic task: Students will make a classroom chart on "why we read."

1.1.3. Plan and lead classroom activities.
Authentic task: Students will chair news time, act as spokesperson for a small group, or introduce a visitor.

1.1.4. Listen to and follow directions to perform a new activity.
Authentic task: Students will playact a new game.

1.1.5. Choose to read for a variety of purposes.
Authentic task: Students will read for enjoyment, to find new ideas, or to confirm ideas.

1.1.6. Choose to write for a variety of purposes.
Authentic task: Students will write to request information, to express gratitude, or for entertainment.

1.1.7. Compose notes and lists to themselves.
Authentic task: Students will write a list of telephone numbers or a reminder note to return library books.

1.1.8. Engage in prewriting discussion.
Authentic task: Students will choose a topic, focus ideas, or clarify purpose.

1.1.9. Use a grid, chart, graph, cluster, or web to organize information.
Authentic task: Students will organize collected facts from researching an animal.

Elementary Intermediate Grades

Students will be able to demonstrate the following:

1.1.10. Describe the broad purposes that are common to communication skills and processes.
Authentic task: Students will advise, command, direct, entertain, inform, persuade, or socialize.

1.1.11. Arrange their own specific purposes that identify the desired result and focus attention.
Authentic task: Students will tune in to the radio news to get information on a specific item.

1.1.12. Arrange their own purposes for listening.
Authentic task: Students will listen attentively to a poem to form sensory images.

1.1.13. Organize their own purposes for speaking.
Authentic task: Students will make a speech to express a personal point of view.

1.1.14. Determine their own purposes for reading.
Authentic task: Students will read a selection to answer specific questions.

1.1.15. Determine their own purposes for writing.
Authentic task: Students will record observations to write a science report.

1.1.16. Arrange their own purposes for viewing.
Authentic task: Students will analyze TV commercials to identify persuasive techniques.

1.1.17. Determine their own purposes for representing.
Authentic task: Students will develop a diagram to organize similarities when comparing two opinions.

1.1.18. Identify the purposes of other people's communication.
Authentic task: Students will recognize propaganda and the desire to convince in a biased presentation.

1.1.19. Recognize the purposes of various media.
Authentic task: Students will infer that television aims to entertain, to inform, and to persuade.

Middle Level or Junior High

Students will be able to demonstrate the following:

1.1.20. Recognize the broad purposes that are common to communication skills and processes.
Authentic task: Students will do controlling, imaging, informing, and socializing.

1.1.21. Identify the audience to which communication is addressed.
Authentic task: Students will communicate with adults, friends, or relatives.

1.1.22. Recognize and focus attention on the desired result of communication.
Authentic task: Students will write a letter of complaint or speak to a group in order to raise funds for a project.

1.1.23. Engage in preparatory activities for listening, speaking, and viewing.
Authentic task: Students will recall prior knowledge of the topic or predict what could be learned about a topic.

1.1.24. Establish a purpose for speaking.
Authentic task: Students will give a formal speech to persuade a group to accept a personal point of view.

1.1.25. Create a purpose for representing.
Authentic task: Students will use a chart to show similarities of themes in U.S. literature.

1.1.26. Recognize persuasive techniques.
Authentic task: Students will recognize bias, propaganda, use of connotation, and use of emotive language.

High School

Students will be able to demonstrate the following:

1.1.27. Employ language strategies and processes that are most likely to elicit the desired results.
Authentic task: Students will choose between a telephone call and a letter to deal with business.

1.1.28 Identify the audience to which a communication is to be directed.
Authentic task: Students will choose peers, adults, or special-interest groups as the appropriate audience.

1.1.29. Select the desired result of a communication.
Authentic task: Students will write a letter of application or a student council letter of request to the principal.

1.1.30. Appraise the difference between active and passive listening by discussing which activities require no effort on the part of the listener and which will demand full attention.
Authentic task: Students will decide that background music is passive listening, and listening for a main idea is active listening.

1.1.31. Develop and apply criteria to evaluate what is heard.
Authentic task: Students will utilize criteria agreed to by the class, such as the main idea, details, and examples to be applied to class speeches.

1.1.32. Identify main ideas.
Authentic task: Students will write down the main ideas after hearing a passage read or will paraphrase a speaker's message orally or in written form.

1.1.33. Distinguish fact from opinion.
Authentic task: Students will, after listening to a reading, list orally or in writing what is fact and what is opinion.

1.1.34. Recognize the influence of the listener's bias or perception.
Authentic task: Students will examine possible preconceived ideas on a topic before the class hears a speech.

1.1.35. Recognize a speaker's purpose and bias.
Authentic task: Students will peruse differences between speeches from the opposing sides on an issue such as capital punishment.

SOURCE: The ELA program scope and sequence, program goal, objectives, and learning outcomes were adapted from *Language Arts English Primary–Graduation Curriculum Guide* (Canadian Ministry of Education, 1992, pp. 18–30).

Each program goal should also list a wide variety of resources, accessible to the staff, to help students accomplish the exit outcomes. Examples of resources include online and mobile devices, applications, software and courseware, textbooks (digital or standard), activities, novels, nonfiction books, anthologies, collections, handbooks, dramas, selected readings from reserved material in the library or classroom, printed handouts, kits, periodicals, transparency sets, video recordings, and audio recordings. The ELA staff should have an updated inventory of materials available that lists where each is located, such as in the classroom, departmental media center, school media center, district media center, regional media center, or state media center.

The program (curriculum) development process described is a design-down, deliver-up model (see Exhibit 10.9). Samples provided of scope and sequence, program goal, objectives for the program goal, learning outcomes, and authentic tasks should enable a school district to develop a performance-based education program. Once a program is developed, teachers can easily develop unit plans and daily lesson plans for their students. It should also be noted that in a technology-based flipped-mastery model—the teacher begins by organizing content around specific objectives (Bergmann & Sams, 2013–2014).

Developing a program's course of study assures continuity of instruction across grade levels and subsequently allows a smoother transition from one grade level to the next. It is a road map for staff and students in a district.

GLOBAL CONNECTIONS: NARROWING THE ACHIEVEMENT GAP

Countries known to outpace the United States in student achievement use a variety of educational and organizational methods but rarely use the approaches to educational reform that we are promoting (Williams & Engel, 2012–2013). Interestingly enough, as society grows both culturally and globally, educators remain concerned as to how the United States is measuring up academically.

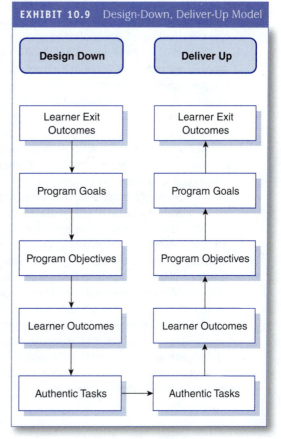

EXHIBIT 10.9   Design-Down, Deliver-Up Model

| Design Down | Deliver Up |

Learner Exit Outcomes → Program Goals → Program Objectives → Learner Outcomes → Authentic Tasks

Authentic Tasks → Learner Outcomes → Program Objectives → Program Goals → Learner Exit Outcomes

Curriculum Tip 10.5

Programs resulting from the recommended, written, supported, taught, tested, and learned curriculum should correlate with the overarching planning cycle involving the following: analysis, design, development, implementation, and evaluation (ADDIE design model) as noted in Chapter 5 (Design Theories and Models, 2014).

Tony Wagner (2008), in his book *The Global Achievement Gap,* related early on how transformations in leadership represent enormous challenges for future educational leaders. He listed a primary challenge as being the ability of educators to prepare students for both analytic and creative thinking. For this reason, Wagner focused on the development of a global achievement gap. Basically, this gap reflects the distance between what our best public schools are teaching and testing, as opposed to what all students need to know in the world today. With an alarming fear of other countries having more success academically, the achievement gap has profound implications not just for work but also for citizenship and lifelong learning. This is especially the case in large cities that are facing serious obstacles to providing a high-quality education to every student (Levin, 2013).

To meet the challenges of curriculum development and narrow the achievement gap, schools are using advances in technology to become globally interconnected. This means school leaders are becoming global leaders as well. A global leader is an individual who is aware of global challenges, world cultures, and the connection between them and the rest of the world. It is crucial, then, for our school leaders to understand globally how other countries develop curriculum, conduct professional development, and handle school-related issues. It is equally imperative for schools to develop a global perspective through integrated online communities, mobile technology, and other communication sources to gather information about other countries and cultures. Thus, by rearranging priorities and developing an effective use of technology, every new 21st-century learner will have an opportunity to learn from a global audience (Blair, 2012). By and large, an increasing number of school leaders are realizing the potential of technology as a powerful resource for enhancing learning on a global scale. Through advanced technology, it is now possible to share information and classroom projects with educators and schools all over the world. As part of that culture of conversation, school leaders will be better able to formulate a broader perspective of world challenges. Moreover, in the process of encouraging staff and students to become global citizens, we can become more interested in using advances in technology to explore civic responsibilities and equity issues, cultural awareness, and the environment. The need for vibrant educational leadership on a global level is here and apparent. Knowing what problems might arise from a worldly perspective and how to deal with complex issues is the reward. Likewise, knowing that this generation of students is more cognizant of world affairs than previous generations will help lead us to an age of global transparency (Whitehead, Jensen, & Boschee, 2013).

LEADERSHIP TRUTHS FOR CURRICULUM LEADERS

Steven Weber (2011), Executive Director of Curriculum and Instruction, Chapel Hill-Carrboro City Schools, Chapel Hill, North Carolina, in an ASCD Edge blog addresses the characteristics needed for curriculum leadership. His experience as a leader in curriculum development and implementation is based on a sound philosophy of experience. Weber introduces the leadership traits with the following statements:

What is a curriculum leader? A second-grade teacher can serve as a curriculum leader. Principals and assistant principals should also be viewed as curriculum leaders. A central office staff member may have the title of Chief Academic Officer or Curriculum Director, but that does not mean they are the only curriculum leader in the school district. Once teachers begin communicating with teachers in the same grade level and make connections with the next level (i.e., middle school and high school transition), students will benefit from increased clarity on the essential learning outcomes.

Curriculum leadership involves working with multiple people to ensure that the curriculum is aligned both horizontally and vertically. "Curriculum development is the essential function of school leadership. Whether the role is carried out by a principal, an assistant principal for curriculum, a team leader, a department head, or by leading classroom teachers, the curriculum defines all other roles in a school" (Wiles, 2009, p. 2). This article addresses ten leadership truths that apply to first-year teachers as well as veteran curriculum directors at the central office level.

Given that many factors will affect curriculum development and implementation, a variety of factors have a large influence which must be of concern to educational planners. The ten leadership truths that Weber (2011) presents in the blog are as follows:

1. Priorities Matter. You Revisit Them Daily

"All learners benefit from and should receive instruction that reflects clarity about purposes and priorities of content" (Tomlinson & McTighe, 2006, p. 6).

2. Curriculum Development Is a Process, Not a Product

Curriculum mapping is an ongoing process that asks teachers to develop curriculum goals; identify essential content, skills, and concepts; and reflect on the taught curriculum. Some school districts make the mistake of diving into curriculum mapping and attempting to complete a product. When teacher teams become satisfied with the product, then the process is at risk. Curriculum development is "an ongoing process that asks teachers and administrators to think, act, and meet differently to improve their students' learning" (Hale, 2008, p. 8).

3. Communication Matters

Curriculum gaps create a barrier for student learning and have a detrimental effect on students' opportunity to learn. Gaps are created by a lack of communication among educators, varying implementation practices, available resources, and decisions about pacing. According to English (2000), "Curriculum design and delivery face one fundamental problem in schools. When the door is shut and nobody else is around, the classroom teacher can select and teach just about any curriculum he or she decides is appropriate" (p. 1).

4. It's Lonely at the Top

John Maxwell (2008) wrote, the statement "It's lonely at the top was never made by a great leader. If you are leading others and you're lonely, then you're not doing it right. What kind of leader would leave everyone behind and take the journey alone? A selfish one. Taking people to the top is what good leaders do." Empowering others is one of the main roles of curriculum leaders. If you are feeling lonely, take a moment to reflect on why no one seems to be following.

5. What Gets Measured Gets Done

Developing curriculum is essential for any school district. However, educators need to know if the curriculum is meeting its intended outcomes. Teachers may indicate that they value 21st-century learning skills, but if the district's benchmark exams and the high-stakes state exam measure lower-order thinking skills and do not measure 21st-century skills, then there will be a temptation to teach to the test. Curriculum leaders understand that curriculum alignment consists of curriculum, instruction, and assessment. Without a method of measurement, then it is highly unlikely that the curriculum will be implemented across classrooms.

6. Alignment Is Critical

Curriculum developers can spend so much time developing curriculum documents that they forget to take time to analyze alignment and have conversations with multiple groups. "Poorly aligned curriculum results in our underestimating the effect of instruction on learning. Simply stated, teachers may be 'teaching up a storm,' but if what they are teaching is neither aligned with the state standards or the state assessments, then their teaching is in vain" (Anderson, 2002, p. 260). If alignment is important for your vehicle, it is even more critical when dealing with children's lives and their future aspirations.

7. Gaps Exist in Every School District . . . Seek Solutions

Jacobs (1997) wrote, "If there are gaps among teachers within buildings, there are virtual Grand Canyons among buildings in a district" (p. 3). Curriculum leaders can conduct a Gap Analysis. Another method is to have ongoing conversations with teams of teachers to analyze common student misunderstandings. Data analysis has become more prominent in public schools over the past ten years. The use of quality data can help schools identify gaps. Curriculum gaps create a disjointed curriculum. In *Toward a Coherent Curriculum: The 1985 ASCD Yearbook,* Stellar wrote, "The curriculum in numerous schools lacks clarity and, more important, coherence. Students move from teacher to teacher and subject to subject along a curriculum continuum that may or may not exhibit planned articulation" (p. v).

8. Curriculum Development Is Never Neutral

If you have ever worked with a team of teachers to develop curriculum maps, align the school district's curriculum, or evaluate curriculum, you understand that curriculum development is a political act. Fenwick English (2000) wrote, "Knowledge is never neutral. The selection of knowledge is fundamentally a political act of deciding who benefits from selecting what in the school's curriculum and who is excluded or diminished" (p. 30).

"Curriculum is always a means to somebody's end. . . . No selection of curriculum content can be considered politically neutral" (English, 2000, p. 53). If you are asked to review curriculum or develop curriculum, then you should be careful to avoid bias. What is good for your own child may not be good for every child. Politics are unavoidable when it comes to curriculum development, but educators can improve the curriculum development process by seeking multiple perspectives.

9. Leadership Is Not a Title

This statement has been made in business leadership books and it holds true in any organization. You may be the Chief Academic Officer or the department chair, but titles don't matter. People matter. Maxwell (1995) wrote, "If you really want to be a successful leader, you must develop other leaders around you. You must establish a team" (p. 2). If curriculum development becomes a matter of pleasing the person with the title, there will be little buy-in and that will have a negative impact on students. "A good leader has the ability to instill within his people confidence in himself. A great leader has the ability to instill within his people confidence in themselves" (Maxwell, 1995, p. 55).

10. The Ultimate Goal Is Student Achievement

According to Wiggins and McTighe (2007), "The job is not to hope that optimal learning will occur, based on our curriculum and initial teaching. The job is to ensure that learning occurs, and when it doesn't, to intervene in altering the syllabus and instruction decisively, quickly, and often" (p. 55). School districts must confront the brutal facts of their current reality in order to improve (Collins, 2001).

A favorite quote on the topic of curriculum leadership is from Allan Glatthorn (1987): "One of the tasks of curriculum leadership is to use the right methods to bring the written, the taught, the supported, and the tested curriculums into closer alignment, so that the learned curriculum is maximized" (p. 4).

Weber (2011) offers a conclusion that sums up leadership for curriculum development and implementation. He states:

> Curriculum development plays a significant role in teaching and learning. Most educators will admit that planning is an essential part of their profession. If curriculum development drives the work of teacher teams, then schools must create time for teachers to collaborate, engage in conflict and provide a process for reflection and revision. Curriculum development should be a priority in schools, rather than something that is handed to teachers as a top-down product. When teachers collaborate to develop the curriculum, they will have co-workers who support them when they come to a fork in the road in instruction. Curriculum leadership is important to the success of a school district and these ten truths can help a leader develop multiple leaders. Curriculum leadership is about empowering those around you to be successful.

References

Anderson, L. W. (2002). Curricular alignment: A re-examination. *Theory into Practice, 41,* 225–260.

Collins, J. (2001). *Good to great: Why some companies make the leap and others don't.* New York, NY: HarperCollins.

English, F. W. (2000). *Deciding what to teach and test: Developing, aligning and auditing the curriculum.* Thousand Oaks, CA: Corwin Press.

Glatthorn, A. A. (1987). *Curriculum renewal.* Alexandria, VA: ASCD.

Hale, J. A. (2008). *A guide to curriculum mapping: Planning, implementing, and sustaining the process.* Thousand Oaks, CA: Corwin Press.

Jacobs, H. H. (1997). *Mapping the big picture: Integrating curriculum and assessment K-12.* Alexandria, VA: ASCD.

Maxwell, J. C. (1995). *Developing the leaders around you.* Nashville, TN: Thomas Nelson.

Maxwell, J. C. (2008). *Leadership gold: Lessons I've learned from a lifetime of leading.* Nashville, TN: Thomas Nelson.

Steller, A. W. (1985). Forward. In J. A. Beane (Ed.), *Toward a coherent curriculum. The 1985 ASCD Yearbook.* Alexandria, VA: ASCD.

Tomlinson, C. A., & McTighe, J. (2006). *Integrating differentiated instruction and understanding by design.* Alexandria, VA: ASCD.

Wiggins, G., & McTighe, J. (2007). *Schooling by design: Mission, action, and achievement.* Alexandria, VA: ASCD.

Wiles, J. (2009). *Leading curriculum development.* Thousand Oaks, CA: Corwin Press.

SUMMARY

The chapter provides an example of the necessary collaborative steps for curriculum development and implementation. The role of each of the constituents (board of education, superintendent, school administrators, and teachers) is displayed in the schematics presented. The chapter also illustrates how to assemble an actualized and effective curriculum that utilizes the key elements shown next.

Recommended → *Written* → *Supported* → *Taught* → *Tested* → *Learned*

The actual results of the curriculum development and implementation process are shown in Chapter 11, Exhibit 11.7.

Throughout this chapter, the reader was made aware of a critical point: *building relationships through teacher involvement.* As part of the collaborative process, and to gain an adequate understanding of the ends and means, every teacher (systemwide) needs to participate in curriculum development for his or her grade level and/or discipline.

APPLICATIONS

1. Why must a curriculum council and program committee have a thorough understanding of the school district's philosophy, vision, mission, and exit outcomes?

2. What characterizes a program philosophy? What characterizes a program rationale statement?

3. What advantages do the Dialogue Technique, the Delphi Technique, the Fishbowl Technique, the Telstar Technique, and the Nominal Group Technique have over other ways groups make decisions?

4. Identify interrelationships that exist between scope and sequence, program goals, objectives, learning outcomes, and authentic tasks.

5. Explain how developing a course of study (curriculum resource guide) facilitates the teacher as content expert.

6. Outline responsibilities for the program committee.

7. Distinguish the responsibilities of the subject-writing committee from those of the program committee.

8. Should the course of study be written by the writing committee during the school year or during the summer months with stipends? Defend your answer.

9. Plan an in-service activity for the staff to accommodate a newly developed course of study.

10. How can teachers become stakeholders of a curriculum with the current state standards and/or the advent of the CCSS?

11. A study by University of Southern California education professor Morgan Polikoff found that many textbooks labeled "CCSS aligned" were, in fact, not. Between 60% and 95% of many textbooks were used for previous standards, indicating the books had not been updated for CCSS. In addition, between 10% and 20% of the material reviewed had nothing to do with CCSS. Is this a problem in your district? Yes or no? Explain.

12. In general, research evidence shows that college and workplace textbooks remain complex while K–12 texts reading texts have become easier. Subsequently, there is a growing and significant difficulty between texts used at the end of high school and those used at the beginning of college. Could this be the reason why remedial education is so prevalent in our colleges and universities? Yes or no? Explain why.

Building Consensus by Committee

Phillip Wright, a first-year curriculum director of a large school district, meets with the superintendent, Dr. Roberta Ellis, to discuss ways to develop an ELA program procedure for adoption.

Searching for some feedback, Wright states, "I need to explore how and when you want me to organize a curriculum committee or committees for the ELA program because the current program is due in the district's five-year curriculum development cycle. For example, I'm thinking of formulating an adoption committee or committees this fall. Do you have any concerns in that regard?"

Dr. Ellis nods her head. "Well, yes, actually, I do have some concerns about organizing committees, especially writing committees, during the school year." Folding her arms across her chest, the superintendent gives a sigh. "I've found hiring substitutes for staff during the year is quite costly—but more important, instructional time lost due to teachers being out of their classrooms is a huge concern because students learn only one third as much with a substitute teacher as they do with their own classroom teacher."

The new curriculum director's eyes widen. "Oh, I didn't realize that," he says demurely. "I'll be happy to establish a writing committee for the summer months. However, the district must pay stipends to teachers participating in committee work."

"Good," says Dr. Ellis and asks, "What process are you using to select teacher representation?"

"Well, my plan is to use the administrative selection method, choosing some strong experienced teachers from each instructional level—you know, primary, intermediate, middle, and high school," shares Wright, continuing to observe his boss for approval, or at least for direction.

Dr. Ellis leans back in her chair. "Well, that's a possibility, but you want to be very careful about whom you select—especially when it comes to strong personalities." The superintendent now focuses her gaze on her new curriculum director and adds, "What sometimes happens is the creation of four armed camps—you know what I mean: no consensus, strife between teachers—basically a lack of cooperation between each other."

"Oh, yeah. Good point."

The superintendent smiles and then decides to share some last words of wisdom. "As effective leaders, *we need to anticipate the need for consensus* and pick some folks who not only know their subject material but who are also flexible and committed to the district's vision and core curriculum beliefs."

"Great idea!" extols Wright, now aware of several crucial points critical to formulating curriculum development committees. After thanking Superintendent Ellis for her input, the curriculum director, with a valise full of notes, begins heading for the door, realizing he has another appointment waiting in his office.

The Challenge

Choosing teacher representation for committees and anticipating the importance of consensus building are both crucial steps toward successful curriculum development. Analyze each of the methods of choosing teacher representation—voluntary, rotation, evolvement, peer selection, and administrative selection—and discuss what challenges a curriculum director might face. Which method do you think is best? What strategies might Phillip Wright use in helping select members for the ELA program committees?

Key Issues or Questions

1. What questions does Phillip Wright need to ask before formulating curriculum committees for the ELA program?

2. What measures does one need to take during the *early planning* phase of committee development?

3. What procedures does one need to implement during the planning phase of curriculum development?

4. What actions does one need to take *after* a curriculum program has been adopted?

5. What is the best method of choosing teacher representation for curriculum committees? Why?

WEBLIOGRAPHY

Effective Schools Research

www.mcrel.org

National Association of Elementary School Principals (NAESP)

www.naesp.org

National Association of Elementary School Principals (NAESP) Leadership Compass

www.naesp.org/leadership-compass-archives-0

National Association of Secondary School Principals (NASSP)

www.nassp.org

Textbooks and Common Core State Standards (CCSS)

http://stateimpact.npr.org/florida/2014/02/26/studies-find-textbooks-are-a-poor-match-for-common-standards

The Flesch–Kincaid Grade Level Reading Formula

www.readabilityformulas.com/flesch-grade-level-readability-formula.php

Types of Curriculum

http://thesecondprinciple.com/instructional-design/types-of-curriculum

REFERENCES

Bambrick-Santoyo, P. (2014). Make students college-ready in high school. *Phi Delta Kappan, 95*(5), 72–73.

Baron, M. A., Boschee, F., & Jacobson, M. (2008). *Performance-based education: Developing programs through strategic planning.* Lanham, MD: Rowman & Littlefield.

Bergmann, J., & Sams, A. (2013–2014). Flipping for mastery. *Educational Leadership, 71*(4), 24–29.

Blair, N. (2012). Technology integration for the new 21st century learner. *Principal, 91*(3), 8–11.

Boschee, F. (1989). *Grouping = growth.* Dubuque, IA: Kendall/Hunt.

Burris, C. C., & Murphy, J. (2013–2014). Everyone can be college ready. *Educational Leadership, 71*(4), 62–66.

Canadian Ministry of Education. (1992). *Language arts English primary–graduation curriculum guide.* Victoria, B.C.: Author.

Dewey, J. (1916). *Democracy and education: An introduction to the philosophy of education.* New York, NY: Macmillian.

Gallagher, K. (2014). Teaching edge sparks the conversation. *Reading Today, 31*(4), 19.

Hewson, K. (2013). Time shift: Developing teacher teams. *Principal, 92*(3), 15–17.

Kizlik, B. (2011). *Definitions of behavioral verbs for learning objectives.* ADPRIMA. Retrieved from http://www.adprima.com/verbs.htm

Levin, B. (2013). Shanghai and Seoul plan higher achievement. *Phi Delta Kappan, 94*(8), 74–75.

Marzano, R. J. (2013–2014). Art & science of teaching: Defusing out-of-control behavior. *Educational Leadership, 71*(4), 82–83.

McAssey, L. (2014). Common core assessments: A principal's view. *Principal, 93*(3), 14–18.

Medin, D. L., & Bang, M. (2013–2014). Culture in the classroom. *Phi Delta Kappan, 95*(4), 64–67.

Plonczak, I., Brooks, J. G., Wilson, G. L., Elijah, R., & Caliendo, J. (2014). STEM studio: Where innovation generates innovation. *Phi Delta Kappan, 95*(5), 52–56.

Prichard, A. (2013–2014). When all else fails, organize and advocate. *Phi Delta Kappan, 95*(4), 44–48.

Protheroe, N. (2011). What do effective principals do? *Principal, 90*(5), 26–30.

Richardson, J. (2010). College knowledge: An interview with David Conley. *Phi Delta Kappan, 92*(1), 28–34.

Wagner, T. (2008). *The global achievement gap: Why even our best schools don't teach the new survival skills our children need—and what we can do about it.* New York, NY: Basic Books.

Waters, J. T., & Marzano, R. J. (2006, September). *School district leadership that works: The effect of superintendent leadership on student achievement* (Working paper). Retrieved from http://www.mcrel.org/pdf/leadershiporganization development/4005RR_Superintendent_Leadership.pdf

Weber, S. (2011, March 20). *Ten leadership truths for curriculum leaders* [Blog post]. Retrieved from http://edge.ascd.org/blogpost/leadership-truths-for-curriculum-leaders

Whitehead, B. M., Jensen, D. F. N., & Boschee, F. (2013). *Planning for technology: A guide for school administrators, technology coordinators, and curriculum leaders* (2nd ed.). Thousand Oaks, CA: Corwin Press.

Wiggins, G. (2013–2014). How good is good enough. *Educational Leadership, 71*(4), 10–16.

Wiles, J. W., & Bondi, J. C. (2011). *Curriculum development: A guide to practice* (8th ed.). Upper Saddle River, NJ: Pearson.

Williams, J. H., & Engel, L. C. (2012–2013). How do other countries evaluate teachers? *Phi Delta Kappan, 94*(4), 53–57.

NOTE

1. The program goal listed (in this revised chapter) was adapted from the *Language Arts English Primary–Graduation Curriculum Guide* (Canadian Ministry of Education, 1992, pp. 19–27). Samples of the nine goals for the ELA program are as follows:

   - Program Goal 1 develops the knowledge, skills, and processes needed to communicate effectively by listening, speaking, reading, writing, and representing.
   - Program Goal 2 develops knowledge, understanding, and appreciation of language and how it is used.
   - Program Goal 3 develops knowledge, understanding, and appreciation of a wide variety of literary genres and media forms.
   - Program Goal 4 develops knowledge, understanding, and appreciation of U.S. and other world literature.
   - Program Goal 5 develops and extends knowledge of self, the world, and our multicultural heritage through language, literature, and media.
   - Program Goal 6 extends capacity for creative thought and expression within the context of language, literature, and media.
   - Program Goal 7 extends capacity for critical thought and expression within the context of language, literature, and media.
   - Program Goal 8 develops the wide variety of strategies for learning.
   - Program Goal 9 develops attributes of wonder, curiosity, independence, and interdependence necessary for lifelong learning.

CHAPTER 11

Aligning the Curriculum

Curriculum alignment is a process of ensuring that the written, the taught, and the tested curricula are closely congruent. This is not always the case, noted Fusarelli (2008), who stated, "There is the common perception that educational leaders ignore research when they make decision about school improvement" (p. 365).

Ignoring important research can be a major roadblock toward formulating congruency between the written, taught, and tested curricula. In too many schools, little correspondence exists between the district curriculum guides, the teacher's instructional plans, and the assessment measures. This problem, however, can be easily addressed by school leaders developing a consistent program of curriculum alignment. Curriculum alignment, based on research and with a focus on a standards-based curriculum, can provide a way to remedy this situation in order to improve achievement for all students.

Questions addressed in this chapter include the following:

- What are the essential elements for curriculum alignment?
- How does one organize a curriculum alignment project?
- What organizational strategies should be used for curriculum alignment?
- What are mastery objectives and curriculum-based tests?
- What is the value of using research in curriculum management?
- How important is professional development in curriculum alignment?
- How can the curriculum alignment project be monitored and evaluated?

> **Key to Leadership**
>
> The function of a principal in a school is to create the conditions for the fullest release of creative talent on the part of individual faculty members and the students. As part of that function, it is important to work collaboratively in formulating curriculum alignment and teacher professional development activities that reflect the elements of high-quality instruction with clear, explicit learning goals.

A RATIONALE FOR CURRICULUM ALIGNMENT

Flexibility is currently at the forefront of reform innovation for schools. It is particularly important when aligning curriculum needed to deliver in ways that helps all students—especially students with previous educational deficits (Raymond, 2014). Clearly, curriculum alignment is a process of ensuring that the *written,* the *taught,* and the *tested* curricula are closely aligned and congruent. A school district's written and assessed curriculum, as aligned with individual state standards or Common Core State Standards (CCSS), should represent a districtwide consensus about instructional objectives and their relative importance for a given group of learners. If collaboratively developed in the manner outlined in previous chapters, it reflects the input of curriculum experts, subject-matter specialists, district administrators, supervisors, and teachers. Because the planned curriculum represents an informed consensus, it should be the determining element in what is taught day-by-day.

Therefore, what is taught and tested needs to encompass the mastery curriculum (as per set standards) as well as what is outlined in the curriculum guide. Keeping with this perspective, district guides should not deal with organic elements (those that do not require structuring) or the enrichment elements (those not essential for all students). Obviously, the alignment process needs to focus only on the mastery curriculum. Because neither organic nor enrichment components are assessed or monitored, the teacher can then have an important measure of autonomy.

PHILOSOPHY STATEMENT

As mentioned in previous chapters, a school's curriculum philosophy and rationale statement must align with individual state standards or CCSS as well as augment the school's vision, mission, and exit (graduation) outcomes. The principal or teacher–leaders guiding the school's

| **Curriculum Tip 11.1** | The alignment process, as part of the curriculum cycle represented by analysis, design, development, implementation, and evaluation (ADDIE model), should not only meet standards but hopefully *exceed* them. |

philosophy hold the responsibility of keeping a shared vision as well as providing the destination and/or direction for the alignment, development, and implementation of the school's comprehensive curriculum. Similarly, the cyclical process of analysis, design, development, implementation, and evaluation (ADDIE model), as noted in Chapter 5, represents a type of curriculum change and guidance that requires careful support throughout the alignment process (Design Theories & Models, 2014). With this understanding, some recommended changes might come from the results of external curriculum audits. An External School Curriculum Audit is a school-based improvement intervention often used as part of a corrective action phase by some schools. These types of audits usually have delineated, interpreted, aligned, and articulated standards for one or more accountability measures for student groups. Recommendations generated from external audits might come in the way of data-driven analysis or a complete change in program design.

ROLE OF THE PRINCIPAL

The processes used in aligning programs and fields of study require exemplary leadership. With that said, the complex, responsive nature of school leadership makes it difficult to predict what each day will bring, and thus, successful principals are those individuals who can comfortably adjust when necessary (Markle & VanKoevering, 2013). It is crucial for 21st-century principals to *first* develop a strong background and knowledge of curriculum; *second,* to fully comprehend and understand the curriculum cycle and alignment process as it pertains to curriculum development; and *third,* to apply solutions needed to improve teaching and learning at all levels.

In meeting today's challenges, school leaders are taking on increasing *collaborative roles* in curriculum alignment as they continue to be reorganized and redirected. Building-level leaders are becoming more knowledgeable and prepared as to what they must do if they are to turn their schools around. Emerging in educational administrative theory are approaches reaffirming the importance of quality leadership in the curriculum planning process. Thus, it is through hard work, commitment, an inquiring mind, and the ability to learn from experiences, as noted in this text, that principals will be able to go from a local perspective to a greater global understanding. As school leaders become more globally attuned and collaboratively interconnected, they will be better able to act as catalysts for curriculum alignment, whether it is a large urban area, rural isolated setting, reservation, or tribal community.

Aligning With Common Core State Standards

The past decade has witnessed considerable interest in curriculum integration and yet, paradoxically, schools are being required at the same time to move to an "accountability" and "standards-based" subject-centered curriculum.

The positive aspect of state standards or CCSS, as stated by Finn and Petrilli (2010), is that they "are the foundation upon which almost everything rests—or should rest" (p. 1). Also, "they should guide state assessments and accountability systems; inform teacher preparation, licensure, and professional development; and *give shape* [emphasis added] to curricula, textbooks, software programs, and more" (p. 1).

In reality, standards are targets, or blueprints, or road maps. They set the destination: what we want our students to know and be able to do by the end of their PreK–12 experience and the benchmarks they should reach along the way. If the standards are vague, watered down, or misguided, they can point our schools down perilous paths. If there are no standards worth following, there is no education destination worth reaching (Finn & Petrilli, 2010, pp. 1–2).

> **Question**
>
> Is having Common Core State Standards the first step toward nationalizing education? The answer is no, because the standards are part of a state-led effort to give all students the skills and knowledge they need to succeed. The federal government was not involved in the development of the standards. Individual states choose whether to adopt these standards. (Council of Chief State School Officers [CCSSO] & National Governors Association [NGA], 2010)

Elements of Common Core State Standards

Because teaching now comes with the responsibility of learning, the following elements of CCSS are provided to enhance understanding of instructional processes. Core elements include the following:

Sequence

A well-organized curriculum states goals in a clear and concise manner. Complex ideas and skills follow simpler ones. Student abilities are considered when determining teaching strategies. Topics are addressed and then covered again in a spiraling curriculum approach, with the learning level advancing with each reteaching. Students develop a richer understanding of the subject area, and there is an appreciation of nuances within the material.

Required Versus Elective

Elements of consistency within the curriculum begin to change as students move from elementary to middle to high school levels. The distinction between mandatory and optional is more evident at high school levels. Students at higher levels are able to pick and choose courses as they relate to graduation and college requirements.

Coordination and Integration

Some curriculum specialists consider subjects as distinct bodies of knowledge to be aligned as standards throughout the curriculum. Other curriculum specialists see subject areas as bodies of knowledge to be interwoven in a thematic scheme. In the latter approach, information can be covered through methods of inquiry and topics can be coordinated and integrated across disciplines. Regardless of which approach is used, the educational task force or district curriculum committee needs to identify mastery objectives within the curriculum.

Assessment and Common Core State Standards

With the implementation of CCSS, many school leaders are focusing on performance-based tests that will measure them—namely Smarter Balanced Assessment Consortium (SBAC) and a second by the Partnership for Assessment of Readiness for College and Careers (PARCC; Dietel, 2011). In addition to measures developed by these consortia, some school districts are formulating their own robust performance tasks and portfolios as part of a multiple-measure system of assessment. This is largely in response to two decades of research that has found when teachers use, score, and discuss the results of high-quality performance assessments over time, both teaching and learning improve (Darling-Hammond, 2014). Keeping with this perspective, multiple measures in addition to CCSS might include the following:

- Classroom-administered performance tasks (e.g., research papers, science investigations, mathematical solutions, engineering designs, and arts performances)
- Portfolios of writing samples, art works, or other learning products
- Oral presentations and scored discussions
- Teacher rating of student note-taking skills, collaboration skills, persistence with challenging tasks, and other evidence of learning skills

Bergmann and Sams (2013–2014) also noted that some school districts are using technology to build integrity into the system through the use of creative strategies such as flipped-mastery strategies and mobile device applications for formative checks as well as summative retakes.

Formative Checks

Formative assessments provide ongoing developmentally appropriate assessments to monitor children's progress and guide as well as improve instructional practice. These assessments are typically linked directly to the classroom instructional program (Jones, 2011). Mobile device applications and verbal checks can be used as formative assessments to monitor student progress on a daily basis as well. During formative checks, teachers can note whether a student has a misconception or was not understanding a crucial point. If goals and benchmarks are not met, students can be given additional instruction, allowed more practice, and, at times, asked to dig deeper through investigation and then reassessed. This type of individualized teaching and learning is probably one the greatest benefits of the flipped-mastery system.

Summative Retakes

In some schools, students can attempt a summative assessment as many times as they need to demonstrate mastery. However, this can be time consuming. To counteract this problem, some districts are using Moodle as a learning management system (LMS). Moodle has the capability of generating thousands of different versions of tests that assess the same objective. If students are having academic challenges, special instruction and interventions can be arranged.

These types of additional assessments allow school leaders and teachers to monitor progress through a data collection process. Moreover, in our accountability-driven culture, finding ways to assess and monitor students to maximize differentiated instruction can be a key to school success. This is especially true for school districts aligning their curriculum with CCSS.

CURRICULUM DESIGN

As part of an overall curriculum planning process, many school districts are currently using a design based on analysis and outcome perspectives—or end-in-mind approach—which can be inverse in nature. This is usually a standards-based alignment, which often accompanies high-stakes testing. Clearly defined steps are followed, and there is a continual link to content standards. Curriculum work is often a collaborative process involving district administrators, classroom teachers, and other faculty, along with outside experts, such as a professor from a local university. This process usually falls into the categories of developing goals, setting benchmarks, defining courses, dividing courses into units, planning units, and formulating specific objectives. Naturally, objectives used in actual instruction are continuously monitored and should tie back to benchmarks previously aligned with individual state standards or CCSS.

Goal-Based Design

Improved public awareness of how alignment and standards can enhance curriculum development is crucial. This often leads to a greater understanding of how curriculum can benefit teachers, students, and citizens. Community appreciation leads to the creation of shared vision and mission statements; joint curriculum committees; appropriate financing programs; infrastructure development; professional development; maintenance and service arrangements; favorable program evaluation; and, finally, successful public relations programs.

A key standard for school jurisdictions to consider is **goal-based design**—the setting of clear and practical goals that will expand the curriculum. This involves administrators coordinating school-based services and resources to best integrate curriculum for students in their schools. With this in mind, envision helping participants become change agents in the teaching learning process, while at the same time, incorporating new strategies into the classroom curriculum. Questions that might be asked include the following:

Curriculum Tip 11.2	Focusing on state standards or CCSS and benchmarks provides an alignment of "what is taught" with "what is written."

- What is the mission of my school?
- What should students be learning?
- What role does activity-based learning play in the curriculum?
- What technology strategies and tools can we use to achieve our curricular objectives?

Successful guiding principles for curriculum planning might include the following:

- Community involvement in planning and implementing the use of an integrated curriculum should be a high priority for school leaders
- The development of quality leadership and planning for effective teaching strategies must receive considerable attention
- Emphasis placed on incorporating learning centers into classrooms
- Curriculum using technology but not being driven by it
- Professional development involving integrated learning that should be made highly practical by having "teachers instruct teachers"
- Planning and implementation phases for the inclusion of new instructional strategies including continual assessment and evaluation standards

Successful curriculum mission statements involving technology might include the following:

- To enhance student learning in all curriculum areas from basic skills through higher thinking skills using state standards or CCSS
- To enhance student global understanding
- To stay abreast of new curricula developments
- To assist the staff in completing routine tasks involving curriculum
- To provide professional in-service on curriculum
- To build student competency in using technology to access and process curriculum information

Unit and Lesson Design

Developing quality lessons is an important aspect of curriculum design. As part of a curriculum alignment process, it is important that teachers have a vision of effective instruction to guide the implementation of their curriculum. Thus, planned and organized units should engage students. In addition, the classroom curriculum should support and challenge students with appropriate questioning and sensemaking strategies. Questioning strategies should enhance the development of students' problem solving, with the teacher emphasizing higher order thinking skills (HOTS).

In that new strategies provide a starting place, it is also crucial that teachers have assistance in formulating and delivering highly effective lesson plans. Keeping with this perspective, it is important for curriculum leaders to provide professional development activities that reflect the elements of high-quality instruction with clear, explicit learning goals. To help guide this along, the American Federation of Teachers has launched a lesson plan site to provide teachers with lessons linked to CCSS (Richardson, 2013). The site is www.sharemylesson.com. Also, the Bill & Melinda Gates Foundation has a CCSS-aligned site at www.betterlesson.com.

Designing Pre-Assessments

Effective pre-assessments help strengthen lesson design and can illuminate where students are now so that teachers can lead students to mastery. Pre-assessment is a way to gather evidence of students' readiness, interests, or learning profiles before beginning a lesson or unit (Hockett & Doubet, 2013–2014). The advent of CCSS makes the intentional use of pre-assessments even more crucial as teachers seek to prioritize, focus, and differentiate instruction for a wide variety of student needs. Pre-assessments must be designed to reveal significant differences in the knowledge, skills, or conceptual understanding for students. With that said, elements of good pre-assessments might include the following:

- Is administered prior to a lesson or unit
- Serves as invitation to learning experience
- Piques students' interest
- Aligns with key lesson or unit goals
- Gauges students' understanding
- Is accessible to all students
- Seeks to discover what students know
- Provides multiple ways of knowing
- Uncovers potential connections between student and content

Attuned and armed with pre-assessment data, teachers can make a proactive, timely, and detailed decision about lessons and instruction that will enable learners to achieve mastery. Pre-assessment, then, can be a catalyst for differentiation as well as a launching point for more effective teaching and learning.

ORGANIZING THE ALIGNMENT PROJECT

An initial step in organizing the alignment of any project is the allocation of responsibilities. If a project is complex, involving several critical stages, it will generally operate more effectively if it involves a wide range of participants. Each district, of course, will develop its own organization and management system for the project; the system outlined next has been derived from an analysis of several successful alignment projects.

One effective way of organizing any alignment process is the appointment of a district-level curriculum alignment committee. This will be a representative group largely responsible for planning and coordinating the project (in larger districts, this committee might evolve into a *task force*). The district curriculum committee can include an appropriate number of representatives from the following constituencies: district administrators, district supervisors, school administrators, teachers, and parents. At the outset, the committee can develop its own planning guide, indicating the steps to be taken, the deadline for each step, and those responsible for each step. Exhibit 11.1 shows a form that can be used to assist in such planning. It lists all the steps in the alignment project and provides space for deadlines and the names of those responsible for each step.

In the discussion that follows, certain assumptions will be made about those providing leadership simply for purposes of illustration; however, each district should develop its own system for allocating leadership responsibilities.

EXHIBIT 11.1 Alignment Project Planning Guide			
Project Step	Deadline	Primarily Responsible	Assists
1. Determine alignment with standards—as well as scope and sequence of project.			
2. Orient school administrators.			
3. Orient teachers.			
4. Orient students and parents.			
5. Revise curriculum guides.			
6. Identify mastery objectives.			
7. Develop curriculum-based assessments.			
8. Correlate mastery objectives with instructional materials.			
9. Develop planning aids.			
10. Help teachers use planning aids.			
11. Monitor teacher use of planning aids.			
12. Develop assessment-reporting materials.			
13. Help teachers use test reports.			
14. Help school administrators use assessment reports.			
15. Use assessment reports in analyzing and evaluating curriculum.			
16. Provide professional development for school administrators.			
17. Provide professional development for teachers.			
18. Monitor and evaluate the alignment project.			

Curriculum Tip 11.3	You should make things as simple as possible, but no simpler.
	—Albert Einstein

Determining the scope of the committee and alignment project should be one of the first decisions made by district administrators. For example, questions to be asked might include the following: Which subjects and what grade levels are to be addressed? This decision will, of course, be affected by such considerations as the size of the district, resources available, and administrators' perceptions of needs.

Likewise, district leaders need to make plans to orient all key groups involved, as well as individuals possibly affected by the alignment project. From a districtwide perspective, one of the first groups to be oriented might be building-level principals. They need to have in-depth preparation to enable them to discharge their own responsibilities as well as to explain the project to others. At various local schools, principals, once trained, can then orient both their own faculties and parent groups along with organizing a building-level curriculum committee.

ORGANIZATIONAL STRATEGIES

A major focus of a curriculum alignment committee is making sure the district or school curriculum aligns with state standards or CCSS. School leaders, along with committee members, will need to work collaboratively to determine a scope and sequence, formulate requirements and electives, and eventually coordinate the entire curriculum.

Identifying Mastery Objectives

Mastery is not an end point but rather an elusive goal that remains forever out of reach (Tucker, 2013). Identifying mastery objectives (as explained in Chapter 1) is a critical task of the district curriculum committee. Mastery objectives are those objectives that are essential for all and require careful structuring. This is largely due to a list of mastery objectives being used in developing curriculum-based tests as well as the alignment of resources and materials. It is therefore essential that the task be done with care and due deliberation. If a district has already developed a curriculum focusing on mastery objectives, then the task is an easier one—especially if objectives are identified for each grade level. But if a district is basing the alignment project on existing guides (that do not embody the mastery approach or individual state standards or CCSS), then the curriculum committee will need to be assigned the task of identifying key objectives.

Once organized, curriculum committee members (or subcommittee) should focus on the critical task of reviewing and revising the guides (standard or digital format). Clearly, even the best guides eventually become outdated; it is obviously unwise to base an alignment project on an inadequate and outdated curriculum. Once necessary revisions are made, members can identify mastery objectives for each grade level—the key skills, concepts, and information that students are expected to master (a sample list is shown in Exhibit 11.2).

EXHIBIT 11.2 Sample Mastery-Objectives List

Grade 5. Social Studies: People of North America

Maps, Globes, and Graphics Skills

1. Locate Canada on a globe.
2. On an outline map of Canada, identify each province.
3. On an outline map of Canada, with locations of cities indicated, identify Montreal, Vancouver, Toronto, Winnipeg, and Calgary.
4. Use the scale on a map to estimate distance between two Canadian cities.
5. Identify major ethnic groups and their relative sizes from the bar graph.

Three types of objectives should probably not be included in the mastery list:

1. *Objectives too difficult to assess with district-made assessments.* Most districts, for example, would probably choose not to assess listening skills, because valid listening tests are difficult to develop, administer, and score. Similarly, most affective outcomes (such as "appreciating poetry") are difficult to measure validly with objectives.

2. *Objectives that are not considered essential for all students.* Many district guides include content that has been identified in this text as enrichment material: objectives that are not really basic for all students but simply broaden the curriculum or challenge the more able.

3. *Objectives that have been emphasized at some previous grade level or that will be emphasized at some future grade level.* While many district guides include objectives that are to be "reviewed" or "introduced," only those objectives to be emphasized at that particular grade level should be identified in the alignment project. It is expected that teachers will review as necessary and will feel free to introduce skills and concepts as the occasion arises.

Once approved by school leaders and curriculum committee members, the preliminary lists of grade-level mastery objectives can then be reviewed by classroom teachers. At the elementary level, reviews can be made by grade-level teams; third-grade teachers, for example, can have an opportunity to review the mastery lists for all areas for which they are responsible. At the secondary level, reviews can be conducted departmentally. For the most part, then, teacher reviews are essential, because teachers will be the ones expected to teach and assess objectives on the final list.

School leaders working collaboratively with other committee members can then undertake a final review of the mastery lists. One of the important questions to be raised at this juncture is whether the skills and concepts can be taught for mastery within the time allotted, or is more time needed? If more time is necessary, how much time should be allotted to mastery objectives?

Developing Curriculum-Based Assessments

Curriculum-based tests (aligned with CCSS and assessments) now play a huge role in the alignment process. In addition, data-enhanced decision making and progress monitoring are helping school leaders and teachers to improve instruction (Aubuchon, 2013). Subsequently, assessment and data collection are becoming such an integral part of narrowing the achievement gap, the following are suggested guidelines as per curriculum-based testing:

1. Determine if assessment aligns with current state standards or CCSS.

2. Determine test scope and frequency. Will assessments be administered in standard or digital format? Will they be administered at the conclusion of each unit, at the end of each semester, or at the end of the school year? More frequent assessment provides school leaders and teachers with formative data that can be used to monitor student progress and take corrective actions.

3. Determine how many forms of each assessment will be required. Larger school systems may require several alternative forms in order to ensure test security. For smaller systems, two forms for each test will probably suffice.

4. Check validity of assessment items as they relate to objectives and benchmarks.

5. Use pilot forms of tests if available.

6. Use a system that provides administrators, teachers, and students with quick retrieval of information required for analysis and understanding of assessment results. School leaders need information about overall achievement; teachers need diagnostic information about individual students and classes; and students need information as it relates to feedback and grades.

7. Monitor assessments to ensure items are valid, that the answers are correct, and that the sampling reflects curricular priorities and standards. Administer pilot forms of the test to groups of students in order to measure test reliability.

Aligning system components through a collaborative process ensures that expectations are not only *written* but also *taught*. Implementing both these strategies is a way to improve teaching practice as well as to improve student learning. As school policymakers continue to ponder which of the many strategies to utilize to meet accountability obligations, we encourage implementing not either, but both strategies presented here. To do less would only result in more of what has plagued education for years.

Focusing on Culture and Social Diversity

As cultural and social backgrounds of PreK–12 student populations vary, it is critical that teachers align instruction to meet all students' needs. Planning instruction that is based on individual student needs, interests, and learning profiles is crucial in differentiating instruction (Parsons, Dodman, & Burrowbridge, 2013). Likewise, taking into account cultural and social diversity when aligning curriculum content, process, and product does help facilitate differentiation. A key, then, for school success, is for school leaders to value formative and summative assessments, emphasize declarative procedures, develop conditional knowledge, and encourage teachers to exercise reflection-on-action as well as reflection-in-action as they relate to social and cultural backgrounds of students and community.

Likewise, it is important to focus on the skills that students need to be successful in school and to possess what many refer to as academic language. According to Zacarian (2013), a partial list of skills needed are as follows:

- Deep cultural knowledge
- The ability to listen, speak, read, and write
- Academic knowledge
- The ability to "think to learn"

These are essential skills that can provide a critical remedy for improving the performance of English language learners (ELLs) and others. What is important, then, is the need for educators to focus on these types of skills if we are to address cultural and social diversity issues in our schools today.

Correlating the Mastery List and Instructional Materials

Once assessments are selected or prepared, curriculum committee members (or subject-matter subcommittee) can turn their attention to instructional materials. By reviewing textbooks or software currently in use (checking content against the mastery list), the committee can establish whether new materials will be required.

With assessments determined, committee members can then collaboratively develop objectives—materials-correlation charts (standard or digital) for each grade. These will be materials that will assist teachers in using instructional resources. If charts are used, the left side of the chart can list mastery objectives. Across the top of the chart are the titles of either texts or software programs. Included will be any new resources to be ordered. Each mastery objective is then keyed to specific passages. A sample correlation chart is shown in Exhibit 11.3. It should be noted that although some companies make correlation charts (standard or digital format), some charts are not sufficiently reliable for use in alignment projects.

Looking back retrospectively, the correlation process accomplishes two important goals: (1) It provides a means for the district to ensure that quality instructional materials are available, and (2) it helps teachers make their instructional plans.

EXHIBIT 11.3 Sample Objectives: Textbook/Software Correlation Chart		
Grade 10. Science: Biology		
Mastery Objective	*Life Sciences*	*Modern Biology*
1. Define ecosystem.	pp. 75–78	pp. 14–18
2. Identify three common air pollutants.	pp. 78–79	pp. 19–20
3. Explain probable causes of acid rain.	pp. 82–83	

Developing Instructional Planning Aids

The next important component of the alignment project is the instructional planning aids. These are materials that will assist teachers in developing and implementing instructional plans. Besides helping teachers plan, they also can facilitate among colleagues about the planning process. Major types of planning aids that play an important role include a yearly planning matrix, a management and monitoring matrix (see Exhibit 11.4), and unit planning guides (standard or digital format).

EXHIBIT 11.4   Management and Monitoring Matrix

Target Area _____   Product _____
1. GOAL _____   End Point _____

3. STATUS TODAY What is the situation today?	4. ACTIVITIES What must be done to get from 4 to 3?	5. LEADERSHIP Who is responsible to initiate or follow through with activities?	6. SCHEDULE What is the time frame for accomplishing each activity being monitored?	2. INDICATORS If the goal were attained, what would really be happening? What would the target area look or be like? List 8 to 10 indicators.
A.				A.
B.				B.
C.				C.
D.				D.

NOTE: This matrix is organized using a backward design, starting with establishing the goals and then moving to the end to establish outcomes (indicators) before working through the other steps.

Making a Yearly Planning Matrix

Teachers will first need help in making tentative plans for the school year, to ensure that all mastery objectives are taught and reinforced and that adequate time has been provided. One way of helping them accomplish these goals is by providing a yearly planning matrix such as the one shown in Exhibit 11.5. The teachers first list the mastery objectives, grouped according to subject matter subdivisions. They then indicate the report or marking period when they plan to teach this objective for mastery and when they expect to reinforce that objective. They then estimate the total number of instructional periods required.

EXHIBIT 11.5 Sample Yearly Planning Guide

Grade 8. English Language Arts (Literature)					
	Report Period				
Mastery Objective	*First*	*Second*	*Third*	*Fourth*	*Total Time Required*
1. Define character.	T		R		2 periods
2. Identify three means of character.	T		R		2 periods
3. Infer character's motivations.	T	R	R		4 periods

NOTE: T = teach for mastery; R = reinforce.

One effective way of using the yearly matrix is as follows:

- The teacher submits the yearly matrix to an instructional leader. The initial entries reflect the teacher's tentative decisions about yearly planning.
- The instructional leader and the teacher confer about the yearly plan, discussing issues of sequencing and time allocation and making any changes they both agree are necessary.
- The yearly matrix is posted in the classroom so that students and classroom visitors can be informed. As the teacher teaches or reinforces a mastery objective, the appropriate entry is marked.
- The teacher is expected to bring the yearly matrix to any supervisory or evaluation conferences.

Developing a Management Planning Matrix

Another design tool is the management planning matrix, which has been developed to help curriculum leaders plan, implement, and evaluate an effective professional development program (Whitehead, Boschee, & Decker, 2013). The matrix design encourages planners not only to develop technology professional development goals but also to formulate measurable indicators of successful in-service. The matrix additionally forces planners to detail activities and leadership roles and to set implementation and evaluation dates. This has been one of the most successful tools used by school leaders in designing effective professional development programs. A management and monitoring matrix can be found in Exhibit 11.5. The example of a yearly matrix thus serves several important purposes.

Creating a Unit-Planning Guide

Teachers will also need help with their unit planning. Two approaches can be used in deriving unit plans from the yearly matrix. In fields such as mathematics and science, where units are built from closely related objectives, the teacher can begin with the yearly matrix, list related objectives in unit clusters, and check to see that the time allocations seem appropriate for that grade level. In this approach, the objectives shape the unit.

In fields such as English and social studies, where several types of objectives are often included in one unit, teachers will need special help learning how to integrate mastery objectives into thematic units. Most teachers will find it helpful to begin by "roughing in" the unit—identifying the unit theme, determining the approximate length of the unit, specifying the major unit generalizations, and identifying the key resources. Next, they turn to the yearly matrix and select appropriate objectives for that unit, checking off each objective as it is included in a particular unit. They then make a final check to be sure that all objectives have been included in at least one unit. Exhibit 11.6 shows one form that can be

---

EXHIBIT 11.6   Sample Unit-Planning Chart

Grade 10. English. Second Report Period

UNIT THEME: The Changing American Family

LENGTH OF UNIT: 10 periods

Thematic Generalizations

1. Understand how the American family is changing
2. Understand reasons for changes

Common Readings

1. *My Antonia*
2. *Life With Father*
3. *Kramer vs. Kramer*
4. Selected articles from current magazines

Mastery Objectives to Be Emphasized

1. Write an expository essay of causal analysis.
2. Identify the author's bias in an essay of opinion.
3. Identify three means of character portrayal.
4. Infer character's motivations.

used in integrating mastery objectives into a thematic unit. In this approach, the unit theme influences the selection of the objectives.

For the most part, these unit-planning guides can play an important role in the supervision process as well. With collaboration as a focus, planning guides can lead to a discussion of curricular priorities, reflect planning approaches, determine instructional methods, and help examine issues of individualization and remediation.

In addition to the yearly and unit planning aids, some district supervisors expect teachers to list, in their daily lesson plans, the mastery objectives to be covered. Other administrators believe teachers should have more flexibility and autonomy in daily planning. The research does not provide any clear guidance here. Although well-structured lessons are usually associated with increased achievement, there is no evidence that the quality of written lesson plans is related to student achievement. Nonetheless, teachers should always aspire to write excellent plans as well as deliver well-structured lessons (for a review of the research on planning and achievement, see Baron, Boschee, & Jacobson, 2008).

In addition, it should be noted that some district supervisors require pacing charts indicating when a given set of objectives should be taught and about how much time should be devoted to each group of outcomes. This approach may or may not be popular. That said, pacing charts can aid discussions between supervisors and classroom teachers as to unit and lesson planning. It can also enhance team and departmental discussions as per content and time allocation.

TURNING TO RESEARCH

Educators need to turn research into practice by discovering the most relevant sources to help improve schools (Tucker, 2012). To be sure, any alignment of curriculum needs to involve an understanding of research. All too often, educators rely on experience and anecdotal information to guide instruction and learning. As a result, it is imperative that educators have a basic understanding of scientific knowledge as it relates to education and what needs to be done to guide instruction.

Two major questions curriculum leaders should ask when selecting and aligning programs are as follows:

1. Does the program comprehensively cover each of the evidence-based skills that students need to be proficient?

2. Has the program or approach been scientifically proven to work with students?

Asking these types of questions is highly important for curriculum leaders at all levels. Research obtained should include information on appropriate methodologies, peer review, converging evidence, and practical application.

There is little doubt that with a market full of descriptions as to best practice and programs that work, school leaders and teachers need to employ research-based strategies in their decision making. Thus, knowing how sources serve different purposes can help administrators and teachers when aligning curriculum. Keeping with this perspective, Bauer and Brazer (2012) noted distinctions between quantitative and qualitative research.

> *Quantitative research* often employs statistical tools for hypothesis testing and are referred to as inferential statistics. These studies depending on "significant level" can serve as a good basis for asserting a specific statistic describes a true relationship. An alternative metric referred to as practical significance, or "effect size," may also be used by school leaders to gauge results. Effect size indicates the strength of an outcome. Results that are not statistically significant or have very small effect sizes may not be meaningful. School leaders, then, often use quantitative research when examining areas of student achievement.
>
> *Qualitative research* (such as case studies) uses words rather than numbers. These studies are generally in the form of a presentation of themes supported by verbatim quotes from research subjects. Qualitative work and mixed methods offer school leaders an opportunity to answer "why" and "how" questions by seeking to understand what subjects think, feel, or believe. Confidence in results is achieved through exhaustive analysis of interviews, observations, and documents as well as the eliminating of plausible alternative explanations.

A major key, then, for school success is for curriculum leaders to apply research (either quantitative or qualitative) to the decision-making process. This allows a successful alignment of curriculum to be predicated on having a clear purpose, knowledge, and resources. Moreover, it is through this understanding of theory and research that school reform can be best achieved.

Using Data-Driven Programs

The curriculum committee should also determine what data and reporting materials will be required in the alignment project. This, of course, is done in consultation with administrators, supervisors, and teachers. Research indicates more effective schools typically use data differently than less effective ones (Protheroe, 2010). Keeping with this perspective, data collection and analysis reports assist curriculum leaders in initializing needed change as well as allowing them to monitor instructional practices successfully. The question then becomes not when to integrate the use of data in school improvement but how. With this in mind, the following key elements of data use have been used in numerous projects:

- *Plan of action.* Expands the definition of data beyond results from state assessments and other traditional indicators. For example, a **planning report** can summarize student performance for each class on the previous year's summative examination. Teachers use the report to determine which objectives need additional review and which students require special attention.
- *Classroom culture of data.* Provides prerequisites and supporting conditions to review the culture of classroom teaching and learning. A classroom diagnostic report can be provided to teachers after each assessment. This gives information

relating to all students in the class. School leaders can then use this data to help analyze and utilize information about district curriculum and how it relates to school communities.

- *Individual student report.* Provides comprehensive information for each student; it also is distributed after each major testing. It gives the student's name and indicates for all objectives the number correct and incorrect. The **individual student report** is made available to teachers, the student, and the student's parents.
- *Data-analysis review.* Allows for a collaborative discussion of data. Some "data conversations" might be whole-school or small grade-level teams. These discussions often provide a practical tool when making decisions over a period of time.

Numerous schools are using comprehensive data and other management tools to facilitate teaching and learning. What is important is having teachers using information databases to find accurate and appropriate knowledge when solving problems (Chesley & Jordan, 2012). Undoubtedly, good and reliable data can lead to amazing results, especially if channeled through well-led teachers. For example, databases in the area of curriculum can do the following:

1. Determine professional development interests and needs

2. Develop a background of skills and usage

3. Identify individuals willing to share ideas and techniques as well as to inventory the type and level of materials and resources used in the classroom

To be sure, with ever-present new advances in data-driven instruction and the advent of CCSS, teachers are now better able to transition schools into digital places of learning. In addition to the CCSS, the National Educational Technology Standards (NETS), developed by the International Society for Technology in Education (ISTE), set a standard of excellence and best practices in learning, teaching, and leading with technology in education (ISTE, 2008). The benefits of using the NETS include the following:

- Improving HOTS, such as problem solving, critical thinking, and creativity
- Preparing students for their future in a competitive global job market
- Designing student-centered, project-based, and online learning environments
- Guiding systemic change in our schools to create digital places of learning
- Inspiring digital-age professional development models for working, collaborating, and decision making

As can be seen, data-driven instruction needs to be a major focus of any curriculum alignment process. Moreover, advances in instruction are continuing to change the way teachers teach as well as the way students learn. But getting data-driven instruction and mastery teaching approaches to take hold requires collaboration and coaching (Goodwin, 2013–2014). This is why professional development and professional learning communities (PLCs) are so important to the alignment process.

PROFESSIONAL DEVELOPMENT AND CURRICULUM ALIGNMENT

Most assuredly, there is no "magic solution" to school improvement, but developing a quality professional development program is a good start (Whitaker, 2013). As part of any curriculum alignment process, everyone on staff should be provided with the in-depth training they will need to implement the project and make it successful. Specific content of any professional development program as it pertains to curriculum alignment will certainly depend on local needs.

Professional development for principals and teacher–leaders includes the following:

- Having a rationale for curriculum alignment
- Orienting teachers and parents about alignment
- Helping teachers use assessment and **data-analysis reports**
- Helping teachers make yearly and unit plans
- Monitoring teacher planning and instruction
- Using alignment to plan instruction for special needs students
- Using assessment and data-analysis reports to evaluate a school's program of studies
- Using the alignment project to make supervision more effective
- Evaluating the alignment project

Professional development specifically for classroom teachers includes:

- Having a rationale for curriculum alignment
- Identifying mastery objectives
- Using mastery objectives in yearly and unit planning
- Using assessment reports to plan instruction and monitor progress
- Using alignment to plan instruction for special needs students
- Locating and using instructional materials
- Teaching for mastery objectives
- Communicating assessment results to students and parents

In order for PLCs to be successful in the school environment, educational leaders must personally commit to the process. This does not mean that the process is theirs alone—quite the contrary. Principals and teachers must develop an awareness of complex social dynamics associated with the school community. They must communicate with both internal and external publics on a continual basis. Adopting any change in a district will affect the organization as a whole. Current attitudes, beliefs, and traditions will have to be addressed. To prevent becoming bogged down by naysayers, one must do his or her best to identify these obstacles and convince everyone that they have something to gain.

As part of a PLC, principals and teachers can take on several roles during the change process. Prior to initiation, participating individuals need to be involved in laying the groundwork by conducting research and building support among publics. They need to collect information through discussions or distribute information among the staff in meetings, blogs, and in newsletters. When the time is right, they will then be prepared to act by framing ideas to other stakeholders. Once the change process is in motion, they must sustain the action by providing momentum. Finally, to keep things on track, the professional learning team must commit to maintaining the process and not grow tired of the challenge.

For the most part, curriculum leaders must rely on proven methods that incorporate a systematic approach to implementing change. Each school district exists in a unique social context. There are easy ways to ensure successful implementation as a step-by-step process for all schools. Moving educational concepts such as PLCs from air-time discussion to real-time existence takes hard work and commitment from the entire staff. When incorporating change into a school district, building principals are bound to experience a few failures along the road to success. This is to be expected. Lovely (2010) said the following:

> The fact of the matter is that professional learning communities are now the engine of high-quality work. Sustaining cohesion among groups that don't readily see eye to eye is a daunting task, since collaboration doesn't come naturally to most educators. (p. 11)

Nonetheless, these failures are part of the learning process and are necessary growing pains. But—that being said—having a PLC plan, focusing on the essential components, and committing to the process can and will help curriculum leaders succeed in implementing change.

On the face of it, community-based learning and PLC models may be better described as the broad set of teaching–learning strategies that enable youth and adults to learn what they want to learn from any segment of the community. This definition provides for learners of all ages to identify what they wish to learn and opens up an unlimited set of resources to support them.

Without question, the basic principles of PLCs provide a firm pedagogical foundation of understanding. With each endeavor, there is a requirement for somewhat different schedules and support arrangements, but in the end there is a measure of school improvement. As part of changing the culture of education, professional development—more specifically, PLCs—are symbolizing an effective means of ensuring successful implementation of new curricula.

MONITORING AND EVALUATING CURRICULUM ALIGNMENT

It is no surprise that evaluating the alignment process is a major part of the curriculum cycle (ADDIE model; Design Theories & Models, 2014). As such, the curriculum alignment process needs to be continually monitored—making sure it is working as planned and summarily evaluated to determine overall effectiveness. Two types of monitoring are required.

First, district administrators should be responsible for overseeing project management, seeking answers to the following questions:

- Have all necessary instructional materials been provided, and are correlation charts accurate?
- Are assessments being administered and scored on schedule?

- Are professional development sessions being conducted as planned, and are they judged by participants to be helpful?
- Are principals and supervisors helping teachers plan effectively, teach to mastery objectives, and use assessment results to modify instruction?

Several methods of reporting can be used to assist with the curriculum alignment process:

- Those responsible for carrying out the steps identified in the planning guide are expected to submit periodic reports, noting dates when key steps were carried out and identifying any problems that developed.
- Time during each professional development session needs to be allotted to identify problems and assess progress. Regularly scheduled administrative and faculty meetings can also be used to assess the progress of the project.
- A representative sample of administrators and teachers need to be interviewed (perhaps once every two months) to survey their perceptions and probe concerns.

Second is the type of monitoring focusing on the teachers' implementation of the project at the classroom level.

- The intent here is for school administrators to ensure everyone is carrying out their responsibilities but doing so in a professional manner that does not create an atmosphere of distrust. This goal can be accomplished if school leaders present the project as a means of assisting teachers through building relationships. All the following activities should, therefore, be carried out in that spirit. First, of course, the submission of the yearly planning matrix will enable the principal and teacher to discuss together such essential matters as the organizing of objectives, the optimal sequencing of instruction, and the allocation of instructional time as a reflection of curricular priorities.
- Also, the unit plans should facilitate professional discussions between supervisors and teachers. The review of those plans will enable the supervisor and the teacher to discuss issues of unit planning, time allocation, instructional methods, assessment of student learning, and remediation strategies.
- Finally, supervisors can focus on outcomes. In pre-observation conferences, they can help the teacher assess what progress already has been made and determine what mastery objectives should be emphasized in the week ahead. The pre-observation conference should also provide both with an opportunity to reflect on assessment concerns: How will student learning be assessed? What will be an acceptable level of student achievement for a given lesson and a series of lessons? In their observations, they can focus on the clarity of objectives and the evidence of student mastery. In the post-observation conference, they can help the teacher use student achievement data as a means of diagnosing instruction.

Such "outcomes-focused supervision" enables supervisors as well as teachers to examine data collaboratively and to concern themselves with the essential issue of student learning—rather than just emphasizing instructional methods. Issues of method are raised only if the data suggest that students did not achieve at the agreed-on level.

The summative evaluation of the alignment project can make use of two measures. First, the perceptions of administrators, supervisors, and teachers should be surveyed at the end of each school year. Exhibit 11.7 shows one type of survey form that can be used. The second, of course, is student achievement. School districts should maintain and carefully analyze results of both curriculum-based and standardized assessments as they relate to benchmarks, noting trends over a multiple-year time period. If the project has been designed carefully and implemented professionally, districts should find that student achievement increases. Using the curriculum development and implementation procedures illustrated in Chapter 10, one of this text's authors saw composite scores in his school

---

EXHIBIT 11.7   Survey of Perceptions of Alignment Project

Directions: Listed here are several statements about our alignment project and its components. Circle the symbol that best represents the extent to which you agree or disagree with the statement:

SA = strongly agree   D = disagree   A = agree   SD = strongly disagree

Statement	Your Perception			
1. The list of mastery objectives helped teachers plan, teach, and assess learning.	SA	A	D	SD
2. Technology-based applications were helpful in planning and using materials.	SA	A	D	SD
3. The yearly planning matrix helped teachers make effective plans for the year.	SA	A	D	SD
4. The unit planning guides helped teachers develop and implement unit plans.	SA	A	D	SD
5. The curriculum-based assessments provided useful information to administrators and teachers.	SA	A	D	SD
6. The alignment project improved the professional climate of the school.	SA	A	D	SD
7. The alignment project seemed successful in improving student learning.	SA	A	D	SD

Please provide brief responses to the two items that follow.

8. The main advantage of the alignment project was _____
_____

9. The alignment project could be improved by _____
_____

Please check below to indicate your professional role; there is no need to sign your name.
___ District administrator ___ District supervisor
___ School administrator ___ Team or department leader
___ Classroom teacher

EXHIBIT 11.8   School District National Percentile Rank

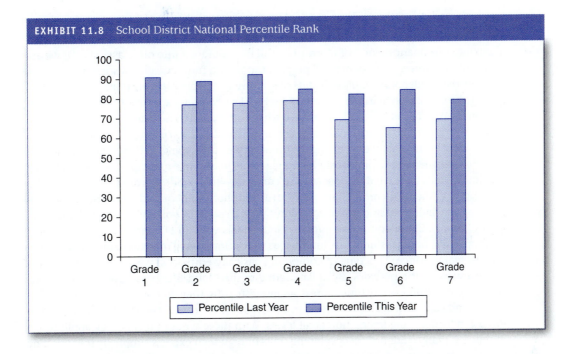

district rise more than 10 percentiles for each grade level in one year due to curricular alignment (see Exhibit 11.8).

UNDERSTANDING THE IMPORTANCE OF CURRICULUM

Due largely to technological innovations, a globally shared vision of educational curriculum is now becoming a reality. And, with this new reality, societies are changing how we view education and curriculum. Along with this change, cultural diversity is becoming a hugely important element. While effective curriculum and instruction worldwide contain many diverse elements, curriculum is now becoming more responsive to individual students. It is with these new developments that an appreciation of contemporary learners necessitates a need to maximize the capacity of each learner and to guide and align the process through a myriad of opinions and perceptions.

Classroom Learning and 21st-Century Technology

According to Hatch (2013), strong networks of relationships increase the chances that teachers can work together to integrate technology and innovative classroom practices. Currently, educators are immersed in a generation where teaching and learning thrives on innovation. As a result, the lives of students today revolve around technological advances in one form or another. A study found that the average American between the ages of 8 and

18 spends 7 hours and 38 minutes per day using media, or 10 hours and 45 minutes if using more than one medium at a time (Rideout, Foehr, & Roberts, 2010). Educators need to tap into this phenomenon of innovation and incorporate it into our classrooms if we are to spark the interest of students and prepare them for a futuristic global society.

Every day, students are exploring and using a variety of technologies in classrooms (Whitehead, Jensen, & Boschee, 2013). Currently, PreK–12 students are accessing and sharing information via Web-based learning, interactive whiteboards, and mobile devices. Both mercurial and date sensitive classroom technology continues to morph and change with the times. One day, classroom students are accessing the Cloud as well as Skyping, and the next day they are Moodling. As mentioned previously, Moodling refers to a course management system (CMS), also known as a LMS, used by educators to create effective online learning sites. In contrast, Skyping is a Microsoft proprietary voice over Internet protocol and software application allowing educators and students to communicate with peers by voice, video, and instant messaging. Finally, Cloud computing provides individuals with an efficient way to get applications up and running faster on the Internet, as well as improving manageability and allowing for less maintenance. This type of computing basically entrusts services with a user's data and software over a network. By collaborating in the Cloud, students have access to their work anywhere and at any time there is an interest. Thus, they do not have to work solely at school and can work wherever they can obtain Internet access. The result is a major step toward individualizing instruction at all levels. With these types of technology applications in schools, many students are developing traits of high-tech experts simply by the way they approach the digital world around them (Cushman, 2012).

Without question, mobile devices are fast becoming a way for teachers to deliver instruction. This is specifically true of iPads and other mobile technology. Whether it is developing math skills, comprehension, or fluency, mobile technology is impacting the way teachers teach and the way students learn (Mulholland, 2011). Walk into any classroom using iPads, or similar devices, and you will find students probably accessing the Cloud and being totally immersed in what they are doing, as well as being highly motivated to do more. With that said, fingers fly with images scrolling across an electronic screen as students navigate a variety of apps and sources. Wrapped in interfaces, technology-loving kids are speaking into microphones, recording themselves, playing back voices, and bringing up interesting photos. This technology-driven classroom is considered to be mobile learning and is occasionally referenced as *m-learning*. Although time will tell, educators are using m-learning as an untethered and more informal approach to instruction. Some teachers even refer to m-learning as "just-in-time" technology because of its overall acquisition speed for students and that it is more "discovery" in nature. Covering the gamut of on-the-spot informational retrieval, m-learning, as well the more common fixed-based electronic learning (*e-learning*), continue to revolutionize classrooms in schools today. What is especially exciting for educators is the speed and instant access to data. Just as importantly, high-speed handheld devices are designed to deliver extra feedback via apps and programs. Moreover, they are not extra work for teachers. By providing untapped opportunities for teachers, student performance can be uploaded, graphed, and screened as an assessment tool. Likewise, teachers and administrators can show parents how students are performing individually and are able to chart what is happening at the school or district level when it is happening. Overall, as shown in Exhibit 11.9, a survey conducted by the MASIE

Center (an international think tank dedicated to exploring the intersection of learning and technology) found a list of the most used technologies in the classroom.

Another plus of mobile technology, especially for administrators and supervisors, is the ease in collecting data for aligning curriculum and staff evaluations. While moving from classroom to classroom, building-level supervisors can document, record, and upload data as needed. Thus, with handheld technology, school leaders are better able to capitalize on the interest, energy, and learning needed to better differentiate teaching and learning in individual classrooms. Not only is this useful in the classroom but these technology advances are also allowing local classrooms to connect with a larger community. As a result, current advances in mobile technology are now providing educators and students everywhere with a long-awaited window to school reform.

But, with that said, caution must also be exercised when integrating technology into the classroom due to some community members expressing concerns over security. Fortunately, the issue of security is being addressed through a series of programs and applications. Systems such as Gaggle (2012) are becoming instrumental in allowing instructors to monitor students by making sure they do not wander on the Internet. Gaggle's control

EXHIBIT 11.9 Technologies Used in the Classroom

Technologies in Classrooms	
Technology	%
Projector/display	85%
Blackboard/whiteboard	80%
Flipchart	78%
Movable furniture	68%
Speakerphone	59%
Microphone/speakers	52%
Wireless	49%
Videoconferencing via Webinar	47%
Flat screen	28%
High-definition projector	28%
Videoconferencing via IP/ISDN	25%
Fixed furniture	25%
Camera or microphone to record class	23%
Dividable spaces	22%
Interactive whiteboard	22%
Videoconferencing via desktop	20%
Document camera	19%
Multiple displays	19%
Audience response systems	13%
Tablet control for instructor	11%
Slide projector	10%
Tablet for every learner	6%
Gaming technology	4%

and filtering system gives administrators and teachers a way to protect students from sending and receiving inappropriate e-mail. Instructors can even place restrictions on student accounts, controlling with whom they communicate. All student mail that is flagged by the filters is redirected to a Google Apps account that will determine if it is allowed to go through or should be blocked. Along with improved security, it is crucial for school leaders to develop an acceptable use policy that addresses mobile electronic devices. When adapting an acceptable use policy, school administrators need to make sure the policy addresses such areas as purpose, responsibility, theft or damage, inappropriate use, as well as sanctions if policy is violated. Regardless of what type of policy is approved, mobile technology appears to be leaving a legacy of individualized learning, especially as it relates to working with both at-risk students as well as gifted and talented students. What really matters then is that handheld devices are a highly motivational learning tool for potentially increasing the "cool factor" for students. The old adage of "If you can't reach them, you can't teach them" seems to readily apply to today's technology.

GLOBAL CONNECTIONS: RUSSIA'S COMMON CORE

Despite facing huge challenges internationally, Russia's education system is moving toward an alignment of outcome-based national standards similar to that of the U.S. CCSS. Russia, according to Lenskaya (2013), saw the need for standards when it finished 14th among 21 participants in the Trends in International Mathematics and Science Study (TIMSS) in 1995. Officials expressed concern about Russian students having difficulty transferring knowledge between disciplines. Not long after, the Russian government adopted new policy guidelines involving competence-based curriculum.

Interestingly enough, the new standards coincidentally overlap with the CCSS used in the United States. Similar to CCSS, the new Russian standards specify the following:

- Goals of education at every key stage
- Core content of the main educational programs
- Maximum workload (lessons per week)
- Main educational outcomes of each key stage
- Main provisions an educational process should meet

These changes in standards have resulted in Russian upper secondary students being able to choose from a variety of school disciplines for the first time. Likewise, the new standards specify expected outcomes for each stage of education in every school discipline, and teachers are to be accountable for helping students achieve prescribed outcomes. Additionally, Russian educators are expecting the CCSS-like standards, and related assessments, to play a significant role in preparing Russian students for challenges in our newly competitive and fast-paced globally connected world.

SUMMARY

This chapter provides a rationale and process for curriculum alignment, which helps ensure that the written, the taught, and the tested curricula are closely compatible. For that reason, curriculum alignment attempts to improve student achievement by remedying the discrepancy that too often exists between state standards and CCSS, district curriculum guides, teachers' instructional plans, and assessment measures in schools.

APPLICATIONS

1. Be prepared to discuss or write about your views on this statement: Curriculum alignment projects are unnecessary attempts by administrators to control teachers and damage the climate of trust essential in effective schools.

2. Using the form shown in Exhibit 11.1 (or your own modification of it), develop an alignment project planning guide that could be used in a school district with which you are acquainted.

3. One of the issues raised in this chapter is the interest in pacing charts. Based on your knowledge of classroom teachers, would you consider such charts helpful or intrusive?

4. The CCSS is, at times, referred to as national standards. If we had national standards for certain subjects, would such a selection change the underlying system? Please explain your response.

5. How would you respond to this question: Since our competency is being judged by students' test scores, due to high-stakes testing, do you feel teaching to the test is necessary?

6. Why are multiple measures needed to address the full depth and breadth of our expectations for student learning?

CASE STUDY   Making Adjustments Via Alignment

A group of third-grade teachers in Portland, Oregon, meet after school to review student achievement test data. The principal happens to arrive at the door of the classroom as the teachers are reviewing the results.

"I think this whole standards movement and emphasis on tests is a way for administrators to control the faculty," says teacher Melody Taylor, revealing anger in her voice.

Principal Barbara Bevington enters the room. "I understand your frustration, Melody," she says calmly. "Nonetheless, I can assure you that I'm not interested in controlling anyone. I'm interested in our school doing the best it can for our students."

Melody looks on disapprovingly, as if she is not buying the principal's sincerity.

Bevington decides to address the group. "What I don't understand is why our students are falling behind in the area of measurement in mathematics. It can't be because of our teachers—we have some of the best teachers in the state," declares the principal, looking approvingly over at Melody, who blushes, embarrassed.

The principal continues. "Math measurement is noted in our district standards as well as being addressed in our textbook, and yet the test data reveal that our students are really struggling in this area." Four of the other teachers are nodding their heads in agreement as they study the data.

Sue Cockrill, another third-grade teacher, adds, "I think I know why our students are doing poorly on measurement. The chapter on measurement is one of the last chapters in our math book, and we usually never get there."

"You're right!" says Melody. "Why don't we move the chapter on measurement up on our schedule? That will ensure that we will cover it."

"Great idea!" says another third-grade teacher, penciling in the change. Everyone smiles.

The principal is beaming. "I am really proud of all of you as a third-grade team. You are really doing some great work in analyzing the test results and adjusting the curriculum accordingly." She then turns and walks back down the hall to her office. Principal Bevington is impressed that through data analysis her teachers were able to identify an area in the standards that is not being met by the local curriculum. She is also proud that Melody Taylor is part of that important team.

The Challenge

Getting teachers to align curriculum to state and federal standards and regulations is a major challenge for school administrators. Analyze the problems and hurdles that Principal Bevington had to overcome. What other strategies can she use to get her teachers to accept mandated changes and to align her school's curriculum?

Key Issues or Questions

1. What are your impressions of Principal Bevington? Did she adequately handle the issue of data analysis and aligning curriculum? Why or why not?

2. What are your impressions of the third-grade teachers in this elementary school?

3. If the principal has another meeting with the third-grade teachers, what should be discussed?

4. What are some possible reasons that Principal Bevington's third-grade curriculum is out of alignment with state and national standards?

5. What are some other innovative approaches that Principal Bevington might use to increase student achievement scores? Identify the strategies and explain why you think they might be effective.

WEBLIOGRAPHY

Assessment and Qualifications Alliance (AQA) of Alberta, Canada

www.ascd.org/publications/educational-leadership/dec13/v0171/num04/How-Good-Is-Good-Enough%C2%A2.aspx

Curriculum Alignment

www.mcrel.org

www.ehow.com/about_6616423_definition-curriculum-alignment.html

www.ascd.org1

Educational Resources Information Center (ERIC)

www.eric.ed.gov

Google Scholar

http://scholar.google.com

High-Stakes Testing

www.apa.org/pubs/info/brochures/testing.aspx

http://en.wikipedia.org/wiki/High-stakes_testing

http://users.manchester.edu/Student/cedavenport/
professionalwebsite/High%20stakes%20
testing%5B1%5D.pdf

Institute for Educational Leadership

www.iel.org

The Massachusetts Comprehensive
Assessment System

www.aps1.net/index.aspx?NID = 711

New Zealand Ministry of Education's
Assessment Online

http://assessment.tki.org.nz/Assessment-tools-
resources/The-New-Zealand-Curriculum-Exemplars

New Zealand Qualifications Authority

www.nzqa.govt.nz/qualifications-standards/
qualifications/ncea

Thomas B. Fordham Institute

http://edex.s3-us-west-2.amazonaws.com/publication/
pdfs/SOSSandCC2010_FullReportFINAL_8.pdf

http://208.106.213.194/doc/20100323_
CommonCoreReview.pdf

What Works Clearinghouse (WWC)

http://ies.ed.gov

REFERENCES

Aubuchon, M. (2013). Raising the bar-Extreme make-over: Staff development edition. *Principal, 92*(3), 34–35.

Baron, M. A., Boschee, F., & Jacobson, M. (2008). *Performance-based education: Developing programs through strategic planning.* Lanham, MD: Rowman & Littlefield.

Bauer, S., & Brazer, D. (2012). Navigating your way through the research jungle. *Principal, 92*(2), 22–25.

Bergmann, J., & Sams, A. (2013–2014). Flipping for mastery. *Educational Leadership, 71*(4), 24–29.

Chesley, G. M., & Jordan, J. (2012). What's missing from teacher prep? *Educational Leadership, 69*(8), 41–45.

Council of Chief State School Officers & National Governors Association. (2010). *Common Core State Standards Initiative.* Retrieved from http://www.corestandards.org

Cushman, K. (2012). Backtalk: How kids get to be "tech experts." *Phi Delta Kappan, 92*(4), 80.

Darling-Hammond, L. (2014). Testing, to, and beyond the common core. *Principal, 93*(3), 8–12.

Design Theories & Models. (2014). *ADDIE model.* Retrieved from http://www.learning-theories.com/addie-model.html

Dietel, R. (2011). Testing to the top: Everything but the kitchen sink. *Phi Delta Kappan, 92*(8), 32–36.

Finn, C. E., Jr., & Petrilli, M. J. (2010, July). Foreword. In S. B. Carmichael, G. Martino, K. Porter-Magee, & W. S. Wilson, *The state of state standards—and the common core—in 2010* (pp. 1–5). Retrieved from http://www.math.jhu.edu/~wsw/FORD/SOSSandCC2010_FullReportFINAL.pdf

Fusarelli, L. D. (2008). Flying (partially) blind: School leaders' use of research in decision making. *Phi Delta Kappan, 89*(5), 365–368.

Gaggle. (2012). Gaggle: Safe online learning tools. Retrieved from https://www.gaggle.net

Goodwin, B. (2013–2014). Simple is not always easy. *Educational Leadership, 71*(4), 78–79.

Hatch, T. (2013). Innovation at the core. *Phi Delta Kappan, 95*(3), 34–38.

Hockett, J. A., & Doubet, K. J. (2013–2014). Turning on the lights: What pre-assessments can do. *Educational Leadership, 71*(4), 50–54.

International Society for Technology in Education. (2008). NETS for teachers 2008. Retrieved from http://www.iste.org/standards/nets-for-teachers/nets-for-teachers-2008.aspx

Jones, J. (2011). Assessing young children's learning and development. *Principal, 90*(5), 12–15.

Lenskaya, E. (2013). Russia's own Common Core. *Phi Delta Kappan, 95*(2), 76–77.

Lovely, S. (2010, January). Generations at school: Building an age-friendly workforce. *American*

Association of School Administrators, 67, 10–16.

Markle, K., & VanKoevering, S. (2013). Reviving Edward Bell. *Phi Delta Kappan, 94*(8), 8–12.

Mulholland, L. (2011). *iPads in the classroom.* Government Technology. Retrieved from http://www.govtech.com/education/iPads-In-The-Classroom.html

Parsons, S. A., Dodman, S. L., & Burrowbridge, S. C. (2013). Broadening the view of differentiated instruction. *Phi Delta Kappan, 95*(1), 38–42.

Protheroe, N. (2010). Schools as effective data users. *Principal, 90*(1), 23–28.

Raymond, M. (2014). To no avail: A critical look at the charter school debate. *Phi Delta Kappan, 95*(5), 8–12.

Richardson, J. (2013). Lesson plans. *Phi Delta Kappan, 94*(8), 7.

Rideout V. J., Foehr, U. G., & Roberts, D. F. (2010, January). *Generation M2: Media in the lives of 8–18 year-olds.* Kaiser Family Foundation. Retrieved from http://www.kff.org/entmedia/upload/8010.pdf

Tucker, C. (2013). Five musts for mastery. *Educational Leadership, 71*(4), 56–60.

Tucker, K. (2012). From the editor: Setting a foundation for STEM. *Principal, 92*(2), 3.

Whitaker, T. (2013). Help teachers be their best: Sow the seeds for duplicating teacher excellence. *Principal, 92*(3), 8–11.

Whitehead, B. M., Boschee, F., & Decker, R. H. (2013). *The principal: Leadership for a global society.* Thousand Oaks, CA: Sage.

Whitehead, B. M., Jensen, D. F. N., & Boschee, F. (2013). *Planning for technology: A guide for school administrators, technology coordinators, and curriculum leaders* (2nd ed.). Thousand Oaks, CA: Corwin Press.

Zacarian, D. (2013). Crossing language barriers. *Principal, 92*(5), 35–38.

CHAPTER 12

Curriculum Evaluation

This desired breath and diversification of curriculum have been reflected through this work. Chapter 6 described a comprehensive assessment model that can be used in improving a program of studies. Chapter 8 emphasized the importance of evaluating new courses of study. Chapter 10 provided a step-by-step on how to develop and implement curriculum. Chapter 11 described the importance of curriculum alignment. The intent of this chapter is to bring all of these approaches into focus and to provide for greater understanding of the evaluation

Questions addressed in this chapter include the following:

- What principles best define curriculum evaluation?
- What curriculum evaluation models are most effective?
- What criteria can be used to develop a curriculum evaluation model?
- How can learning experiences be organized for effective instruction?
- How can the effectiveness of learning experiences be evaluated?
- How can a field of study be evaluated?
- How can effective teaching be identified?

Key to Leadership

Curriculum evaluation represents the summation of the written, the supported, the taught, the tested, and the learned curriculums. Therefore, the process of evaluation is essentially the procedure for determining to what extent the educational objectives are actually being realized by the program of curriculum and instruction.

process. To that end, it begins by proposing a broad definition of the term *curriculum evaluation*. It then describes several evaluation models. It concludes by proposing a comprehensive and eclectic process that can be used to evaluate a **field of study,** which is perhaps the most difficult curricular element that evaluators face.

CURRICULUM EVALUATION DEFINED

Evaluations, when done wisely, involve timely and approximate professional development for both teachers and principals (Connelly, 2013). Therefore, the stakes for designing effective evaluation systems have never been higher, especially as ratings are used more and more to impact compensation and promotion. Well-designed measurement systems allow teachers to ask questions and engage in discussions, and also encourage principals to seek feedback from stakeholders—teachers, students, even parents—on their own performance.

Authentic Assessment

The primary purpose of assessment in schools should be to educate (and motivate) students about the real world of adult challenges (Wiggins, 2011).

> Assessment should better replicate or simulate what mathematicians, scientists, and historians *do,* not just what they know. The term "authenticity" refers less to the particular challenge or question and more to the realism of the setting—the audience, purpose, constraints, and opportunities. Wiggins adds that the goal of schooling is transfer; the goal is not to get good at school and prove through assessment that you learned what was taught. On the contrary, in a truly modern assessment, the challenge is to look *forward,* not backward: We must determine if the student is ready for *future* challenges in which they must transfer prior learning. We should look at whether the student can draw creatively and effectively on their repertoire when handling a novel challenge, not merely, determine what they learned. (p. 63)

EVALUATION MODELS

In charting a course for educational reform, Common Core State Standards (CCSS) and the Next Generation Science Standards (NGSS) have been developed with increased rigor as a primary goal. This has led to a demand for equally rigorous assessments (Chappuis, 2014). Keeping with this perspective, as an authentic tool, curriculum evaluation should be concerned with assessing the value of a **program of study** (all the planned learning experiences over a multiyear period for a given group of learners), a field of study (all the planned learning experiences over a multiyear period in a given discipline or area of study), and a **course of study** (all the planned learning experiences for a period of 1 year or less in a given field of study). All three levels of curriculum work are important. But substantive differences still exist between evaluating a program of study and a field of study, and differences of scope exist between evaluating a field of study and a course of study. With this in mind, evaluation specialists have proposed an array of models, an examination of which can provide useful background for the process presented in this work.

Tyler's Objectives-Centered Model

One of the earliest curriculum evaluation models, which continues to influence many assessment projects, was that proposed by Ralph Tyler (1950) in his monograph *Basic Principles of Curriculum and Instruction*. As explained in this work and used in numerous large-scale assessment efforts, the Tyler approach moved rationally and systematically through several related steps:

1. Begin with the behavioral objectives that have been previously determined. Those objectives should specify both the content of learning and the student behavior expected: "Demonstrate familiarity with dependable sources of information on questions relating to nutrition."

2. Identify the situations that will give the student the opportunity to express the behavior embodied in the objective and that evoke or encourage this behavior. Thus, if you wish to assess oral language use, identify situations that evoke oral language.

3. Select, modify, or construct suitable evaluation instruments, and check the instruments for objectivity, reliability, and validity.

4. Use the instruments to obtain summarized or appraised results.

5. Compare the results obtained from several instruments before and after given periods in order to estimate the amount of change taking place.

6. Analyze the results in order to determine strengths and weaknesses of the curriculum and to identify possible explanations about the reason for this particular pattern of strengths and weaknesses.

7. Use the results to make the necessary modifications in the curriculum. (as cited in Glatthorn, 1987, p. 273)

The Tyler model has several advantages: It is relatively easy to understand and apply. It is rational and systematic. It focuses attention on curricular strengths and weaknesses, rather than being concerned solely with the performance of individual students. It also emphasizes the importance of a continuing cycle of assessment, analysis, and improvement. As Guba and Lincoln (1981) pointed out, however, it suffers from several deficiencies. It does not suggest how the objectives themselves should be evaluated. It does not provide standards or suggest how standards should be developed. Its emphasis on the prior statement of objectives may restrict creativity in curriculum development, and it seems to place undue emphasis on the preassessment and postassessment, ignoring completely the need for formative assessment. Similarly, Baron and Boschee (1995), in their book *Authentic Assessment: The Key to Unlocking Student Success,* stress that "we are encountering fundamental changes in the way we view and conduct assessment in American schools" (p. 1). And "sixty years have passed since we experienced such a deep-seated and thoughtful reevaluation of our assessment methods" (p. 1).

Stufflebeam's Context, Input, Process, Product Model

These obvious weaknesses in the Tyler model led several evaluation experts in the late 1960s and early 1970s to attack the Tyler model and to offer their own alternatives. The alternative that had the greatest impact was that developed by a Phi Delta Kappa committee chaired by Daniel Stufflebeam (1971). This model seemed to appeal to educational leaders because it emphasized the importance of producing evaluative data for decision making; in fact, decision making was the sole justification for evaluation, in the view of the Phi Delta Kappa committee.

To service the needs of decision makers, the Stufflebeam model provides a means for generating data relating to four stages of program operation: **context evaluation**, which continuously assesses needs and problems in the context to help decision makers determine goals and objectives; **input evaluation**, which assesses alternative means for achieving those goals to help decision makers choose optimal means; **process evaluation**, which monitors the processes both to ensure that the means are actually being implemented and to make the necessary modifications; and **product evaluation**, which compares actual ends with intended ends and leads to a series of recycling decisions.

During each of these four stages, specific steps are taken:

- The kinds of decisions are identified.
- The kinds of data needed to make those decisions are identified.
- Those data are collected.
- The criteria for determining quality are established.
- The data are analyzed on the basis of those criteria.
- The needed information is provided to decision makers. (as cited in Glatthorn, 1987, pp. 273–274)

The context, input, process, product (CIPP) model, as it has come to be called, has several attractive features for those interested in curriculum evaluation. Its emphasis on decision making seems appropriate for administrators concerned with improving curricula. Its concern for the formative aspects of evaluation remedies a serious deficiency in the Tyler model. Finally, the detailed guidelines and forms created by the committee provide step-by-step guidance for users.

The CIPP model, however, has some serious drawbacks associated with it. Its main weakness seems to be its failure to recognize the complexity of the decision-making process in organizations. It assumes more rationality than exists in such situations and ignores the political factors that play a large part in these decisions. Also, as Guba and Lincoln (1981) noted, it seems difficult to implement and expensive to maintain.

Scriven's Goal-Free Model

Michael Scriven (1972) was the first to question the assumption that goals or objectives are crucial in the evaluation process. After his involvement in several evaluation projects where so-called side effects seemed more significant than the original objectives, he began to question the seemingly arbitrary distinction between intended and unintended effects. His goal-free model was the outcome of this dissatisfaction.

In conducting a goal-free evaluation, the evaluator functions as an unbiased observer who begins by generating a profile of needs for the group served by a given program (Scriven is somewhat vague as to how this needs profile is to be derived). Then, by using methods that are primarily qualitative in nature, the evaluator assesses the actual effects of the program. If a program has an effect that is responsive to one of the identified needs, then the program is perceived as useful.

Scriven's main contribution, obviously, was to redirect the attention of evaluators and administrators to the importance of unintended effects—a redirection that seems especially useful in education. If a mathematics program achieves its objectives of improving computational skills but has the unintended effect of diminishing interest in mathematics, then it cannot be judged completely successful. Scriven's emphasis on qualitative methods also seemed to come at an opportune moment, when there was increasing dissatisfaction in the research community with the dominance of quantitative methodologies.

As Scriven himself noted, however, goal-free evaluation should be used to complement, not supplant, goal-based assessments. Used alone, it cannot provide sufficient information for the decision maker. Some critics have faulted Scriven for not providing more explicit directions for developing and implementing the goal-free model; as a consequence, it probably can be used only by experts who do not require explicit guidance in assessing needs and detecting effects.

Stake's Responsive Model

Robert Stake (1975) made a major contribution to curriculum evaluation in his development of the responsive model, because the responsive model is based explicitly on the assumption that the concerns of the stakeholders—those for whom the evaluation is done—should be paramount in determining the evaluation issues. He made the point this way:

> To emphasize evaluation issues that are important for each particular program, I recommend the responsive evaluation approach. It is an approach that trades off some measurement precision in order to increase the usefulness of the findings to persons in and around the program. . . . An educational evaluation is a responsive evaluation if it orients more directly to program activities than to program intents; responds to audience requirements for information; and if the different value perspectives present are referred to in reporting the success and failure of the program. (Stake, 1975, p. 14)

Stake recommended an interactive and recursive evaluation process that embodies these steps:

- The evaluator meets with clients, staff, and audiences to gain a sense of their perspectives on and intentions regarding the evaluation.
- The evaluator draws on such discussions and the analysis of any documents to determine the scope of the evaluation project.
- The evaluator observes the program closely to get a sense of its operation and to note any unintended deviations from announced intents.
- The evaluator discovers the stated and real purposes of the project and the concerns that various audiences have about it and the evaluation.
- The evaluator identifies the issues and problems with which the evaluation should be concerned. For each issue and problem, the evaluator develops an evaluation design, specifying the kinds of data needed.
- The evaluator selects the means needed to acquire the data desired. Most often, the means will be human observers or judges.
- The evaluator implements the data-collection procedures.
- The evaluator organizes the information into themes and prepares "portrayals" that communicate in natural ways the thematic reports. The portrayals may involve videotapes, artifacts, case studies, or other "faithful representations."
- By again being sensitive to the concerns of the stakeholders, the evaluator decides which audiences require which reports and chooses formats most appropriate for given audiences. (as cited by Glatthorn, 1987, pp. 275–276)

Clearly, the chief advantage of the responsive model is its sensitivity to clients. By identifying their concerns and being sensitive to their values, by involving them closely throughout the evaluation, and by adapting the form of reports to meet their needs, the model, if effectively used, should result in evaluations of high utility to clients. The responsive model also has the virtue of flexibility: The evaluator is able to choose from a variety of methodologies once client concerns have been identified. Its chief weakness would seem to be its susceptibility to manipulation by clients, who in expressing their concerns might attempt to draw attention away from weaknesses they did not want exposed.

Eisner's Connoisseurship Model

Elliot Eisner (1979) drew from his background in aesthetics and art education in developing his "connoisseurship" model, an approach to evaluation that emphasizes qualitative appreciation. The Eisner model is built on two closely related constructs: connoisseurship and criticism. Connoisseurship, in Eisner's terms, is the art of appreciation—recognizing and appreciating through perceptual memory, drawing from experience to appreciate what is significant. It is the ability both to perceive the particulars of educational life and to understand how those particulars form part of a classroom structure. Criticism, to Eisner, is the art of disclosing qualities of an entity that connoisseurship perceives. In such a disclosure, the educational critic is more likely to use what Eisner called "nondiscursive"—a language that is metaphorical, connotative, and symbolic. It uses linguistic forms to present, rather than represent, conception or feeling.

Educational criticism, in Eisner's formulation, has three aspects. The descriptive aspect is an attempt to characterize and portray the relevant qualities of educational life—the rules, the regularities, the underlying architecture. The interpretive aspect uses ideas from the social sciences to explore meanings and develop alternative explanations—to explicate social phenomena. The evaluative aspect makes judgments to improve the educational processes and provides grounds for the value choices made so that others might better disagree.

The chief contribution of the Eisner model is that it breaks sharply with the traditional scientific models and offers a radically different view of what evaluation might be. In doing so, it broadens the evaluator's perspective and enriches his or her repertoire by drawing from a rich tradition of artistic criticism. Its critics have faulted it for its lack of methodological rigor, although Eisner has attempted to refute such charges. Critics have also argued that use of the model requires a great deal of expertise, noting the seeming elitism implied in the term *connoisseurship*.

Bradley's Effectiveness Model

Bradley's (1985) book *Curriculum Leadership and Development Handbook* provides 10 key indicators that can be used to measure the effectiveness of a developed curriculum. These indicators include: *vertical curriculum continuity; horizontal curriculum continuity; instruction based on curriculum; curriculum priority; broad involvement; long-range planning; decision-making clarity; positive human relations; theory into practice approach;* and *planned change.*

Bradley's indicators are more than mere curriculum markers. They represent working characteristics that any complex organization might exhibit in order to be responsive and responsible to its clients. Further, these indicators can be oriented to meet the needs of any school district—from large to small—and it can focus on a specific evaluation of a district's curriculum area, such as reading, English language arts (ELA), math, or any content area designated.

DEVELOPING AN ECLECTIC APPROACH

Although the Tyler, Stufflebeam, Scriven, Stake, Eisner, and Bradley models, noted previously, appear to have sharp differences, there is evidence of congruence that exists within each. While the models propose to differ in many of their details, several commonalities emerge. These include *study the context, determine client concerns, use qualitative methods, assess opportunity cost* (what other opportunities the student is missing by taking this course), *be sensitive to unintended effects,* and *develop different reports for different audiences.*

By using these commonalities, along with insights generated from analyzing other models, it is possible to develop a list of criteria that can be used in both assessing and developing evaluation models. Such a list is shown in Exhibit 12.1. Districts with sufficient resources to employ an expert consultant can use the criteria to assess the model proposed by the consultant; districts developing a homegrown process can use the criteria to direct their own work.

The criteria will obviously result in an eclectic approach to evaluation, one that draws from the strengths of several different models. Such an eclectic process has been used successfully in evaluating a field of study; this same process also can be used to evaluate a course of study with the scope of the evaluation reduced.

EXHIBIT 12.1   Criteria for a Curriculum Evaluation Model

An effective curriculum evaluation model does the following:

1. Can be implemented without making inordinate demands upon district resources
2. Can be applied to all levels of curriculum—programs of study, fields of study, courses of study
3. Makes provisions for assessing all significant aspects of curriculum—the written, the taught, the supported, the tested, and the learned curricula
4. Makes useful distinctions between merit (intrinsic value) and worth (value for a given context)
5. Is responsive to the special concerns of district stakeholders and is able to provide them with the data they need for decision making
6. Is goal oriented, emphasizing objectives and outcomes
7. Is sensitive to and makes appropriate provisions for assessing unintended effects
8. Pays due attention to and makes provisions for assessing formative aspects of evaluation
9. Is sensitive to and makes provisions for assessing the special context for the curriculum
10. Is sensitive to and makes provisions for assessing the aesthetic or qualitative aspects of the curriculum
11. Makes provisions for assessing opportunity cost—the opportunities lost by those studying this curriculum
12. Uses both quantitative and qualitative methods for gathering and analyzing data
13. Presents findings in reports responsive to the special needs of several audiences

---

EVALUATING A FIELD OF STUDY

"How good is our K–12 science curriculum?" The answer to this question comes from evaluating a field of study—a multigrade sequence of learning experiences in one discipline, subject area, or field. Such evaluations are almost always made for a single purpose—to identify strengths and weaknesses in order to plan for improvements. The process of evaluating a field of study includes five important phases: preparing for the evaluation, assessing the context, identifying the evaluation issues, developing the evaluation design, and implementing the evaluation design.

Preparing for the Evaluation

Preparations for the evaluation include three major steps: setting the project parameters, selecting the project director and the evaluation task force, and preparing the evaluation documents.

In setting the project parameters, district administrators in consultation with the school board should determine both the purpose and the limits of the project. They should, first of all, be clear about the central purpose of the review, because purpose will affect both issues to be examined and methods to be used. In identifying the limits of the project, they should develop answers to the following questions:

- How much time will be allocated, and by what date should the evaluation be completed?
- What human, fiscal, and material resources will be provided?
- Which fields will be evaluated?
- What constituencies will be asked for input? Specifically, will parents, community representatives, and students be involved?

With those parameters set, the project director and evaluation task force should be selected. The project director should be a consultant or a member of the district staff who has considerable technical expertise in curriculum evaluation. The task force should function as an advisory and planning group, making recommendations to and monitoring the performance of the project director. It should probably include a total of 10 to 20 individuals, depending on the size of the district, and have adequate representation from these constituencies: school board, school administrators, teachers and other faculty members, and parents and community organizations. If administrators wish, and if it is felt that their input can be useful, secondary students can be included.

The project director and the task force can then begin to assemble the documents necessary for the program review. The following documents will typically be needed:

- A statement of the curriculum goals for that field
- A comprehensive description of the community and the student body
- A list of all required courses in that field, with time allocations and brief descriptions of each course
- A list of all elective courses in the field, including time allocations, course descriptions, and most recent enrollment figures
- A random selection of student schedules
- Syllabi or course guides for all courses offered
- Faculty schedules, showing class enrollments

Other materials, of course, will be required as the review gets under way, but the previously listed materials are important at the outset.

Assessing the Context

The next stage in a comprehensive evaluation of a field of study is to assess the context. While this stage is obviously of critical importance for an outside evaluator, it is also essential in district-directed projects. The context assessment stage enables the evaluators to identify both the salient aspects of the educational environment that impinge on the field of studies and the critical needs of the learners. In assessing the context, the evaluators typically should seek answers to the following questions:

1. What are the prevailing attitudes, values, and expectations of the community?

2. What significant aspects of the school district impinge on the field of study: size, leadership, organizational structure, fiscal resources?

3. What are the special characteristics of school facilities that impinge on or constrain this field of study?

4. What are the special characteristics of the student body: scholastic aptitude, achievement, home background, ethnic identity, social and physical development?

5. What are the special characteristics of the faculty: experience, educational values, overall competence, educational background?

6. What is special about the school organization: nature of leadership, organizational structure?

The context assessment should result in a report that calls attention to the salient aspects affecting the field of study and identifies the special needs of the learners.

Identifying the Evaluation Issues

The next step in the process is to identify the evaluation issues, to be sure that the evaluation is sensitive to the special concern of the stakeholders and will provide the information needed. Here, the distinctions between the several aspects of the curriculum are essential: the written, the supported, the taught, the tested, and the learned curricula all subsume quite different assessment issues.

Also, each of these five must be assessed if the results are to be at all valid. In too many curriculum evaluations, the team evaluates only the written curriculum (the official course guides) and the learned curriculum (the results on achievement tests). No valid inferences can be drawn from such an assessment, because the other three important components have been ignored. Suppose, for example, that the students in a particular district do not perform well on measures of critical thinking in social studies, even though district guides include such units. District administrators cannot be sure about the causes of the problem. It might well be that teachers have chosen not to teach those units because they lack the training and materials necessary. Only a comprehensive assessment can yield the information needed to make improvements.

As shown in Exhibit 12.2, those five components subsume more than 50 different issues. Obviously, not all these issues will be used in every evaluation. Here, it is essential for the evaluation team to identify the issues by surveying and interviewing stakeholders. That list of issues can be used to survey such constituencies as board members, school administrators, faculty, and parents, using a form similar to the one shown in Exhibit 12.3. The responses can then be analyzed to determine which issues should be evaluated, given the constraints previously identified. The surveys, of course, should be supplemented with interviews of key individuals to provide supplementary data.

EXHIBIT 12.2   Evaluation Issues: Field of Study

The Written Curriculum

Goals

1. Are the goals of this subject clearly and explicitly stated and readily accessible to those who need to refer to them?
2. Are those goals congruent with relevant curricular goals of the school district?
3. Are the goals in accord with the recommendations of experts in the field?
4. Are the goals understood and supported by parents?
5. Are the goals understood and supported by school administrators?
6. Are the goals understood and supported by classroom teachers?
7. Are the goals understood and supported by students?

Scope and Sequence of Level Objectives

1. Have the goals of this field been analyzed into a set of grade-level (or achievement level) objectives that identify the important concepts, skills, and attitudes to be attained?
2. Are those level objectives sufficiently comprehensive so that they adequately reflect the goals of this field?
3. Are those level objectives clearly displayed in some form (such as a scope-and-sequence chart) that facilitates understanding and use?
4. Are the level objectives in accord with and do they reflect the recommendations of experts in the field?
5. Does the grade placement of objectives reflect the best current knowledge of child development?
6. Does the grade placement of objectives provide for sufficient reinforcement without undue repetition?
7. Is the grade placement of objectives appropriate in relation to their difficulty for learners at that level?
8. Are the objectives appropriately distributed over the grades so that there is balance between the grades?

Written Course Guides

1. Are there written course guides for this field covering all grade levels?
2. Are those guides readily available to administrators, teachers, and parents?
3. Does the format of the guides facilitate revision and amplification?
4. Do the guides clearly specify grade-level objectives in a format and manner that facilitate use?
5. Do the guides make appropriate distinctions between mastery, organic, and enrichment outcomes and focus primarily on the mastery outcomes?
6. Do the guides indicate clearly the relative importance of the mastery outcomes and suggest time allocations that reflect their importance?

(Continued)

EXHIBIT 12.2 (continued)

7. Do the guides suggest ways of organizing the objectives into learning units, without requiring a particular type of unit organization?

8. Do the guides recommend (but not mandate) teaching–learning activities that seem likely to lead to the attainment of the relevant objectives?

9. Do the teaching and learning activities recommended reflect the best current knowledge about teaching and learning with technology, and are they qualitatively excellent?

10. Do the guides suggest appropriate evaluation processes and instruments?

11. Do the guides recommend appropriate instructional materials and other resources?

The Supported Curriculum

Time

1. Has the school district clearly specified time to be allocated to this field of study at each level of schooling?

2. Does the time allocated to this field seem appropriate in relation to the district's goals, the goals of the field of study, and the recommendations of experts?

3. Do school master schedules and administrative guidelines on time allocation appropriately reflect district allocations?

Materials

1. Is the quantity of instructional materials and technology adequate in relation to student enrollments?

2. Are the learning objectives of the instructional materials consonant with the objectives of the written course guides?

3. Do the instructional materials reflect the best current knowledge in this field of study?

4. Are the instructional materials free of gender bias and ethnic stereotyping?

5. Are the instructional materials written at an appropriate level of difficulty?

6. Are the instructional materials designed and organized in a manner that facilitates teacher use?

7. Do the instructional materials reflect sound learning principles, providing adequately for motivation, explanation, application, reinforcement, and enrichment?

Professional Development

1. Does the district provide ongoing professional development programs that help the teachers use the curriculum guides effectively and involve teachers in improving the guides?

The Taught Curriculum

1. Do the teachers allocate time to this field of study in accordance with district and school guidelines?

2. Do the teachers allocate time to the several components of this field of study in a way that reflects curricular priorities?

3. Do the teachers teach for the objectives specified for that grade?

4. Do the instructional methods used by the teachers reflect the best current knowledge about teaching that field of study and are they qualitatively excellent?

5. What unintended effects does this curriculum have on teaching?

The Tested Curriculum

1. Does the district provide curriculum-based assessments that adequately reflect and correspond with the objectives stated in the course guides?

2. Are such tests valid and reliable measures of performance?

3. Does the district make use of standardized tests or CCSS-related assessments that provide data on achievement in this field of study?

4. Do any formalized assessments used by the district adequately reflect and correspond with the objectives stated in the course guides?

The Learned Curriculum

1. Do pupils believe that what they are learning is useful and meaningful?

2. Do pupils achieve the specified objectives at a satisfactory level?

3. What unintended learning outcomes are evidenced?

4. What are the opportunity costs for pupils involved in this field of study?

Formative Aspects

1. By what processes was this field of study developed, and did those processes provide for appropriate input from all constituencies?

2. What specific provisions are there for continuing input from those constituencies?

3. What specific provisions are there for revising and modifying the program of studies?

EXHIBIT 12.3   Survey Form—Evaluation Issues: Mathematics

Directions: As you probably are aware, our school district will soon begin to evaluate the mathematics curriculum in our district. Listed next are the questions we might ask in such an evaluation. Tell us how important you think each question is. Read each question, and then circle one of the following symbols:

VI: I think this question is very important.

I: I think this question is important.

LI: I think this question is less important.

Your responses will help us decide which questions to study.

Question	Your Response		
1. Are the goals of this subject clearly and explicitly stated and readily accessible to those who need to refer to them?	VI	I	LI

Developing the Evaluation Design

With the evaluation issues identified, the project director and the task force should cooperatively develop the evaluation design. One historical and yet useful framework for such a design was proposed by Worthen (1981). For each evaluative question (or evaluation issue, to use the terminology employed here), identify the information required, the sources of information, and the methods for collecting that information. Thus, in an example used by Worthen, if the evaluation proposes to answer the question, "Do student attitudes demonstrate that the curriculum is producing the desired results?" the attitudes of students with regard to the values and concepts taught constitute the information required. Students are the source of information, and the methods employed might include a comparative design using attitude scales and simulated situations requiring an attitudinal response.

In identifying the methods for collecting information, evaluators should be certain to include qualitative approaches. As noted previously, current evaluation theory gives strong emphasis to such qualitative methods as interviews and observations in assessing curriculum impact.

Those decisions—about the issues, the information required, the sources of information, and the methods for collecting information—should form the basis of a detailed evaluation plan, which would also include the specific tasks to be undertaken, the names of those responsible for each task, and the deadline for accomplishing the task.

Curriculum Tip 12.1	Curriculum evaluation is an attempt to toss light on two questions: Do planned courses, programs, activities, and learning opportunities developed and organized actually produce desired results? How can the curriculum offerings best be improved?

PURPOSE OF EVALUATION: MEASURING EFFECTIVENESS VERSUS DEVELOPING TEACHERS

Regardless of what form evaluation ultimately takes, focusing on individual student growth and achievement with a nurturing environment will ensure success (Chapko, 2013). Unfortunately, many believe teacher evaluation systems have not accurately measured teacher quality. Although efforts to move quickly in designing and implementing more effective teacher evaluation systems are laudable, educators need to acknowledge a crucial issue—that measuring teacher effectiveness and developing teachers are different purposes with different implications (Marzano, 2012).

Noted author Charlotte Danielson (2010–2011) agreed with Marzano and believes there are two fundamental purposes of evaluation. These are as follows:

To ensure teacher quality. Teacher quality is represented by good teaching, a shared understanding of what is good teaching, and skilled evaluators. With this in mind, Danielson's Framework for Teaching can be used as a reference.

To promote professional development. Teacher evaluation is best served through professional conversations between teacher and colleagues as well as between teachers and supervisors following formal or informal observations.

The challenge, however, is merging these two purposes of teaching evaluation and creating procedures that yield valid and reliable results. This involves a commitment to teaching and professional learning that is represented through the evaluation process. Danielson (2010–2011) noted that systems based on ensuring quality must be valid, reliable, and defensible whereas systems designed to promote professional learning are likely to be collegial and collaborative. Previous attempts to merge quality assurance with professional learning were based on organization and skill development and were represented largely by clinical supervision and cognitive coaching. Danielson argued that it is best when requirements for the two purposes of quality teaching and professional development are embedded in the design of the system themselves.

Curriculum Tip 12.2	Effective school leaders become adept at obtaining "teacher buy-in" as well as conveying expectations of how teaching and learning can be enhanced via the curriculum.

To make evaluation systems more meaningful, participants must use processes that not only are rigorous, valid, and reliable but also engage teachers and supervisors in those activities that promote learning—namely self-assessment, reflection on practice, and professional conversation. Such an approach provides the vehicle for teacher growth and development by providing opportunities for professional conversation around agreed-on standards of practice.

Leadership and Evaluation

A major factor in any evaluation process is quality of leadership. One of the most important aspects of that leadership role is for educational planners to understand the process of evaluation and how it should be administered (Radoslovich, Roberts, & Plaza, 2014). Creating this level of evaluation process means leaders will have to convey knowledge of curriculum as well as instructional strategies. For that reason, school leaders must become adept at obtaining teacher buy-in as well as conveying expectations of how teaching and learning can be enhanced via the curriculum. There is a special need for leadership and more understanding as to the process of evaluation and how it relates to the development of effective curriculum.

Role of the Principal in Evaluation

The principal's role in the evaluation process is not only assessing outcomes and making adjustments but also assisting teachers in improving their practice. With this in mind, an ultimate goal is to guide state and district practices, inform federal and state policy, and link evaluation to professional development necessary for building the capacity of principals.

Building a capacity for principals not only helps teachers create great classrooms but also helps principals create and sustain great schools (Connelly, 2013). Unfortunately, a variety of models of evaluation have individual uniqueness that support district missions and goals, but their overall effect is providing only a process where teachers are involved in their own learning to improve their practice. In contrast, many newly developed systems have incorporated the concept of differentiation that relies on multiple activities, procedures, and timelines to support different levels of groups and teaching experience. This type of differentiation adjusts the pattern of evaluations, which may include a more formal or comprehensive process for new teachers annually, and a different formal process for more experienced teachers, and then a process conducted on a multiyear basis for tenured and those deemed to be superior or master teachers.

The Principal and Evaluation Design

According to Gassenheimer (2013), research supports that professional learning programs should be designed to set the stage for participants' collegial learning and to provide guidance about future learning opportunities.

In a 2010 report titled "Evaluating Principals: Balancing Accountability With Professional Growth" (New Leaders for New Schools, 2010), several statements should trigger a significant professional discussion on the role of the principal as a leader. The quotes noted for further discussion are as follows:

- Effective principals are those who boost academic achievement for all students, increase the effectiveness of their teaching staffs, and consistently take leadership actions shown to improve outcomes for students.
- Principal and teacher quality account for nearly 60% of a school's total impact on student achievement and principals alone for 25% (New Leaders for New Schools, 2010).
- The principal's impact is so significant because of the leadership action principals take to create the schoolwide conditions that support student learning—especially those that directly influence teacher effectiveness, including hiring, professional development, evaluation, and retention or dismissal.

From the onset, principals who are leaders of schools in a global society are expected to increase teacher quality and effectiveness and must become proficient in their ability to become an instructional leader. It has been estimated that evaluation of instruction and evaluating quality and effectiveness should be at least 70% workload that principals do to increase student achievement and teacher effectiveness, with the remaining 30% focused on their demonstration of effective practices and leadership actions (New Leaders for New Schools, 2010). Likewise, local school systems need to establish policies to ensure that building-level administrators are competent in their ability to perform evaluation tasks. The Sioux Falls School District in Sioux Falls, South Dakota, is an example of such a system (see Appendix B in the Sioux Falls School District 49–5 [2008] *Professional Evaluation Staff Handbook*). School districts need to create the conditions for principal and teacher effectiveness to take place. By having competent building instructional leaders who are skillful in evaluating quality instruction and effectiveness will have a significant impact on both the teacher and student.

Understanding Effective Teaching

Research supports the notion that principals must have the skills and work in collaboration with faculty and staff to improve their professional practice. It is with this in mind that Exhibit 12.4 provides a school district's indicators of effective teaching that becomes a guide for principals in their evaluation process. Principals need to master instructional strategies that will aid the teacher in looking at their teaching practices and challenge them to evaluate themselves in ways that will stretch them in new domains of instruction and strategies. New domains are those areas where digital-age students have established practices of learning but appear to be foreign to faculty who have not been involved with new teaching practices, such as some mobile learning applications and other media that are coming into the teaching arena. Most assuredly, the classroom is changing, and thus, it is imperative that both principals and teachers embrace new standards of teaching practices that meet the needs of students in a global society.

EXHIBIT 12.4 Indicators of Effective Teaching

Indicators

SECTION 1—PLANNING FOR INSTRUCTION

A. Plan instructional tasks that are meaningful and related to learning goals

- plans for learning needs and abilities of each student
- prepares plans which correlate with specific instructional objectives
- plans instructional activities that communicate high level of expectation
- selects instructional methods (models) and learning activities that are compatible with
- content, learning styles, and student abilities
- constructs a variety of learning activities
- develops extended and enriched activities to challenge students beyond the required curriculum
- plans evaluation procedures consistent with instructional objectives

SECTION 2—IMPLEMENTING INSTRUCTION

A. Implements District curriculum

- uses approved district curriculum
- uses resource and supplemental materials that relate to the curriculum

B. Maintains a strong instructional focus utilizing the elements of effective instruction

- introduces the lesson
- states the lesson objective/goal

(Continued)

EXHIBIT 12.4 (continued)

- uses variation in voice, movement, and pacing to focus attention during lesson
- models/demonstrates
- checks for understanding
- includes guided and/or independent practice
- summarizes lesson

   C. Communicates a high level of expectation
   D. Communicates clear learning goals to students
   E. Adapts instruction to meet the needs of all students
   F. Addresses various learning styles
   G. Sequences content at an appropriate pace
   H. Uses appropriate level of questioning to promote understanding

- solicits student participation
- extends student's responses/contributions or probes for deeper understanding
- provides ample time for students to respond to teacher questions and to consider
- content

   I. Relates lesson content to prior and future learning
   J. Requires students to summarize information in written and/or verbal form

   K. Appropriately recognizes and reinforces individual student effort
   L. Represents knowledge/information non-linguistically through a variety of methods

- Could include use of methods such as graphic organizers, physical models, mental
- pictures, drawings and pictographs, or kinesthetic activities

   M. Organizes students in cooperative or ability groups when appropriate
   N. Requires students to analyze and apply knowledge
   O. Displays enjoyment, humor, and enthusiasm for teaching and expects students to enjoy learning

SECTION 3—EVALUATING INSTRUCTION

   A. Conducts ongoing assessments for learning

- provides specific and immediate feedback related to student learning
- monitors students' performance as they engage in learning activities
- solicits responses or demonstrations from specific students for assessment purposes
- monitors and communicates student progress at regular intervals

   B. Provides re-teaching and/or interventions when appropriate

SECTION 4—CLASSROOM MANAGEMENT

   A. Has established appropriate classroom rules and procedures that are clearly understood by all students
   B. Effectively and consistently enforces rules and follows procedures
   C. Redirects students naturally and immediately without disrupting others

    D.   Is well-organized and has all materials, equipment, etc., ready for immediate use

    E.   Carries out smooth and effective transitions (e.g., from one activity to another, as students enter and leave the room)

    F.   Maximizes time on purposeful instructional tasks

    G.   Begins and ends class period with focus on learning

    H.   Has established a positive learning environment

- respects and shows sensitivity to individual needs and concerns
- provides opportunities for the student to assume responsibility and develop
- independence
- avoids sarcasm and negative criticism
- establishes and maintains positive rapport with students
- establishes a trusting environment that fosters risk taking
- treats students in a professional teacher-student manner
- recognizes individual and cultural diversity of students

SECTION 5—DEMONSTRATES PROFESSIONALISM

    A.   Participates in ongoing professional growth

- stays current in content and instructional strategies
- incorporates technology
- seeks and/or participates in opportunities such as Innovative and Experimental
- Programs, Summer Research, local, state and federal grants

    B.   Participates in school/professional and/or community organizations or events

    C.   Completes routine assigned tasks and complies with District requirements

- completes required paperwork
- monitors budget if required by position
- meets established timelines
- follows District and building policies and procedures
- demonstrates support of District goals

    D.   Promotes the education profession

- serves on building or District committees
- volunteers for extra duty assignments
- serves as a teacher, trainer, presenter, or mentor to others
- serves as a positive role model in the school environment

    E.   Communicates effectively and professionally with colleagues, parents and students

- initiates communication with parents about student performance and/or behavior
- when appropriate
- conducts parent-teacher conferences in accordance with District policy
- reports student progress to parents and students
- maintains confidentiality unless disclosure is required by law
- develops and maintains supportive, flexible, and cooperative relationships with
- colleagues, parents, and students

SOURCE: Sioux Falls School District 49–5 (2008, pp. 13–15)

In addition to the indicators for effective teaching, the Sioux Falls School District 49–5 in Sioux Falls, South Dakota, has identified effective indicators for the following professional staff: school library or media staff, speech and language therapy staff, school psychologists or psychometrists, school social workers, school nurses, and school counseling. These additional indicators are in the Sioux Falls School District 49–5 (2008) *Professional Evaluation Staff Handbook* in Appendix A.

Along with Exhibit 12.4, Indicators of Effective Teaching, instructional leaders (principals) should become familiar with Danielson's (2007) *Framework for Teaching,* which outlines four domains. Domain 1 identifies the planning and preparation for teaching, followed by Domain 2, which identifies classroom environment, followed by Domain 3 on instruction, and finally Domain 4, which establishes professional responsibilities. The principal who understands Danielson's effective teaching research and develops a skill set that encompasses such areas as effective listening, observation with a best practice knowledge base, questioning and discussion skills, collaborative and relationship building skills, and effective communications skills will have a formula to establish an effective evaluation component to their practice of being an effective instructional leader.

To be an effective instructional leader, the principal must have a positive attitude when embarking on the evaluative process. Due to the fact that the teaching process is a complex and often misunderstood and misevaluated process, the principal has to establish a credible and reliable process and relationship with their faculty. It is very easy to observe a teaching segment and become critical of what you are observing, but it is a little more difficult to provide researched best practice feedback for the teacher and then have a constructive, not destructive, feedback conversation. Catching the teacher performing a best practice teaching moment and providing feedback is a relationship-building experience. When the observable moment or evidence of poor practice is evident, hopefully the previous positive conversations will be a bridge for future growth and not a barrier for continued failure.

Relationship building with expertise and integrity is the cornerstone for movement into a successful evaluation process. Therefore, the principal must establish their credibility as an instructional leader and that is based on their understanding of best practice research. Principals must "walk the talk," and when teachers realize that the principal is not there to catch them doing something wrong, but to help them perform better, the result will be a stronger performance in the classroom by the teacher and the student.

Measuring for Success

As a key strategy in facilitating reform, CCSS summative assessments are represented by two consortia—the Partnership for Assessment of Readiness for College and Careers (PARCC) and the Smarter Balanced Assessment Consortium (SBAC). Although there are differences across the two consortia in assessment design, each will contain a performance-based component and an end-of-the-year component to help measure student performance. Both PARCC and the SBAC—as well as professional organizations, nonprofits, and publishers—have developed many supports to help schools implement the CCSS and the aligned assessments. Some of these supports include Internet sites containing highly detailed curriculum modules with mid-module and end-of-module assessments, professional development kits for teachers and principals, a library of videos that exemplify the shifts in instruction, and a library of resources for families (Doorey, 2014).

Bridging Cultural Knowledge

As CCSS demands rigor as well as better assessment and evaluation, it also creates opportunities to build bridges between where students are and where they need to be. This is especially the case as it applies to cultural issues that are often subtle and elusive. As noted by Dong (2013–2014), classroom teachers can use improved assessment and monitoring practices to help bridge knowledge gaps and address English language learner (ELL) cultural needs. Research has shown relatedly that assessing language learners' prior knowledge—which includes their previous learning history, native language, cultural and life experiences, and any understandings they have about the topic at hand—is a key ingredient of learning. The key, then, is using instructional and assessment materials that connect to students' home cultures and help increase their understandings and motivation for learning.

Assessing Teaching and Learning

Determining how new programs enhance the integration of curriculum as well as curriculum content is a way to measure the effectiveness of teaching practices. For example, expectations for student learning achievement are directly tied to the development of a culturally sensitive as well as differentiated curriculum. Thus, the formulation of learning objectives is certainly an important component in assessing student growth. The design of the curriculum, then, should provide students with the essential knowledge and skills, via information technology, that can be applied across the curriculum.

Focusing on Student Performance

According to Robert Marzano (2012), an evaluation system that fosters teacher (and student) learning will differ from one whose aim is to measure teacher competence. With this in mind, it is essential for administrators to focus the direction of any new program or initiative on student performance. The key, then, is to create a more symbiotic relationship between teacher and students as well as a connection between student performance and the curriculum. In doing so, correlations between student performance and changes in the classrooms will become more evident. This means that appropriate mechanisms and administrative structures will need to be made so that student performance can be measured and assessed in relevant ways. The key here is that we want teachers, students, administrators, and the external community to see that teaching is having a positive impact on student achievement and that students are performing better because of changes enacted within the school.

According to Tomlinson (2014), formative assessments can improve both teaching and learning. Both in its alignment with current content goals as well as its immediacy in providing insight about student understanding, formative assessments can help teachers make near-term adjustments that hopefully will increase student performance. As part of this process Tomlinson lists 10 principles associated with best practices as they relate to formative assessment:

1. Help students understand the role of formative assessment.

2. Apply clear know, understand, and do (KUD) practices.

3. Make room for student differences.

4. Provide instructive feedback.

5. Make feedback user-friendly.

6. Assess persistently.

7. Engage students with formative assessment.

8. Look for patterns.

9. Plan instruction around content requirements and student needs.

10. Repeat the process.

Using these types of formative assessment strategies as part of an evaluation plan can maximize individual student growth. Moreover, by qualitatively assessing each learning experience, teachers are better able to channel instruction for the next learning experience.

Value-Added Assessment

Value-added assessment (VAA) is a highly controversial technique of using test data to determine the value that teachers add to the learning of each student. With this in mind, many questions remain unanswered as schools forge ahead into greater uses of performance assessments—potentially even linking them to teacher and principal evaluations (Dietel, 2011). Di Carlo (2012) noted the following:

> Value-added models are a specific type of *growth model,* a diverse group of
> statistical techniques used to isolate a teacher's impact on his or her students'
> testing progress while controlling for other measurable factors, such as student
> and school characteristics that are outside of the teacher's control. (p. 38)

From a historical perspective, VAAs were designed to focus on how test data can help each child academically. Theoretically, this type of assessment makes it possible to isolate the impact of individual teachers and to respond with appropriate rewards or corrective training. Former University of Tennessee statistician William Sanders, who helped pioneer value-added research, noted that this method offers a way to ensure that as few children as possible suffer a disadvantage in learning. Sanders (as cited in Holland, 2001) believed that "under effective teachers, students could make gains no matter what their ability or achievement levels were when they started" (p. 3).

Value-Added Assessment Format

- Each spring, students take a norm-referenced state test in five core subjects (math, science, reading, language, and social studies). Nonredundant test items are added each year in an attempt to discourage blatant "teaching to the test."
- Each fall, districts receive a report card broken down by school and grade showing progress in each subject in the context of three-year averages. The system records

student achievement gains in scale score points and in the form of comparisons to local, state, and national averages. School and district reports are reported to the public.

- Each teacher receives a report card—one that is not released to the general public—showing the year-to-year progress of his or her students. Supervisors also receive these reports.

Not everyone believes the value-added model (VAM) is a good thing. For example, Linda Darling-Hammond (Darling-Hammond, Amrein-Beardsley, Haertel, & Rothstein, 2012), the Charles E. Ducommun Professor of Teaching and Teacher Education at Stanford University, has reservations about VAMs. She noted that VAM for individual teacher evaluation is based on the belief that measured achievement gains for a specific teacher's students reflect that teacher's "effectiveness." This attribution, however, assumes that student learning is measured well by a given test, is influenced by the teacher alone, and is independent from the growth of classmates and other aspects of the classroom context. None of these assumptions is well supported by current evidence. For example, research concludes that value-added models are inconsistent and do not actually measure teacher "effectiveness" but rather rely on statistical controls for past achievement to parse out the small portion of student gains.

EVALUATION PROGRAM GUIDELINES

The field of education is ever-changing, and so the best of plans must change as well. Due to the scope of most educational programs, it is critical that the evaluation process be viewed as ongoing. With that said, statewide educational agencies should review and evaluate school programs and curriculum in their states at a minimum of every three years. This type of review process helps to identify standards and interconnection issues that should be evaluated and addressed. It will also identify the success stories and research that is needed to validate the cost and implementation of new programs.

Guidelines for program evaluation are listed here:

- Indicators of success for any programs should be developed at the onset of any project.
- Indicators of success should relate to the original vision of the project as well as to the mission statement.
- An evaluation component for professional development should be a major component of any curriculum plan.
- A feedback process for information should be incorporated in the evaluation plan.
- Clear indicators of success expressed in terms of student outcomes should drive improvement efforts.
- Assessment should derive from multiple sources of data, both quantitative and qualitative.

Evaluation Checklist

Evaluation checklists are helpful to educational planners trying to gauge the success of their school and district programs. The checklist shown in Exhibit 12.5 is easy to administer and provides a quick assessment of program components.

EXHIBIT 12.5	Evaluation Checklist
Check ✓ if yes	Curricular Program Components
	Does the curriculum provide evidence of administrative and school board support?
	Does the curriculum plan incorporate a mission statement?
	Does the curriculum plan establish a task force or advisory committee?
	Does the curriculum plan facilitate the involvement of parents and the community?
	Does the curriculum design allow for research development?
	Does the curriculum plan utilize student learner outcomes as a measure?
	Does the curriculum plan have an evaluation tool that provides for the collection of qualitative data?

EVALUATION STRATEGIES FOR SUCCESS

Successful school administrators use the following strategies in developing assessment and evaluation (Whitehead, Jensen, & Boschee, 2013).

Setting Goals and Indicators

The evaluation and assessment process must be linked to the original mission statement and objectives of the district. Indicators of successful curriculum integration for the purposes of evaluation should be established during the early planning stages of any program.

Identifying Target Populations

Successful evaluation and assessment procedures should focus on targeting specific external and internal population groups. Parents and community-related organizations and businesses represent external groups. Trustees, administrators, teachers, and students represent internal target groups. Data collection needs to specifically focus on these target areas and how they relate to curriculum practices.

Educational Research Centers

Educational research centers found on university campuses can do an orderly investigation of a subject matter for the purpose of adding to knowledge. Within the realm of educational planning, many things are always changing: the structure of the education system, curriculum, textbooks, and modes of teaching, among others. These changes may lead to an improvement, or a worsening, in the quality of an educational system. The educational planner working within this kind of environment must be able to undertake assessments of the effects of major changes and then provide policy advice that will consolidate and extend the postproductive courses of action and also intercept and terminate existing practices that are shown to be damaging and wasteful.

Regardless of the process used to evaluate curriculum, planners need to be willing to use data to make changes and adjustments where necessary. They must understand that curriculum improvement and instructional improvement are interconnected and that a change in one area will probably elicit a change in another area. Problems and concerns can misrepresent issues at hand, making evaluation an important tool. With higher quality and more detailed information available, school leaders will be able to focus more on how curriculum planning can help teachers with student achievement.

Implementing the Evaluation Design

If current trends continue, comprehensive evaluation systems can be an effective way to support the professional growth of teachers and administrators (Murphy, Goldring, & Porter, 2014). With that said, and once a design is developed, the evaluation team can move expeditiously to implement the design and report the results. Two matters should be stressed here: First, the implementation process should be flexible. If new issues develop or if additional data sources become apparent, they should be built into a revised design and incorporated into the implementation process. Second, the results should be reported in ways that will accommodate the special needs of the several audiences. Thus, several reports might be envisioned: a summary written in plain language for the public, an action plan presented to the board and school administrators, and a detailed report for the broader educational community.

Once people know, firsthand, and are able to measure the benefits of effective curriculum planning and evaluation, the public support for funding will become viable. Indicators of success used to measure the impact of student achievement in schools will be a determining factor. It is hoped that future research will be based on these indicators to give educational planners a more complete picture as to the impact of curriculum changes on teaching and learning as well. A key, then, to the success of any curricular program in the future is the ability of school leaders to develop awareness and understanding through the implementation of an effective evaluation program. Throughout the entire evaluation process, the focus for administrators should be on combining appropriate strategies with measurable results indicating positive correlations with teaching and learning.

TECHNOLOGY AND EVALUATION: THE FINAL PIECE OF THE PUZZLE

Despite many challenges—orchestrating major shifts in teaching, instituting new assessments, and facilitating professional development—building principals report new changes are offering great rewards (Alfred, Johnson, Yuen, & Sternberg, 2012). For example, measuring student access and maintaining equity is a way of assessing the impact of technology in schools. Likewise, student learning outcomes can include measures of how well students learn, think, reason, and solve complex problems through the use of technology in the classroom. Program attendance, graduation rates, standardized testing, teacher-made pre- and posttests, observation, portfolios, grades, and the degree of student participation can also provide indications of program success. Finally, teacher and student use of technology can be documented by logging the number of times an individual uses some type of digital source. A log of all Internet queries and messages sent and received can be noted. This data can be graphed and shared with the community to show how technology is being used in classrooms.

For the most part, innovative schools are using technology to make assessment and evaluation an integral part of the instructional design and development process. Built into this technology initiative are procedures for school leaders to monitor and evaluate the direction and implementation of the plan. When appropriate technology is used to facilitate teaching and learning, it becomes an established part of a school. The development of a statewide electronic communication network infrastructure will help assist school leaders in best using and sharing information gained through meaningful program evaluation.

The single biggest barrier to widespread school technology implementation continues to be basic awareness of the measurable benefits. Unprecedented support for school technology is spurring an investment of billions of dollars, but the lack of research and quality measurement has led to unclear results. The key issue is establishing more effective and accurate ways in which we can measure the real benefits of educational technology and measure the true associated costs in money and time spent learning to use these technologies. Sociological acceptance and adoption of the use of these new communications technologies continues to represent a challenge as well.

Another concern is the lack of quality leadership in establishing strong evaluation and assessment agendas and programs and supporting teachers. Authors Williams and Engel (2012–2013) noted that if one understands the teaching process, then building the nation's teaching capital calls for hiring teachers with potentially good teaching traits and providing support to teach well. As part of that support, administrators need to assist teachers with technology integration. Thus, there is a special need for leadership and more understanding as to the process of evaluation and how it relates to technology development in schools. Quality leadership is a key component to the success of any educational technology implementation process. One of the most important aspects of that leadership role is that educational planners understand the process of evaluation and how it should be administered.

The rapid changes occurring in technology also pose a challenge to establishing effective evaluation programs. Technology capabilities have continued to change faster than educational researchers can keep up. For example, initial evidence on the use of technology applications in the classroom showed that drill and practice activities were successful in reinforcing skills. Now, with continued advances in mobile devices and applications being used extensively in classrooms, teachers are becoming even more creative in their approach to integrating technology. Subsequently, it has been difficult for researchers to complete large-scale, controlled studies that lead to solid conclusions because by the time their research is published, new technologies are providing new opportunities for teachers and students.

Of concern is the need to better align technology standards and guidelines with current teaching and curriculum evaluation frameworks. Fortunately, the move toward CCSS and the work of numerous states in developing new multimeasure frameworks for teaching and evaluation is helping to fill this gap (Depascale, 2012). As part of this evaluative process, there appears to be increased interest in determining possible links between technology integration and characteristics of high performing schools. To be sure, administrators, teachers, and parents want to know and understand the impact that technology has made on district goals relating to student learning, professional development, and curricular content.

Connectivity

Many states are concerned that a number of school technology applications and programs are not being used—or used wisely. Thus, some technology planners are monitoring student use as per a connectivity rate. A school's connectivity rate can be formulated by calculating the number of minutes students are actually using their technology device divided by the number of applications provided. This can be tracked daily and averaged at the end of the month. A school's connectivity rate can become an important factor when administrators are allocating technology funding or competitive grants.

Integrated System Assessments

A popular way to access student achievement and performance is through the use of integrated data-based systems. For the most part, integrated data programs allow individual students to learn and work at their independent challenge levels but, at the same time, are able to digitally track student performance. These data-based approaches also have a teacher management component that provides diagnosis, adjustment, and evaluation features. Information collected from these databases can then be used as part of a larger program evaluation process.

Technology and Student Achievement

Today's educators must provide a learning environment that takes students beyond the walls of their classrooms and into a virtual world of endless opportunities. But, according to Walmsley (2014), we must teach children how to balance the benefits of operating in the virtual world as well as in face-to-face situations. It is hoped that technology standards will do just that by ensuring digital-age students be empowered to learn, live, and work successfully today and tomorrow. As innovations in technology dramatically change our society, educators need to demonstrate the skills and behaviors of digital-age professionals. Competence with technology is the foundation. Societies are changing, expectations are changing, teaching is changing, and educators must take the lead to move into a global society.

Widely adopted and recognized in the United States—and increasingly adopted in countries worldwide—the National Educational Technology Standards (NETS) integrate educational technology standards across all educational curricula. While most educational standards apply to a specific content area, the NETS are not subject-matter specific but rather a compendium of skills required for students to be competitive and successful in a global and digital world.

Digital-Age Learning

"As foundational technology skills penetrate throughout our society, students will be expected to apply the basics in authentic, integrated ways to solve problems, complete projects, and creatively extend their abilities" (International Society for Technology in Education [ISTE], 2008). The standards identify several higher order thinking skills (HOTS) and digital citizenship as critical for students to learn effectively for a lifetime and live productively in our emerging global society. These areas include the ability to do the following:

- Demonstrate creativity and innovation
- Communicate and collaborate
- Conduct research and use information
- Think critically, solve problems, and make decisions
- Use technology effectively and productively

It is evident that technology skills for educators and students will change the way they teach, the way they work, and the way they learn in an increasingly connected global and digital society. Rapid advances in technology are putting new demands on educators and students. Subsequently, teachers play a key role in determining how well technology is used in their schools.

Digital-Age Teaching

The rapid advances in technology are putting new demands on classroom teachers and students. Consequently, workable standards are needed to provide a framework for teachers to use as they transition schools from Industrial Age to Digital Age places of learning. NETS, developed by the ISTE (2008), consist of the following standards:

- Facilitate and inspire student learning and creativity
- Design and develop digital-age learning experiences and assessments
- Model digital-age work and learning
- Promote and model digital citizenship and responsibility
- Engage in professional growth and leadership

Digital-Age Leadership

Regarding digital-age leadership, school principals "play a critical role in determining how well technology is used in [their] schools" (ISTE, 2008). Don Knezek (ISTE, 2008), ISTE CEO, so amply stated the following:

Integrating technology throughout a school system is, in itself, significant systemic reform. We have a wealth of evidence attesting to the importance of leadership in implementing and sustaining systemic reform in schools. It is critical, therefore, that we attend seriously to leadership for technology in schools.

In that school principals play a pivotal role in determining how well technology is used in their schools, NETS for Administrators enable us to define what building-level leaders need to know and be able to do in order to discharge their responsibility as leaders in the effective use of technology in our schools. NETS, developed for administrators, especially principals, by the ISTE (2008), consist of the following standards:

- Visionary leadership
- Digital age learning culture
- Excellence in professional practice
- Systemic improvement
- Digital citizenship

There is little doubt that for principals to create and sustain a culture that supports digital-age learning, they must become comfortable collaborating as co-learners with colleagues around the world. In today's digital learning culture, it is less about staying ahead and more about moving forward as members of dynamic learning communities.

Data Collection

Formulating excellence in schools means creating routines for educators to collect data on the process and results of teaching (Halverson, Kelley, & Shaw, 2014). Data collection, then, can be a major key to finding out how technology is being used to impact teaching and learning. Given the nature of school reform associated with digital change, a number of national marketing companies are now collecting data on technology use. These commercial marketing firms collect information on school technology and sell that information to technology manufacturers. They conduct mail and telephone surveys of schools throughout the nation, determining what type of high-tech equipment is being used and how it is being used. Results are supplemented by information from departments of education and other surveys. State and school leaders, upon request, may obtain this information after a certain amount of time.

State and school leaders do have to be careful in placing too much emphasis on data collected by marketing companies. One of the weaknesses of this data is that it is usually based on small-sample populations. This can generate misleading statistics that tend to favor the direction of the company sponsoring the survey. Another problem is that district administrators do not always take surveys seriously or rush through them without real consideration. As a result, some states are collecting their own data because they feel that schools take government surveys more seriously and the results will be more accurate. In addition, these surveys have an educational and student achievement focus on technology and are less likely to have a hidden technological agenda like that found in market research.

This data is also public property and can be shared more easily among districts and states for comparison studies.

Technology Plan Assessment

To help anchor standards, it is crucial for leadership to work collaboratively with students and community members to establish a set of guidelines and expectations that involve integrating digital literacy and citizenship into the curriculum (Tarte, 2014). Keeping with this perspective, an assessment of the technology plan should reveal the quality of change that occurred during the actual implementation process. Assessment indicators need to reveal the quality of change rather than just a snapshot of current conditions. The evaluation process should help determine if the school's vision of technology truly reflects a focus on student learning. School leaders must examine and review the technology plan to make sure that it encourages teachers to use current research and academic development practices in their classrooms. The following questions can provide direction during a review of a technology plan:

- Does the technology plan address the meaningful involvement of community members, parents, and other stakeholders who have shown an interest in developing and promoting informational technology?
- Should the technology plan be changed to increase community involvement?
- Does the technology plan facilitate instruction?
- Do action steps in the plan reflect the alignment of up-to-date technological practices with student-learning patterns?
- How effective is the technology plan in accounting for student performance?
- Are objectives for student performance responsive to the learning needs of students?
- Are student achievement goals being met?

In sum, an evaluation of the technology plan should reveal a dynamic perspective of growth in the area of technology use.

Professional Development and Evaluation

Often a strong association exists between effective leadership and the evaluation of professional development programs. Effective professional development programs can be evaluated as well as analyzed by using indicators of success developed early in the project. Objectives of any quality professional development program involving the use of technology should be consistent with the school district's shared vision. Indicators of professional development success can be measured through the staff's ability to do the following:

- Understand and follow school vision and goals as shown by surveys and documents.
- Get involved in a variety of technology workshops and conferences.
- Access district operating and informational systems.
- Use data collection and multimedia.

- Demonstrate an ability to access Cloud and use of mobile technology.
- Identify technology resources involving support and service.
- Use emerging technology to support to instruction.
- Understand equity and legal issues involving the use of technology.
- Evaluate and assess student performance and outcomes.

Classroom Technology Environment

Decision making about technology has to be a shared responsibility with both classroom teachers and technicians (Johnson, 2013). Classrooms must be designed technologically to foster active involvement of students in the learning process. Lessons should be based on high expectations and an application of HOTS whenever applicable. From an evaluation standpoint, the pace of learning should take into account learning styles of children and stages of growth and development. Application of instruction should be based on individual needs of the students and allow them to explore and investigate new forms of informational technology.

The amount of student writing, as well as the completion rate of projects, can be used to measure positive changes. Pointedly, there appears to be a trend of student attendance rates going up in classrooms using technology. Students participating in interactive technology seem to want to come to school. Attendance rates can easily be cross-correlated with classrooms using interactive technology to give administrators a feel as to whether technology may be having an effect on attendance.

Another indicator of technology success in the classroom is teacher and parent support. Teacher and parent support of technology can be monitored via questionnaires or surveys as well as by the collection of positive correspondence. In addition, minutes from board of trustee meetings can provide documentation of positive feelings toward technology and thus reflect possible organizational climate changes.

Equity Issues

Monitoring multicultural and equity issues as they relate to technology planning and implementation is a key to reforming education. On the other hand, an equity problem can arise due to a lack of technology. Wealthier school districts almost certainly have an advantage over economically deprived urban and rural schools when it comes to accessing technology. This has a tendency to create a situation referred to as "pockets of excellence." That said, thousands of rural and economically disadvantaged schools need to upgrade equipment and programs if they are to keep up with emerging technologies. Hopefully, with more research and support, better access, and additional funding, all of these rural and disadvantaged schools will be able to address this problem.

GLOBAL CONNECTIONS: EVALUATION AND ACCOUNTABILITY

A variety of countries are known to have outpaced the United States in student achievement as well as the area of evaluation and assessment. After researching evaluation approaches in Finland, Korea, Japan, Singapore, and Canada, Williams and Engel (2012–2013) determined the following:

1. Teacher evaluation is used for both accountability and instructional improvement in most school systems. However, teacher evaluation systems are organized differently depending on the model of accountability.

2. There is a growing trend to use student test results and metrics to inform accountability for schools, principals, and teachers, instructional improvement in classrooms, and schools, and reform at the system level.

3. In particular, standardized testing of students, a primary and growing component of teacher evaluation in the United States, is generally administered and used differently in other countries.

Additionally, Williams and Engel (2012–2013) found four primary approaches to accountability: professional, organizational, market, and parental or community.

- *Professional accountability.* Results from practitioner identification with the profession and a corresponding internalized obligation to uphold, even advance, its standards. *Finland's* teacher evaluation system is based almost entirely on professional accountability, in which teachers are accountable to each other, the school, the children, and their parents.
- *Organizational accountability.* Relates to the structures, norms, incentives, and sanctions of the formal institutions. *Mexico's* system is heavily influenced by socioeconomic status and thus represents organizational accountability.
- *Market accountability.* A result of consumer selection among competing services. This approach calls for schools to complete to provide the best services demanded by parents and students. *Singapore's* teacher evaluation is an example.
- *Parental or community accountability.* An attempt to describe the informal, bottom-up accountability resulting from parental and societal pressure on schools, teachers, and students to do well. *Japan's* program represents a parental or community accountability approach.

Interestingly enough, as per evaluation approaches, the *United States* relies most heavily on market accountability—although organizational, professional, and parental accountability are also present.

SUMMARY

This chapter brings approaches of curriculum leadership into a global focus and provides for greater understanding of the evaluation process. To that end, it proposes a broad definition of the term *curriculum evaluation*. It also describes several effective evaluation models. The chapter proposes a comprehensive and eclectic process that can be used to evaluate a field of study as well as technological applications. In addition, challenges to curriculum leadership are addressed.

APPLICATIONS

1. Choose one of the issues identified for the field of study evaluation. Use one of the frameworks noted in the chapter in developing a design for that issue.

2. Select one of the models described, and write a detailed explication and critique of that model.

3. Suppose a classroom teacher posed this to you: I want to evaluate my own course. I don't know much about statistics. Can you tell me how to evaluate it in a way that won't take too much time? Write the answer you would give that teacher.

4. Using the evaluation checklist in Exhibit 12.5, evaluate a classroom curricular program in your school.

5. If you answered no to any of the curriculum development indicators in Bradley's effectiveness model from Exhibit 12.4, explain how you would make it or them positive (yes).

6. In the following chart that is provided, identify the elements from each of the curriculum development models that address Bradley's effectiveness model.

Models	Place the item number(s) from Bradley's effectiveness model in this column.
Tyler's objectives-centered model	
Stufflebeam's context, input, process, product (CIPP) model	
Scriven's goal-free model	
Stake's responsive model	
Eisner's connoisseurship model	
Overall, what elements from Bradley's effectiveness model were not addressed?	

CASE STUDY   Teaching to the Test

A school trustee shares with Kathy Peterson, district superintendent, that one of the school district teachers is teaching to the test.

"I understand that one of our sixth-grade teachers is teaching to the test in Principal Harris's building," says board trustee Ron Dawson.

Superintendent Peterson smiles. "It would be a problem if we were talking about a norm-referenced standardized test as the evaluative tool. Fortunately, it is my understanding that the sixth-grade teacher is referring to our criterion-referenced assessments that are currently based on CCSS. In this case, we want the teachers to analyze the items and adjust their curriculum to benchmarks on the test—so, in effect, she is teaching to the test."

Trustee Dawson looks as though he is slightly confused.

Peterson continues, "Not only is she teaching to the test but she has also developed a computerized grading system that has the capability of providing e-mail reports to parents. This way, the parents can also help address the acquisition of certain basic skills. The result is that we have basically wrapped the testing process into our curriculum evaluation process."

"And how is that?" Ron Dawson asks.

"Well, at a push of a button, your sixth-grade teacher can average and total any student's grade at any time. If parents walk through the door, she can tell them exactly how their child is doing. She also has an electronic portfolio of every student as part of the evaluative process."

Trustee Dawson likes the idea of having the district's teachers addressing basic skills that are on the state test. "This concept of teaching to the test—a criterion-referenced test—is what we should have been doing all along," he says enthusiastically.

The Challenge

Using electronic testing and setting benchmarks is proving to be a successful evaluation strategy for Principal Harris. What are some other novel or innovative ways that Principal Harris can use to evaluate and assess student achievement as well as his overall school curricula?

Key Issues or Questions

1. What are some major differences between electronic testing and regular testing? Do you feel that electronic online testing is worth the cost? Why or why not?

2. How might Principal Harris deal with resistance from teachers who oppose the use of electronic testing and data analysis?

3. If the principal meets with other teachers about using a data-analysis approach, what should be discussed?

4. What future role will online electronic testing have in evaluating a field of study?

5. What are some other technological approaches that Principal Harris might use to assess student achievement? Identify the strategies, and explain why you think they might be effective.

WEBLIOGRAPHY

Assessment vs. Evaluation
www.teachervision.fen.com/assessment/new-teacher/48353.html

Curriculum Audit
http://files.eric.ed.gov/fulltext/ED505923.pdf

Curriculum Evaluation
http://tyrannyofthetextbook.wordpress.com/2011/09/03/rubrics-for-evaluating-curriculum
www.mcrel.org
www.naesp.org
www.ascd.org

Educational Resources Information Center (ERIC)
www.eric.ed.gov

Google Scholar
http://scholar.google.com

National Center for Education Statistics
http://nces.ed.gov

National Center for Educational Achievement
www.nc4ea.org

Research Center for Leadership in Action
http://wagner.nyu.edu/leadership

Value-Added Assessment (VAA)
www.cgp.upenn.edu/ope_value.html#13

What Works Clearinghouse (WWC)
http://ies.ed.gov/ncee/wwc

REFERENCES

Alfred, H. C., Johnson, J., Yuen, K., & Sternberg, D. (2012). At the center of the common core: Principals share solutions, tips, and top resources for school-level implementation. *Principal, 92*(1), 8–11.

Baron, M. A., & Boschee, F. (1995). *Authentic assessment: The key to unlocking student success.* Lanham, MD: Rowman & Littlefield.

Bradley, L. H. (1985). *Curriculum leadership and development handbook.* Englewood Cliffs, NJ: Prentice Hall.

Chapko, M. A. (2013). Fear and loathing of the evaluation bandwagon. *Principal, 92*(3), 42–43.

Chappuis, J. (2014). Thoughtful assessment with the learner in mind. *Educational Leadership, 71*(6), 20–26.

Connelly, G. (2013). Redesigning evaluations to build capacity. *Principal, 92*(3), 52.

Danielson, C. (2007). *Enhancing professional practice: A framework for teaching* (2nd ed.). Alexandria, VA: ASCD.

Danielson, C. (2010–2011). Evaluations that help teachers learn. *Educational Leadership, 68*(4), 35–39.

Darling-Hammond, L., Amrein-Beardsley, A., Haertel, E., & Rothstein, J. (2012). Evaluating teacher evaluation. *Phi Delta Kappan, 93*(6), 8–15.

Depascale, C. A. (2012). Managing multiple measures. *Principal, 91*(5), 6–12.

Di Carlo, M. (2012). How to use value-added measures right. *Educational Leadership, 70*(3), 38.

Dietel, R. (2011). Testing to the top: Everything but the kitchen sink? *Phi Delta Kappan, 92*(8), 32–36.

Dong, Y. R. (2013–2014). The bridge of knowledge. *Educational Leadership, 71*(4), 30–36.

Doorey, N. (2014). The common core assessments: What you need to know. *Educational Leadership, 71*(6), 57–60.

Eisner, E. W. (1979). *The educational imagination: On the design and evaluation of school programs.* New York, NY: Macmillan.

Esselman, M., Lee-Gwin, R., & Rounds, M. (2012). Rightsizing a school district. *Phi Delta Kappan, 93*(6), 56–61.

Gassenheimer, C. (2013). Best practice for spreading innovation: Let the practitioners do it. *Phi Delta Kappan, 95*(3), 39–43.

Glatthorn, A. A. (1987). *Curriculum leadership*. New York, NY: HarperCollins.

Guba, E., & Lincoln, Y. (1981). *Effective evaluation*. San Francisco, CA: Jossey-Bass.

Halverson, R., Kelley, C., & Shaw, J. (2014). A CALL for improved school leadership. *Phi Delta Kappan, 95*(6), 57–60.

Holland, R. (2001, December). *Indispensable tests: How a value-added approach to school testing could identify and bolster exceptional teaching*. Retrieved from http://www.lexingtoninstitute.org/education/schooltesting.htm

Johnson, D. (2013). Good technology choices: A team effort. *Educational Leadership, 71*(1), 80–82.

Marzano, R. J. (2012). The two purposes of teacher evaluation. *Educational Leadership, 70*(3), 14–19.

Murphy, J., Goldring, E., & Porter, A. (2014). Principal evaluation takes center stage. *Principal, 93*(3), 20–24.

New Leaders for New Schools. (2010). *Evaluating principals: Balancing accountability with professional growth*. Retrieved from http://www.nlns.org/evaluating-principals.jsp

Radoslovich, J., Roberts, S., & Plaza, A. (2014). Charter school innovations: A teacher growth model. *Phi Delta Kappan, 95*(5), 40–46.

Scriven, M. (1972). Pros and cons about goal-free evaluation. *Evaluation Comment, 3*(4), 1–4.

Sioux Falls School District 49-5. (2008, May). *Professional evaluation staff handbook*, 13–15.

Stake, R. E. (Ed.). (1975). *Evaluating the arts in education: A responsive approach*. Columbus, OH: Bobbs-Merrill.

Stufflebeam, D. L. (1971). *Educational evaluation and decision making*. Itasca, IL: Peacock.

Tarte, J. (2014). 10 tips to avoid tech integration frustration. *Principal, 93*(3), 50–51.

Tomlinson, C. A. (2014). The bridge between today's lesson and tomorrow's. *Education al Leadership, 71*(6), 11–14.

Tyler, R. W. (1950). *Basic principles of curriculum and instruction: Syllabus for Education 305*. Chicago: University of Chicago Press.

Walmsley, A. (2014). Unplug the kids. *Phi Delta Kappan, 95*(6), 80.

Whitehead, B. M., Jensen, D. F. N., & Boschee, F. (2013). *Planning for technology: A guide for school administrators, technology coordinators, and curriculum leaders* (2nd ed.). Thousand Oaks, CA: Corwin Press.

Wiggins, G. (2011). Moving to modern assessments. *Phi Delta Kappan, 92*(7), 63.

Williams, J. H., & Engel, L. C. (2012–2013). How do other countries evaluate teachers? *Phi Delta Kappan 94*(4), 53–57.

Worthen, B. R. (1981). Journal entries of an eclectic evaluator. In R. S. Brandt (Ed.), *Applied strategies for curriculum evaluation* (pp. 58–90). Alexandria, VA: ASCD.

PART IV

Current Trends in the Curriculum

To understand the genre of curriculum, a close examination of the trends in the specific subject areas is important. The purpose of Part IV is to examine trends in the subject fields and across the curriculum, as well as to focus on trends linking individualizing the curriculum and needs of special students and global and diversity education.

CHAPTER 13

Current Developments in the Subject Fields

Certainly, many developments and trends in PreK–12 education are altering the landscape for curriculum work in subject areas—but Common Core State Standards (CCSS) are perhaps one of the most pronounced. Although history shows it is often hard to predict which changes will have a substantial impact on schools and which will turn out to be nothing more than fads, it is worthwhile to assess current trends, especially in subject areas, as part of curriculum renewal. This chapter will examine those developments in the subject areas that ordinarily constitute the common curriculum: English language arts (ELA), reading, or writing; social studies; mathematics; science; foreign language; the arts; and physical and health education. In each case, the discussion begins with a review of the recent history of that field—starting with the curricular reform movement of the post-*Sputnik* era—and concludes with a description of current trends and standards.

Questions to be addressed in this chapter include the following:

- What are some of the trends and issues involved in ELA (reading and writing), mathematics, science, foreign language, arts education, and physical education?
- How is technology affecting the delivery and implementation of curriculum in subject areas?

Key to Leadership

Successful curriculum leaders are finding that a multitiered approach involving high-quality classroom instruction combined with targeted, small-group interventions enhances learning.

Just as the CCSS set a high bar for all students across subject matter areas, they also set a high bar for all subject matter teachers (Dong, 2013–2014). Subsequently, one of the best ways to understand general developments in the curriculum is to examine trends as well as individual success in specific subject areas. While certain innovations transcend the discipline, most of the important changes seem to take place and are worked out in the subject areas themselves.

Just as the CCSS set a high bar for all students across subject matter areas, they also set a high bar for all subject matter teachers (Dong, 2013–2014). Subsequently, one of the best ways to understand general developments in the curriculum is to examine trends as well as individual success in specific subject areas. While certain innovations transcend the discipline, most of the important changes seem to take place and are worked out in the subject areas themselves.

DEVELOPMENTS IN ENGLISH LANGUAGE ARTS, READING, AND WRITING

All across the United States, literacy has become a high priority. During this millennium, public attention is being sharply focused on education and particularly on ELA instruction. Policymakers and parents see direct evidence that our country's future depends on the education of its workforce, and they worry that schools are not as effective as they need to be. According to Schmoker (2012), schools can make a profound difference if they increase the amount of purposeful close reading, discussing, and writing that students do in school. To that end, and with the global economy increasingly demanding high levels of literacy from both workers and managers, a series of questions has become part of a national conversation: How can we break the cycle of failure? What will it take to help all children achieve academically? What kinds of changes in curriculum and instruction will increase student achievement? How can schools ensure that every child learns to read and write well?

Looking toward the increasing role of CCSS, the International Reading Association (IRA) revised criteria for developing and evaluating preparation programs for reading professionals in 2010. The *Standards for Reading Professionals* (IRA, 2010) describe what candidates for the reading profession should know and be able to do in professional settings. The standards are performance based, focusing on the knowledge, skills, and dispositions necessary for effective educational practice in a specific role. Also, the standards are the result of a deliberative process that drew from professional expertise and research in the reading field. The six standards are illustrated in Exhibit 13.1.

Curriculum Tip 13.1	Things are not always as they appear. In regards to the subject of reading, an important step for curriculum leaders is to draw valuable lessons from the relationship between current educational research and practice in general.

EXHIBIT 13.1 Progression of Standards Across the Role	
Standard	*Descriptor*
1. Foundational knowledge	*Candidates understand the theoretical and evidence-based foundations of reading and writing processes and instruction.* Individuals who enter the reading profession should understand the historically shared knowledge of the profession and develop the capacity to act on that knowledge responsibly. Elements of the Foundational Knowledge Standard set expectations in the domains of theoretical and practical knowledge, and in developing dispositions for the active, ethical use of professional knowledge.
2. Curriculum and instruction	*Candidates use instructional approaches, materials, and an integrated, comprehensive, balanced curriculum to support student learning in reading and writing.* This standard recognizes the need to prepare educators who have a deep understanding and knowledge of the elements of a balanced, integrated, and comprehensive literacy curriculum and have developed expertise in enacting that curriculum. The elements focus on the use of effective practices in a well-articulated curriculum, using traditional print, digital, and online resources.
3. Assessment and evaluation	*Candidates use a variety of assessment tools and practices to plan and evaluate effective reading and writing instruction.* The assessment and evaluation standard recognizes the need to prepare teachers for using a variety of assessment tools and practices to plan and evaluate effective reading and writing instruction. The elements featured in this standard relate to the systematic monitoring of student performance at individual, classroom, school, and system wide levels. Teacher educators who specialize in literacy play a critical role in preparing teachers for multifaceted assessment responsibilities.
4. Diversity	*Candidates create and engage their students in literacy practices that develop awareness, understanding, respect, and a valuing of differences in our society.* The diversity standard focuses on the need to prepare teachers to build and engage their students in a curriculum that places value on the diversity that exists in our society, as featured in elements such as race, ethnicity, class, gender, religion, and language. This standard is grounded in a set of principles and understandings that reflect a vision for a democratic and just society and inform the effective preparation of reading professionals.
5. Literate environment	*Candidates create a literate environment that fosters reading and writing by integrating foundational knowledge, instructional practices, approaches and methods, curriculum materials, and the appropriate use of assessments.* This standard focuses on the need for candidates to synthesize their foundational knowledge about content, pedagogy, the effective use of physical space, instructional materials and technology, and the impact of the social environment to create an environment that fosters and supports students' traditional print, digital, and online reading and writing achievement. This standard recognizes that candidates must create a literate environment that meets the diverse needs of students and facilitates connections across content areas as well as with the world outside the school.

6. Professional learning and leadership	*Candidates recognize the importance of, demonstrate, and facilitate professional learning and leadership as a career-long effort and responsibility.*
	The standard is based on a commitment by all reading professionals to lifelong learning. Professionals learn in many different ways, for example, individual learning through activities such as reading, pursuing advanced degrees, and attending professional meetings. The elements featured in this standard include an emphasis on positive dispositions, individual and collaborative learning, the ability to design and evaluate professional learning experiences, the importance of advocacy, and a need for knowledge about adult learning and school leadership. Also, learning is often collaborative and occurs in the workplace through grade-level meetings, academic team meetings, workshops, study groups, and so forth.

SOURCE: Adapted from the IRA (2010). Used with permission.

ENGLISH LANGUAGE ARTS

Historically, before the advent of CCSS, four developments in English curricula appear to be significant.

First, developing a widespread interest in the composing process and concomitant attention to diverse types of writing. Motivated primarily by the widely disseminated National Writing Project, the developers of English curriculum guides stress the importance of an inclusive writing process that gives due attention to prewriting and revision, rather than focus solely on the final product and emphasize varied forms of writing for real audiences and purposes.

Second, providing a more comprehensive and diversified view of the students' response to literature. While previous curriculum guides stressed the interpretive and evaluative responses, other approaches encourage students to respond personally and creatively to the work studied. The intent is to help students find personal meaning in literature, not to develop young literary critics.

Third, focusing on the teaching of critical thinking in English. As part of a general nationwide interest in teaching thinking (see Chapter 14), curriculum leaders and experts urge English teachers to see thinking as central to all classroom uses of language.

Fourth, integrating ELA. While such interest can be traced back to *English for Social Living* by Roberts, Kaulfers, and Kefaurer (1943), the emphasis on *Standards for the English Language Arts,* by the IRA and National Council of Teachers of English (NCTE; 1996), resulted in the formation of the measures described earlier to "develop the language skills [students] need to pursue life's goals and to participate fully as informed, productive members of society" (p. 3).

Curriculum Tip 13.2	Students should research and write from a multitude of perspectives and approaches.

EXHIBIT 13.2 Framework for Common Core State Standards Planning and Implementation

1. *An integrated model of literacy.* The ELA—listening, speaking, reading, and writing—should be integrated with each other and across the curriculum. Students are asked to read and/or listen to texts read aloud and respond critically through discussion and writing. Response may take the form of written or oral explanation and argument. Emphasis is placed on critical thinking, problem solving, and collaboration with peers.

2. *A cumulative model of expectations.* Instruction should address grade-specific standards in tandem with the broader goals of college and career readiness. Sometimes referred to as spiraling, similar standards are expressed with increasing complexity from grade to grade, providing an ongoing and cumulative progression of mastery that is refined and applied at increasingly higher levels for various purposes and in a variety of contexts.

3. *Shared responsibility for students' literacy development.* Teachers in self-contained classrooms are generally responsible for the integration of curriculum. However, grade-level planning among groups of teachers can facilitate the process. In departmental settings, content area teachers and ELA or literacy teachers need to plan and work together, thus providing a more coherent program to support students' ability to apply what they learn about language and literacy to actual content under study.

4. *Research and media skills blended into the standards as a whole.* Critical thinking with texts in all forms of media and technology is emphasized. Texts may be oral or written and make sure of a variety of types of media and graphics. Forms may be combined for a specific goal or purpose. An equal balance of literary and information texts is desirable.

5. *Greater use of on-grade-level texts.* Emphasis is placed on helping students become proficient in reading complex texts independently and in a variety of content areas. Models of instruction should include complex texts for reading aloud to students, for closely guided or interactive instruction to build background knowledge, vocabulary, and concepts; and to model how good readers approach difficult texts. Texts representing a range of complexity should also be available for independent reading and response.

In that CCSS plays such a large role in education today, an ELA literacy checklist is provided to assist readers (International Center for Leadership in Education, 2012).

Trends in English Language Arts

One of the major trends in ELA is the implementation of CCSS. Exhibit 13.2 provides a curriculum framework as noted by Strickland (2012) for the planning and implementation of CCSS.

English Language Arts Common Core State Standards Literacy Checklist

Literacy Checklist	Exceeding	Meeting	Developing	Beginning	Absent
1. Literacy is an important priority throughout the school.					
2. There are clear, measurable goals for levels of student reading.					

3. A standard measure of reading, such as Lexile, is used to describe aspects of reading achievement.					
4. Literacy development is addressed in all disciplines.					
5. Student literacy levels are measured continuously, and the data are compared to literacy achievement goals of the school.					
6. Teachers have convenient access to data about student reading levels.					
7. Professional development opportunities are available to support an interdisciplinary approach to literacy.					
8. Teachers select rigorous and relevant instructional materials to appropriately challenge students.					
9. Teachers use effective instructional strategies pertaining to vocabulary to improve reading in their content areas.					
10. Teachers know the reading level requirements for postsecondary opportunities, including college, employment, and personal use.					
11. Instructional coaches are available to assist teachers in improving strategies related to reading.					
12. Teachers personalize instruction to accommodate different levels of reading in the classroom.					
13. The school media center/library is aligned with reading-level information and is an integral part of the literacy program.					
14. Students are expected to engage in complex texts across all disciplines.					
15. State assessments in all subjects have been analyzed based on student reading levels.					
16. Teachers break tradition by emphasizing informational texts and literary non-fiction.					
17. Teachers emphasize analytical writing, quarterly research, and the expectation that students analyze texts, cite textual evidence, and be able to cite sources.					
18. Teachers provide opportunities for students to develop comprehension and collaboration through speaking and listening.					
19. Teachers require students to present to a variety of audiences utilizing digital media, visual and quantitative data.					
20. Students are expected to be able to answer a range of text-dependent questions based only on the text presented.					

SOURCE: International Center for Leadership in Education (2012).

For the most part, standards (whether individual state standards or CCSS) can provide clarity about what students are expected to learn in ELA; they help teachers zero in on the most important knowledge and skills; they establish shared goals among students, parents, and teachers; they help states and districts assess the effectiveness of schools and classrooms; and they give all students an equal opportunity for high achievement. In reality, the impetus to hold students, teachers, schools, and districts accountable for results is gaining momentum daily.

Critical Literacy

From a historical perspective, critical literacy is rooted in the work of Paulo Freire (1921– 1997), the Brazilian educationalist, who left a significant mark on thinking about progressive practice (McDaniel, 2004). Critical literacy has developed into a way to encourage English teachers and their students to adopt a questioning stance and to work toward changing themselves and their worlds. That said, the approach goes beyond **critical thinking skills** by promoting a certain version of reality for both teacher and student.

Despite a greater focus on informational text, there continues to be a strong trend toward the implementation of critical literacy in classrooms today. With some certainty, ELA teachers continue to look for ways to incorporate critical literacy as well as capture children's imaginations in and out of the classroom.

REALITIES IN READING

Cummins (2013) shared that as we pursue helping students meet the CCSS, there will be a lot of push in the field to engage students at various levels. Although reading in the strictest sense is one of the ELA (usually construed to cover reading, writing, speaking, and listening), it has so much importance, especially in the early grades, that it is given separate consideration as a curriculum field. Gathering and collecting student data continues to generate much interest among educators. Having more information helps reading teachers focus on what techniques and strategies are successful and which are not. As part of this process, a statistical procedure called meta-analysis synthesizes data from a number of studies as to "what works" in classrooms. Evidence from many successful schools and from multiple research studies seems to show that a *multitiered approach* involving high-quality classroom instruction in combination with targeted, small-group interventions can substantially reduce the proportion of students who struggle to read (Lyon, Fletcher, Torgesen, Shaywitz, & Chhabra, 2004). For the most part, teachers using this approach are better able to obtain additional information as they develop blended learning environments. Knowing what works encourages students to become part owners of what they read and begin charting their own path (Patterson, 2012).

Curriculum Tip 13.3	Regardless of expert tutoring or the use of small-group instruction, most reading researchers seem to agree that a strong exposure of teachers to a variety of approaches and different types of instruction is highly beneficial.

Trends in Reading

The 21st-century challenge in education will be to assess curricular and technology credibility in a systematic and sustained way (Abilock, 2012). With this in mind, the art of planning and building successful technology programs to enhance reading will continue to involve a number of important factors and target areas. The following target areas provide a brief overview of individual elements needed for a successful technology outline. In most cases, these target areas provide concise categories as a guideline for school leaders and technology coordinators.

In any technology initiative, the needs of reading students can be placed above any other factor being considered. The present interest in mobile technology and mobile learning, or *m-learning,* often derives support from viewpoints that take into account the importance of student needs. Teaching and learning are two distinctly complex and yet complementary entities. Therefore, they must be considered simultaneously when deciding how technology will be brought into the classroom or the school (Whitehead, Boschee, & Decker, 2013). When considering what effects technology has on the teaching and learning as it relates to reading, the following should be addressed:

- Carefully consider how new technology applications will affect teaching and learning in the area of reading. Make sure to have a purpose that reflects teaching and learning when bringing technologies into the school and into classrooms.
- Determine how new technology used in reading will coexist with other technologies used throughout the school district.
- Explore and manage bandwidth issues.
- Evaluate applications and purchases as well as coordinate them to student needs.
- Consider features like durability, maintenance, access, and speed.
- Evaluate projected purchases to determine which programs and applications will best complement, support, and expand the teaching of reading.
- Evaluate planned purchases for user friendliness. Use is important because ease of use reduces the learning curve and helps ensure that the program will be used.
- Determine the simplest approach that will effectively integrate technology into the teaching and learning of reading. Making technology transparent allows stakeholders to support the process more readily.
- Establish dialogues with teachers to evaluate classroom space as it relates to new technology.
- Determine the amount of use teachers will make of the new technology.

For more information on the reading research community, browse through a few of the following Internet sites:

- *The IRA (International Reading Association).* This is a professional membership organization with members and affiliates in 99 countries. The organization's mission is to promote high levels of literacy by improving the quality of reading instruction, disseminating research and information about reading, and encouraging the lifetime reading habit. At the IRA Web site (www.reading.org), you can find sample archives of selected articles from *The Reading Teacher, Journal of Adolescent & Adult Literacy,* and *Reading Research Quarterly,* as well as the IRA peer-reviewed online journal *Reading Online.*
- *Education Commission of the States.* The "Reading/Literacy" section of this site (www.ecs.org) includes links to Common Strategies to Improve Student Reading,

A Consumer's Guide to Evaluating a Core Reading Program Grades K–3, and Preventing Reading Difficulties in Young Children.
- *Council for Learning Disabilities*. This organization's Web site (www .cldinternational.org) contains a collection of Infosheets designed to support the translation of research into practice.

Recommendations for Curriculum Leaders

Reading is one of the most important learning processes around the world. Teachers globally face a continual challenge as to the difficult task of improving student reading skills. Although phonics, word reading, and reading fluency are building blocks of literacy, reading comprehension is the ultimate goal for most readers. It is for this reason that schools worldwide need to support all students by explicitly teaching the active comprehension processes that skilled readers use. According to Van Keer and Vanderlinde (2013), reviews of research affirm that monitoring and regulating skills, as well as applying relevant reading strategies, helps improve comprehension. More specifically, research underscores that the best way to ensure improved literacy among students is to directly and explicitly teach comprehension strategies. To narrow the gap between reading research and the reality of instruction, teachers of reading need two primary as well as complementary cornerstones:

- Explicit instruction in reading strategies
- The act of creating opportunities to engage in meaningful peer interaction and collaboration

Of similar importance to these cornerstones is the role of the school library in improving reading comprehension scores. More evidence is revealing that a well-stocked and well-staffed library plays a key role in student achievement. This is largely due to school libraries offering students resources for both conducting research and reading for fun. Well-stocked school libraries can, therefore, do much to help nonproficient readers.

For the most part, predominant reading styles of nonproficient readers are visual, tactile, and kinesthetic. It is, therefore, important for school administrators and curriculum leaders to provide as many intervention strategies as possible. Whether it is through a focus on reading throughout the curriculum, small-group instruction, expert tutoring, a multitiered approach, professional development, or just an awareness of the problem, leaders need to address the issue of improving reading as well as writing.

Curriculum Tip 13.4	Successful curriculum leaders realize that the writing process is itself made up of a number of processes. As an act of making meaning, it assumes recursive movement through five major processes: prewriting, drafting, revising, editing, and publishing.

EXPANDING A CULTURE OF WRITING

With the advent of CCSS, there is a greater focus on engaging students in analyzing complex and informational texts (Ehrenworth, 2013). This new emphasis on ELA and writing standards reflects an effort to improve schools across the country. It should be noted, however, that from a historical perspective—regardless of the new standards—writing has always been at the forefront of school improvement. The MIT Online Writing and Communication Center (1999) noted the following:

> Writing is critical to the educational process—it is a process that involves at least five distinct steps: prewriting, drafting, revising, editing, and publishing. It is known as a recursive process. While you are revising, you might have to return to a prewriting step to develop and expand your ideas.

Exhibit 13.3 provides descriptors for each step to be used in writing and in teaching the writing process.

It is important then to realize that writing is an increasingly complex and yet multifaceted activity. The multifaceted aspect of writing is further demonstrated in Exhibit 13.4. IRA/NCTE offer several principles that should guide effective teaching practice.

EXHIBIT 13.3 The Writing Process	
Steps	*Descriptors*
Prewriting	Prewriting is anything you do before you write a draft of your document. It includes thinking, taking notes, talking to others, brainstorming, outlining, and gathering information (e.g., interviewing people, researching in the library, assessing data). Although prewriting is the first activity you engage in, generating ideas is an activity that occurs throughout the writing process.
Drafting	Drafting occurs when you put your ideas into sentences and paragraphs. Here, you concentrate on explaining and supporting your ideas fully. You also begin to connect your ideas. Regardless of how much thinking and planning you do, the process of putting your ideas in words changes them; often, the very words you select evoke additional ideas or implications. Don't pay attention to such things as spelling at this stage. This draft tends to be writer-centered: It is you telling yourself what you know and think about the topic.
Revising	Revision is the key to effective documents. Here, you think more deeply about your readers' needs and expectations. The document becomes reader-centered. How much support will each idea need to convince your readers? Which terms should be defined for these particular readers? Is your organization effective? Do readers need to know X before they can understand Y? At this stage, you also refine your prose, making each sentence as concise and accurate as possible. Make connections between ideas explicit and clear.
Editing	Check for such things as grammar, mechanics, and spelling. The last thing you should do before printing your document is to spell-check it. Don't edit your writing until the other steps in the writing process are complete.
Publishing	The writer shares what has been written with the intended audience. [This step was added by the authors.]

SOURCE: Adapted from MIT Online Writing and Communication Center (1999).

Writing to Learn

As is the case with many other things people do, getting better at writing requires doing it—a lot. This means actual writing, not merely listening to lectures about writing, doing grammar drills, or discussing readings. The more people write, the easier it gets and the more they are motivated to do it. (NCTE, 2004)

To help forge a more vibrant system, **writing to learn** can be greatly enhanced through collaboration and sharing. It is a discovery activity in which the text emerges as the student writes (Thompson, 2011). As part of individual state standards and CCSS, teachers are expanding the writing process, making sure students are exposed to informational text.

EXHIBIT 13.4 National Council of Teachers of English/International Reading Association Language Arts Standards (Revised 2012)

1. Students read a wide range of print and nonprint texts to build an understanding of texts, of themselves, and of the cultures of the United States and the world; to acquire new information; to respond to the needs and demands of society and the workplace; and for personal fulfillment. Among these texts are fiction and nonfiction, classic and contemporary works.
2. Students read a wide range of literature from many periods in many genres to build an understanding of the many dimensions (e.g., philosophical, ethical, aesthetic) of human experience.
3. Students apply a wide range of strategies to comprehend, interpret, evaluate, and appreciate texts. They draw on their prior experience, their interactions with other readers and writers, their knowledge of word meaning and of other texts, their word identification strategies, and their understanding of textual features (e.g., sound–letter correspondence, sentence structure, context, graphics).
4. Students adjust their use of spoken, written, and visual language (e.g., conventions, style, vocabulary) to communicate effectively with a variety of audiences and for different purposes.
5. Students employ a wide range of strategies as they write and use different writing process elements appropriately to communicate with different audiences for a variety of purposes.
6. Students apply knowledge of language structure, language conventions (e.g., spelling and punctuation), media techniques, figurative language, and genre to create, critique, and discuss print and nonprint texts.
7. Students conduct research on issues and interests by generating ideas and questions and by posing problems. They gather, evaluate, and synthesize data from a variety of sources (e.g., print and nonprint texts, artifacts, people) to communicate their discoveries in ways that suit their purpose and audience.
8. Students use a variety of technological and information resources (e.g., libraries, databases, computer networks, video) to gather and synthesize information and to create and communicate knowledge.
9. Students develop an understanding of and respect for diversity in language use, patterns, and dialects across cultures, ethnic groups, geographic regions, and social roles.
10. Students whose first language is not English make use of their first language to develop competency in the ELA and to develop understanding of content across the curriculum.
11. Students participate as knowledgeable, reflective, creative, and critical members of a variety of literacy communities.
12. Students use spoken, written, and visual language to accomplish their own purposes (e.g., for learning, enjoyment, persuasion, and the exchange of information).

With this in mind, Johnston (2012) offered the following five principles of writing.

1. *Context matters.* Context affects feedback. When students are fully engaged, teachers can provide ample differentiated feedback only when necessary. This is largely because students who are working on something personally and socially meaningful know when they need assistance.

2. *Teachers are not the sole source of feedback.* In writing, feedback or assistance can come from other students as well as the teacher. Part of students' ELA development should involve learning how to give feedback to others—how to respond to other learners. As part of growth in writing, classroom talk becomes reflective.

3. *Focus on a writing process that empowers students.* Responsive classroom writing communities use three key practices.

    - Listening
    - Noticing significant decisions that authors make
    - Causal process feedback (feedback on student choices that affect final product)

4. *Be positive without praise.* Positive feedback about individual writing motivates students and gives them the tools to improve. Rather than simple praise, teachers might frame positive comments into questions such as "How did you do that?" or "How does it feel to have completed your first poem?" These types of comments go a long way in creating independent driven writers.

5. *Shift focus on how students see themselves.* For young writers, feedback sets in motion conversations that affect how a student might make sense of themselves. Using nonjudgmental comments focusing more on the process of writing, rather than the writer, have a greater chance of success. For example, a teacher might say, "You found a way to solve the problem. Are there any other ways you can think of to solve it?"

Johnston's principles share an innovative perspective to writing. Likewise, these principles are very much in line with CCSS.

Trends in Writing Across the Curriculum

According to Shanahan (2013), current "writing standards define informational/explanatory writing as text that conveys information accurately to increase readers' knowledge of subject, to help readers better understand a procedure or process, or to provide readers with an enhanced comprehension of a concept" (National Governors Association [NGA] Center for Best Practices & Council of Chief State School Officers [CCSSO], 2010, p. 23). Subsequently, CCSS recommends a shift from an emphasis on personal writing to one on academic writing. Along with this shift, CCSS is relying on two consortia to assist with implementation. They include the Partnership for Assessment of Readiness for College and Careers (PARCC) and the Smarter Balanced Assessment Consortium (SBAC).

- PARCC indicates that informational texts and literary nonfiction should include subgenres of exposition, argument, and functional text in the form of personal essays; speeches; opinion pieces; essays about art or literature; biographies; memoirs; journalism; and historical scientific, technical, or economic accounts (including digital sources) written for a broad audience.

- Similarly, the SBAC states the following:

  ○ Grades 3–5 categories include biographies and autobiographies; books about history, social studies, science, and the arts; technical texts, including directions, forms, and information displayed in graphs, charts, or maps; and digital sources on a range of topics.

  ○ Grades 6–12 categories include subgenres of exposition, argument, and functional text in the form of personal essays; speeches; opinion pieces; essays about art or literature; biographies; memoirs; journalism; and historical, scientific, technical, or economic accounts (including digital sources written) for a broad audience (Shanahan, 2013, p. 12).

These changes in writing standards (**writing across the curriculum**) move students to embrace a vision of what is possible, formulate strategic options for getting there, build the necessary knowledge, and develop the persistence needed to be a successful writer. Much in the same way, Johnston (2012), shared a process that encourages teachers to involve their students in meaningful writing projects. So, in the end, new standards are designed to give students an opportunity to practice imagining themselves as authors, write independently, and become more successful (Thompson, 2011).

DUAL IMMERSION PROGRAMS IN ENGLISH LANGUAGE ARTS

Dual immersion programs are an important part of any ELA curriculum. Subsequently, effective dual immersion programs need administrators, teachers, parents, and students who consider bilingualism a positive attribute rather than a linguistic, cognitive, and academic liability. According to Soderman (2010), providing second language experiences and knowledge about other cultures is paramount to any country's ability to remain competitive and is critical to economic success, national security, and international relations. Research reveals several cognitive advantages to having early exposure to a second language. They include the following:

- *Children are driven to higher levels of cognitive flexibility than are unilingual children in educational settings.* Learning a new language is greater than simply acquiring a vocabulary and workable syntax. It is a problem-solving, "knowledge-assembly" task in which children are required to pay greater attention to the context, interact flexibly with others, and decide over and over what is relevant and what is not.
- *Children become more aware of the meta-linguistic structures of language.* As dual language learners become more adept at both languages, they increase their abilities to reflect on the unique structures and features of each language and to manipulate them verbally and in their writing.
- *Young language learners are more likely to develop naturalistic prosody and phonology, the music and rhythms unique to particular languages.* Human beings

gradually lose the capacity to "hear" certain sounds in languages they do not experience at a younger age.

- *Young children are fully able to handle bilingualism without becoming developmentally delayed in language or become "language confused."* Children usually acquire language on the same developmental schedule in each language.

As can be seen, dual immersion programs are becoming an important part of an expanding global awareness and the transforming of education worldwide. To that end, each child needs the ability to think and express themselves in more than one language. This enhances an understanding of others and provides the confidence needed to move fluidly from one culture to another. To speak more than one language fluently—better yet, to be able to read and write fluently in more than one language—provides children with a key to the future.

HISTORY–SOCIAL STUDIES

School districts across the United States continue to work in establishing new and improved academic standards in the area of history–social studies. This involves developing new frameworks, standards, and assessments for history–social studies content and skills that all students should learn. These new frameworks will provide guidance for educators to implement standards and assessments that will generate information about student achievement and solidify integrity and accountability throughout the educational system (Fogo, 2011).

Several studies of the past status of the field suggested a somewhat discouraging picture at the time of the present work (the following synthesis is drawn from Ponder, 1979; Shaver, Davis, & Helburn, 1979; Superka, Hawke, & Morrissett, 1980). First, the discipline-centered projects of the post-*Sputnik* era do not seem to have made a lasting impact; even generous estimates suggest that they were being used in only 20% of the nation's school districts. Second, despite a widely held belief that there was little uniformity in the social studies, a standard organizational pattern had firmly taken hold. Exhibit 13.5 shows the sequence of what Superka and colleagues (1980) called "a virtual nationwide curriculum held rather firmly in place by state laws, district requirements, textbook offerings, and tradition" (p. 365).

Despite improvements in texts, the taught curriculum had changed very little. The whole class lecture–recitation method dominated, and students were tested primarily on their ability to remember and reproduce information. Experience-based curricula and inquiry learning were rare. Teachers were the final arbiters of the curriculum actually delivered, and those teachers tended to support a somewhat traditional view of the field. Today, with the new social studies standards and differentiated teaching utilized in the classroom, the social studies curriculum should be exhilarating.

Revised National Curriculum Standards for Social Studies

The nation's foremost social studies organization released its revised national standards, *National Curriculum Standards for Social Studies: A Framework for Teaching, Learning, and*

EXHIBIT 13.5 Dominant Organizational Patterns for Social Studies

K—Self, school, community, home

1—Families

2—Neighborhoods

3—Communities

4—State history, geographic regions

5—American history

6—World cultures, Western Hemisphere

7—World geography or history

8—American history

9—Civics or world cultures

10—World history

11—American history

12—American government

Assessment, on September 17, 2010, Constitution Day. The revised curriculum standards are centered on the following 10 themes:

1. *Culture.* Social studies programs should include experiences that provide for the study of culture and cultural diversity.

2. *Time, continuity, and change.* Social studies programs should include experiences that provide for the study of the past and its legacy.

3. *People, places, and environment.* Social studies programs should include experiences that provide for the study of people, places, and environments.

4. *Individual development and identity.* Social studies programs should include experiences that provide for the study of individual development and identity.

5. *Individual groups and institutions.* Social studies programs should include experiences that provide for the study of interactions among individuals, groups, and institutions.

6. *Power, authority, and governance.* Social studies programs should include experiences that provide for the study of how people create; interact with; and change structures of power, authority, and governance.

7. *Production, distribution, and consumption.* Social studies programs should include experiences that provide for the study of how people organize for the production, distribution, and consumption of goods and services.

8. *Science, technology, and society.* Social studies programs should include experiences that provide for the study of relationships among science, technology, and society.

9. *Global connections.* Social studies programs should include experiences that provide for the study of global connections and interdependence.

10. *Civic ideals and practices.* Social studies programs should include experiences that provide for the study of the ideals, principles, and practices of citizenship in a democratic republic. (National Council for the Social Studies, 2010)

According to Steve Goldberg, president of the National Council for the Social Studies and social studies department chair at New Rochelle High School, New York, "This is one of the best frameworks for preparing your students to be college, career and citizenship ready" (National Council for the Social Studies, 2010).

Trends in History–Social Studies

To prepare students for history–social studies assessments tied to CCSS, teachers need tools and tests that help students analyze primary and secondary sources and develop written historical arguments. According to Breakstone, Smith, and Wineburg (2013), a mini-industry of how-to guides, curriculum maps, and professional development workshops has sprouted up over the years. In history–social studies courses, students are expected to analyze primary and secondary sources, cite textual evidence to support arguments, consider the influence of an author's perspective, corroborate different sources, and develop written historical arguments—crucial skills if students are to succeed in college and beyond.

With the advent of CCSS, schools, textbook publishers, and software companies are attempting to "integrate" history–social studies into the teaching of reading as well. As a result, new trends in this area appear to be focusing on a technique that engages students at multiple levels. This new focus is bringing a broadening scope to the teaching and learning of both history and social studies. For example, clustering, brainstorming, mind maps, and other types of graphic organizers are being used throughout classes today. New perspectives are causing history and social studies teachers to rethink their approach to teaching. Classroom teachers are now finding that achieving a high standard in the learning of history can go well beyond the basics. Students are no longer just focusing on "learned facts" but are learning how to think in a different and deeper way.

As part of demystifying history–social studies instruction, there is now renewed interest in not just giving dates, places, and names but giving students opportunities to question, investigate, and make personal connections to the lives of people they are studying. Moreover, students are now using historical thinking skills to examine rich content. "Inspired history" is allowing students to make a connection to the past as well as to open ideas and thinking about how to address the future.

Curriculum Tip 13.5	History and social studies need to come alive for students. Finding ways to engage students appears to be the key to successful curriculum planning.

From a historical perspective, Alan Stoskopf (2001) advocated early on a set of historical thinking skills that helps students learn about history. These skills include point of view, credibility of evidence, historical context, causality, and multiple perspectives.

- *Point of view.* Relates to how an author's personal background and status influences what is written. How is the point of view of the author being interpreted?
- *Credibility of evidence.* Is the source reliable? Where did it originate, and for what purpose was it used at the time?
- *Historical context.* How does one see the past on its own terms? Are current values obscuring what really happened?
- *Causality.* How does one avoid seeing past events as caused by one factor? Complex history should not be reduced to a single driving force.
- *Multiple perspectives.* How does one weigh different interpretations of the same event? There is a need to search for the ideas and opinions of different historical individuals to gain a more sophisticated understanding of the past.

Building understanding is becoming a major factor in revolutionizing how history and social studies is taught. To be sure, the skills noted by Stoskopf are still being integrated into history and social studies units today. Likewise, the role of technology is becoming hugely important in this field as well. For example, **Worker Education and Training Program (WETP)** advocates are using geographical, mapping, and history-based software applications, as well as age-appropriate simulations with elementary students. This allows these students to expand their understanding of the world beyond themselves and their families. Simulations offer students the opportunity to participate in historical events or major decision-making events by virtue of role playing. Whether studying the 50 states or debating the pros and cons of declaring U.S. independence from England, students can find a wealth of excellent technology-based applications to make exploring social studies themes exciting (North Central Educational Regional Laboratory, n.d.).

As part of transforming history–social studies instruction, more teachers and students are using WebQuest (2014). A WebQuest is an inquiry-oriented activity in which most or all of the information used by learners is drawn from the Web. WebQuest allows students to use selected Internet resources to find specific information about their topics. Resources are previously organized into subject-based Web sites by either a student or a teacher. These new ways of addressing history and social studies are forcing teachers to rethink how they should teach. They are forcing a rethinking of dominant assumptions of how history is written and how it is taught. Likewise, in keeping with the mission of change, pedagogy is broadening and expanding history and social studies to include narratives relating to such fields as social, economic, and cultural histories.

MATHEMATICS

Shumway and Kyriopoulos (2013–2014) noted how CCSS is bringing attention to how students are understanding mathematics content. Such understanding is difficult to assess through a typical paper-and-pencil assessment or standardized test because students can follow procedures to obtain the correct answer without understanding the number relationships behind the procedure. With this mind, getting the right answer in math class is not enough if students do not know why the answer is the right one. Moreover, to assess mastery of practice standards, classroom teachers need to explore how students are arriving at their solutions.

EXHIBIT 13.6	Curriculum Trends in Mathematics
Year	*Emphasis*
1944: Post–World War II Plan	The National Council of Teachers of Mathematics (NCTM) created a postwar plan to help World War II have a lasting effect on math education. Grades 1 through 6 were considered crucial years to build the foundations of math concepts, with the main focus on algebra. In the war years, algebra had one understood purpose—to help the military and industries with the war effort.
1989: Curriculum and Evaluation Standards for School Mathematics	The controversial 1989 NCTM Standards called for more emphasis on conceptual understanding and problem solving informed by a constructivist understanding of how children learn. The increased emphasis on concepts required decreased emphasis on direct instruction of facts and algorithms. This decrease of traditional rote learning was sometimes understood by both critics and proponents of the standards to mean elimination of basic skills and precise answers, but the NCTM has refuted this interpretation.
2000: Principles and Standards for School Mathematics	The controversy surrounding the 1989 standards paved the way for revised standards that sought more clarity and balance. The new standards were organized around six principles (equity, curriculum, teaching, learning, assessment, and technology) and 10 strands that included five content areas (number and operations, algebra, geometry, measurement, and data analysis and probability) and five processes (problem solving, reasoning and proof, communication, connections, and representation).
2006: Curriculum Focal Points	In the Curriculum Focal Points, NCTM identified what it believed to be the most important mathematical topics for each grade level, including the related ideas, concepts, skills, and procedures that form the foundation for understanding and lasting learning. In the focal points, NCTM made it clear that the standard algorithms were to be included in arithmetic instruction.
2010: Common Core State Standards (CCSS)	The Council of Chief State School Officers (CCSSO) and the National Governors Association (NGA) Center for Best Practices collaborated to establish consistent and clear education standards for mathematics, known as the CCSS, which would better prepare students for success in college, career, and the competitive global economy. The CCSS, adopted by a number of states, support the fundamental principle that every school-age child shall have an opportunity to develop the knowledge base and analytic skills needed to excel in a career or in a postsecondary academic setting. The standards also seek to make certain that what children learn is not based solely on where they might live. However, several states have balked at adopting the CCSS if they are made mandatory. Some state officials say they want assurances the so-called national standards will not dilute existing state frameworks.

SOURCE: Excerpts were adapted from Klein (2003) and Common Core State Standards Initiative (2010).

Trends in Mathematics

If trends in the subject areas are strongly influenced by the widely disseminated pronouncements of professional associations, then, as shown in Exhibit 13.6, trends in mathematics are relatively easy to identify.

For the most part, CCSS in mathematics were built on progressions: narrative documents describing the progression of a topic across a number of grade levels informed both by research on children's cognitive development and by the logical structure of mathematics. These documents were spliced together and then sliced into grade-level standards.

Regardless of any changes to standards, teachers across the country are pushing their students to think like mathematicians—to justify their ideas, communicate with peers, and construct arguments. According to Schifter and Granofsky (2012), these are the necessary steps for students to take as they develop enduring understandings about mathematics. Equally important is for teachers to know it is the interplay of the Standards for Mathematical Practice and the content standards that make CCSS a more robust set of guidelines. Additionally, it is important for teachers to promote the eight Standards for Mathematical Practice that identify mathematical "habits of mind" that educators should seek to develop at all levels. These practices—such as constructing viable arguments, critiquing the reasoning of others, and communicating with precision—often take years to develop but are essential for success in mathematics.

Schifter and Granofsky (2012) also emphasized the importance of choosing tried and true ways of teaching and learning mathematics. For example, there are many strong CCSS-aligned curricula available for elementary, middle, and high school adoptions. Additionally, schools must prioritize teacher professional development into two main areas:

- First, teachers will need to understand both the mathematical content and the conceptual challenges that students deal with when they encounter that content.
- Second, teachers require support with the Standards for Mathematical Practice—both in thinking about how to teach with them and in learning how to identify evidence of these practices in student work.

It is in this milieu of reform that teachers and principals need to know how state standards or CCSS can best be accomplished. For example, educators must be attentive to the nuances and complexity of the English language even when teaching math (Barrow, 2014). In addition, there should be an extension of mathematical understanding, practice, and peer collaboration that needs to happen first. But, with that said, when it comes to teaching mathematics, teachers need time and space to teach. If courses are already aligned to standards, then teachers will be better able to put their energy into other important issues—such as preparing lessons, analyzing their students' work, and collaborating with colleagues.

Curriculum Tip 13.6	Mathematics teachers are now asking these questions: What do my students understand? How do I know they understand?

Most assuredly, teachers are changing the way they teach mathematics. Along with CCSS, the National Council of Teachers of Mathematics (NCTM) continues to emphasize the important role of communication in helping children construct understanding of mathematical concepts and develop connections between their informal knowledge and the abstract symbolism of mathematical concepts. One of the trends in mathematics is the move toward a vertical approach to math instruction. Regardless of whether schools are using CCSS or individual state standards, vertical mathematics teams offer an opportunity for teachers to grow professionally, for leadership to grow among the faculty, and for schools to change their perspective of teaching and learning of mathematics.

Key Strategies

The following are strategies that contribute to successful vertical mathematics teams as provided by Gojak (2012):

- *Vertical team should span three to four grade levels.* Spanning grade levels provides teachers the opportunity to look at the students' mathematics experiences by examining how topics develop from one grade to the next. Other mathematics intervention specialists or Response to Intervention (RTI) teachers should be included in this process. Grade-level groups can be organized to share knowledge from team meetings.
- *Development of mathematics across grades needs to involve more than just building skills.* For example, teams should expand their knowledge from being solely skill oriented to creating a foundation of conceptual understanding of key mathematics topics. This leads to a deeper understanding of mathematical concepts and supports the development of mathematical skills.
- *Providing time to be a team.* To function effectively, teams of teachers need time to meet and work during the school day. Meeting times can be arranged through a combination of early-release days and in-school activities monitored by faculty who are not involved in mathematics instruction.
- *Develop a mathematics focus.* As part of a collaborative effort, teams can determine other topics to explore for the school year. Leadership can then plan an agenda for each vertical team to meet as well as find materials to support the work of the teachers.
- *Work from expectations to opportunities—then to implementation.* When examining state standards, teams can determine expectations for a topic across multiple grades and levels. This includes looking at grade levels before and after the span of the vertical team to determine where students are coming from and where they are going with that topic.

As part of the process, an analysis can be made of both conceptual understandings and associated skills that are part of student expectations. This is an opportunity for collective teams as well as leadership to better understand the entire vertical progression of the topic, including concepts and skills, connections between grade levels, and each teacher's role in supporting student growth. Although vertical math teams represent only one example of trends in mathematics, it is nevertheless a powerful strategy. While the work of vertical teams can follow different structures, what is important is that it provides school leaders and teachers with professional learning opportunities to build a cohesive mathematics program across grade levels and across the district.

The Equity Principle

Excellence in mathematics requires an **equity principle**—high expectations and strong support for all students.

All students, regardless of their personal characteristics, backgrounds, or physical challenges, must have an opportunity to study and learn mathematics. This does not mean that every student should be treated the same, but all students need access each year they are in school to a coherent, challenging mathematics curriculum taught by competent and well-supported mathematics teachers.

Far too many students—especially students who are poor, not native speakers of English, disabled, female, or members of minority groups—are victims of low expectations in mathematics. For example, tracking has consistently consigned disadvantaged groups of students to mathematics classes that concentrate on remediation or do not offer significant mathematical substance. The equity principle demands that high expectations for mathematics learning be communicated in words and deeds to all students.

Some students may need more than an ambitious curriculum and excellent teaching to meet high expectations. Students who are having difficulty may benefit from such resources as after-school programs, peer mentoring, or cross-age tutoring. Students with special learning needs in mathematics should be supported by both their classroom teachers and special education staff. Keeping with this mission, an excellent resource for understanding mathematical standards can be found at http://standards.nctm.org (NCTM, 2004).

SCIENCE

Producing students who think, write, and speak like scientists and mathematicians is a key to making schools successful in our global world (Fisher & Blachowicz, 2013). Unfortunately, the recent history of science curricula provides a paradigmatic example of federal influence in curricular matters and therefore deserves a close examination. Along with more states moving toward CCSS, a national report by the National Research Council developed standards that help serve as a foundation for what is taught in elementary school through high school, replacing decade-old standards. Physicist Helen Quinn said the following:

> Science education in the U.S. lacks a common vision of what students should know and be able to do by the end of high school; curricula too often emphasize breadth over depth, and students are rarely given the opportunity to experience how science is actually done. (National Academies, 2011b)

The framework for science, as shown in Exhibit 13.7, consists of a limited number of elements in three dimensions: (1) scientific and engineering practices, (2) crosscutting concepts, and (3) disciplinary core ideas in science (National Research Council, 2011). According to the National Academies (2011a), the *Framework for K–12 Science Education* (National Research Council, 2011) is intended as a guide for those who develop science education standards, those who design curricula and assessments, and others who work in K–12 science education. Also, the "three dimensions within the framework should not be taught separately from one another. Rather, they should be integrated in standards, assessment, curricula, and instruction" (National Academies, 2011a).

From a historical perspective, studies by Piaget and others since the 1970s have led to the constructivist philosophy, which focuses on the framework that students carry into learning situations. Constructivism says that learners bring their personal experiences into the classroom, and these experiences have a tremendous impact on their views of how the world works. Students come to learning situations with a variety of knowledge, feelings, and skills, and this is where learning should begin. This knowledge exists within the student and is developed as individuals interact with their peers, teachers, and the environment. Learners construct understanding or meaning by making sense of their experiences and fitting their own ideas into

---

EXHIBIT 13.7 Framework for K–12 Science Standards

Dimension 1: Scientific and Engineering Practices

1. Asking questions (for science) and defining problems (for engineering)
2. Developing and using models
3. Planning and carrying out investigations
4. Analyzing and interpreting data
5. Using mathematics and computational thinking
6. Constructing explanations (for science) and designing solutions (for engineering)
7. Engaging in argument from evidence
8. Obtaining, evaluating, and communicating information

Dimension 2: Crosscutting Concepts That Have Common Application Across Fields

1. Patterns
2. Cause and effect: mechanism and explanation
3. Scale, proportion, and quantity
4. Systems and system models
5. Energy and matter: flows, cycles, and conservation
6. Structure and function
7. Stability and change

Dimension 3: Core Ideas in Four Disciplinary Areas
Physical Sciences

PS 1. Matter and its interactions
PS 2. Motion and stability: Forces and interactions
PS 3. Energy
PS 4. Waves and their applications in technologies for information transfer

(Continued)

EXHIBIT 13.7   (Continued)

Life Sciences

LS 1.   From molecules to organisms: Structures and processes

LS 2.   Ecosystem: Interactions, energy, and dynamics

LS 3.   Heredity: Inheritance and variation of traits

LS 4.   Biological evolution: Unity and delivery

Earth and Space Sciences

ESS 1.   Earth's place in the universe

ESS 2.   Earth's systems

ESS 3.   Earth and human activity

Engineering, Technology, and the Application of Science

ETS 1.   Engineering design

ETS 2.   Links among engineering, technology, science, and society

---

SOURCE: Reprinted with permission from *Box ES-1, A Framework for K–12 Science Education: Practices, Crosscutting Concepts, and Core Ideas,* 2011 by the National Academy of Sciences, Courtesy of the National Academies Press, Washington, DC.

reality. Likewise, children construct thoughts, expectations, and explanations about natural phenomena to make sense of their everyday experiences. Constructivists believe that actual learning takes place through accommodation, which occurs when students change their existing ideas in response to new information. Constructivism allows students to learn by asking questions and forming their own opinions.

As shared by Olson and Mokhtari (2010), decades of research in science education indicate that students learn better when teachers begin instructional sequence with more concrete representations; then scaffold toward more abstract representations; and finally, return to concrete experiences. This process is represented by a *learning cycle* that has three stages:

1. *Exploration.* Students are presented with a challenge question to explore, a phenomenon to observe, or some other guided experience. A common elementary classroom example involves students given a battery, a bulb, and several wires and asked to find as many ways as possible to light an incandescent bulb.

2. *Concept development.* Students discuss various observations. They also pose questions and provide possible explanations and solutions. Likewise, students can generate challenges or clarifications. Going back to the prior example in the elementary class, students might illustrate a wiring configuration used to light the bulb on chart paper (or digital source).

3. *Application.* Students use new ideas in a more complex setting—solve a new challenge, or test ideas. Using the elementary class battery, wire, and bulb activity, some students might identify both series and parallel circuits. Additionally, they can discuss the classroom lighting system or similar electrical circuits in their school.

As noted in the battery and lightbulb activity, using an inquiry or discovery approach, along with scaffolding, to teach science can be very effective. To be certain, however, neither exploration nor inquiry-based learning is a new technique. But it does stand in contrast to the more traditional lecture format of teaching.

At the heart of inquiry-based learning is the aspect of asking questions. The goal is not to ask just any questions but to ask ones that children honestly care about. Teachers using an inquiry approach find that it melds easily with technology. However, finding ways to use technology to facilitate the inquiry approach takes time—a lot of time. This means faculty and staff need more opportunities to consider how best to adapt science content and pedagogy to an online format. In addition, staff members need ongoing access to technology and to professional development that meets their individual needs.

Without question, technology is becoming an important and powerful tool in helping teachers lead their students through the inquiry process. As part of that process, inquiry-based instructional strategies and scaffolding strategies can lead to student investigations that, in turn, lead to great conceptual understanding. However, implementing and sustaining this type of new science curriculum is not without great challenges. As with any meaningful change, it will need dedicated leaders who can focus on the importance of teaching science. School districts also need to foster discovery and inquiry methods along with high-quality professional development. Thus, finding new and improved ways of teaching science is important, and making connections between a district's science curriculum and current developments in state and national standards could prove to be very rewarding.

Trends in Science

In analyzing trends in science, it appears that science education in the United States continues to face many challenges. As noted by the National Research Council (2011), "Too often, standards are long lists of detailed and disconnected facts, reinforcing the criticism that our schools' science curricula tend to be a mile wide and an inch deep" (p. 1). Moreover, despite a continued sense of urgency to better prepare students, much of the discourse on improving science education has focused on the latter end of a student's academic career, overlooking the opportunity to set an early foundation (Tucker, 2012).

This concern over science instruction seems to beg the question as to what is the best way to teach science. Much of the answer lies not only with CCSS but also with the Next Generation Science Standards (NGSS). As noted by Stewart, Willard, and Wesson (2012), NGSS standards are largely based on "A Framework for K-12 Science Education: Practices, Crosscutting Concepts, and Core Ideas" (National Research Council, 2011). A number of states are already involved in the development of the NGSS, and it continues to grow in popularity. In addition to life science, earth and space science, as well as physical science, NGSS standards relate to technology, engineering, and the application of science as a fourth content area. Specifically, the NGSS has a strong focus on scientific and engineering practices, which are combined with core disciplinary ideas to form performance expectations. Also outlined in NGSS are expectations for students to understand important ideas about engineering design such as knowing that "a solution needs to be tested—and then modified on the basis of the test results—in order to improve it." Additionally, students are expected to understand links that involve engineering, technology, science, and society. As part of this trend, the National Science Teachers Association and many other professional organizations are now marshalling resources to bring science, technology, engineering, and mathematics (STEM) into classrooms as an integrated whole.

SCIENCE, TECHNOLOGY, ENGINEERING, AND MATHEMATICS

STEM is becoming an important part of schooling. According to Rosen (2012), STEM initially evolved out of a partnership between educational leaders and business to share a common vision of excellent teaching and learning in math and science. Educators, early on, quickly realized how STEM aligns well to the business world's need for people who can apply knowledge and work collaboratively. As a result, business leaders are becoming highly invested in our nation's youngest learners. This is best evidenced by the major focus of Change the Equation (CTEq), a nonprofit, nonpartisan, CEO-led initiative that is mobilizing the business community to improve the quality of PreK–12 STEM learning in the United States. As part of the STEM emphasis on math and science learning, business and schools are focusing on the following:

- More time for science in classrooms
- Professional development for teachers of math and science
- Hands-on learning
- After-school programming

As it continues to gain momentum, STEM curriculum is becoming a unifying force in promoting inquiry and curiosity. This is largely due to more students wanting to understand and learn more about areas of science and mathematics. STEM also provides success for English language learners (ELLs) in the areas of math and science. For example, Sotomayor (2013) provided six strategies for assisting ELLs with STEM curriculum:

- *Differentiate and individualize learning.* STEM integrates technology into instruction—as well as into every subject area.
- *Mix modalities.* A technologically infused curriculum addresses diverse learning styles.
- *Connect concepts to the real world.* Students are taught to connect concepts and apply them to real-world situations.
- *Use data to inform instruction.* Data is used to differentiate instruction and to address individual student needs.
- *Extend communication beyond the classroom.* Teachers use Moodle and other Web-based programs.
- *Encourage student exploration.* Curriculum provides students with opportunities to explore online while promoting inquiry and curiosity.

It is not surprising, then, that amidst a national backdrop of calls for enriching and deepening educational practices in science that some schools are already embedding STEM into every subject. Moreover, because of STEM, many more students are now being engaged in authentic, real-world, expeditionary learning.

Curriculum Tip 13.7	Inquiry and scaffolding teaching strategies are providing a pathway for the enrichment of many disciplines.

FOREIGN LANGUAGE

As noted by Nelson Mandela, education is the most powerful weapon we can use to change the world (Richardson, 2014). Keeping with this understanding, there seems to be a growing realization that we live in a "global village" where the price of oil from the Middle East affects employment levels in Texas. In such a global village, competence in a foreign language would seem to be a vital necessity.

In relation to a statement of philosophy, the recommendations from Education for Global Leadership (2007) are as follows:

- Teaching international content across the curriculum and at all levels of learning to expand U.S. students' knowledge of other countries and cultures
- Expanding the training pipeline at every level of education as well as addressing the paucity of Americans fluent in foreign languages, especially critical, less-commonly taught languages
- National leaders—political leaders as well as the business and philanthropic communities and the media—should educate the public about the importance of improving education in languages other than English and international studies.

Recent studies indicate, however, that only about one fourth of the nation's students are studying a foreign language. The discussion that follows examines some current trends in language study.

Trends in Foreign Language Education

Trends in foreign language education can perhaps best be analyzed by dividing them into curricular approaches and instructional approaches, although such a division is in some ways misleading, especially with respect to foreign language.

Curricular Approaches

Several new approaches to the design and development of curricula have appeared in recent years. The first approach is termed *problem-posing education,* a foreign language curriculum with an existentialist emphasis.

The second curricular approach gaining attention, at least from leaders in the profession, is the functional-notional syllabus. Influenced greatly by the theories of psycho- and sociolinguistics, the functional-notional syllabus is predicated on the importance of two closely related aspects of language: the functions of language (such as requesting

information, giving instructions, clarifying the order of events) and the notions or semantic meanings (concepts such as time, quantification, possession, modality). Thus, the
functional-notional syllabus stresses the purposes for which learners need the language
and the notions or concepts involved with those purposes.

A third approach to curriculum development might be termed the *proficiency approach*.
These are curricula developed around the proficiencies identified by the American Council
on the Teaching of Foreign Languages (1982). The council's guidelines describe in specific
terms six proficiency levels in speaking, reading, listening, and writing: Level 0, no functional ability; Level 1, elementary survival-level proficiency; Level 2, limited working proficiency; Level 3, professional working proficiency; Level 4, full professional proficiency;
Level 5, the proficiency of a native speaker.

Instructional Approaches

Two quite different instructional approaches have attracted the attention of foreign language specialists: immersion programs and "Suggestopedia."

Immersion programs were first developed in Canada in response to the concerns of English-
speaking parents in Quebec. Teachers use the target language to teach regular school subjects:
The second language is not another subject but is instead the medium of instruction. In early
total immersion programs, all instruction for the first three or four grades is presented in the
target language; the native language is not introduced until second or third grade. By the end of
elementary school, each language is used to teach about half the curriculum.

Suggestopedia, first developed by Lozanov in 1978, is an instructional method that
attempts to involve both conscious and unconscious faculties by using intensive time periods (three- or four-hour sessions five days a week), a secure group atmosphere (ideally, six
males and six females with a highly skilled teacher), rhythmic breathing exercises, and
baroque music. Its instructional procedure consists of three parts: a review of the previous
day's work through conversation, games, and skits; new material introduced using dialogue
in familiar situations; and a "séance" that aims at unconscious memorization using yogic
breathing and baroque music.

Students in U.S. classrooms are culturally, linguistically, ethnically, and socioeconomically
diverse (Hammerberg, 2004), and it is important that educators understand the current methods
of comprehension instruction taught to students from diverse backgrounds. Professionals need
to deepen their understanding of the impact of culture and language on the instructional and
assessment process (Santos, 2004). In any educational field, a close relationship exists between
assessment and instruction. In light of current brain-based research and the current educational
climate, policymakers and national organizations often initiate new trends in standards and
assessment to bring about changes in instructional objectives and approaches at the classroom
level. As these instructional objectives and approaches change, updated assessment practices
are needed to reflect the changes. This interactive relationship between assessment and instruction, in which each influences the other, has characterized the foreign language field during the
past two decades (Santos, 2004). Since the early 1980s, the focus of foreign language instruction
has moved away from the mastery of discrete language skills, such as grammar, vocabulary, and
pronunciation, to the development of communicative proficiency—that is, the ability to communicate about real-world topics with native speakers of the target language. Widely termed the

proficiency movement. this change has developed in tandem with changes in how students' foreign language skills are assessed.

The traditional assessment tools of earlier decades—usually discrete-point tests that focused on individual skills—evaluated students' knowledge *about* the language, not what they could *do with* the language. Although discrete-point tests are still used in many circumstances, particularly for large-scale standardized assessments, many of the newer assessment measures and techniques are performance based; that is, they require students to demonstrate knowledge and skills by carrying out challenging tasks. This enables teachers to measure what the students can actually do in various communicative contexts using the target language.

Current trends are finding that in teaching foreign languages it is most effective to use drama, art, music, and physical movement as well as reading, writing, and grammar usage. Students, for the most part, should have the opportunity to teach some aspect of what they learn. For example, many schools have developed "little buddy" programs. These programs are designed for older students to teach an aspect of the weekly theme or what the younger students (buddies) are learning in English.

Because of these principles of instruction and types of teaching strategies, leaders in the field, such as Stephen Krashen (comprehensible input) and Blaine Ray (Teaching Proficiency Through Reading and Storytelling [TPRS]), are changing the face of foreign language instruction in schools (Schutz, 2007). Many believe the TPRS approach is making pure book memorization less useful.

Changes in foreign language assessment in recent years can be divided into two main categories based on their catalysts: National assessment initiatives have widely influenced classroom instruction in a top-down approach; local assessment initiatives, which have appeared in response to curricular and instructional changes, may be seen as bottom-up initiatives. Top-down and bottom-up influences on foreign language assessment will undoubtedly continue. The publication of the national foreign language standards (National Standards in Foreign Language Education Project, 1996) means that attainment of these standards will need to be assessed (see Exhibit 13.8).

It will take time before the real extent of the impact of enforceable curriculum standards on multicultural education and foreign language is known (Bohn & Sleeter, 2000). To many curriculum leaders, standards make visible the expectations for learning that otherwise might be implicit. At the same time, teachers of foreign language or multicultural education are not looking for a quick fix.

The best way to face the challenge of assessing attainment of national goals may be by using alternative assessments developed in specific instructional contexts. ELLs are capable of high levels of conceptual understanding. While many ELL students have difficulty writing in English, they can speak with a level of sophistication not reflected on written assignments (Cox-Petersen & Olson, 2007). Given the wide variation among foreign language students, teachers, courses, and contexts, an assessment tool or procedure that works well in one

| **Curriculum Tip 13.8** | Teachers must be given time to examine their own views on foreign language and diversity education as well as be able to relate those views to standards that are adopted. |

EXHIBIT 13.8 Standards in Foreign Language Education

Statement of Philosophy

Language and communication are at the heart of the human experience. The United States must educate students who are linguistically and culturally equipped to communicate successfully in a pluralistic American society and abroad. This imperative envisions a future in which ALL students will develop and maintain proficiency in English and at least one other language, modern or classical. Children who come to school from non-English backgrounds should also have opportunities to develop further proficiencies in their first language.

Standards for Foreign Language Learning

Communication

Communicate in Languages Other Than English

Standard 1.1: Students engage in conversations, provide and obtain information, express feelings and emotions, and exchange opinions.

Standard 1.2: Students understand and interpret written and spoken language on a variety of topics.

Standard 1.3: Students present information, concepts, and ideas to an audience of listeners or readers on a variety of topics.

Cultures+

Gain Knowledge and Understanding of Other Cultures

Standard 2.1: Students demonstrate an understanding of the relationship between the practices and perspectives of the culture studied.

Standard 2.2: Students demonstrate an understanding of the relationship between the products and perspectives of the culture studied.

Connections

Connect With Other Disciplines and Acquire Information

Standard 3.1: Students reinforce and further their knowledge of other disciplines through the foreign language.

Standard 3.2: Students acquire information and recognize the distinctive viewpoints that are only available through the foreign language and its cultures.

Comparisons

Develop Insight Into the Nature of Language and Culture

Standard 4.1: Students demonstrate understanding of the nature of language through comparisons of the language studied and their own.

Standard 4.2: Students demonstrate understanding of the concept of culture through comparisons of the cultures studied and their own.

Communities

Participate in Multilingual Communities at Home and Around the World

Standard 5.1: Students use the language both within and beyond the school setting.

Standard 5.2: Students show evidence of becoming lifelong learners by using the language for personal enjoyment and enrichment.

SOURCE: American Council on the Teaching of Foreign Languages (n.d.).

situation may be totally inappropriate in another. To evaluate students' progress and proficiency effectively, teachers need to learn about and gain competence in the use of a variety of assessment measures and procedures to discover what works best for them in each of the changing contexts in which they teach and with the full range of students in their classes.

The Internet can also be a valuable tool in aiding assessment and instruction of foreign languages in U.S. classrooms. Diane Vitaska (2002), a French teacher, uses the Internet to research cultural aspects of France in her classroom. Students can create a PowerPoint presentation, a brochure, or a newsletter as a Web page. LCD projectors are used to help students view computer images on a screen. Digital cameras can be used to help students develop personalized notebooks or practice language skills. Some teachers of foreign languages are using mobile videoconferencing labs with a webcam and speaker microphone to connect U.S. classrooms to classrooms in Europe. As can be seen, technology can be used in a plethora of ways to aid the teaching and assessing of students in foreign language classes.

EDUCATION IN THE ARTS

Over the years, the arts have had to struggle for a place in the school's curriculum. Ever since the Committee of Fifteen's report (National Education Association [NEA], 1895/1969), the arts usually have been defined as "minor" subjects taught only an hour or two a week up to Grade 8 and then offered as electives at the high school level.

Trends in Art Education

Teaching for Artistic Behavior (TAB) is a grassroots movement gaining popularity in a number of schools (Hathaway & Jaquith, 2014). But this was not always the case. In the past and in traditional art programs, a teacher was often assigned a project designed to teach various concepts of skills. These assignments generally resulted in a predetermined product. In contrast, TAB educators set up their classrooms like artists' studios with materials, equipment, and resources embedded into multiple studio centers, each with a particular media focus such as painting or ceramics. Due to increasing classroom teacher interest, the TAB concept is expanding across the nation.

Art, like every discipline, should be infinite in scope. It is not enough, nor should it be, for curriculum to rest neatly within a narrow precept of elements and principals of design. With that said, during the 1950s and 1960s, art education was conceived rather narrowly as including only the visual arts and music. Children in the elementary grades were assisted by art and music specialists who emphasized performance (drawing and singing, primarily) as a way of making those subjects interesting. At the junior high level, units and courses in art appreciation and music appreciation were introduced, usually emphasizing the study of the great masters as a means of teaching students some elementary aesthetic principles. At the high school level, students majoring in art spent five or more periods a week in art studies. The emphasis on performance continued: Many suburban high schools offered courses called "band," "orchestra," and "chorus," in which students spent most of their time preparing for public performances.

This patchwork arts curriculum, which seemed to lack any organizing principle or governing theory, was the target of two major reform efforts during the 1970s, both supported with the federal funds that seemed so abundant in that decade. When federal funds were no longer available, the local districts found it possible to support these exemplary projects for only a few more years.

The lack of continued federal funding for projects in the past decade has not deterred leaders in the field from their continued efforts to strengthen education in the arts and to reassert the importance of the arts at a time when the rest of the profession seems obsessed with the academic curriculum.

Those efforts seem to have found expression in three related developments. The first is an attempt to broaden the field. Rather than limiting the arts to the visual arts and music, current thinking stresses the multiple nature of aesthetic expression. While such an expanded understanding of the nature of the arts seems theoretically desirable, practitioners have expressed reservations about the difficulties of finding the time, money, and staff to support such a diversified and comprehensive program.

The second development is an attempt to formulate and promulgate a new rationale for the arts. In previous years, those advocating the arts tended to speak in terms that connoted a subtle elitism: The arts refine the aesthetic sensibilities and help people appreciate the finer things in life. The tendency in the current period is to defend the arts as an essential and unique way of knowing—one that is basic for all students.

Finally, there seems to be a resurgence of interest in interdisciplinary humanities courses in which the arts play a central role. Such courses enjoyed a period of brief popularity in the early 1960s; during that period, these courses tended to emphasize literature and history and gave only scant attention to the fine arts. After this, there seemed to be a concerted effort, through the development of standards, to position the arts more centrally in such interdisciplinary courses.

For example, National Standards for Arts Education were developed in 1994 by experts in education and the arts. These standards describe what a child with a complete, sequential education in the arts should know and be able to do at various grade levels in each artistic discipline. The 1997 National Assessment for Educational Progress was developed in coordination with these national standards.

Standards in the arts (dance, music, theater, visual arts) continue to be developed to provide a guide and resource to states and school districts that want to develop their art programs. Most states have standards in place for arts education, and still, other states are in the process of developing arts standards. State-by-state summaries of arts education standards and other policies are available from each state educational agency (Americans for the Arts, 2009).

As Reeves (2007) aptly noted, the stark choice between academics and the arts is a false dichotomy. Teachers need to regard literacy not as a diversion from their primary subjects but as a useful way of helping students think about their subjects. We write in music and art class because those subjects are worth writing about.

Curriculum leaders need to encourage content-area teachers to integrate the arts into their classes. This will ensure that every student receives opportunities to excel not only academically but also in the arts.

| **Curriculum Tip 13.9** | Curriculum leaders are urging the approach to the teaching of art along three broad avenues: universals, the community, and the individual. |

In reviewing the literature, Donovan Walling (2001), director of publications and research at Phi Delta Kappa, stated that the changing priorities of schools, coupled with high standards, high-stakes testing, and the ascendancy of math and science, are pushing art education back to the heart of education.

The arts have had a long struggle finding an appropriate place in the school curriculum. With the passage of the Goals 2000: Educate America Act, the national goals were written into law, naming the arts as a core, academic subject—as important to education as English, mathematics, history, civics and government, geography, science, and foreign language. The published standards were discipline specific to dance, music, theatre, and the visual arts. The five general standards shown below for the visual arts illustrate their placement.

What Students Should Know and Be Able to Do in the Arts

Research findings demonstrate that young people interested in the arts may also exhibit increased motivation to learn in other subject areas as well. Hence, it comes as no surprise that there are many routes to competence in the arts disciplines. For example, students may work in different arts at different times. Moreover, their study may take a variety of approaches, and their abilities may develop at different rates (Johnson, 2014). Competence means the ability to use an array of knowledge and skills. Terms often used to describe this array include *creation, performance, production, history, culture, perception, analysis, criticism, aesthetics, technology,* and *appreciation.* Competence means capabilities with these elements themselves and an understanding of their interdependence; it also means the ability to combine the content, perspectives, and techniques associated with the various elements to achieve specific artistic and analytical goals. Students work toward *comprehensive* competence from the very beginning, preparing in the lower grades for deeper and more rigorous work each succeeding year. Essentially, the standards ask that students know and be able to do the following by the time they have completed secondary school:

- *They should be able to communicate at a basic level in the four arts disciplines—* dance, music, theatre, and the visual arts. This includes knowledge and skills in the use of the basic vocabularies, materials, tools, techniques, and intellectual methods of each arts discipline.
- *They should be able to communicate proficiently in at least one art form,* including the ability to define and solve artistic problems with insight, reason, and technical proficiency.
- *They should be able to develop and present basic analyses of works of art* from structural, historical, and cultural perspectives and from combinations of those perspectives. This includes the ability to understand and evaluate work in the various arts disciplines.
- *They should have an informed acquaintance with exemplary works of art from a variety of cultures and historical periods* and a basic understanding of historical development in the arts disciplines, across the arts as a whole, and within cultures.
- *They should be able to relate various types of arts knowledge and skills within and across the arts disciplines.* This includes mixing and matching competencies and understandings in art-making, history and culture, and analysis in any arts-related project. (National Council for Arts Education, n.d.)

According to the National Coalition for Core Arts Standards (NCCAS, 2014), PreK–12 standards in dance, music, theatre, and visual arts will be available on the website (http://nccas.wikispaces.com) in March 2015. The new, voluntary grade-by-grade standards are intended to affirm the place of arts education in a balanced core curriculum, support the 21st-century needs of students and teachers, and help ensure that all students are college and career ready.

These standards primarily address general principles and are open to interpretation. Discipline-based art education follows these standards and is often found in school curricula today. One of the originators of discipline-based art was Dwaine Greer, whose aim was to develop mature students who are both comfortable and familiar with major aspects of the disciplines of art (Walling, 2001, p. 628).

New trends in educational art are favoring aesthetics, art history, and art criticism. Complementary interest in extending art education through interdisciplinary studies—across all disciplines—appears to be currently driving the process. Walling (2001) noted several questions that pertain to this movement:

- How should we define "universals," and who should have a say in the definition?
- What traditions characterize the "community," and how can they be incorporated into the art curriculum?
- How will the "individual" be recognized, and how will individual differences be accommodated, validated, and valued?

No matter how art educators address these questions, a move continues today to incorporate technology into the art curriculum. Two themes appear here: The first incorporates creation of art using the computer to produce and manipulate images, and the second uses the computer to investigate the visual arts. Teachers and students are finding a plethora of ways to use the computer and Internet in the field of visual arts. So many Web sites about art exist that it takes a considerable amount of time to review them all. There is little doubt that technology is fast becoming a major factor in how art is viewed and integrated into the local school curriculum.

PHYSICAL EDUCATION AND HEALTH

Schools are continuing to take an important step toward helping children become healthy. This is best evidenced by cutting-edge research that is currently helping tackle the obesity epidemic, motivating children and their families to maintain a physically active lifestyle. As part of this dramatic process of change, physical education and health teachers are assuming a key role in leading school wellness initiatives and physical education programs (National Association for Sport and Physical Education, 2014).

Trends in Physical Education

In today's fast-paced and complex society, school leaders need to be champions for health and fitness. We need to lead by example, and we need to find ways to make physical activity accessible to all students and their families (Cote, 2014). As a key strategy to improving health, physical education classes now teach students to add physical activity to their daily lives and exposes them to content and learning experiences that develop the skills and desire to be active for life (see Exhibit 13.9). In addition to physical activity improving muscular strength and endurance, flexibility, and cardiovascular endurance, it helps children establish self-esteem and set and achieve goals.

The National Content Standards publications define what a student should know and be able to do as result of a quality physical education program. States and local school districts across the country use the National Standards to develop or revise existing standards, frameworks, and curricula (National Association for Sport and Physical Education, 2014).

To meet the physical education standards displayed in Exhibit 13.9, the National Association for Sport and Physical Education (2011) recommends the following:

- Instruction periods totaling a minimum of 150 minutes per week for elementary students and 225 minutes per week for middle and secondary students
- High-quality physical education specialists who provide a developmentally appropriate program
- Adequate equipment and facilities (p. 2)

A New Vision for Physical Education

Preparing students to make healthy decisions about physical activity, health, and nutrition is the hallmark of quality physical education and health programs across the United States. As shared by Vandertie, Corner, and Corner (2012), school districts need to deliver physical education programs that arm kids with the knowledge and skills to make healthy choices long after they leave physical education class. Making healthy decisions is a skill much like learning to swim or clearing a hurdle, which means that students need intentional instruction to develop that skill. That said, activities should involve smaller groups of students to provide more participation for all. Likewise, student choice can drive involvement as well.

EXHIBIT 13.9 *Physical Education Standards*

Standard 1—The physically literate individual demonstrates competency in a variety of motor skills and movement patterns.

Standard 2—The physically literate individual applies knowledge of concepts, principles, strategies and tactics related to movement and performance.

Standard 3—The physically literate individual demonstrates the knowledge and skills to achieve and maintain a health-enhancing level of physical activity and fitness.

Standard 4—The physically literate individual exhibits responsible personal and social behavior that respects and others.

Standard 5—The physically literate individual recognizes the value of physical activity for health, enjoyment, challenge, self-expression, and/or social interaction.

SOURCE: National Association for Sport and Physical Education (2014).

In much the same way, teachers need to collaborate to offer multiple options to students, enabling them to be involved in activities they enjoy rather than being required to participate in a single activity chosen by a teacher.

Evidence reveals that a high-quality physical education program should parallel whole-child education. While the main focus is on physical development (psychomotor), it also addresses the knowledge (cognitive) and social (affective) aspects of the child. With this realistic information about the value of high-quality physical education programs, school districts nationwide still limit the physical education activities of students at all levels. In addition to the subject field standards, educators need to incorporate global education and diversity education into the subject fields. To accomplish this, curriculum leaders and teachers must consider actions that have the greatest impact on individual learning in physical education worldwide.

COMMON CORE STATE STANDARDS AND MULTICULTURAL EDUCATION

When it comes to deepening understanding and facilitating instruction in various subject fields, CCSS appears to be helping educators connect informational text and elevate expectations for students across grade levels. For example, Silva, Delleman, and Phesia (2013) noted that both Spanish and English informative texts use main ideas to introduce topics, but there are significant rhetorical differences. Compared to Spanish texts, English texts are more likely to vary in sentence length, restrict paragraph content to one narrow main idea, and provide concrete support for main ideas. Likewise, Silva and colleagues believe that second language learners' familiarity with the rhetorical schemata of their first language may hinder an ability to process and retain information presented in a second language. As a result, involving English language learners (ELLs) in a task that asks them to analyze discourse and examine the rhetorical schema of English written texts can help overcome this obstacle.

Regardless of approach, making sure all students can read and understand a variety of texts in different subject areas is a highly complex matter. With this in mind, several questions have been posed over the years. First, "Why do we need to address diversity in our schools?" This question was answered years ago by Richards, Brown, and Forde (2006, p. 40). They noted that "more and more students from diverse backgrounds were populating 21st century classrooms, and efforts were mounting to identify effective methods to teach these students." Additionally, they noted, "the need for pedagogical approaches that are culturally responsive" (p. 4), which requires teachers to educate students with varying cultures, languages, abilities, and many other characteristics.

A second question often posed is "What is culturally responsive pedagogy?" Richards and colleagues (2006) again perceived culturally responsive pedagogy as the following:

> [Teaching that] facilitates and supports the achievement of all
> students. . . . Culturally responsive pedagogy comprises three dimension: (a)
> institutional, (b) personal, and (c) instructional. The institutional dimension
> reflects the administration and its policies and values. The personal dimension
> refers to the cognitive and emotional processes teachers must engage in to
> become culturally responsive. The instructional dimension includes materials,
> strategies, and activities that form the basis for instruction. (p. 4)

The key is incorporating diverse ideas and cultures into a collective vision of change and reform. But, for the most part, it is still clear today that no single template of actions can be placed on an educational system to make multicultural education compatible with the many diverse groups. However, with the advent of CCSS, more is being done to address this situation.

> Good schools, like good societies and good families, celebrate and cherish diversity.
>
> —Deborah Meier

TECHNOLOGY AND EXPONENTIAL CHANGE

School leaders need an open dialogue about concerns, responsibilities, and priorities that are essential for successful technology integration (Johnson, 2013). Subsequently, along with multicultural and diversity issues, a major question for school leaders today is, How can we best move our schools and curriculum into the realm of 21st-century learning? Finding the answer to this question definitely has major political, economic, and social implications. To be sure, education is changing, and our mandate is to prepare students for a globally connected world. Moreover, one cannot sidestep the importance of technology as we prepare students for dynamically shifting environments. This poses a series of politically charged conundrums such as envisioning a shift from textbooks to Web-based learning, brick-and-mortar classrooms, lectures, worksheets, standardized tests, bells, career focused curriculum, etc. The list is endless, and the implications are extraordinary and wide-ranging.

Most assuredly, research is confirming the large number of youth engaging in interest-driven practices with digital media (Lam, 2013). With that said, many adolescents are showing an interest in music, fan fiction, and fan art by connecting with peers and other adults across the world. This research has led some scholars to advocate "Connected Learning" (http://connect edlearning.tv/what-is-connected-learning) to harness different support structures across online and offline spaces. The idea is to draw from the power of digital networks to connect multiple sets of resources across school, home, community, and the rest of the world.

Shifts of this magnitude are forcing administrators, curriculum leaders, and teachers to rethink digital aspects of student learning. Basically, 21st-century technology has the ability of connecting individual students to master course material at their own pace (Whitehead, Jensen, & Boschee, 2013). With extended digital learning and individualized instruction, the delivery of course content can be adjusted to the individual abilities of the student. When this occurs, the focus of school will shift away from achievement based on age and grade level to the mastery of content and skills. Likewise, with learning being both virtual and physical, the essence of what teachers must do in the future will be based on helping students learn career-related skills, knowledge, attitudes, and behaviors (Jukes, McCain, & Crockett, 2010–2011).

GLOBAL CONNECTIONS: TEACHING CONTENT ACROSS CULTURES

Pointedly, U.S. students in the 21st century must become globally literate. Many of the individual state standards and CCSS contain some global and international implications;

however, many issues related to global and international studies still need to be addressed, enhanced, and expanded. According to Munson (2011), many nations are setting their instructional sights on far more than basic skills. In nearly all of the top-performing countries, the study of the arts, literature, history, geography, civics, reading, science, foreign language, and mathematics is compulsory. In contrast, only a number of states in the United States require students to take a foreign language.

Munson (2011) listed some examples of what other countries are asking their students—both in standards and on national, state, and provincial examinations—to know and be able to do:

- To meet the learning objectives in the visual arts national curriculum framework, fourth graders in *Hong Kong* visit an artist's studio, study Picasso's *Guernica,* and analyze the works of modernist sculptor Henry Moore.
- In *Finland,* fifth and sixth graders are required to study the effects of the French Revolution and how the invention of writing changed human life. For example, they trace a topic, such as the evolution of trade, from prehistory until the 19th century.
- Seventh graders in *South Korea* are expected to know and understand the concept of supply and demand, as well as equilibrium price theories, property rights, and ways to improve market function.
- *Japanese* seventh to ninth graders conduct experiments to find out that pressure is related to the magnitude of a force and the area to which the force is applied.
- *Canadian* eighth graders (from the province of Ontario) are expected to create musical compositions, conduct a group of musicians, and know musical terms in Italian.
- *Dutch* twelfth graders must know enough about the Crimean War to be able to put seven events (relating to the war) in chronological order.

As can be seen from Munson's list, students internationally are required to deepen their knowledge and their understanding of various subject areas. More research is emerging to suggest that U.S. educators equally need to incorporate a deeper understanding of content as it relates to the centerpiece of classroom discussions. Much of this research confirms that on a global level, nations that score competitively on the Program for International Student Assessment (PISA) put content before skills. Perhaps this is an issue worth considering by school leaders in the United States.

SUMMARY

This chapter examines general developments in the curriculum by analyzing trends in specific subject areas, because even though innovations transcend the discipline, most of the important changes take place and are worked out in the subject areas themselves. Many current developments and trends in PreK–12 education are altering the landscape for curriculum work, and it is worthwhile to assess current trends as part of curriculum renewal. It is for this reason that the authors include some of the trends and issues involved in the subject areas of ELA, reading, mathematics, social studies, science, foreign language, the arts, and physical education. Finally, the chapter includes some ways that technology is impacting the delivery and implementation of curriculum in schools worldwide.

Other areas in education that are currently developing standards are vocational studies and technology or mobile learning. Vocational studies such as shop, family and consumer science, and mechanics are important to career opportunities for today's students. Technology and Web-based instruction is constantly changing. Curriculum should be developed for these areas and updated on a regular basis. Technology-based curriculum and education is discussed in greater depth in the next chapter.

APPLICATIONS

1. An analysis of the curriculum trends suggests quite clearly that the ideal curriculum proposed by national commissions is always far ahead of the taught curriculum delivered in the classroom. In a well-organized essay that draws from your own experience and your knowledge of the research, explain why it seems difficult to change the taught curriculum.

2. Select one of the fields discussed. By analyzing how it has changed and is changing now, project the major changes that might occur during the next 10 years. Write a summary of your projections.

3. Based on a close reading of this chapter and your own observations, determine which of the fields seems to have experienced the greatest changes. Write a brief essay in which you explain why this particular field seems to have changed more than the others.

4. Knowing that constructivism is linked to the higher achievement of students in science, how can this strategy be implemented into other areas of the curriculum?

5. A high-quality physical education program is critical to educating the whole child. Explain why many school districts fail to allocate the time recommended for such a program.

6. Access the Global Education Checklist at www.globaled.org/fianlcopy.pdf, and complete the self-assessment instrument to measure your school's or school district's degree of success in the different areas in question regarding global education. Based on the needs assessment, develop some action plans for the development of specific goals, resources needed, and time and participation required. Note: If the Web site is inactive, contact the American Forum for Global Education via e-mail (info@globaled.org) or telephone (212–624–1412) to secure the self-assessment instrument.

7. From the tips for improving diversity education provided in Exhibit 13.8, identify those that exist in your school or school district. If some tips are missing in your school or school district, what should be done to make them a reality?

CASE STUDY   What Is Taught Versus What Should Be Taught

When planning and developing curriculum, sometimes what is taught in the classroom is not what was proposed as the district's curriculum. As an example, a school principal has been having differences with several teachers who do not want to follow the district's proposed curriculum, one that meets individual state standards or CCSS, which matches national recommendations.

This situation is a major concern for Dave Anon—the superintendent in charge of a number of small, rural schools in the Southwest—who has Principal Bob Huerta on the phone.

"Bob, I asked for curriculum surveys from your teachers, and I found that what they are teaching in their classrooms does not follow our district's curriculum scope and sequence," says Dave Anon. "For example, I noted on the surveys that the teachers are not covering geometry in the fourth grade. Our district math curriculum is based on national recommendations and specifically requires that geometry be taught at that level."

"Yes, I know," states Principal Huerta. "I have several fourth-grade teachers who feel the previous series is better than the newly adopted series." There is silence on the phone. Bob Huerta can sense that the superintendent is upset.

"Bob, I e-mailed you a month ago that our math scores are down and we need to align our elementary curriculum with state standards. I specifically noted that your fourth-grade students are not doing well on math test items related to geometry."

"It is a concern," says Principal Huerta. "I am trying my best to get this resolved."

"Well, you need to get this situation under control. It is crucial that our teachers follow the curriculum that we have outlined and as recommended in CCSS," notes the superintendent. "How do you plan to address this problem?"

The Challenge

Good communication and an understanding of curriculum applications between the district office and a local school is a critical issue. What else can Superintendent Anon do to improve communication with his principals, as well as with his teachers and local parents?

Key Issues or Questions

1. What are your impressions of Superintendent Anon and Principal Huerta? Do you think the issue of communication will be resolved? Why or why not?

2. How do you feel about technology and its impact on teaching and learning?

3. What are some areas in ELA and reading that have changed dramatically with the advent of CCSS? Explain your answer.

4. What are some areas in mathematics and science that have changed dramatically with the advent of CCSS? Explain your answer.

5. What are some areas in social studies and art that have changed dramatically with the advent of technology? Explain your answer.

WEBLIOGRAPHY

Annenberg Foundation: Math in Daily Life
www.learner.org/interactives/dailymath

Differentiated Curriculum
www.teach-nology.com/edleadership/curriculum_
development/differentiation

Google Lit Trips
www.googlelittrips.org

International Reading Association (IRA)
www.reading.org

www.reading.org/General/CurrentResearch/
Standards/ProfessionalStandards2010.aspx

The K–12 Mathematics Curriculum Center
www2.edc.org/mcc

Learning First Alliance
www.learningfirst.org

National Core Art Standards
http://nccas.wikispaces.com.#sthash.v3vnRMtf.dpuf

National Council of Teachers of Mathematics
(NCTM) Curriculum Focal Points
www.nctm.org/focalpoints

National Reading Styles Institute
www.nrsi.com

National Science Resources Center
www.nsrconline.org

National Science Teachers Association
www.nsta.org

National Standards for Arts Education
www2.ed.gov/pubs/ArtsStandards.html

Progressions Framework in Mathematics
www.nciea.org/publications/Math_LPF_KH11.pdf

Reading Recovery Council of North America
www.readingrecovery.org

Science News for Students
https://student.societyforscience.org/sciencenews-
students

The History Place
www.historyplace.com

The National Academies (Framework for K–12
Science Education)
www7.nationalacademies.org/bose/Standards_
Framework_Homepage.html

REFERENCES

Abilock, A. (2012). How can students know whether the information on line is true or not. *Educational Leadership, 69*(6), 70–74.

American Council on the Teaching of Foreign Languages. (1982). *ACTFL provisional proficiency guidelines.* Hastings-on-Hudson, NY: Author.

American Council on the Teaching of Foreign Languages. (n.d.). *National standards for foreign language education.* Retrieved from http://www.actfl.org/i4a/pages/index.cfm?pageid = 3392

Americans for the Arts. (2009). *Standards for arts education.* Retrieved from http://www.americans forth earts.org/public_awareness/artsed_facts/004.asp

Barrow, M. A. (2014). Even math requires learning academic language. *Phi Delta Kappan, 95*(6), 35–38.

Bohn, A. P., & Sleeter, C. E. (2000). Multicultural education and the standards movement: A report from the field. *Phi Delta Kappan, 82*(2), 156–159.

Breakstone, J., Smith, M., & Wineburg, S. (2013). Beyond the bubble in history/social studies assessments. *Phi Delta Kappan, 94*(5), 53–57.

Common Core State Standards Initiative. (2010). *About the standards.* Retrieved from http://www.corestan dards.org

Cote, P. (2014). Champions for fitness. *Principal, 93*(3), 52.

Cox-Petersen, A., & Olson, J. K. (2007). Alternate assessments for English language learners. *Principal, 87*(2), 32–34.

Cummins, S. (2013). What students can do when the reading gets rough. *Educational Leadership, 71*(3), 69–72.

Dong, Y. R. (2013–2014). The bridge of knowledge. *Educational Leadership, 71*(4), 30–36.

Education for Global Leadership. (2007, November 1). *Business and academic leaders endorse CED foreign language studies project.* Retrieved from http://www.ced.org/projects/educ_forlang.shtml

Ehrenworth, M. (2013). Unlocking the secrets of complex text. *Educational Leadership, 71*(3), 16–21.

Fisher, P. J., & Blachowicz, C. L. Z. (2013). A few words about math and science. *Educational Leadership, 71*(3), 46–51.

Fogo, B. (2011). Making and measuring the California history standards. *Phi Delta Kappan, 92*(8), 62–66.

Gojak, L. (2012). A vertical approach to math instruction. *Principal, 92*(2), 13–15.

Hammerberg, D. D. (2004). Comprehension instruction for socioculturally diverse classrooms: A review of what we know. *Reading Teacher, 57*(7), 648–661.

Hathaway, N. E., & Jaquith, D. B. (2014). Where's the revolution? *Phi Delta Kappan, 95*(6), 25–29.

International Center for Leadership in Education. (2012). *Common core readiness rubrics: Literacy check list.* Rexford, NY: Author.

International Reading Association. (2010). *Standards for reading professionals: Revised 2010.* Retrieved from http://www.reading.org/General/CurrentResearch/Standards/ProfessionalStandards2010.aspx

International Reading Association & National Council of Teachers of English. (1996). *Standards for the English language arts* (updated in 2010). Retrieved from http://www1.ncte.org/library/files/Store/Books/Sample/StandardsDoc.pdf

Johnson, D. (2013). Good technology choices: A team effort. *Educational Leadership, 71*(1), 80–82.

Johnson, K. (2014). Arts-science approach for gifted learners. *Principal, 93*(3), 42–43.

Johnston, P. (2012). Guiding the budding writer. *Educational Leadership, 70*(1), 64–67.

Jukes, I., McCain, T., & Crockett, L. (2010–2011). Education and the role of the educator in the future. *Phi Delta Kappan, 92*(4), 15–21.

Klein, D. (2003). A brief history of American K–12 mathematics education in the 20th century. In J. M. Royer (Ed.), *Mathematical cognition* (pp. 175–225). Greenwich, CT: Information Age.

Lam, W. S. E. (2013). What immigrant students can teach us about new media literacy? *Phi Delta Kappan, 94*(4), 62–65.

Lozanov, G. (1978). *Suggestology and outlines of Suggestopedia.* New York, NY: Gordon & Breach.

Lyon, G. R., Fletcher, J. M., Torgesen, J. K., Shaywitz, S. E., & Chhabra, V. (2004). Preventing and remediating reading failure: A response to Allington. *Educational Leadership, 61*(6), 86–88.

McDaniel, C. (2004). Critical literacy: A questioning stance and the possibility for change. *Reading Teacher, 57*(5), 472–473.

MIT Online Writing and Communication Center. (1999). *The writing process.* Boston: Massachusetts Institute of Technology.

Munson, L. (2011). What students really need to learn? *Educational Leadership, 68*(6), 10–14.

National Academies. (2011a, July 11). *Conceptual framework for new science education standards.* Retrieved from http://www7.nationalacade mies.org/bose/Standards_Framework_Home page.html

National Academies. (2011b, June 19). *Report offers new framework to guide K–12 science education, calls for shift in the way science is taught in the U.S.* [Press release]. Retrieved from http://www8.nationalacademies.org/onpi news/newsitem.aspx?RecordID=13165

National Association for Sport and Physical Education. (2011). *Physical education is critical to educating the whole child.* Reston, VA: Author.

National Association for Sport and Physical Education. (2014). *National PE standards.* Retrieved from http://www.shapeamerica.org/standards/pe

National Coalition for Core Arts Standards. (2014). *Next generation national visual arts standards.* Retrieved from http://www.arteducators.org/research/nccas

National Council for Arts Education. (n.d.). *Summary statement: Education reform, standards, and the arts.* Retrieved from http://www2.ed.gov/pubs/ArtsStandards.html

National Council for the Social Studies. (2010). *New standards.* Retrieved from http://www.socialstudies.org/standards

National Council for the Social Studies. (2014). *Themes of Social Studies.* Retrieved from http://www.social studies.org/standards/strands

National Council of Teachers of English (n.d.). *Language arts standards.* Retrieved from http://www.ncte.org/standards/ncte-ira

National Council of Teachers of English. (2004). *NCTE beliefs about the teaching of writing.* Retrieved from http://www.ncte.org/positions/statements/writingbeliefs

National Council of Teachers of English/International Reading Association. (2012). *NCTE/IRA standards for the English language arts.* Retrieved from http://www.ncte.org/standards/ncte-ira

National Council of Teachers of Mathematics. (2004). *Principles and standards for school mathematics.* Reston, VA: Author. Retrieved from http://standards.nctm.org/document

National Education Association. (1969). *Report of the Committee of Fifteen.* New York: Arno Press. (Original work published 1895 by New England Publishing)

National Governors Association Center for Best Practices & Council of Chief State School Officers. (2010). *Common Core State Standards for English language arts and literacy in history/social studies, science, and technical subjects.* Washington, DC: Author. Retrieved from www.corestandards.org/assets/ELA%20Standards.pdf

National Research Council. (2011, July). *A framework for K–12 science standards: Practices, crosscutting concepts, and core ideas*. Retrieved from http://www.nap.edu/openbook.php?record_id = 13165&page = 3

National Standards in Foreign Language Education Project. (1996). *Standards for foreign language learning: Preparing for the 21st century.* Yonkers, NY: Author. Retrieved from ERIC database. (ED394279)

North Central Educational Regional Laboratory. (n.d.). *Integrating technology into the curriculum: Technology in social studies.* Retrieved from http://www.ncrel.org/tplan/guide/int7.htm

Olson J. K., & Mokhtari, K. (2010). Making science real. *Educational Leadership, 67*(6), 56–62.

Patterson, G. (2012). Blended education for high-octane motivation. *Phi Delta Kappan 94*(2), 14–18.

Ponder, G. (1979). The more things change: The status of social studies. *Educational Leadership, 36*(7), 515–518.

Reeves, D. (2007). Leading to change/academics and the arts. *Educational Leadership, 64*(5), 80–81.

Richards, H. V., Brown, A. F., & Forde, T. B. (2006). *Addressing diversity in schools: Culturally responsive pedagogy.* Tempe, AZ: National Center for Culturally Responsive Educational Systems.

Richardson, J. (Ed.) (2014). Highlighted & underlined: A notebook of short but worthy items. *Phi Delta Kappan, 95*(6), 7.

Roberts, H. D., Kaulfers, W. V., & Kefaurer, G. N. (Eds.). (1943). *English for social living.* New York, NY: McGraw-Hill.

Rosen, L. (2012). STEM gets a boost from business. *Principal, 92*(2), 6–8.

Santos, R. M. (2004). Ensuring culturally and linguistically appropriate assessment of young children. *Young Children, 59*(1), 48–50.

Schifter, D., & Granofsky, B. (2012). The right equation for math teaching. *Principal, 92*(2), 16–20.

Schmoker, M. (2012). Can schools close the gap? *Phi Delta Kappan, 93*(7), 70–71.

Schutz, R. (2007). *Stephen Krashen's theory of second language acquisition.* Retrieved from http://www.sk.com.br/sk-krash.html

Shanahan, T. (2013). Tackling Informational text: You want me to read what? *Educational Leadership, 71*(3), 10–15.

Shaver, J. P., Davis, O. L., Jr., & Helburn, S. W. (1979). The status of social studies education: Impressions from three NSF studies. *Social Education, 43*(2), 150–163.

Shumway, J. F., & Kyriopoulos, J. (2013–2014). Mastery multiplied. *Educational Leadership, 71*(4), 73–76.

Silva, J., Delleman, P., & Phesia, A. (2013). Preparing English language learners for complex reading. *Educational Leadership, 71*(3), 52–61.

Soderman, A. K. (2010). Language immersion programs for young? Yes . . . but proceed with caution. *Phi Delta Kappan, 91*(8), 54–61.

Sotomayor, K. (2013). Ten to teen: Teaching STEM to English-language learners. *Principal, 92*(3), 40–41.

Stewart, B., Willard, T., & Wesson, K. A. (2012). The impact of next generation science standards. *Principal, 92*(2), 18–19.

Stoskopf, A. (2001). Reviving Clio: Inspired history teaching and learning (without high-stakes testing). *Phi Delta Kappan, 82,* 468–473.

Strickland, D. S. (2012). Planning curriculum to meet the common core state standards. *Reading Today, 29*(4), 25–26.

Superka, D. P., Hawke, S., & Morrissett, I. (1980). The current and future status of the social studies. *Social Education, 44*(5), 362–369.

Thompson, C. L. (2011). A dose of writing reality: Helping students become better writers. *Phi Delta Kappan, 92*(7), 57–61.

Tucker, K. (2012). Setting a foundation for STEM. *Principal, 92*(2), 3.

Vandertie, J., Corner, A. B., & Corner, K. J. (2012). The new P.E. *Phi Delta Kappan, 93*(7), 21–25.

Van Keer, H., & Vanderlinde, R. (2013). A book for two: Explicitly taught reading comprehension strategies paired with peer tutoring can boost reading skills for elementary school students. *Phi Delta Kappan, 94*(8), 54–58.

Vitaska, D. (2002). The new language classroom. *Media & Methods, 39*(1), 10–13.

Walling, D. R. (2001). Rethinking visual arts education: A convergence of influences. *Phi Delta Kappan, 82*(8), 626–631.

WebQuest. (2014). What is a WebQuest? Retrieved from http://webquest.org

Whitehead, B. M., Boschee, F., & Decker, R. H. (2013). *The principal: Leadership for a global society.* Thousand Oaks, CA: Sage.

Whitehead, B. M., Jensen, D. F. N., & Boschee, F. (2013). *Planning for technology: A guide for school administrators, technology coordinators, and curriculum leaders* (2nd ed.). Thousand Oaks, CA: Corwin Press.

CHAPTER 14

Current Developments Across the Curriculum

After years of test-driven, high-stakes accountability, many educators and policymakers in the United States are looking forward to developing a more balanced approach to curriculum planning. Rather than maintaining a system that uses narrow measures of student achievement to sanction poorly performing schools, the push is now to implement next-generation learning goals that challenge learners and develop higher order thinking skills (HOTS; Darling-Hammond, 2014). In addition, curriculum planners are working with changes that best integrate new advances in technology as well as incorporate listening, speaking, and thinking skills into and throughout the curriculum. Such changes will require both a different perspective on curriculum change as well as different processes for planning and implementation.

Questions addressed in this chapter include the following:

- What are some of the curriculum changes that are improving listening, speaking, and thinking skills?
- What changes have taken place in technology use in our schools?

Key to Leadership

Meeting the needs of advanced learners, struggling learners, or students with different learning styles can be achieved through the use of technology. Innovative technology programs can help students gauge their progress and become more self-paced.

THINKING SKILLS

The synergy that occurs between creativity and critical thinking allows powerful learning to occur (Moeller, Cutler, Fiedler, & Weier, 2013). It is not a surprise that a major movement for reform includes the concerted effort to improve critical thinking skills throughout the disciplines. A major focus area for improving thinking skills is the engagement of students with technology and content. High-quality lessons involving thinking skills generally invite students to interact purposefully with content as part of their mobile learning experience. Thus, by building on their previous knowledge and real-world examples, various strategies are used to engage students in firsthand experiences. This is one of the best ways to get students thinking.

Curriculum Tip 14.1	Critical thinking is the skillful application of a repertoire of validated general techniques for deciding the level of confidence you should have in a proposition in the light of the available evidence. —Francis Bacon (1605)

In reviewing the literature, another major strategy involving the integration of thinking skills is the concept of **metacognition,** or thinking about thinking. In the research literature, metacognition is usually presented as a conscious and deliberate mental activity—we become aware that we do not understand a paragraph we read or a statement we hear (Martinez, 2006). Studies in metacognition have led to a number of applications in teacher-directed learning. Some of these focus on teaching students to relate academic success to personal effort rather than to chance. Other applications emphasize the teaching of self-regulation. Students learn the efficient management of their own participation, studies, and assignments. Other applications emphasize teaching students learning strategies, processes, and systems that they can apply to a range of tasks and situations—in other words, teaching students how to think and learn. Some individual teachers believe engaging students is not enough—they must be involved in a critical thinking process as well.

Curriculum Tip 14.2	We need to teach not only the facts but teach how the facts relate to our global world.

Still another question that seems to divide the profession is whether thinking skills are more usefully perceived as a set of general processes that transcend the disciplines or as content-specific skills that should be anchored in a discipline. If thinking is a set of general processes, then these processes can best be taught in separate thinking courses. If thinking is subject specific, then it is best taught within the context of a discipline.

Common Core State Standards (CCSS) make sure students are refining their thinking skills (Gardner & Powell, 2013–2014). In all fairness, thinking skills, and more specifically critical

Curriculum Tip 14.3	The most basic premise in the current thinking skills movement is the notion that students *can* learn to think better if schools concentrate on teaching them *how* to do so.

thinking skills, have been an important focus of many schools for years. Very early on, Glatthorn (1985) had some success in using a critical thinking approach. He proposed that after reviewing theory and research on thinking, teachers in each secondary department are first asked to select one of the following units of study as being most appropriate for each grade level they teach: controlled problem solving (using algorithms and heuristic strategies for solving convergent problems with one right answer), open-ended problem solving (using systematic strategies to find the optimal solution to an open-ended problem), information processing (storing, retrieving, and evaluating information), reasoning (the systematic application of logic), evaluating (using critical thinking processes to evaluate products and individuals), analyzing persuasive messages (including critical analysis of the mass media), mastering disciplinary inquiry (learning the special inquiry processes and truth tests used in a discipline), making moral choices (making ethical judgments), and using thinking in making other life choices (especially college and careers). These particular unit topics, focusing as they do on more general processes that are relatively simple to link to a given discipline, seem to appeal to most teachers as both important and subject relevant. After each departmental team reaches a consensus on the units to be developed, the team works together to organize discipline-based instructional materials focusing on the general processes identified. They are thus able to produce a graded series of units that, while lacking professional sophistication, is likely to be used.

With that phase of the project accomplished, they turn their attention to specific thinking skills that were not incorporated into the units. They review a comprehensive list of such specific skills as classifying and making inferences and identify those they think should be taught. In teams, they decide whether each skill so identified would be better taught in an "integrated" or a "focused" lesson (see Exhibit 14.1 for a form that can be used to assist teachers in making these decisions). In an *integrated* lesson, as the term is used here, a content objective (such as being able to describe Cortez's first meeting with Native Americans) is the objective of the lesson; the thinking skill (in this case, perhaps, contrasting) is taught as part of that lesson. In a *focused* lesson, a thinking skill, such as evaluating sources for bias, is the objective of the lesson. Subject content is merely the carrier.

Effective Schools Process

Along with Glatthorn's approach to aiding critical thinking skills as noted previously, Taylor (2002) shared six correlates of effective schools developed by Ronald Edmonds and John Frederickson. The six correlates are as follows:

1. Clearly stated and focused school mission

2. Safe and orderly climate for learning

EXHIBIT 14.1   Identifying Specific Thinking Skills

The following critical thinking skills are often taught in school subjects. Consider that skill and its importance in the subject and grade level you teach. Indicate your preference for teaching that subject by putting an X in the appropriate column. A focused lesson is one in which the thinking skill represents the main objective of that lesson. An integrated lesson is one in which a subject-matter concept or skill represents the main objective; the thinking skill is taught in the process of teaching that concept or skill. "Not Appropriate" means that you do not think that particular skill is appropriate for your subject or grade level.

Skill	Focused	Integrated	Not Appropriate
1. Finding and defining problems			
2. Representing problems in an appropriate symbol system			
3. Organizing facts and concepts in a systematic way			
4. Inferring a conclusion from what is stated			
5. Locating and evaluating sources			
6. Synthesizing information to reach a conclusion			
7. Distinguishing between observations, assumptions, and inferences			
8. Classifying logically			
9. Making predictions			
10. Interpreting nonliteral material			
11. Identifying persuasive messages and techniques			
12. Applying logical operations of negation, disjunction, and conjunction			
13. Making and using analogies			
14. Determining likely causes			
15. Explaining cause-and-effect relationships			
16. Avoiding misleading use of language			
17. Avoiding statistical fallacies			
18. Other:			

3. High expectations for students, teachers, and administrators

4. Opportunity to learn and student time-on-task

5. Instructional leadership by all administrators and staff members

6. Positive homeschool relations

The **effective schools process** is considered by many a tried-and-true process of school change that can create schools in which all children make progress and are ready for study at the next grade level. To complement the effective schools process, a number of districts are developing and using instructional design. This process can help schools restructure the delivery and assessment of classroom instruction and integrate thinking skills into the curriculum. If school leaders are to formulate an instructional design process, it is also important to involve three distinct thinking skills strategies: *independent thinking, self-managed learning,* and *self-directed learning* (Gibbons, 2004, p. 466).

Independent thinking requires students to address subsets of related questions and develop essential skills outlined in the curriculum. Requirements include inquiry into essential questions that students pose for themselves. These pursuits are supported by a number of excellent instruments, practices, and services.

Self-managed learning requires that students have outcomes to achieve. Students make their own timetables; work alone; work with others; attend seminars, workshops, and labs; work online; and use other resources to help them in their self-regulated efforts.

Self-directed learning requires that each day of the week is set aside for independent activities, regular education, trips, or challenging exercises. This may include the Walkabout Program, logical inquiry, creativity, practical applications, or community activities. Students present their accomplishments to their peers, teachers, parents, and other adults at graduation. Individual work is supported by an adviser. When focusing on the classroom restructuring process, it is important to place an emphasis on the integration of thinking skills. As part of this process, we find the development of activities in processing information, inventing and expanding on ideas, and examining and evaluating facts and processes to be an essential part of every discipline. Similarly, thinking skills should be deeply embedded in all strands of the communication arts. Students must think to respond to literature, to write, to speak, to use media, to listen, and to read. In short, thinking skills provide students with the means to make the most effective use of all areas of their education.

Curriculum Tip 14.4	Higher-order thinking skills (HOTS) concentrate on the top three levels of Bloom's taxonomy: analysis, synthesis, and evaluation (see Exhibit 10.4 on the levels of action verbs).

It is important, in planning curricular strategies, to introduce thinking skills, to reinforce them throughout the content levels, and to build more complex processes on the foundation of skills introduced earlier. Students should be encouraged to "think about their thinking"—examining the thinking skills and strategies they apply to interpret literature and media, choose language, make an appeal in advertising, or follow directions.

LISTENING SKILLS

Listening is the first source of communication. By developing competent listening skills, one expands vocabulary, develops sentence structures, and begins to discriminate what is heard. Speaking, reading, and writing are built on this foundation. Students come to school with some degree of competence in listening, acquired "naturally" in the developmental process. Consequently, listening is often the most neglected area of instruction in the communication arts curriculum. The International Listening Association came out with the following information:

- 45% of a student's day is spent listening
- Students are expected to acquire 85% of the knowledge they have by listening
- Only 2% of the population ever received formal listening instruction (Learning Ally, 2011)

Many educators have assumed that listening skills can be developed by telling students to listen and periodically reminding them they are not listening. Also, teacher education programs, textbooks, digital sources, communication research, and assessments give little assistance in listening instruction.

In spite of this neglect, the importance of listening has been thoroughly documented. For example, a White Paper sponsored by the research committee of the International Listening Association (2008) supports the notion that using meta-analysis, practical significant differences were noted between the treatment and control groups in the comprehension modes of listening and reading. The effect size in reading (.9953) was considered a large difference, while the effect size for listening (.3747) was considered a small difference. The effect size data indicate that treatment of listening skills training improved listening and reading comprehension. This is consistent with research on the benefits derived from expertise in one comprehension mode carrying over to another language arts strand. The overall conclusion of the study revealed that more time should be spent on listening skill development.

Listening is a skill that can be improved through direct instruction and practice. It requires conscious planning by the teacher to include listening activities and requires practice by the student. Here are some easy tips to start helping students become better listeners:

> I like to listen. I have learned a great deal from listening carefully. Most people never listen.
>
> —Ernest Hemingway

- Address communication needs of students that arise from real-life situations.
- Involve direct teaching of listening strategies and practice of those strategies in a variety of listening situations.
- Include listening in all communication contexts, including interpersonal, small group, public communication, and mass communication.
- Integrate with the teaching of all the other communication arts strands.
- Be interdisciplinary across the curriculum.
- Be incorporated in cocurricular programs that aid students in refining their listening skills.
- Be sensitive to the diversity of culturally appropriate listening behaviors.

Teaching listening skills may not seem necessary, but according to statistics, studies, and state standards, it is. Listening is a skill that students can use in every subject, and it will benefit them throughout their lives.

SPEAKING SKILLS

Children enter school with some basic competence in speaking, but without social contact and modeling, speech may not develop as it should. A child's self-concept is largely formed through interaction with significant people in the child's environment. The role of the teacher is to help students improve and refine their speaking skills in a variety of situations. Good speaking skills are important to students for their success in school and in the workplace. Employers frequently identify oral communication skills as the most important skills considered for initial employment, retention, and promotion. An average of 30% of our communication is spoken, and speech is second only to listening in frequency of use in everyday life. Speech has an important place in the curriculum.

Given the importance of speech and the position it often has had in the curriculum, districts developing speaking curricula should keep in mind the following statements. Instruction in speaking should (a) address the communication needs of students that arise from everyday situations; (b) provide direct instruction, supervised practice, constructive feedback, and more practice in a variety of situations rather than offering only opportunities to speak; (c) include all communication contexts (e.g., intrapersonal, interpersonal, group, public, and mass communication); (d) be integrated with the teaching of all the other communication arts strands; (e) be interdisciplinary and across the curriculum; (f) offer opportunities for cocurricular programs that aid students in refining their speaking skills; and (g) be sensitive to the diversity of culturally appropriate speaking behaviors.

ENGLISH LANGUAGE LEARNER EDUCATION

Not surprisingly, school populations are changing. Many students are now English language learners (ELLs) and represent a wide array of diverse language and cultural backgrounds. Broadening our view of ELL students is crucial in this time of changing populations, changing demographics, and new census data. For example, as noted by Soto (2014), there are different kinds of ELLs: newcomers who are highly literate, educated, but under-schooled; long-term ELLs who have been in the country six years or longer; and ELLs progressing predictably through the developmental sequence. Thus, it is imperative to tailor instruction and professional development to the specific needs of the ELLs at a school site. Additionally, it should be noted that sociolinguists study language in its social contexts and thereby study the varieties spoken by subgroups based on *geographic region, ethnicity, age, educational background, and job description.* A common theory among sociolinguistics is that essentially "we are what we speak." Some students speak stigmatized or marginalized dialects and languages, while others speak the valued form, yet many communicate effectively in their subgroup. What makes dialects different from on another is their unique use of lexicon, their unique syntax, and their unique accent (O'Neal & Ringler, 2010).

According to data from the U.S. Department of Education, the population of ELLs grew significantly from 2001 to 2010 and continues to grow rapidly (Zacarian, 2013). With a growing level of urgency about this increasing population, educators are now looking closely at what is being used to design, implement, and make data-based decisions about programming for ELLs as well as to ensure that the programming works.

As part of this process, four common descriptors of ELLs are provided.

1. *The languages of English learners.* Many state regulations call for schools to employ bilingual programming when there is a critical mass of speakers from the same language group.

2. *Country of origin.* While many ELLs come from countries other than the United States, research indicates that the majority of elementary-aged ELLs are born in the United States.

3. *Level of English language development (ELD).* In addition to the number of languages and counties of origin, ELLs range in English development from those at the beginning stages to those close to being proficient. Each state provides a means for measuring and describing the state of ELD for each ELL.

4. *Performance on high-stakes tests.* The achievement gap between ELLs and the general student population is significant and growing. In response, educators are analyzing the performance of ELLs on state tests to determine who needs to improve, what needs to improve, and how improvements will be accomplished.

Knowledge of research regarding ELLs is becoming increasingly important. Likewise, this research needs to focus on instructional strategies of ELL students as well as the importance of educator roles in developing effective programs. Along this line, Protheroe (2011) shared examples of various strategies.

Examples of effective ELL strategies include the following:

- A focus on oral language development, such as opportunities to practice English in the classroom, building on students' background knowledge
- Cooperative learning
- Explicit instruction in the elements of English literacy
- Differentiated instruction
- The use of graphic organizers as a comprehension strategy
- A focus on academic language

Teachers using these strategies also need to carefully consider characteristics of the ELL students being served, as well as local school and community resources relevant to ELL instruction. When making decisions about instructional models, programs, and practices curriculum leaders and teachers might address a number of questions.

Examples of ELL instructional questions include the following:

1. How long have students lived in the United States (e.g., are they recent immigrants, second generation)?

2. What kinds of language resources are available to the students at home or in their community?

3. How long should students receive instruction in their primary language?

4. What should be the relative emphasis between promoting knowledge and skills in the primary language and developing English language proficiency?

5. What are the experience levels of teachers?

6. How much experience do the teachers have working with ELL students?

With the advent of CCSS, it is important for school leaders and teachers to be sensitive to ELL needs and issues as they relate to standards. For example, Silva, Delleman, and Phesia (2013) noted that without explicit instruction, Spanish-speaking ELLs exhibit little awareness of the rhetorical characteristic of informative text in English. Likewise, second language learners' familiarity with the rhetorical schemata of their first language can hinder their ability to process and retain information presented in their second language. These issues can be eased by scaffolding the steps students use to process and analyze argumentative discourse. Scaffolding includes the following:

1. Identifying support for main ideas

2. Recognizing bias

3. Distinguishing arguments (issues)

4. Evaluating relative strength of arguments (issues)

5. Drawing conclusions based on evidence

As can be seen, being mindful of ELL issues and creating and implementing tasks that both support and challenge multicultural learners is a key component of school success. Along with technological advances, CCSS, and new ways of improving schools, school leaders and teachers must develop a better understanding as to the varieties of English: regional dialects, nonstandard, and marginalized varieties. It is with insightful curriculum planning, technological advances, and explicit support for native languages that schools can best help ELL students in the future.

LEADERSHIP FOR SOCIALLY DIVERSE GROUPS

Addressing prejudice in the classroom is as crucial to our youth's education as learning to read (Shields 2014). With that said, social issues can be politically challenging for many schools. One area of special note is gender bias as well as lesbian, gay, bisexual, and transgender (LGBT) student concerns. Despite progress, schools continue to struggle with how to increase diversity awareness in schools. According to Wright (2010), most of the research on this population revolves around three themes: the history of LGBT students and educators, the climates they have faced and currently face in schools, and individual school experiences.

As a result of the established values and attitudes that many youth acquire from their parents and society in general, the research, according to Pace (2005), does the following:

> Portrays a bleak picture for gay and lesbian students. The majority of the literature is of a quantitative nature and often reveals many challenges for these students, including verbal and physical harassment, low self-esteem, poor grades, and a particularly high risk of suicide, among other dangers. (Abstract)

According to Pace's (2009) research conducted with eight gay and lesbian students, some of the wishes or desires of those students include the following:

- If you decide that you're going to be a teacher, or if you want to be a person who is in the school, then you need to be there for everybody. (p. 22)
- It's not just about strengthening gay and lesbian students, but there is a need for changes in school policy. (p. 41)
- A strong bond with parents along with a diverse and open school helps to traverse the difficult path for gay and lesbian students. (p. 60)
- Diverse sexual orientation should be openly addressed in classes (N. J. Pace, personal communication, September 13, 2012).

Basically, school leaders and teachers have an obligation to support and enhance the self-esteem of all students regardless of their sexual orientation. Conceivably, the most compelling reason for schools to address sexual orientation straightforwardly is that young people are asking. Silence on these issues communicates values just as loudly as responding would. Along with more awareness, more positive steps are being taken to help LGBT teachers and students. In the past decade, school leaders have increasingly included gender bias and particularly LGBT concerns into teaching and learning about diverse populations. Likewise, more school leaders and faculty members are working toward making a significant contribution to the safety and well-being of LGBT students and educators.

ACCOMMODATING DIVERSITY

A careful look around the country, as well as around the globe, reveals that communities are embracing educational change. For example, technology innovations are helping to enhance differentiated teaching and learning. Through a variety of new applications and programs, individual instruction can be more self-paced, and assessment tools can better gauge student progress. As will be discussed in Chapter 15, this is particularly beneficial when either modifying curriculum or accommodating students with special needs.

In a first-step move, visionary school leaders are now refocusing district and state efforts on how technology can best enhance a variety of students' academic and social needs, especially through cloud computing (Damani, 2011–2012). What is even more interesting is that with all these changes, students are matriculating into upper grades with more technical skills as well as a greater desire to learn. More to the point, these reforms are generating greater interest on the part of parents, teachers, and students as to the real-world relevancy of educational technology.

All of these changes are causing technology planners and school leaders to rethink how schools approach teaching and learning. Given the circumstances, perhaps we have reached a tipping point in how schools address reform—especially on how school planners, administrators, board members, trustees, and teachers are reassessing the ways technology can impact instructional delivery. In keeping with this perspective, educational leaders are now compelled to ask some penetrating questions:

- How can technology best be integrated into educational programs to help diverse learners?
- Will educationally related technological approaches have the impact we expect?
- Is redirecting our technological program worth the effort?
- Are there technological advances on the horizon that will render our current use obsolete in the not-too-distant future?
- Where can we go to get the best advice about meeting our technological needs as they relate to diversity and multicultural education?

INNOVATION AND 21st-CENTURY LEARNING

The role and importance of technology in the curriculum is a given educational reality. With this reality, the challenge facing educational leaders and teachers is to tune into the future direction of education and better synchronize learning with modern, technological pedagogies and curriculum. One justification for this is that with information literacy and global awareness a part of our daily lives, it is important, if not crucial, for educational reform to become a priority, especially when connecting technology to learning. In order to meet these demands, administrators and teachers must understand changing environments in technology and pay keen attention to innovative ways of leading schools. Sharing leadership, as well as sharing a vision of technology, is paramount if we are to meet the ever-increasing local and global demands placed on our schools. Understanding that this new reality is upon us, educators worldwide are coming to realize that learners of the 21st century are different and do require modern learning experiences.

Technology and Pedagogy

What is extraordinary is the capability of technology in augmenting educational reform in terms of pedagogies. To prove this point, models emerging from research, in the areas of leadership and technology, show that technology is becoming a driver of student growth and achievement (Lytle, 2012). This alters the philosophies that teachers hold about the nature of instruction. One of the realities seen in the literature, from a philosophical level, is how many educators continue to depend on the foundational pedagogies of Piaget, Bruner, and Vygotsky, for example. The struggle here is that their pedagogies are based on a non-technological educational space. This creates a unique philosophical conflict between how learning is conceived and how learning happens when technology is added to the equation. What is required, perhaps, are modern technological pedagogies that are consistent with the technological educational space we now inhabit. A key, then, is researching and discovering how future educators will be able to learn to adapt to tomorrow's pedagogical challenges and opportunities.

Redefining the Culture of School

New advances in technology are helping to redefine the culture of schools. In this regard, innovative administrators, teachers, and technology planners are blending an assortment of data-driven assessment processes into the rubric of school change. Furthermore, there is a host of Web-based applications providing high-quality lesson content as well as digitized assessment item banks that can be used to create individual student assessments. With all of this happening, the result has been an increase in teachers currently using standards-aligned formative and summative tests, quizzes, and study guides in classrooms. Thus, with game-changing technology applications in place, every teacher and every school leader has, or will have, an ability to improve how students learn. This is the essence of school reform.

Technology Linked to Student Achievement

When all is said and done, it will be individual teachers who determine the success or failure of technology in the classroom. Keeping with this perspective, it is the interaction between a teacher and student that truly accentuates learning in a technological environment. Technology is a proven tool that can help lower dropout rates, enhance student achievement, provide access to information around the world, and raise students' self-esteem. In every class, teachers must contend with a variety of learners, such as the fast-paced learner, the less-motivated learner, students with learning difficulties, and the list goes on. With technology in the classroom, teachers have access to tools that have the potential for providing learning experiences relevant to each of these unique learners.

A classroom is a very complex setting in which to work, and technology, for many teachers, only makes matters more complicated. In order to have a successful technology plan, technology coordinators and school leaders need to be conscious of the realities that can hinder the process of bringing technology into the 21st-century classroom. Once school leaders seriously consider these realities, they will have the necessary knowledge to counter the negative impact of these barriers. There has been ample research in this area leading to the following variables negatively impacting technology integration (Hew & Brush, 2007).

- *Lack of resources.* Teachers need the right technology that is linked with the vision and mission for technology in the local district and school.

- *Limited knowledge and skills.* This is where professional development is so important. Teachers need proper training and knowledge to help them take full advantage of the potential that technology has for reforming the educational experience for students.
- *Poor visioning institution.* Leaders in schools must have a desire to create 21st-century schools. Technology change can only happen if meaningful school reform occurs and school leaders support a technologically literate school culture.
- *Negative attitudes and beliefs.* So many schools are plagued by outdated or defiant attitudes with people saying it can't be done, I don't want to change, or I can't see the vision. All school members must learn to see the vision and urgency for bringing technology into schools in meaningful and purposeful ways.
- *Weak assessment strategies.* Empirical assessment is such a huge driver of decisions related to educational reform. In this sense, some schools are nervous about the risks associated with giving technology a more dominant part in the learning experience of students with the fear that student achievement will go down during the integration phase. At the same time, empirical assessment can cause educators to use technology purely for data collection and assessment and lose sight of its ability to positively impact teaching and learning.
- *Inability to see broad application.* A dilemma within education is that there is a culture that says technology is only effective in certain subject areas and is not relevant across the entire curriculum.

The other big challenge facing schools are educators who do not have a clear understanding of what a 21st-century school looks like and what kind of learning happens in them. Once educators catch the vision of this, then school reform linked with technology integration will be a natural path of school reform. Under this reality, the proper context will exist for the creative potential of technology to truly impact student achievement and curricular design.

Curriculum Tip 14.5	Review your school's technology plan to ensure that it is developing well-rounded, adept, intuitive, and culturally aware students.

Impact of Technological Advances

Along with focusing on student achievement, educational leaders must realize the overall impact of technology on schools. This is especially the case due to educators having a sense of greater ownership as well as having their work on permanent display for the world to see. Naturally, these changes continue to be hugely significant. Keeping with this perspective of a culture of change, educators worldwide are finding advancements in technology can potentially impact schools in at least 10 major areas (Whitehead, Jensen, & Boschee, 2013).

Impact areas include the following:

1. *Increased student writing.* Simply measuring the amount that students are using technology applications to write reveals one positive impact of technology. Students are writing more compositions and doing so more often. Many teachers now find that students are producing three times the amount of written documents than they did before digital learning became available. Teachers who carefully watch students find that it often appears to be easier for their pupils to use a mobile device than a pen or pencil to write. The direct result is that students are writing more often and with seemingly greater ease.

2. *Higher quality student writing.* Analysis of student writing by numerous researchers has shown that word processing–related programs help students become more effective writers. This is not surprising to anyone who uses digital media to any degree.

3. *Enhanced cooperative learning.* Teachers using mobile technology are finding this format greatly enhances and supports cooperative learning strategies. When collaborative learning is linked with technology, it is known to have a strong positive influence on student achievement.

4. *Enhanced integration of curriculum.* Instructors having access to cloud computing as well as mobile devices are finding technological applications are making it easier to integrate history–social studies, literature, math, and science into a more coordinated series of learning experiences for students. A practical example of this is when students use applications to create content integrated presentations using material from several disciplines. In addition, maps, graphs, tables, and illustrations from a variety of subject areas can be easily shared or incorporated into student projects and visual presentations.

5. *Greater range of learning applications.* Teachers are finding the use of technology helps accommodate different ways students learn. This is best evidenced by research noting certain cognitive skills are strengthened, sometimes substantially, by the use of mobile devices and the Internet (Carr, 2011).

6. *Increased applications of cross-age tutoring.* Students using mobile technology now have easy access to information across grade levels. As a result, teachers are finding that older students can work with younger students on cooperative or tutorial projects anytime, anywhere.

7. *Increased teacher communication.* Instructors using mobile technology are finding it easy to communicate with colleagues. Today's technological advances create greater possibilities for exchanging information and sharing on local, state, national, as well as global levels.

8. *Greater parent communication.* New technology innovations are proving to be a promising link between home and school. Parents anywhere and at any time can readily receive updated reports on student performance, homework assignments, as well as school activities.

9. *Enhanced community relations.* Bringing the school and community together provides another compelling reason for implementing technology into schools. In many school districts, community residents and local business members often participate in campus training and professional development programs using school technology. As a result, adult education classes are on the rise. In addition, students and teachers across the country are helping civic groups as well as small businesses become more attuned to the latest up-to-date technological advances.

10. *Enhanced global learners.* Never before have educators and students been able to develop a better understanding of other cultures and people than is possible today. Many schools are now using technology applications to access information from all parts of the globe. As one considers this phenomenon, it becomes increasingly evident that technology in schools is paving the way for students, teachers, and citizens to enter into a community of global learners.

PROFESSIONAL DEVELOPMENT AND TECHNOLOGY

A reality of reform in schools is for school leaders to increase the role of technology in professional development. Many groups, societies, and organizations have thought intently about this issue and have provided public school leaders with the means to help them make informed decisions about technology, collaborative learning, and professional development in their schools. Utilizing these public sources of data can help local leaders bring strategy to their school technology reform.

For instance, the Office of Educational Technology within the U.S. Department of Education has produced a national education technology plan called "Transforming American Education: Learning Powered by Technology 2010." When referencing professional development, there are some goals from the technology plan that educational leaders can consider as they work with their teachers. The overall plan sets a vision of a model of learning powered by technology with goals and recommendations in five essential areas: learning, assessment, teaching, infrastructure, and productivity.

- *Learning goal.* All learners will have engaging and empowering learning experiences both in and out of school that prepare them to be active, creative, knowledgeable, and ethical participants in our globally networked society.
- *Assessment goal.* Our education system at all levels will leverage the power of technology to measure what matters and use assessment data for continuous improvement.
- *Teaching goal.* Professional educators will be supported individually and in teams by technology that connects them to data, content, resources, expertise, and learning experiences that enable and inspire more effective teaching for all learners.
- *Infrastructure goal.* All students and educators will have access to a comprehensive infrastructure for learning when and where they need it.

- *Productivity goal.* Our education system at all levels will redesign processes and structures to take advantage of the *power* of technology to improve learning outcomes while making more efficient use of time, money, and staff.

In relation to this technology plan and setting a strategic direction for your school's technology reform, educational administrators and teacher–leaders can work through the worksheet shown in Exhibit 14.2 to help bring a strategic focus to professional development.

EXHIBIT 14.2 Strategic Professional Development				
Teaching and Learning Powered by Technology for the 21st Century				
Educational Need	*Are your teachers/ administrators skilled in this?*		*Relevant to your school?*		*Suggested ideas/ opportunities for professional development (if needed)*
	Yes	*No*	*Yes*	*No*	
Students need to learn using multimedia content.					
Students need skills in participating and collaborating in online social networks.					
Students need technology to help with personalized learning experiences.					
Students need to be engaged in learning through small and large groups within a local and global community.					
Students need access to a global set of educators such as parents, experts, mentors, and teachers.					
Students need resources that aid in 24/7 and lifelong learning.					
Students need 21st-century skills of: • Critical Thinking • Problem Solving • Collaboration • Multimedia Communication					

(Continued)

EXHIBIT 14.2   (Continued)

Students need exposure to technology that professionals use to help solve real-world problems.					
Teachers need technology based assessments to both diagnose and modify: • Conditions of learning • Instructional practices • Level of knowledge • Problem-solving abilities					
Teachers need technology-based assessments to determine what students have learned.					
Teachers need relevant student data at the right time and in the right form.					
Teachers need training to help them manage assessment data.					
Teachers need training to help them analyze relevant data.					
Teachers need training to help them act upon results of assessment data.					
Teachers need technology to help them transition into connected teaching.					
Teachers need to be fully connected to school learning data.					
Teachers need technology to help them: • Create • Manage • Engage • Support students in their learning both inside school and out of school					
Teachers need access to resources that improve their own instructional practices.					

Teachers need to see education as a team activity where they are connected with online learning communities including: • Students • Fellow educators • Professional experts • Members of relevant learning communities • Parents					
Teachers need professional development that is: • collaborative • coherent • continuous • convenient • enabled by online resources and opportunities					
Teachers need professional development that exposes them to: • exceptional technology educators • technology learning systems • self-directed learning programs					
Schools need technology infrastructure that is: • always on • available to students • available to educators • available to administrators regardless of location or time of day					
Schools need technology infrastructures that allow for capturing and sharing knowledge in: • multimedia formats • still and moving images • audio • text					

(Continued)

EXHIBIT 14.2 (Continued)					
Schools need technology that enables an integration of in- and out-of-school learning.					
Schools need technology infrastructures that ensure the security and privacy of educational data.					
Schools need an interdisciplinary team of professionals to oversee learning that is powered by technology.					

SOURCE: Whitehead et al. (2013).

As can be seen, school leaders can use this information as a means to begin developing collaborative learning, differentiated instruction, and professional development initiatives for the school year. For example, principals can use a nominal group technique to determine where the faculty rate their professional development needs. For this process, you first of all generate a list of the professional development needs that are "relevant to your school." This can be done on a whiteboard or on several large pieces of paper. From here, each faculty member is given 10 smaller circle stickers and then asked to place them next to the items he or she feels is most relevant to his or her professional development needs. There are no rules regarding how the stickers can be placed. For example, one faculty member could put all ten of their stickers next to one item, or five next to one item and five stickers next to another item, or any other combination. Next, you tally up the stickers next to each item on the list. This will give you a list of the areas that faculty deem as related to their most pressing professional development needs related to technology and the curriculum. You can then begin to fill out the last column of the chart related to "suggested ideas for professional development" on the items that were ranked the highest. This can then be used to define the strategy for professional development in your school for that given academic year.

Applying strategy and focus to collaborative learning through technology and professional development in your school is essential to having meaning and purpose behind your efforts. You want to have a vision about how teachers will be connected with technology and how they can use that to empower collaborative learning in the 21st century. The following conceptual model from the Transforming Education through Technology Plan is a good image of how these various components can be used to direct professional development in your school.

Setting Priorities

One of the most important keys to school reform is enhancing collaborative learning through professional development. The key here is that in an age of global interconnectedness, we

GRAPHIC 14.1   Collaborative Learning Through Professional Development

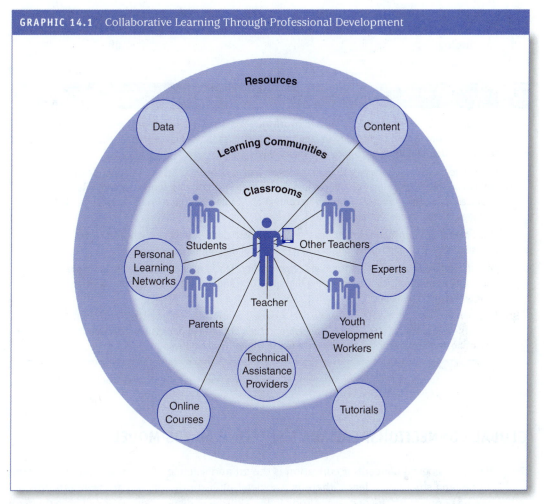

SOURCE: U.S. Department of Education, Office of Educational Technology (2010).

cannot afford to work at less than stellar levels when it comes to teaching and learning. According to Sterling and Frazier (2011), leaving teachers on their own to determine how to teach is not an effective way to support staff and is unfair to students. The key, then, is helping teachers fully understand and appreciate the powerful role technology plays in collaborative learning and unlocking student potential.

Within the priorities of 21st-century learning, the focus on collaborative learning and technology-based professional development is to assist as many teachers as possible to become digitally literate. This is best evidenced in Exhibit 14.3. By incorporating these components into their educational life, the teacher is able to process information from a variety of sources and formats so that he or she can draw upon his or her own conclusions and create a personal knowledge path about the relationship between technology and learning. In doing so, teachers will be able to empower their students with the skills, knowledge, and dispositions necessary to be successful in a global reality dominated by technology.

EXHIBIT 14.3 Core Competencies for Digitally Literate Teachers

1. *Facilitate and inspire student learning and creativity.* Teachers use their knowledge of subject matter, teaching, learning, and technology to facilitate experiences that advance student learning, creativity, and innovation in both face-to-face and virtual environments.

2. *Design and develop digital age learning experiences and assessments.* Teachers design, develop, and evaluate authentic learning experiences and assessment incorporating contemporary tools and resources to maximize content learning in context and to develop the relevant knowledge, skills, and attitudes related to content area.

3. *Model digital age work and learning.* Teachers exhibit knowledge, skills, and work processes representative of an innovative professional in a global and digital society.

4. *Promote and model digital citizenship and responsibility.* Teachers understand local and global societal issues and responsibilities in an evolving digital culture and exhibit legal and ethical behavior in their professional practices.

5. *Engage in professional growth and leadership.* Teachers continually improve their professional practice, model lifelong learning, and exhibit leadership in their school and professional community by promoting and demonstrating the effective use of digital tools and resources.

SOURCE: International Society for Technology in Education. *NETS for Teachers.* Retrieved online http://www.iste.org/standards/nets-for-teachers

---

GLOBAL CONNECTIONS: CANADA'S SHIFTING MINDS MODEL

The pedagogical concept of education is the art and science of helping students to learn. In helping students to learn, there is a societal philosophy that we are trying to provide young people with the necessary knowledge, skills, and dispositions that will help them to be healthy, informed, and productive citizens. In so doing, the work of education is to envision the future and see what learners will need five, ten, or even twenty years into the future so that they can engage in their world. Educators must clearly understand that today's learning is in response to tomorrow's reality.

Keeping with this perspective, the following material discusses a *Canadian model* for conceiving the 21st-century educational experience and the dispositions viewed as essential within our educational enterprise. School administrators, curriculum leaders, and teachers can consider these frameworks as they design technology plans based upon local contexts, teacher abilities, and student needs. Through this, it is hoped that educational leaders will develop a better understanding of how teaching, learning, and technology come together in the 21st-century school and classroom. In the following model, the elements that directly bring technology into 21st-century learning have been highlighted (bold and italicized) to bring these competencies to the forefront of the discussion.

Shifting Minds—A 21st-Century Inspired Vision for Canada's Public Education Systems

	21st-CENTURY COMPETENCIES—Shifting Minds	
21st-Century Competency	Targeted Outcomes	Rationale
Creativity, Innovation and Entrepreneurship	Creativity: The ability to apply creative thought processes to create something of value. Innovation and Entrepreneurship: The capacity to create and apply new knowledge in innovative and entrepreneurial ways to create new products or solve complex problems. The capacity to invent new problem solving heuristics when all standard protocols have failed (Dede, 2010).	Today's economic, social, environmental, and financial challenges are increasingly complex and require creative, innovative, and entrepreneurial thinking to solve problems and keep apace of the ongoing and escalating demand for new and innovative solutions and products. For success in school, work, and life, people must be able to use creativity in order to adapt, generate new ideas, theories, products, and knowledge.
Critical Thinking	A deep understanding of and capacity to apply the elements and processes associated with critical thinking and problem solving. *The ability to acquire, process, interpret, rationalize, and critically analyze large volumes of often conflicting information to the point of making an informed decision and taking action in a timely fashion.*	*The knowledge and digital era is demanding people with higher order thinking skills [HOTS];* the ability to think logically and to solve ill-defined problems by identifying and describing the problem, critically analyzing the information available or creating the knowledge required, framing and testing various hypotheses, formulating creative solutions, and taking action.
Collaboration	The ability to interact positively and respectfully with others in creating new ideas and developing products. The ability to lead or work in a team and to relate to other people in varying contexts, including capacity to resolve and manage conflict. *The capacity for sensitivity to the issues and processes associated with collaborating across cultures. The ability to collaborate across networks, using various information and communication technologies.*	Importance of interpersonal capabilities is higher and the skills involved more sophisticated than in the industrial era. *Social media has created a dominant impact on the collaboration dynamic that occurs outside schools.*

SOURCE: Shifting Minds—A 21st-Century Inspired Vision for Canada's Public Education Systems. C21 Canada (2012).

(Continued)

(Continued)

Communication	High-level literacy skills, including strength in a person's mother tongue with multi-lingual capacity a definite asset. *The ability to use technology to develop 21st-century competencies in the context of core subjects.* *The capacity to communicate using a variety of media and technologies.* *The ability to access, analyze, integrate, and managing large volumes of information.* *The capacity to effectively use social media to communicate and resolve challenges.* *The ability to critically interpret and evaluate ideas presented through a variety of media and technologies.* Highly developed cooperative interpersonal capabilities.	*Communication is more complex and sophisticated and work is often occurring with peers located halfway around the world.* Learning science reinforces constructivist models of building understanding and making meaning which are built on human interactions.
Character	Learners will develop 21st-century life skills, such as: • Life-long and learner • Leadership, responsibility, and accountability • Self-directed, adaptable and resilient • Tolerant, ethical and fair • Personal productivity • Interpersonal (people) skills • Mental and physical well being • Proficiency in managing personal relationships.	The knowledge economy and social environment is highly complex, fast paced, multi-cultural, and stressful in nature, demanding people with highly developed interpersonal traits and strength of character. Collaborating to learn requires social emotional learning skills including self- awareness, social awareness, self- regulation, relationship skills.

Culture and Ethical Citizenship	The capacity to comprehend Canada's political, social, economic and financial systems in a global context. The ability to appreciate cultural and societal diversity at the local, national and global levels. The ability to critically analyze the past and present and apply those understandings in planning for the future. The capacity to understand key ideas and concepts related to democracy, social justice, and human rights. Disposition and skills necessary for effective civic engagement. The ability to understand the dynamic interactions of Earth's systems, the dependence of our social and economic systems on these natural systems, our fundamental connection to all living things, and the impact of humans upon the environment. The capacity to consider the impact of societal and environmental trends and issues.	Canadians place value on the history and culture that shapes our country and its people. Aboriginal communities in particular wish to see their culture reflected in Canadian education policy, programs and services. The increasingly global nature of the economic social, environmental, and financial sectors means cross-cultural interactions, creating both opportunities and challenges that require unique competencies and skill sets. Canadians must be global citizens, with a clear identity of their own history and culture along with sensitivity and respect for diverse identities and cultures as impacted upon our sustainability.
Computer and Digital Technologies	*The capacity to use computers and digital resources to access information and create knowledge, solutions, products, and services.* *The capacity to use social media for learning.*	*The 21st century is a technology and media-driven environment and digital literacy is an essential competency for both learners and teachers.*

SYSTEM REDESIGN PRIORITIES—*Shifting Minds*	
System Element	*Priorities for Action*
Curriculum	Learning outcomes and associated activities must be relevant to engage the 21st-century digital learner. The number of learning outcomes must be reduced substantially to increase instructional time and allow for depth of understanding. Learning outcomes must be rationalized across subject areas to reduce redundancy while strengthening cross-curricular relationships. Higher levels of learner performance in literacy and numeracy performance must be achieved. Twenty-first-century competencies must be infused throughout all learning outcomes. Assessment regime(s) must be complementary to 21st-century learning outcomes and pedagogical practices. Digital technology must be harnessed to ensure data generation dynamic and timely, and able to be mined effectively and efficiently to allow timely adjustments and interventions. Roles within education systems must be rationalized and clarified to enhance efficiency of program delivery.
Pedagogy	Teaching practices and assessment methods must change to align with 21st-century models of learning. Teachers must achieve fluency in using new technologies to engage and support student learning; Personalized learning opportunities must be offered to all students; Learners must have individualized access to the Internet and digital resources; Teachers must offer project based learning opportunities to students reflecting the student's passion and interest areas. Teachers must embrace collaborative teaching models (e.g., professional learning communities [PLCs]); The application of social media to learning must be achieved; Complementary standards and assessments must be realized; Flexibility in instructional time allocations must be attained to support anytime anywhere learning.
Learning Environment	Learning spaces must be flexible and offer opportunities for both personalized and collaborative learning. Mobile learning opportunities should be integrated with other learning delivery models, where appropriate. Learning environments must be ICT rich with adequate technical support and infrastructure Design standards must support anytime, anywhere learning opportunities. Online learning, blended learning, and virtual schools must be pursued as viable and relevant options to meeting the needs of many learners. Networks must be designed to facilitate a seamless transition between digital devices to access the internet. Assistive technologies to support the full range of learners, including gifted learners and learners with learning or physical disabilities, must be ubiquitous.

Governance	Creating a 21st-century model of learning requires a strategic and focused approach by governments and educators, and an alignment of purpose within the system. Leadership must be a shared responsibility of all education partners and stakeholders, demanding highly collaborative and communicative design and implementation processes. Creativity and innovation in the classroom is best promoted when central education agencies are responsible for policy (learning outcomes and resources) and schools are empowered and resourced to be creative and innovative in the delivery of learning (student performance and engagement). School leaders must model 21st-century skills in daily decision making, develop school improvement plans reflecting 21st-century learning goals and support procedures and practices which promote the shift in mindset required to achieve 21st-century learning in school.
Citizen Engagement	Parental and community engagement in the transformation process is a pre-requisite to success. Community engagement is essential to offer students both in-school learning supports and authentic learning opportunities outside the classroom. Societal awareness of and support for the return on investment benefits (economic, social, environmental, financial, and personal) of 21st-century models of learning are essential for successful transformation.

SOURCE: System Redesign Priorities, C21 Canada (2012).

Strategies for Success

Most assuredly, if schools are to be successful in our globally interconnected world, it is evident that all educators and learners must be skilled in the use of technology. This is especially important in that research on raising achievement consistently points to an effective teacher as the most crucial element in a student's success (Routman, 2012). Therefore, to bring about change and establish equity in our schools, factors such as proper professional development programs, technical support, and time for learning must be provided simultaneously.

Successful School Technology Strategies

- Community involvement in planning and implementing the use of technology in schools should be a high priority for school leaders.
- Developing quality technological leadership and planning for effective technology use must receive considerable attention.
- Finances for technology and other forms of school technology should become a line item in the general budget of all school districts.
- Emphasis should be placed on incorporating handheld mobile technology into all classrooms.
- Professional development involving technology should be made highly practical by encouraging teachers to teach other teachers.
- Planning and implementation phases for new technology should include assessment and evaluation standards.
- A well-planned public relations program should be a priority of every school district.

GRAPHIC 14.2   Conceptual Model of Shifting Minds

SOURCE: C21 Canada (2012).

Looking back retrospectively, the successful integration of technology is becoming a critical component of curriculum development. Thus, by incorporating innovative ideas and strategies into a collective vision, school leaders and teachers can—and will—improve the overall nature of education as we know it. Furthermore, there is no question that in our rapidly changing world, the economic vitality of our communities will depend more and more on students being able to turn information into usable knowledge (Goudvis & Harvey, 2012). Just as importantly, individual students will be better able to build knowledge, solve problems, and share cultural successes with a larger global community.

SUMMARY

This chapter addresses curricular changes that transcend all disciplines. The major curricular changes include incorporating thinking, speaking, and listening skills; developing a diverse learning environment; and integrating technology throughout the curriculum. Transcending disciplines to address these elements requires both a different perspective on curriculum change and different processes for planning and implementation.

APPLICATIONS

1. Develop an outline of a professional development program in technology for your school. Using the professional development worksheet as well as Canada's Shifting Minds Model, discuss the major components of your program.

2. The HOTS concentrate on the top three levels of Bloom's taxonomy: analysis, synthesis, and evaluation. Review the curriculum guides or units or daily lesson plans in your school or district and identify several HOTS.

3. If you were charged with the responsibility of developing a district curriculum in critical thinking, would you recommend developing separate courses, integrating critical thinking into existing courses, or using both approaches? Provide a rationale for your recommendation.

4. Consider the four uses of technology in relation to the curriculum: technology applications as developer, technology applications as deliverer, technology applications as tools, and technology applications as the curriculum. As you assess the needs of a school system with which you are familiar, how would you prioritize these four approaches? What systematic processes would you use in making such a determination?

5. Nearly every piece of printed material you see anywhere, anytime was created by technology. And nearly all well-paying or high-paying jobs now require the ability to use mobile devices. Generally, that is why we teach technology literacy. Since technology literacy curriculum varies from school district to school district, at what grade level(s) should technology literacy be taught? What are some of the grade-appropriate technology literacy activities in your school or district?

6. Politicians often are afraid their votes against ELL education will be perceived as hostile to minorities. This is ironic, since a READ Institute survey showed that 81 % of Hispanics wanted their children to learn English first; only 12 % wanted their children taught in Spanish. ProEnglish supports state initiatives to end ELL education and believes the federal government should stop funding ELL education programs exclusively and leave such decisions to states and local school districts. While ProEnglish endorses the teaching of second languages, it believes the first responsibility of our public school system is to teach children English. Should students spend one full school year intensively learning English? Why? (See https://www.proenglish.org/projects/bilingual-education.html.)

CASE STUDY   Developing and Sharing Strategies

This case study provides an example of how a teacher–leader solves the problem of a colleague who is not using the writing-to-learn project—a district-mandated curriculum program.

"I've noticed that some of our fifth-grade students are not using the school district's writing-to-learn project," states teacher–leader Bill Drucker. "Is there a reason that we are not using this program?"

Fifth-grade teacher Pam Hollenbeck looks up from her desk. "That's correct. I just don't have the time to work this program into my schedule. There are so many other subjects during the day that I cannot get to it."

"I realize that time is a concern," sighs the teacher–leader. "Nevertheless, according to our curriculum and district policy in regards to that curriculum, we will have to find a way to incorporate the writing-to-learn project. It's a mandatory project."

Mrs. Hollenbeck realizes her colleague is concerned and quickly comprehends the seriousness of the situation. "Well, I suppose I can incorporate a writing-to-learn project in social studies."

"Yes," answers Drucker, giving a sigh of relief. "A writing-to-learn project in social studies would be great!"

Now smiling, Hollenbeck adds, "One of my students is participating in a writing-to-learn project involving a great story on Seaman, Captain Lewis's dog. This is the Newfoundland dog that accompanied the men throughout the Lewis and Clark expedition." She continues, "As part of the writing-to-learn project, my students can also make a PowerPoint presentation of the story. Also, since the fourth grade is developing a unit on Montana history, this could be sent to all fourth-grade teachers in the district."

"Yes, I heard something about that from the fourth-grade teachers. They loved it!" he says, smiling. "It is really great that we can share materials with other grades!"

The Challenge

Teacher Pam Hollenbeck uses technology successfully to improve student writing and thinking skills. What specific steps can teacher–leader Drucker take to get other teachers to use Hollenbeck's ideas and strategies? What kind of resistance might he encounter from other teachers and staff?

Key Issues or Questions

1. Is it possible to bring a school facing the problem of unsatisfactory student writing levels up to national standards with the use of technology? Why or why not?

2. What are your impressions of Pam Hollenbeck's program in this Montana school? Can this program be replicated in other states using their own history as a guideline?

3. What are some of the problems that educators face as they begin using technology in the classroom?

4. What other innovative technology strategies can be used to improve student writing and thinking skills? How can teacher–leaders and principals best initiate these strategies?

5. How does technology use in middle and high schools differ from that in an elementary classroom setting?

WEBLIOGRAPHY

Center for Implementing Technology in Education

www.cited.org

International Society for Technology Education (ISTE) National Educational Technology Standards

www.iste.org/docs/pdfs/20–14_ISTE_Standards-T_PDF.pdf

Internet4Classrooms: Grade-Level Content Skills

www.internet4classrooms.com/grade_level_help.htm

National Council of Teachers of English (NCTE)

www.ncte.org

National Staff Development Council: "Data-in-a-Day Technique Provides a Snapshot of Teaching That Motivates"

http://learningforward.org/docs/jsd-spring-2001/ginsberg222.pdf?sfvrsn = 2

National Writing Project

www.nwp.org

BBC News: "Teachers Face Handheld Revolution"

http://news.bbc.co.uk/1/hi/uk_politics/4230832.stm

Technology in Education Resource Center

www.rtec.org

Topmarks Educational Search Engine

www.topmarks.co.uk

REFERENCES

Carr, N. (2011). The juggler's brain. *Phi Delta Kappan, 92*(4), 8–14.

C21 Canada. (2012). *A 21st century vision of public education for Canada.* Retrieved from http://www.c21canada.org/wp-content/uploads/2012/05/C21-Canada-Shifting-Version-2.0.pdf

Damani, B. (2011–2012). Tell me about: How you are doing more with less: Going to the cloud. *Educational Leadership, 69*(4), 94–95.

Darling-Hammond, L. (2014). Testing to, and beyond the common core. *Principal, 93*(3), 8–12.

Gardner, N. S., & Powell, R. (2013–2014). The common core is a change for the better. *Phi Delta Kappan, 95*(4), 49–53.

Gibbons, M. (2004). Pardon me, didn't I just hear a paradigm shift? *Phi Delta Kappan, 85*(6), 461–467.

Glatthorn, A. A. (1985). *Teaching critical thinking: A teacher-centered process.* Unpublished manuscript, University of Pennsylvania, Philadelphia.

Goudvis, A., & Harvey, S. (2012). Teaching for historical literacy. *Educational Leadership, 69*(6), 52–57.

Hew, K. F., & Brush, T. (2007). Integrating technology into K-12 teaching and learning: Current knowledge gaps and recommendations for future research. *Educational Technology Research and Development, 55*(3), 223–252.

International Listening Association. (2008). *Priorities of listening research: Four interrelated initiatives*

[White paper]. Retrieved from http://www.listen.org/Resources/Documents/White_Paper_PrioritiesResearch.pdf

Learning Ally. (2011). *History and overview of listening.* Retrieved from http://www.learningthrough listening.org/Listening-A-Powerful-Skill/The-Science-of-Listening/History-and-Overview-of- Listening/91/

Lytle, J. H. (2012). Where is leadership heading. *Phi Delta Kappan, 93*(8), 54–57.

Martinez, M. E. (2006). What is metacognition? *Phi Delta Kappan, 87*(9), 696–699.

Moeller, M., Cutler, K., Fiedler, D., & Weier, L. (2013). Visual thinking strategies = creative and critical thinking. *Phi Delta Kappan, 95*(3), 56–60.

O'Neal, D., & Ringler, M. (2010). Broadening our view of linguistic diversity. *Phi Delta Kappan, 91*(7), 48–52.

Pace, N. J. (2005). *Come out, stay out, stand out: Eight stories of gay and lesbian high school students* (Unpublished doctoral dissertation). University of Northern Iowa, Cedar Rapids, Iowa.

Pace, N. J. (2009). *The principal's challenge: Learning from gay and lesbian students.* Charlotte, NC: Information Age Publishing.

Protheroe, N. (2011). Effective instruction for English-language learners. *Principal, 90*(3), 26–29.

Routman, R. (2012). Mapping a pathway to school-wide highly effective teaching. *Phi Delta Kappan, 93*(5), 56–61.

Shields, D. L. (2014). Deconstructing the pyramid of prejudice. *Phi Delta Kappan, 95*(6), 20–24.

Silva, J., Delleman, P., & Phesia, A. (2013). Preparing English language learners for complex reading. *Educational Leadership, 71*(3), 52–56.

Soto, I. (2014). Experience ELL shadowing. *Principal, 93*(3), 32–35.

Sterling, D. R., & Frazier, W. M. (2011). Setting up uncertified teachers to succeed. *Phi Delta Kappan, 92*(7), 40–45.

Taylor, B. O. (2002). The effective schools process: Alive and well. *Phi Delta Kappan, 83*(5), 375–378.

U.S. Department of Education, Office of Educational Technology. (2010). *Transforming American Education: Learning Powered by Technology,* Washington, DC: Author.

Whitehead, B. M., Jensen, D. F. N., & Boschee, F. (2013). *Planning for technology: A guide for school administrators, technology coordinators, and curriculum leaders* (2nd ed.). Thousand Oaks, CA: Corwin Press.

Wright, T. E. (2010). LGBT educators' perceptions of school climate. *Phi Delta Kappan, 91*(8), 49–52.

Zacarian, D. (2013). Crossing language barriers. *Principal, 92*(5), 34–38.

CHAPTER 15

Individualizing the Curriculum

Plato may have been one of the first writers to recommend individualization through tracking. In his *Republic,* Plato made clear his belief that children should be directed toward the roles of philosopher, guardian, or artisan based on their talents. While contemporary educators reject such a deterministic differentiation, the search for curricula that respond to individual differences continues. Therefore, this chapter reviews previous attempts to respond to individual student needs as well as current approaches to differentiated instruction.

Questions addressed in this chapter include the following:

- What early attempts were made to individualize curriculum?
- What is differentiated instruction, and how does it help students with diverse academic needs?
- What are some examples of current individualized programs, and why are they considered to be successful?
- What individualized adaptive approaches are being used in gifted education, and are they considered successful?
- What are some examples of specialized curriculum, and how are they enhancing the concept of individualization?

Key to Leadership

In truly individualized instruction, the method of teaching is suited to student capabilities.

DIFFERENTIATED INSTRUCTION

The research is clear: students in today's classrooms vary greatly in background, cultures, language proficiency, educational skills, and interests. To best meet students' diverse needs, teachers must differentiate their instruction (Parsons, Dodman, & Burrowbridge, 2013). That said, the standards-based expectations for many schools still seem to mandate a cookie-cutter approach to education. All students, regardless of abilities, background, and interests, are expected to learn a common set of standards. However, both research and the experiences of educators make it clear that a significant number of students will fail to learn the specified knowledge and skills, unless focused attention is paid to the instructional needs of individual students. To surmount the cookie-cutter approach, "differentiated instruction applies a way to teaching and learning that gives students multiple options for taking information and making sense of ideas" (Hall, Strangman, & Meyer, 2011). Although it might seem like a daunting task, differentiated instruction is (a) *not* a recipe for teaching, (b) *not* an instructional strategy, and (c) *not* what a teacher does when he or she has time. Rather, it is a unique way of teaching and learning.

From a historical perspective, attempts to individualize education in the United States go back to colonial times, a period they characterize as individualized instruction by default (Grinder & Nelsen, 1985). One hundred youngsters would be seated in a large ungraded classroom, working on exercises, while one teacher monitored their work. The need to educate large numbers of children in a more systematic manner led 19th-century educational reformers to institute graded classrooms, each with a teacher in charge, presenting a standard program. While this self-contained graded classroom has persisted as the norm for at least 100 years, during this time, numerous attempts have been made to break out of the constraints imposed by traditional educational approaches. Rather than presenting a comprehensive historical review of such attempts, the discussion that follows concentrates on successful inroads being made by differentiated instruction.

In reflecting on core aspects of curriculum over the years, a few key elements seem to have guided differentiated instruction. For example, Tomlinson (2001) and Tomlinson and McTighe (2006), renowned educators and authors, identified three elements of the curriculum that can be differentiated: content, process, and products (see Exhibit 15.1). These are described in the following three sections. Additional guidelines for forming an understanding of and developing ideas around differentiated instruction are listed in Tomlinson's publications.

Content

- *Several elements and materials are used to support instructional content.* These include acts, concepts, generalizations or principles, attitudes, and skills. The variation seen in a differentiated classroom is most frequently in the manner in which students gain access to important learning. Access to the content is seen as key.
- *Align tasks and objectives to learning goals.* Designers of differentiated instruction view the alignment of tasks with instructional goals and objectives as essential. Goals are most frequently assessed by many state-level, high-stakes tests and frequently administered standardized measures. Objectives are frequently written

EXHIBIT 15.1   Process of Planning and Implementing Differentiated Instruction

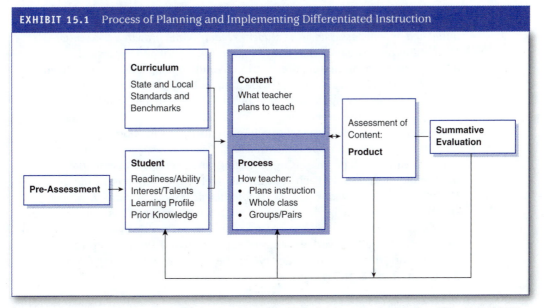

in incremental steps resulting in a continuum of skills-building tasks. An objectives-driven menu makes it easier to find the next instructional step for learners entering at varying levels.

- *Instruction is concept focused and principle driven.* The instructional concepts should be broad-based, not focused on minute details or unlimited facts. Teachers must focus on the concepts, principles, and skills that students should learn. The content of instruction should address the same concepts with all students, but the degree of complexity should be adjusted to suit diverse learners (Tomlinson, 2001; Tomlinson & McTighe, 2006).

Process

- *Flexible grouping is consistently used.* Strategies for flexible grouping are essential. Learners are expected to interact and work together as they develop knowledge of new content. Teachers may conduct whole-class introductory discussions of big ideas followed by small-group or paired work. Student groups may be coached from within or by the teacher to complete assigned tasks. Grouping of students is not fixed. As one of the foundations of differentiated instruction, grouping and regrouping must be a dynamic process, changing with the content, project, and ongoing evaluations.
- *Classroom management benefits students and teachers.* To effectively operate a classroom using differentiated instruction, teachers must carefully select organization and instructional delivery strategies (Tomlinson, 2001; Tomlinson & McTighe, 2006).

Products

- *Initial and ongoing assessment of student readiness and growth are essential.* Meaningful preassessment naturally leads to functional and successful differentiation. Incorporating preassessment and ongoing assessment informs teachers so that they can better provide a menu of approaches, choices, and scaffolds for the varying needs, interests, and abilities that exist in classrooms of diverse students. Assessments may be formal or informal, including interviews, surveys, performance assessments, and more formal evaluation procedures.
- *Students are active and responsible explorers.* Teachers respect that each task put before a learner will be interesting, engaging, and accessible to essential understanding and skills. Each child should feel challenged most of the time.
- *Various expectations and requirements for student responses.* Items to which students respond may be differentiated so that different students can demonstrate or express their knowledge and understanding in different ways. A well-designed student product allows varied means of expression and alternative procedures and offers varying degrees of difficulty, types of evaluation, and scoring (Tomlinson, 2001; Tomlinson & McTighe, 2006).

NOTE: In her text, *How to Differentiate Instruction in Mixed-Ability Classrooms* (Chapter 7), Carol Tomlinson (2001) identified 17 key strategies for teachers to meet the challenge of designing and managing differentiated instruction successfully.

Traditionally, differentiation has not meant providing separate, unrelated activities for each student but just the opposite—providing interrelated activities that are based on student needs. With this in mind, Bosch (2008) listed two questions that deal with "how" a teacher can make differentiation work.

Question #1

How should a general education teacher differentiate curriculum in response to the learner's needs? A teacher should be guided by the general principles of differentiation shown in Exhibit 15.2.

Curriculum Tip 15.1	**Adaptive curricula** are educational processes that arrange the conditions and materials of learning so that they fit individual learner differences.

Question #2

How should a teacher differentiate curriculum in response to *high-ability learners?* The following principles should guide the teacher with high-ability learners:

- Present content that is related to broad-based issues, themes, or problems.
- Integrate multiple disciplines into the area of study.

EXHIBIT 15.2 General Principles of Differentiation

Principles	Descriptors
Respectful tasks	A classroom teacher ensures that students' learning is respected. The teacher does this by assessing the readiness level of each student by evaluating competency in the skills and concepts included in the local curriculum standards, expecting and supporting continual growth in all students by providing challenging curriculum, offering all students the opportunity to explore skills and understanding at appropriate degrees of difficulty, and offering all students tasks that are equally interesting, important, and engaging.
Flexible grouping	Teachers link learners with essential understandings and skills at appropriate levels of challenge and interest. This could mean that students are working in groups on a variety of tasks at the appropriate depth, complexity, and speed for those involved.
Ongoing assessment and adjustment	Throughout units, teachers use assessments to yield an emerging picture of those students who understand key ideas and can perform targeted tasks. Then the teacher shapes the next lesson to fit again the needs of individual students. Assessments need not be formal "tests" but may come from activities such as group discussions, journal or portfolio entries, skills inventories, homework assignments, or interest surveys.

SOURCE: Bosch (2008). Permission granted for use by Bruce Passman, State Director, Kansas State Department of Education, 120 S.E. 10th Avenue, Topeka, Kansas 66612.

- Present comprehensive, related, and mutually reinforcing experience within an area of study.
- Allow for in-depth learning of a self-selected topic within the area of study.
- Develop independent or self-directed study skills.
- Focus on open-ended tasks.
- Develop research skills and methods.
- Integrate basic skills and higher-level thinking into the curriculum.
- Encourage the development of products that challenge existing ideas and produce "new" ideas.
- Encourage the development of products that use new techniques, materials, and forms.
- Encourage the development of self-understanding.
- Evaluate student outcomes by using appropriate and specific criteria through self-appraisal, criterion-referenced, and or standardized instruments. (Bosch, 2008)

In summation, when differentiating the content, the educator considers what students already know and adapts the curriculum content to be presented accordingly.

TYPES OF INDIVIDUALIZED INSTRUCTION

Given a vision of curriculum development it would be useful to clarify the concept of individualized instruction. Here, it seems wise to substitute the clearer term *adaptive* for the more ambiguous *individualized*. Largely because of the vague and conflicting connotations associated with the latter term, specialists in the field often refer to *adaptive* curricula and *adaptive* instructional practices. From a historical perspective, the following represent types of individualized instruction.

Elective Courses

John Dewey, in his book *Democracy and Education,* referred to active student engagement as an essential factor of learning and education (Mahatmya, Brown, & Johnson, 2014). Unfortunately, not everyone agreed with Dewey at the time—especially during the early years of schooling. For example, during the first century of U.S. education, instructors seemed concerned solely with identifying the common curriculum for all students; electives, as such, were not even considered. Even though Charles Eliot was chairperson of the Committee of Ten, he was not able to persuade the committee that electives were desirable; the only option provided in their recommendations was substituting bookkeeping and commercial arithmetic for algebra (see Committee of Ten, 1893). The first official statement recommending elective courses was the *Cardinal Principles of Secondary Education,* published by the Commission on the Reorganization of Secondary Education in 1918. In their formulation of the ideal program, the commission recommended a balance between the constants (those courses to help all students achieve essential goals), curriculum variables (special courses determined by the student's specific educational and career goals), and free electives (courses chosen in response to special interests).

For the past 90 years, the debate over what constitutes the best balance of these three components has continued unabated. The debate has not been informed by rational analysis and too often has produced prescriptions that reflect only the participants' biases about the need to control the education of the young:

> While some high schools have long offered a smorgasbord of electives, many began cutting back in the late 1970s and '80s under a back-to-basics movement. They eliminated even more after the No Child Left Behind law (NCLB) in 2001, to focus on bringing all students up to minimum federal and state standards. (Hu, 2008, p. A21)

Today, the move toward adapting instruction is no exception and continues with the development of Common Core State Standards (CCSS), mobile technology, and data driven assessments.

Curriculum Tracking

Along with adapting instruction, the process of tracking students has come into focus. Unfortunately, many tracking and pacing guides have been developed with an incomplete understanding of the role that diagnostic assessment information plays in effective teaching (Chappuis, 2014). That said, a particularly difficult decision for educators is how best to balance comprehensive (one-school-for-all) versus "selective" schooling.

Curriculum tracking—that is, sorting students into somewhat rigid tracks based on career and educational goals—was probably first formally recognized as a desirable practice by the Committee of Ten. Their report recommended four tracks that differentiated instruction chiefly by the language studied: Classical, Latin Scientific, Modern Languages, and English. The committee was quite explicit about the relative qualities of those four: "The programs called respectively Modern Languages and English must in practice be distinctly inferior to the other two" (Committee of Ten, 1893, p. 48). Thus, the practice of tracking and the status accorded to certain tracks have continued for almost 100 years; all that changes are the number of tracks and their names. However, things are changing. Some high schools now provide for only three tracks (if any), determined primarily by educational and career goals: college preparatory, general, and vocational or technical.

For the most part, then, many schools have eliminated tracked classes and have adopted a universal accelerated program and instituted heterogeneous grouping, with dramatic results. Using this type of curriculum reform, high achievers seem to be doing better, and more students are excelling. Ultimately, "just one question might best serve diverse learners, their teachers, and their society. What can we do to support educators in developing the skill and the will to teach for each learner's equity of access to excellence?" (Tomlinson, 2003, p. 7). With this in mind, Exhibit 15.3 notes some of the principles that can help liberate students from stereotypical expectations and provide equity of success to excellence.

Minicourses

In following adaptive instructional practices, many school districts in the past gave students content options within a field of study by developing minicourses lasting from 6 to 18 weeks. Rather than taking English II, students could choose from an array of offerings with titles such as "Women in Literature," "The Mass Media," and "The Search for Wisdom." While such minicourses were more often developed in the fields of English and social studies, they could also be found in science and mathematics; in fact, many schools prided themselves on offering more than 200 minicourses.

Similar to elective courses, the minicourse approach was highly popular with teachers because it enabled them to develop and teach courses relating to their special interests and knowledge. Most schools using a minicourse curriculum reported high levels of student satisfaction. Most of these courses seemed poorly designed, however. They were produced with a small overall conceptualization of a particular field and gave scant attention to important skills and concepts. Thus, the claim that this *smorgasbord curriculum* contributed to the decline in academic achievement seems warranted, even though no persuasive empirical evidence was apparent on this point.

Open Classrooms

Another creative aspect to school reform, open classrooms, came into vogue during the late 1960s and early 1970s. This led educators to respond to individualized instruction in

EXHIBIT 15.3	Principles for Fostering Equity and Excellence in Academic Diversity
Principles	Descriptors
Good curriculum comes first.	The teacher's first job is always to ensure a coherent, important, inviting, and thoughtful curriculum.
All tasks should respect each learner.	Every student deserves work that is focused on the essential knowledge, understanding, and skills targeted for the lesson. Every student should be required to think at a high level and should find his or her work interesting and powerful.
When in doubt, teach up!	Good instruction stretches learners. The best tasks are those that students find a little too difficult to complete comfortably. Be sure there is a support system in place to facilitate the student's success at a level that he or she doubted was attainable.
Use flexible grouping.	Find ways and time for the class to work as a whole, for students to demonstrate competence alone, and for students to work with varied groups of peers. Using only one or two types of groups causes students to see themselves and one another in more limited ways, keeps the teacher from "auditioning" students in varied contexts, and limits potentially rich exchanges in the classroom.
Become an assessment junkie.	Everything that a student says and does is a potential source of assessment data. Assessment should be an ongoing process, conducted in flexible but distinct stages, and it should maximize opportunities for each student to open the widest possible window on his or her learning.
Grade to reflect growth.	The most we can ask of any person—and the least we ought to ask—is to be and become their best. The teacher's job is to guide and support the learner in this endeavor. Grading should, in part, reflect a learner's growth.

SOURCE: Adapted from Tomlinson and Edison (2003).

several ways. First, open-classroom teachers felt less constrained by district curriculum guides and fashioned curricula that they believed responded to the special needs and interests of their pupils. While elementary teachers in open classrooms all taught English language arts (ELA), social studies, mathematics, and science, they chose content that they believed would be most meaningful to their pupils and that content typically involved the integration of several subject fields. Second, pupils had some options about their use of time: They could work in special learning centers any time during the day—unlimited by bells and artificial distinctions between subjects—and they could spend as much time as they needed. They also had some choice about activities and materials; the learning centers were usually provisioned with a rich assortment of materials for learning. Finally, there was an atmosphere of informality, which advocates believed was truly individualized: Pupils could talk together and move about the room as necessary.

Despite its uniqueness, the open-classroom movement was short-lived, succumbing to conservative pressures for more teacher control and higher achievement in the basics. Its rapid demise was probably unfortunate.

Self-Paced Instruction

During the 1960s and 1970s, there was also much interest in several varieties of self-paced instruction, commonly referred to as *individualized learning*. While these programs varied in their details, they shared several common characteristics:

- The curriculum is analyzed into several components, arranged in a tightly controlled sequence.
- The learner is assessed and placed appropriately along that sequence.
- Students work on self-instructional packets or lessons, usually in isolation in order to achieve clearly specified objectives.
- Students obtain feedback about progress and remediates where necessary.

In an ideal world, students master content at their own pace and move on when they have done so. Basically, all students are self-starters and theoretically are genuinely interested in all subjects. This, of course, is not realistic. In most such programs, only the pace of learning—and, concomitantly, the time spent on learning a particular set of objectives—is adapted to learner needs; every other important element is controlled and standardized. That said, using new Web-based forms of instruction today, innovative teachers are providing some new ways of keeping learners challenged, highly motivated, and, more importantly, on track (Bergmann & Sams, 2013–2014).

Another innovative approach involves Autonomy-Oriented Education (AOE), whereby teachers are in the best position to make informed decisions about a student's education. They should be given as much autonomy as possible when it comes to choosing instructional strategies, designing lessons, and providing academic support. Stringent regulations, tougher job requirements, greater administrative oversight, or more burdensome teacher evaluation procedures can stifle the instructional creativity and responsiveness of teachers, which could produce a variety of negative results, including lower student performance or higher job dissatisfaction and attrition rates among teachers.

Critics of teacher autonomy tend to cite evidence that teaching quality is uneven, and that problems such as achievement gaps or low graduation rates indicate that measures need to be taken to improve the effectiveness of teachers and public-school instruction. (The Glossary of Teacher Education Reform, 2014)

National Association of Early Childhood Specialists in State Departments of Education

Keeping with the concept of improving adaptive curricula, the National Association for the Education of Young Children (NAEYC) and the National Association of Early Childhood Specialists in State Departments of Education (NAECS-SDE; 2009) drafted a series of indicators that best reflect adapted curriculum. These indicators include the following:

- Children are active and engaged.
- Goals are clear and shared by all.

- Curriculum is evidence-based.
- Valued content is learned through investigation and focused, intentional teaching.
- Curriculum builds on prior learning and experiences.
- Curriculum is comprehensive.
- Professional standards validate the curriculum's subject-matter content.
- The curriculum is likely to benefit children. (p. 1)

When reviewing the indictors that were just noted, it is important to realize the overarching need to create an individualized and integrated curriculum that meets the needs of all children. Such a curriculum will be able to focus on a capacity to support learning and development for children living in poverty, children with disabilities, children whose home language is not English, and children who need to be academically challenged.

Adaptive Learning Environments Model

The **adaptive learning environments model (ALEM)** was created at the Learning Research and Development Center of the University of Pittsburgh. As an adaptive program, it is designed to address individual student needs. With that said, this program is not to be construed as a mass-customized learning (MCL) model (Wilson, 2014). In the views of its developers, ALEM is an attempt to combine prescriptive or direct instruction with those aspects of open education that have been found to be effective. ALEM is a rather ambitious model that attempts to restructure the school environment, not simply alter the instructional system.

Learning-Styles Models

Learning-styles models have been around for some time. According to Marie Carbo (2007), even the slowest and most reluctant readers are able to read well when taught according to their individual learning styles. With this in mind, learning-styles models are built on the assumptions that learners differ significantly in their styles of learning, that those styles can be assessed, and that knowledge of styles can help both teachers and learners. Moreover, students who voluntarily read for their own pleasure improve their reading skills and their test scores at a much faster rate than those who do not. Keeping with this perspective, Carbo provided five effective reading strategies:

1. *Change negative perceptions.* Youngsters benefit from high-interest, challenging reading materials; structured choices; powerful modeling of texts; increasingly difficult stories; hands-on skill work; opportunities for mobility; and opportunities to work in groups.

2. *Reduce stress.* When we reduce the stress associated with reading, students become excited about reading and learning experiences.

3. *Use powerful modeling reading methods.* Modeling methods help struggling readers bypass the decoding process, read fluently, and concentrate on meaning.

4. *Use Carbo recordings*. These recordings have enabled students to read challenging reading materials with ease and to make high gains in reading fluency, vocabulary, and comprehension.

5. *Provide student-responsive environments*. Young children—and at-risk readers, in particular—tend to be global, tactile, and kinesthetic learners. These children prefer and do well in classrooms that allow for movement, have some comfortable seating and varied lighting, and enable students to work with relative ease in different groupings. (pp. 43–45)

What else can educators do once a student's learning style has been identified? Many learning-styles advocates recommend a matching strategy: Find the student's preferred learning style and then provide learning experiences that match that style.

What does the research say about the usefulness of the learning-styles models? First, a considerable body of evidence supports the aspects of cognitive style, especially, play an important role in learning. Here, the dimension of field independence and field dependence is perhaps the most studied. The field-dependent person, in perceiving phenomena, is less able than the field-independent person to keep an item separate from its context.

For additional information on learning styles, see the following Web resources:

- National Reading Styles Institute, titled Research Update, at www.nrsi.com
- Education Northwest at educationnorthwest.org
- The Center for Comprehensive School Reform and Improvement at www.centerforcsri.org (Carbo, 2007, p. 24)

Cooperative Learning Models

During these challenging times in education, dedicated teachers continue to look for better ways and ideas to meet the many challenges they face in school. This is especially the case as student populations dramatically change. With that said, cooperative learning models appear to provide teachers with effective ways to respond to diverse student bodies by promoting academic achievement and cross-cultural understanding.

As part of the cooperative learning process, a team-assisted approach allows students to be assigned to four- and five-member heterogeneous teams and given a test to determine placement. During the individualized portion of the program, they work on prepared curriculum materials that include an instruction sheet, several problem sheets, a practice test, and a final test. Students are encouraged to work on their units in teams, helping one another and assisting with the practice tests. Teams then receive scores, with special recognition for high performance.

Mastery Learning Models

Effective transfer of learning done with creativity and grace is the essence of mastery. It is in this vein that the issue of getting students to mastery must be addressed locally by overhauling the quality of local grading and testing to calibrate them with wider-world standards (Wiggins, 2013–2014). As explained previously in Chapter 2, mastery learning principles were first enunciated by Benjamin Bloom; they since have been adapted in several different approaches. In a review of literature, Guskey (2010) analyzed the **mastery learning models** and found most applications stem from the work of Bloom (1971, 1976, 1984), who considered how teachers might adapt the most powerful aspects of tutoring and individualized instruction to improve student learning in general education classrooms. According to Guskey (2010), "Bloom suggested that although students vary widely in their learning rates and modalities, if teachers could provide the necessary time and appropriate learning conditions, nearly all students could reach a high level of achievement" (p. 52).

Core elements of mastery learning are evident in many more recently developed instructional models and interventions. Moreover, research has consistently linked these elements to highly effective instruction and student learning success. As noted by Guskey (2010), core elements for mastery learning are presented in Exhibit 15.4.

EXHIBIT 15.4 Elements That Mastery Learning and Other Interventions Share	
Elements	*Descriptors*
Diagnostic pre-assessment with pre-teaching	Most mastery learning models stress the importance of administering a quick and targeted pre-assessment to all students before beginning instruction to determine whether they have the prerequisite knowledge and skills for success in the upcoming learning sequence.
High-quality, group-based initial instruction	Every description of mastery learning, as well as other interventions such as Understanding by Design (UbD) and RTI (Response to Intervention), emphasizes the importance of engaging all students in high-quality, developmentally appropriate, research-based instruction in the general education classroom.
Progress monitoring through regular formative assessments	Another element of mastery learning that many other interventions share is the use of regular formative assessments to systematically monitor student progress and give students prescriptive feedback. These brief classroom assessments measure the most important learning goals from an instructional unit and typically are administered after a week or two of instruction. They reinforce precisely what students were expected to learn, identify what they learned well, and describe what they need to learn better.
High-quality corrective instruction	High-quality corrective instruction is not the same as "reteaching," which often consists simply of restating the original explanations louder and more slowly. Instead, mastery learning teachers use corrective instruction approaches that accommodate differences in students' learning styles, learning modalities, or types of intelligence. Some teachers engage students in peer tutoring or cooperative learning groups. Others use paraprofessional instructional aides.

Second, parallel formative assessments	In mastery learning, assessments are not a one-shot, do-or-die experience; instead, they are part of an ongoing effort to help students learn. So, after corrective activities, mastery learning teachers give students a second, parallel formative assessment that helps determine the effectiveness of the corrective instruction and offers students a second chance to demonstrate mastery and experience success. RTI similarly requires frequent assessment of student learning progress to check on the effectiveness of intervention strategies.
Enrichment or extension activities	These activities should enable successful learners to explore in greater depth a range of related topics that keenly interest them but lie beyond the established curriculum. Many teachers draw from activities developed for gifted and talented students when planning enrichment activities, including challenging academic games and exercises, various multimedia projects, and peer tutoring. They are also a part of classrooms implementing differentiated instruction (Tomlinson & McTighe, 2006). The challenge for teachers in implementing enrichment or extension activities is to ensure that these activities engage students in truly valuable learning experiences. Having successful learners simply bide their time, doing more, harder problems or completing busywork while others are engaged in corrective instruction would be highly inappropriate. Enrichment activities must provide these students with opportunities to pursue their interests, extend their understanding, and broaden their learning experiences.

SOURCE: Adapted from Guskey (2010).

ENHANCING TEACHING AND LEARNING

Without question, differentiation of teaching and learning is enhanced as teachers adapt their instruction during lessons. Indeed, the perspectives and techniques previously discussed in this chapter are helpful for supporting teachers in thinking about different ways to offer content, engage students in learning, and provide opportunities for varied end products. As noted by Parsons et al. (2013), teachers who effectively differentiate instruction show the following attributes:

- Consistently assess student progress in multiple ways
- Are very knowledgeable about effective pedagogy and how students learn
- Are highly reflective
- Possess these career goals: college preparatory, general, and vocational/technical

Curriculum Tip 15.2	Merging individual instruction with standardized assessment, formal assessment, and teacher evaluation completes the curriculum cycle—what is taught directly correlates with what is written.

There remains little doubt that with today's technological advances and a focus on mobile learning, schools have an untapped possibility of helping individual students be successful learners. All students, regardless of skills or background, deserve equitable access to an engaging and rigorous curriculum. To help make this a reality, Tomlinson and Javius (2012) shared the following seven principles for enhancing differentiated teaching:

1. *Accept that human differences are not only normal but also desirable.* Each person has something of value to contribute to the group, and the group is diminished without their contribution. Culturally and economically sensitive teachers take into account the power of race, culture, and economic status in how students learn.

2. *Develop a growth mind-set.* Providing equity of access to excellence increases the capacity of each individual learner to succeed. The greatest barrier to equitable learning is often not what a student knows but what a teacher expects.

3. *Work to understand students' cultures, interests, needs, and perspectives.* Students are often shaped by their backgrounds. How they learn is molded by a variety of factors, including culture, gender, environmental preferences, and personal strengths or weakness. Differentiated teaching means respecting these factors and making needed changes to accommodate diversity.

4. *Create a base of rigorous learning opportunities.* Differentiating instruction allows students to form a conceptual understanding of the disciplines, connect what they learn to their own lives, address significant problems using essential knowledge and skills, collaborate with peers, examine varied perspectives, and create authentic products for meaningful audiences.

5. *Understand that students come to the classroom with varied points of entry into a curriculum and move through it at different rates.* For intellectual risk-taking to occur, students need to feel safe to explore a full range of cultural, racial, and economic backgrounds. Differentiated teaching means monitoring student growth so that when students fall behind, misunderstand, or move beyond expectations, a variety of adjustments and instructional changes are made to enhance success.

6. *Create flexible classroom routines and procedures that attend to learner needs.* Teaching styles and approaches operate flexibly enough to make room for a range of student needs and differences. In differentiated teaching, this flexibility is a prerequisite for complex student thinking and student application of content.

7. *Be an analytical practitioner.* Teachers applying differentiated instruction focus on procedures, practices, and pedagogies to address the needs of each student. This involves noticing student strengths and weaknesses as well as providing positive feedback when needed.

| **Curriculum Tip 15.3** | Awareness and a willingness to restructure and realign the classroom curriculum is the key to developing successful adaptive change. |

Special Needs: Accommodations and Modifications

Schools today continue developing concepts centering on mainstreaming or inclusion in schools. This approach advocates that special education children be allowed to remain in the regular classroom. Individuals supporting these students work together collaboratively to develop an awareness of the benefits of inclusion and how it may have a positive impact on mildly handicapped learners.

As explained in Chapter 4, Public Law 94–142 was landmark legislation that radically changed how the schools were to provide for special students. And yet, under various curriculum programs and assessments, accommodations and modifications for students with disabilities continue to be perceived as not having not been adequately addressed. With this in mind, McLaughlin (2012) posited six principles for schools to consider in implementing state standards or CCSS as per student with disabilities. These six principles include the following:

- *Recognize that students with disabilities are a diverse group and require individualized educational planning.* A student with a learning disability (LD) is likely to have different needs than a student with a visual impairment, and that student has different needs than a student with autism.
- *Distinguish between accommodations and modifications.* Providing multiple means for students to learn the standards, as well as express what they know, or can do, is consistent with the concept of accommodations. An accommodation can be a device, practice, intervention, or procedure.

  ○ Accommodation: This is a device, practice, intervention, or procedure provided to a student with a disability that affords equal access to instruction or assessment but does not change the content being taught, nor does it reduce learning or achievement expectations.
  ○ Modification: This is a device, practice, intervention, or procedure provided to a student with a disability that affords equal access to instruction or assessment but may change the core content or performance expectation.

- *Support an environment, and set expectations that teachers will understand and use evidence-based practices.* An important factor is providing opportunities for general and special education teachers to share knowledge about evidence-based practices or interventions, as well as how to apply these to actual instruction. Common features of instructional interventions include providing explicit, intensive instruction and frequent monitoring of individual student learning.
- *Augment end-of-year state assessments with a schoolwide assessment program that can measure progress and growth.* Assessing student progress is essential. A list of assessment consortia includes Race to the Top, Partnership for Assessment of Readiness for College and Careers (PARCC), Smarter Balanced Assessment Consortium (SBAC), Dynamic Learning Maps (DLM) Alternate Assessment Consortium, and National Center and State Collaborative (NCSC). Additionally, the English Language Proficiency Assessment Consortia and Assessment Service Supporting ELs (or English Learners) Through Technology Systems (ASSETS).

- *Understand and support the alignment of individualized education programs (IEPs) with CCSS.* An IEP that is based on standards is one in which individual educational goals are directly linked to grade-level content standards. These IEPs define an individual plan of accommodations and supports that are designed for each child and intended to enable the child to meet the standards.
- *Hire and support the best special educators.* Good practice is employing graduates of accredited professional preparation programs who have mastered the specialized skills for safe and effective practice, including empirical research, disciplined inquiry, informed theory, and have the wisdom of practice for their area of expertise.

As noted, these six principles provide an excellent understanding as to how to adapt curriculum for students with special needs. Perhaps the most important element is having a talented and team-oriented staff that is dedicated to coordinating; cooperating; and collaborating with colleagues, parents, and administrators (Schlepp, 2012).

Section 504

There has been some confusion in educational circles as to the application of Section 504 under the Individuals with Disabilities Education Act (IDEA). Recently, the Americans with Disabilities Act Amendments Act (ADAAA) developed a broader eligibility standard that went into effect January 1, 2009. According to Zirkel (2011), principals and special services directors need to take a leadership role in building-level implementation of Section 504 for students not eligible under IDEA. This involves having available (a) a grievance procedure for disability-related complaints from parents, students, employees, and others; (b) a procedural safeguards notice that includes provision for an impartial hearing; and (c) a designated coordinator for Section 504/Americans with Disabilities Act (ADA).

Cross-Cultural Comparisons in Special Education

Cross-cultural comparisons of inclusionary practices provide a unique opportunity to question our perceptions of disability and the nature of special education programs. With that said, a major goal of education is to transmit cultural values from one generation to the next. This is especially the case in that society's values are often reflected in its classroom practices, particularly as they relate to special needs as well as nondisabled children.

There are, however, nuances of difference between countries. According to Linn (2011), Portugal, as well as other European nations, mandate full inclusion (with rare exceptions) for students with disabilities. In contrast, the United States, more specifically the IDEA, specifies that students with special needs can be removed from the general education setting only if they fail to achieve, as measured by formal assessments, despite documented supports, aids, and services. The primary goal, then, of inclusion for students identified with special needs in the United States appears to focus on academic achievement. This differs with Portugal. Unlike teachers in the United States, who may have 10 or more students with special needs in their class, teachers in Portugal typically have only one or two students with an identified disability, and often the size of these inclusive classrooms is controlled. A key word here is *identified*. In Portugal, only students with low-incidence disabilities—such as intellectual and developmental disability, autism, and physical disabilities—are recognized as needing special education. Students with high-incidence disabilities are currently not identified by the Portuguese special education system. In addition, instruction for students with LDs—or any student with a disability, identified or not—must be done with significantly less resources than in U.S. classrooms. Likewise, teachers in Portugal receive far less support in terms of specialized instruction or material for the special needs student as do U.S. teachers.

Adaptive Programs for the Gifted

Keeping with a perspective of addressing special needs of U.S. students, curriculum leaders have long contended that what is taught must reflect the needs of the learner as well as the recommendations of scholars in various academic fields. Unfortunately, schools are narrowing the curriculum because they are under considerable pressure to show adequate yearly progress. Subsequently, any balanced curriculum should highlight the interconnectedness of various fields of knowledge.

For example, the field of gifted education, like the fields of special education and child psychiatry, is experiencing rapid change. These changes are influenced by dramatic ideological, political, economic, and cultural shifts and by recent technological advances.

Curriculum Tip 15.4	Most adaptive models can be used in educating the gifted and talented.

Focusing on gifted traits provides educators with a way to understand how we can create conditions that will stimulate more people to use their gifts in socially constructive ways. With this mind, Renzulli (2011) stated the following:

Major changes have taken place in gifted education over the past three decades, and my 1978 article on what is now popularly referred to as the Three Ring Conception of Giftedness has frequently been cited as the starting point for a broadened conception of giftedness. Subsequent work by leading scholars such as Paul Torrance, Robert Sternberg, Howard Gardner, David Lohman, and Benjamin Bloom have reinforced the argument for 1) using an expanded set of criteria to examine high levels of potential in young people, and 2) viewing giftedness as something we can develop in far more students than previously identified by using an IQ cutoff score approach. This article wasn't very popular with the conservative gifted education establishment when it was published, but it's had a remarkable impact on identification and programming practices and is now the most widely cited publication in the field.

Although most scholars and researchers have embraced a more flexible approach to identifying students for special program services, regulations and guidelines for identification in several states continue to place major emphasis on IQ or other cognitive ability tests. The reasons for the gap between current theory and regulatory practices are threefold. First, there is an "administrative tidiness" with a test cutoff system that avoids using what many consider subjective information. Second, parents of traditionally served and mainly middle-class students generally oppose opening the door to young people from different cultural backgrounds or those who show their potentials in nonconventional ways. Third, state departments of education that reimburse districts based on a "head count" of identified students want to control the amount of funds allocated to gifted programs.

If I were rewriting this article today, my experience over the years would lead me to emphasize three recommendations. First, I would recommend using local (school level) rather than national or state norms when looking at decisions based on cognitive ability or achievement test scores. Low-income and minority students continue to be underrepresented in gifted programs. The only way to include the highest potential students from schools serving low-income and minority group students is to avoid making comparisons with amalgamated norm groups. Second, I'd recommend that state reimbursement formulas be based on total district enrollments. This approach would allow schools with lower achievement levels to compete for funds that traditionally have gone to higher socioeconomic status districts. At the same time, it would guarantee that funding agencies can set an upper limit on total funds available for gifted programs in any given state's budgets. Finally, I'd recommend that weighting systems be developed to help achieve equity for all three sets of characteristics in the Three Ring Conception of Giftedness. Currently, there still tends to be disproportional emphasis on test scores at the expense of criteria that reflect creativity and task commitment. Developing high levels of creative talent and high motivation among all of our young people is essential for the continued economic and cultural advancement of our country. (p. 61)

Parallel Curriculum for the Gifted

An inescapable truth is that gifted learners vary. Their abilities may be strong in one area and weak in another. Their capabilities may appear easy to some and difficult to others. A gifted student may find easy what a talented student finds difficult. With this in mind, some schools are moving to parallel curriculum models.

The concept of a parallel curriculum takes its basic definition from paralleling other forms of curriculum. For example, the overall or umbrella curriculum spans and parallels four different curriculum approaches for the gifted learner: **core curriculum, connective curriculum, curriculum of practice,** and **curriculum of identity** (Tomlinson et al., 2002). The core curriculum parallels a discipline, while the connective curriculum makes connections within and across times, cultures, places, and disciplines. The curriculum of practice guides gifted learners in understanding and applying the facts, concepts, principles, and methodologies of the discipline. The curriculum of identity guides gifted students to understand their own strengths, preferences, values, and commitment. Teachers who use a parallel curriculum approach do so by creating a challenging and overarching curriculum as well as a framework for thinking.

Compacting

Curriculum **compacting** was first developed by Joseph Renzulli at the University of Connecticut. Once demonstrating a level of proficiency in the basic curriculum, compacting allows a student to exchange instructional time for other learning. Compacting is designed to help advanced or gifted learners maximize their use of time for learning. According to noted author Carol Tomlinson (2001), compacting has three stages.

> *Stage 1:* The teacher identifies gifted and talented students who are candidates for compacting and assesses what they do and do not know. Students who are compacting are exempt from whole-class instruction and activities in content areas they have already mastered.

> *Stage 2:* The teacher notes any skills or understandings covered in the study in which the student did not demonstrate mastery. The teacher then lays out a plan to make certain the student achieves those goals and meets those objectives. The plan may require the student to work with other individuals in the classroom.

> *Stage 3:* The teacher and student design an investigation or study for the student to engage in while others are working with the general lessons. Project parameters, goals, timelines, procedures for completing tasks, and criteria for evaluation are determined at that time.

Compacting helps gifted or accelerated learners avoid having to go over mastered material while offering them a chance to challenge themselves in the classroom. This provides for invigorating and productive learning in school.

Discovery Method

The **discovery method** (occasionally referred to as the Socratic method) is often used by teachers when working with gifted and talented students, but it can certainly apply to all students. When children are exposed to the wonders of science, the doors to discovery are opened for them. The more we encourage our children to explore and appreciate the world through the lens of a discoverer, the more likely they will be to understand the value of global diversity (Connelly, 2007). Likewise, through a process of inductive and deductive reasoning, students can become better able to "discover" a deep understanding of a problem, hopefully leading to greater motivation or different levels of learning.

It is noted by a few that certain skills are not amenable to discovery learning. In mathematics, for example, students often are required or need to follow a series of specific steps to reach the solution to a problem. It is better to demonstrate those steps and then provide opportunities for the students to alter the steps or change them in some way. The key to the success of the discovery-oriented approach probably lies with the teacher and the student. Both the teacher's and student's awareness and interest in the problem will lead to a point of understanding or a point of discovery.

Brain-Based Learning

Brain-based learning follows the belief that there are connections between brain function and educational practice. Brown (2012) noted that a child's brain structure and chemistry change every day and that environment and experiences in the classroom and throughout school can have a profound impact on these changes. Based on this information, four elements were developed to teach children to make smart decisions in a systematic, intentional, and sequential way. These four elements include the following:

- Instructional strategies increase the brain's capacity to learn and change the emotional state of learners.
- Enriched environments encourage optimal learning conditions in school, at home, and in the community.
- Deficit correction and cognitive enhancement builds the foundation for critical thinking.
- Evaluation tools provide feedback to learners, teachers, parents, and community members.

Additional research shows that certain cognitive skills are strengthened sometimes substantially by our use of technology and the Internet (Carr, 2010–2011). For example, brain functions that help to quickly locate, categorize, and assess disparate bits of information in a variety of forms are, coincidentally, very similar to the ones performed best by technology applications. Thus, a teacher's ability to give sufficient examples relating to the students' experiences and to involve gifted and talented students in experiences makes the abstract concepts of brain-based learning at least a bit more understandable. According to Patricia Wolfe (2001), many of our strongest neural networks are formed by actual experience. It is often possible to take advantage of this natural proclivity by involving students in solving authentic problems in their school or community. In addition to the obvious benefits of engaging in authentic problem solving, teachers report that it also enhances students' motivation, sense of efficacy, and self-esteem.

Special Pace: Acceleration

Acceleration as an adaptive strategy that helps gifted students advance and master academic content at a highly accelerated rate. Thus, a gifted 10-year-old might be placed in a ninth-grade science class, or a very intelligent middle school student might be studying mathematics normally taught in high school. Likewise, high school students preparing for and taking Advanced Placement (AP) classes and examinations for college entrance are experiencing a similar type of acceleration.

To be sure, classroom technology along with access to the Internet can provide an alternative to advancing students into another grade level. Accessing the Internet to build Web sites or to obtain information globally allows gifted and talented students a way to enhance and accelerate learning and still remain in their classrooms. For example, a student using an educational hypermedia system might be given an assignment that relates specifically to his or her knowledge of the subject. This might involve using an adaptive electronic encyclopedia or a virtual museum trip to help direct a pathway for further learning. Clearly, hypermedia, as well as similar programs, have proven to be an excellent way for classroom teachers to use technology in building an accelerated program for gifted and talented learners.

Special Curricula

It is crucial when formulating special curricula for the gifted and talented to develop materials that clarify specific learning goals that are linked to state standards or CCSS. Moreover, it is sometimes necessary to supplement standards with more detailed descriptions of goals and objectives so that teachers and administrators understand what students are expected to know and what they are expected to do. Curricular modifications for the gifted have in general taken two forms: offering special subjects and providing for enrichment activities. In many school districts, gifted students can study subjects ordinarily not included in the curriculum by following independent study programs or by receiving group instruction in a special program. The Philosophy for Children program has been used by many school districts for such purposes, with generally successful results.

From a historical perspective, several enrichment models have been used in programs for the gifted. Two of those that seem in extensive use are Renzulli's (1977) and Renzulli, Reis, and Smith's (1981) **Triad/Revolving Door Identification Model (RDIM) program** and Meeker's (1985) **Structure of the Intellect (SOI)** model. Interestingly enough, these programs are still in use today.

Triad/RDIM Program

The Triad/RDIM program combines the enrichment triad model originally proposed by Renzulli (1977) with a relatively recent approach to selection, the RDIM (Renzulli et al., 1981). The enrichment triad model is based on three types of enrichment activities for the gifted. Type I activities are general exploratory activities in which learners explore areas of personal interest. Type II activities are group-training activities, consisting of materials and instructional techniques designed to develop critical and creative thinking skills. Type III activities are individual or small-group investigations, in which students have an opportunity to investigate real problems through research and inquiry.

RDIM begins by identifying a pool of the top 15% to 20% of the student population. All these students are exposed to Type I and Type II activities on a regular basis. As these students work on these enriching activities, teachers remain alert for students who demonstrate signs of interest, creativity, task commitment, and advanced ability. As a student is so identified, the teacher encourages the student to move into a Type III activity, using either the resources of the regular classroom or the special "resource room" until the project is completed.

On the basis of implementation studies in 30 Connecticut schools, Reis and Renzulli (1984) were able to identify several key features that account for successful programs:

thorough orientation of teachers, parents, and administrators; extensive planning by the local school team; in-service and administrative support; schoolwide enrichment teams composed of the principal, the resource teacher, classroom teachers, parents, and in some cases a student; development in the entire staff of a sense of ownership of the program; detailed orientation of the students; communication with prime interest groups; program flexibility; and evaluation and program monitoring.

The triad/RDIM program seems to be a productive means for providing interesting learning experiences. The obvious question arises again, however: Why for only the top 20%?

Meeker's Structure of the Intellect Model

Over the course of several decades, the structure of the intellect (SOI) model of intelligence has come to represent a three-dimensional cube. The three dimensions are the five *operations* of the intellect, the five *contents* of the intellect, and the six *products*. Of these 120 possible intellectual abilities that result from the intersection of these three dimensions, 96 have been substantiated through testing. Meeker, Meeker, and Roid (1985) validated 26 of those factored abilities as necessary for successful learning. Those 26 intellectual abilities have been used to develop several tests that have been useful in identifying potentially gifted students, especially minority students. For example, blacks, Hispanics, and Native Americans score higher on some SOI measures than do white students. Also, the SOI model has been useful in diagnosing and prescribing for the developmental needs of the gifted.

Meeker and her associates (1985) also noted that the SOI model can be used to develop curricula and instructional strategies. Their analysis identified 90 specific thinking skills and suggested how they can be linked with school subjects in a developmental sequence. For example, the analysis identified four reasoning skills essential for ELA or reading: concept formation, differentiating concepts, comprehending verbal relations, and comprehending verbal systems. Four enrichment reasoning skills were also identified: memory for implied meanings, using analogical ideas, creative interpretations, and creative "grammatics." Additionally, special material was developed for individual and group tasks designed to improve cognition, memory, convergent production, divergent production, and evaluation.

In general, most curricula for academically challenged students have emphasized the development of the basic skills, along with expressing a broader concern for improving social skills, helping learners manage their own behavior, and improving their cognitive skills. It is important, however, to avoid a "scattershot type of curriculum" when planning units and lessons for challenged learners. Scattershot approaches have insufficient planning, the objectives are not tied to goals, and goals are not tied to the school mission statement, which is generally based on individual state standards or CCSS. This form of curriculum planning is often unreliable and is hit or miss at best. It is important to have a focused and well-planned curriculum when developing and implementing cognitive skills for academically challenged learners.

PreK and Early Childhood

A child's experiences in their early years can make a difference in their academic success. As noted by Frede and Barnett (2011), institutionalized preschool education is found to increase school-appropriate behavior and cognitive abilities. Studies also find that as preschool participation rates move toward universal coverage, average test scores rise. Additionally, research finds that national achievement test scores rise with the level of public expenditure on preschool education and with the quality of preschool education as measured by teacher qualifications.

State and local PreK programs vary widely from place to place. Some states have highly effective PreK programs that are based on high standards and that are adequately funded. Others are barely better than subsidized child care. Early childhood programs found to produce the largest gains have had well-educated, adequately paid teachers who exhibit high expectations for children's learning and development. Teachers in these programs work with a well-defined curriculum under strong supervision.

Frede and Barnett (2011) offered 10 research-based, practice-tested action steps for school leaders wanting to improve PreK programs. They include the following:

1. *Develop an Early Childhood Advisory Council.* This involves reaching out to local preschool programs, child care centers, Head Start agencies, university experts, social service agencies, and parent groups.

2. *Establish PreK inclusion classes.* This requires the conversion of PreK special education classes into inclusion classes.

3. *Offer school-based PreK classes.* Elementary schools need to offer space to local agencies or Head Start as a way to incorporate PreK classes on site.

4. *Research effective PreK programs.* Becoming knowledgeable about what is working in other school districts and other agencies is essential to success.

5. *Revise teacher evaluation and coaching tools.* Using research-based teaching practices for PreK is paramount for effective implementation.

6. *Hire qualified preschool teachers.* Making sure PreK teachers have experience with preschoolers is important.

7. *Guarantee a diverse classroom composition.* Children benefit greatly from multicultural integration.

8. *Provide dual-language classrooms.* Non-English speakers can learn English, but, just as importantly, English speakers can become bilingual.

9. *Design professional development expressly for PreK programs.* Ongoing, classroom-specific, in-service education is critical to overall school success.

10. *Institute other schoolwide practices to meet individual needs.* Including PreK children in assemblies and programs provides background experience. Including them on the playground and in cafeterias is also extremely helpful in building confidence.

On the whole, the 10 steps above will help school leaders and teachers formulate effective PreK programs in their districts.

From a historical perspective, researcher Barbara Taylor (Taylor, Pearson, Clark, & Walpole, 1999) found a combination of school and teacher factors to be the most important elements in beating the odds in teaching all children how to read. Factors to use in **early intervention** include the following:

- Schools with strong links to parents
- Collaboration of teaching staff
- Shared system for assessing oral reading fluency, accuracy, and text level
- Extensive professional development on instructional practices

An emphasis on one-on-one instruction is also an important factor. Others include the following:

- Small-group instruction
- Time for independent reading
- Communication and reading with parents
- Applying word identification
- Asking higher-level questions

These early intervention strategies are still in use today. According to Taylor, they have been especially effective in large urban poverty environments.

Since the relationships between poverty environments and developmental learning problems have been clearly established, most early intervention programs have focused on the children of the poor. Increasingly, such programs have attempted to reach infant children and their parents, on the theory that *the earlier, the better.*

Value-Added Early Learning

The state of Pennsylvania has a state-funded quality PreK system that includes education programs based both in public schools and in the community (Dichter, 2011). This system establishes Learning Standards for Early Childhood that are central to the state's agenda. These are research-based standards for infants, toddlers, preschoolers and Grades K through 2, and explicitly connect and align to the standards for Grades 3 through 12 (although they go beyond PreK–12 for the domains of development). Additionally, the Early Childhood Education Career Lattice was created to ensure coherence across the early education programs and to build a pathway for professionals to work in both public school and community settings.

Early Intervention Programs

For early intervention programs, any formal assessment tool or method used should meet established criteria for validity and reliability. For example, the American Educational Research Association, American Psychological Association, and National Council on Measurement in Education (1999) define validity and reliability as follows:

- Validity is the degree to which a test measures what it is supposed to measure. Because tests are only valid for a specific purpose and assessments are conducted for so many different reasons, there is no single type of validity that is most appropriate across tests.
- Reliability refers to the consistency, or reproducibility, of measurements. A sufficiently reliable test will yield similar results across time for a single child, even if different examiners or different forms of the test are used. Reliability is expressed as a coefficient between 0 (absence of reliability) and 1 (perfect reliability). Generally, for individualized tests of cognitive or special abilities, a reliability coefficient of .80 or higher is considered acceptable (American Educational Research Association, American Psychological Association, & National Council of Measurement in Education, 1999).

Reading Test

In order to initiate a good reading instructional program, a performance baseline and ceiling must be determined. The Gray Oral Reading Test, Fifth Edition (GORT-5) provides a baseline for reading that can be determined through assessment.

One of the most widely used measures of oral reading fluency and comprehension in the United States, the Gray Oral Reading Test (GORT) series, has been updated and improved (see Exhibit 15.5). Two equivalent forms (Form A and Form B) each contain 16 developmentally sequenced reading passages with five comprehension questions each. An optional miscue analysis system allows reading specialists to analyze reading errors and tailor interventions to specific students' needs.

Spelling Test

For ages 6 through 18 years of age, the Test of Written Spelling–Fifth Edition (TWS-5) is an accurate and efficient instrument that uses a dictated-word format to assess spelling skills in school-age children and adolescents. It has two forms that can be administered in 20 minutes either individually or in groups. Each form contains 50 spelling words drawn from eight basal spelling series and graded word lists. The TWS-5 provides percentiles, standard scores, age, and grade equivalents. The Answer and Record Form offers a convenient way to record and keep track of scores, summarize the results, and indicate any comments and recommendations.

The results of the TWS-5 can be used for three specific purposes:

- To identify students whose scores are significantly below those of their peers and who might need interventions designed to improve spelling proficiency
- To document overall progress in spelling as a consequence of intervention programs
- To serve as a measure for research efforts designed to investigate spelling

The TWS-5 was normed on a representative sample of 1,634 students from 23 U.S. states. The analyses show no gender or racial bias in the TWS-5 items. Test reliability was studied in various ways: coefficient alphas, alternate form (immediate administration), test–retest, alternate form (delayed administration), and interscorer. All coefficients are over .90, which

EXHIBIT 15.5 Features and Benefits of the Gray Oral Reading Test

Features	Benefits
Updated norms	New normative data were collected in 2008–2010, and norms have been extended upward to age 23 years, 11 months.
Easier and more efficient administration	Basal and ceiling rules have been streamlined to allow for hassle-free administration.
Revised items	The comprehension questions were completely revised, and studies show that the items are passage-dependent.
New psychometrics	Additional studies showing evidence of the test's reliability and validity were added.
Test Structure	**Technical Information**
The GORT-5 produces four scores and a composite score. • The Rate score is derived from the amount of time in seconds taken by a student to read a story aloud. • The Accuracy score is derived from the number of words the student pronounces correctly when reading the passage. • The Fluency score is a combination of the student's Rate and Accuracy scores. • The Comprehension score is the number of questions about the stories that the student answers correctly. The open-ended format ensures that the items are passage-dependent. • The Oral Reading Index (ORI) is a composite score formed by combining students' Fluency and Comprehension scaled scores.	• For both forms, average internal consistency reliability coefficients exceed .90. • The alternate forms reliability coefficients for the ORI exceed .90. The average test-retest coefficients for the ORI for the same form (i.e., Form A to A, Form B to B) exceed .85. • The average test-retest coefficient for the ORI for different forms (i.e., Form A to B, Form B to A) is .85. • Correlations of the GORT-5 scores with those of other well-known reading measures are large or very large in magnitude. • Studies indicate that the GORT-5 is able to accurately identify students with reading difficulties.

SOURCE: Wiederholt and Bryant (2013).

indicates the test's high reliability. Additional studies confirmed the TWS-5 content-description, criterion-prediction, and construct-identification validity. Especially encouraging are the new studies of the test's sensitivity, specificity, and receiver operating characteristic (ROC)/area under the curve (AUC).

These assessments by GORT-5 and TWS-5 are supported in the 15th edition of the *Mental Measurements Yearbook* by Buros (Plake, Impara, & Spies, 2003). They provide teachers with valid and reliable information needed to develop appropriate lessons and improve instruction for all students, including students with disabilities. The progress of the students can be monitored by ongoing benchmarks through reading and spelling assessments.

Additionally, because of the diverse backgrounds prevalent in classrooms today, literacy instruction must be carefully assessed. Through these assessments, a literacy program can be designed to meet the individual needs of each student. The importance of having students read in their zone of proximal development (ZPD) has been defined by Vygotsky (1978) as "the distance between the actual developmental level as determined by independent problem solving and the level of potential development as determined through problem solving under adult guidance, or in collaboration with more capable peers" (p. 86).

Therefore, through formal assessment, identifying their ZPD and designing a reading and spelling program to foster growth in their specified ZPD is essential to guide instruction. As shown in Exhibit 15.6, the information gained from appropriate assessment enables teachers to provide exceptional students with improved access to the curriculum.

When a formal assessment is chosen based on research that proves reliability and validity, a structured plan for reading and other subjects can be implemented for student success. The following format will ensure the success of a reading plan for each student: implementation of a reliable and valid formal reading assessment, adequate teacher training regarding the student(s) scores from the formal assessment, integration of the scores to the chosen curriculum for the students, students' understanding of their personal reading ability, and parental understanding of the scores and process for increasing their students' reading scores.

An example of a Coaching Lesson Plan for Reading and a sample of the results utilizing the plan are shown in Exhibits 15.7 and 15.8.

EXHIBIT 15.6   Teacher Responsibility and Benefits of Valid and Reliable Skill Level Assessment

Teacher Responsibility	Benefits
Identify skills that need review.	Assessment provides teachers with information on what skills students have and have not mastered. It is needed to help teachers know the skill levels of their students, since students have varying experiences and knowledge.
Monitor student progress.	A teacher can learn which students need review before covering additional content and which students are ready to move forward.
Guide teacher instruction.	Through consistent assessment, a teacher can make informed decisions about what instruction is appropriate for each student.
Demonstrate the effectiveness of instruction.	The information gained from assessment allows teachers to know if all students are mastering the content covered. It is important for teachers to use instructional time effectively, and this can be done when teachers are knowledgeable about what their students are ready to learn and what they already know. Therefore, the information gained from assessment allows a teacher to create appropriate instruction for their students.
Improve instruction.	It provides teachers with information on how instruction can be improved.

SOURCE: Adapted from DeBruin-Parecki (2004).

EXHIBIT 15.7   A Coaching Lesson Plan for Reading

Coach's Name: Sandra Hague Student's Name: Andrew

Grade Level/Zone of Proximal Development (ZPD): 2.2–3.2

Day /Date: September 1, 2014

Step 1: 3:30–3:40 P.M. Fluency Development Repeated Reading Comprehension: Oral Retelling **********************	Andrew will read an 83-word passage from *Cowgirl Kate and Cocoa* (Silverman, 2008) three times so I can measure fluency progress. We need to work on all three areas of Andrew's fluency—rate, accuracy, and prosody. Andrew will be asked to retell the first chapter of *Cowgirl Kate and Cocoa* (Silverman, 2008) using *first, next, then,* and *last.* Andrew will be reading in his zone of proximal development (ZPD).
Step 2: 3:40–4:00 P.M. Word Study/Vocabulary Goals: At the end of the lesson, Andrew will be able to successfully read and spell two syllable words that contain the VCe pattern. **********************	** Two syllable words with a long vowel spelled with the Vowel-Consonant-e (VCe) pattern by speaking and writing words that contain this type of long vowel pattern. Andrew will learn words that have VCe make the long vowel. Some of the words I will say and have Andrew write, and others I will write and have Andrew pronounce. ** We will begin by reading chapter two of *Cowgirl Kate and Cocoa: School Days* (Silverman, 2008). Comprehension questions will be asked as each page is read based on Bloom's taxonomy.
Step 3: 4:00–4:20 P.M. Comprehension Strategies Guided Oral Reading **********************	
Step 4: 4:20–4:25 P.M. Writing **********************	** I will ask Andrew to complete a written retelling of the first chapter of *Cowgirl Kate* using *first, next, then,* and *last* as sentence starters. I will make sure he tells me what he is going to write before allowing him to write four sentences. We will edit this together after he is done writing.
Step 5: 4:25–4:30 P.M. Coach Read Aloud Frindle (Clements, 1996)	** I will be reading a book one to two grade levels above Andrew's ZPD. There will be questions utilizing Bloom's taxonomy as I read aloud to Andrew.

EXHIBIT 15.8   Sample of Results Using the Gray Oral Reading Test, Fifth Edition

Second Grade	11–05–2013	1–21–2014	3–18–2014	5–13–2014
Rate	2.4	3.4	4.4	4.7
Accuracy	4.4	5.0	5.4	6.7
Fluency	3.2	4.0	5.0	5.4
Comprehension	4.2	5.0	5.7	6.4
ZPD	3.0—4.0	4.0—5.0	4.5—5.5	5.5—6.5

NOTE: ZPD = zone of proximal development; one of the authors, a current school principal, is using the Gray Oral Reading Test, Fifth Edition (GORT-5) to enhance the reading ability of students in the school.

Reading Recovery

What Works Clearinghouse (WWC) is "a central and trusted source of scientific evidence for what works in education" and publishes intervention reports that assess research on beginning reading programs. WWC evaluations translate effect sizes from research into improvement index scores to reflect the average change in a student's percentile rank that can be expected if the student has the intervention.

In 2007, 2008, and in July 2013, the WWC, a central and trusted source of scientific evidence for what works in education, examined research on Reading Recovery and accepted studies that met its evidence standards. Reading Recovery received positive or potentially positive ratings across all four domains: alphabetics (phonics and phonemic awareness), fluency, comprehension, and general reading achievement. Among all programs reviewed, Reading Recovery received the highest rating in general reading achievement.

Reading Recovery, Reading for Success, and other interventions are now being used extensively in schools. Of all the early literacy interventions being used, Reading Recovery is the most well known and most widely implemented. An independent review of experimental research by the WWC (2007, 2008, 2013), a branch of the U.S. Department of Education and the Institute of Education Sciences (IES), clearly determined Reading Recovery to be an effective intervention based on scientific research.

The hallmark of Reading Recovery is its accountability for student outcomes. The goal of Reading Recovery is to reduce dramatically both the number of students in first grade who are at risk of literacy failure and the cost of these learners to the school district.

Curriculum Tip 15.5	Response to Intervention (RTI) and similar programs may very likely affect every classroom and every teacher in the nation.

Response to Intervention

The Response to Intervention (RTI) program is a tiered model of instruction that allows teachers to target students' individualized learning needs and provide more focused instruction in areas of concern, as well as strengths (McAssey, 2014). RTI is proving to be highly successful for students requiring more intensive structure in their learning. William Bender and Cara Shores (2007), in their book *Response to Intervention: A Practical Guide for Every Teacher,* noted that many students respond better on an individual basis to various educational interventions. Most of the early work required by the RTI procedures for a particular child takes place in the general education classroom.

The following guidelines outline the RTI process:

1. Make certain that the reading curriculum utilized in the general-education classrooms is a research-validated instructional curriculum and that teachers are trained in the use of that curriculum. If those conditions are met, then the "Tier-One" intervention may become merely a "progress monitoring" of the child's

progress on a weekly basis, and not a separate instructional intervention that must be implemented.

2. Train faculty in interventions that have a sound scientific base, in order to ensure treatment fidelity. In that sense, implementation of RTI can benefit all students.

3. Use content experts as the independent observers for Tier One and Tier Two. In the case of reading disability, use a reading teacher, a master-level general education teacher, or a school psychologist with expertise in instruction for those observations.

4. Using persons who would be spending time assessing the child under the traditional discrepancy-based paradigm (i.e., a school psychologist) as the observer offers the option of replacing one set of eligibility duties of that person with another. In effect, then, no additional resources are needed and fewer resources will be required because the eligibility determination no longer requires such extensive individualized assessment.

5. Use a different observer for the Tier-One and Tier-Two interventions when possible. In that fashion, more educators have actually seen how the student responds to intervention, and thus more will be qualified to suggest additional instructional ideas.

6. For Tier-Two interventions, develop systems whereby students who need a Tier-Two intervention may join in small-group instruction that is already ongoing in the school. For example, many Tier-One programs and/or various early intervention programs in reading or math involve small-group instruction (as is required in Tier Two). Thus, for Tier-Two interventions, students may be assigned to those groups for one grading period, and their progress may be charted either daily or weekly.

7. Prior to Tier-Three interventions, an eligibility committee must meet and formally determine that the child has not been responsive to instruction in Tier One and Tier Two. The committee meeting is called for whenever a student is unresponsive to Tier-One and Tier-Two interventions, and the Tier-Three intervention takes place under the rubric of more advanced services.

SOURCE: Bender and Shores (2007, p.41).

NOTE: Tiers One, Two, and Three refer to levels of instruction.

SOCIAL AND ECONOMIC CONSIDERATIONS

Along with a focus on individualized instruction and early child education, other social and economic considerations continue to come into purview. For example, many individual students are rethinking what it means to go to school and, thus, are getting their education online. Seeing this as an issue, some school districts are meeting this challenge and now offer technology-rich online and self-directed instruction. In addition, SDE are promoting and supporting such educational experiences.

In a radical rethinking of what it means to go to school, states and districts nationwide are launching online public schools that let students from kindergarten to 12th grade take some—or all—of their classes from their bedrooms, living rooms, and kitchens. Other states and districts are bringing students into brick-and-mortar schools for instruction that is largely technology-based and self-directed (Banchero & Simon, 2011).

Not to be outdone, the state of Virginia has already authorized a number of new online schools, and Florida began requiring all public high school students to take at least one online course. This is largely to prepare them for college cyber courses. In Georgia, a new app lets high school students take full course loads on their mobile devices (Banchero & Simon, 2011). According to the Evergreen Education Group (2011), more than 250,000 students nationwide have participated in full-time virtual educational experiences. This has increased by 40% over the past three years. Another two million plus students take at least one class online. Along with this increasing phenomenon, many states and local districts now run their own online schools. In addition, there are increasing numbers of for-profit corporations that can provide monitoring of student performance. These for-profit educational corporations have lobbied to expand online public education, and they are having success. From a socioeconomic perspective, this is all a part of an increasing interest in digital education. Fueled by declining budgetary resources and parental dissatisfaction with their children's educational experiences, more students are turning to online learning.

Advocates note that online schooling can save individual states money, offer curricula customized to each student, and give parents more choice in education. But, that said, there is always some form of controversy. A few states have found that students enrolled full-time in virtual schools may not learn how to get along with others or participate in group discussions. Additionally, critics worry about these students often scoring significantly lower on standardized tests and making less academic progress from year to year than their peers. In addressing these criticisms, advocates of full-time cyber schools say that the disappointing results are partly because some of the students had a rough time in traditional schools and arrived in their new school testing well below grade level in one or more subjects.

Whether schools offer a successful virtual or hybrid educational experience, students in the future will likely be impacted in some way. Their experience will be very different from the brick-and-mortar model that most of us have had in our educational careers. The question school leaders need to ask might be this: Are virtual schools and online learning experiences making a difference, positively or negatively, in educating the youth that will lead in the future?

Focusing on Social Media and Ethical Issues

Research seems to suggest that social media and e-mentoring are helping to define various generations such as *generation Y, millennials, net generation,* and *iGeneration.* For example, Rosen (2011) referred to the *iGeneration* as the group who heavily used such digital technologies as iPhone, iPod, iPad, Wii, and iTunes. Interestingly enough, regardless of the label, social networking technology uniquely offers new generations an opportunity to interact with an expansive universe of team members, family, and friends (Richardson, 2011).

There are, however, some drawbacks to using social networking websites. Gross and Acquisti (2005) shared four areas where social networking can cause individuals both personal and professional harm. First, it must be understood that when making postings on various types of websites, individuals are making public statements and not *private* postings. Second, when posting a statement or story, it is important to note the post is and remains a digital footprint and is accessible to the rest of the world. To remove a statement or story, one needs to go through the website policy process for removing information. Third, the Internet is an open unlimited international community in which many people have access. Thus, personal responsibility is a critical aspect of being safe on the Internet. Fourth, there is another angle to consider: the privacy of others. "Privacy" is a complicated matter in American law. It evokes everything from the right to family planning through Fourth Amendment search and seizure, to torts, or civil rights (Hodge, 2006). Clearly, then, school leaders and staff need to be aware that if they post an alleged fact about someone that proves incorrect, the message writer may be liable for damages under either defamation or libel. Moreover, if one posts photographs or information about someone that can be construed to be an "invasion of their privacy" or "false light," or "misappropriation of likeness," they may also be liable for a tort under the broad rubric of "privacy."

To be sure, even though social networks are a great innovation allowing users to express their humanity and an opportunity to create new communities, the freedom of the Internet does not suggest individuals can act with impunity. Since we live in a society in which expression is judged in legal policy and even personal ways, it is important to remember the consequences of that expression no matter how ephemeral or fun in the moment it might seem to be. What matters most for educators is to be fully aware and realize that anything posted about them or anyone else, given caching technologies, might prove to be a liability to an ongoing sense of identity over the longer course of history. Behind every device, behind every new program, behind every technology is a law, a social norm, or a business practice that warrants thoughtful consideration (Whitehead, Boschee, & Decker, 2013).

Social Ramifications of Cyberbullying

In our newly developing digital world, the age-old problem of bullying is taking on a whole new agenda that is hidden behind digital screens and cell phones. The term *cyberbullying* is harassment over the Internet or via other technologies. Teasing, name-calling, and making threats thrive on social media networks as well as text messaging on cell phones and in e-mails. A research study sponsored by the Pew Research Center titled *Teens, Kindness and Cruelty on Social Network Sites* reported that 9 out of 10 teens say they have witnessed cruelty by their peers on social networks (Lenhart, Madden, Purcell, & Zickuhr, 2011). The survey of 800 children between the ages of 12 to 17 found cyberbullying cuts across all ages and backgrounds. Some 15% of teen social media users who were participants in the Pew Research Center sponsored research indicated that they have experienced such harassment themselves (Guess, 2011).

As part of creating a sense of responsibility, schools are now paying closer attention to cyberbullying experiences (Guess, 2011). Therefore, it is important for educational leaders worldwide to not only address the cyberbully issue but also to have counselors available to assist targeted students. Having a plan as well as an authentic problem-based solving approach to help and assist victims of cyberbullying can be just as important as catching the culprit. Students engaged in authentic problem-based learning are encouraged to apply their knowledge to questions they have about why things happen in their world and thus are better able to discuss social ramifications often associated with specific issues—such as cyberbullying. Pew Research has identified some areas of interest for school leaders that involve negative impacts of cyberbullying. A substantial number of teens report specific negative outcomes from experiences on social network sites. For example, teens who use social media say they have experienced at least one of the following negative outcomes:

- Twenty-five percent of social media teens have had an experience on a social network site that resulted in a face-to-face argument or confrontation with someone.
- Twenty-two percent have had an experience that ended their friendship with someone.
- Thirteen percent have had an experience that caused a problem with their parents.
- Thirteen percent have felt nervous about going to school the next day.
- Eight percent have gotten into a physical fight with someone else because of something that happened on a social network site.
- Six percent have gotten in trouble at school because of an experience on a social network site.

Understanding that technology is constantly evolving, lawmakers are racing to keep up with policies and punishments for cyberbullying. As schools and administrators struggle to keep up with the changes, they must stay on top of this issue for the safety of students who are trying to become young adults in a global environment that is constantly changing (Whitehead et al., 2013).

DIGITAL CITIZENS: A NEW CULTURE OF THE 21st CENTURY

As part of social and economic concerns, technology safety and control is shifting from being the sole responsibility of school administrators, teachers, and technology coordinators to a model of shared responsibility among educators, students, and families. This is directly in line with the philosophical basis of 21st-century learning where the educational focus is on helping students to become digitally literate. In one sense, they become digital learners who are aware of and understand the norms of appropriate and responsible technology use. Taking it further, technology and academic plans in schools should address helping young learners to become digital citizens.

Nine Themes of Digital Citizenship (digitalcitizenship.net)

1. *Digital access: Full electronic participation in society.* Technology users need to be aware of and support electronic access for all to create a foundation for digital citizenship. Digital exclusion of any kind does not enhance the growth of users in

an electronic society. All people should have fair access to technology no matter who they are. Places or organizations with limited connectivity need to be addressed as well. To become productive citizens, we need to be committed to equal digital access.

2. *Digital commerce: Electronic buying and selling of goods.* Technology users need to understand that a large share of market economy is being done electronically. Legitimate and legal exchanges are occurring, but the buyer or seller needs to be aware of the issues associated with it. The mainstream availability of Internet purchases of clothing, cars, food, etc., has become commonplace to many users. At the same time, an equal amount of goods and services that are in conflict with the laws or morals of some countries are surfacing (which might include activities such as illegal downloading, pornography, and gambling). Users need to learn about how to be effective consumers in a new digital economy.

3. *Digital communication: Electronic exchange of information.* One of the significant changes within the digital revolution is a person's ability to communicate with other people. In the 19th century, forms of communication were limited. In the 21st century, communication options have exploded to offer a wide variety of choices (e.g., e-mail, cell phones, text messages). The expanding digital communication options have changed everything because people are able to keep in constant communication with anyone else. Now everyone has the opportunity to communicate and collaborate with anyone from anywhere and anytime. Unfortunately, many users have not been taught how to make appropriate decisions when faced with so many different digital communication options.

4. *Digital literacy: Process of teaching and learning about technology and the use of technology.* While schools have made great progress in the area of technology infusion, much remains to be done. A renewed focus must be made on what technologies must be taught as well as how they should be used. New technologies are finding their way into the workplace that are not always used in schools (e.g., videoconferencing, online sharing spaces such as wikis). In addition, workers in many different occupations need immediate information (i.e., just-in-time information). This process requires sophisticated searching and processing skills (i.e., information literacy). Learners must be taught how to learn in a digital society. In other words, learners must be taught to learn anything, anytime, anywhere. Business, military, and medicine are excellent examples of how technology is being used differently in the 21st century. As new technologies emerge, learners need to learn how to use that technology quickly and appropriately. Digital citizenship involves educating people in a new way—these individuals need a high degree of information literacy skills.

5. *Digital etiquette: Electronic standards of conduct or procedure.* Technology users often see this area as one of the most pressing problems when dealing with digital citizenship. We recognize inappropriate behavior when we see it, but before people use technology, they do not learn digital etiquette (i.e., appropriate conduct). Many people feel uncomfortable talking to others about their digital

etiquette. Often rules and regulations are created, or the technology is simply banned to stop inappropriate use. It is not enough to create rules and policy; we must teach everyone to become responsible digital citizens in this new society.

6. *Digital law: Electronic responsibility for actions and deeds.* Digital law deals with the ethics of technology within a society. Unethical use manifests itself in form of theft and/or crime. Ethical use manifests itself in the form of abiding by the laws of society. Users need to understand that stealing or causing damage to other people's work, identity, or property online is a crime. There are certain rules of society that users need to be aware of in an ethical society. These laws apply to anyone who works or plays online. Hacking into others information; downloading illegal music; plagiarizing; creating destructive worms, viruses, or creating Trojan Horses; sending spam; or stealing anyone's identify or property is unethical.

7. *Digital rights and responsibilities: Those freedoms extended to everyone in a digital world.* Just as in the U.S. Constitution where there is a Bill of Rights, there is a basic set of rights extended to every digital citizen. Digital citizens have the right to privacy, free speech, etc. Basic digital rights must be addressed, discussed, and understood in the digital world. With these rights also come responsibilities as well. Users must help define how the technology is to be used in an appropriate manner. In a digital society, these two areas must work together for everyone to be productive.

8. *Digital health and wellness: Physical and psychological well-being in a digital technology world.* Eye safety, repetitive stress syndrome, and sound ergonomic practices are issues that need to be addressed in a new technological world. Beyond the physical issues are those of the psychological issues that are becoming more prevalent such as Internet addiction. Users need to be taught that there are inherent dangers of technology. Digital citizenship includes a culture where technology users are taught how to protect themselves through education and training.

9. *Digital security (self-protection): Electronic precautions to guarantee safety.* In any society, there are individuals who steal, deface, or disrupt other people. The same is true for the digital community. It is not enough to trust other members in the community for our own safety. In our own homes, we put locks on our doors and fire alarms in our houses to provide some level of protection. The same must be true for the digital security. We need to have virus protection, backups of data, and surge control of our equipment. As responsible citizens, we must protect our information from outside forces that might cause disruption or harm.

GLOBAL CONNECTIONS: POSITIVE IMPACT WORLDWIDE

Along with a culture of new digital citizens, education and schools around the world continue to improve. According to Levin (2012–2013), many positive educational developments are happening globally. He noted that 50 years ago, *Korea* and *Singapore* were poor countries with significant illiteracy. Now they, and others, are becoming better educated and much wealthier. The same scenario applies to *China,* which has multiplied its university enrollment sixfold in the last decade. Levin added that countries already doing reasonably well in educational terms have experienced even more improvements—*Finland* and *Poland* are examples. *Chile* has also made serious efforts in improving education even among very poor populations.

Overall, from a global perspective, education outcomes are better now than they have ever been. The challenge, however, before the educational community worldwide, is that expectations are rising faster than outcomes. As a result, the achievement gap never seems to get smaller.

But there is action—and action leads to improvement. The success noted by a host of countries represents just a partial list of the total success story. A key here, then, is that educators across the globe are becoming internationally interconnected through 21st-century technology. This high level of connectivity is leading to a deepening awareness and deliberate action on the part of improving school curriculum globally.

APPLICATIONS

1. Some have argued that all learning is individualized: The learner makes individual meaning out of what is learned. They continue by disparaging the need for any type of individualized or adaptive instruction, contending that group-paced learning can be just as effective. How would you respond to such an argument?

2. Does effectively teaching 30 students in one classroom require teachers to develop 30 lessons, each tailor-made for every student? Or should teachers "aim for the middle" and hope to reach most students in a given lesson? Select one and defend your answer.

3. Identify a subject or grade level you know well. Which of the adaptive approaches do you think would work best? Explain your choice and the reasons supporting it.

4. Some have suggested that knowledge about learning styles will produce an "educational revolution." Others are much less sanguine about the possibilities, pointing out that the research so far has not yielded significant gains for learning styles adaptations. As you review the models described in this chapter and analyze the research findings, what position do you take regarding this issue?

5. If teachers adhere to the principles shown in Exhibit 15.2, differentiation can liberate students from stereotypical expectations and experience and provide equity of success to excellence. What should be done in the school district where you are employed to make differentiation a reality?

6. Suppose you were not limited by laws, such as Public Law 94–142, that mandate mainstreaming or inclusion. As an educational leader, would you use mainstreaming or inclusion in your school? On what grounds would you justify your position?

7. What is the reason(s) for only using tests to measure reading and spelling that are valid and reliable?

8. How would you justify and present adding a Reading Recovery or similar program to the board of education?

9. What are some of the social and ethical drawbacks of network media in education? Discuss in detail how you as a teacher or administrator would address these concerns in your school.

10. List and discuss the nine themes of digital citizenship. Pick three of the themes, and note how each one might be applied in your school.

CASE STUDY   Response to Intervention Issues

Maintaining academically challenged students in the regular classroom can be rewarding, but it can also pose some difficulties. The following is an example of how one teacher–leader handled a problem for a colleague.

Mr. Rusk, a new sixth-grade teacher, meets with one of the teacher–leaders, Susan Thomas.

Shortly after entering Thomas' classroom, Rusk nervously walks around a few desks and appears to be very frustrated and down. "I want to visit with you about a student in my classroom," he says quietly.

"Well, I'm glad you came to me," shares Thomas smiling, hoping to ease the tension.

"So what can we do about these kids who are really struggling in math?" Rusk asks, wanting an answer but not expecting much. "I have a student who is just not getting fractions."

"Well, that's a tough situation," shares Susan, showing concern. "We just started using an RTI program here at school. Maybe this kid would qualify. What do you think?"

"Gosh, hadn't thought of that," notes Rusk, now embarrassed he hadn't thought about RTI.

Thomas smiles and reaches for her scheduler buried deep in her purse. "Let me get things started. I'll schedule him in for testing right away. Also, let me check around and see who is already doing some RTI interventions. Maybe they can help."

"Sounds like a plan!" Rusk says, breaking into a big grin and pleased to have Thomas as a friend.

The Challenge

Making sure the school addresses the needs of all students and follows federal guidelines is a critical component of any curriculum across the country. How can programs like RTI be helpful in addressing student academic needs?

Key Issues or Questions

1. What are your impressions of Susan Thomas and how she dealt with the issue of RTI? Did the teacher–leader adequately address Mr. Rusk's concerns? Why or why not?

2. What are your beliefs about RTI? How much in-service should schools provide regarding RTI guidelines?

3. If a principal meets with a teacher about RTI, what should be discussed? When should the teacher be first involved in the discussion?

4. What are your feelings on state or federal mandated programs? Do you feel that RTI is a viable option for academically challenged students?

5. What are some innovative approaches that principals and teacher–leaders might use to address RTI concerns? Identify specific strategies and explain why you think they might be effective.

WEBLIOGRAPHY

Assessment and Qualifications Alliance (AQA), Alberta, Canada: Find Past Papers and Mark Schemes
www.aqa.org.uk/exams-administration/exams-guidance/find-past-papers-and-mark-schemes

Association for Positive Behavior Support
www.apbs.org

The Center for Comprehensive School Reform and Improvement: Differentiating Instruction
www.centerforcsri.org

Council for Children with Behavioral Disorders
www.ccbd.net

Learning Generation report on promoting the use of technology in special-education classrooms
http://familiestogetherinc.com/wp-content/uploads/2011/08/COMPUTERTECHNEEDS.pdf

Massachusetts Department of Elementary and Secondary Education: The Massachusetts Comprehensive Assessment System
www.doe.mass.edu/mcas/testitems.html

New Horizons for Learning
www.newhorizons.org/spneeds/inclusion/teaching/sax.htm

OpenEd Resource Catalog
www.opened.io

PBS Misunderstood Minds: Resources for Instructional strategies
www.pbs.org/wgbh/misunderstoodminds

Reading Recovery
http://readingrecovery.org/reading-recovery/teaching-children/basic-facts

Six Seconds: Emotional Intelligence for Positive Change
www.6seconds.org/school

SMART Education: Online Strategies to Help Teach Special Education Students
http://gettingsmart.com/2014/05/5-ways-new-tools-schools-transforming-special-education

REFERENCES

American Educational Research Association, American Psychological Association, & National Council of Measurement in Education. (1999). *Standards for educational and psychological testing*. Washington, DC: American Psychological Association.

Banchero, S., & Simon, S. (2011, November 12). My teacher is an app. *The Wall Street Journal*. Retrieved from http://online.wsj.com/article/SB10001424052970204358004577030600066250144.html

Bender, W. N., & Shores, C. (2007). *Response to intervention: A practical guide for every teacher*. Thousand Oaks, CA: Corwin Press and Council for Exceptional Children.

Bergmann, J., & Sams, A. (2013–2014). Flipping for mastery. *Educational Leadership, 71*(4), 24–29.

Bloom, B. S. (1971). Mastery learning. In J. H. Block (Ed.), *Mastery learning: Theory and practice* (pp. 47–63). New York, NY: Holt, Rinehart, & Winston.

Bloom, B. S. (1976). *Human characteristics and school learning*. New York, NY: McGraw-Hill.

Bloom, B. S. (1984). The search for methods of group instruction as effective as one-to-one tutoring. *Educational Leadership, 41*(8), 4–17.

Bosch, N. (Ed.). (2008). Differentiated curriculum. *A different place*. Retrieved from http://adifferent place. org/differentiated.htm

Brown, L. B. (2012). Bringing brain research into teaching. *Principal, 91*(3), 34–35.

Carbo, M. (2007). Best practices for achieving high, rapid reading gains. *Principal, 87*(2), 42–45.

Carr, N. (2010–2011). The juggler's brain. *Phi Delta Kappan, 92*(4), 8–14.

Chappuis, J. (2014). Thoughtful assessment with the learner in mind. *Educational Leadership, 71*(6), 20–26.

Clements, A. (1996). *Frindle*. New York, NY: Scholastic, Inc.

Commission on the Reorganization of Secondary Education. (1918). *Cardinal principles of secondary education*. Washington, DC: Government Printing Office.

Committee of Ten. (1893). *Report of the Committee of Ten on secondary school students*. Washington, DC: National Education Association.

Connelly, G. (2007). Opening the doors to discovery. *Principal, 87*(2), 68.

DeBruin-Parecki, A. (2004). Evaluating early literacy skills and providing instruction in a meaningful context. *High/Scope Resource: A Magazine for Educators, 23*(3), 510.

Dichter, H. (2011). Value-added early learning. *Principal, 90*(5), 16–19.

Evergreen Education Group. (2011). *Keeping pace with K-12 online learning: An annual review of policy and practice*. Retrieved from http://kpk12.com

Frede, E. & Barnett, W. S. (2011). Why pre-k is critical to closing the achievement gap. *Principal, 90*(5), 8–11.

The Glossary of Teacher Education Reform. (2014, September 12). *Teacher autonomy*. Retrieved from http://edglossary.org/teacher-autonomy

Grinder, R. E., & Nelsen, E. A. (1985). Individualized instruction in American pedagogy. In M. C. Wang & H. J. Walberg (Eds.), *Adapting instruction to individual differences* (pp. 24–43). Berkeley, CA: McCutchan.

Gross, R., & Acquisti, A. (2005). *Information revelation and privacy in online social networks. Workshop on privacy in the electronic society*. Retrieved from http://portal.acm.org/citation.cfm?id = 1102214

Guess, K., (2011, November 20). Schools paying closer attention to cyberbullying. *The WCF Courier*, pp. A1, A6. Retrieved from http://wcfcourier.com/news/local/schools-paying-closer-attention-to-cyber-bullying/article_29497291-c2c7-5fc2-8fda-6d8fb6f5907a.html

Guskey, T. R. (2010). Lessons of mastery learning. *Educational Leadership, 68*(2), 52–57.

Hall, T. (2002). *Differentiated instruction*. Wakefield, MA: National Center on Accessing the General Curriculum. Retrieved from http://cast .org/publications/ncac/ncac_diffinstruc.html

Hall, T., Strangman, N., & Meyer, A. (2011). *Differentiated instruction and implications for UDL implementation*. Retrieved from http://aim .cast.org/learn/historyarchive/backgroundpapers/differentiated_instruction_udl

Hodge, M. J. (2006). The Fourth Amendment and privacy issues on the 'new' Internet: Facebook.com and MySpace.com. *Southern Illinois University Law Journal, 31*, 95–122.

Hu, W. (2008, October 27). High schools add electives to cultivate interests. *New York Times*, p. A21. Retrieved from http://www.nytimes.com/2008/10/27/education/27electives.html

Lenhart, A., Madden, M, Purcell, K., & Zickuhr, K. (2011). *Teens, kindness and cruelty on social network sites: How American teens navigate the new world of digital citizenship*. Washington, DC: Pew Research Center. Retrieved from www.pewinternet.org

Levin, B. (2012–2013). Staying optimistic in tough times. *Phi Delta Kappan, 94*(4), 74–75.

Linn, M. I. (2011). Inclusion in two languages: Special education in Portugal and the United States. *Phi Delta Kappan, 92*(8), 58–60.

Mahatmya, D., Brown, R. C., & Johnson, A. D. (2014). Student-as-client. *Phi Delta Kappan, 95*(6), 30–34.

McAssey, L. (2014). Common core assessments: A principal's view. *Principal, 93*(3), 14–17.

McLaughlin, M. J. (2012). Access for all: Six principles for principals to consider in implementing CCSS for students with disabilities. *Principal, 92*(1), 22–26.

Meeker, M. N. (1985). SOI. In A. L. Costa (Ed.), *Developing minds: A resource book for teaching thinking* (pp. 187–192). Alexandria, VA: ASCD.

Meeker, M. N., Meeker, R., & Roid, G. (1985). *The basic SOI manual.* Los Angeles, CA: WPS.

National Association for the Education of Young Children & National Association of Early Childhood Specialists in State Departments of Education. (2009). *Where we stand on curriculum assessment and program evaluation.* Retrieved from http://www.naeyc.org/files/naeyc/file/positions/StandCurrAss.pdf

Oaksford, L., & Jones, L. (2001). *Differentiated instruction abstract.* Tallahassee, FL: Leon County Schools.

Parsons, S. A., Dodman, S.L., & Burrowbridge, S. C. (2013). Broadening the view of differentiated instruction. *Phi Delta Kappan, 95*(1), 38–42.

Plake, B. S., Impara, J. C., & Spies, R. A. (Eds.). (2003). The fifteenth mental measurements yearbook (Buros Mental Measurements Yearbook). Lincoln, NE: Buros Center.

Reis, S. M., & Renzulli, J. S. (1984). Key features of successful programs for the gifted and talented. *Educational Leadership, 41*(7), 28–34.

Renzulli, J. S. (1977). *The enrichment triad model: A guide for developing defensible programs for the gifted.* Mansfield Center, CT: Creative Learning.

Renzulli, J. S. (2011). *Kappan* classic: More changes needed to expand gifted identification and support. *Phi Delta Kappan, 92*(8), 61. Retrieved from http://www.kappanmagazine.org/content/92/8/61.full?sid = 78eacd5c-d9fc-45e0-a6dd-3494ddfce425

Renzulli, J. S., Reis, S. M., & Smith, L. H. (1981). *The revolving door identification model.* Mansfield Center, CT: Creative Learning.

Richardson, J. (2011). Tune in to what the new generation of teachers can do. *Phi Delta Kappan, 92*(8), 14–19.

Rosen, L. D. (2011). Teaching the iGeneration. *Educational Leadership, 68*(5), 10–15.

Schlepp, D. (2012). An inclusionary model of support. *Principal, 91*(5), 32–36.

Silverman, E. (2008). *Cowgirl Kate and Cocoa.* Boston, MA: Houghton Mifflin Harcourt.

Taylor, B. M., Pearson, P. D., Clark, K. F., & Walpole, S. (1999, September 30). *Beating the odds in teaching all children to read* (CIERA Report No. 2–006). Ann Arbor: Center for the Improvement of Early Reading Achievement, University of Michigan School of Education.

Tomlinson, C. A. (2001). *How to differentiate instruction in mixed-ability classrooms* (2nd ed.). Alexandria, VA: ASCD.

Tomlinson, C. A. (2003). Deciding to teach them all. *Educational Leadership, 61*(2), 6–11.

Tomlinson, C. A., & Edison, C. C. (2003). *Differentiation in practice: A resource guide for differentiating curriculum, Grades 5–9.* Alexandria, VA: ASCD.

Tomlinson, C. A., & Javius, E. L. (2012). Teach up for excellence: All students deserve equitable access to an engaging and rigorous curriculum. *Educational Leadership, 95*(1), 28–33.

Tomlinson, C. A., Kaplan, S. N., Renzulli, J. S., Purcell, J., Leppien, J., & Burns, D. (2002). *The parallel curriculum: A design to develop high potential and challenge high-ability learners.* Thousand Oaks, CA: Corwin Press.

Tomlinson, C. A., & McTighe, J. (2006). *Integrating differentiated instruction and understanding by design: Connecting content and kids.* Alexandria, VA: ASCD.

Vygotsky, L. S. (1978). *Mind in society: The development of higher psychological processes.* Cambridge, MA: Harvard University Press.

What Works Clearinghouse. (2007, March 19). *WWC intervention report: Reading Recovery.* Washington, DC: U.S. Department of Education, Institute of Education Sciences.

What Works Clearinghouse. (2008). *A summary of changes to the WWC handbook.* Washington, DC: U.S. Department of Education, Institute of Education Sciences.

What Works Clearinghouse. (2013). *Does the What Works Clearinghouse work?* Washington, DC: U.S. Department of Education, Institute of Education Sciences.

Whitehead, B. M., Boschee, F. & Decker, R. H. (2013). *The Principal: Leadership for a global society.* Thousand Oaks, CA: Sage.

Wiederholt, J. L., & Bryant, B. R. (2013). Gray Oral Reading Tests–fifth edition (GORT-5). Retrieved from http://www4.parinc.com/products/Product.aspx?ProductID = GORT-5

Wiggins, G. (2013–2014). How good is good enough? *Educational Leadership, 71*(4), 10–16.

Wilson, M. (2014). Personalization: It's anything but personal. *Educational Leadership, 71*(6), 73–77.

Wolfe, P. (2001). *Brain matters: Translating research into classroom practice.* Alexandria, VA: ASCD.

Zirkel, P. A. (2011). The "New" section 504. *Principal, 91*(1), 54–55.

Glossary

Academic Scientism. This describes the academic period from 1890 to 1916 that derives from two influences: the academic and the scientific. The academic influence was the result of systematic and somewhat effective efforts of colleges to shape curriculum for basic education; scientific influence resulted from the attempts of educational theorists to use newly developed scientific knowledge in making decisions about the mission of the school and the content of the curriculum.

Acceleration. Acceleration is an adaptive strategy that helps gifted students advance through the grades and master advanced academic content at a rapidly accelerated rate.

Adaptive curricula. Adaptive curricula and instructional practices are educational processes that arrange the conditions and materials of learning so that they fit individual learner differences.

Adaptive learning environments model (ALEM). This model is an attempt to combine prescriptive or direct instruction with those aspects of open education that have been found to be effective.

Affective education. The affective education movement emphasized the feelings and values of the child. While cognitive development was considered important, it was seen only as an adjunct to affective growth.

Anticipatory set. An anticipatory set helps students develop a mental set that allows them to focus on what will be learned.

Authentic tasks. Authentic tasks are assignments given to students designed to assess their ability to apply standard-driven knowledge and skills to real-world challenges.

Benchmarks. Benchmarks are points along a path toward learning a new skill or set of skills.

Bilingual programs. In bilingual programs, the goal is to develop proficiency in both the formal language as well as a secondary language.

Brain-based learning. Brain-based learning follows the belief that there are connections between brain function and educational practice.

Charter schools. Charter schools are non-sectarian public schools of choice that operate with freedom from many of the regulations that apply to traditional public schools.

Child-centered curriculum. A child-centered curriculum is an approach whereby the child is the beginning point, the determiner, and the shaper of the curriculum. Although the developing child will at some point acquire knowledge of subject matter, the disciplines are seen as only one type of learning. Elements of child-centered curricula include affective education, open education, and developmental education.

Committee of Fifteen. The Committee of Fifteen, commissioned by the National Education Association in the early 1890s, was appointed to make recommendations for elementary school curriculum.

Committee of Ten. The Committee of Ten, commissioned by the National Education Association (NEA) in 1893, was appointed to make recommendations for high school curriculum.

Common Core State Standards (CCSS). The CCSS are a set of high-quality academic expectations in English language arts (ELA) and mathematics that define the knowledge and skills all students should master by the end of each grade level in order to be on track for success in college and career.

Community-based learning model. A community-based learning model is an approach based around an interdisciplinary theme that integrates educational experiences and closely parallels the way people learn. A community-based learning model makes it possible for teachers to draw on external communities that promote divergent thinking.

Compacting. Once a student has demonstrated a level of proficiency in the basic curriculum, compacting allows the student to exchange instructional time for other learning.

Conceptual empiricists. Conceptual empiricists are those who derive their research methodologies from the physical sciences in attempting to produce generalizations that will enable educators to control and predict what happens in schools.

Conformists. Conformists are individuals who believe that the existing order is a good one—the best of all possible worlds.

Connective curriculum. Connective curriculum makes connections within and across times, cultures, places, and disciplines.

Content-oriented theories. Content-oriented theories are concerned primarily with specifying the major sources that should influence the selection and organization of the curriculum content.

Context evaluation. Context evaluation continually assesses needs and problems in the context to help decision makers determine goals and objectives.

Cooperative development. Cooperative development is an option usually provided only to experienced and competent teachers; it enables small groups of teachers to work together in a collegial relationship for mutual growth. It is intended to be a teacher-centered, teacher-directed process that respects the professionalism of competent teachers.

Cooperative learning models. These are models that provide teachers with effective ways to respond to diverse students by promoting academic achievement and cross-cultural understanding and ways to have students work in groups to reinforce concepts taught by the teacher.

Core curriculum. This curriculum is based on the concept there is a uniform body of knowledge that all students should know. Core curriculum parallels a discipline.

Core curriculum movement. The core curriculum movement is a movement that assumes there is a uniform body of knowledge that all students should know.

Correlating curricula. Correlating curricula is a process of aligning contents of two or more subjects. It is an interdisciplinary approach whereby teachers are organized into teams to plan for correlated lessons.

Course of study. A course of study is all the planned learning experiences for a period of one year or less in a given field of study.

Critical thinking skills. Critical thinking skills are skills that provide a set of information and belief based on intellectual commitment.

Curriculum alignment. Curriculum alignment is a process of ensuring that the written, taught, and tested curricula are closely congruent.

Curriculum-development team (CDT). A curriculum-development team is a team comprising administrators, teachers, and parents who review and plan curriculum for a district.

Curriculum evaluation. Curriculum evaluation is the assessment of the merit and worth of a program of studies, a field of study, or a course of study.

Curriculum framework. Curriculum framework is an organized plan, set of standards, or list of outcomes defining the recommended curricula.

Curriculum guides. Curriculum guides have components that include specific learning objectives and the activities suggested for each objective. It is intentionally designed to meet district and state standards and is used to aid teachers in planning and developing teacher plans and strategies for specific subject areas.

Curriculum-objectives notebook. The curriculum-objectives notebook is a loose-leaf notebook that contains the following: a summary of the research on how to teach a given subject, a copy of the scope-and-sequence chart in reduced form, and a list of the objectives for those grade levels taught by the teacher to whom the guide is issued.

Curriculum of identity. Curriculum of identity guides students in coming to understand their own strengths, preferences, values, and commitment by reflecting on their own development through the lens of contributors and professionals.

Curriculum of practice. Curriculum of practice guides gifted learners in understanding and applying the facts, concepts, principles, and methodologies of the discipline.

Curriculum planning. Curriculum planning is the specification and sequencing of major decisions to be made in the future with regard to educational curriculum. Specific details of the curriculum-planning process are determined by the level and nature of curriculum work; designing a field of studies, improving a program of studies, and developing a course of study involve quite different processes.

Curriculum-scenario book. The curriculum-scenario book is a collection of learning scenarios—a practical account—to help determine what mix of learning activities, learning materials, and learning objectives can result in quality learning experiences.

Curriculum specialists. The term *curriculum specialists* is used to designate administrators or supervisors with responsibility for and training in curriculum development.

Curriculum theory. Curriculum theory is a way of noting philosophy of certain approaches and strategies to the development and enactment of curriculum. Theory is often considered a formalized, deductively connected bundle of laws that are applicable in specifiable ways to their observable manifestations.

Data-analysis report. The data-analysis report is a way of summarizing and aggregating results from individuals or groups about curriculum and school communities. If, however, an evaluation has been conducted that employs a control group, or measures changes in program participants over time, then it might be appropriate to employ *inferential* analysis, in which a decision is made about whether the particular results of the study are "real." A data-analysis report provides data to analyze and utilize information.

Descriptive curriculum. Descriptive curriculum is curriculum not merely based on what ought to happen but on what is actually happening in the classroom.

Developmental Conformism. Developmental Conformism (1941–1956) is a period marked by rather intensive interest in the educational implications of child and adolescent development. Dewey, among others, had long been concerned with delineating and responding to the stages of growth in children and youth. Two trends, developmental abilities and needs of youth and a concern with conformity, were the focus during this 15-year period.

Developmental education. Developmental education is a term referring to any curriculum theory that stresses the developmental stages of child growth as the primary determiners of placement and sequence.

Diagnostic–prescriptive models. These are models that structure the field of study as series of sequential nongraded levels of learning. It is an approach that represents observation, planning, teaching, obtaining feedback, monitoring, and revising instruction.

Differentiated professional development. Differentiated professional development is essentially a reconceptualization of the supervisory function, one that attempts to broaden the practitioner's view of supervision.

Discipline-based curriculum. This model uses the standard disciplines as the fields or organizing centers of learning.

Discovery method. The discovery method allows students to "discover" how to perform a skill or tactic rather than being directly taught the skill or tactic.

Diversity education. Diversity education is a process that permeates all aspects of school practices, policies, and organization as a means to ensure the highest levels of academic achievement for all students. It should prepare students to live, learn, and work in a pluralistic world by fostering appreciation, respect, and tolerance for people of other ethnic and cultural backgrounds.

Dynamic knowledge. Dynamic knowledge refers to metacognitive strategies, cognitive processes, thinking skills, and content-area procedural knowledge. In dynamic knowledge, curricula and teachers no longer serve solely as static knowledge options but assist in the development of a knowledge base that is student centered and enhances effective thinking on the part of the individual learner.

Early intervention. Early intervention is a system of coordinated services that promotes the child's growth and development and supports families during the critical years. Early intervention services for eligible children and families are federally mandated through the Individuals with Disabilities Education Act (IDEA).

Effective schools process. Effective schools process is a way of creating schools in which all children make progress and are ready for study at the next grade level.

Elective models. Individuals advocating elective models view the curriculum as a multipath network.

Elements of lesson design. These are the basic underpinnings of a lesson design.

English language learners (ELLs). Active learners of the English language who may benefit from various types of language support programs.

Enrichment curriculum. Throughout the year, each classroom teacher provides a number of special experiences and activities. These range from special programs and projects in the classroom to field trips and class excursions.

Equity principle. This involves teachers having high expectations and strong support for all students being able to learn.

Field of study. A field of study is all the planned learning experiences over a multiyear period in a given discipline or area of study.

Futurists. Futurists are individuals who, rather than being attuned to the present problems of the society, look to the coming age.

Goal-based design. Goal-based design is the setting of clear and practical goals that will expand the curriculum.

Goal-based model. A goal-based model is a curriculum model that aligns the district's educational goals with appropriate curricular fields. This model provides organizing strategies to determine the locus of control in decision making and what organizational structures are needed.

Heart of education. The basic essence of teaching and learning.

Hidden curriculum. The hidden curriculum is the unintended curriculum—what students learn from the school's culture and climate. It includes such elements as the use of time, allocation of space, funding for programs and activities, and disciplinary

policies and practices. For example, if an elementary school allocates 450 minutes each week to reading and 45 minutes to art, the hidden message to students is that "art doesn't matter."

Independent practice. This is the process of assigning independent practice of a process or skill, used to reinforce understanding.

Individual student report. An individual student report provides comprehensive information for each student; it also is distributed after each major testing. It gives the student's name and indicates the number correct and incorrect for all objectives.

Input. This is the process of giving students information about the knowledge, skill, or process they are to achieve.

Input evaluation. Input evaluation assesses alternative means for achieving determined goals to help decision makers choose optimal means.

Integrated curriculum. Integrated curriculum is a teaching method that attempts to break down barriers between subjects to make learning more meaningful.

Intensive development. This is an intensive and systematic process in which a supervisor, administrator, or expert teacher works closely with an individual teacher in an attempt to effect significant improvement in the essential skills of teaching.

Intentional curriculum. Intentional curriculum is the set of learnings that the school system consciously intends, in contradistinction to the hidden curriculum, which by and large is not a product of conscious intention. It has the following components: the written, the supported, the taught, and the tested.

Interdisciplinary courses. Interdisciplinary courses are those courses related to and characterized by participation of two or more fields of study. They are courses of study that either integrate content from two or more disciplines (such as English and social studies) or ignore the disciplines totally when organizing learning experiences.

Knowledge-centered curricula. This term refers to curricula advocating a knowledge-centered approach whereby disciplines or bodies of knowledge are the primary determiners of what is taught.

Learned curriculum. The learned curriculum is the bottom-line curriculum—what students learn. Clearly, it is the most important of all.

Learning scenarios. Learning scenarios are sequences of concepts from domain knowledge represented by series of activities. As the learning process proceeds, the scenarios are changed dynamically to better suit actual learner characteristics.

Learning-styles models. Learning-styles models are built on the assumptions that learners differ significantly in their styles of learning, that those styles can be assessed, and that knowledge of styles can help both teachers and learners.

Lesson. A lesson is a set of related learning experiences typically lasting from 20 to 60 minutes, focusing on a relatively small number of objectives.

Limited English proficiency (LEP). Limited English proficiency is employed by the U.S. Department of Education to refer to English language learners (ELLs) who lack sufficient mastery of English to meet state standards and excel in an English-language classroom.

Mainstreaming/inclusion. This approach advocates that special education children be allowed to remain in the regular classroom whenever appropriate.

Mastery curriculum. Mastery curriculum proposes that students work on a subject until they demonstrate mastery of it, which may be indicated by a grade of 90% or better on each and every assignment. Although most students complete their coursework on a time frame similar to that in conventional schools, the mastery curriculum can accommodate students who may need more time on a particular subject or who want to speed up their progress.

Mastery learning models. Mastery learning models have six features in common: clearly specified learning objectives; short, valid assessment procedures; current mastery standards; a sequence of learning units; provision of feedback on learning progress to students; and provision of additional time and help to correct specified errors of students failing to meet the mastery standard.

Merit. The term *merit* refers to the intrinsic value of an entity—value that is implicit, inherent, and independent of any applications.

Metacognition. Metacognition is usually presented as a conscious and deliberate mental activity—we become aware that we don't understand a paragraph we read or a statement we hear.

Modeling. Modeling is demonstrating a process or skill.

Modern Conservatism. This is the academic period from 2000 to the present, evidenced by a move toward accountability. This period is marked by profound independence of the mind, intellectual equalitarianism, and distrust of traditional values. The No Child Left Behind Act (NCLB) and Response to Intervention (RTI) are typical federal programs of this time.

Naturalistic process. The naturalistic process attempts to be sensitive to the political aspects of curriculum making, places greater emphasis on the quality of the learning activities, attempts to reflect more accurately the way curricula actually have been developed, and takes cognizance of the way teachers really plan for instruction.

Needs assessment. Needs assessment is a process used to obtain accurate, thorough data as to the strengths and weaknesses of a school and community to determine the academic needs of all students as well as to contribute to the improvement of student achievement.

Open education. A child-centered curriculum movement that emphasized the social and cognitive development of the child through informal exploration, activity, and discovery. Open education was an approach emphasizing a rich learning environment, one that modeled the use of concrete and interactive materials organized in "learning centers."

Permanent scaffolding. A scaffold is a temporary support offered to a student to help him or her grasp a concept or master a skill. Since a scaffold is temporary by definition, teachers should be testing continually for independent mastery by removing these scaffolds, much like parents take off the training wheels of a child's first bike.

Planning report. A planning report summarizes student performance for each class on the previous year's summative examination.

Prescriptive curricula. Prescriptive curricula can be defined as what "ought" to happen in curriculum. It often takes the form of a plan, an intended program, or some kind of expert opinion about what needs to take place in the course of study.

Privatistic Conservatism. This was the academic period from 1975 to 1989, evidenced by substantially reducing federal spending, strengthening local and state control, maintaining a limited federal role in helping states carry out their educational responsibilities, expanding parental choice, reducing federal judicial activity in education, and abolishing the Department of Education.

Process evaluation. Process evaluation monitors the processes both to ensure that the means are actually being implemented and to make the necessary modifications.

Process-oriented theories. Process-oriented theories are concerned primarily with describing how curricula are developed or recommending how they should be developed. Some process-oriented theories are descriptive in nature; others are more prescriptive.

Product evaluation. Product evaluation compares actual ends with intended ends and leads to a series of recycling decisions.

Proficiency movement. A proficiency movement is the commitment of educators to the concept of developing student and skill proficiency.

Program of study. A program of study represents all the planned learning experiences over a multiyear period for a given group of learners.

Progressive Functionalism. The era of Progressive Functionalism, which lasted from approximately 1917 to 1940, was characterized by the confluence of two seemingly disparate views: the progressive, child-centered orientation of the followers of John Dewey, and the functional orientation of curriculum scientists.

Radicals. Radicals are individuals who regard society as critically flawed and who espouse curricula that would expose those flaws and empower the young to effect radical changes.

Rating. As per this text, the term *rating* is used in this sense: the process of making formative and summative assessments of teacher performance for purposes of administrative decision making.

Recommended curriculum. This is a curriculum recommended by individual scholars, professional associations, and reform commissions; it also encompasses the curriculum requirements of policymaking groups, such as federal and state governments.

Reconceptualists. Reconceptualists are individuals who view education more as an existential experience. They emphasize subjectivity, existential experience, and the art of interpretation in order to reveal the class conflict and unequal power relationships existing in the larger society.

Reformers. Reformers are individuals who see society as essentially sound in its democratic structure but want to affect major reforms in the social order.

Response to Intervention (RTI). RTI is a multi-tier approach to the early identification and support of students with learning and behavior needs.

Romantic Radicalism. This was the academic period from 1968 to 1974, evidenced by "rights," not responsibilities, being the dominant slogan: Black people, handicapped individuals, homosexuals, women, and non-native groups all asserted their rights to liberation and to greater power. Educational reform was viewed as a political process.

Scholarly Structuralism. This was the academic period from 1957 to 1967, evidenced by educational leaders being convinced that rational, technological approaches could solve the schools' problems.

School vouchers. School vouchers are government grants aimed at improving education for the children of low-income families by providing school tuition that can be used at public or private schools. The thought behind school vouchers is to give parents a wider choice of educational institutions and approaches; it is also assumed that competition from private schools will pressure public schools into providing a better education for their students.

Scope and sequence matrix. Scope and sequence matrix is a set of PreK–12 learning objectives that reflect local, state, and national standards.

Self-directed development. Self-directed development is a way for teachers to identify a small number of professional-growth goals for the year and work independently in attempting to accomplish those goals.

Society-centered curricula. These are curricula that are based on the concept of social order being the starting point and the primary determiner of the curriculum.

Standard curriculum guide. Most often used by districts, its main components are the specific learning objectives and the activities suggested for each objective.

Standards and outcome statements. Standards and outcome statements define knowledge and skills students need to possess at critical points during their education.

Structure of the Intellect (SOI). This model of intelligence is represented by three dimensions: the five *contents* of the intellect (visual, auditory, symbolic, semantic, behavioral), the six *products* of the intellect (units, classes, relations, systems, transformation, implications), and the five *operations* (evaluation, convergent production, divergent production, memory, cognition).

Structure-oriented theories. Structure-oriented theories are generally concerned with components of curriculum and their interrelationships. Primarily analytical in their approach, educators espousing structure-oriented theories often seek to describe and explain how curricular components interact within an educational environment.

Supported curriculum. The supported curriculum is reflected and shaped by the resources allocated to support or deliver the curriculum.

Taught curriculum. The taught curriculum is the one that teachers actually deliver. Researchers have pointed out that there is enormous variation in the nature of what is actually taught, despite the superficial appearance of uniformity.

Technological Constructionism. This was the academic period from 1990 to 1999, evidenced by the development of a standards-based and technological reform movement that gained support at national, state, and local levels.

Technological Functionalism. Making the rise of modern technology functional in today's classrooms. Functionalism focuses on how technology contributes to the teaching and learning process.

Technological process. The technological process describes any curriculum-development model that emphasizes the importance of defining terminal learning objectives early in the process and then identifies the steps needed to accomplish those objectives.

Tested curriculum. The tested curriculum is the one embodied in tests developed by the state, school system, and teachers. The term *test* is used broadly here to include standardized tests, competency tests, and performance assessments.

Traditionalists. Traditionalists view curriculum as notions of class, teacher, course, units, and lessons. They are individuals concerned with the most efficient means of transmitting a fixed body of knowledge in order to impart the cultural heritage and keep the existing society functioning.

Triad/Revolving Door Identification Model (RDIM) program. A triad/RDIM program is based on three types of enrichment activities for the gifted: general exploratory activities, group training activities, and individual or small-group investigation activities.

Types of curricula. The 11 types of curriculum (as defined by Leslie Wilson) are the overt, explicit, or written curriculum; societal curriculum; hidden or covert curriculum; null curriculum; phantom curriculum; concomitant curriculum; rhetorical curriculum; curriculum-in-use; received curriculum; internal curriculum; and e-curriculum.

Unit of study. A unit of study is a subset of a course of study that constitutes one education unit; it includes the amount of contact hours and/or material covered for completion.

Value-oriented theories. Value-oriented theories are based on the precept that central to the human condition is a search for transcendence, the struggle of the individual to actualize the whole self. Educators espousing a value-oriented philosophy tend to question their assumptions, to aspire to more worthy goals, and to reconceptualize the enterprise of curriculum making.

Walkthroughs. A walkthrough is "the practice of principals or other instructional leaders spend[ing] only minutes observing classrooms to form an impression about the quality of teaching and learning occurring" (Pitler & Goodwin, 2008, p. 9 [see Chapter 9]).

Ways of knowing. This is an educational approach espousing the view that there are multiple ways of knowing, not just one or two.

Worker Education and Training Program (WETP). This model program, under the auspices of the National Institute of Environmental Health Sciences, was given major responsibility for initiating a training grants program under the Superfund Amendments and Reauthorization Act of 1986. It encourages innovation for training difficult-to-reach populations by addressing issues such as literacy, appropriate adult education techniques, training quality improvement, and other areas unaddressed directly by the private sector. The program enhances rather than replaces private-sector training responsibility by demonstrating new and cost-effective training techniques and materials.

Worth. *Worth* refers to the value of an entity in reference to a specific context or application. Worth varies from one context to another. For example, a curriculum may have a certain worth for teaching a particular child in a given year.

Writing across the curriculum. Writing across the curriculum can be defined as a comprehensive program that transforms the curriculum, encouraging writing to learn and learning to write in all disciplines. Also, writing and thinking are closely allied because learning to write well involves learning particular discourse conventions. Therefore, writing belongs in the entire curriculum, not just in a course offered by the English department.

Writing process. The writing process represents the complex act of creating written communication, specifically planning, drafting, revising, editing, and publishing.

Writing to learn. A writing-to-learn program is an approach that implies that students have something to say and that the process of writing provides at once a way for them to discourse and communicate.

Written curriculum. The written curriculum indicates a rationale that supports the curriculum, the general goals to be accomplished, the specific objectives to be mastered, the sequence in which those objectives should be studied, and the kinds of learning activities that should be used.

Index

About the Authors

Allan A. Glatthorn (1924–2007) was a Distinguished Research Professor of Education (Emeritus) at East Carolina University, Greenville, North Carolina. He formerly was a member of the faculty at the University of Pennsylvania Graduate School of Education. During his 55 years working in education, he served as a teacher, principal, supervisor, and professor. He was also the author of more than 20 books in the field of curriculum and supervision and consulted with more than 200 school districts, assisting them in developing and implementing their curricula.

Floyd Boschee has an extensive background in teaching and educational administration. He served as a teacher, coach, and school administrator in the public schools and as a professor and chairman of departments of education at the collegiate level. Dr. Boschee is professor emeritus in the Division of Educational Administration, School of Education, at the University of South Dakota and a former school board member of the Vermillion School District, Vermillion, South Dakota. During his tenure as a university professor, he consulted with school districts on reorganization; published numerous articles in major educational journals; and conducted workshops on curriculum development and implementation, the teaching and learning process, and school administrator evaluations. He is the author or coauthor of 13 books in the fields of school administration and curriculum and instruction.

Bruce M. Whitehead is an NAESP Nationally Distinguished Principal and has served for over 30 years as a principal for School District # 4 in Missoula, Montana. He also serves as an adjunct professor for the University of Montana. His career includes appointments to numerous national and international committees as well as becoming President of the Montana Association of Elementary School Principals and the Montana State Reading Association. He also served as the chairman of Montana's first Governor's Task Force on Technology as well as being an NCATE Advisor. As a co-author of 10 books and numerous articles in the field of education, Dr. Whitehead is a recipient of the University of Montana's highest honor, the Montana Distinguished Alumni Award. Additional honors include the International Reading Association's Presidential Service Award, NASA Explorer Schools Leadership Award, National Milken Foundation's Outstanding Educator Award,

John F. Kennedy Center's Award for Arts in Education, Outstanding Contributions to Saudi Arabian Education, and Japan's International Soroban Institute Award.

 **Bonni F. Boschee** is the principal of the Volga Christian School, Volga, South Dakota. Prior to the principalship position, she was a professor of language arts and also served as chair of the Graduate Program at Northern State University, Aberdeen, South Dakota. Dr. Boschee was also an elementary school teacher for 15 years in the Rapid City School District, Rapid City, South Dakota, where she was active in curriculum development and implementation and a K–12 administrator. Her research findings on homeschooling were presented at the state and national levels and published in a national journal. She currently is piloting a literacy program to enhance reading scores at Volga Christian School.

◎SAGE research**methods**

The essential online tool for researchers from the world's leading methods publisher

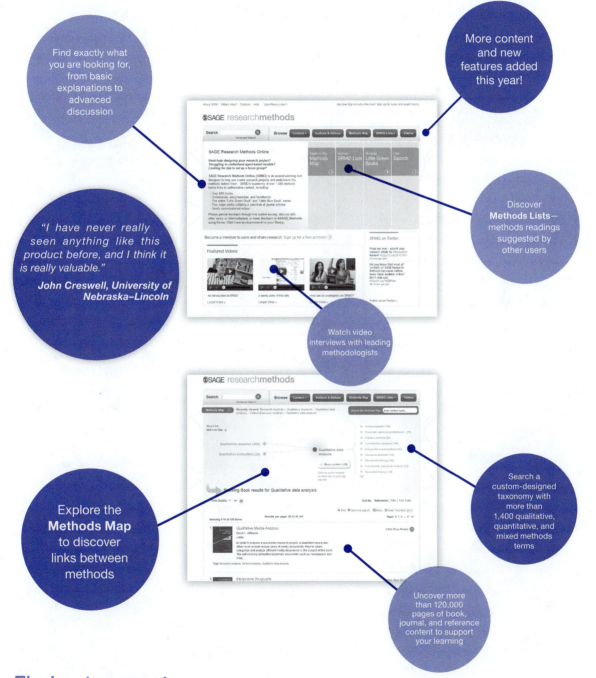

More content and new features added this year!

Find exactly what you are looking for, from basic explanations to advanced discussion

Discover **Methods Lists**— methods readings suggested by other users

"I have never really seen anything like this product before, and I think it is really valuable."

John Creswell, University of Nebraska–Lincoln

Watch video interviews with leading methodologists

Explore the **Methods Map** to discover links between methods

Search a custom-designed taxonomy with more than 1,400 qualitative, quantitative, and mixed methods terms

Uncover more than 120,000 pages of book, journal, and reference content to support your learning

Find out more at
www.sageresearchmethods.com